BTEC
FIRST

endorsed for BTEC

INFORMATION AND CREATIVE TECHNOLOGY

PEARSON

Published by Pearson Education Limited, Edinburgh Gate, Harlow, Essex, CM20 2JE.

www.pearsonschoolsandfecolleges.co.uk

Text: © Pearson Education Limited 2013
Typeset by Phoenix Photosetting, Chatham, Kent, UK
Original illustrations © Pearson Education Limited
Illustrations by Tim Ellis and Phoenix Photosetting
Cover design by Pearson Education Limited and Andrew Magee Design
Front cover photo: Getty Images: Don Farrall

First published 2013

16 15 14
10 9 8 7 6 5 4 3

British Library Cataloguing in Publication Data
A catalogue record for this book is available from the British Library

ISBN 978 1 446901 87 8

Printed in Slovakia by Neografia

Websites
There are links to relevant websites in this book. In order to ensure that the links are up to date, that the links works, and that the sites aren't inadvertently links to sites that could be considered offensive, we have made the links available on our website at www.pearsonhotlinks.co.uk. Search for the title BTEC First in Information and Creative Technology Student Book or ISBN 978 1 446901 87 8.

Copies of official specifications for all Pearson qualifications may be found on the website: www.edexcel.com

A NOTE FROM THE PUBLISHER

In order to ensure that this resource offers high-quality support for the associated BTEC qualification, it has been through a review process by the awarding organisation to confirm that it fully covers the teaching and learning content of the specification or part of a specification at which it is aimed, and demonstrates an appropriate balance between the development of subject skills, knowledge and understanding, in addition to preparation for assessment.

While the publishers have made every attempt to ensure that advice on the qualification and its assessment is accurate, the official specification and associated assessment guidance materials are the only authoritative source of information and should always be referred to for definitive guidance.

BTEC examiners have not contributed to any sections in this resource relevant to examination papers for which they have responsibility.

No material from an endorsed book will be used verbatim in any assessment set by BTEC.

Endorsement of a book does not mean that the book is required to achieve this BTEC qualification, nor does it mean that it is the only suitable material available to support the qualification, and any resource lists produced by the awarding organisation shall include this and other appropriate resources.

Contents

Acknowledgements

The publisher would like to thank the following for their kind permission to reproduce their photographs:

(Key: b-bottom; c-centre; l-left; r-right; t-top)

Alamy Images: Alex Segre 245, Ingram Publishing 200tr; **Bananastock:** Robert Harding 311; **Brand X Pictures:** Morey Milbradt 229t; **Corbis:** Aurora Photos / Peter Essick 365, © Colin Anderson / Blend Images 209, Image Werks 421; **Creatas:** photolibrary.com 388; **Datacraft Co Ltd:** 149; **Digital Stock:** 201t, 201b; **Digital Vision:** 202; **Getty Images:** PhotoDisc 113; **Glow Images:** Image 100. Corbis 240, OJO Images 261; **Imagestate Media:** John Foxx Collection 363, 428; **Mary Evans Picture Library:** 116; **MIXA Co Ltd:** 372; **Pearson Education Ltd:** Coleman Yuen 230cr, Gareth Boden 302, 376, Ian Wedgewood 108, Jon Barlow 33, 193, 208, 229b, 285, 420, 455, Jules Selmes 46, 178, 184b, Martin Beddall 165, MindStudio 230tl, Naki Photography 88, Sophie Bluy 230tr, Steve Shott 212, Stuart Cox 119, Studio 8 230cl, 328; **PhotoDisc:** 25, 200tl, 203, 226, Kevin Peterson 266; **Photolibrary.com:** Corbis / Guy Cali 231, Fanatic S. Photos India 41b; **Photos.com:** Aleksei Vasileika 377, Jupiterimages 2, Todd Arena 3; **Shutterstock.com:** archerix 81, Diego Cervo 228r, Dmitriy Shironosov 84 (Banner), Kheng Guan Toh 303, Losevsky Photo and Video 224, Luchschen 148, MIhai Simonia 4 (Banner), Ocsi Balazs 270 (Banner), Paul Matthew Photography 112, photoprince 179, pkchai 91, ra3rn 162c, rangizzz 244 (Banner), Ryan Carter 48 (Banner), Scorpp 152 (Banner), Stanislav Popov 235; **The Kobal Collection:** 20th Century Fox 120r, David FIlms/Jasin Boland 122, Studio Ghibli 120l, Walt Disney Productions 117; **Veer/Corbis:** Alliance 47, cienpies 380 (Banner), Coprid 162t, Deklofenak 213, entropic 182 (Banner), gunnar3000 424 (Banner), IKO 167, iofoto 335, kariiika 184t, kgtoh 267, Kheng Ho Toh 306 (Banner), Konstantin Sutyagin 183b, kovaleff 329, kuzma 212 (Banner), nruboc 182, Ragsac 48, rainerplendl 52, rudi1976 228l, sergej 117 (Banner), Sergej Khakimullin 241, Serghei Platonov 162b, Spectral-Design 342 (Banner), stillfx 41t, Take A Pix Media 227, Wavebreakmediamicro 414, Wong Sze Fei 183t; **www.imagesource.com:** 53, 230br

Cover images: *Front:* **Getty Images:** Don Farrall

All other images © Pearson Education

Picture Research by: Jane Smith

Microsoft product screenshots reprinted with permission from **Microsoft Corporation**.

Adobe product screenshots reprinted with permission from **Adobe Systems Incorporated**.

Every effort has been made to contact copyright holders of material in this book. Any omissions will be rectified in subsequent printings if notice is given to the publishers.

About this book

This book is designed to help you through your BTEC First Information and Creative Technology qualification.

About your BTEC First Information and Creative Technology

Choosing to study for a BTEC First Information and Creative Technology (I&CT) qualification is a great decision to make for lots of reasons. You will learn about the online world and technology systems, develop the skills to create and work with digital assets including audio and graphics, and have the opportunity to develop apps and work with other software. This qualification will help to make you technology savvy, equipping you with the skills valued by employers in any career you wish to pursue, but will particularly prepare you for a career using I&CT. In addition, a BTEC First Information and Creative Technology qualification can help you to progress to the next level of study.

About the authors

Eddie Allman spent over 20 years working in industry and commerce before moving into education later in his career. He taught vocational computing, mainly BTEC, for over 10 years, during which time he became involved in writing, moderating and verifying. Now largely retired, Eddie serves on the 'Ask the Expert' team.

Ben Elson has 6 years' experience of teaching BTEC Level 3 Creative Media (Interactive Media & Games Development). He coordinates assessment and quality assurance across the College, and has a focus on moving students onto relevant Higher Education. He has also run a photography business, and his specialist fields include 3D design and animation, video production, photography and computer game design.

Alan Jarvis has been teaching in further education for over 18 years and has delivered BTEC courses in IT at Levels 2 and 3. He been involved in verifying and been an author of several student books and teaching resources, including previous editions of this book. His specialist fields include computer hardware, programming and robotics.

Richard McGill is a highly skilled programmer, hardware guru and networking expert who has worked in FE as a course team leader and lecturer for over 25 years. He has collaborated on many textbooks and course support materials using the wealth of knowledge he has gained from teaching and verifying.

Allen Kaye has taught Computer Science and Business from Level 1 to degree level. He was heavily involved in the emerging national IT scene as Treasurer and later Chair of the North London branch of NAITFE and NILTA. Allen has been part of the author team on a number of student and teacher resources, and has written a number of computing articles for specialist publications.

Daniel Richardson has been lecturing in sixth form and further education for several years on a wide variety of BTEC First and National IT units. He is currently an ICT programme leader and lead internal verifier for a sixth form college. He has been an author of many textbooks on the subject.

Neela Soomary has been working in education for over 20 years, delivering BTEC courses in IT at Levels 2 and 3, along with a wide range of other courses. She currently works as a freelance assessor and verifier for several training providers on Apprentice programmes. She has been an author of several student books and teaching resources.

Paul Winser has been in education for over 15 years and has delivered BTEC courses in IT from Level 2 to Level 5. He has been an author for several student and teacher resources. Paul is a member of the British Computer Society and the Chartered Management Institute. His specialist fields include software development, web design, computer hardware and software, and computer networking.

How to use this book

This book contains many features that will help you use your skills and knowledge in work-related situations, and assist you in getting the most from your course.

These introductions give you a snapshot of what to expect from each unit – and what you should be aiming for by the time you finish it.

How this unit is assessed

Learning aims describe what you will be doing in the unit.

A learner shares their experience in relation to the unit.

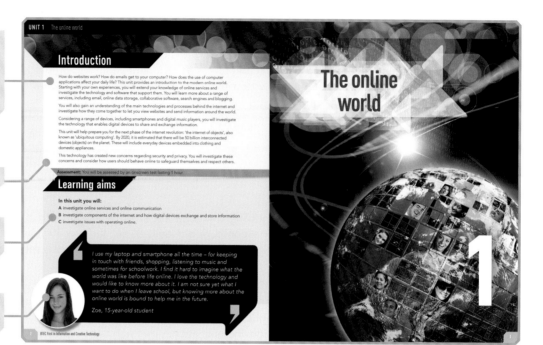

Features of this book

There are lots of features in this book to help you learn about the topics in each unit, and to have fun while learning! These pages show some of the features that you will come across when using the book.

Learning aims references show which parts of the BTEC you are covering on these pages.

Getting started with a short activity or discussion about the topic.

Key terms appear in blue bold text and are defined either within the text or in a key term box on the page.

Also see the glossary for definitions of important words and phrases.

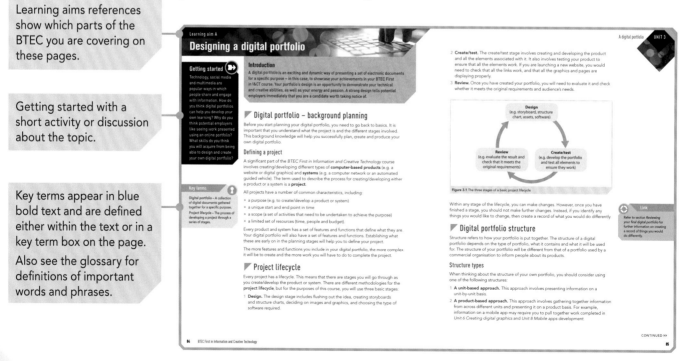

Activity 3.11

Review the user feedback and make a note of any feedback that caused you to make modifications, as well as any that could lead to future modifications.

Carefully consider what improvements could be made to your portfolio.

Keep your notes, as they may help you in your final assessment.

> Activities will help you learn about the topic. These will be done in pairs or groups, or sometimes on your own.

Assessment activity 4.4

| 1C.6 | 2C.P6 | 2C.M5 | 2C.D4 |

Barry is very happy with your animation. But how do you think it went? Look back over the design process and the finished product to see if you could make any improvements.

- Compare your final animation with your design brief.
- Does the animation include the key points Barry wanted it to? Explain how.
- Do you think your animation will appeal to Barry's target audience?
- Where there any problems you experienced when sourcing graphics or audio for the animation?
- Identify some areas where you could improve your animation.

Tips

- Explain why you made any changes.
- Refer back to the feedback you received from other people to consider what further improvements you could make.

> Activities that relate to the unit's assessment critera. These activities will help you prepare for your assignments and contain tips to help you achieve your best results. (For all units **except** Unit 1 and Unit 2.)

Just checking ✔

1 Name five examples of digital products.
2 What is the purpose of using graphics?
3 Why is the selection of digital images so important?

> Use these to check your knowledge and understanding of the section you have just covered.

Someone who works in the Information and Creative Technology industry explains how this unit of the BTEC First applies to the day-to-day work they do as part of their job.

WorkSpace

▶ Sally Blake

Sound archivist

I work as a sound archivist at a museum in London. It's a fascinating job in general, but even more so for someone like me who is interested in history and enjoys a challenge!

The museum has a large collection of historical audio recordings, all of which are held on a variety of analogue media, such as gramophone records, reel-to-reel tapes and cassette tapes. Some of the very old recordings were made on wax cylinders and magnetic wires. Most of these recordings are in such poor condition that they will soon decay to the point where we can no longer save them.

Because some of the tapes are in such poor physical condition (due to age, dust and mould), they have to be cleaned up before we can even try to play them. I have a range of analogue playback equipment connected to my computer, including reel-to-reel and cassette tape players and gramophone turntables. Once I have converted the recording to digital format, I then have to adjust the recording to achieve the best possible result. I also have to update the file's metadata and add in details of what the recording is and when it was made. This enables historians to search for information relevant to their research.

Some of the material is really fascinating. The project I'm currently working on involves the recollections of a solider from World War I, recorded on a gramophone record in the 1920s, shortly after the war ended.

Think about it

1 What sort of skills (both technical and other skills) do you think Sally needs to do her job?

2 What challenges does she face in her day-to-day work?

3 What do you think she likes best about her job?

This section also gives you the chance to think more about the role that this person does, and whether you would want to follow in their footsteps once you've completed your BTEC.

167

BTEC Assessment Zone

You will be assessed in two different ways for your BTEC First Information and Creative Technology qualification. For most units, your teacher/tutor will set assignments for you to complete. They may take the form of projects where you research, plan, prepare, and evaluate a piece of work or activity. The table in the BTEC Assessment Zone explains what you must do in order to achieve each of the assessment criteria. Each unit of this book contains a number of assessment activities to help you with the assessment criteria.

> The table in the BTEC Assessment Zone explains what you must do in order to achieve each of the assessment criteria, and signposts assessment activities in this book to help you to prepare for your assignments

Assessment criteria

Level 1	Level 2 Pass	Level 2 Merit	Level 2 Distinction
Learning aim A: Design a digital portfolio			
1A.1 Identify the audience and purpose for the design of a digital portfolio. **Assessment activity 3.1, page 17**	**2A.P1** Describe the audience and purpose for the design of a digital portfolio. **Assessment activity 3.1, page 17**	**2A.M1** Produce detailed designs for a digital portfolio, including: • alternative solutions • detailed storyboard of the layout and content of pages • a detailed structure chart with complete navigation routes • fully referenced sources for the ready-made assets. **Assessment activity 3.1, page 17**	**2A.D1** Justify the final design decisions, explaining how the digital portfolio will: • fulfil the stated purpose • meet the needs of the intended audience. **Assessment activity 3.1, page 17**
1A.2 Produce designs for a digital portfolio, with guidance, including: • outline storyboards of the layout and content • a list of ready-made assets to be used. **Assessment activity 3.1, page 17**	**2A.P2** Produce designs for a digital portfolio, including: • a timeline for the project • a storyboard of the layout and content of pages • a structure chart indicating navigation routes • a list of ready-made assets to be used, including sources. **Assessment activity 3.1, page 17**		

> Activities in this book will show you the kinds of task you might be asked to do to meet these criteria when your tutor sets an assignment.

A Questions where the answers are available and you have to choose the answer(s). *Tip: Always read carefully to see how many answers are needed and how you can show the right answer.*

Examples:

Which of the following is an online commerce service? Select the correct answer. [1]

A Train timetable

B Online tax return

C Online auction website

D Instant messaging

Answer: C

What name is given to the device that directs the traffic over the internet? Select the correct answer. [1]

A Modem   C Client

B Server   D Router

Answer: D

> Unit 1 and Unit 2 of your BTEC are assessed by an on screen exam. The BTEC Assessment Zone in these units will help you to prepare for your exam by showing you some of the different types of questions you will need to answer.

Study skills

▋ Planning and getting organised

The first step in managing your time is to plan ahead and be well organised. Some people are naturally good at this. They think ahead, write down commitments in a diary or planner and store their notes and handouts neatly and carefully so they can find them quickly.

How good are your working habits?

Improving your planning and organisational skills

1 Use a diary to schedule working times into your weekdays and weekends.

2 Also use the diary to write down exactly what work you have to do. You could use this as a 'to do' list and tick off each task as you go.

3 Divide up long or complex tasks into manageable chunks and put each 'chunk' in your diary with a deadline of its own.

4 Always allow more time than you think you need for a task.

▋ Sources of information

You will need to use research to complete your BTEC First assignments, so it's important to know what sources of information are available to you. These are likely to include the following:

Take it further

If you become distracted by social networking sites or texts when you're working, set yourself a time limit of 10 minutes or so to indulge yourself. You could even use this as a reward for completing a certain amount of work.

Key term

Bias – People often have strong opinions about certain topics. This is called 'bias'. Newspaper or magazine articles, or information found on the internet, may be biased to present a specific point of view.

Remember!

Store relevant information when you find it – keep a folder on your computer specifically for research – so you don't have to worry about finding it again at a later date.

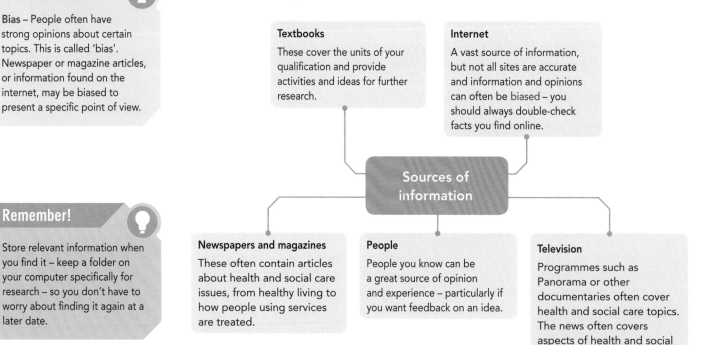

Textbooks
These cover the units of your qualification and provide activities and ideas for further research.

Internet
A vast source of information, but not all sites are accurate and information and opinions can often be biased – you should always double-check facts you find online.

Sources of information

Newspapers and magazines
These often contain articles about health and social care issues, from healthy living to how people using services are treated.

People
People you know can be a great source of opinion and experience – particularly if you want feedback on an idea.

Television
Programmes such as Panorama or other documentaries often cover health and social care topics. The news often covers aspects of health and social care such as the NHS.

Organising and selecting information

Organising your information

Once you have used a range of sources of information for research, you will need to organise the information so it's easy to use.

- Make sure your written notes are neat and have a clear heading – it's often useful to date them, too.
- Always keep a note of where the information came from (the title of a book, the title and date of a newspaper or magazine and the web address of a website) and, if relevant, which pages.
- Work out the results of any questionnaires you've used.

Selecting your information

Once you have completed your research, re-read the assignment brief or instructions you were given to remind yourself of the exact wording of the question(s) and divide your information into three groups:

5 Information that is totally relevant.

6 Information that is not as good, but which could come in useful.

7 Information that doesn't match the questions or assignment brief very much, but that you kept because you couldn't find anything better!

Check that there are no obvious gaps in your information against the questions or assignment brief. If there are, make a note of them so that you know exactly what you still have to find.

▌ Presenting your work

Before handing in any assignments, make sure:

- you have addressed each part of the question and that your work is as complete as possible
- all spelling and grammar is correct
- you have referenced all sources of information you used for your research
- all work is your own – otherwise you could be committing **plagiarism**
- you have saved a copy of your work.

Key term

Plagiarism – If you are including other people's views, comments or opinions, or copying a diagram or table from another publication, you must state the source by including the name of the author or publication, or the web address. Failure to do this (when you are really pretending other people's work is your own) is known as plagiarism. Check your school's policy on plagiarism and copying.

Introduction

How do websites work? How do emails get to your computer? How does the use of computer applications affect your daily life? This unit provides an introduction to the modern online world. Starting with your own experiences, you will extend your knowledge of online services and investigate the technology and software that support them. You will learn more about a range of services, including email, online data storage, collaborative software, search engines and blogging.

You will also gain an understanding of the main technologies and processes behind the internet and investigate how they come together to let you view websites and send information around the world.

Considering a range of devices, including smartphones and digital music players, you will investigate the technology that enables digital devices to share and exchange information.

This unit will help prepare you for the next phase of the internet revolution: 'the internet of objects', also known as 'ubiquitous computing'. By 2020, it is estimated that there will be 50 billion interconnected devices (objects) on the planet. These will include everyday devices embedded into clothing and domestic appliances.

This technology has created new concerns regarding security and privacy. You will investigate these concerns and consider how users should behave online to safeguard themselves and respect others.

Assessment: You will be assessed by an onscreen test lasting 1 hour.

Learning aims

In this unit you will:

A investigate online services and online communication

B investigate components of the internet and how digital devices exchange and store information

C investigate issues with operating online.

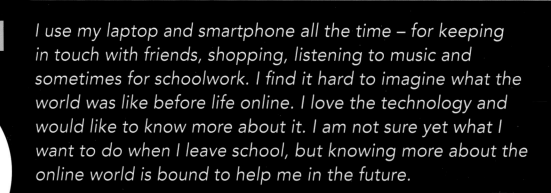

I use my laptop and smartphone all the time – for keeping in touch with friends, shopping, listening to music and sometimes for schoolwork. I find it hard to imagine what the world was like before life online. I love the technology and would like to know more about it. I am not sure yet what I want to do when I leave school, but knowing more about the online world is bound to help me in the future.

Zoe, 15-year-old student

The online world

1

Online services 1

Introduction

Every time that you connect to the internet, you are using online services. If you are passing information to other people or exchanging information with them, then you are using online communications. Online services and online communications can be used on any type of equipment: desktop computer, laptop, palmtop, mobile telephone or tablet.

In this section you will look at the use of online services and investigate the use of online document systems.

How online services can be used

Table 1.1 provides a summary of the different online services that are available. It lists some examples of everyday uses of these services and the advantages of using each service.

You will notice that there are overlaps between many of the services; for example, 'conferencing' could appear in both the 'Communication' and 'Business' sections.

Table 1.1 Examples of online services

Service	Types	Example uses	Benefits
1. Communication	Email, messaging, news groups, social networks, conferencing, blogs, vlogs	Talking to friends on Skype™. Using social networking applications like Facebook or Google+ to exchange information.	Instant responses to someone who is remote from you, at no additional cost to your broadband fees. Socialising.
2. Real-time information	Timetables, news, sport updates, weather reports, travel news	Checking an airport website for estimated arrival times of flights.	Provides up-to-date information when picking people up from an airport. Companies can use real-time information about customers' reactions to an advertisement to improve the effectiveness of the advert.
3. Commerce	Banking, auctions, online sales and purchases, publishing	Selling something through a service such as ebay™ or Amazon®.	Allows users to carry out transactions seamlessly (without the need to use physical money) and globally.
4. Government	Tax returns, e-voting, applications for grants or benefits	Applying for your first provisional driving licence.	Saves time and is more convenient – saves you a visit to the post office and means can take your time filling in the form and can easily amend any errors.

continued

Table 1.1 (*continued*)

Service	Types	Example uses	Benefits
5. Education	Online learning, online training, manufacturers' online tutorials	Using the Microsoft® training package for Windows® 7.	Allows you to do training from the comfort of your own computer and at your own pace.
6. Virtual learning environment (VLE)	VLEs such as Moodle	Your school or college may use a VLE for you to access lecture notes and assignments, and for you to submit assignment work.	Cost-effective for the school/college and allows the school/college to track the submission of learners' work.
7. Business (different types of organisations)	Business networks, collaborative working, video conferencing	Using a price comparison website is an example where you touch on business usage.	Allows you to get the best price for purchases.
8. Entertainment	Multi-user games, radio and TV players, video streaming	Playing a game with other people over the internet.	Enhances the gaming experience by allowing you to play against people you may not know.
9. Download services	Music, films, new software, software upgrades, games	Downloading music from a service such as iTunes® or Amazon®.	Makes purchasing easier and more affordable.

Activity 1.1

Think about how you use the internet and online services.

Working independently, list all the online services you use and provide examples of how you use each service. Swap your list with a partner and compare your lists. Discuss the different types of services you have both listed.

Working in small groups, discuss which services are most popular and why you think this is. Decide which services are most important for:

- businesses
- schools and colleges
- people wanting to communicate with friends and family.

Assessment tip

The uses and benefits of different types of online services is an important topic. Make sure you read Table 1.1 carefully and include it in your revision.

? Did you know?

Skype™ was bought by Microsoft® in 2011. Over 600 million people use Skype™ to communicate with each other.

↗ Take it further

Lots of industries use real-time information to track services. For example, train and bus companies use real-time information to inform passengers about arrival and departure times. Find out how real-time information is used by different industries and what it is used to track.

Online services 2

Introduction

Online advertising is a means of promoting products and services using the internet. It can be used to spread marketing messages widely to customers. Online data storage is another example of an online service.

Online advertising

Online advertising uses a number of methods to promote products and services. The most commonly used methods include:

- **Search engine results pages.** Companies can register with the bigger search engines (Google™, Bing, Yahoo!) so that their websites appear high up in a list of keyword searches or pay for links that appear when a user does a search.
- **Banner and pop-up advertisements.** These are advertisements that appear at the top of web pages or pop up on web pages. These are often animated to capture attention.

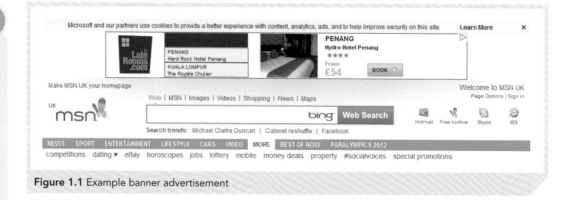

Figure 1.1 Example banner advertisement

- **Email marketing.** Uses email to send advertisements to customers (both potential customers and existing customers). However, customers often see this type of marketing as **spam** if it is sent as **unsolicited bulk emails**.

Online advertising is becoming a very popular means of promoting products and events, but it isn't always effective. In order to ensure that online advertising is effective, companies need to make sure that it:

1 Captures the attention of the target market through the use of design features (colour, layout, graphics, animation, for example in a banner advertisement) and is easily accessible.

2 Retains consumers' interest, for example by directing consumers to additional interactive information about a product, such as a video demonstration of the product. The speed with which the information loads is also important to make sure that consumers don't lose interest.

Link

Refer to section *Worldwide web 2* for futher information on search engines.

Did you know?

Forty-seven per cent of consumers expect an e-commerce page to load in two seconds or less. This is a key factor in user loyalty. For more information about this, see the press release from Akamai Technologies. (You can access this web page by going to www.pearsonhotlinks.co.uk and searching for this title.)

Google™ found that moving from a page displaying 10 results loading in 0.4 seconds to a page displaying 30 results loading in 0.9 seconds decreased traffic and ad revenues by 20 per cent.

Discussion point

Discuss in a small group what effect the increase in online advertising is likely to have on television.

Consider revenue, output, quality of advertising, etc.

Pay-per-click advertising

Pay-per-click (PPC) advertising is a form of online advertising. It involves websites or web pages hosting ads for other companies. If a surfer clicks on an ad, they will be redirected to the advertiser's website. The website or web page provider will receive a payment for every ad that is clicked on.

Pay-per-click advertising uses what is known as an **affiliate model**. Advertisements or links to a company's website are placed on other websites (affiliates) and in return the affiliate site receives a percentage of the income from any customer that clicks through. Google™ AdWords™, Yahoo! Search Marketing and Microsoft® adCenter are all big players in this field.

Online data storage

Data storage is another type of online service. Many organisations are providing facilities for you to store and back up your data on their computers, and to make files available to share with others. The current term used for online data storage is 'cloud storage'.

Data backup is a method of making copies of files. These copies can then be retrieved if disaster recovery is needed.

Assessment tips

Revise the features of online advertising, including the pay-per-click model.

Make sure you understand the features of online data storage.

Just checking

1　List three different ways of advertising online. Explain the differences between each type.

2　What is 'pay-per-click' advertising?

3　What is another term for online data storage?

Key terms

Spam – Junk email where identical messages are sent to a number of recipients.

Unsolicited bulk emails – Emails that are sent to a large number of people who haven't requested them.

Affiliate model – An 'affiliate' website is one that is attached to another company's website via a link. The affiliate website receives a percentage of the revenue from customers clicking through from their website to the other company's website.

Research

Find out more about pay-per-click advertising and how companies use it. Produce a short leaflet which describes the pay-per-click structure and gives reasons for and against this form of advertising. You can find helpful information on sites including Google™ AdWords™ and Pay Per Click Universe. (You can access these websites by going to www.pearsonhotlinks.co.uk and searching for this title.)

Link

Data backup is dealt with in more detail in the *Online documents* section.

File access, types of access and sharing of files are also dealt in the *Online documents* section.

Online documents

Introduction

Online documents (such as text documents, spreadsheets, presentations, graphics and forms) are any documents that are held on a computer but can be accessed, edited and shared from anywhere. Services which allow this include Live Documents, Microsoft® Office® Live and Google™ Docs.

Key terms

Upload – When you upload a file you move it from one system to another system. For example, you can upload files from your computer to a web page.

Download – This is when you move files from a system to your personal computer.

Algorithm – A mathematical step-by-step sequence used to work out calculations or carry out instructions.

Link

Unit 2 Technology systems provides an introduction to computer systems. The background knowledge from Unit 2 will be helpful in this section.

Compressing files

Working with online documents means that local files frequently need to be **uploaded** for sharing or **downloaded** to be used for local processing. Files may be extremely large, which can cause problems with transmission (delivery) in terms of speed and network usage. To reduce this problem, files have to be compressed (i.e. reduced in size) before transmission and then expanded after transmission. A common method of doing this is to convert them to zip files (.zip format).

Zip files are basically stores of data files which may have been compressed. There are many different **algorithms** for doing the compression – with most compression software supporting several of these. The last item in a zip file is an index, which shows the placement of each of the data files and allows other files to be added. Quite often the zip file will also contain some program code (a sequence of instructions) to allow the files within the zip file to be unzipped (known as self-extracting files).

There is a wide range of software available for zipping files – one of the most popular of these is WinZip.

Activity 1.2

1 Practise zipping and unzipping files: first single files and then multiple files.
2 Write a short instruction guide on how to do this. Aim your guide at people who are not particularly computer literate – so be sure to explain each step and what functions need to be carried out.

The advantages of using online software

The biggest advantage of using online document software is that you can allow many people to share a version of a document and work on it at the same time as other people (known as collaborative working). You can also access content:

- anywhere there is an available internet connection
- via different devices (e.g. PC, smartphone, tablet)
- on different operating devices (e.g. Windows® and Mac®).

Online documents can also have automatic backup. Backing up files means that you save a copy of the file at a known point in time. This means that you can always go back to that version if you lose or corrupt the present version.

Some software programs will automatically make a copy of the file you have open and are working on at set time intervals. In Microsoft® Word® you can set how often you would like the file to automatically backup (every 30 minutes, every 60 minutes, etc.). Automatic backup of online documents is just an extension of this concept.

Activity	1.3

Consider how file sharing can impact on collaborative working practices.

What are the advantages and disadvantages of using:

- online document sharing software
- standalone software

when working on a collaborative project?

Controls over online documents

Version control

Version control is important when users are sharing documents online, as all users need to be working from the most up-to-date version of the same document. One of the simplest ways of implementing version control is to allow just one user to open a document, or part of the document, for update at any one time. When one user has the document open and someone else tries to access it, the document will be **locked**. It is only unlocked when the original user has completed updating the file and has closed it again.

Other methods of version control include the software allocating the latest version number, showing the time and identity of the person making the changes. If, for any reason, a document does become corrupt (damaged) or is missing important updates, it is possible to roll back to a commonly agreed version number.

Levels of access and file permissions

The system administrator within an organisation can control the levels of access users have to a particular document. They can allocate access to individuals or particular groups of documents by using **file permissions**. Some users may only be able to read documents, but not edit them. Other users may be allowed to read and edit documents, some may be allowed to add new documents and some will be allowed to delete documents.

File permissions can be used to restrict access to certain documents and to restrict what can be done to them. An example within an accountancy business is shown in Figure 1.2.

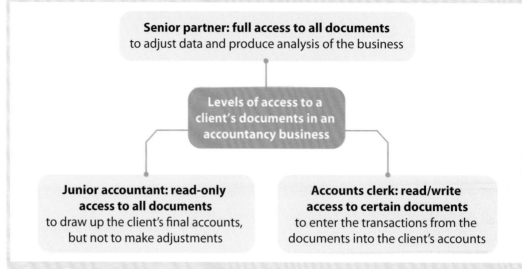

Figure 1.2 Examples of different levels of access required

- **Read-only access.** This allows a user to look at and read a document, but not to change it. A university lecturer could use a Word® document to create a test for their class. If they set the document as 'read-only', then the class will not be able to make any changes to the wording.
- **Read/Write access.** This allows a user to look at and read a document, but also to make changes to it.
- **Full control.** This allows users to retrieve a document, read it, edit it, add a new document or delete or archive an existing document. Full control is usually given to people who administer the system. They may be senior people within the organisation or senior administrators who report directly to senior management.

Activity 1.4

Using the internet to help you, make some brief notes on the reasons why particular protection levels need to be allocated to various users of an online document system.

Assessment tips

You need to know about compressing files.

Revise the advantages of using online software as compared to standalone software.

Make sure you understand the controls that are used with online documents.

Just checking

1 Name a common format for compressing files.
2 What is the main advantage of using online software?
3 List two different methods of controlling online documents.

Online communication 1

Getting started

Technology has changed the ways people communicate with each other. Find out what the most common forms of communication were 50 years ago, 100 years ago and 150 years ago. How do these methods compare with modern forms of communication?

Key terms

Online community – A virtual community which exists only online. It may be open to anyone (e.g. a bulletin board) or restricted by interest (e.g. various scientific communities).

Network of friends – A group of people who jointly keep in regular contact online. This may be a specific network, such as The National Youth Science Forum, or it may be more general, like a group of friends keeping in touch through Facebook.

Virtual world – An online community which meets in a computer-generated world, for example the large multi-player online games.

Netiquette – Short for 'internet etiquette' or 'network etiquette'. It is a set of conventions covering the use of networks used to interact with other people. The conventions are designed to prevent people causing annoyance or offence to others.

Chat – In this context, refers to any kind of online real-time communication over the internet.

Chatroom – Large-scale interactive conferencing with many people involved in the same conversation at the same time.

Introduction

One of the most common reasons for using the internet is to communicate. In this section you will find out about some of the different ways people communicate online.

Contemporary social media

People with common interests tend to gather together to exchange views and put forward ideas. Often this takes the form of a club such as a sports club or a society such as a historical society. However, the internet has had a dramatic impact on the way people communicate and share information.

Online communities

People who are computer literate, and have the equipment, can form groups or 'societies' online. These groups are known as **online communities** and they provide a place for people with similar interests to come together and exchange views. Where the community involves a group of people who keep in up-to-date contact with each other, they may be referred to as a **network of friends**.

Sometimes the communities exist in a **virtual world** online. This is an unreal world created by the computer. Popular examples include SecondLife, Twinity and Habbo. The *World of Warcraft* virtual world is another popular example of a large interactive gaming virtual world which supports multi-player gaming.

Communicating online requires a special behaviour or etiquette, known as **netiquette**. This is a set of rules designed to prevent abusive behaviour online. If a user breaks netiquette, then other users can report them.

Information exchanges

Online communities make use of contemporary social media to publish, access and exchange information. They use several online tools to do this:

- **Web logs (blogs).** These are frequently updated online journals with diary-like entries that allow people to express their thoughts and feelings and give details of their daily activities. Typically, a blog includes text, photos and sometimes video.
- **Microblogging sites.** These are sites that allow users to create and exchange very short text entries. A popular example of this type of site is Twitter™.
- **Wikis.** These are websites that provide information that visitors to the site can extend and edit. They allow users to share information and are useful for research. The best-known example of a wiki is Wikipedia, the online encyclopaedia that can be updated by contributors.
- **Chatrooms.** Online communication within communities is sometimes referred to as **chat**. Some of the large interactive communities where people take part in the same conversation or type of chat at the same time are known as **chatrooms**.

CONTINUED ▶▶

Discussion point

Find examples of online communities. What do you think the purpose of these communities is? What do you see as being the advantages and disadvantages of these communities?

Research

Find examples of netiquette from different sectors. As a starting point, you could look at the Core Rules of Netiquette on the Albion website. (You can access this website by going to www.pearsonhotlinks.co.uk and searching for this title.)

Create a set of netiquette rules for your college. There should be at least ten.

Key term

Profile – A user profile is a collection of personal data about a specific person. This may include biographical information, lists of interests and photographs.

Remember

One of the problems with wikis is that it is sometimes difficult to know how reliable and accurate contributions are. The sites are open to abuse from malicious contributors.

Podcasts

Podcasts are a series of audio or video files that can be downloaded from the internet. If video is published in episodes like a blog, this process is known as a vlog (video blog). YouTube is an example of a video-sharing website where individuals can share vlogs.

Virtual learning environments

A school community may make use of a virtual learning environment (VLE) to distribute resources, support learning and assess progress online. A VLE is an education system based on web facilities. The system is a virtual world that mirrors the real world of education – it contains learning materials, tests, projects, lectures/lessons and allows interaction between teachers and learners. The system also records and tracks learners' progress and performs other class management functions.

Sometimes the system can work in real time. Learners can communicate using microphones and speakers, or by text exchanges. At other times learners can be left to work at their own pace to meet specified deadlines. Lectures and lesson notes, as well as exercises, are all held on the system and can be accessed by learners.

Learners 'hand in' their work to their teacher electronically using the VLE. Teachers assess the work online and give feedback electronically via the VLE.

Social networking websites

Social networking sites, such as Facebook, Twitter™, LinkedIn, Google+ and MySpace, allow members of the online community to interact and communicate by setting up a **profile**. Users can then add links to friends' profiles and post personal information, including photographs, videos, favourite music and blog entries.

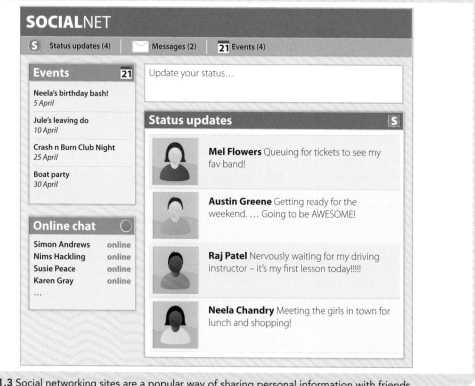

Figure 1.3 Social networking sites are a popular way of sharing personal information with friends

Online communication 2

Introduction

Online technology has radically impacted on the way people communicate. Not only has it changed the speed with which people communicate, but it has also had a positive impact on people's finances, as instant messaging and internet telephone services such as Skype™ are often cheaper than telephone calls.

Research

Some of the first social networking sites included Friendster, MySpace and Bebo.

How do these sites compare with Facebook and Google+? What features are different? Are people using social networking sites differently now compared with when they first started?

Did you know?

Instant messages can also include basic images, the most common of which are faces that show different expressions. These are referred to emoticons. Smiley faces are represented as :) and sad faces are represented as :(. You can also use emoticons to express a range of other expressions, such as laughing, crying, winking, happiness and anger.

Take it further

In pairs, create a series of instant messages to each other. You should use both text and emoticons in your messages.

Implications of online communication

Social networking

Social networking websites have changed the way that we communicate. They allow people to communicate interactively in real time anywhere in the world. Groups of like-minded people can share information, opinions and interests cheaply, normally for the cost of a broadband connection. Social networking provides a great way of staying in touch with friends and business contacts.

Instant messaging

Instant messaging provides a way to exchange textual messages as an alternative to the telephone and at a fraction of the cost. As messages are sent in real time, responses can be received instantaneously.

However, instant messaging does have its disadvantages:

- Emotions are better expressed in person and can sometimes be miscommunicated within an instant message that is sent quickly.
- Viruses can be spread by instant messaging.

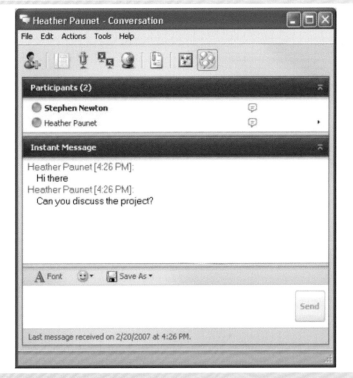

Figure 1.4 Instant messaging is used by businesses as well as by people socially

CONTINUED ▶▶

Voice over Internet Protocol (VoIP)

Voice over Internet Protocol (VoIP) allows people to interact in real time using voice and/or video messaging, and is available between any two points in the world. For internet-only conversations, there is no additional cost at either end. Skype™ is an example of a service that uses VoIP.

Being able to contact relatives and business colleagues on the other side of the world at relatively low cost is the biggest benefit. VoIP software is often used by businesses for online conferences and meetings. This reduces travel costs, travel time (and therefore loss of productivity while travelling) and the cost of hiring a venue.

As with all new technology, VoIP has its limitations:

- **Reliability.** VoIP service is dependent on the quality and reliability of your broadband service and may not work if there is a power cut.
- **Voice quality.** Voices can sometimes be distorted or there may be long pauses between questions and answers.
- **Security.** As with all internet technologies, identity theft, viruses, spamming and phishing are all potential threats.

Link

Refer to section *Data exchange 1* for more information on Voice over Internet Protocol (VoIP).

Activity 1.5

1 Set up a wiki web page with content about online communities and explaining what a social networking site involves.
2 Invite a partner to join your wiki and ask them to add information about instant messaging.
3 Update the content of the wiki, making any changes or corrections that you think are necessary.
4 Review your wiki. Consider how useful it has been for sharing information and note any limitations or difficulties you have experienced.

Just checking

1 Give three examples of social media used online.
2 What does the term 'netiquette' mean?
3 What are the benefits and limitations of using VoIP?

Cloud computing and ubiquitous computing systems

Introduction

Exciting and relatively new technologies allow computing to be a seamless part of our everyday lives. **Cloud computing** allows users to save their files to 'the cloud' rather than their own computer so they can access their files anywhere, even on the move.

Ubiquitous computing, or 'the internet of objects', describes how computers are embedded into all sorts of objects we use in our daily lives, such as cars, kitchen appliances and even clothes.

Did you know?

The term 'cloud' is often used as a metaphor for the internet. The exact origin of the term cloud computing is unclear, but many people believe it comes from diagrams of computing and communications systems, which used clouds to represent networks.

Key terms

Cloud computing – This is when a computer uses services provided by another organisation's computer systems.

Servers – A computer hardware system which acts as a host for other computers on the same network.

Cloud storage – This is when a computer's storage, access and retrieval facilities are hosted by another computer system.

Research

Research how cloud computing and storage work and what they are used for. You could start by looking at the How Stuff Works website. (You can access this website by going to www.pearsonhotlinks.co.uk and searching for this title.)

Then produce a poster that provides details about cloud computing and storage, and their uses.

Cloud computing and cloud storage

Cloud computing means using computer services on another organisation's computers, which are known as hosts. The services are provided by organisations known as hosting companies.

Some well-known hosting companies for cloud computing include Amazon®, Microsoft®, Google™ and RackSpace. Cloud users can access software, data and storage on the host computers, which will be at a remote location. Users do this through a web browser or mobile app, without ever directly accessing the **servers** that the information is stored on.

Cloud storage is related to cloud computing – it is where only the storage, access and retrieval facilities are provided by the host provider, often via the internet.

The benefits to the customer and some concerns about cloud computing and storage are shown in Figure 1.5.

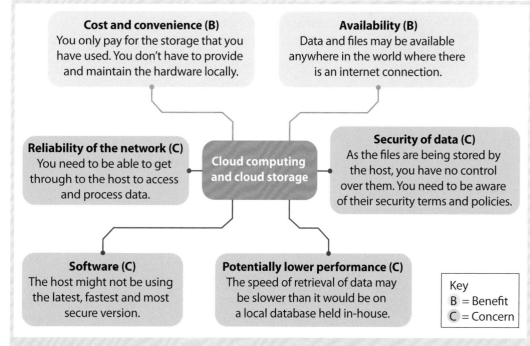

Cost and convenience (B)
You only pay for the storage that you have used. You don't have to provide and maintain the hardware locally.

Availability (B)
Data and files may be available anywhere in the world where there is an internet connection.

Reliability of the network (C)
You need to be able to get through to the host to access and process data.

Cloud computing and cloud storage

Security of data (C)
As the files are being stored by the host, you have no control over them. You need to be aware of their security terms and policies.

Software (C)
The host might not be using the latest, fastest and most secure version.

Potentially lower performance (C)
The speed of retrieval of data may be slower than it would be on a local database held in-house.

Key
B = Benefit
C = Concern

Figure 1.5 Benefits of, and concerns about, cloud computing and storage

CONTINUED ▶▶

Ubiquitous computing systems

Ubiquitous means 'existing everywhere'. Processors can be embedded in any device, including clothing, appliances, vehicles, buildings and people, to connect them to the internet so that the data generated by the processors will be readily available.

Radio frequency identification (RFID)

Currently, objects within a ubiquitous computing environment usually contain **radio frequency identification (RFID)** chips. RFID is a technology that uses radio waves to transfer data to a tag on a person or an object so that the person/object can be identified and tracked. These tags contain information that is stored electronically and can be transmitted. It is similar to the bar code systems used in supermarkets, but unlike a bar code, RFID does not need to be scanned. An example of how RFID is used is the cat flaps that only open for the animal that has the correct chip in its collar.

Applications of ubiquitous computing

Currently, there are computing systems in place that monitor shelf and warehouse stock. This technology is used by many industries (supermarkets, book and DVD suppliers, car part manufacturers, etc.). When the stock reaches a certain minimum level, an order is automatically placed with the appropriate supplier electronically. This is usually done by a process in which the tills feed product sales to a central computer, which then calculates the present stock. Currently, manual checks still have to be made to allow for 'shrinkage' (loss due to theft or damage).

However, there are now experimental systems involving products that contain RFID. The RFIDs register when any product leaves the premises.

Some futuristic examples of ubiquitous computing include:

- a car that can inform the owner when it needs servicing, book itself into the garage and place orders for any parts needed
- a refrigerator that can monitor its contents, compile an order as food is used and add the items to the user's online shopping account.

Assessment tips

Make sure you understand the terms 'cloud computing' and 'cloud storage'.

You also need to understand the concept of ubiquitous computing.

Just checking

1 What do the terms 'cloud computing' and 'cloud storage' mean?
2 Give three advantages and three disadvantages of cloud computing/storage?
3 What does the acronym RFID stand for? What is it used for?

The internet

Introduction

There is more to the internet than just the worldwide web. In the following sections you will find out about some of the other things you can do on the internet, including email, data exchange and the use of wireless networks.

There are many specialist terms associated with the internet. You need to be able to recognise these and understand what they mean.

Key internet terms

The internet is simply a worldwide computer **network** that uses standardised communication **protocols** to transmit and exchange data.

The internet has a whole vocabulary of its own. Table 1.2 explains some of the terms that you need to be familiar with.

Table 1.2 Important internet terms

Term	Definition
Point of Presence (PoP)	An access point to the internet. Normally, it is a location that contains all of the hardware that allows internet users access to the internet. An Internet Service Provider (ISP) may operate several PoPs in their area to allow good access to the internet.
Network Access Point (NAP)	An interchange between networks within the internet. It allows ISPs to interconnect with each other.
Internet Protocol (IP)	The protocol used to route packets of information across the internet. A packet is an individual unit of data that is carried across a network, including the internet. It is made up of a header which identifies the packet and a body which is the actual data message. It is one of the functions of the Transmission Control Protocol (TCP) to organise an internet message into packets.
Transmission Control Protocol (TCP)	The protocol that takes data from a user's application program and passes it to the IP for transfer across the internet. The reverse operation is performed at the destination computer, where the TCP reassembles the data (from individual packets) and forwards them to the user's application program. The close relation of the TCP with the IP means that the terms are usually used in combination as TCP/IP.
File Transfer Protocol (FTP)	A standard protocol that allows files to be transferred between two computers on a TCP-based network. It is commonly used to download programs to your computer from other servers and to upload web pages that you have created to the server that is hosting them on the internet.
Internet Service Provider (ISP)	Direct connection to the internet would be very costly and so ISPs provide a cost-effective gateway for people and organisations to get onto the internet. In the UK there are many ISPs – some of the most popular ISPs are BT (British Telecom), Virgin Media and Sky.
ISP services	As well as providing a gateway to the internet, ISPs normally provide additional services such as email. Many also provide web space for the development of websites, technical support and troubleshooting.

CONTINUED ▶▶

▶ Internet infrastructure

The internet is essentially a huge client–server system of interconnected computers that uses a wide range of hardware. Some of the main components of the internet's infrastructure are described in Table 1.3.

Table 1.3 Internet infrastructure

Infrastructure term	Description
Server	A computer or program that runs purely to serve the needs of other computers. It runs special server software to service the requirements of the users (clients). There are several types of servers, including file servers and printer servers on a local area network (LAN), and web and email servers that manage communication with the internet.
Client	A computer that uses the services provided by the server.
Router	A piece of hardware that connects two or more networks. In relation to the internet, data from the ISP is sent into the network and the router then directs the data packets to the correct destinations. The router also handles data travelling in the other direction. Routers can be described as 'directors of traffic' for the networks.
Connecting backbone	The main connecting data routes between large networks on the internet and smaller networks in local regions.

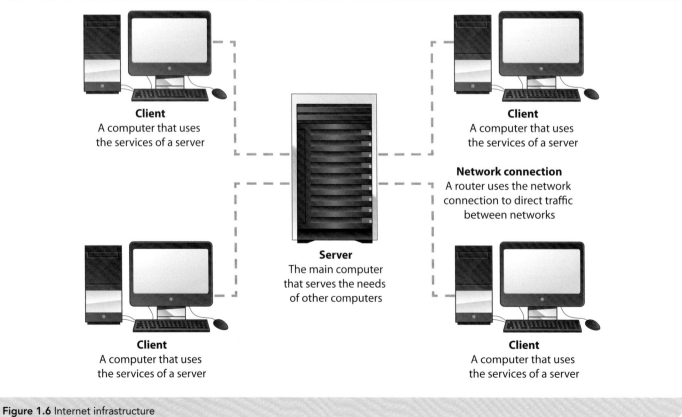

Figure 1.6 Internet infrastructure

Internet connection methods

There are three methods for connecting to the internet, as described in Table 1.4.

Table 1.4 Internet connection methods

Connection method	Description	Advantages	Disadvantages
Wireless	Used by wireless-enabled devices (computers, mobiles, smartphones, etc.) to log in to the internet. Wireless is exactly what it says; there are no wires to connect.	Not fixed to a stationary computer. Can be used wherever there is a wireless hub that is accessible.	Need to have access to a wireless hub. Can be less secure than wired connections. Tends to have slower data transmission speeds than wired broadband methods.
Broadband	A wired connection to a broadband supplier. Normally the connection is via a network card in the computer. Cable users have an **ethernet** connection from their computer to the network.	Broadband connections can give better reception and are usually faster than dial-up.	Requires a base that is wired in, so it is less flexible than wireless.
Dial-up	A wired connection via a conventional telephone line, which needs a modem to convert signals to and from analogue for transmission.	Can use existing telephone circuits, which is useful in some areas.	Older technology gives poor reception at times. The conversion from digital to analogue signals can cause errors. Tends to be slower than other connection methods.

Bandwidth and transmission rate

Bandwidth is a measure of the available capacity of a network (to carry data) measured in **bits** per second.

The transmission rate is a measure of the number of pieces of information that have been transferred during a specific time period, usually measured in bits per second.

A high bandwidth means more information can be carried in a given time, so a higher transmission rate is achieved. Insufficient bandwidth can result in websites and servers appearing to run very slowly.

Key terms

Ethernet – An ethernet cable is used to connect a user to a network.

Bandwidth – A way of measuring how much data can be carried over a network.

Bit – The amount of data transferred within a unit of time (i.e. bits per second).

Assessment tip

You need to know the infrastructure terminology used with the internet.

Just checking

1 What do the abbreviations IP, TCP and FTP stand for? What is each of these protocols used for?

2 Name the four main components of the internet infrastructure.

3 Explain the term 'bandwidth'.

Worldwide web 1

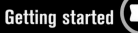

Getting started

The worldwide web (or WWW) and the internet are not the same thing. The WWW is a subset of the internet. The WWW consists of web pages that can be accessed using a web browser, whereas the internet is the network on which all the information sits.

What services are considered part of the internet but not part of the WWW?

Did you know?

Tim Berners-Lee developed the worldwide web in 1991.

Key terms

Hyperlink – A link (which can be text or a graphic) that takes you to another web page or location within a document.

Web server – It is the job of a web server to deliver web pages to users' computers.

Hypertext markup language (HTML) – A computer language used to create web pages.

Wizard – A sequence of dialog boxes that lead the user through a series of well-defined steps.

HTML element – An individual component of an HTML document.

Introduction

The worldwide web (or WWW) consists of millions of web pages linked together, plus the content that appears on those pages (such as text and images).

What is the worldwide web?

The content of the worldwide web is held on individual web pages, which are gathered together to form websites of associated information.

Web pages are connected using hyperlinks. A **hyperlink** is a link that, when clicked on, takes the website reader to another web page on the website or to a different website.

Websites are held on a computer called a **web server**, which is connected to the internet and delivers web pages to users' computers. When an internet user wants to look at a web page from a specific website, it is the web server's job to deliver (download) those pages to the user's computer.

Web pages are viewed through web browsers. These are software application programs that allow internet users to access, retrieve and view information on the internet. Internet Explorer® and Firefox® are two examples of web browsers that you can use. It is the web browser that reads document files written in **Hypertext Markup Language (HTML)** and translates them into viewable web pages.

HTML

HTML is a computer language used to create web pages. You can create HTML directly in the language itself or by using authoring software (such as Adobe® Dreamweaver® or Microsoft® Expression®), which uses templates and **wizards** to create HTML code. HTML files usually have a filename with .htm or .html as the file extension, for example **document.htm**.

HTML is a language that relies on a series of tags. Tags usually operate in pairs, as shown in the example in Table 1.5. There is an opening tag such as <body>, <bp> or <p>, and an end tag. End tags are identified by the '/' character at the beginning of the tag. For example: </body> closes the section of program called 'body'; </bp> closes the bullet point tag and </p> ends the paragraph 'p'.

Tags that don't operate in pairs include <img> (used to tag an image) and header tags (e.g. <h1>).

The content between each pair of tags is called an **HTML element**. The language is written as a series of elements. Gradually the elements build up to describe a web page. Table 1.5 gives a small, simplistic example.

Table 1.5 HTML structure

Example of html code	Description
<html>	An opening tag for the program
<body>	An opening tag for the section
<h1>This is a heading </h1>	Heading tag, content – element
<p>This is a paragraph</p>	Paragraph tag, content, end tag – element
</body>	End tag for the section
</html>	End tag for the program

Link

Refer to *Unit 13 Website development* for further information on the use of HTML in creating web pages.

In Table 1.5, the whole code is enclosed within the <html> </html> tags, which define this code as an HTML program. Then the section of working code in the example is written between the <body> and </body> tags.

Within this there are two HTML elements:

- A web page heading enclosed between the <h1> and </h1> tags. The example code in Table 1.5 will show 'This is a heading' as a heading on the web page.
- This is followed by a paragraph of text which is enclosed between the <p> and </p> tags. The example would show 'This is a paragraph' below the heading.

The whole web page is built up by writing these elements. There are tags used to colour the website, position objects such as text, graphics and media on the website and to do all of the other formatting that we see on websites.

Research

Explore how to write HTML code. There are lots of helpful examples on the internet. You could try the HTML Tutorial on the W3Schools website. (You can access this web page by going to www.pearsonhotlinks.co.uk and searching for this title.)

Try writing some HTML code using the examples given.

Create a small leaflet of the essential features of HTML.

```
<html>
<head>
<title> Music is my life </title>
</head>
<body>

<h1> Why music is good for the soul </h1>

<p> I love music. Every single type of music.
Music has the power to take you to new places. </p>

<p> My favourite old-style artist is Elvis Presley.
Here is a link to his website – check him out!
<a href="http://www.elvis.com/"> Elvis Presley</a>. </p>

<p> Although I love Elvis, I really hope to marry
Harry from One Direction some day. </p>

</body>
</html>
```

Figure 1.7 HTML code can be used to write simple web pages, such as your own music blog

Assessment tips

You need to know what the worldwide web is, and how it differs from the internet.

You need to be aware of the terminology used when talking about the worldwide web.

You need to know the role of HTML and hyperlinks in creating a web page.

Worldwide web 2

Introduction

As the worldwide web is made up of millions of web pages, each page must have a unique identity, so that it can be found by individual web browsers. This section looks at how web pages are identified and how **search engines** work.

URLs

Web pages are searched for using a **uniform resource locator (URL)**, which is a string of characters that identify a particular web page on the internet. Every web page has a unique URL.

URLs are made up of three components. An example is shown in Figure 1.8.

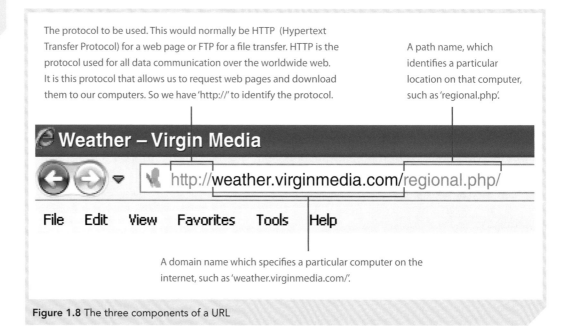

The protocol to be used. This would normally be HTTP (Hypertext Transfer Protocol) for a web page or FTP for a file transfer. HTTP is the protocol used for all data communication over the worldwide web. It is this protocol that allows us to request web pages and download them to our computers. So we have 'http://' to identify the protocol.

A path name, which identifies a particular location on that computer, such as 'regional.php'.

Weather – Virgin Media

http://weather.virginmedia.com/regional.php/

File   Edit   View   Favorites   Tools   Help

A domain name which specifies a particular computer on the internet, such as 'weather.virginmedia.com/'.

Figure 1.8 The three components of a URL

Search engines

If you don't know the name of a particular web page or want to find web pages on a particular topic, you can use a search engine to find it. Search engines such as Google™ and Yahoo! allow you to enter a description of what you are looking for and the search engine will search its indexes (databases of web pages) and find matching items. The items are normally presented in ranking order, with the most popular or relevant search results showing at the top of the list.

Search engines work by retrieving information from the HTML of web pages and storing this on an indexed database. An automated web browser (which is known by different names, including crawler, spider and bot) is used to follow every link in a website. Each page is analysed as it is found, and relevant data is extracted and stored on the search engine's index database.

When you enter a word or short phrase as a query, the search engine looks at its index and displays a list of the 'best matches', together with a short extract from each web page. With most general queries, there will be many hundreds or even thousands of matches, so the search engines operate a ranking system for their indexes. The ranking system is used to try to make the results of the searches relevant. However, as search engines are commercial businesses, other companies can pay money to improve their position in the ranking system.

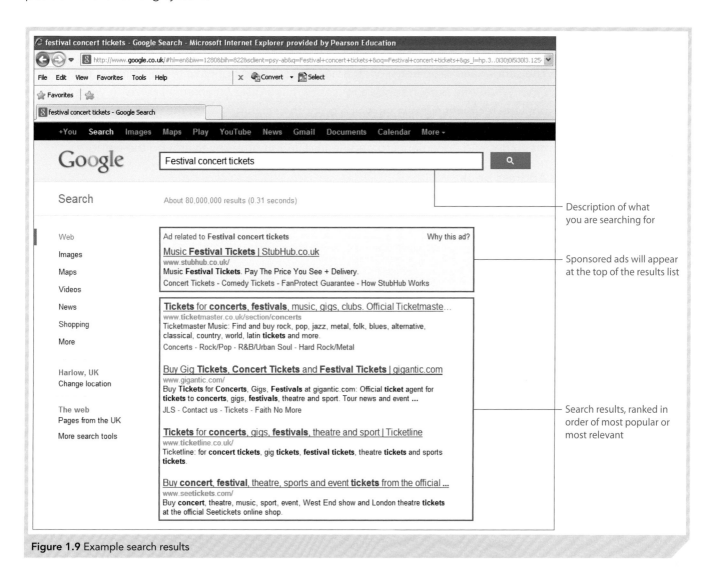

Figure 1.9 Example search results

Just checking

1 What do the acronyms HTML and URL stand for?

2 Give three examples of tags used in HTML code. Why do tags always have to come in pairs?

3 What are the three components that make up a URL?

Email

Getting started ▶

Get together in small groups and discuss the different email providers you all use. Compare and contrast the different features.

Key terms 🔑

Store and forward system – When an email is sent, it is stored on an email server and remains there until the recipient accesses their email account. It is at this point that the server forwards the message to them.

Address book – An email tool that allows you to store the names, email addresses and other contact details of people.

Attachment – A file or document that you attach and send with an email.

CC – Stands for carbon copy. You can copy in additional email recipients using this field.

BCC – Stands for blind carbon copy. You can copy in people to emails – but hide their identify and email address from other recipients – by entering them in this field.

Did you know? ❓

The term carbon copy dates back to when typewriters were used. In order to make copies of a letter or memo, a sheet of carbon paper was inserted under the original version and a sheet of blank paper was placed under the carbon paper. As a letter or memo was typed, a copied version would be transferred via the carbon paper to the blank sheet of paper.

Introduction

Email is short for 'electronic mail'. It is a system used to send digital messages from user to user.

▶ Using email

The sender and recipient(s) of an email message do not have to be online at the same time. When one person sends a message, it is stored on an email server. It waits in store until the recipient signs in, at which point the server forwards the message to them. The system is known as a **store and forward system**. This is of great benefit when sending messages and documents to people in different time zones around the world.

Address book

Within your email program, you can create a list of people's contact details (including name, email address, company name, phone numbers). This is known as an **address book.**

Attachments

You can send a message and attach files to it (such as photos, documents, spreadsheets). These files are known as **attachments**.

Multiple recipients

You can send the same message to a number of people. You can copy people in to the email using the **CC** (carbon copy) field. Recipients who are entered in this field will be visible to everyone the email is sent to. If you want to include a recipient on an email – but you don't want other people to see that the email has been sent to them – then you add them into the **BCC** (blind carbon copy) field.

1 – To field – where you enter recipients' email addresses
2 – Cc field
3 – Bcc field

Figure 1.10 The different email fields

Benefits and drawbacks of email

Email has undoubtedly changed the way individuals and companies communicate with each other on a global scale. There are many benefits and drawbacks of email, for example speed of delivery is a benefit and **hacking** is a drawback.

Benefits of email include:	Drawbacks of email include:
✓ Speed of delivery.	✗ Privacy and security. People can **hack** into your emails and read material that should not be available to them. Some of that material may pose a risk to your security, that of your employer or even that of the nation.
✓ Cost. Unlike the conventional mail system, there is no additional cost to the standard broadband charges.	
✓ Instant delivery on a global scale.	
✓ Delivery to multiple recipients.	✗ Internet access. The fact that both sender and recipient(s) have to have email accounts can be a problem. Some people do not have access to the internet (or choose not to use it), so you cannot assume that everyone has an email account.
✓ Attachments (e.g. documents and audio and video files).	
✓ Having a record of the correspondence between users.	
✓ Webmail providers (including Hotmail and Gmail) tend to store emails on a remote provider, meaning that you can access them anywhere via a web browser.	✗ Sometimes a lack of interactivity may be a problem. In situations where an instant reply or interactive discussion is needed, email does have limitations if the participants are not online at the same time.
	✗ Spam.
	✗ Viruses.
	✗ Phishing scams.

Key term

Hack – To use illegal means to access someone's email account or computer system.

Link

Refer to *Possible threats to data 1* for further information on phishing.

Emails can be sent instantaneously to multiple recipients on a global scale

CONTINUED ▶▶

◢ Email protocols

A separate system of protocols has been devised for use purely by email. An email protocol is a set of rules that allows computers to send and receive emails from a network. There are three basic protocols used by email, which are compared in Table 1.6.

Table 1.6 Email protocols

Protocol	Acronym	Description
Simple Mail Transfer Protocol	SMTP	The internet standard used for sending messages across IP networks in server-to-server transfers. Also used by email users to send a message to an email server.
Post Office Protocol 3	POP3	Used to retrieve emails from an email server over a TCP/IP connection. This is the most widely used email retrieval protocol. Normally users download emails to their local computer using POP3 – this deletes them from the email server.
Internet Message Access Protocol	IMAP	This is the other popular email retrieval protocol. Normally users work on the emails as they reside on the email server using IMAP and do not download them.

Research

Create a table of the important characteristics of:

- the internet
- the WWW
- email.

Include the history of each of these and the important developments, together with the names of some of the people responsible for the developments.

Activity 1.6

1 Carry out the following tasks:
- Add the email addresses of five friends to your email address book.
- Send the same email to these five friends.
- Ask each person to send a reply.
2 Carry out the following tasks:
- Create a group using the five email addresses in your address book.
- Send out an email to the group and add an attachment.
- Ask the members in your group to reply to the email and include an attachment.
3 Make notes about how you did each activity.

Discussion point

Businesses need to compete on an international scale and often people expect businesses to operate 24/7. Discuss how email helps businesses to achieve this. What are the advantages and disadvantages of this?

Assessment tip

You need to be able to describe what email is and how it is used. Don't forget the email protocols.

Just checking

1 What is a 'store and forward' system?
2 Give two benefits and two drawbacks of email.
3 Describe the differences between the three email protocols SMTP, POP3 and IMAP.

Data exchange 1

Key terms

Data – Any kind of information that has been formatted in a specific way. Different types of data include audio, video, images and monitoring signals, as well as text.

Devices/components – Used as a generic term to mean computers, peripheral hardware, mobile telephones, manufacturing plant, environment monitors and many other things.

Peripheral – Any device, such as a printer, attached to a computer to expand its functionality.

Codec – A device or program used to encode or decode data.

Internet packets – A formatted block of data sent over networks and the internet. A packet contains the addresses of the sender and destination, the data itself and error checking.

Introduction

Data exchange is the term used to cover all methods of passing data (including audio, video, images and text) between devices/components (computers, peripheral hardware, mobile phones, manufacturing machinery, environment monitors) and users over a network.

One network where data is exchanged is, of course, the internet, but data exchange takes place on networks of all types. This section looks at some of the ways in which data is exchanged over networks.

Voice over Internet Protocol (VoIP)

VoIP is a group of internet protocols that provides a means of sending voice and multimedia communication over the internet rather than by public telephone networks. Real-time communication has become more and more common, with communication by Voice over Internet Protocol (VoIP) growing in popularity.

Any computer system that has microphone input, speaker or headphone output and a broadband connection can be used to transmit and receive voice communication using this system. The addition of a webcam will allow multimedia transmission (the simultaneous transmission of video and audio). When many users have these facilities, web meetings and conferencing can be set up.

The software required to run a VoIP system consists mainly of an encoding and decoding program, which is often called a coder/decoder program (**codec**). This program is used, where necessary, to digitise an analogue voice signal, then compress it and split it into **internet packets** for transmission. It then performs the reverse at the receiving end.

VoIP is available over desktop and laptop computers, as well as many other internet devices such as smartphones. One of the most popular VoIP systems is Skype™.

Assessment tip

VoIP is important – revise everything you can about it.

Wireless networks

Wireless networks are another means by which data can be exchanged between a computer and a network, including the internet. A wireless network is any network servicing computers or other devices (e.g. mobile phones) in which the connections do not use cables of any kind. Wireless communication usually uses radio waves, but infrared communication is also used.

In wireless networking, all devices using the network need to have a wireless network interface card through which they gain access to the network. The card is used to transmit data across the network and to receive incoming data from the network.

The network itself will contain routers (see Table 1.3) and network access points (see Table 1.2).

Wireless networks have many advantages – probably the most important is mobility; people are no longer tied to desks and wires.

CONTINUED ▶▶

Alternative transmission methods

Table 1.7 introduces some of the methods of transmission used, and describes some of the benefits and limitations of each method.

Table 1.7 Alternative transmission methods

Type	UTP/STP	Coaxial	Fibre optic	Infrared	
Details	Unshielded twisted pair (UTP) cables are basic pairs of cables twisted together. Shielded twisted pair (STP) cables are similar but have a foil shielding.	Solid wire core separated from a copper-braided outer cable by a plastic insulation sheath. The inner cable transmits the data and the outer cable connects to earth.	Glass or plastic cables that use total internal reflection of light to transmit data. Normally uses LED or laser visible light, although infrared has also been used.	Short range data transmissions using infrared light (just beyond visible light). This is the same technology as is used in TV handsets.	
Maximum data transfer rate	250 **Mbps**	1000 Mbps (or more for Category 7 cable)	2.4 **Gbps** (higher has been achieved in laboratory testing)	4 Mbps	
Maximum range	100 m	100 m	50 km	100 m	
Benefits	Twisting cancels out some interference. Very low cost and adaptable.	Fast and reliable.	Fast. Works over long distances. Little interference.	Tends to be reliable.	
Limitations	Slower and with less capacity than other cables, and can only be used over short distances. Susceptible to noise.	Costs more than UTP/STP. Susceptible to noise.	Complex connection and termination equipment.	Short range. Devices must be in a direct line of sight. Can suffer from external interference.	
Example of how it is used	Analogue telephone network.	Connection to cable TV networks. Aerial/dish connection to TV.	The cable networks use fibre from their source to the distribution panels in the street. From there they use coaxial cable to individual households.	Keyboard, printer, mouse to processor unit. Handsets.	

continued

Type	**Microwave**	**Satellite** – (high frequency, 1 to 50 GHz range, radio signals)
Details	Short wavelength radio transmissions working at very high frequencies.	Data is transmitted from Earth to a satellite, which relays it to the relevant receiving station back on Earth.
Maximum data transfer rate	300 Gbps	Huge
Maximum range	100 m	Between about 500 km to 36,000 km
Benefits	Signal degrades very little over long distances.	Can increase the distance a network can reach.
Limitations	Devices must be in a direct line of sight. Can be affected by rain, pollen and **sun spot activity**. Can suffer from external interference.	Expensive.
Example of how it is used	Earth to satellite communication. Bluetooth.	Global communication systems.

Key terms

Mbps – Stands for megabits per second. A medium with a transmission rate of 1 Mbps can transmit approximately one million bits per second.

Gbps – Stands for gigabits per second. A medium with a transmission rate of 1 Gbps can transmit approximately one thousand million bits per second.

Sun spot activity – From time to time there is the equivalent of a huge wave of flame released from the surface of the Sun. This releases millions of charged particles, some of which hit the Earth. These can cause disruption to data transmissions.

Geostationary satellite – A satellite orbiting the Earth at a height of 35,786 km and at the same speed that the Earth is rotating. It therefore appears to be stationary above a single point on the Earth's surface.

Data exchange 2

Introduction

Devices on a network use a variety of methods to communicate with each other and to transmit data. This section looks at these methods in more detail, and explains client-side and server-side processing.

Transmission modes

There are three common modes of transmission:

1 **Simplex transmission:** sends data in one direction only. A radio broadcast is a good example of simplex transmission.

2 **Half-duplex transmission:** allows two-way transmissions, but the devices don't transmit at the same time. A system being used to monitor and control manufacturing processes can use half-duplex transmissions. It will send a message to the control computer, which will respond with new settings, but they cannot both send messages at the same time. Some network systems use half-duplex to maximise bandwidth.

3 **Full duplex transmission:** allows two-way communication at the same time. The telephone system, land or mobile, is an example of a full duplex system.

Parallel and serial transmission

Parallel transmission

In parallel transmission, a number of bits of data are transmitted simultaneously over an equal number of wires/channels. This allows the bits in a whole **byte** of information to be transmitted together. It has a short range, with an absolute maximum of around 5 metres.

Parallel transmission used to be popular for connecting printers to computers, but it is rarely used these days in computing because of its cost and limited range.

Serial transmission

In serial transmission, bits are transmitted one at a time over a single wire/channel. This reduces the cost of the cable, but gives a slower rate of data transfer. There is also some additional complexity, as bytes have to be disassembled into individual bits for transmission and then reassembled after receipt. Serial transmissions can be used over large distances.

Universal serial bus (USB)

Universal serial bus (USB) is a serial transmission method that was introduced to make many of the connections to a computer look the same. Nowadays, USB is used in a wide variety of devices, such as mobile telephones, memory sticks and MP3 players. USB ports also supply power to some devices.

The maximum theoretical transmission rate for USB 2.0 is 480 Mbps, but this is shared among all devices on a USB hub, so the rate for each device will be less than this.

Key terms

Byte – In computing and telecommunications, a byte is a unit of digital information which commonly consists of eight bits. (See page 19 for a definition of bits.)

Universal serial bus (USB) – A higher-speed serial connection standard that supports low-speed devices (e.g. mice, keyboards, scanners) and higher-speed devices (e.g. digital cameras).

Did you know?

There has been some increased usage of parallel approaches in radio frequency (RF) transmissions. Parallel buses are still used within central processing units (CPU).

Further details can be found in *Unit 2 Technology systems*.

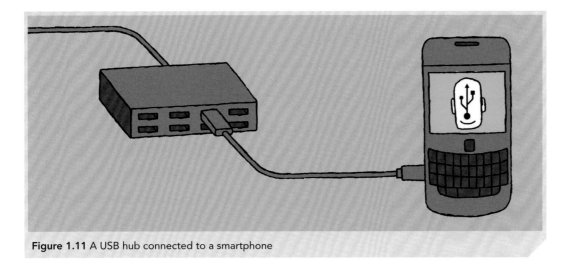

Figure 1.11 A USB hub connected to a smartphone

Bi-directional transmission

Bi-directional transmission has several meanings within data communication, but it is essentially about transmitting in both directions. Most recently, the term has been applied to fibre optics. Using the current technology, light passes in one direction only, so you have to add extra fibres to the bundle to carry a signal in the opposite direction.

Client-side processing

Client-side processing is the use of a scripting language to create code that provides interactivity on web pages. The important point is that the interaction takes place within the web page and the code is downloaded to the user's computer when the web page is opened by the user's browser.

A good example of a client-side interaction is a roll over (often called a mouseover), where some code is triggered when you move the mouse over a particular part of the web page. This might be something simple like the display of an advertisement, or it could be a demand for some data entry (e.g. filling in your details on a social networking website).

Benefits of client-side processing include:

✓ **Speed:** The interaction may be faster once the code has been downloaded with the page.
✓ **Security:** It is more secure (than server-side processing) as all the action takes place in the downloaded page and nothing comes from the browser, which could cause corruption or security problems.

Disadvantages of client-side processing include:

✗ **It is browser specific:** Not all scripts work the same way on all browsers, so you may have to create different versions depending on the browsers used.
✗ **Computer speed:** It can be affected by the speed of your own computer. As all of the activity is taking place on a downloaded web page, the speed of the download and the speed of processing will depend on your computer system. If the processing is complex or resource hungry, it may run slowly or cause other programs to run slowly on your system.

CONTINUED ▸▸

? Did you know?

A lot of research has been carried out to try to develop bi-directional transmissions using light, as this would give a cost reduction of at least two (i.e. it would halve the cost).

Key term

Client-side processing – When the interaction between a web page and code occurs directly on a user's computer.

Discussion point

There are many examples of client-side scripts on the web. Have a look at the JavaScript (a computer language) examples on the University of York website. (You can access the relevant web page by going to www.pearsonhotlinks.co.uk and searching for this title.)

- Discuss in a small group how you could use client-side scripting.
- List examples of client-side processing.
- Write some simple scripts.

Key term

Server-side processing – When the interaction between a web page and a computer is processed through a server.

Research

There are lots of good examples of server-side scripting on the web. Identify three examples.

Have a look at these examples and search for other material using a suitable web search engine.

Create a leaflet listing examples of some of the server-side processes.

Server-side processing

Server-side processing involves the use of scripts that reside and are run on another computer on the internet (the web server). Information is submitted to a server, which processes it to provide results in the form of a web page.

A good example of server-side processing is the submission of a search through a search engine. The search engine matches the word or phrase against an index of website content on the web server using scripts.

Benefits of server-side processing include:

✓ **Efficiency:** Complex code may run more efficiently, as it does not have to be downloaded on to the user's computer.

✓ **Browser independent:** The code is browser independent, so it can be run on any web browser.

✓ **Speed:** Performance is affected only by the speed of the web server. As all of the processing is done on the web server, the speed of your own computer is only significant for the downloading of the web pages. All of the other processing takes place on a highly resourced and speedy server.

Disadvantages of server-side processing include:

✗ **Security:** The exchange of data over the network may present security risks.

✗ **Overloading:** A server needs to be able to cope with large volumes of users.

Assessment tip

Learn the difference between server-side and client-side processing, including examples of each.

Just checking

1 Name three methods of transmitting data over a network, and give examples of what each is used for.
2 What does VoIP stand for and what is it used for?
3 Explain the difference between client-side and server-side processing.

WorkSpace

▼ Samia Matthews

Technical support technician

I took a holiday job with my current company before I started the BTEC National Diploma. I'd already taken the BTEC First Diploma in IT and I was keen to continue my studies. Part-way through the summer, the company offered me an apprenticeship as an alternative way of pursuing my education and earning some money at the same time. That was two years ago. When I complete the apprenticeship, the company is going to give me a job and help me continue with my education.

I work as part of a team, dealing with IT queries from staff members. Not everyone in the team is an expert in every field: each of us has developed knowledge in specialised areas, but we also need to have good all-round general technical knowledge. My specialist areas include threats to data, especially online threats, and I continually have to update my knowledge by attending courses and by doing lots of background reading. Some of the most up-to-date courses are provided by manufacturers and suppliers of hardware and software.

I work closely with a senior technician and between us we ensure that all the company's systems are equipped with the latest security software and that it is kept up to date. Any sign of a virus, or any form of sustained attack, means that we take priority action to identify and remove the problem. If we're unable to remove it, then we contain it and limit the damage until removal is possible. I like the adrenalin rush caused by a major security alert, even though most of these prove to be false alarms.

I really love my job. Down the line, I hope to progress to a managerial post in the technical support field.

Think about it

1 Why is it important for Samia to keep her skills and knowledge up to date?
2 What skills and qualities has Samia developed?
3 What do you think the benefits of taking an apprenticeship are?

Data storage 1

Getting started

What types of data do you think can be held on computer systems?

Choose four different sectors (e.g. healthcare, the media, leisure and tourism and the financial sector), and discuss in small groups the types of data each sector might need to store. Compare and contrast each sector's needs.

Do you think the same type of database could be used for each sector?

Introduction

The term data storage covers all of the many ways in which data is held. For the purposes of this unit, it means holding data on a computer system. The main way that we hold data on a computer is by using a database. This is simply a collection of data that is usually organised in some way. It is important that you understand not only what databases can do, but also how they are structured.

Database structure

A **database** is a system for managing a collection of data. Data about a particular type of thing – for example, customers or products – is stored in a **table**. You can think of a table as a grid. Every row in the table holds information about a single item; this is also called a **record**. Every column holds information about a property of the items in the table, such as a customer's name or an item's price – these properties are called **fields**.

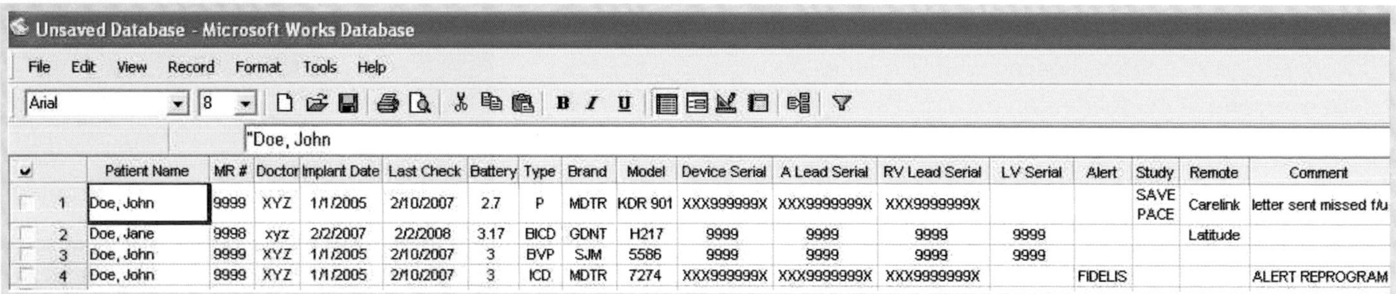
Unsaved Database - Microsoft Works Database

File Edit View Record Format Tools Help

"Doe, John

✔	Patient Name	MR #	Doctor	Implant Date	Last Check	Battery	Type	Brand	Model	Device Serial	A Lead Serial	RV Lead Serial	LV Serial	Alert	Study	Remote	Comment
1	Doe, John	9999	XYZ	1/1/2005	2/10/2007	2.7	P	MDTR	KDR 901	XXX999999X	XXX9999999X	XXX9999999X			SAVE PACE	Carelink	letter sent missed f/u
2	Doe, Jane	9998	xyz	2/2/2007	2/2/2008	3.17	BICD	GDNT	H217	9999	9999	9999	9999			Latitude	
3	Doe, John	9999	XYZ	1/1/2005	2/10/2007	3	BVP	SJM	5586	9999	9999	9999	9999				
4	Doe, John	9999	XYZ	1/1/2005	2/10/2007	3	ICD	MDTR	7274	XXX999999X	XXX9999999X	XXX9999999X		FIDELIS			ALERT REPROGRAM

Figure 1.12 Example of a table displayed in a Microsoft® database program

Link

Unit 10 Database development takes the subject further than in this short section.

Data types

Every field (column) in a database is set up to hold a certain type of data. The main data types are:

- **Text** (also called **characters** or **strings**): sequences of letters, numbers and other symbols. Someone's name would be a text field. A field that can accept multi-line text is often called a **memo** field.
- **Number:** represents a numerical value. A product's price or the number of items left in stock would be stored as numbers. This would enable you to produce a report summing up the prices of all the products you had sold, which wouldn't be possible if they were stored as text.
- **Date/time:** stores dates or a combination of dates and times.
- **Logical** (also called **Boolean** or **Yes/No**): represents a value that is either true or false. For example, when a customer opens an account with an online company, they might be asked whether they are happy to receive marketing material. Their answer could be stored in a logical field (true if they are happy to receive marketing information, false if they are not).

Did you know?

One of the reasons that data is displayed as a table is because people were familiar with the table format from printed information such as timetables and bank statements.

Relationships between database tables

A benefit of databases is the ease with which the information they hold can be accessed.

All tables have a **primary key**. The primary key is used to organise and sort data. The primary key is the unique identifier of each record in the table. The tables may themselves hold fields that are primary keys in other tables (**foreign keys**), which can be used to access associated information from many tables in one query.

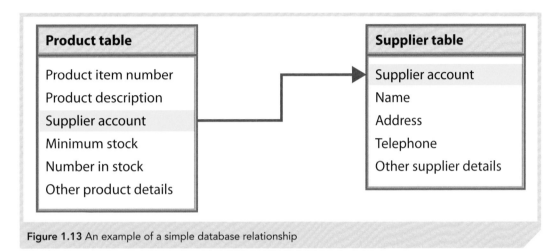

Figure 1.13 An example of a simple database relationship

In the example shown in Figure 1.13, the primary key of the product table is the product item number, as each product in the database has a unique number.

The primary key of the supplier table is the supplier account number, which is also held as a foreign key in the product table.

This allows you to find a product in the product table and at the same time find the supplier's details in the supplier table, and to display all of the information you want about both items.

This link using a foreign key is known as a relationship, and you can build up any number of relationships between different tables.

Relationships can be one-way (as shown in Figure 1.13), two-way, one-to-many or many-to-one. Many-to-many relationships also exist in some databases but are extremely complex to provide.

Key terms

Database – A collection of data stored in a structured way.

Table – A two-dimensional representation of data in a database.

Record – A group of selected data that is associated in some way.

Field – A single piece of data within a record.

Primary key – A single unique key used to identify each record in a table.

Foreign key – A field that can be used to cross-reference and access associated information across many tables.

Link

You can find further information on database structures and relationships in *Unit 10 Database development*.

Just checking

1 What are the main data types held within fields?
2 Explain what a primary key is.
3 Explain what a foreign key is.

Data storage 2

Introduction

Databases are simply collections of data held in a central place. How they are organised and how users engage with them can vary a lot, depending on what the information is and how it needs to be used.

Link

Refer to section *Worldwide web 2* for more information on search engines.

Refer to section *Cloud computing and ubiquitous computing systems*.

Online databases

Online databases are databases that are accessible using a network, including the internet. They are very different to local databases as they have to be accessed, and possibly updated, by millions of users. Normally, these databases will have thousands of rows of information. Usually, people find information in online databases by using a search engine.

Special database software is available to help users build online databases. Some of the basic software is free, but you will usually have to pay for upgrades to do more sophisticated things. The more sophisticated software usually incurs a charge (for example, KeepandShare, Vectorwise, Microsoft® Office® 365, Alventis™).

Quite often the data is held by a hosting service, which also supplies the software as part of cloud storage on the internet.

These online databases hold many different types of information, from databases of cartoons to databases of financial information.

id	Datetime	Magnitude	Region	Latitude	Longitude
1	*Edit column* 10 01:4	1.3	Northern California	38.83	-122.8	0
2	10 01:3	1.7	Greater Los Angeles area, California	34.03	-117.2	9.5
3	*Delete column* ...10 01:3	1.1	Central California	36.65	-121.28	6.3
4	Thursday, August 26, 2010 01:3	1	Southern California	33.43	-116.56	9.3
5	Thursday, August 26, 2010 01:2	2.9	Island of Hawaii, Hawaii	19.4	-155.43	10.8
6	Thursday, August 26, 2010 01:0	1.4	Central Alaska	63.25	-150.67	150.3
7	Thursday, August 26, 2010 00:5	1.2	Southern California	33.46	-116.58	12.8
8	Thursday, August 26, 2010 00:4	3.8	Anguilla region, Leeward Islands	18.04	-63.63	154.9
9	Wednesday, August 25, 2010 2:	1.5	Baja California, Mexico	32.44	-115.4	7.1
10	Wednesday, August 25, 2010 2:	1.4	Central California	36.58	-121.12	9.7
11	Wednesday, August 25, 2010 2:	1.5	Southern California	32.68	-115.88	8
12	Wednesday, August 25, 2010 2:	1.2	Northern California	38.83	-122.8	1.6
13	Wednesday, August 25, 2010 2:	5.2	Tonga	-21.85	-174.49	10
14	Wednesday, August 25, 2010 2:	1.3	Northern California	38.56	-122.46	8.7
15	Wednesday, August 25, 2010 2:	1.7	Central Alaska	64.77	-146.89	3.1
16	Wednesday, August 25, 2010 2	3.1	Fox Islands, Aleutian Islands, Alaska	52.89	-169.45	0
17	Wednesday, August 25, 2010 2	1.5	Baja California, Mexico	32.4	-115.55	0.1
18	Wednesday, August 25, 2010 2	1.4	Southern California	34.03	-116.99	15.1

Welcome | Earthquakes ×

Edit | Save Design | Rename | Create Forms | Rows per Page: 25 ▾

Page 1 of 45 | Displaying rows 1 - 25 of 1113

Figure 1.14 Online database can be used in many ways, such as tracking earthquakes

Database management systems

Database management systems (DBMS) are the programs that allow you to create any database that you need and to use the databases you have created.

The DBMS allows you to create, maintain, search and sort data on a database. It allows different users to access the database at the same time, and can provide different levels of access to the data.

Structured Query Language (SQL)

Structured Query Language (SQL) is a high-level language that is used to undertake this management activity. It is normally in two parts:

1 **Data Definition Language (DDL):** This is the part that is used to define the database structure.

2 **Data Manipulation Language (DML):** This is the part used to add, delete, change and query the data that is held in the database structure.

SQL is the language that generates the code used by the DBMS.

Remember

A **database** is a collection of data that is usually structured. A **DBMS** is the software that allows you to make use of that data.

Link

Refer to section *Online documents* for further information on access levels and file permissions.

Activity   1.7

W3Schools has a web page where you can try out some SQL commands for yourself. To access the relevant page, go to www.pearsonhotlinks.co.uk and search for this title.

Try out the example queries.

Write down any other useful queries you come up with.

Assessment tips

You need to know all of the terminology associated with databases, including the purpose of a DBMS.

You are required to know about online databases.

Just checking ✔

1 Give three examples of data types that can be used in a database field.

2 Give an example of how an online database might be used.

3 Explain the difference between a database and a database management system (DBMS).

Possible threats to data 1

Getting started

In small groups, research some examples of high-profile companies who have had their systems hacked. Answer the following questions.

• Why do you think that company was targeted?

• What do you think were the intensions of the hacker(s)?

• How did the company respond to the attack?

• Do you think it is possible to create a secure network that will never be hacked? If so, how would you go about creating this?

Key term

Malware – A hostile, intrusive or annoying piece of software or program code.

Introduction

Online facilities, whether on public or private networks, are vulnerable to attacks from determined individuals. There have been many high-profile examples of people hacking into secure government systems and of newspaper journalists hacking people's mobile phones. It is extremely difficult to keep the hacker out if they are very determined, but there are things we can do to prevent access by the opportunist. This section also looks at why secure network access is important for individuals, businesses and society.

Types of threats

Threats to computer systems come in many forms.

• **Opportunist threats.** People who find an unattended computer that has been left logged in to a system may view, steal or damage information, programs or even hardware.

• **Computer viruses.** These are small programs that can replicate themselves and spread from computer to computer. They are never beneficial; usually they will make some changes to the system they infect and, even if they do no real damage, they are undesirable. They arrive by attaching themselves to files or email messages.

• **Other malware.** Examples of **malware** include: computer worms (essentially a computer virus that does not need to attach itself to a file or message); Trojan horses, which appear as some benign program allowing a hacker full access to a system; spyware; adware; and various other nasties. Malware is never beneficial.

• **Phishing.** This is a type of threat that attempts to gain access to passwords, financial details and other such privileged information. Often this is done by email messages pretending to come from trusted websites, instant messaging or social networks. Normally, they try to divert you to a website that looks authentic and that asks for information about you.

• **Accidental damage.** This may be caused by a natural disaster (e.g. flooding), mischief or accidental mishap, and can result in losing all of a computer's data.

From: SecureBank
Subject: Online Security Message
To: Account Holder
📎 1 Attachment, 56 KB

🔒 SecureBank

Dear Account holder,

It has been reported to our online security team that there has been a false SecureBank message sent to all our customers. We are trying to rectify and protect all our online customers accounts from any unwanted transactions. We have programmed our Security and Database systems to alert us when any unauthorised transactions are about to take place. We require you to register your details on to our upgraded security system to avoid your account from being disabled by our security systems. A confirmation of this will be sent to your residential address after 7 days of registering. We want to assure you that your account will be safe guarded by our new security systems immediately after you register.

To do this you are required to click on the secure link below :

[www.securebank.co.uk]

Customer Service,
SecureBank Online Banking

Important

Failure to update your account within 24hrs might lead to your account being suspended and online access will be restricted.

Thank You.

Figure 1.15 Example of a phishing email

Importance of security

Computer/technology systems are under constant threat of attack and the threats are continuous and ever-changing. All computers and systems are vulnerable to attack and it is impossible to provide 100 per cent protection.

An attack could result in some form of loss (data or financial) to an individual, organisation and/or society. Examples include:

- Organisations that trade online have to build up a reputation for being secure organisations with secure network access. If this reputation is damaged, potential customers might be put off, costing the organisation money.

- When an organisation's secrets are spread to competitors or to the wider public, any particular advantage the organisation has will be lost. An example is when an organisation has been doing research on a new product, and the results of that research find their way to a competitor.

- Identity theft could cause problems when trying to obtain loans and with other contractual agreements.

- Disclosure of information could cause legal problems. A company can be sued by its customers if it sells their personal information or fails to protect it properly. The obligations of organisations to protect customers' data are covered by the Data Protection Act (1998). Organisations that store people's personal information have to register with the Information Commissioner's Office (ICO) and must undertake to treat the information responsibly.

Research

Find out more about the Data Protection Act by looking at websites such as the Information Commissioner's Office: Guide to data protection. To access this web page, go to www.pearsonhotlinks.co.uk and search for this title.

Find out what a company's legal obligations are regarding storage and use of personal data. Write a list of the rules.

Case study

In April 2011, the gaming giant, Sony®, has its PlayStation Network hacked in what is thought to be the largest internet security break-in to date.

Sony® revealed that the data for approximately 77 million users had been stolen during the attack. Users' data that was stolen included:

- usernames
- passwords
- credit card details
- security answers
- purchase history
- address.

Research this attack.

1. How do you think online networks can protect users' data from attacks of this kind?

2. How do you think an attack of this scale has affected:
   - the general public's confidence in online networks?
   - the security protocols of companies who trade online?
   - the internet as a whole?

Possible threats to data 2

Introduction

As you learned about in section *Possible threats to data 1*, there are ways in which information can be damaged, stolen or lost by malicious action or accidental events. There are many things you can do to limit the possibility of this happening. This section looks at some of the measures you can take to protect your data and your personal safety online.

Preventative and remedial actions

It is important to protect both IT systems and their data. Using the following can help:

- **Physical barriers.** These include turning off computers and locking offices when the systems are unattended to prevent damage by people, the environment (e.g. fire, flooding, electrical interference) or theft.

- **Password control of access.** Passwords are sequences of characters, known only to the computer user, which allow access to a computer, network or application. Passwords should always be strong so that it is hard for someone else to guess them or work them out.

- **Access levels.** These can be set up to allow individuals to have access to only specific levels of an application and to prevent unauthorised users from accessing particular data.

- **Anti-virus software.** This is set up to intercept computer viruses before they can become resident on the computer. The software can isolate the virus, remove it and sometimes repair any damage. Equivalent security programs exist for other types of malware.

- **Firewall.** This is a piece of software that monitors all data arriving at your computer from the internet and all data leaving your computer. It stops anything that it thinks is harmful or unwanted (such as viruses, spam, Trojan horses and hackers).

- **Encryption.** This is used to codify data so that it cannot be read by anyone who does not have the key to the code. An algorithm, sometimes known as a cipher, is applied to the data at the transmission end and the reverse is applied at the reception end.

- **Backup and recovery.** Making a backup of data is the only way of recovering from a total data disaster. Many individuals and organisations back up data to Flash® solid state storage devices or magnetic tape at night. The tapes are stored safely in a separate place, so that they are not destroyed by any disaster that could destroy the master system (fire, earthquake, etc.). Many types of backup exist, including:
  - full system backup of all data held for a specific purpose
  - incremental backups of files or data that have been changed since the last full backup – this is faster than running a full backup every time
  - backups to removable media, such as a removable hard drive (if you have a large amount of data), USB sticks, CDs and DVDs.

It is also possible to back up data across a network (or across the internet) to a server in a completely separate location (for example, backing up data to the cloud).

Personal safety

The dangers of **identity theft** and of revealing too much personal information on social networks and via instant messaging are often reported in the news.

These threats can affect both your security and your reputation. Think about who has access to the information you put online. Before you put photos on your social networking profile, think about who might see them and whether you would mind. You might not want your employer or teacher to see something that might be embarrassing or harmful to your reputation.

Use security settings to protect your privacy and identity. Remember that not everyone is who they claim to be. Criminals access social networking sites trying to find out information about people. This may put you at risk of identity theft and password theft if you have revealed too much information about yourself. Be careful not to reveal information that you might use in a password, such as your pet's name.

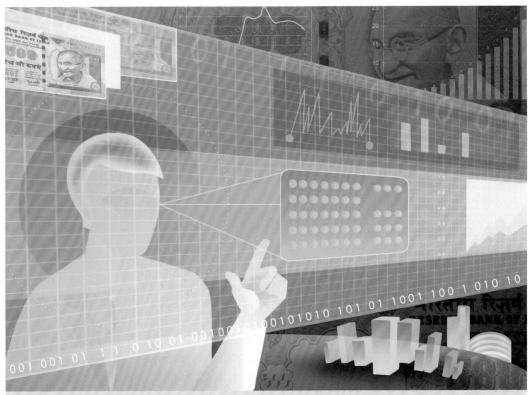

Think about the type of information you want to share with others over the internet

Key term

Identity theft – When someone steals your personal details in order to use them to open bank accounts and get credit cards, loans, a passport or a driving licence in your name.

Discussion point

Discuss the ways that companies and government use to access your personal information via online services. Discuss the pros and cons of this.

Reflect

Technology can be used to monitor individuals' movements and communications. For example, burglars could see from a public social network site that someone is away on holiday and break into their house. Similarly, if you send unencrypted email, it can potentially be read by other people.

Can you think of any other examples?

Remember

Emails and email attachments can contain viruses. It is important to run up-to-date anti-virus software.

Assessment tip

Make sure you know the methods that can be used to protect and restore data.

Just checking

1 Give three examples of threats to computer systems.
2 Give the methods that you can use to reduce the threats you listed in question 1.
3 How can you help to prevent identity theft when using social networking sites?

Assessment Zone

This section has been written to help you to do your best when you take the assessment test. Read through it carefully and ask your tutor if there is anything that you are still not sure about.

How you will be assessed

You will take an onscreen assessment using a computer. This will be set over about 15–20 screens and have a maximum of 50 marks. It will last for 1 hour.

There will be different types of questions in the test:

Disclaimer: These practice questions and sample answers are not actual exam questions. They are provided as a practice aid only and should not be assumed to reflect either the format or coverage of the real external test.

A Questions where the answers are available and you have to choose the answer(s). *Tip: Always read carefully to see how many answers are needed and how you can show the right answer.*

Examples:

> Which of the following is an online commerce service? Select the correct answer. [1]
>
> **A** Train timetable
>
> **B** Online tax return
>
> **C** Online auction website
>
> **D** Instant messaging
>
> **Answer:** C

> What name is given to the device that directs the traffic over the internet? Select the correct answer. [1]
>
> **A** Modem   **C** Client
>
> **B** Server   **D** Router
>
> **Answer:** D

B Questions where you are asked to give a short answer worth 1–2 marks. *Tip: Look carefully at how the question is set out to see how many points need to be included in your answer.*

Examples:

> What is the main reason for zipping files? [1]
>
> **Answer:** To compress them (i.e. make them smaller)

> What is Transmission Control Protocol (TCP)? [2]
>
> **Answer:** The protocol that takes data from a user's application and passes it to the Internet Protocol for transmitting across the internet. It controls the reverse process at the receiver.

C Questions where you are asked to give a longer answer – these can be worth up to 8 marks. *Tip: Plan your answer – think about how many points you need to make. Check through your answer – you may need to use the scroll bar to move back to the top.*

Example:

> Explain what client-side processing is. What are the benefits and the disadvantages of this type of data exchange? [6]
>
> **Answer:** Client-side processing enables interactivity within a web page. When a user opens the web page, the code is downloaded to the user's computer.
>
> Advantages include speed of interactivity and security. Once the code has been downloaded to a user's computer, the interactive elements should run quickly. Because the web pages are downloaded, the chances for corruption are reduced.
>
> A disadvantage is that the scripting language that creates the code might not work on every browser. This means you would need to create different browser versions. The download time can also be affected by your computer's ability to download and process data. Complex or large amounts of interactivity might make web pages slow to load, and can also cause other programs to run slowly.

Many questions will have images. Sometimes you will be asked to click to play a video or animation. You can do this as many times as you want.

Sometimes you may be asked to do a calculation – you can use the calculator provided in the onscreen test system if you need to.

Hints and tips

- **Use the pre-test time.** Make sure you have read the instructions, tested the function buttons, adjusted your seat and that you can see the screen clearly.
- **Watch the time.** The screen shows you how much time you have left. You should aim to take about 1 minute per mark. Some early questions will take less time than this and some later questions will take you longer.
- **Plan your longer answers.** Read the question carefully and think about the key points you will make. You can use paper or the onscreen note function to jot down ideas.
- **Check answers at the end.** You should keep moving through the questions and not let yourself get stuck on one. If you are really unsure of an answer or cannot give an answer, then you can use the onscreen system to flag that you need to come back to that question at the end.
- **Read back your longer answers.** Make sure you view the whole answer if you are checking back. There is no spell check facility.
- **Do you find it harder to read onscreen?** Talk to your teacher about how the system can be adjusted to meet your needs; for example, by changing the font size or colour.

How to improve your answer

Read the two student answers below, together with the feedback. Try to use what you learn here when you answer questions in your test.

Question

Give four examples of how data can be threatened and an example of how each threat can be minimised. (8 Marks)

Student 1's answer

> Opportunist threats, which can be prevented by turning a machine off, virus threats by installing anti-virus software, phishing by using a firewall and accidental damage by doing regular backups

Feedback on student 1

The learner has not read the question, which asks for specific examples of 'how data can be threatened' and not generic types of threats. In effect, they have not answered the question and they have not indicated how the data can be threatened. They might possibly get a couple of marks for the minimisation (anti-virus software and firewall perhaps) but that would be quite generous.

Student 2's answer

> People may enter an office and find a computer already logged into a particular program. They could use the software to amend or delete records or files used by that program, which may not be detected until much later.
>
> Always log off when you leave your computer, and set up an appropriate auto logoff time if this function is available.
>
> Viruses are small programs that can arrive as email attachments and that run once the attachment is opened. They can do all sorts of damage, including deleting or amending data files or records. This may not be spotted at the time and will cause problems later.
>
> Up-to-date anti-virus software will scan emails, attachments and files for known viruses and will delete or isolate them.
>
> Trojan horses are programs that appear to be from a trusted person or website. When they are activated, often by diverting you to a look-alike website, they give a hacker control of your computer so that they can find out your passwords, bank details, etc.
>
> Installation of firewall software will intercept and prevent these attacks.
>
> A natural disaster such as a fire is capable of totally destroying all files on a computer system.
>
> Making regular backups of files will allow the data to be loaded on a different computer and brought up to date with missing transactions. It will provide continuity of operation.

Feedback on student 2

Four specific threats to data have been identified and described in sufficient detail to show why they are threats. It is clear the learner understands the nature of the threats.

The 'remedies' have also been well described, again showing knowledge of the nature of the problems.

Full marks for this answer.

Assess yourself

Question 1

Which of the following terms is not a method of online information exchange? [1]

A Blog

C Cloud

B Wiki

D Podcast

Question 2

What do you understand by the term 'netiquette'? [2]

Question 3

State what the acronym VoIP stands for and give an example of a service that uses it. Describe one way in which it may be used and give two examples of limitations to the service [5]

Answers

1) C

2) A set of rules that govern the behaviour of people using the internet.
Or something similar: one point for knowing they are rules/conventions on behaviour, and one point for knowing that they have to do with networks/the internet. A definition of network etiquette or internet etiquette would be worth one point.

3) Voice over Internet Protocol (1 mark) and an example is Skype™ (1 mark). It can be used by companies with many locations to hold video conferences over the internet (1 mark, but any acceptable use is valid). Limitations include quality of voice and video (1 mark) and an unreliable service from a network provider (1 mark, also anything similar or additional such as security problems could be used).

Introduction

Technology systems are involved in many of the objects we use every day, from laptop computers to smartphones. This unit provides a first look at how the main building blocks of technology systems work.

A computer is a programmable machine for completing arithmetic and logical operations (called processes) on digital data. A technology system will contain at least one computer, which interacts with other devices and components in a system. You will explore the common hardware devices that make up technology systems, including touch screens, printers and components such as the processor, buses and memory, which are the internal building blocks of a computer.

The different devices in a technology system communicate with each other using a network. This unit covers the purposes of different types of computer network and the different methods for transferring data around a network.

A technology system is nothing without the software that brings it to life. You will explore many different types of software, including operating systems, utility programs and productivity applications. You will also undertake an introduction to programming that will help you to discover the excitement of creating your own computer programs.

Assessment: You will be assessed by an onscreen test lasting 1 hour.

Learning aims

In this unit you will:

A understand how the components of technology systems work together

B understand how data flows between internal components of a computer and is processed to provide information

C understand different types of software.

I enjoyed how this unit introduced me to networking. The best thing though, was finding out about how binary and programming work. I want to be a programmer so it was great to see what goes into designing and writing code.

Samantha, 16-year-old would-be IT computer programmer

Technology systems

Applications of technology systems and issues

Introduction

Technology systems are used by most organisations in every type of sector for many different purposes. Some examples are given in this section, but see what others you can find out about. This section also explores some of the issues involved with using technology systems, such as environmental and safety concerns. The final part of this section gives some information about why organisations need to plan and develop their technology systems.

Uses in different sectors

Depending on the type of organisation, they may use their technology systems to store information, keep accounts, plan, draw, do calculations, send email, access the internet or produce documents. Here are some examples of uses in different sectors:

- **Construction sector:** uses technology systems to plan projects, create architect drawings (using CAD) and to track spending.
- **Finance sector:** uses technology systems to follow the prices of stocks and shares and to calculate the effects of interest rates on loans and savings.
- **Health sector:** uses technology systems to scan patients and in life support systems to monitor heart beats, breathing and other processes.
- **Manufacturing sector:** uses **computer aided design/computer aided manufacture (CAD/CAM)** systems to design parts for production and to control robots and other machines on the production lines. Robots are good at production tasks because they are fast, accurate, never get tired of repetitive tasks and can work in dangerous conditions.
- **Retail sector:** uses technology to track sales at tills, using **point of sale (PoS)** systems that automatically update stock records and produce reports. The retail sector also uses the internet to advertise and sell products.

Key terms

Computer aided design/ computer aided manufacture (CAD/CAM) – A technology system used to design component parts on a computer and to send the design to robotic tools that manufacture the parts. CAD systems are also used to create plans for buildings. The plans are printed out using an inkjet plotter onto large pieces of paper.

Point of sale (PoS) – Computerised tills that communicate with a database to keep track of stock. The information stored in the database updates with every item sold.

Computer aided design systems are used by lots of industries including engineering, manufacturing and architectural design

Issues involved in the use of technology systems

Environmental issues

Technology systems can be good for the planet and help **sustainability** by reducing the need for travel. Video conferencing enables people from different locations around the world to meet.

Technology systems can also be bad for the planet, as hardware devices consume power. Many technology systems are left switched on 24/7, creating heat and wasting electricity.

For example, online shopping reduces the need to travel to shops. However, delivering the products ordered online uses a similar amount of energy.

Computer security and copyright

All computers in technology systems are at risk of attack from sources that do not have authorised access to the system. Attacks commonly occur for the advantage of others, such as for financial gain or to obtain sensitive information. **Malware**, such as a computer virus, worm, spyware or Trojan horse, is a common form of attack.

The privacy of personal and sensitive data contained within computers or entered into a website and transferred across the internet is also an issue.

Computer security is used by individuals and organisations to protect their computers from attack and to safeguard their privacy. Typical security measures include using secure passwords, which are used to authenticate user IDs, and by setting different levels of access to system servers and folders for different users.

The internet contains a massive amount of information, which you are able to view and download. Often this information is protected by copyright, so you can be breaking the law by downloading music, artwork, photographs or other material such as documents.

Developing technology systems

There are many reasons why organisations (and perhaps individuals) want to improve and develop new technology systems. These include:

- **Competitive advantage.** The objective is to gain advantage over competitors by using technology. For example, by using advanced technologies Rolls-Royce is able to monitor the performance of their jet engines while in flight, in real time. They are able to charge their customers for this service as it reduces their staff and maintenance costs, and helps prevent service disruption.
- **Reduced costs.** Cost savings can be made by developing the system so that fewer people are needed to operate it or to save time and distance by using the system to plan routes for deliveries.
- **Improved performance.** This can be achieved by developing systems to deliver results more quickly, by making it easier for staff to use the systems and by providing a more satisfying experience for customers.

Reflect

Health and safety is important in all workplaces. Health and safety issues regarding technology systems include:

- Positioning and laying out equipment so it does not cause users any strain or discomfort. There are several laws that ensure organisations make their technology systems safe for staff.

- Technology systems hold a lot of information that must be protected, as it can be disastrous to individuals or to an organisation if other people are able to access it. Security measures such as passwords are needed to authenticate anyone trying to gain access to information such as bank details or customer information. Within technology systems, there are usually different levels of access for different users, to prevent unauthorised users from seeing sensitive information such as personal details of other staff members.

Key terms

Sustainability – Using resources in such a way that we meet the needs of the present generation without affecting the ability of future generations to meet their needs. Sustainability involves protecting the environment so that we will continue to have the water, food and other resources that we need.

Malware – Software that is created to harm computers and/or technology systems. Malware includes: spyware, viruses, worms and many others that are able to infect your computer to damage how it works or to obtain sensitive information.

Link

See *Unit 1 The online world* for further information on computer security.

Just checking

1 Give three examples of the uses of technology systems in different sectors, e.g. finance and construction.
2 What are the environmental benefits and drawbacks of using technology?
3 Give three reasons why an organisation might want to develop and improve its technology systems.

Computer hardware devices

Introduction

The term hardware is used to describe any of the physical devices and components used within a technology system. It includes different types of computer and other digital devices, for inputting and outputting data and for data storage. This section also explores the specialised devices used in two important sectors of the economy, retailing and manufacturing. You could explore other sectors of the economy too.

Hardware devices

You need to know the features and uses of the hardware devices shown in Table 2.1.

Link

The features described in Table 2.1 are covered in more detail within this unit.

Table 2.1 Features and uses of hardware devices

System	Features	Key uses
Personal computer (PC)	Processor type, e.g. single core, dual core, or quad core Processor speed, e.g. 1.6 or 2.6 GHz Amount of Random Access Memory (RAM), e.g. 4GB or higher Type of operating system, e.g. Windows®, OS X or Linux Network connectivity, e.g. wireless or wired Storage size, e.g. 160 GB, and type, e.g. solid state device	Running apps such as word processing and spreadsheets
Server	Powerful computer with lots of RAM and disk space	Controlling a network
Laptop	Portable computer	Mobile computing
Tablet	Touch screen computer	Web browsing
Games console	Computer designed for gaming with high-quality graphics card	Gaming
Programmable digital devices	Anything with digital control, for example a microwave oven	Controlling hardware

Key terms

Force feedback device – A device used to provide you with touch output from a computer device. A games controller uses this technology when it vibrates. An area for future development is a device to give surgeons feedback when carrying out an operation remotely using a robot arm.

Actuators – Motors that can be controlled by a technology system such as a motor used to move part of a robot arm.

Solid state drive (SSD) – A data storage device.

Optical media – CDs, CD-ROMs and DVDs are examples of optical media disks.

Hardware devices are also used by technology systems for:

- **Inputting:** to accept information and commands into the system. Input devices include keyboard, mouse, sensors, touch screen, microphone, scanner and digital camera.
- **Outputting:** to transfer information out of the system. Output devices include printers, speakers, **force feedback devices**, **actuators**, screens, projectors, robot arms and other control devices.
- **Storage:** to hold information when the hardware device or system is turned off. Storage devices include **solid state drives (SSD)**, **optical media** such as DVDs and magnetic media such as hard disks.

Link

Refer to section *Internal components of a computer 1* for more information on storage.

There are many different types of printer, including the following:

- Inkjet printers are used in many homes and small offices. They are cheap to buy, reasonably cheap to operate and produce good-quality colour output, but are poor at large volume printing.
- Laser printers are used in many homes and businesses. They are cheap to buy, reasonably cheap to operate and are good at large volume printing. They are often black and white but colour laser printers are also available.
- Impact dot-matrix printers are used on some shop counters to print multi-part stationary, which can be separated into copies for customer and shop. These are often more expensive to buy, are loud and have poor print quality, but they are very cheap to run.

1 Make a list of the printers in your school or college, including their types.
2 For each printer, say why that type of printer has been used in that room/department.

Automated systems

In addition to the traditional hardware devices associated with computer systems, different sectors are using specialist devices to help improve the efficiency and productivity of their businesses.

Automated technology systems (also known as automated computer systems) monitor and perform activities on our behalf. Examples include central heating systems that regulate our environment and robots that explore the universe.

Automated systems are commonly used in supermarkets, factories and many other places. Two examples are given in Table 2.2.

> **Key term**
>
> **Automated system** – A system that uses technology and control systems. It doesn't usually require human intervention.

Table 2.2 Examples of automated systems

Automated system	What is it?	Input devices	Output devices
Self-service checkout	You have probably used a self-service checkout in your local supermarket to scan your own purchases and to pay for your shopping.	• Scales to weigh the goods before and after scanning • Scanner to read bar codes on your shopping and loyalty card • Payment inputs from cards, coins or notes	• Screen and speakers to explain how to use the checkout • Payment receipt printer and a device to give money as change
Production line	Hardware components such as robots and controlling software can be combined to form an automated system in a production line to make cars and other products.	• Optical sensors to locate product components • Pressure sensors to feel product components	• Controlling robots to manufacture components

CONTINUED ▶▶

Automated technology systems can be used to control robotic arms in manufacturing plants

Other devices

Other devices used to capture and store data in a technology system include:

- magnetic strip readers, used to read some loyalty and other cards.
- optical character readers (OCR) to scan a document into text.
- optical mark readers (OMR) to input survey and multiple choice forms.
- **radio frequency identification systems (RFID)**, known as smart labels, are used like bar codes on products for automatic identification and tracking. The technology uses radio-frequency electromagnetic fields to transfer data. Some smart labels require no battery, as they are powered by the electromagnetic fields used to read them.

Just checking

1 Give three types of storage devices used in technology systems.
2 Explain what an 'automated technology system' is.
3 What is RFID?

WorkSpace

▶ Dan Sheppard

Estate agent

I'm based in Bristol, but my company operates out of ten towns in the South West. It's really important that each location is connected so that staff can communicate easily and share information reliably and quickly. We're very proud of our network system as it meets our needs very well, looks professional and our clients find it informative and easy to use.

Our biggest branch holds details of all the properties we currently have for sale or rent on the main network file server. This information is made available to all other computers on the LAN in this shop and through our WAN to the branches, so agents can show them to clients or make changes.

The routers all have fast optical broadband connections, giving a very responsive system with little lag in showing photos of our properties. Our routers are configured into a WAN, with each branch able to access information held on our server quickly and securely.

Digital cameras have had a huge impact on the way property is now bought and sold. This technology instantly transformed the ease and speed of accepting new properties into our portfolio and displaying them on our systems. We like to print paper copies of our properties for branch wall displays, as well as showing them on our website. We also advertise on every house hunting website we know of to reach as many potential clients as possible.

Our website has a nice, simple form that clients can complete for more information or to arrange a visit to any of the properties. The system looks great, is quick to search and allows potential clients to contact us easily.

Think about it

1 How do you think property details and images were entered on to the system before digital cameras were used?

2 How do you think the networked system works?

3 What security measures do you think have been used to keep the information secure?

Computer networking and transferring data

Link

Unit 1 The online world and *Unit 11 Network development* provide more guidance and explanation of computer networks and the technology that underpins them, as well as data transfer.

Introduction

Computers in technology systems can communicate with one another by sending messages and transmitting data over a network. An introduction to computer networks and transferring data is given in this section, as they form an important part of technology systems. However, the underpinning knowledge of how the technology of networking and data transfer work is not explained here, as these are covered in other units.

Networks are everywhere, and there are different types for different purposes. This section explores the main types of networks and their uses, as well as the different ways in which data is transferred over networks.

Types of network

There are four main types of network that you will come across:

1 **Local area network (LAN).** Connects computers and other devices such as printers together at a single location, such as a business premises or a home.

2 **Wide area network (WAN).** Used by organisations to connect their LANs together into a single network covering anywhere in the world.

3 **Personal area network (PAN).** Used to connect your devices together; for example, to synchronise your computer, including your email, with your mobile phone.

4 **Mobile broadband.** Uses **3G mobile phone technology** to connect your laptop (using a **dongle**), netbook or phone to the internet.

Key terms

3G mobile photo technology – 3G stands for third generation and refers to technology which supports fast data-transmission speeds and increased network capacity and networks through a smart phone. 3G supersedes 1G and 2G mobile phone technology and precedes 4G technology.

Dongle – A small hardware device that plugs into the USB to provide functionality such as connecting to Wi-Fi.

Activity 2.2

For each of the four types of network, write down three examples of users that the network would be suitable for. For example, a wide area network would be suitable for a supermarket chain wishing to connect all their branches to head office.

Uses of network systems

Sharing

Networks are used to share resources and data, so that anyone who is logged onto the network and has authorisation to access them can do so.

Networked resources include printers, the internet and your document space on a network server. For example, shared data is held on the network of an organisation so that staff can see and change information about clients and for other collaborative work such as working on documents.

Entertainment

Networked systems provide the infrastructure to connect with people or online services anywhere in the world. You can stream films or listen to radio stations live hundreds or thousands of miles away, or you can join in online gaming communities and play with other players from different parts of the country or the world. You can also get up-to-the-second news updates and updates from friends via social networking or microblogging sites (e.g. Facebook, Google+ and Twitter™).

Online gaming is a form of entertainment that uses networked systems to connect to the other players through the internet. One popular online game is *Unreal Tournament*.

Many people enjoy LAN parties, where people bring their computers together to play games such as *Need for Speed* using a local area network.

Communication

Networks are great for communication – email, instant messaging and video conferencing are available for users to share ideas and reduce the need for travel.

Benefits of networking computers

Networking computers can save money by allowing people to share resources. Networks can enhance how people work by improving communications and giving them the ability to share documents.

Employees can access networks from home and many other places, so people have less need to attend the workplace. This saves organisations time and also reduces the pollution caused by commuting to and from the workplace.

Synchronising data

If you have similar information on different devices, you will need to **synchronise** this data using Bluetooth, Wi-Fi, infrared or cable to connect the devices. The devices can be connected to form a PAN to update older information to the most recent.

Synchronising data can bring calendars on two different devices up to date by making appointments and reminders the same on both. Other data that might need synchronising could be texts, email messages, music, videos, **podcasts** or anything else held on these devices.

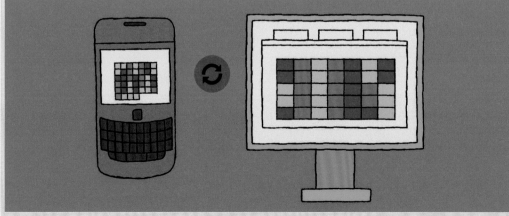

Figure 2.1 You can synchronise the calendar on a desktop with the calendar on a mobile phone

Key terms

Synchronise – In this context, it means making the same data available using different devices. If you're using different devices, then each time you use a new device the data will need to 'sync' (i.e. update) so that you are using the most up-to-date version of the data.

Podcast – A download from the BBC, Apple® and many other providers in the form of video or audio. Once you have downloaded a podcast, you can play it at any time on your mobile phone or computer.

CONTINUED ▶▶

Physical methods of transferring data

Physical methods of transferring data between devices use **cabled topology** to connect the devices together. Cabling must always meet the requirements for specified users and purpose. Cabled methods include:

- **Optical fibre.** Used for very fast connections between **switches** in a network and to bring broadband to buildings and business premises. Optical fibre cables are great for very fast connections, but not very good for places where the cable might be moved, such as a connection to a workstation.
- **Unshielded twisted pair (UTP).** Used widely to connect computers and printers to switches in LANs with CAT6 or CAT5 cabling. UTP is a great all-rounder for cabled LANs, but is poor at very high speeds.
- **Coaxial cables (coax).** Used to connect homes to optical broadband systems. Older networks used copper coaxial cabling, which was a lot slower; this has mostly been replaced by UTP. Coax is good for short distances, but poor for longer stretches.

Wireless methods of transferring data

Wireless transfer methods include Wi-Fi and Bluetooth.

Wi-Fi

Wi-Fi is a very common technology built into every laptop for connection to LANs. Many printers have built in Wi-Fi for connection to a wireless network and so they are easily positioned without a network cable. Some desktop computers have built in Wi-Fi. Other computers that need a wireless connection can have a Wi-Fi network card installed or Wi-Fi devices can connect via the USB (universal serial bus) port.

Wi-Fi needs a wireless access point (WAP), which is often part of a router and acts like a switch to connect the wireless devices together.

Bluetooth

Bluetooth is a short-range, fairly slow wireless technology that is built into most mobile phones. It is used to connect mobile phones to headsets and for data transfers such as MP3 music between phones and computers.

Activity   2.3

Create a table with three columns.
- In the first column list the different physical methods of transferring data.
- In the second column give the benefits of each method.
- In the third column give the drawbacks.

Just checking

1 Name the four main types of network and state where they are commonly used.

2 What does the term 'synchronise' mean?

3 Explain the difference between Wi-Fi and Bluetooth.

Internal components of a computer 1

Getting started ▶▶

Imagine there is a computer in front of you. There are components you can see (external) and components you can't see (internal). Create two lists with the following titles: External components and Internal components. Under each heading write down as many components as you think of.

Which of the internal components on your list have the greatest effect on the computer's performance? Explain why you think this is.

Once you've completed this unit, go back to your lists and add in any components you missed out initially.

Key terms 🔑

Machine code – A computer programming language consisting of binary or hexadecimal instructions that a computer can respond to directly.

RAM – Stands for random access memory.

Link 🔗

Refer to section *Internal components of a computer 2* for further information on bytes.

Introduction

A computer is made up of different components. These components can be internal (e.g. CPU, RAM or hard drive) or external (e.g. keyboard, mouse, webcam). This section looks at the internal components and how these can have an impact on a computer's performance.

At the heart of a technology system is at least one computer. This section provides an introduction to how the internal components of a computer work. Computers include PCs, laptops, mobile devices and other programmable devices like the Raspberry Pi™.

Main components of a computer

A computer is made up of many elements. Table 2.3 describes the main components.

Table 2.3 The main components of a computer

Component	Description
Motherboard	The main printed circuit board (PCB) where all the other system components plug in.
Central processing unit (CPU)	Each computer has at least one CPU or microprocessor, which runs instructions contained in computer programs and undertakes input/output operations to other parts of the computer and/or technology system. The CPU has many parts, including the arithmetic and logic unit (ALU), control unit and registers.
Arithmetic and logic unit (ALU)	This completes basic calculations (arithmetic) and comparisons (logic). Comparisons are used in sorting and searching operations.
Control unit	Each **machine code** instruction is extracted from memory, decoded and run, calling on the ALU when necessary. The output is either written to the register for fast recall as part of subsequent instructions or back to main memory. The control unit is there to make the rest of the computer hardware do whatever is the result of the completed instruction.
Registers	There are several types of register within the CPU that are used to store a small amount of data in the form of bytes. This is useful for the ALU so it can work out a calculation from two bytes held in registers. Registers are also used to hold addresses in RAM so the CPU knows where the next machine code instruction will come from and where to send the results of a calculation.
Memory	The **RAM** is used to hold all the programs that have been started and all opened documents, so the CPU can access them. A large amount of RAM allows you to have lots of applications open at the same time and to edit large files such as music or video easily.

continued

Research

The components inside a computer have a huge impact on the performance and the cost. Processors are continually being developed, with new models regularly entering the marketplace that offer improved performance, often with high price tags. AMD and Intel have been in competition for decades to produce the best processor products, typically found in PCs and laptops.

Visit an independent website that tests and reports on computer hardware, such as Tom's Hardware. (You can access this website by going to www.pearsonhotlinks.co.uk and searching for this title.)

Use the link at the bottom of the home page to jump to the processor charts pages.

Find one processor each from AMD and Intel with similar performance. What is the price of each? Which is the more expensive and why do you think this might be?

Key term

Central processing unit (CPU) – The part of a computer that controls the entire system and processes the data.

Discussion point

How does each of the components of a computer affect performance?

How does that affect the user experience?

Table 2.3 (*continued*)

Graphics card (or video card)	This is used to make visual images that can be displayed on a monitor.
Sound	Hardware used to drive (send sound signals to) speakers is usually built into the motherboard.
Heat dispersal	The fan and heat sink are needed by the CPU and other hot parts of the computer so they don't burn out.
Storage devices	A solid state or magnetic drive is needed to keep programs and documents when the computer is switched off. You will need a large storage device if you want to keep large files such as videos.
Optical drive	An optical drive uses laser light to read data from CDs and DVDs. The optical drive is used to install new software and to make backups.

Processing digital data

Figure 2.4 shows the hard disk of a computer, which is the storage device used to load programs (apps) into RAM so the **central processing unit (CPU)** can run them.

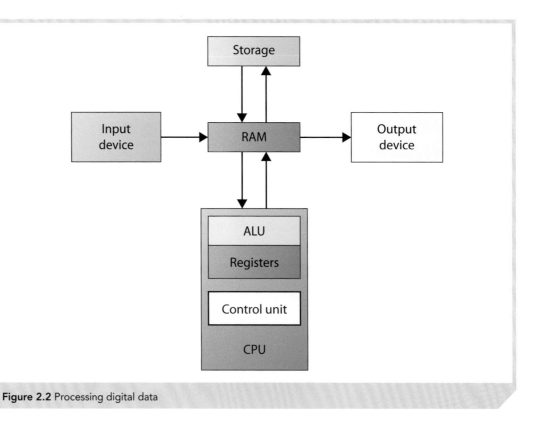

Figure 2.2 Processing digital data

The storage device is also used for documents – these are copied into RAM when opened or to storage when saved.

The CPU and **graphical processing unit (GPU)** (which processes visual images) have a massive effect on a computer's performance. These run all the instructions and complete the calculations.

The speed at which instructions and calculations within the CPU and GPU occur and the synchronisation of all the components within the processor are regulated by a clock. A microprocessor requires a fixed number of clock cycles to execute each instruction. The **clock speed** is typically measured in either megahertz (MHz) or gigahertz (GHz). In general, the faster the clock speed, the more instructions the processor can execute per second and the higher the performance of the computer.

Processors often have **multiple processing cores**. Each core is able to run code independently, so more cores mean that more code is being processed at the same time. Therefore, programs run faster and the user experience is improved.

Cache memory

Cache memory is used between faster and slower devices to let them work more quickly together. The fast device writes or reads to/from the cache memory and the slower device updates as quickly as it can. For example, the processor has cache memory to speed up access to the slower RAM, which means that the processor isn't idle while it waits for RAM to respond to an instruction. Also, slower hard disks have a cache memory to speed up disk access between the RAM and the hard disk.

Powerful microprocessors generate lots of heat. Without a heat sink and fan heat dispersal system to cool them down they would quickly burn out.

The **power supply unit (PSU)** must produce enough power (watts) for all the components in the computer.

Data buses

A data bus is simply a circuit that connects one part of the motherboard to another. The more data a bus can handle at one time (capacity), the faster it allows information to travel between components and the better the performance of the computer. There are many types of bus that are used for transferring data within a computer (internal buses) and for transferring data between computers (external).

Key terms

Graphical processing unit (GPU) – A key component that supports the delivery and quality of graphics.

Clock speed – How quickly a component works – the faster the better!

Multiple processing core – Where multiple cores (central processing units) read and execute program instructions simultaneously.

Cache memory – A fast memory that is used as a data buffer between the CPU and RAM.

Power supply unit (PSU) – Every computer system unit has a PSU that plugs into the mains electricity socket. It converts mains electricity into low voltage electricity for the computer components. Every PSU produces the same voltage, but may produce a different amount of power (wattage). For example, a 600 W PSU is more powerful than a 400 W PSU.

Just checking

1 List the main components of a computer.
2 What is machine code?
3 How is data processed?

Internal components of a computer 2

Introduction

This section will look at how the features of memory and storage devices affect performance and the user experience.

Memory and storage

The performance of memory and storage devices comes from their speed and storage capacity. Faster speed and lots of storage space make for a better user experience.

Computer memory

Computer memory, like cache, Random Access Memory (RAM) and Read-Only Memory (ROM), is **solid state**, which means that they are microchips with no moving parts. The different types of computer memory are used for different purposes.

RAM is used to store programs and data that that the CPU is processing and that the user has accessed. PCs, laptops and some game consoles generally use **dynamic RAM**. This uses a type of transistor (an electrical component contained within microprocessors) that needs a constant electrical power source to store data. Therefore, when a computer is switched off, any data stored within RAM is lost (deleted).

Mobile phones, digital cameras and some games consoles devices generally use **static RAM (flash memory)**. This technology uses a type of transistor that retains its state (on or off), so it stores data, even after the power supply is disconnected.

Static RAM is more expensive and physically larger than dynamic RAM, but it uses less power and is faster, which makes it more suitable for smaller portable devices.

<div class="key-terms">

Key terms

Solid state – A component with no moving parts such as a solid state drive (SSD).

Dynamic RAM – Or DRAM, is a type of memory that contains programs in use.

Static RAM – Or SRAM, is a type of memory that stores data, and which doesn't need to be continually refreshed.

Flash memory – A type of memory which can be deleted and reprogrammed in blocks of memory.

</div>

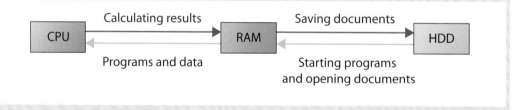

Figure 2.3 The interaction between CPU, RAM and HDD

ROM

Read-Only Memory (ROM) is memory that keeps the contents when the power is switched off. PCs have ROM on the motherboard to keep setup information such as the boot sequence to control whether the computer starts with the hard drive (normal) or the DVD drive (to reinstall the operating system).

Storage devices

Storage devices are used to keep data and documents saved from RAM, so when the computer is switched off they are kept safe for another time. They are also used to keep programs for loading into RAM when they start so the CPU can run them.

- **Hard disk drives (HDD).** These are magnetic media, as they use tiny magnetic spots on a disk surface to store data. The disk spins round using circular tracks to organise the magnetic spots, with a read/write head moving over the disk surface between tracks to use them.

- **Solid state drives (SSD).** These store data in flash memory microchips, which contain transistors that retain their state (on or off) and store the data, even when there's no electrical power supply. Although currently HDD are generally cheaper and can have larger capacities, this is beginning to change and SSD is becoming increasingly popular and more common. They are the same physical size as a HDD, with the same connections and functions, but they do not have any moving parts so are a lot faster, quieter and more reliable than HDD.

  A USB drive is a similar storage device using flash memory, but it is slower and less reliable than SSD.

- **Optical drives.** Items such as DVDs and CDs are used to install new software and to make backups of hard disks.

A hard disk drive uses tiny magnetic spots on a disk surface to store data

The overall performance of a computer is dependent on a number of different factors, including clock speed, memory size, word size, number of processors, bus capacity and storage type. Therefore, it is the combination of the performance of different components and hardware devices that determines the overall performance and cost of the computer.

Mobile devices

We use a wide range of technology devices and systems to communicate and share data. While the components are similar, how the components are used and perform can differ a little. The features on a mobile device affect both the performance and user experience. More powerful features provide a better experience but reduce the **battery life**.

Modern mobile devices use **system on a chip (SoC)** technology to combine the CPU and GPU onto a single **chip**. This has many benefits, including making the device smaller, easier to manufacture, faster and needing less power.

The battery life for a mobile device is important, as people need to be able to use it for at least a day and preferably for a week or more. Recharging batteries takes time, inconveniences the user and reduces mobility. Designers therefore take a lot of care to design mobile devices with just the right mix of processing power and battery life.

The amount of electrical power the processing consumes is not such an issue with a **traditional platform** such as a desktop PC, as mains electricity is plentiful and there is little extra cost involved in running a powerful computer. The size and weight are also less of a concern than for mobile devices, which need to be portable and convenient to use.

Link

Refer to section *Analogue and digital data* for further information on data types.

Key terms

Battery life – How long the battery lasts in a mobile device.

System on a chip (SoC) – This is a single chip (integrated circuit) containing all the computer circuits an embedded device such as a microwave needs to control it.

Chip – A microchip, often called a chip, is an integrated circuit (IC). The IC is a single component that can be soldered onto an electronic circuit board to connect the chip to the rest of the device.

Traditional platform – A computer system using mains power with system unit, keyboard, mouse, screen and hard drive.

Analogue and digital data

Introduction

Analogue data occurs in the natural world and changes constantly with time. Examples include the human voice, temperature and musical instruments.

Digital data is a representation of a sequence of discrete values or numbers, such as digital clocks and Morse code. It is digital data that computers process in the form of binary numbers, as explained in this section.

Key terms

Analogue data – Also referred to as analog data, is data represented by an electrical signal, and in the case of an ordinary internet user, travels down standard telephone lines.

Digital data – Data transmitted or stored using bits and bytes.

Encrypt – To protect data using a series of codes or passwords.

Bit – A place where either of the two digits 0 and 1 are kept. Bits are usually grouped into eight to make a byte. A byte is really useful, as there are 256 different ways the 8 bits can be arranged.

There is a need to convert analogue signals, such as the human voice, to digital signals so that computers can process and interact with the natural world.

Digital transmissions are able to check for errors, so that there is no change or distortion in the data being transmitted. Sometimes computers **encrypt** digital transmissions to make them more secure, so if anyone is able to intercept the transmission they will not be able to understand the data.

Binary

Digital data in any computer is represented using binary notation, which uses only two digits: 0 and 1. The use of binary notation works very well in every part of a computer, which is why binary numbers represent all data within a computer. Here are some examples of how binary notation is represented in different hardware devices:

- In RAM, binary notation is represented in transistors (electrical components contained within microprocessors) as with electrical charge (1) or without electrical charge (0).
- In a hard disk drive, binary notation is represented in the magnetised surface of the disk as North (1) or South (0).
- In a DVD, binary notation is represented in the reflective surface of the disk to a laser as reflective (1) or not reflective (0).

Binary is a base 2 number system composed of 1s and 0s, whereas the number system that we use in everyday life is called denary (base 10). In order for a computer to process data from the natural world, it converts data, such as denary numbers and text, into binary values. This is why it is important for you to understand the process.

In binary, each digit represents an increasing power of 2, with the rightmost digit representing 2^0, the next digit representing 2^1, then 2^2, and so on. The smallest single unit of information possible in a computer is a binary value, of either 0 or 1, which is called a **bit**.

Table 2.4 shows the binary equivalents of denary (base 10) numbers:

The binary column headings always start on the right with 1, then each column heading to the left is double the number to the right of it.

To calculate the denary equivalent of any binary number, just add together the numbers in the heading row for every bit with a value of 1. For example, from Table 2.4, you can work out that the binary number 1001 = 9 (8+1).

Table 2.4 Binary equivalents of denary numbers 0–10

Denary number	Binary number			
	8	4	2	1
0	0	0	0	0
1	0	0	0	1
2	0	0	1	0
3	0	0	1	1
4	0	1	0	0
5	0	1	0	1
6	0	1	1	0
7	0	1	1	1
8	1	0	0	0
9	1	0	0	1
10	1	0	1	0

Converting binary numbers

You can see that binary notation increases in size by the power of two: 1, 2, 4, 8, 16, 32, 64 and so on. This is an important concept in computing, as computer memory is designed using binary logic. It is also used to determine the size of data that a processor can process most efficiently and the number of bits used to represent memory addresses. Early processors were typically 8-bit or 16-bit, whereas today many processors are 32-bit or 64-bit and therefore have more memory.

Word and word length

A **word** is the term used to describe the number of bits – for example, 32-bits – used by a particular processor. A word is basically a fixed sized group of bits (binary data) that is handled as a group by the instruction set and the CPU (for example, for the registers). A processor usually runs instructions that are a fixed length, typically corresponding with the word size or a fraction/multiple of a word in each clock cycle.

The size of the word length is important in the processor design, as it affects the processing power of a computer. In general, the larger the word length the greater the processing power of the microprocessor and the more memory that can be addressed. For example, in a memory subsystem such as the data bus between the CPU and RAM, the amount of data transferred in a clock cycle is typically a word. Therefore, the larger the word length the greater the amount of data that is transferred per clock cycle, so the greater the processing power of the computer.

Remember

For assessment you should be able to convert binary numbers into denary numbers and vice versa from zero up to ten. You should know that there are eight-bits in a byte.

Key terms

Byte – A unit of digital data made up of 8 bits.

Word – A fixed-sized group of bits (binary data) that is handled as a group by the instructions set and the CPU.

CONTINUED ▸▸

Key terms

American Standard Code for Information Interchange (ASCII) – The system used in most computer systems to hold alphabetic and numeric characters. In this system, 01000001 (value 65) is used for A, 01000010 (value 66) is used for B, and so on.

Binary format – This format uses just two digits, 0 and 1. (The 'bi' part of 'binary' means two, as in a bicycle with two wheels.) Everything in a computer is in binary format, with groups of eight 1s and 0s held as bytes.

ASCII

ASCII is a system used to represent characters in a **binary format**. It uses byte values 48–57 to represent the numbers 0–9, byte values 65–90 to represent the upper case letters A–Z, byte values 97–122 to represent the lower case letters a–z and other byte values for punctuation and other uses. You can see the ASCII character set used on a PC in the **Character Map** program in **Accessories** under **System Tools**.

You should know how characters can be represented in binary format.

Binary units

The byte is used to describe the size or capacity of memory and data storage. Table 2.5 gives the different multiples of bytes used to show the magnitude of the units.

Table 2.5 The different units used to measure the memory and data storage of hardware devices

Unit	Approximate number	How number is calculated	Accurate number
Kilobyte (Thousand bytes)	1000	1024	1024
Megabyte (Million bytes)	1,000,000	1024 x 1024	1,048,576
Gigabyte (Thousand million bytes)	1,000,000,000	1024 x 1024 x 1024	1,073,741,824
Terabyte (Million million bytes)	1,000,000,000,000	1024 x 1024 x 1024 x 1024	1,099,511,627,776
Petabyte (Thousand million million bytes)	1,000,000,000,000,000	1024 x 1024 x 1024 x 1024 x 1024	1,125,889,906,842,620

Remember

Each byte consists of 8 bits, each of which could be 0 or 1.

Because computers use binary, magnitudes are used as the approximate values, so a megabyte is 1,048,576 bytes but is thought of as a million.

Just checking

1 What are 'analogue' and 'digital' data?
2 Convert the denary number 75 to binary.
3 Convert the binary number 1100100 to denary.

Different types of computer software

Introduction

Software brings technology systems to life so that you can use them as a tool for work, research, gaming and much more. Different types of computer software have different purposes. For example, an operating system is software used to connect applications to the hardware. Modern operating systems include Windows®, Linux and OS X, all of which use the mouse to help control the computer.

Software

Software is any program that can run on a computer containing a microprocessor. When a program runs, it directs the operation of the technology system by controlling the processing and peripheral devices.

There are two main categories of software:

1 **Off-the-shelf.** These programs are usually cheaper than custom-made software. They are instantly available, well tested and bug-free, with good support available from books and the internet. For example, the Microsoft® Office® suite of applications and Adobe® Photoshop®.

2 **Custom-made.** These programs are written specially for a client to meet a specific need. Custom-made (also known as bespoke) programs usually take weeks or months to write but will deliver exactly what the client specified. Some organisations commission custom-made software to solve a specific problem, such as carrying out financial transactions or a robot control program for an automated car production line.

Operating systems

The role of the operating system is to link the hardware with the user and any program running on the computer. The operating system has many functions, including:

- **managing files** by copying, renaming and deleting them and using folders
- **managing hardware** by loading programs, allocating them resources and using drivers to link to specialist hardware such as a video card
- **allocating resources** by sending keyboard/mouse inputs to programs, as well as accessing other resources such as printing and the hard disk
- **handling security issues**, such as restore points (to return system files and settings back to an earlier state), backups and access to files when multiple users share a PC.

Utility applications

Operating systems may include **utility applications**, which are small programs designed to improve system performance. Here are some examples of utility applications:

- **Disk defragmenters.** These make hard disks run faster. Deleting a file makes a gap on the drive, which can be reused when another file is saved. If the new file is too big for a gap it fragments to another gap. Eventually, loading files makes the read–write head move to several places, slowing the drive down. Defragmentation rewrites files, bringing them together to make the hard disk run faster.

CONTINUED ▸▸

Key terms

Operating system – The software that runs on computers and manages the computer hardware.

Utility application – A program which supports an app or operating system function.

Disk Defragmenter

Volume	Session Status	File System	Capacity	Free Space	% Free Space
(C:)	Analyzed	NTFS	74.53 ...	46.44 GB	62 %

Estimated disk usage before defragmentation:

Estimated disk usage after defragmentation:

| Analyze | Defragment | Pause | Stop | View F |

■ Fragmented files ■ Contiguous files ☐ Unmovable files
☐ Free space

Figure 2.4 An example of a disk defragmenter application cleaning up the system

- **Software firewalls.** These stop unwanted traffic from the internet entering the computer.
- **Anti-virus software.** This tries to prevent malware from entering a computer. It also scans the computer and connected devices to check that no malware has gained access.

User interface

There are two common ways users can interface with computer operating systems and other applications, either using a GUI or a **command line interface (CLI).**

Accessibility and ease of use are a lot better with a GUI than with a CLI for the following reasons:

- The mouse is easy to use for controlling the computer.
- A GUI can be configured to magnify the screen, speak documents to you or recognise your voice commands.
- A GUI has drop-down menus, which list all the available choices. All the user needs to do is to click on the choice they want.
- There is often a search box, where you can type in the name of a document or a key word within a document that you need to find. The operating system will then find the file for you, instead of you having to manually search through folders and files.
- A GUI uses icons to click on, so you can easily start an action with the mouse.

Key term

Command line interface (CLI) – Used by older systems such as DOS, where you had to type commands into a prompt.

Mobile devices

Mobile devices, such as phones, have operating systems that are optimised for user interface, accessibility and ease of use. The user interface is usually a touch screen with voice recognition, which the operating system needs to control and make easy to use.

Accessibility on, mobile devices can be further enhanced with onscreen readers and magnifiers to make parts of the screen larger.

The operating system for a modern mobile phone might be Android, BlackBerry, iPhone OS, Symbian or Windows® Mobile.

◤ Productivity applications

Productivity applications are software programs written to improve the efficiency and effectiveness of everyday tasks.

- Home office programs include word processor, spreadsheet, database and presentation software, which can be purchased individually or as a suite.
- Graphics software is used to make and edit pictures.
- CAD (computer aided design) software is used to design components and buildings.
- Multimedia software is used to combine sound and images into cartoons or videos.
- Web-authoring software is used to create, edit and upload web pages.

Did you know?

The benefits of using a suite of productivity applications include saving money and a common approach to using the applications – each application in a suite is controlled in a similar way, making it easier to learn to use them.

Some common types of software applications are listed in Table 2.6.

Table 2.6 Software applications and their uses

Software application	Typical tasks
Word processor	Business letters, reports, coursework
Spreadsheet	Cash flows, what-if analysis, charts
Database	Storing records of staff, stock and customers
Presentation	Creating presentation slides and rolling displays
Graphics	Creating logos and editing photographs
CAD package	Producing accurate drawings and floor plans
Multimedia	Making animations
Web-authoring	Creating websites

Software installation and upgrades

There are some factors you need to consider before installing or upgrading an operating system or productivity application to ensure it will work. You should make sure that any application you wish to install is compatible with your operating system.

Table 2.7 Software installation factors

Hardware technology systems	This is the computer specification, particularly the CPU, video system, amount of RAM and free disk space. If any of these are not good enough for the new software, the installation will fail.
Accessibility features	If these are important to the user, they should be checked to ensure they are included in the software before it is installed.
Cost of the software	An organisation needs to check the full cost of the software before installation. The full cost will be the cost of the licences needed for all the computers plus the cost of setting the software up, training staff and paying for any support and maintenance.
Speed	This is important, especially when new software will be run on older hardware. Slow software adversely affects the user experience and reduces productivity.
Security features	These are important in a new operating system and include firewalls, malware management and setting user permissions. An organisation needs to understand the security features, so they can be set up to best protect the system and support the users.

Remember

If you need to use new software with a particular application or hardware, you should check compatibility first to be sure they will work together.

Training and support can add a lot to the cost of software, as they involve paying for the time of expensive specialist IT professionals who provide users with advice and guidance.

Setting user permissions controls how much the system is protected from users logging onto the system and making configuration changes.

Just checking

1 Give four functions of a computer operating system.

2 What do GUI and CLI stand for? Explain the difference between them.

3 What type of program is a disk defragmenter? What does it do?

Introduction to computer programming concepts

Introduction

Now you have investigated the different types of software program that bring computers to life. The next step is to understand the computer programming concepts, constructs (programming building blocks) and techniques needed to create your own programs.

In this section you will discover that computer programming is a very creative process and by the end of the unit you should start to appreciate the excitement and power of creating your own computer programs to solve problems and perhaps to entertain.

Link

Other units in your *BTEC First Information and Creative Technology* course develop practical programming skills. These include *Unit 8 Mobile apps development, Unit 12 Software development, Unit 16 Automated computer systems* and *Unit 23 Software systems development*. Also, *Unit 19 Computational thinking* provides you with more tools and techniques to develop creative and well-designed software programs.

Key term

Hierarchical structure – An arrangement of items or data is a tree-like structure, which ranks the most important item or data in layers.

Programming concepts

Professional programmers use specialised skills and creativity to write programs. Some people find programming easy and great fun. The programming concepts you need to understand are described below.

Hierarchical structures

There is a **hierarchical structure** for software in a computer system. Figure 2.5 illustrates how the different types of programs work together to control the computer hardware.

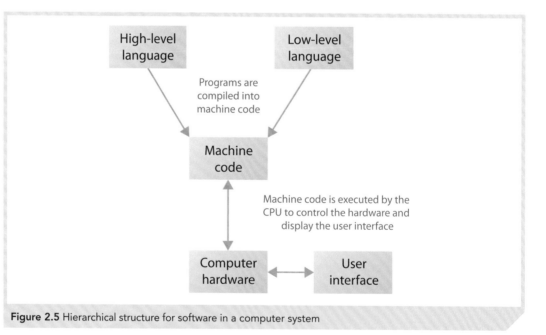

Figure 2.5 Hierarchical structure for software in a computer system

Application software package

This is the end result of programming. When an application is running, the user interface is what you see and interact with by typing or using buttons. Application software packages are created by programming with a high-level programming language, and are used to solve problems and to entertain.

High-level programming language

A high-level programming language is one that is quite close to natural human language (rather than computer language, also known as machine code). This is what most programmers use to write programs. Examples of high-level programming language are C# (pronounced as 'C sharp'), C++, Java and Visual Basic.

Microsoft® Office® applications, including Excel®, also offer high-level programming functionality using VBA (Visual Basic for Applications). This allows users to add automation to Office® documents by creating macros. For example, a user might program an Excel® macro to go through data, hiding rows that are not wanted and making visible the rows that are.

High-level programming languages are compiled into machine code so that the computer can understand and run it.

Low-level programming language

These languages are close to machine code and therefore need less changes before a processor can actually run them (compared with high-level programming languages). Low-level programs are written using an assembler, which is simply a programming environment designed to help write these programs.

Each simple command you type into the program you are writing gets assembled into the equivalent machine code instruction. This is different from a high-level language, where a single line of code could compile into hundreds of lines of machine code that the processor will run to action that line of the code.

Machine code

This is the actual binary code that the CPU can understand. Before any program you write can run on a computer, it must be translated (compiled or assembled) into machine code.

Hardware

The hardware is controlled by software as the CPU decodes each machine code instruction to carry out actions such as adding two numbers together, displaying part of the user interface on the screen or loading a document into RAM from the disk.

Link
See *Unit 9 Spreadsheet development* for more information on macros.

Remember
High-level programming languages have very powerful constructs (further details about this are given at the end of the unit) and techniques to help you produce your app code.

Did you know?
Machine code is in binary format, so if you could see it in memory, it would just be 1s and 0s grouped into bytes.

Just checking

1 Describe the hierarchical structure of software in a computer system.
2 What are the differences between high- and low-level programming languages?
3 What is the relationship between a low-level programming language and machine code?

Characteristics of high-level and low-level programming

Introduction

Most programmers use a high-level programming language to write their programs. High-level programs have much clearer structures when repeating code or making decisions.

Low-level programs usually have a very large number of lines of code because each instruction only does a small action, so it can be difficult to see the overall structure among so much detail.

This section will discuss the characteristics of high-level and low-level programming.

Characteristics of high-level programming languages

High-level programming languages are powerful and easy to understand.

Programs written in a high-level language are much closer to spoken language than low-level, as well as being a lot more intuitive to use.

High-level programming languages have several ways of working, including:

- **Imperative code.** This is used in most languages, both older and modern. In this type of code, each program statement is a step towards handling the inputs, processing and outputs.
- **Procedural programs.** These have definite start and end points. These languages were normal before GUI operating systems, as they usually have a single starting point then follow a sequence. Modern programs respond to events so can have many start points within the code.
- **Event-driven programs.** These respond to events such as a mouse click. These are the current approach for modern programming because they need to produce responses to the great variety of events that GUI operating systems provide.
- **Object-orientated programs (OOP).** These view programs as a collection of objects, such as a database record, and not as a list of tasks as in procedural programming. Each object can be viewed as an independent 'machine' with a distinct role or responsibility, which is capable of receiving messages, processing data and sending messages to other objects. These concepts are difficult to understand without more experience and they are not covered within the *BTEC First in Information and Creative Technology* course.

Characteristics of low-level programming languages

Assembly language is written using an assembler, which helps the programmer by checking for errors in the **mnemonics** before compiling the program into machine code.

Machine code is binary bytes, so could be written without an assembler by typing binary numbers direct into memory. However, this would be very difficult, as the programmer would only see the program as numbers. The mnemonic abbreviations in assembly languages make understanding the program much easier.

An introduction to designing a computer program

Introduction

Programs need to be designed so they meet the intended requirements and to help ensure they function correctly. The design for the program is used to create a test plan to make sure that every part of the program works as intended. One of the common approaches to designing computer programs is to create a flow chart. In this section you will learn about the symbols used in flow charts so that you can create your own.

Link

Unit 12 Software development and *Unit 19 Computational thinking* explore other approaches to designing a program.

Flow charts

You can use a flow chart to help design a program. A flow chart is a diagram that shows how a program works and the routes that can be taken through it.

A flow chart shows where the program starts, where decisions are taken, processing operations, inputs and outputs.

Some of the symbols you will use in flow charts are shown in Figure 2.16 and Table 2.8.

Table 2.8 Flow chart symbols

Process	Used to represent any calculation or general processing operation carried out by the program.
Terminator	Shows where the program starts and finishes.
Decision box	Used in any place where the program makes a test to decide on a choice of directions to run the next code.
Data (Input/ Output)	Represents any part of the program that takes data in or shows, prints or outputs data.
Connector	Also known as a flow line. These lines connect other parts of the flow chart to show the routes the program can take. Flow lines usually have an arrow at one end to show the direction the program takes. If there is no arrow, the direction will be either downwards or to the right.

Process   Terminator   Decision box   Data (I/O)   Connector

Figure 2.6 Flow chart symbols

CONTINUED ▸▸

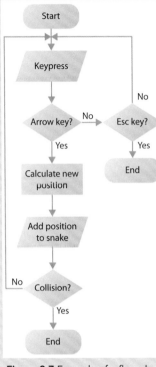

Figure 2.7 Example of a flow chart for a Snake game program

The example flow chart in Figure 2.7 shows a Snake game program which responds to an arrow key to change the direction of the snake or the Esc key to complete the program. Other keys are ignored. The game is over if there is a collision.

- The program accepts any key press.
- The first decision is whether an arrow key was used. If false, the program tests for the Esc key, either ending at that point or looping back to wait for another key press.
- If an arrow key was used the program calculates the new position for the snake.
- The snake occupies the new position.
- The program tests the new position for a collision. If true the program ends, otherwise the program loops back to wait for another key press.

Activity 2.4

A flow chart to convert marks to grades

Create a flow chart to show how a program could be used to calculate the overall grade for you and other learners completing the *BTEC First Award in Information and Creative Technology* qualification.

The overall grade is calculated from the unit points.

- All level 2 grades must have 24 points from core units.

The grades are awarded as follows:

- Level 2 Distinction* for 90 or more points
- Level 2 Distinction for 84–89 points
- Level 2 Merit for 66–83 points
- Level 2 Pass for 48–65 points
- Level 1 for 24–47 points, including 12 or more points from core units
- Unclassified for 23 or fewer points
- Unclassified if any unit is not completed and does not report an outcome.

The core units are:

- Unit 1 The online world
- Unit 2 Technology systems
- Unit 3 A digital portfolio.

Just checking

1 Can you draw the following flow chart symbols?
- a process
- a decision box
- a terminator
- data
- a connector

2 What is the purpose of a flow chart when programming?

Writing computer programs

Introduction

Computer programming constructs and techniques are the basic building blocks of a computer program. They are used by professional software developers to produce effective and accurate software and also help with maintaining the software.

This section introduces the basic constructs and some techniques used in computer programming. This knowledge and understanding will help you to discover the fun of writing your own simple programs.

Programming terms

Variables

Variables are used to hold data when the program runs. You can think of a variable as rather like a box with a name on it. You can put data into the box, move it to another box or change it

Before a variable is used it should be declared so the program knows the name of the variable, the type of data expected to be kept there and how much of the program can use the variable.

This is an example of a **declaration** statement in Visual Basic:

Dim QuizScore As Integer

In this statement, a variable named QuizScore is declared to be used to hold whole numbers (integers).

The position of the declaration statement in the program defines the **scope** of the variable. The scope can be local or global:

- A local variable has the declaration inside the **subroutine** where it can be used. The variable is then local to that subroutine and cannot be used elsewhere in the program.
- A global variable has the declaration outside of all the subroutines at the start of the program. The variable can then be used anywhere in the program.

Some programming languages need global variable declaration statements to be in a module alongside other parts of the program, such as forms.

An **assignment** statement in a program is where a variable has a value put inside it or where the value already held there is changed. The following assignment statement will put a value of 20 inside a variable named VAT:

VAT = 20

When a value is assigned to a variable, it will be kept there and can be used by the program. A variable can hold a value that can change (vary).

A **constant** is like a variable in that it can be referenced by a program many times, but the value of a constant is specified only once. A constant is often used to represent a value which will not change in that program, for example Pi (π) or gravity.

CONTINUED ▶▶

Input and output

A program needs input to get information or control from the user. The program then uses this impact to produce the required results.

Input could be a number typed into a text box that is then used by a calculation to work out a result. There are lots of other possible inputs, including form combo boxes, buttons and many other form objects.

Subroutines

Programs usually have subroutines to structure the code into small sections. Each subroutine is there for a particular part of the program.

Modern programs naturally structure themselves into subroutines, as a new one is created every time an **event handler** is added to a control.

Annotations

Professional software developers always annotate their code when writing programs to allow for maintenance. Annotations are comments written into the code to explain what parts of the program are there for.

Annotating code is useful for a programmer who has been asked to edit or maintain code, as the original developer's comments will help them understand how it works. Original authors can also use their own annotations as reminders if they need to maintain the code.

Data types

Programs need to use data for calculations, comparisons and for output to various devices. The best programs will always use the most appropriate data types to make the most effective use of memory and to ensure that only the correct types of data are allowed to be input.

A variable can be declared to have a data type, including:

- **Character** – allows any single letter or number.
- **String** – allows any combination of letters, numbers and spaces.
- **Integer** – for whole numbers.
- **Real** – for numbers with both whole parts and fractional parts.
- **Boolean** – can only hold true or false.

An example of each of these data types is given in Table 2.9.

Table 2.9 Examples of data for the different data types

Variable data type	Typical data held in the variable
Character	R
String	RJ Macey
Integer	356
Real	3.24
Boolean	TRUE

> **Key term**
>
> **Event handler** – The event handler for an object is the code that runs when that event occurred. A button will have an event handler for the click event, with code that runs when the user clicks on the button.

Data structures

Programs allow the use of data structures with variables, including records and simple arrays. These are defined below:

- A record data structure contains fields to store information in a similar way to a database table.
- An array data structure is a variable with many parts, in simple terms they can be thought of as tables with a number of rows and columns. The array has a number inside brackets (called a subscript), which is used to identify an item in the array that is required. For example, an array named Customer(100) that has just one column and 100 rows, so Customer(12) would be the contents of item number 12 in the list 0 to 99.

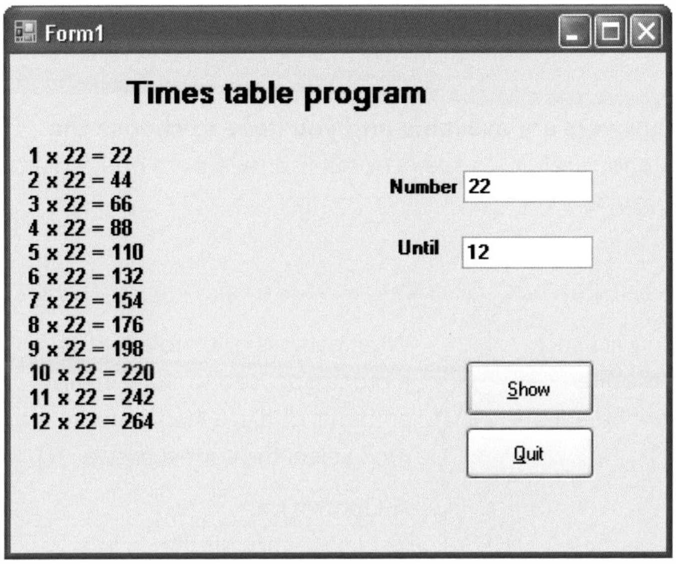

```
Private Sub btnShow_Click(ByVal sender As System.Object, ByVal e As System.EventArgs)
Handles btnShow.Click
    Dim Y As Integer
    Dim TableFont As Font = New Font("Arial", 10, FontStyle.Bold, GraphicsUnit.Point)
    Dim myBrush As New SolidBrush(Color.Black)
    Me.CreateGraphics.Clear(Me.BackColor)
    For Y = 1 To CInt(txtUntil.Text)
        Me.CreateGraphics.DrawString(Y & " x " & txtNumber.Text & " = " & Y * _
        CDbl(txtNumber.Text), TableFont, myBrush, 10, Y * 15 + 40)
    Next Y
End Sub
```

Figure 2.8 The code for a simple program and the resulting program

Just checking

1 What is the difference between a global variable and a local variable?

2 What data can be held in a variable that is declared to be a 'String'?

3 Why do programmers annotate their code?

Assessment Zone

This section has been written to help you to do your best when you take the assessment test. Read through it carefully and ask your tutor if there is anything that you are still not sure about.

How you will be assessed

You will take an onscreen assessment, using a computer. This will be set over about 15–20 screens and have a maximum of 50 marks. It will last for 1 hour.

There will be different types of questions in the test:

Disclaimer: These practice questions and sample answers are not actual exam questions. They are provided as a practice aid only and should not be assumed to reflect either the format or coverage of the real external test.

A Questions where the answers are available and you have to choose the answer(s). *Tip: Always read carefully to see how many answers are needed and how you can show the right answer.*

Examples:

Which of the following is used to synchronise your mobile phone and computer? Select the correct answer. [1]

A LAN

B PAN

C VAN

D WAN

Answer: B

What name is given to a part of a processor used to store small amounts of data when code is run? Select the correct answer. [1]

A Control unit

B Arithmetic & logic unit

C Register

D Core

Answer: C

B Questions where you are asked to give a short answer worth 1–2 marks. *Tip: Look carefully at how the question is set out to see how many points need to be included in your answer.*

Examples:

What is the main reason for using cache memory? [1]

Answer: To speed up a slower device, e.g. hard disk.

Describe the role of the processor in a computer system. [2]

Answer: The processor is the brain of the system. It runs the programs and controls the hardware. All the calculations and decisions are carried out within the processor.

C Questions where you are asked to give a longer answer – these can be worth up to 8 marks. *Tip: Plan your answer – think about how many points you need to make. Check through your answer – you may need to use the scroll bar to move back to the top.*

Example:

> Explain with examples the benefits of developing technology systems to an organisation. [6]
>
> **Answer:** Competitive advantage is when an organisation is able to provide better or different services than its competitors. Technology systems can provide better user experiences for both employees and customers, and can give an organisation a competitor advantage. A website which allows customers to make a booking and payment online is more likely to generate business than a website which requires customers to ring and speak to a person to make bookings.
>
> A developed system will also require less people to operate within that part of the business, meaning that business costs will be lower. For example, a computer-based payroll system that tracks employees' working hours is more time-efficient and cost-effective than a paper-based system. A paper-based system requires information to be copied across from time cards, whereas a computer-based system doesn't and the data is easier to access and use.
>
> This type of technology system can improve business performance, as processes are done more quickly and efficiently. It is also more satisfying for the people involved in the work. A developed system could also include new hardware, making software run faster, which can also help employees to achieve more in their working day.

Many questions will have images. Sometimes you will be asked to click to play a video or animation. You can do this as many times as you want.

Sometimes you may be asked to do a calculation – you can use the calculator provided in the onscreen test system if you need to.

Hints and tips

- **Use the pre-test time.** Make sure you have read the instructions, tested the function buttons, adjusted your seat and that you can see the screen clearly.
- **Watch the time.** The screen shows you how much time you have left. You should aim to take about 1 minute per mark. Some early questions will take less time than this and some later questions will take you longer.
- **Plan your longer answers.** Read the question carefully and think about the key points you will make. You can use paper or the onscreen note function to jot down ideas.
- **Check answers at the end.** You should keep moving through the questions and not let yourself get stuck on one. If you are really unsure of an answer or cannot give an answer, then you can use the onscreen system to flag that you need to come back to that question at the end.
- **Read back your longer answers.** Make sure you view the whole answer if you are checking back. There is no spell check facility.
- **Do you find it harder to read onscreen?** Talk to your teacher about how the system can be adjusted to meet your needs; for example, by changing the font size or colour.

How to improve your answer

Read the two student answers below, together with the feedback. Try to use what you learn here when you answer questions in your test.

Question

Identify three software utility applications, each with an example of the benefit it can bring to a computer system. (6 Marks)

Student 1's answer

> Utility apps are great software that can be good for your computer. They are often used by technicians to help fix or maintain a computer system, as this type of software can do things the techie would not be able to do or find out themselves. The technician's job would be a lot more difficult without this essential type of software app.

Feedback on student 1

The learner has not read the question, which asks them to identify three utility applications, each with an example of the benefit it can bring to a computer system and not generic writing about this type of utility. The learner has not answered the question asked and they haven't indicated any actual utility app specific benefits.

Student 2's answer

> Software utility apps are used by technicians to help find problems and to maintain computer systems.
>
> **Disk defragmenters** are there to help hard disks run faster. As we use a hard disk we are always saving or deleting work. Each time a file is deleted from a disk there will be a gap (space) left which can be reused. If another file is saved here and is too big for the gap it fragments into another gap. This will slow the drive down as it needs to get files from several places, not just one. Defragmentation remakes the disk, bringing files together and so making the hard disk run faster
>
> **Software firewalls** are there to stop potentially damaging content from the internet entering the computer. Without a firewall a computer would quickly get lots of malware installed, risking the user's work and security.
>
> **Anti-virus software** is there to find and get rid of any malware that gets through the firewall or gets installed in other ways, such as from a pen drive. Anti-virus software can regularly scan the computer to make sure no malware has got hold of the system.
>
> Without software utility apps a technician would find it a lot harder to keep an organisation's computer systems working well.

Feedback on student 2

Good introduction and summary to this work.

Three software utility applications have been identified and described in sufficient detail to show the learner understands their usage.

This is a good example as it clearly states each utility and the benefits they can add to a computer system.

Full marks would be awarded for this answer.

Assess yourself

Question 1

Which of these will lose their data when the power is disconnected? [1]

A HDD   C ROM

B RAM   D SD

Question 2

What is an operating system? [2]

Question 3

Explain what analogue data and digital data are, and provide and example of each. [4]

Answers

1) B

2) An operating system is the software used to link the hardware with apps and the user. The operating system has many functions including managing files, hardware, allocating resources and handling security.

3) Analogue data is real-world data with smooth changes between values *(1 mark)*. An example is sound which can have any number of differences in volume *(1 mark)*. Digital data is used inside a computer system and is based on numbers obtained from sampling analogue sound *(1 mark)*. Analogue sound that is sampled into digital sound would be held inside a computer system as a collection of numbers *(1 mark)*.

Introduction

In this digital age, the web is an ideal home to share and showcase your work. A digital portfolio is a collection of your work that you can shape onscreen and make available to anyone with a computer and internet connection.

Digital portfolios come in many forms, depending on the information they contain, the person providing them and the target audience. They may be:

- simple collections of files of varying types with a simple user interface for a specific purpose, such as the information held by estate agents on the different types of properties they are selling
- a virtual learning environment (VLE), such as Moodle, which teachers use to store a portfolio of lecture notes, exercises and assignments
- sophisticated databases and associated interfaces, such as some of the medical diagnostic and treatment portfolios.

A digital portfolio is an exciting way to demonstrate your talent and achievements. Not only can you share information in real time on a global scale, you can also connect with new audiences and include multimedia elements within your portfolio.

In this unit you will learn how to create a digital portfolio that uses web pages to show examples of your work. You will also learn about the lifecycle of a project, and gain an understanding of how to design, create and review your digital portfolio. For the purposes of assessment, you will need to design your portfolio to support an application, whether for a job, college, further training or higher education.

The work that you include must cover something from **all** the units in the *BTEC First in Information and Creative Technology* course, and you could also include work you have undertaken outside education, such as from hobbies or a part-time job.

Assessment: You will be assessed by a series of assignments set by your teacher.

Learning aims

In this unit you will:

A design a digital portfolio

B create and test a digital portfolio

C review the digital portfolio.

A digital portfolio

3

BTEC
Assessment Zone

This table shows what you must do in order to achieve a **Pass**, **Merit** or **Distinction** grade, and where you can find activities to help you.

Assessment criteria

Level 1	Level 2 Pass	Level 2 Merit	Level 2 Distinction
Learning aim A: Design a digital portfolio			
1A.1 Identify the audience and purpose for the design of a digital portfolio. **Assessment activity 3.1, page 95**	**2A.P1** Describe the audience and purpose for the design of a digital portfolio. **Assessment activity 3.1, page 95**	**2A.M1** Produce detailed designs for a digital portfolio, including: • alternative solutions • detailed storyboard of the layout and content of pages • a detailed structure chart with complete navigation routes • fully referenced sources for the ready-made assets. **Assessment activity 3.1, page 95**	**2A.D1** Justify the final design decisions, explaining how the digital portfolio will: • fulfil the stated purpose • meet the needs of the intended audience. **Assessment activity 3.1, page 95**
1A.2 Produce designs for a digital portfolio, with guidance, including: • outline storyboards of the layout and content • a list of ready-made assets to be used. **Assessment activity 3.1, page 95**	**2A.P2** Produce designs for a digital portfolio, including: • a timeline for the project • a storyboard of the layout and content of pages • a structure chart indicating navigation routes • a list of ready-made assets to be used, including sources. **Assessment activity 3.1, page 95**		
Learning aim B: Create and test a digital portfolio			
1B.3 English Prepare portfolio content, with guidance. **Assessment activity 3.2, page 97**	**2B.P3** English Prepare portfolio content and save in appropriate file formats, using folders, demonstrating awareness of purpose. **Assessment activity 3.2, page 97**	**2B.M2** English Select and refine a range of portfolio content and save in appropriate file formats, using a logical folder structure and demonstrating awareness of the audience. **Assessment activity 3.2, page 97**	**2B.D2** English Refine the portfolio to improve navigation and include commentaries that justify the choice of content. **Assessment activity 3.3, page 105**
1B.4 Create a functional digital portfolio, with guidance. **Assessment activity 3.3, page 105**	**2B.P4** Create a functional digital portfolio, including: • home page and section pages • context pages. **Assessment activity 3.3, page 105**	**2B.M3** English Develop the portfolio demonstrating awareness of the audience, using: • a range of suitable assets on the web pages • consistent navigation • commentaries to explain the content. **Assessment activity 3.3, page 105**	
1B.5 Test the digital portfolio for functionality, with guidance. **Assessment activity 3.4, page 108**	**2B.P5** Test the portfolio for purpose and functionality on a different system and browser, and take appropriate action. **Assessment activity 3.4, page 108**	**2B.M4** Gather feedback from others and use it to improve the portfolio, demonstrating awareness of audience and purpose. **Assessment activity 3.4, page 108**	

Assessment criteria			
Level 1	Level 2 Pass	Level 2 Merit	Level 2 Distinction
Learning aim C: Review the digital portfolio			
1C.6 Identify how the final portfolio is suitable for the intended purpose. **Assessment activity 3.5, page 111**	**2C.P6** Explain how the final portfolio is suitable for the intended audience and purpose. **Assessment activity 3.5, page 111**	**2C.M5** Review the extent to which the final portfolio meets the needs of audience and purpose, considering feedback from others. **Assessment activity 3.5, page 111**	**2C.D3** Evaluate the final digital portfolio against the initial designs and justify any changes made, making recommendations for further improvement. **Assessment activity 3.5, page 111**

English   Opportunity to practise English skills

How you will be assessed

The unit will be assessed by a series of internally marked tasks. You will be expected to show an understanding of the design and development of digital portfolios. The tasks will be set in the context of designing and creating your own digital portfolio, which you can use to apply for courses or employment. For example, you might be given a scenario in which you are asked to describe the purpose of your portfolio or plan out the content using a structure chart.

Your assessments could be in the form of:

- an illustrated report explaining the purpose of your portfolio and identifying who the audience is
- a structure chart listing all your content and assets
- a storyboard showing the content and running order of your portfolio
- a report containing screenshots of your home page, section pages and content pages
- a test report and feedback from user testing.

Learning aim A

Designing a digital portfolio

Getting started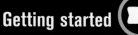

Technology, social media and multimedia are popular ways in which people share and engage with information. How do you think digital portfolios can help you develop your own learning? Why do you think potential employers like seeing work presented using an online portfolio? What skills do you think you will acquire from being able to design and create your own digital portfolio?

Key terms

Digital portfolio – A collection of digital documents gathered together for a specific purpose.

Project lifecycle – The process of developing a project through a series of stages.

Introduction

A **digital portfolio** is an exciting and dynamic way of presenting a set of electronic documents for a specific purpose – in this case, to showcase your achievements in your BTEC First in I&CT course. Your portfolio's design is an opportunity to demonstrate your technical and creative abilities, as well as your energy and passion. A strong design tells potential employers immediately that you are a candidate worth taking notice of.

Digital portfolio – background planning

Before you start planning your digital portfolio, you need to go back to basics. It is important that you understand what the project is and the different stages involved. This background knowledge will help you successfully plan, create and produce your own digital portfolio.

Defining a project

A significant part of the *BTEC First in Information and Creative Technology* course involves creating/developing different types of **computer-based products** (e.g. a website or digital graphics) and **systems** (e.g. a computer network or an automated guided vehicle). The term used to describe the process for creating/developing either a product or a system is a **project**.

All projects have a number of common characteristics, including:

- a purpose (e.g. to create/develop a product or system)
- a unique start and end point in time
- a scope (a set of activities that need to be undertaken to achieve the purpose)
- a limited set of resources (time, people and budget).

Every product and system has a set of features and functions that define what they are. Your digital portfolio will also have a set of features and functions. Establishing what these are early on in the planning stages will help you to define your project.

The more features and functions you include in your digital portfolio, the more complex it will be to create and the more work you will have to do to complete the project.

Project lifecycle

Every project has a lifecycle. This means that there are stages you will go through as you create/develop the product or system. There are different methodologies for the **project lifecycle**, but for the purposes of this course, you will use three basic stages:

1 **Design.** The design stage includes flushing out the idea, creating storyboards and structure charts, deciding on images and graphics, and choosing the type of software required.

2 **Create/test.** The create/test stage involves creating and developing the product and all the elements associated with it. It also involves testing your product to ensure that all the elements work. If you are launching a new website, you would need to check that all the links work, and that all the graphics and pages are displaying properly.

3 **Review.** Once you have created your portfolio, you will need to evaluate it and check whether it meets the original requirements and audience's needs.

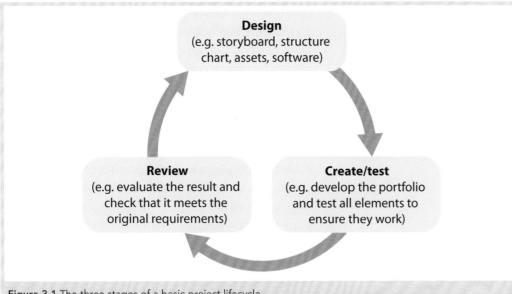

Figure 3.1 The three stages of a basic project lifecycle

Within any stage of the lifecycle, you can make changes. However, once you have finished a stage, you should not make further changes. Instead, if you identify any things you would like to change, then create a record of what you would do differently.

Digital portfolio structure

Structure refers to how your portfolio is put together. The structure of a digital portfolio depends on the type of portfolio, what it contains and what it will be used for. The structure of your portfolio will be different from that of a portfolio used by a commercial organisation to inform people about its products.

Structure types

When thinking about the structure of your own portfolio, you should consider using one of the following structures:

1 **A unit-based approach.** This approach involves presenting information on a unit-by-unit basis.

2 **A product-based approach.** This approach involves gathering together information from across different units and presenting it on a product basis. For example, information on a mobile app may require you to pull together work completed in *Unit 6 Creating digital graphics* and *Unit 8 Mobile apps development*.

Link

Refer to section *Reviewing your final digital portfolio* for further information on creating a record of things you would do differently.

CONTINUED ▸▸

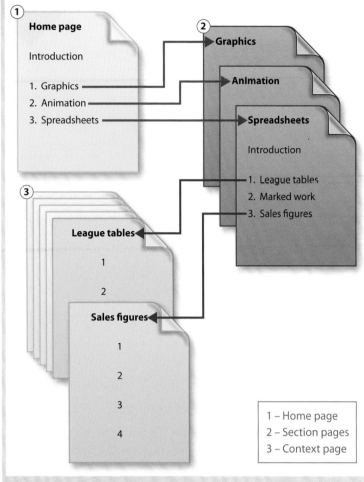

Figure 3.2 A digital portfolio's structure should include a home page, sections pages and context pages

1 – Home page
2 – Section pages
3 – Context page

Page types

Every digital portfolio should contain the following three types of pages.

1. Home page

The **home page** is the first page in a portfolio. There is usually a brief introduction to the whole portfolio on this page. Navigation to the section pages in the portfolio is controlled from this page. If your portfolio is going to contain samples of your work on graphics, animation and spreadsheets, you should be able to go to each of these sections from the home page. People looking at the portfolio will normally return to this page when they have finished a section.

2. Section pages

A **section page** starts each new section of the portfolio. Each section page should contain a brief description of the section. There may be one section page each for graphics, animation and spreadsheets. There will be navigation controls to the context pages within each section so that the user can navigate to animations (or graphics or spreadsheets) you have created and supporting work, such as your design documentation.

3. Context pages

The **context pages** are the areas of the portfolio that contain the work you have created in the other units. The context pages will contain a brief description of the pieces of evidence that you have collected and information about how you collected it. They will include navigation links to each item of evidence and back to the section pages and home page.

Structure chart

You need to create and include a structure chart to show how your pages will be linked together. You could use your work in Activity 3.3 to create this.

There are many different ways you can create a structure chart, including a basic block diagram, a navigation chart or a storyboard. An example of a basic structure chart for the graphics section of a portfolio is shown in Figure 3.3. You would use a similar structure for the other sections, such as those dealing with the animation and spreadsheet units.

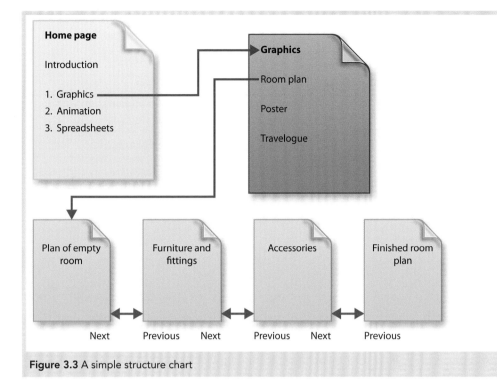

Figure 3.3 A simple structure chart

Once you have completed your structure chart, it is good practice to set up a similar folder structure. As you complete your work, you can save the content into the relevant folder. You will then be able to easily locate all the relevant information when you come to create your portfolio.

Timeline

A timeline is used to try to predict the total time needed to complete the project and the time needed to complete key stages of the project. It also indicates what you should be working on when. It should help you manage your time, so you don't spend too much time on any one activity! There are many ways that you can do this. Your timeline should identify the different project stages, as well as showing which tasks can be done at the same time and which must wait for a previous stage to finish.

> ### Activity 3.1
>
> Using sheets of paper, create a simple design for a home page and try different combinations of colours and fonts.
>
> Decide which you think are the best three combinations.
>
> Show these to a small group of people and see what they think.
>
> Keep the examples and notes of comments for when you start to design your portfolio.

> ### Just checking
>
> 1 What are the three stages of a basic project lifecycle? What happens during each stage?
> 2 What are the three types of pages you need to include in your digital portfolio?

Link

Refer to section *Folder structure and storage* for more on folders.

Discussion point

What do you understand by the term digital portfolio?

Discuss this in small groups and present your findings to the rest of your class.

Collate the findings of all of the groups and produce a definition.

User interface

Introduction

A user interface is a program designed to let people (users) interact with a system. It controls the user's display (screen) and allows the user to exchange information with the system through a series of controls, including buttons, commands and type-in fields.

Simple ways of inputting include data input forms, buttons and mouseovers. Simple forms of output include printouts and tabulations, diagrams and sound.

The design of your user interface for your digital portfolio is very important. You will need to sketch out your web pages to show how they will look and what they will contain.

Audience and purpose

The design of your user interface needs to reflect the target audience. How your portfolio looks and how easy it is to navigate will create an impression on your audience.

The people who will be looking at your portfolio could be managers in the organisation you are applying to: for example, the Human Resources Manager, the Technical Manager or the division's Director. All these people may be looking at different things; for example, your ability to communicate, your grasp of technical skills and whether your experience would fit in with their needs.

During your initial design stage, produce a short paragraph describing the purpose of the portfolio. This will help you define its purpose. Make sure your paragraph sets out the following:

- why you are creating the portfolio
- what you hope the portfolio will achieve
- what attributes your portfolio is likely to have. Will it be easy to use or very detailed? Explain why you have chosen to have these attributes.

Figure 3.4 You will need to explain why you have designed your portfolio in a particular way to prospective employers

Activity   3.2

Create a list of people who you think are likely to see your portfolio. Beside each person, write a short sentence outlining what you think they want/expect to see.

Make a list of the work you would like to include in the portfolio.

List the formats of this work.

Write a few brief notes about how these items will help support your application.

Keep copies of this work, as your notes may help you with your assessment.

Navigation

Good navigation is essential to allow users to move around your digital portfolio easily. If your portfolio is arranged in sections, your home page should include a **hyperlink** to each section, and each section should include hyperlinks to all the topics relating to that section. This navigation should work whether the user is moving forwards or backwards through sections.

Hyperlinks are normally positioned within a **navigation bar**. The location of the navigation bar requires some thought – although users need to find and access it easily, it shouldn't take over your page's design. It should also allow easy access to all pages in your digital portfolio, without having to keep going back through the home page.

Hyperlinks often appear as text. Users will click on this to 'jump' (move) to another page. If you prefer, you can also set up menus, images and buttons to provide the navigation.

Whichever navigation scheme you decide to use, it is important that you use it consistently within your portfolio. If you use a navigation bar or menu, make sure you position it in the same place on every page, as this will make it easier for users to navigate through your portfolio.

Page formatting

This is where you think about how the web pages will look. You will need to decide on a style for the web pages to provide some **consistency** and **continuity**.

Colour scheme

What colour scheme are you going to use? The colour scheme you choose must be accessible to everyone. Here are some examples of the types of things that you will have to consider:

- Red and yellow is an exciting combination, but not one that people can look at for long periods.

  This is an example of red on yellow.

- The combination of red and green causes problems for people who are colour blind.

Link

Refer to section *Page formatting* for more information on internal hyperlinks and navigation bars.

Key terms

Hyperlink – A link (which can be text or a graphic) that takes you to another web page or location within a document.

Navigation bar – A section of a web page that contains hypertext links, which connect you to other parts of the website.

Consistency – When all similar pages look similar throughout the portfolio (e.g. all section pages have the same format).

Continuity – When sections flow without major interruptions such as big changes in format or colour.

CONTINUED ▸▸

- White on cyan has been found to be a combination that is easily readable, but is it a pleasing combination?

  Cyan is a type of blue. Some early home computers used this combination.

- Black on white is the most usual combination, but does it really make an impact?

The use of too many colours can result in the reader losing concentration.

Fonts and sizes

Once you have decided on a colour scheme, you will need to decide on fonts and sizes for your text.

- Scripts have their place but can be very annoying to read.

  How easy do you find it to read this font?

- Headings are important, as they direct the reader to things that they are interested in. You need to use different fonts or different sizes of a font for headings.

- **Bold**, *italic* and <u>underline</u> need to be used with care. Just use them to highlight occasional words or phrases that have particular significance. In this student book, for example, you will find that the key terms (important words) and the illustration caption numbers use bold. This helps these features to be easily identifiable from the remainder of the text.

- You need to select readable font sizes, but ones that do not take up too much space. If people cannot easily read material, they are likely to ignore it.

Activity 3.3

Draw a neat, hand-drawn draft of your section pages to show the layout of your portfolio.

Draw a draft of a diagram showing how your home page will be linked to the section pages.

Add the linkages to the context pages to your diagram and note how you will link between context pages.

Note what type of link (e.g. buttons, menus, etc.) you are going to use and what your navigation bar will look like.

Keep this diagram to help you with your design work.

Just checking

1. Name three things you need to consider when planning your colour scheme.
2. Why are consistency and continuity important?
3. What is a navigation bar and why is it used?

WorkSpace

▶ Tim Symmons

Team leader: interface design

After getting distinctions in my National Diploma, I went to university to continue my education in Information Technology. In my second year I could pick specialist options, and I chose Human–Computer Interaction (HCI). I became fascinated by this developing area, from the design aspects to the psychology and science behind it, and I felt that this was a field in which I could carve out a career.

My first job was a junior designer within a large team of software designers. At first, I was given fairly small tasks, including roughing out designs, which more experienced designers would develop. Gradually, more interesting and technical work began to come my way. I had an interest in designing system interfaces for users, and my manager spotted that I had a talent for this and encouraged this specialism.

Initially, my work dealt with websites, but gradually I became involved in more general software interfaces. Currently, I'm involved with designing HCIs for people with various disabilities, using different types of hardware and software. HCI technology is a huge field and the ever-expanding range of hardware (e.g. smartphones and tablets) and disciplines makes it extremely exciting. Part of what I do involves translating computer sensible information into human sensible information, and the reverse.

It's important to be receptive to new things and to have an aptitude for innovative design. You have to be able to look at a problem and ask questions about how people work, what the computer needs, and how best to provide the environment for both to talk to each other.

There are great opportunities in this field to be involved in pioneering, cutting edge work and also to progress your career and develop your skills and knowledge base.

Think about it:

1 What is HCI?

2 What skills and characteristics do you think are needed for this type of job?

3 Consider all of the computer applications you use. What do you know about the number and type of interfaces they have?

Digital portfolio content

Introduction

Now that you have thought about how your portfolio will look, it is time to consider what it will contain. The portfolio is going to support an application for a job or for a place at college or in higher education, so you want to include your best pieces of work that showcase your talents and achievements.

Your digital portfolio must cover work from every unit of the course; you should select the most appropriate pieces that demonstrate a range of talents and skills (e.g. project planning, communication, creative flair, formatting techniques, asset selection), as potential employers will be looking for these.

Key terms

Multimedia files – Files that contain a mixture of digital images, sound or moving images.

Storyboard – A sequence of sketches or images. Storyboards are used to plan out photo or video shoots, as well as to plan sequences in TV programmes and films.

Assets – Things of value that you want to include in your portfolio. Digital assets can include images, sound and video.

Digital images – Diagrams, drawings, still photographs and clip art held electronically.

Audio files – Any files containing sounds, speech and/or music.

Moving images – Any images with movement (cartoons, video, film, etc.).

Compression – A method of reducing the size of files.

Compression ratio – The approximate percentage by which a file is reduced in size.

Link

For more information on how storyboards are used, see *Unit 4 Creating digital animation*, *Unit 7 Creating digital video* and *Unit 13 Website development*.

What to include in your portfolio

You need to think about what content to include in your portfolio and what your selection of web pages will look like. You will also want to think about how the user interface, formatting and colour schemes fit together with the content.

You also need to consider:

- how you will combine files of different formats into your portfolio
- what you can do to limit the size of **multimedia files**, which can be large (tens of megabytes in size)
- how you will get your audience to move systematically through your portfolio.

Storyboard

A **storyboard** is a graphical representation of the 'story' being told. In the case of a digital portfolio, the storyboard will be a set of sketched web pages presented in a logical sequence that is determined by the structure chart.

The storyboard will contain a number of panels. Each panel will represent a web page, including the method you have chosen for the user interface. You need to create a storyboard for your preferred design solution, which may include some details of alternative design solutions. Your storyboard should contain a minimum of eight panels and should include the following elements:

1 a sketch of the home page, containing basic notes about the main features and functions and how these relate to the audience and purpose

2 sketches of a few section pages, containing basic notes about the main features and functions and how these relate to the audience and purpose

3 sketches of several context pages and how the user will move between them, with notes about the main features and functions, as well as how these relate to the audience and purpose.

The actual content of the storyboards will depend on what work you are going to include in your portfolio.

Digital assets

The term digital **assets** refers to any type of graphic/image, audio clip, video clip or animation sequence. Throughout your course, you will produce assets that you could include in your digital portfolio and they include several different file formats.

How are you going to include these different assets in your portfolio? How will they support your application?

Digital images can have a variety of different file formats, for example:

.bmp   .jpg   .tif   .psd

.gif   .tng   .png   .psp

Each one has its own characteristics and purpose. Digital photographs, drawings, clip art, illustrations, full colour images, black and white images and so on may all have different file types.

Do you have many images that between them use lots of different file formats? If you do, you should save them in just one or two different formats. This will make it a lot simpler to compile and use your portfolio.

Audio files also have different formats. Some of the most popular include:

.wav   .tta   .mp3   .mpeg

Moving images have a variety of formats that you will need to consider. The following file extensions represent some of the more common formats:

.avi   .asf   .asx   .flv   .mov

File sizes and compression

The files used to hold digital media tend to be extremely large. One thing that you can do to reduce the size of these files is use a technique called **compression**.

Compression is performed in different ways, usually depending on the type of file being compressed:

- **TIFF** files tend not to use compression at all and are always large.
- **JPG** files analyse the image and discard the information that the eye is least likely to notice. It is often possible to set the compression ratio for .jpg files.
- **GIF** format reduces the number of colours and abbreviates information for repeating groups.

Compression methods are automatic within file types, although you can set the **compression ratio** (and therefore the file size) within some types.

Link

See *Unit 6 Creating digital graphics* for more information on digital image formats and vector and bitmap images.

Did you know?

Some file formats cannot be read by some web browsers (TIFF is problematic for web use), so make sure you use file types that can be accessed by everyone.

Vector images and bitmapped images tend to use different file formats, so you can usually tell which type an image is from its file extension.

Some file formats cannot handle large numbers of colours (GIF reduces the number of colours in colour-rich images), so for photos a different file format (such as JPG or PNG) might be more appropriate.

Remember

You will be using web pages for your portfolio, so use image formats that most web browsers can handle, such as GIF and JPG.

Documents library			Arrange by: Folder ▾
Email attachment			
Name	Date modified	Type	Size
LargeFile	16/08/2011 22:19	Word 2007 Docu...	9,284 KB
LargeFile	19/08/2011 09:11	Compressed (zipp...	9,118 KB

Figure 3.5 Example of a compressed file

CONTINUED ▸▸

Accessibility

Accessibility is a term used to describe how easily people can access the portfolio. It also refers to whether or not all members of your target audience can use your portfolio.

- Can they open the portfolio and find their way around it?
- Can they understand the content of your digital portfolio?
- Can they see and read the content? You will need to consider this for people with visual or auditory impairments.

You should include details of the folders in which you will store the relevant files, even if these are automatically allocated by the software you are using. People who will be reading the portfolio will also need instructions on how to start running the portfolio.

Web accessibility

When creating web pages, it is very important to think about user accessibility, and whether the content is accessible to people of all abilities and disabilities. Things to consider include:

- **Font and screen colour.** The colour combination of red and green is difficult for some people to read, as are similar colours when layered together (e.g. a pink font against a red background).
- **Size of text.** Some users might need to adjust the size of text to make the text larger and easier to read.
- **Audio.** Some users might have visual impairments, making it hard to read text on a screen, so including image descriptions that can be used by screen readers can help users engage with a page.
- **Flashing effects.** Where possible, you should avoid these or make them optional so that users who are prone to seizures caused by these effects are not put at risk.

When pages are correctly designed, developed and edited, all users can have equal access to information and functionality.

Sources table

In your storyboard, you will have identified buttons, pictures, audio clips and other assets that you want to include in your digital portfolio. These will be either original (made by you) or ready-made (made by another person or third party).

As part of your design documentation, you need to create a sources table identifying all the ready-made assets you are going to include, together with their formats and details of the folder structure in which you will store the relevant files. You may also want to include original assets in the table. (The work you completed in Activity 3.2, will help you to produce this.)

Remember that you do not need to create a sources table for any assets you have included as part of an alternative design.

Activity   3.4

Make detailed notes of what digital images your portfolio will include and what formats they are in at the moment.

Make similar notes about any audio files, moving image files and multimedia files you will be using.

Decide on the file formats you are hoping to use for these files.

Note any thoughts or concerns you have about accessibility.

Discussion point

In a future project you may need to include people with sight problems, hearing problems or mobility problems in your target audience.

Discuss with your peer group and teacher how you could make provisions for this.

Alternative design ideas

It is important to think of alternate design ideas so that you can be confident that your overall design solution (everything that forms part of your design) is fit for the intended purpose and audience.

For the digital portfolio, your alternative design ideas are likely to focus on different approaches to particular aspects of the design, such as an alternative structure (e.g. organised by theme or organised by course unit), a different style or positioning of a menu bar or font type.

You should identify and describe the alternative design ideas on your storyboard. With all of your alternative ideas, you will need to explain why you have decided not to use them.

You could also briefly describe a completely different design solution, but you do not need to produce a storyboard for this.

Assessment activity 3.1 | 1A.1 | 1A.2 | 2A.1 | 2A.P2 | 2A.M1 | 2A.D1 |

Your teacher has asked you to create a digital portfolio to showcase your digital skills to potential employers or colleges.

* Describe what your digital portfolio will be about.
* Consider who will be looking at your portfolio. How might they expect it to look? What would they expect it to include? Find examples of good digital portfolios and explain how you will make your portfolio suitable for your intended audience.
* Create a plan outlining the stages of the project.
* Design your portfolio.
* Come up with some alternative ideas for elements of your design.
* Review your designs and explain why you selected them and how they are suitable for your intended audience.

Tips
* Include as much as detail as you can about each element.
* When considering your designs, take each element in turn, describe the options you came up with and select the best one. Explain why you choose that option over the other ones.

Creating and testing a digital portfolio

 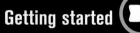
Introduction

Now you need to take the designs you have been working on and use them to create your digital portfolio. There are four basic stages in the actual creation process:

1 preparing the content
2 using tools and techniques for page formatting
3 building content into web pages
4 including images and objects.

This section covers preparing the content. The other stages will be covered later.

Preparing the content

There are many different pieces of software available for creating web pages. The software that you use will usually be determined by what your school or college has available. This section only deals with the generic aspects of creating web pages and does not include specific techniques or specific software.

Folder structure and storage

A folder structure and suitable storage are very important to ensure that the content you have selected to include in your portfolio is stored in a logical place. Therefore, when you come to create your digital portfolio, you will be able to find it easily. Remember to back up all content, as you don't want to lose any work if a software or computer error occurs.

If you start the course by designing your digital portfolio, then it is a good idea to set up a folder structure that is similar to the portfolio structure at the same time. The advantage of this approach is that as you create suitable content, you can store it in an appropriate folder for when you come to create your digital portfolio.

If you are developing the portfolio at the end of the course, your teacher should have already asked you to store your work in an appropriate folder structure.

To create links from your web pages that work, you will need to group together only the information that you are actually going to use into the appropriate folders in your structure.

Figure 3.6 is a diagram of a type of folder structure that you could use.

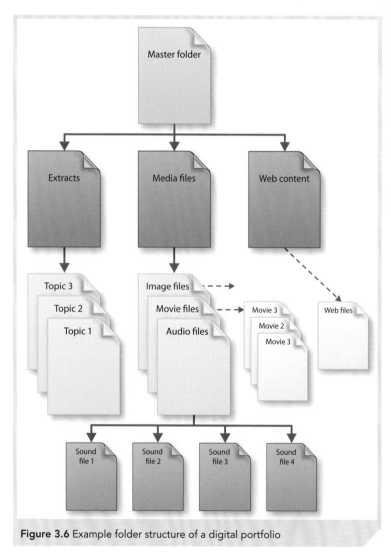

Figure 3.6 Example folder structure of a digital portfolio

Gathering and preparing extracts and other content

During the design stage, you will have identified the material that you want to include in your portfolio. This material, known as assets, can include some, or all, of the following:

- text extracts from coursework
- pictures
- video files
- diagrams
- extracts from projects
- audio files
- multimedia files.

You should gather all this information together into a single folder so that it is separate from other data on your computer. Having all the data in one folder will allow you to check that you have got everything you need.

Selecting material from that collected

When you have gathered together all the information you would like to include in your portfolio, you may find that you have too much material. You will need to **refine** your selection and focus on material that:

1 has a specific purpose – in this case, your purpose is to show your audience what you can do and what sort of person you are

2 provides information in a way that interests your audience and really shows off your achievement and potential – an employer will be looking for specific **characteristics** from applicants and you need to show to the best of your ability that you have these

3 does not duplicate information elsewhere in your portfolio.

File conversions

You will need to check that your assets (including digital assets) have been saved in the correct format for use within your portfolio. Your audience will also need to be able to view the assets, so think about file sizes (as large files could cause a delay with pages loading/opening) and formats. You did some preparatory work on this in Activity 3.4, when you identified the best formats for the different types of file.)

You will need to check:

- if the software you have allows you to save the file in the format you have selected
- whether the file can be converted to the format you have selected
- how to convert the file using another software application if a simple saving system will not work
- that the selected format will work within your proposed portfolio.

Key terms

Refine – To make things better in some way. This could be by careful selection of things (as in this case) or by changing things so they work better (e.g. a computer program) or by making things easier to read or access.

Characteristics – The properties that someone or something has. Usually these are things that are useful in certain types of work or situations. Characteristics that are not useful are known as negative characteristics.

Link

Refer to section *Digital portfolio content* for more information on file formats.

Remember

You should only include file types in your portfolio that typical users will be able to open.

Assessment activity 3.2   *English* | 1B.3 | 2B.P3 | 2B.M2 |

Your next step is to prepare all of the material you want to include in your digital portfolio. Carefully choose which material you are going to include and put it in appropriate folders so you know where it will go in your portfolio. You should be able to justify why you have decided to include each piece.

Tips
- Make sure you have a good reason for including each piece of material.
- Make sure you use a clear folder structure so you don't lose any material.

Page formatting

Introduction

Page formatting refers to all the basic formatting information (fonts, colours, line spacing and headings) that you need to add to your templates before you include content. You are likely to use whatever web page authoring software you have available to create page templates for your web pages. You will have to decide on some basic features that will be consistent throughout your finished portfolio, and include these in your templates.

Key terms

Authoring software – A program used to create, edit and delete web pages.

Templates – Web pages that contain just the basic structure you want. You can then slot content into these templates to form the finished web pages. (Templates can also be used for items such as text documents, spreadsheets and slides.)

Tables

Sometimes information looks better when it is organised in a table because people can easily see and compare information from different sources.

Look at and compare the following two examples. Example 1 uses text, while Example 2 uses a table format to display the same information. Which format do you think makes things clearer and is easier to read?

Example 1

'I received a distinction for my work on spreadsheets, which received very good comments from my teacher. My merit for **Animation** received good comments from my teacher but I missed one part of the **Distinction** and didn't have time to add it, although I could have done. My **Graphics** work was marked as excellent, and my teacher commented that it "was some of the best work I've seen".'

Example 2

Unit	Title	Grade	Comment
4	Animation	M	Good work but missed one D criterion
6	Graphics	D	Excellent work
9	Spreadsheets	D	Very good work

If you are going to use tables, you will need to decide on the fonts and headings you will use, and how the text will be aligned within the cells.

Fonts

Fonts were discussed in the section *User interface*. You need to choose fonts that are easy to read and use a variety of sizes to represent different levels of heading.

In this Student Book, you will find the following types of headings and text:

Main heading

Section heading

Subheading

Content text

You will need to have a similar scheme for your portfolio. It will help your audience to know where major sections start and finish.

Alignment

Alignment is to do with the boundaries of your content in relation to the edges of a page: where something starts, where it ends and whether it lines up on the left, on the right or in the centre. You can apply alignment to text on a page, in a box or in a table, and also to digital assets.

This text is aligned on the left.	This text is aligned in the centre.	This text is aligned on the right.

Colour

In your design work, you played around with colour combinations to try to find a combination that suits your particular portfolio. Within the software you are using to create web pages, you can set up templates that use your chosen colour scheme as a standard.

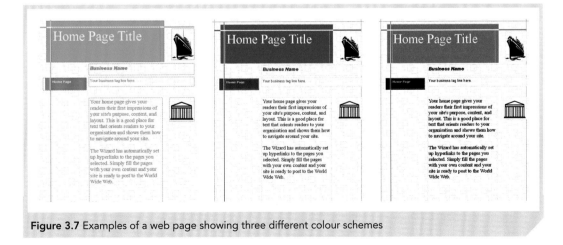

Figure 3.7 Examples of a web page showing three different colour schemes

If you are going to include boxes with important information that you want your audience to notice, using a different colour scheme for these boxes will help to make the information stand out.

CONTINUED ▶▶

Line spacing

You can use line spacing for effect. Normal blocks of text are single spaced, with the next line of text appearing on the next possible line with no space between. This paragraph is printed using single line spacing.

Sometimes a spacing of 1.15 lines can help with readability, especially where a difficult colour combination is being used. This paragraph is printed using 1.15 spacing.

Increased line spacing is often used between paragraphs, before and after headings, and sometimes between items in a list. It can also be used to make text more easily readable, for example when producing notes for giving a talk or presentation.

Double spacing can help things to stand out in the text, but if it is used too frequently, it can make things more difficult to read. You should, therefore, use it with care. Line spacing greater than double spaced is rarely used, as it can look clumsy.

Bullets and numbered lists

Bullets and numbering are very good for highlighting lists of things. For many lists, bullets will provide better outcomes on web pages, although you can use numbering in menus. Bullets are used for many of the lists in this chapter.

Activity 3.5

It is important that your digital portfolio looks consistent. Using templates is a very good way of ensuring that your portfolio has a consistent look and layout.

1 Research what templates are provided in your authoring software. What other standard templates can you find?

2 Select a number of templates that you would like to use in your portfolio. Practise adding the following different formatting options to these templates:

- tables
- fonts
- line spacing
- bullets and numbered lists
- alignment
- headings
- colour schemes.

Just checking

1 Why is it important to use a folder structure for the material you will be using in your portfolio?

2 Why are different styles of headings important? What do they tell you? Give an example of three different types of heading.

3 What does 'alignment' mean?

Page content

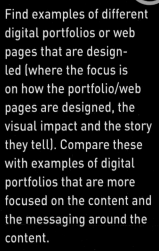

Introduction

There is no point in having a beautifully designed portfolio unless it also contains good content. You will need to consider why you are including each piece of content and make sure it is of the highest quality you can produce.

Text

The text you include on your pages needs to explain the content to your audience. Each piece of content should include an introduction to explain what it is and why you have included it. The introduction should lead your audience into the content by including the reasons the work was undertaken, and which of your characteristics it demonstrates.

In addition to introductions, you may need to add some text to provide a link between the various pieces of work included.

Images

Images can include photographs, drawings, illustrations, clip art or diagrams.

It is often said that a picture is worth a thousand words, but this is only true when the picture adds something to the work as a whole. The images you select must add something extra to the text, or provide further explanation or clarification of the text. You could also include an image used as a logo to help give a consistent look and feel to the presentation of your portfolio.

You may need to write captions for some of the images used to make sure that they fully explain the text.

Sound and video

If you are going to use sound clips and video clips, then like images, they must have a real purpose. They have to add something special to the rest of the content, or demonstrate something that the text and images on the web page cannot.

As your portfolio is in support of an application, you might choose to include audio or video of a presentation that you have given to demonstrate your presentation skills. (The ability to present and effectively communicate information is highly valued by employers, and are key skills that they look for.)

If you include audio files, you could also look at including a transcript (a written version of what is contained in the audio file). An audio file will give your audience an idea of your expressiveness when speaking to people.

Video will show not only your vocal control, but also your body language during a presentation. You could also include video of you performing a practical activity to demonstrate your practical skills.

While audio and video clips are very useful, you should not include too many. If you are going to use more than one clip, you should make sure they are varied to prevent them from becoming monotonous.

CONTINUED ▶▶

Lines and shapes

Lines and simple shapes can be used to great advantage to divide sections of information on a website. They can also add to the consistent image that you want to portray in your portfolio.

You can use simple shapes such as rectangles to produce text boxes for highlighting specific pieces of text. You can use lines as dividers to separate different types of information in your text.

Figure 3.8 Different ways of presenting hyperlinks within a web page

Internal hyperlinks

Hyperlinks control the navigation from web page to web page. There are many ways of presenting hyperlinks and some have been mentioned already in section *User interface*. Popular ways include:

- a text menu in which the user clicks on the text
- graphics with mouseover and click states
- buttons
- drop-down menus
- navigation bars.

How you use hyperlinks is important from a user's perspective. It needs to be consistent and made easy for users, so that they are able to easily spot hyperlinks within different sections of your portfolio. To provide consistency across your portfolio, you should aim to apply the same style and positioning of hyperlinks across your portfolio. For example, have all text hyperlinks the same colour and have the navigation bar in the same location on each of your pages.

Navigation bars

This is the area of a web page that contains the hyperlinks. Navigation bars take up room and may, therefore, limit the space available for you to place your actual content. It is usual practice for every navigation bar to have at least one link to take users to the level above, as well as ones to the levels below. Normally, there is also a link that takes users to the home page.

Activity	3.6

Using some of the templates you created in Activity 3.5, create a few sample web pages that include a number of the page content features covered in this section.

Keep notes of what you have done and save the pages you create, as they may be useful for Assessment activity 3.3.

Visual assets: images and objects

Introduction

Web pages do not just contain text – they also contain assets (graphics, audio, tables, hyperlinks and moving images). In fact, assets cover everything other than text. Within this unit, the terms 'images' and 'objects' have also been used when speaking about visual assets. The careful use of images and objects can make your portfolio more interesting and useful.

An object could be almost anything other than text that you want to include; diagrams, spreadsheets, graphics, tables and hyperlinks are all objects. In fact, many people would argue that the term 'object' includes images.

Earlier in this unit, you looked at how you can use assets within your portfolio's content and formatting. This section will deal with images and objects from the point of view of incorporating them into your web pages. It is worth bearing in mind that too many objects and images can be more difficult to cope with than too few.

Position

The position of an image or object on a web page needs a lot of thought. It can be positioned top, middle or bottom or left, middle or right, but there are many combinations of these simple positions that you can use.

Starting the content of a web page with an image or other object is not always effective unless it immediately introduces the subject visually. It is often better to have some headings and a little text and then include an image or object.

The image is of elephants going to a river on the Serengeti plains in Tanzania. It was taken using an old Sony 3.2. megapixel digital camera. Not the sharpness of image perhaps of more modern cameras, or even of good quality mobile leading edge at the country was waiting around some of the there was still a lushness to the rains, of course, the whole area becomes it is much more  'phones, but quite time. Although the for the autumn rains, rivers and waterholes sufficient water to give vegetation. After the vegetation across the green and prolific, and difficult to find animals at that time because they disperse throughout the area. During the dry season they tend to congregate within close proximity to water, and are thus much easier to find.

Figure 3.9: Positioning an image in the middle of text or a web page can make it difficult to read the information

Images in the centre of the page are rarely suitably placed. The page looks far more interesting when the image is offset. Positioning a logo is also difficult – you need to decide if it should go in a header, footer, side panel or within the main body of the page.

You will have thought about some of these issues at the design stage, but it is only at the creation stage that you get to see what your web pages really look like. Don't be afraid to make changes to your design if you have good reason to do so. Remember to make a note of the change and the reason(s) for it on your design documents.

CONTINUED ▶▶

▶▶ CONTINUED

Link

See *Unit 6 Creating digital graphics* for more information on cropping images, resolution and pixelation.

Key terms

Crop – To remove parts of an image so that only the bit you want will remain.

Resolution – Refers to the amount of information an image holds. The greater the resolution aspect, the better quality the image is.

Pixelated – When an image is enlarged so much that it appears blurry.

Landscape orientation – When the width of a page or image is greater than its height (i.e. it is short and wide).

Portrait orientation – When the height of a page or image is greater than its width (i.e. it is tall and thin).

Crop and size

Sometimes when you choose an image, you might only want to use part of it. This is possible – you just need to **crop** the image. Cropping is a form of cutting. You select the part you'd like to keep and then you use the crop tool to cut away the rest of the image. If you are using the cropped image on a website or printing it out, then you need to make sure that the **resolution** is still OK and that your photo hasn't become blurry and **pixelated**.

Alignment

Alignment of text was covered in section *Page formatting*. Alignment is just as important with objects and images as it is with text.

You can align objects and images horizontally:

- with the left-hand edge of the page or sub-area of the page
- with the right-hand edge of the page or sub-area of the page
- in the centre across the page.

You can also align objects and images vertically:

- at the top of the page
- at the bottom of the page
- in the centre down the page.

As with text alignment, you should think carefully about the most appropriate alignment.

Orientation

You will need to decide whether the images or objects fit the page better in **landscape** or **portrait orientation**. A web page is usually portrait orientation, but that does not necessarily mean that the images have to be portrait orientation within the page.

The orientation will mainly be determined by the natural orientation of the image or object you are inserting. Photographs are usually clearly either portrait or landscape. The same is true for most things, such as spreadsheet pages, charts and diagrams. Occasionally, objects could be either portrait or landscape and then you need to use your judgement as to which looks better on your page.

The image is of elephants going to a river on the Serengeti plains in Tanzania. It was taken using an old Sony 3.2. megapixel digital camera. Not the sharpness of image perhaps of more modern cameras, or even of good quality mobile 'phones, but quite leading edge at the time. Although the country was waiting for the autumn rains, around some of the rivers and waterholes there was still sufficient water to give a lushness to the vegetation. After the rains, of course, the vegetation across the whole area becomes green and prolific, and it is much more difficult to find animals at that time because they

Figure 3.10 Text flowing around an image

Text wrapping

There are various effects that you can apply to text to control how it interacts with nearby images. This is known as text wrapping.

You can set text to:

- flow around an image
- appear to the left and/or right of an image
- start above and continue below an image, with no text down the sides of the image

- flow behind an image (for example, if some of the image is transparent)
- appear in front of an image.

When you are creating your portfolio and adding images, remember:

- It is much more difficult to read and concentrate on text that runs down both sides of an image. It is better to have text to the left or right of an image rather than on both sides.
- An image behind text may cause problems both with identifying the image and with reading the text. You should use this option with care.
- Most people will read text from left to right, so if the image is more important than the text, you might like to position it on the left. If the text is more important, you will probably want to position the image to the right of the text.

Resolution

The resolution (dots per inch) of an image or object (visual asset) is important so that the audience is able to identify what it is showing. However, the resolution will largely be determined by the object being used. If you are presenting objects with a very high resolution, consider using low-resolution thumbnail images that link to the higher-resolution originals. These lower-resolution thumbnails will be smaller (and faster to load) than the originals.

One thing that you can influence is the sizing of objects – you can increase the size of an image until it is out of focus or decrease its size until it can no longer be identified.

Activity 3.7

Using some of the work you produced in Activities 3.5. and 3.6, include some images and objects to add clarity to your pages.

Keep notes of what you have done and save the pages you create, as they may be useful for Assessment activity 3.3.

Assessment activity 3.3   *English* | 1B.4 | 2B.P4 | 2B.M3 | 2B.D2 |

- Develop your digital portfolio, keeping the needs of your audience in mind at all times. Make sure it has appropriate pages, which are easy to navigate around, and a range of assets, such as images and videos, etc.
- Write commentaries to explain your content.

Tips
- During development, keep asking yourself, 'How could this be improved?'. This will help you develop your portfolio.
- Make notes on every decision you make to help you explain your choices.

Testing your digital portfolio

Getting started

Testing is a broad term. In small groups, discuss what you think is meant by 'testing'. Write down the different steps you think the testing process involves – and at the end of this section, revisit your list and add in any missing stages.

Introduction

Testing your portfolio is important as it will allow you to identify and correct any errors, as well as make further refinements before you release it to your audience. You should carry out testing when you complete a section of the digital portfolio and at the point that your whole portfolio is complete.

What tests should I complete?

You need to undertake the testing of your digital portfolio in a logical fashion. There are many ways of doing this, and an example test checklist is shown in Figure 3.11.

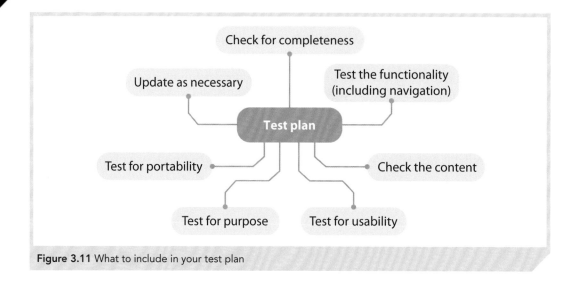

Figure 3.11 What to include in your test plan

Audience and purpose

Part of the testing process involves checking whether your portfolio is suitable for your audience and if it meets its purpose. Ask yourself the following questions:

1 Does it contain everything I wanted to show the audience?
2 Does it contain everything that the audience would want to know about me and my work?
3 Does it showcase my work in the best possible (appropriate) way?

Completeness

Checking for completeness involves making sure that all the things you want to include, together with the commentaries and any additional text, are present in the portfolio.

Go through the lists of assets you made in Activity 3.2 and make sure they are all present in the portfolio folder structure. If you have missed anything, make sure you put it into place before you continue.

Remember

Your portfolio must be complete in itself. Your audience will not be able to access any information that is not in your folder structure.

Functionality and navigation

Test every pathway through your portfolio. Check that all the hyperlinks work correctly and take you to the expected content. No link should escape being tested. If there are problems, now is the time to correct them.

Content

- Check that the content is effective (i.e. well suited to its purpose and audience).
- Check that every page contains what you expect it to contain. Occasionally, content can end up on the wrong page.
- Check every page for errors: spell check and proofread all the text.
- Make sure that assets (including images and objects) have the correct captions. It is surprising how often there are errors within captions.
- Check that there are sensible descriptions for links to other pages, particularly on the home page and the section pages. They should give users a good idea of what will be on the page that is being linked to.

Usability

Testing for usability means testing how easy the portfolio is to use. You should ask the following questions:

- Is the user interface pleasing to look at?
- Is it easy to find information on the pages?
- Can you understand what you have to do just by looking at the pages?
- Is the content eye-catching and consistent in layout?
- Does the content immediately make sense?
- Are there any sudden changes in style?
- Overall, is the portfolio straightforward to use?

Get other people to test your portfolio and give you feedback. Make notes as you go through and make any necessary amendments.

Portability

Portability refers to the portfolio being used on different systems. Test your portfolio on another system using a different browser.

If it does not work on a different system or browser, then you need to work out what you can do to fix this. If the solution is simple (for example, replacing a component that requires Internet Explorer® with one that works in all web browsers), then you can fix it. If the solution is not easy to implement, you could issue a note with the portfolio that states the system requirements it will run on.

Remember

Your portfolio is designed to help you get a job or a place on a course.

Your audience is your prospective employers or admissions tutors, and they will not want to have to spend time learning how to use your portfolio; any difficulty and they will just not bother.

You need to make an immediate impact.

Your portfolio needs to contain everything the audience is likely to want to see.

Key term

Portability – This is when you can view or use your portfolio across different systems, meaning that your portfolio is 'portable' and can viewed on systems using different browsers.

CONTINUED ▶▶

Get feedback from a range of people to ensure your portfolio is fit for purpose

Test users

It is a good idea to get someone else to test your portfolio and feed back to you on their experiences. You could arrange for a test user (whether a friend, family member or another learner) to test your portfolio to ensure that it is fit for purpose and audience and that it is easy to find and access information. This should happen at several times during the development – so after you have completed each section – and it should happen before you complete the portfolio.

The test user should do a 'walk through' of the portfolio, taking on the role of a user. They should note down their findings and recommendations. At this stage, this does not need to be a formal process (e.g. creating a questionnaire), but following the testing you should have an informal discussion with your test user. You could record the discussion or write down the key points following the discussion.

You should use this feedback to refine your portfolio, noting any instances where you have chosen not to implement any feedback and why you have chosen not to do so.

Assessment activity 3.4 | 1B.5 | 2B.P5 | 2B.M4

Now you need to test your portfolio.

- Check that it works as it should on different browsers and systems.
- Ask other people to test it. See if they can navigate around it easily to find what they are looking for. You should record any comments they make.
- Look at the results of your tests and the user feedback. You should try to fix any problems that were encountered, and improve your portfolio in line with the user's suggestions where possible.

Tips

- Keep a log of the tests you do, and record the results of each action as you go along.
- If a user comments that they have a problem, ask them questions to find out exactly what is at the source of the problem. For example, if they can't find a file, find out whether it's not where it should be (uploading or functionality issues), or whether they were looking for it in a different place (in which case you might want to rethink your structure).

Reviewing your final digital portfolio

CONTINUED ▶▶

Getting started

When you get to the end of a project, it can be very hard to review your own work objectively. This is why it is so important to establish at the start of a project what the purpose is and what the audience's requirements are.

In the *Getting started* section of *Page content*, you looked at a number of different types of digital portfolios. Select one and write down what you think its purpose and audience requirements are. Does the portfolio deliver on these?

Introduction

You should undertake a review of your final portfolio once you have finished it. Reviewing involves taking a critical look at what you have produced and comparing it to what you expected to produce, as well as what your audience actually needed. Reviewing is an extremely difficult skill that is usually only fully developed after many years of practice. It is a good idea to start practising your reviewing skills at every level of your work.

What to include in your review

Your review process should include the following stages:

1 Check how closely the finished portfolio fits the original purpose.
2 Consider whether the finished portfolio meet the needs of the audience.
3 Evaluate the design documentation.
4 Evaluate any changes made during the development of your portfolio.
5 Carry out basic user testing (getting users to review the portfolio).
6 Incorporate users' feedback.
7 Suggest further improvements that could be made, and explain why these improvements are necessary.

Reviewing for purpose

This involves going back to the beginning and looking at the reasons why you produced the portfolio in the first place. What was its purpose?

The purpose could have been to provide evidence of who you are and what you can do to support a job application to an IT company. You now need to look at your finished portfolio and compare it against that original purpose.

Activity 3.8

Ask yourself: 'Have I provided all the information I can to showcase my skills, talent and abilities to this employer?' If the answer is no, then ask yourself, 'What have I missed?'

Ask yourself: 'Could I have provided more information, or different information, that would have been better?' If the answer is yes, then ask yourself, 'What would have been better?'

Keep notes of everything you do in this part of the review, as they may help you with your final assessment.

Reviewing for audience

Having considered the purpose of the portfolio, you now need to go back and think about what the audience expected.

The audience for your portfolio may be prospective employers who may come from different areas of the business to which you are applying. You need to think about the things these people may want to find out and compare what you have produced against their expectations. Figure 3.12 shows three examples of what different people might be looking for.

Figure 3.12 What different people within an organisation might be looking for in a potential employee

Activity 3.9

Ask yourself: 'If I were one of the people likely to see this portfolio, would it provide all the information I need?' If the answer is no, then ask yourself, 'What have I missed?'

Repeat this for a selection of people who may be involved in appointing staff.

Keep notes of everything you do in this part of the review, as they may help you with your final assessment.

Reviewing the development

This is a review of the processes you went through, not the outcomes or the product. To do this you need to go through all of the actions you have taken, and decide whether each step:

- went well and would not need to be changed in a future development
- went acceptably, but would possibly need thinking about in future
- went badly and should have been done a different way.

This is a very useful activity that you can use for reviewing other projects that you undertake in the future.

Activity 3.10

Review all of the stages of making a portfolio and decide which have gone well, which have gone badly and which are merely acceptable.

Note practices you would not change and practices that need some modification.

Keep your notes, as they may help you in your final assessment.

Reviewing user feedback

This is a more formal review of the portfolio, where you ask test users to review what you have produced. The test users should **not** have been involved in the development or earlier testing of the portfolio. They should review the portfolio to determine if it would meet the needs of the intended audience and purpose, and how easy it is to use.

There are numerous methods you could use to gather the test users' feedback. One method could be a questionnaire. This method supports continuity as a questionnaire will contain pre-determined questions – meaning that all test users will be asked the same questions.

You should use the feedback to explain how your portfolio meets the needs of the intended audience and purpose, and it will help you make recommendations for further improvement.

Suggested improvements

At the end of the review you should be in a position to suggest some further improvements to the portfolio. You should justify why each improvement is needed. Remember – you don't need to implement the recommendations, but it is important to record them. It is possible that these suggestions may lead to the start of a development cycle to update the product.

Activity 3.11

Review the user feedback and make a note of any feedback that caused you to make modifications, as well as any that could lead to future modifications.

Carefully consider what improvements could be made to your portfolio.

Keep your notes, as they may help you in your final assessment.

Assessment activity 3.5

1C.6 | 2C.P6 | 2C.M5 | 2C.D3

Now it's time to evaluate your portfolio.

- Compare your finished portfolio to your original designs – does it look exactly as you originally planned, or have you made any changes? If so, explain what changes you made, and why.

- Consider how well it meets the needs you identified for your audience. Use the feedback you gathered from other people as part of your testing.

- Describe how you could improve on your final portfolio.

Tip

Whatever format you choose for your evaluation, make sure it is presented clearly. Think about the structure, and tackle one element at a time, making sure you include reasons for decisions you made.

Introduction

Animation is used for a wide variety of purposes, including various forms of entertainment, advertising and simulation. Many films and games contain amazing visual effects created using computer animation. Most of us have enjoyed watching cartoons ranging from short children's TV programmes to full-length animated feature films.

Although almost all animation is now created using digital techniques, animation has a long history that pre-dates computers. Animation is an exciting and fast-moving area that provides opportunities to combine creative and technical skills. However, it also requires patience and attention to detail.

Assessment: You will be assessed by a series of assignments set by your teacher.

Learning aims

In this unit you will:

A understand the applications and features of digital animation products

B design a digital animation product

C create, test and review a digital animation product.

> *Completing this unit was challenging as it required quite a lot more patience and skills than I first thought, but it was really exciting to see the final result. I am proud of the animation I produced and it really made all the effort I put into it worthwhile.*
>
> *Wendy, 16-year-old animator*

Creating digital animation

4

BTEC
Assessment Zone

This table shows what you must do in order to achieve a **Pass**, **Merit** or **Distinction** grade, and where you can find activities in this book to help you.

Assessment criteria			
Level 1	**Level 2 Pass**	**Level 2 Merit**	**Level 2 Distinction**
Learning aim A: Understand the applications and features of digital animation products			
1A.1 Identify the intended purpose and features of two animation products. **Assessment activity 4.1, page 121**	**2A.P1** Explain the intended purpose and features of two different animation products. **Assessment activity 4.1, page 121**	**2A.M1** Review how the products are fit for purpose and their intended effect on the audience. **Assessment activity 4.1, page 121**	**2A.D1** Discuss the strengths and weaknesses of two animation products. **Assessment activity 4.1, page 121**
Learning aim B: Design a digital animation product			
1B.2 Identify the audience and purpose for the design of an animation. **Assessment activity 4.2, page 124**	**2B.P2** Describe the audience and purpose for the design of an animation. **Assessment activity 4.2, page 124**	**2B.M2** English Produce a detailed animation product design, including reasons why alternative ideas have been discarded. **Assessment activity 4.2, page 124**	**2B.D2** English Justify the final design decisions, explain how they will: • fulfil the stated purpose and requirements of the brief • meet the needs of the audience. **Assessment activity 4.2, page 124**
1B.3 Produce an outline design for an animation product, with guidance. The design must include an outline storyboard. **Assessment activity 4.2, page 124**	**2B.P3** English Produce designs for an animation product of at least 30 seconds duration. The design must include: • description of requirements from the brief • a storyboard • a list of ready-made assets • audio. **Assessment activity 4.2, page 124**		
Learning aim C: Create, test and review a digital animation product			
1C.4 Prepare assets for the animation, with guidance. **Assessment activity 4.3, page 147**	**2C.P4** Prepare original and any ready-made assets for the animation product demonstrating awareness of purpose, with sources of assets listed. **Assessment activity 4.3, page 147**	**2C.M3** Prepare assets for the animation product demonstrating awareness of audience, with all sources of assets fully referenced. **Assessment activity 4.3, page 147**	**2C.D3** Maths Refine assets to create a high-quality animation product. **Assessment activity 4.3, page 147**

Assessment criteria

Level 1	Level 2 Pass	Level 2 Merit	Level 2 Distinction
1C.5 Maths	**2C.P5** Maths	**2C.M4** Maths	
Edit assets to create an animation product of at least 20 seconds, testing the product for functionality with guidance. **Assessment activity 4.3, page 147**	Edit assets to create an animation of at least 30 seconds which includes audio. Test the product for functionality and purpose against the original requirements, making any necessary improvements to the product. **Assessment activity 4.3, page 147**	Gather feedback from others on the quality of the product and use it to improve the product, demonstrating awareness of audience and purpose. **Assessment activity 4.3, page 147**	
1C.6	**2C.P6**	**2C.M5**	**2C.D4**
Identify how the final animation product is suitable for the intended purpose. **Assessment activity 4.4, page 147**	Explain how the final animation product is suitable for the intended audience and purpose. **Assessment activity 4.4, page 147**	Review the extent to which the final animation product meets the needs of the intended audience and the purpose, considering feedback from others and any constraints. **Assessment activity 4.4, page 147**	Evaluate the final animation product and the initial design and justify any changes made, making recommendations for further improvement. **Assessment activity 4.4, page 147**

Maths   Opportunity to practise mathematical skills   English   Opportunity to practise English skills

How you will be assessed

This unit will be assessed by a series of internally marked tasks. You will be expected to show that you understand the features of animation products and the processes involved in creating them. The tasks will be based on a scenario for which you will need to develop an animation of between 30 seconds and two minutes in length that meets a particular brief. For example, the brief could be from a charity that has commissioned you to produce an animation about a health-related issue.

Your assessment could be in the form of:

- a report or magazine article on the use and purposes of animation products
- written design documentation and prototypes for the animation you will be developing
- the completed digital animation product
- annotated and updated design documents
- written review documentation showing your completed test plan and the responses to feedback you have gathered
- a written evaluation report giving details of the strengths and weaknesses and improvements made.

Types of animation

Getting started

With a couple of your classmates, brainstorm the different types of animations you have seen at the cinema, on TV, in games or on the internet. What types can you identify? What are the key features of each type?

Introduction

Animation uses a series of images shown in quick succession to create the illusion of movement. In this section you will be introduced to the different types of animation (including traditional methods and digital-based methods) and the ways you can use different techniques and methods to achieve the illustration of movement.

Flick or flip book

These are one of the simplest forms of animation. Drawings of the steps of a person or object in motion (such as a person running) are created on successive pages of a book. By flicking through the pages you can create the illusion of movement.

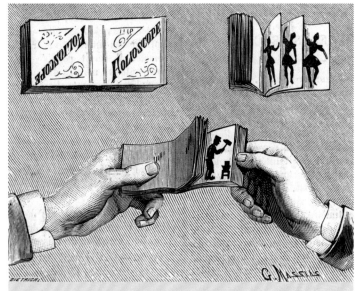

Figure 4.1 A simple flip book animation

Activity 4.1

Use a book or note pad that has at least 30 sheets of paper. For every one second of animation you will need at least five sheets of paper. Starting at the bottom sheet, draw your first character in the bottom corner of the sheet near the edge of the page. A simple stick person is fine. On the next sheet up, draw the next step of your animation. This should be aligned with the previous one, but you need to make a very minor change to your drawing, such as a slight raise of the foot. Once you have completed about 30 sheets, quickly flick through them and your character should appear to move.

Cel animation

Cel animation is the traditional technique that was used up until the 1990s to make animated cartoons, such as *Tom and Jerry*, and feature-length films. With this technique, each frame of the animation is drawn and painted by hand. Moving characters are drawn on transparent sheets (called cels) and placed over fixed backgrounds. Each set of cels (foreground action and fixed background) is then photographed. Normally 12 or 24 drawings are required for each second of the film.

Stop motion

In this technique, actual models of the characters and backgrounds are used. These are photographed and then moved by a small amount for each frame, creating the illusion of motion. Well-known examples include the *Wallace and Gromit* films. Stop motion has also been used to create special effects in films such as *Star Wars* and *RoboCop*. Although largely replaced by computerised techniques, stop motion is still used in some projects.

Cut-out animation

Cut-out is one of the earliest techniques used to make animated films. It is similar to cel animation but the characters and backgrounds are made from paper or card. Today, a similar look can be created using computer techniques that replace the paper or card cut-outs with computer-drawn images.

Computer-generated imagery (CGI)

Many action, science fiction and fantasy films include special effects created using **CGI**. It is used because the quality is often better and the effects are more controllable than, for example, using models. Another use is for crowd scenes, because it allows more flexibility than other methods and avoids the hire of expensive extras (actors).

The film *Tron Legacy* features animation using cutouts

Adobe® Flash® animation

Adobe® Flash® software is relativity easy to use to create simple 2D animations and it is widely used to create animation for web pages. For this reason, Adobe® Flash® is used for the example animations in this unit.

Other types of animation

Motion capture is widely used in computer games to capture, for example, the movements of athletes and martial artists. It is also used in live action films to create computer-generated creatures, including Gollum in *Lord of the Rings*, the Na'vi in *Avatar* and Clu in *TRON Legacy*. During the filming of these sequences, actors wear reflective markers on their body and face that are tracked by software and used to animate the computer-generated characters.

Other types of animation, including rotoscoping and skeletal animation, are covered later in this unit.

Key terms

CGI – Images or life-like characters created using computerised technology.

Did you know?

The actor Oliver Reed died in 1999 while making the film *Gladiator*. CGI was used to include his character, Proximo, in scenes filmed after his death.

Link

See section *2D animation techniques* for information on other types of animation.

Just checking

1 What are the different types of animation that can be used to create the illusion of movement?

2 What is the difference between cel and cut-out animation?

3 What are some of the advantages of using computer-generated imagery?

Applications of digital animation

Introduction

We are all familiar with children's cartoons, but animation is used in many other ways too. In some cases, such as the animations used in films for special effects, they are designed to appear to be real live action rather than an animation.

How animation is used

Let's look of some of the different ways in which computer animation can be used. The most obvious is in the creation of animations for entertainment.

Some uses for animation

Children's cartoons for television and full-length animated feature films may be the first use that you think of. However, animation is often used in adverts and in music videos. It is also used to create simulations, such as what happens during an earthquake or how a spacecraft will land on Mars.

Animations are widely used on the internet and for mobile content, ranging from simple animations to liven up web pages to the complex animations used in games.

Creating effects

Animation can be used to create scenes that would be impossible, very difficult or very expensive to reproduce with live action. For example, it can be used to produce monsters, aliens or animals that can talk.

Animation can be used to create an atmosphere or mood in a film that cannot easily be produced with live action. Children's cartoons, for example, can have a silly, crazy feel that is exciting, fast moving and totally unrealistic. This may include animals or inanimate objects (such as cars or trains) that have human features and characteristics and may involve them interacting with real humans.

Animations can also show how something works (or will work) more clearly than could be done with words or still images (for example the Mars landing animation). This is called a simulation.

Animation may be aimed at many different types of audience. It can be used to make people laugh, make them sad, educate them or to produce many other effects. When designing an animation product, you will need to consider who the audience is and what kind of effect you want to have on them.

Did you know?

You can watch an animation of the way the Mars spacecraft Curiosity was expected to land on the planet. Using the internet, go to YouTube and search for **'Mars Science Laboratory Curiosity Rover Animation'**. This project was launched in 2011 and Curiosity landed on Mars in August 2012.

Activity 4.2

Imagine you are considering making a short animated film. You want to target the film at a particular audience but you haven't yet decided who that audience is. Brainstorm a list of the different sorts of things you might include in the animation to appeal to the following audiences (one example has already been included for you).

- Young children (e.g. bright colours)
- Teenage boys
- Teenage girls
- Adults (aged 21–40)
- Older adults (aged 40–60)

WorkSpace

▶ Simon Jones

Junior animator

I have been working as a junior animator at an animation company in Bristol for two years.

I was lucky to get a job here as there is a lot of competition in this industry. I got into animation at school and I went on to study Computer Animation at University, but after I completed my degree it took me almost a year to find a paid job in animation.

During that time, before I got a paid job, I created a number of showreels (example animations) that showcased my skills. In the end, that is what really helped me get a job. However, I also needed to demonstrate I had very good knowledge and skills in using Flash®.

I spend most of my working hours creating Flash® animations for children's TV. I work from rough storyboards that the designers produce. I have to work quickly and accurately, and I need good drawing and design skills. I always have to work to quite tight deadlines, as the TV shows have to be completed and fit into a schedule. If I get behind with anything, I just have to stay late and get the work done!

The work can be quite tough and some aspects of it can be a bit tedious, but I get a tremendous kick out of seeing animations I have created shown on the TV.

In the future, I'm hoping to progress to become a designer. I've got some great ideas that I think will make amazing animations.

Think about it

1 What skills, qualifications and experience did Simon need to get a job as an animator?

2 What challenges does he face in his day-to-day work?

3 What does he like best about his job?

Features of digital animation

 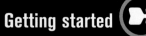
Introduction

Animating a drawing creates the illusion of movement or life. This section explores some of the features used to add realism to animations.

2D and 3D models

Characters and backgrounds are created using simple graphic images. Two-dimensional (2D) animation (Figure 4.2) is easy to create, but has a flat look and lacks realism. With 3D animation (Figure 4.3), textures and lighting effects can be added to give the impression of depth. Although more complex to create, 3D animations are more realistic and are often used in applications, for example in games, where realism is important.

Figure 4.2 *Spirited Away*, the Japanese animated fantasy film, uses 2D animation

Figure 4.3 The feature film *Ice Age* uses 3D animation to create realistic characters

Link

For more detailed information on bitmap and vector images and how to edit them, see *Unit 6 Creating digital graphics*.

Image type

Bitmaps and vector images are file types used in animation software to provide characters and backgrounds. Bitmaps are used for images such as photos where realism is important, whereas vector images are used more for non-realistic images such as diagrams or cartoon characters.

Did you know?

Drawing 24 frames for every one second of film is expensive. Therefore, almost all hand-drawn animation is done by 'shooting on twos', where each frame is shown twice, making only 12 different frames per second. Many low budget films are created using 'shooting on fours', with only six different frames per second.

Frames per second (fps)

Both live action and animated films are made up of consecutive still images that produce the illusion of movement. The number of different images displayed per second is known as the frame rate. Various frame rates are used in TV and video, ranging from 24 fps up to 60 fps. Traditional hand-drawn animation is designed to be played at 24 fps. This is also the default frame rate used in Flash®.

Resolution

Resolution is a measure of the number of pixels in a bitmap image. The more pixels there are in an image of a given size, the better the quality of the image. However, more pixels also make a larger file size. Computer animations can be made up of thousands of different images, creating very large files, so it is important to have in mind the size (resolution) that the animation is likely to be viewed at.

Link

You can find more about image type and resolution in *Unit 6 Creating digital graphics*.

Timing and length

In a live action film, scenes are played out naturally. In an animated film, the animators have to pay special attention to the timing of scenes as they create them so that they appear realistic when played back. For this unit you are only required to create a short animation of at least 30 seconds, but this will probably be made up of 720 or more frames. Animation software such as Flash® helps you by creating many of the frames for you, but you will still need to plan how long each part of the animation will take.

Special effects

You can use various special effects to create the illusion of movement, adding realism to your characters. These include:

- **rendering** – using colour fill and shading
- **morphing** – using a shape tween to change one shape into another
- **camera angles** – using different shots to create an effect or mood
- **motion blur/fade** – used to make movement look more realistic.

Audio

Most animations include a soundtrack. The simplest form of soundtrack consists of just music. More sophisticated versions include sound effects, music and speech. Details of how to add audio files are given later in this unit in section *Audio*.

Link

Recording and editing audio is covered in detail in *Unit 5 Creating digital audio*.

Assessment activity 4.1   1A.1 | 2A.P1 | 2A.M1 | 2A.D1

Your friend Barry is a DJ. He has asked for your help in advertising his business. Barry likes the idea of including an animation on the website he's planning, but he does not know enough about this area and he wants you to explain the options.

Pick two different digitally animated products to evaluate and prepare a short document to help you explain animation to Barry. Your document should cover the following:

- What is the animation for?
- Who is the animation meant to appeal to?
- How does the animation appeal to the desired audience? For example, what style and approach has the animator used?
- How successful are the animations? Do they appeal to the correct audience?
- Explain the strengths and weaknesses of each animation.

Tips

- Identify some key features and take each one in turn to consider the animations.

- Think about how the features, style and approach of each animation differs, and how these elements affect the audience watching the animation and impacts on the animation's success.

Designing your animation

Getting started

Before starting on your own animation you should look at several examples of short animations for inspiration. However, don't forget that it is also good to develop your own ideas.

Introduction

This section asks you to think about what animation you are going to create and who you are creating it for.

What goes into the design?

Before you can start designing your animation you will need to think about some of the following issues.

Intended audience, purpose and user requirements

Make sure you are clear about the purpose of your animation. For example, are you using it to amuse or educate your intended audience?

You must clearly identify your intended audience and ensure that you include features that will appeal to them. You will need to think about the story your animation will tell, what colours and characters you will use, and the type of language and tone you will use in the soundtrack.

In some situations you may have a client brief to work from. This should outline the intended purpose and audience for the animation and identify things such as the length and format of the animation.

Storyboards

A very useful way for you to try out your first design ideas is by making **storyboards**.

Storyboards are often used by professional filmmakers when they are designing scenes in both animated and live action films. A storyboard is a series of drawings that allows you to see what the final product will look like. You should produce a storyboard for each **keyframe**. A keyframe is when there is a significant change in your animation, such as a character starting to move.

Remember

Your final product for assessment of this unit only needs to be 30-seconds long (although it can of course be longer). Look for a storyline that is short and punchy rather than long and complex.

Key terms

Storyboard – A series of drawings used to show how a final product will look.

Keyframe – A keyframe marks the start and end points of any significant change within an animation.

Did you know?

The storyboard technique was developed in the 1930s by the Walt Disney Studio. Storyboards continue to be used for both live action and animated films to this day.

Storyboards are very useful for planning out sequences

Storyboards are working documents. They do not have to be well drawn and can end up quite messy, with handwritten notes and arrows showing direction of movements.

Prototypes

Prototyping can be a very useful technique in developing your designs and ideas for your animation. A prototype is a version of your animation that may not be complete or fully polished but it gives you an idea of how a design concept may work. With some animation techniques being rather complex and time-consuming, you can also use a prototype to test out the feasibility of an idea that you have. You may well produce a number of different prototypes to test out and refine different ideas.

Activity   4.3

A charity supporting young mothers has asked you to produce a short animation. The purpose is to encourage young mothers to think about the dangers of smoking, and how secondary smoking may harm the health of their children. (Secondary smoking is where a non-smoker, such as a small child, inhales smoke because someone close to them is smoking.)

The charity's Director would like the animation to be thought-provoking rather than entertaining. She would like it to emphasise the love that exists between a mother and her child, while contrasting this with the potential dangers that a mother exposes her child to by smoking.

Sketch out your prototype ideas to help plan the animation sequence

- Produce two prototype sketches to show to the charity's Director.

Documenting ready-made assets

Your animation may contain **graphic assets**, such as characters and backgrounds. You should produce a list (also known as a sources table) of where these assets come from, especially if you have downloaded them. For example, you may draw assets just for this unit, or you may be creating some in another unit, such as *Unit 6 Creating digital graphics*, or you may be using ready-made assets from the internet.

Key term

Graphic assets – The digital images used in a product. You can create the graphic assets yourself or use ready-made assets from other sources, but you must have the right to use them.

CONTINUED ▶▶

Alternative design ideas

You are unlikely to arrive at your final design without considering some alternatives. These might be ideas for completely different approaches to the animation, or ideas about different features within the animation. For example, you might consider a number of different characters or backgrounds for your animation. You need to keep a record of these alternative design ideas, as you will need to explain the alternatives you considered and the reasons for your final choices to obtain the higher grades.

| **Assessment activity 4.2** | *English* | 1B.2 | 1B.3 | 2B.P2 | 2B.P3 | 2B.M2 | 2B.D2 |

Barry was impressed by your introduction to animation and he would like you to come up with a design for a digital animation product for his DJ business.

For the last year, Barry's booking have been for parties, weddings and special occasions. He would like to attract new clients looking to hire a DJ for corporate events and themed nights. He wants to promote that fact that he can cater for all musical tastes, play at any venue and that he can make every party fun for all the guests.

- Identify the key points that Barry would like the animation to convey.
- Consider the type of clients Barry wants to appeal to. Who are they? How will you make your animation appeal to this audience?
- Create a plan outlining the elements which need to be included in your design.
- Come up with some ideas for the design of the animation. Think about which ones will be most appropriate for your purpose, and make notes on your designs to indicate which ones you will use, with reasons why.
- Make sure your animation is at least 30 seconds long.
- Review your designs and explain why you selected them and why they are suitable for your audience.

Tips

- Your designs should be clearly laid out to explain what is happening at different points in the animation.
- Include as much useful detail as you can about how things will work, which options you choose, etc. – it will help you when you come to evaluate your finished product.
- Always think about who the animation needs to appeal to when choosing visuals and audio tracks.

Creating the animation

Getting started

In small groups, discuss what assets you are planning to include in your digital animation. How are you planning to keep track of these assets and the different formats they are in? Does your animation software support the current format of these assets? Do you need to convert any assets to a different format? If so, how are you planning to do this?

Introduction

Once you have completed the design phase, it is time create your animation. The first stage of this process is preparing your assets. Assets include everything from audio clips and video footage, to digitally created or hand-drawn graphics you have created or sourced elsewhere. You will need to check whether your animation software can support the formats of your assets.

Preparing assets

Your assets are a very important part of your animation, and it is vital that you spend time organising and preparing them to be included in the animation.

Gathering ready-made digital assets

With ready-made assets such as clip art, it may simply be a case of finding the suitable image on the internet and importing it into your animation software. Many internet sites provide copyright-free clip art, which you can use to create characters, backgrounds or other objects. There are also sites that provide copyright-free music, which you can use as background music and sound effects for your animation.

Hand draw or use graphics-editing software to create original assets

To create assets yourself, you can either hand draw them and scan them into the computer or use graphics-editing software to draw and edit the images from scratch. Which method you use depends partly on your artistic ability and on the style you want your animation to have. Hand-drawn pictures tend to look just that, and you will need some artistic ability. Alternatively, you can further edit your drawings once you have scanned them into the computer.

Importing original and ready-made assets

Ready-made assets you identify may be in a variety of graphic, video or audio file formats. You will need to check that the animation software you are using supports each of these formats. Table 4.1 lists some common formats.

Link

Creating and editing graphics images is covered in *Unit 6 Creating digital graphics*.

Table 4.1 Common video, graphics and audio formats

Video/graphics formats	
.tga	Bitmap graphics format often used for backgrounds or textures. Cannot be directly imported into Flash® so would need converting to another format, such as BMP or JPG.
.jpg	Very widely used compressed bitmap graphics format. Can be directly imported into Flash®.
.dpx	Bitmap graphic format sometimes used for scanned images. Cannot be directly imported into Flash® so would need converting to another format, such as BMP or JPG.
.iff	File interchange format. Cannot be directly imported into Flash® so would need converting to another format, such as BMP or JPG.

continued

Table 4.1 (continued)

.avi	Microsoft® video file format. Can be directly imported into Flash®.
.png	Very widely used compressed bitmap graphics format. Can be directly imported into Flash®.
.ac (AC3D)	Proprietary 3D graphics file format.
.obj (Wavefront)	Open 3D graphics file format.
.lwo (Lightwave)	Lightwave is a high-end 3D graphics product used to produce high-quality 3D graphic images.
.mov (QuickTime)	QuickTime is a widely used video format originally developed by Apple® but also supported by the Windows® operating system. Can be directly imported into Flash®.
.mp4 and .mpg	MPG and MP4 are widely used open standards for video formats. Can be directly imported into Flash®.
Audio formats	
.wav	Wave files are uncompressed digital audio files. Can be directly imported into Flash®.
.au	Audio file format developed by Sun Microsystems, and often used on Unix and Linux systems. Cannot be directly imported into Flash® so would need converting to another format, such as MP3.
.mp3	Very widely used compressed audio file format. Can be directly imported into Flash®.
.aiff	Audio format developed by Apple® and widely used on their systems. Cannot be directly imported into Flash® so would need converting to another format such as MP3.

With graphic images it is probably best to import them into the Flash® library. That way you can include them in any frames as and when they are needed.

Discussion point

Why is it important to make sure that you do not use copyright materials without permission?

How to import graphic images into Flash®

Step 1 Go to the **File** menu in Flash® and choose **Import**. This will pop out a submenu, where you should choose **Import to library**.

Step 2 Then select the file you wish to import.

Remember to keep a table of all the ready-made assets you use, with their sources. This is required for your assessment and also helps you to demonstrate that you have used copyright-free assets.

Just checking

1 QuickTime is a format created by which well-known computer company?
2 When importing graphics into Flash, where is the best place to store them?
3 What is the name of the most widely used compressed audio format?

Editing tools and techniques

Introduction

To complete this unit, you will need to create assets for your digital animation using graphics-editing software.

In order to create and prepare both vector and bitmap images, you will need to understand and be able to use the different editing tools and techniques available in the graphics-editing software. This section looks at some of these tools and techniques.

Vector-editing tools and techniques

You can use vector-editing tools to help you with:

- text
- lines and curves
- shading, colour fills, gradients and patterns
- layering.

Let's look at some simple examples of editing vector graphics in Flash®. The software featured in the 'How to' guides and screenshots is Adobe® Photoshop®.

How to draw shapes

To draw a simple rectangle:

Step 1 Select the **Rectangle** tool from the toolbar on the left of the screen.

Step 2 Click in the stage area and use your mouse to drag out a rectangle shape on the stage (see Figure 4.4).

To draw other shapes:

Step 1 Click and hold on the **Rectangle** tool and a menu will pop out. From this menu, you can select other shapes, such as an ellipse or polygon.

Step 2 To select a shape you have already drawn, use the **Selection** tool and click on the shape. The **Properties** panel will show you the fill colour and line style and allow you to edit them. (Flash® calls the line style the stroke of the selected shape.)

Step 3 As you create a drawing made up of different shape, it is a good idea to group the shapes together so they can be treated as a single drawing object.

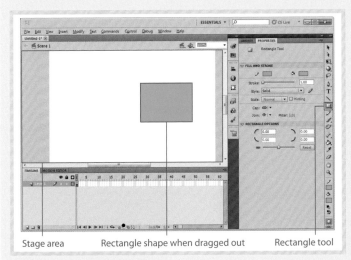

Stage area   Rectangle shape when dragged out   Rectangle tool

Figure 4.4 Drawing a rectangle

CONTINUED ▶▶

How to group shapes

Step 1 Select the **Selection** tool in the toolbar on the left.

Step 2 Drag out a **marquee** over the whole collection of shapes to select them all.

Step 3 From the **Modify** menu in the menu bar, choose **Group**.

Step 4 If you later decide you need to edit an individual part of a grouped object, you can ungroup it by choosing **Ungroup** from the **Modify** menu.

Step 5 Once you have grouped a set of shapes, you can fill, scale, rotate and flip it.

Text

Text is just as important as your graphics. You can edit the size, font, colour and position of your text.

How to add text to a Flash® drawing

Step 1 Click the **Text** tool in the toolbar on the right.

Step 2 Click on the stage at the point where you want the text to appear.

Step 3 Type in some text.

Step 4 The **Properties** panel on the right allows you to choose the font, size, colour and many other attributes of the text. See Figure 4.5.

Figure 4.5 Adding text

Layers

Layering is a very important graphics drawing technique for animation.

Key term

Layering – Layers are like transparent sheets layered on top of each other. Layers are shown in Flash® in the timeline. Graphic objects on the top layer will appear in front of those in lower layers. Parts of a drawing or character you want to animate must be on separate layers. Layering is when you place layers over the top of each other.

How to create a new layer

Step 1 Right click the existing layer in the timeline at the bottom of the Flash® screen (see Figure 4.6).

Step 2 Choose **Insert new layer**.

Step 3 Double click the layer name and change it to something meaningful.

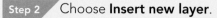

Figure 4.6 Flash® layers

Shapes are added to the currently selected layer. The pupils of the eyes need to be animated (see Figure 4.5), so a separate layer called 'Eyes' has been added and the pupils drawn on that layer. The rest of the face is drawn on the 'Face' layer. Note that the 'Eyes' layer is shown above the 'Face' layer; if this was not the case, the pupils would be hidden behind the face. You can change the order of a layer by dragging it above or below another layer in the timeline.

Photo-editing tools and techniques

You can use photo-editing tools to:

- select and remove parts
- crop and resize images
- use shape fill (texture and solid), colour gradient and outline
- scale, rotate, reflect and distort layers.

How to select and remove parts of an image

Step 1 Using photo-editing software (e.g. Adobe® Photoshop®), choose the **Selection** tool.

Step 2 Select the area you want to remove by dragging out a **marquee** over it.

Step 3 From the **Edit** menu, choose **Cut**.

How to crop and resize images

Step 1 Choose the **Crop** tool.

Step 2 Drag out a **marquee** over the area you want to keep.

Step 3 Right click on the image and choose **Crop**.

Step 4 To resize an image, choose the **Image** menu and select **Image size.**

Step 5 From the dialog box that appears, adjust the image size. Click **OK** to close the dialog box, and your image will be resized.

How to use shape fill (texture and solid), colour gradient and outline

Step 1 Draw or select the shape you require.

Step 2 Choose the required settings for the shape fill and outline from the **Shape** menu.

CONTINUED ▶▶

How to scale, rotate, reflect and distort layers

Step 1 To rotate an entire image, choose the **Rotate canvas** option.

Step 2 To reflect, distort or apply other transformation to an object, first select the layer the object is on.

Step 3 Using the **Move** tool, select the object. Make sure you have the **Show transform controls** option selected in the top toolbar.

Step 4 Either use the handles on the object to transform it or right click on the object and choose the transformation you require.

You can import various types of bitmap (photo) graphics files into Flash® by choosing the **Import** option under the **File** menu. However, the photo-editing facilities inside Flash® are quite limited, so you should edit the file first in a photo-editing package, such as Adobe® Photoshop®. In particular, you should ensure you resize the image close to the size it will be when used in your animation to avoid creating very large files.

Once you have imported a bitmap, you can resize and rotate it by selecting it with the **Free Transform** tool.

In general, vector graphics will occupy much less file space than bitmaps, so it is wise to use vector graphics for all the characters in your animation. Using bitmap graphics for your characters would create an animation with a very large file size. However, you can use bitmap images as backgrounds as these probably don't change very often in the animation so the size issue is not as important.

Link

Photo editing is covered in detail in *Unit 6 Creating digital graphics*.

Activity 4.4

Use the vector-editing facilities in Flash® to create a simple character with a face, limbs and body. Place the main parts of the body and face on different layers so you can animate them later.

Create a background using bitmap-editing software and place this on the bottom layer behind the layers of your character.

Just checking

1 What technique do you use so you can animate parts of your scene separately?
2 Why is it better to use vector graphics instead of bitmap graphics for the characters in your animation?
3 Should you use bitmap graphics at all? If so, when should you use them?

2D animation techniques

Getting started ▶▶

Research the Academy Award for Best Animated Feature and look at all of the animated features nominated over the last ten years. Discuss in groups the different types of animation techniques and software you think were used to create some of these animated features.

Introduction

Your design will probably have defined the animation techniques (cut-out, rotoscoping or skeletal animation) you will use and what your keyframes will look like. To actually create the animation, you will now need to set up those keyframes in your animation software and then use techniques such as tweening to create the intermediate frames.

A number of different techniques can be used to create 2D animations. Your choice of technique will depend of the type and style of animation you are creating. In this section, we will look at cut-out animation, rotoscoping and skeletal animation.

In this section, you will use animation-editing software to create a range of 2D animation techniques.

Cut-out animation

If you find drawing your characters on the computer difficult, you can use the cut-out technique and hand draw them. Then scan them into the computer. However, it is best to draw and scan each part of the character you want to animate separately, then you can easily import each part of the character onto a separate layer.

Rotoscoping

Another method to add more realism to the movement of your characters is rotoscoping. This involves tracing over the frames of a video. Although it produces realistic animation, it is a lengthy process that requires patience. For a five-second video, shooting on twos (one tracing for every two frames), you will need to trace 60 frames.

First you need to record a short video of some kind of movement and then import it into Flash®:

Link ◉

Recording and editing video is covered in *Unit 7 Creating digital video*.

How to import a video into Flash®

Step 1 Go to the **File** menu and choose **Import**, then **Import video**. You will then see the dialog box shown in Figure 4.7.

Step 2 Choose the video you want to import by clicking the **Browse** button. Click the option **Embed FLV in SWF and play in timeline**.

Step 3 Click **Next** and you will see the **Embedding** dialog box. Turn off the **Include audio** check box, unless you want to include the audio track from the video, and then click **Next**. You will then see the **Finish importing video** dialog box. Click **Finish**. The first frame of the video will then be shown.

Step 4 Rename the layer the video is on to 'Video', then add another layer and call it 'Drawing'.

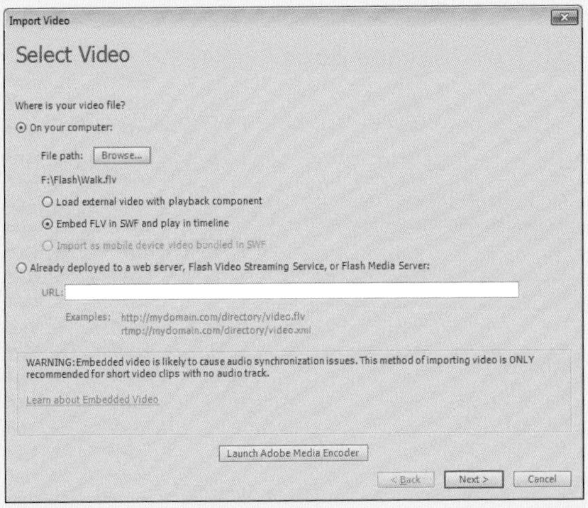

Figure 4.7 Import video dialog box

continued

▶▶ CONTINUED

Step 5 Find the first frame you want to use and insert a **blank keyframe** in the **Drawing** layer. Then, using the **Brush** tool, draw around the moving object. The example shown in Figure 4.8 is a video of fingers walking.

Figure 4.8 Tracing around a moving object

Step 6 Now move forward two frames (you are 'shooting on twos' here) and insert another blank keyframe in the **Drawing** layer. Draw around the moving object in this frame of the video.

Step 7 Continue through every two frames of the video, inserting a blank keyframe and drawing around the moving object. Once you have completed about 24 frames (tracing 12 of them) you can use the playhead to preview your animation. Hide the video layer to see how it looks without the video behind the animation.

Skeletal animation

You can use skeletal or bone animation in Flash® to animate connected parts of an object, such as a character's arms and legs.

How to animate parts of an object

Step 1 Create a limb by drawing the different parts and converting each part of the drawing into a symbol. Right click on the **Drawing** shape and choose the **Convert to symbol** option. Figure 4.9 shows a series of ellipse shapes arranged to look like the arm of a cartoon character.

Step 2 Click the **Bone** icon in the toolbar on the left.

Step 3 Click on the top of the arm, then drag down to the top of the lower arm section. This will create a coloured 'bone' within the arm.

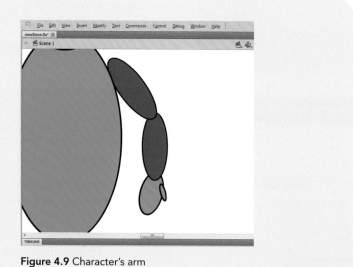

Figure 4.9 Character's arm

continued

Step 4 Now click again with the **Bone** icon on the top of the lower arm (where the first bone ends) and drag down to the joint with the hand. The arm should now have two bones inside it, as shown in Figure 4.10.

Note that the limbs with the bones are automatically placed on a new layer called Armature_2.

Step 5 If you now click the **Selection** tool and drag the hand across the stage, the rest of the limbs will also have bones.

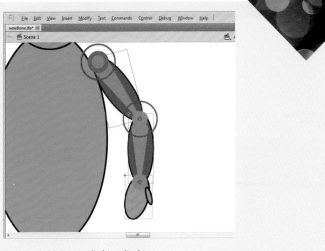

Figure 4.10 Bones linking limbs

How to create movement

To bend a limb without moving the other limbs or the hand:

Step 1 Move the mouse over the limb, press and hold the **Shift** key and then drag with the mouse.

To animate the arm:

Step 1 First make sure you have the arm positioned in its starting pose.

Step 2 Right click in the Armature_2 Layer in the timeline at frame 50 and choose **Insert pose**.

Step 3 Now position the limb in the required ending pose. Note that any drawing on Layer1 will not be visible on this frame until you insert a keyframe for Layer1. See Figure 4.11.

Step 4 If you now move the playhead back and forth, you will see that the arm animates from the stating pose to the ending one in frame 50. Inserting a keyframe for Layer1 at frame 50 will show the rest of the character's body throughout the animation.

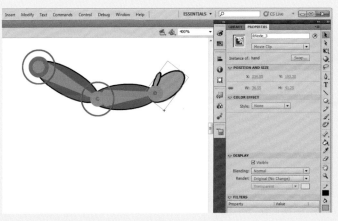

Figure 4.11 Final pose

Just checking

1 What is the first step in creating a 'cut-out' animation?

2 What is the name of the animation technique where you trace over the frames of a video?

3 When might you need to use the technique of bone animation?

Animation processes 1

Introduction

Animation can be a tedious and time-consuming process. Fortunately, animation software like Flash® provides a number of tools to make it easier.

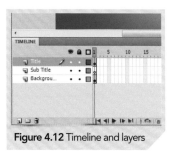

Figure 4.12 Timeline and layers

The timeline and keyframes

The timeline in Flash® is where you control how the movie plays and what is displayed on the stage at any time. The timeline is divided into frames and layers. When editing any part of your animation, it is very important to check which frame and layer you currently have selected. You need to insert keyframes into the timeline when something changes in your animation. In Figure 4.12 a series of text titles for an animation is being created. The two titles are on separate layers, with the colour background on another layer below them so it appears behind the text.

So that the titles will appear for a certain length of time, frames must be added further down the timeline.

How to add timings to titles

Step 1 Insert a keyframe at frame 96, by right clicking in that frame and choosing **Insert Keyframe**.

Step 2 To have the background appear along with the main title, insert a keyframe at frame 96 for that layer too.

Step 3 The subtitle is needed on the screen for two seconds, after which it will be replaced by another subtitle.

Step 4 Add a keyframe to the **Sub title** layer at frame 48. This will mean the subtitle will not show after frame 48.

Step 5 Add another layer above the **Background** layer and insert a keyframe in that layer at frame 49. Flash® automatically adds frames so that the new subtitle shows to the end of the sequence (see Figure 4.13).

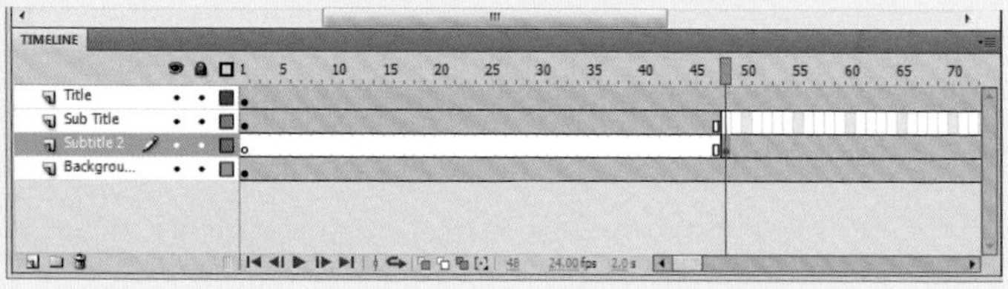

Figure 4.13 Completed sequence

You can remove frames or keyframes by right clicking on them and choosing **Clear frame**. You can also copy and paste frames by right clicking on them and choosing the appropriate option.

Tweening

Tweening, also known as in-betweening, is a process in which intermediate frames are created between two images to give the impression that the first image changes to the second one.

In section *Editing tools and techniques* you created a vector drawing of a happy face. The pupils of the eyes were placed on a separate layer from the rest of the face. Now you can animate the pupils so they look from one side to the other.

How to create a motion tween

Step 1   Make sure you have the **Eyes** layer selected.

Step 2   Select the two pupils. Click the **Select** tool in the toolbar on the right, then click on one pupil, and hold down the **Shift** key and click the other.

Step 3   From the **Modify** menu, choose **Convert to symbol**. This will display the **Convert to Symbol** dialog box, as shown in Figure 4.14.

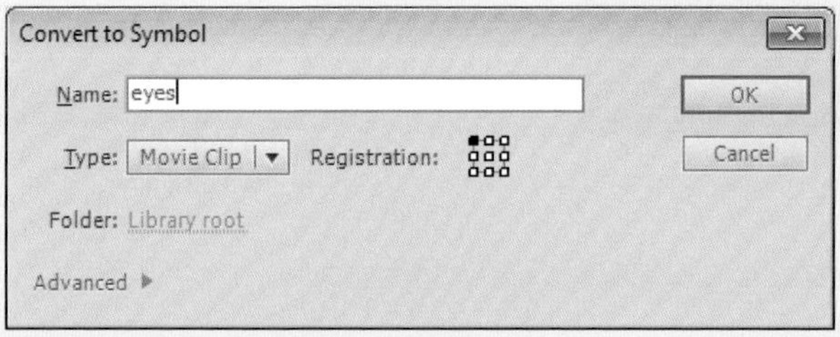

Figure 4.14 Converting to a symbol

Step 4   Right click the **Eyes** symbol and chose **Create Motion Tween**.

Step 5   Flash® will automatically create a 24 second sequence in the timeline. If you want the animation to be longer or shorter than this, drag the blue selected layer backwards or forwards. The timeline will jump forward to the end of the tween, as shown in Figure 4.15.

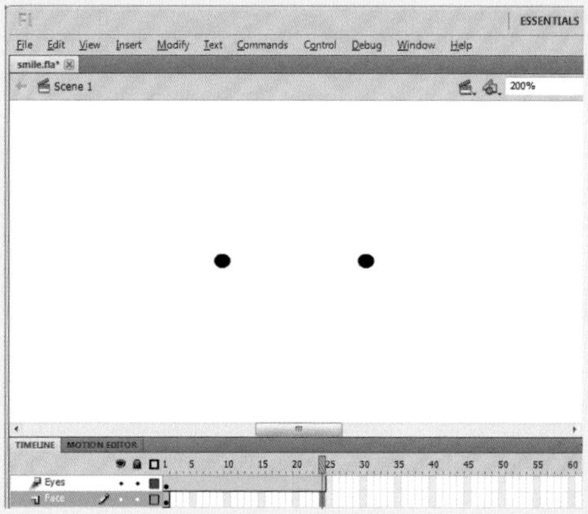

Figure 4.15 Creating a motion tween

To be able to see the rest of the face at the end of the tween, you need to create a keyframe on the **Face** layer.

How to create a keyframe

Step 1   Right click the frame in the **Face** layer at the end of the tween (frame 24) and choose **Insert Keyframe**. Your animation should now look like Figure 4.16.

Step 3   If you drag the playhead up and down the timeline, you will see you have created an animation of the eyes moving from one side to the other.

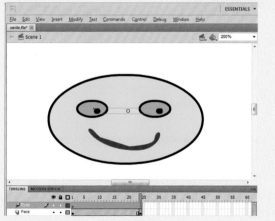

Figure 4.16 Keyframe for the Face layer

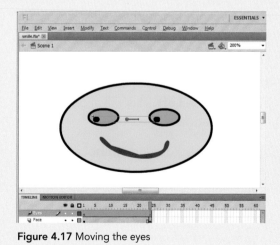

Figure 4.17 Moving the eyes

Step 2   Now select the **Eyes** layer again. Make sure the playhead is at the end of the tween. Click on one of the pupils and drag them to the left side of the eyes. See Figure 4.17.

CONTINUED ▶▶

▶▶ CONTINUED

Camera angles, pan and zoom

To create a **camera pan** or **zoom** effect, you will need to create a background that is bigger than the stage, like that shown in Figure 4.18.

Key terms

Camera pan – Where the camera moves (usually horizontally) across a scene.

Zoom – Where a camera starts with a wide view of a scene (sometimes called a wide angle shot) and then moves in to focus on a small part of the scene.

Remember

Remember: the stage is what will be displayed when you play the completed animation, but you can place items off the stage.

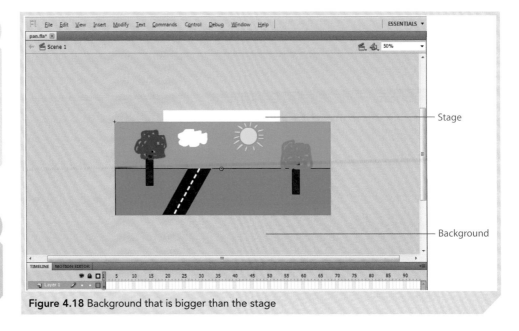

Figure 4.18 Background that is bigger than the stage

How to create a camera pan effect

To create a camera pan effect you need to convert the background to a symbol.

Step 1 Go to the **Edit** menu, choose **Select All**, then right click on the selected images and choose **Convert to symbol**.

Step 2 With the background symbol still selected, go to the **Modify** menu, choose **Align** and then select **Align to stage**.

Step 3 Go to the **Modify** menu again, choose **Align** and this time choose **Left**. This will align your background to the left edge of the stage.

Step 4 Right click the background symbol and choose **Create Motion Tween**, which will create a 24 frame (1 second) tween.

Step 5 Drag the end of the tween in the timeline to frame 48 (this will make the camera pan last 2 seconds).

Step 6 Click in frame 48 in the timeline and, using the same technique as before, align the background to the right edge of the stage. The result is shown in Figure 4.19.

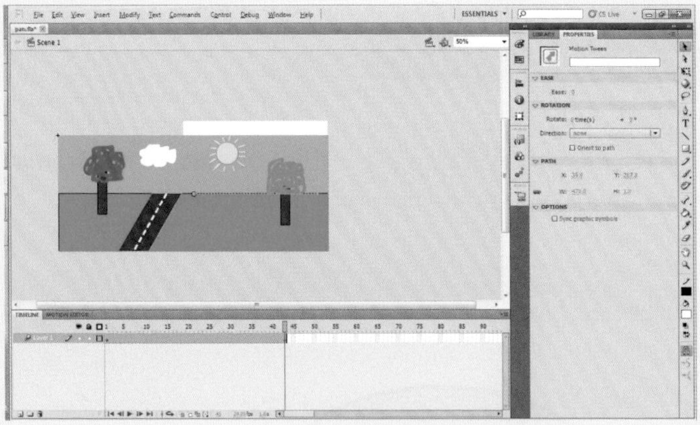

Figure 4.19 Final frame aligned to the right of the stage

Now if you use the playhead to run through your animation, the background looks as if it is moving from right to left. However, if you choose the **Control** menu and the **Test Scene** option, the animation will play as the user would see it (with only the stage shown). This gives the impression that a 'camera' is panning across the scene.

How to create a zoom effect

Step 1 First add in another layer called **Zoom**.

Step 2 Insert a blank keyframe in the new layer at frame 49.

Step 3 The background symbol does appear in the frame so click in frame 48 on the **Pan** layer, right click and choose **Copy frames**.

Step 4 Go back to frame 49 in the **Zoom** layer, right click and choose **Paste frames**. This frame is still part of the Pan Tween so right click on the background symbol (in frame 49) and choose **Remove tween**. Now right click on it again and choose **Create motion tween** to start the new zoom effect.

Step 5 Drag the tween bar (coloured blue) in the timeline up to frame 96 (to make a 2 second zoom).

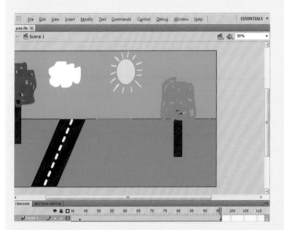

Figure 4.20 Blank keyframe in the Zoom layer at frame 49

Step 6 With the playhead still on frame 96, click the **Transform** tool in the toolbar on the right, then click the background symbol and drag the scale handle on the top left to make the background scale up.

Step 7 Use the **Modify, Align, Right** options to realign the background to the right edge of the stage. See Figure 4.21.

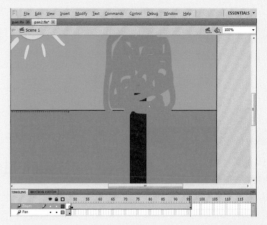

Figure 4.21 Background scaled to give a zoom effect

Step 8 If you use the **Test Scene** option again, you will see that the 'camera' now appears to pan across the scene and then zooms in.

If you want to use different camera angles (perhaps during a dialogue between two characters, you want to show one character talking, viewed from one angle, then swap to a view of the other character from a different camera angle), you can simply move the background and characters relative to the position of the stage without any tweening. This will create the impression of a sudden change of camera angle/position.

Just checking ✔

1 What is it called when a camera moves sideways across a scene?

2 Give an example of when you might want to use different camera angles in a scene.

3 What do you have to convert the parts of your drawing to before you can use them in a skeletal animation?

4 In an animation design, what shows the timings when events happen?

5 What is the marker used at the start and end of a sequence of animation?

6 If you draw an animation and scan it in, what is this process called?

Activity 4.5

Extend the background you created earlier or make a new one that is much wider than the stage. Add the character you created earlier at one side of the stage. Pan across the stage and then zoom in on your character.

Animation processes 2

Introduction

In this section we will look at a number of other animation software tools which you can use to achieve a wide range of effects.

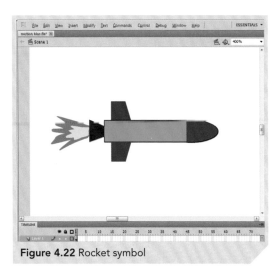

Figure 4.22 Rocket symbol

Transition effects

Transition effects refer to:

- motion blur
- fade in/out
- morphing.

Motion blur

You can add motion blur to moving objects to make them look more realistic. Figure 4.22 shows a drawing of a rocket. This has been created by grouping together various shapes and then made into a symbol. In the following examples we will add a blur filter to this rocket symbol.

How to add a blur filter to the rocket

Step 1 Make sure you have the rocket symbol selected, then click on the **Properties** tab to display the Properties pane, on the right. At the bottom of the pane, click the **Add filter** button.

Step 2 Select a **blur filter**. The blur filter setting allows you to define how much blur you want to add on the horizontal (X) axis and the vertical (Y) axis. Since the rocket will be flying horizontally across the stage, the X blur has been set to 25 and the Y blur to 0. The quality has been set to medium; setting it too high may make the animation play slowly. See Figure 4.24.

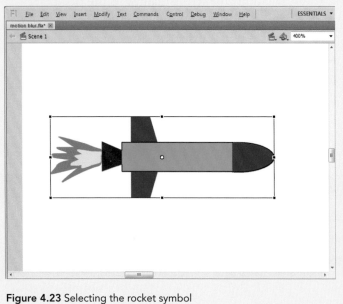

Figure 4.23 Selecting the rocket symbol

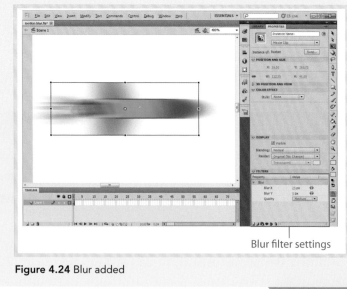

Blur filter settings

Figure 4.24 Blur added

continued

Step 3   Insert another layer in the timeline (above the existing one) and drag another copy of the rocket symbol from the library onto the new layer. Place it over, but slightly ahead of, the blurred rocket. Your screen should now look like Figure 4.25.

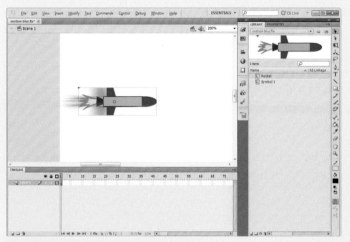

Figure 4.25 Another rocket symbol added

Step 4   Now right click in frame 1 of each layer and choose **Create motion tween**. This will insert a keyframe in frame 24 of each layer.

Step 5   Click in frame 24 and move both the blurred rocket and the non-blurred one across to the right of the stage, as shown in Figure 4.26.

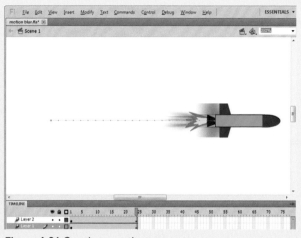

Figure 4.26 Creating a motion tween

If you now play the animation, the blur follows the rocket. However, you can make the effect more realistic by removing the blur from the first and last frames, when the rocket is not moving.

How to remove the blur when the rocket is not moving

Step 1   In the layer that contains the blurred rocket, click on frame 1 and drag it to the right to frame 2. This will leave a blank keyframe in frame 1 when the rocket is not moving.

Step 2   Do the same in the last frame, but this time drag the frame to the left, to frame 23 (see Figure 4.27). Now there is no blur shown until the rocket starts moving.

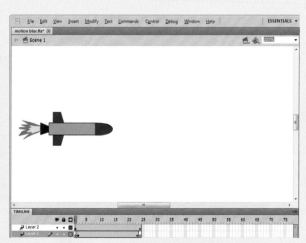

Figure 4.27 Timeline adjusted

Fading in and out

You can fade in or out any photo or graphic object (including text). Simply convert the object to a symbol (movie clip), then create a tween.

How to create fade in and out

Step 1 Click in the first frame of the tween then, with the selection tool, click on the symbol.

Step 2 In the **Properties** panel, click the **Color Effect** drop down and choose **Alpha** (see Figure 4.28).

Step 3 Move the slider to 0% (the symbol seems to disappear but its selection box is still visible).

Step 4 Click in the last frame of the tween and click on the symbol again, then move the **Alpha** slide back up to 100%. The symbol will then fade in.

Step 5 To fade a symbol out, just set the **Alpha** to 100% in the first frame of the tween and 0% in the last.

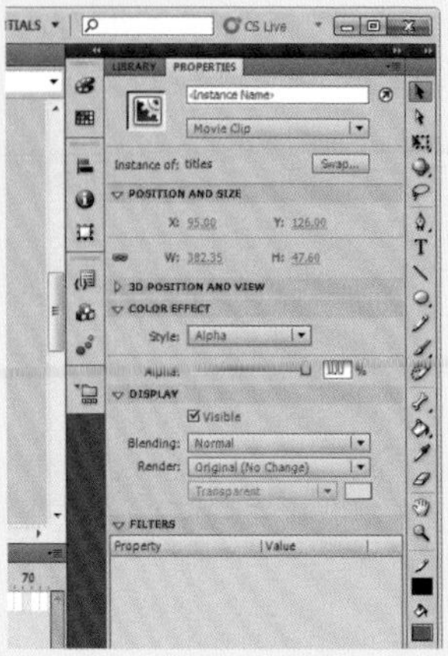

Figure 4.28 Adjusting the Color Alpha setting

Morphing

You can morph one shape into another using a shape tween. Unlike a motion tween, a shape tween can only be used on graphic shapes, not symbols or bitmaps.

How to morph one shape into another shape

Step 1 Draw a shape and then add a keyframe in the shape's layer about 30 frames on.

Step 2 Modify the shape in the new keyframe, then right click in the layer on the timeline and choose **Create shape tween**. The shape will then smoothly morph from its original version to the modified one.

Activity   4.6

Create a short animation that demonstrates motion blur and fading in and out. For example, you could create some movie titles that fade in and out and create a motion blur for a racing car or other moving object.

▶ Rendering

Adding rendering effects to fill colours can help make your animations look more realistic. Shading is an example of such an effect, and is quite easy to apply.

The character shown in Figure 4.29 has a solid fill applied to his face. However, the side of his face nearest to the Sun should be lighter than the other side.

Figure 4.29 Character with solid fill

How to add rendering effects

Step 1 First make sure the character's head is selected.

Step 2 Click the **Colour palette** and from the drop-down choose **Linear gradient.**

Step 3 Adjust the **Colour panel** to give the right colours, as shown in Figure 4.30.

This gradient runs from left to right with the darker side towards the Sun, which is the opposite of what we want.

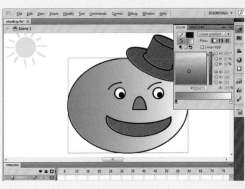

Figure 4.30 Applying a linear gradient

How to adjust the gradient

Step 1 First click and hold on the **Free transform** tool in the toolbar until the submenu pops up, and choose the **Gradient transform** tool.

Step 2 A box will appear around the character's face with a **Rotate** icon in the top right. Move your mouse pointer over the **Rotate** icon until it changes shape, then drag the gradient until the light part is facing the Sun, as shown in Figure 4.31.

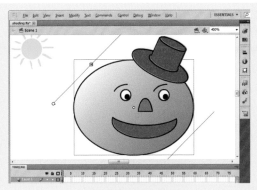

Figure 4.31 Gradient aligned to the Sun

Activity   4.7

Add shading effects to the characters in your animation.

Audio

You can add an audio file to your animation.

How to add audio to your animation

Step 1 Choose **Import** from the **File** menu, then **Import to library** from the submenu.

Step 2 Select the audio file you want to use. This will import the audio file into your library.

Step 3 Create a layer for the audio and insert a keyframe where you want the audio to start, then drag the audio file from the library to the stage.

Step 4 To make the sound play, you will also need to add a keyframe further along the timeline where the sound will stop playing. See Figure 4.32.

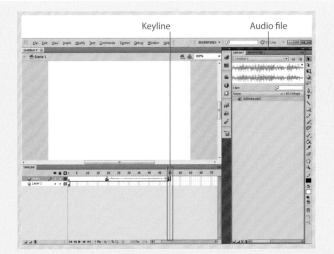

Figure 4.32 Audio file added to the timeline

CONTINUED ▶▶

Activity 4.8

Create a simple audio track to accompany your animation, using the techniques explained in Unit 5. Start off with a simple music track and then try to add some sound effects to your animations.

Lip sync

Link

Editing audio clips is covered in *Unit 5 Creating digital audio.*

Synchronising animated mouth movements with an audio speech track is known as lip sync and requires practice and patience. You will need to record the speech, starting off with a short recording of just a few words. You also need to have your cartoon face drawn.

How to add synchronised animated mouth movements

Step 1 Create a number of different mouth shapes to use with your face and save them in the library. Start off with just a few mouth shapes, as shown in Figure 4.33.

Step 2 Now import the sound file onto its own layer on the timeline.

It is useful to be able to clearly see the audio wave form in the timeline.

Step 3 Right click on the **Audio** layer name and choose **Properties**.

Step 4 From the **Properties** dialog, choose 300% in the **Layer height** drop-down menu. You can play sections of the audio by dragging the playhead along the timeline.

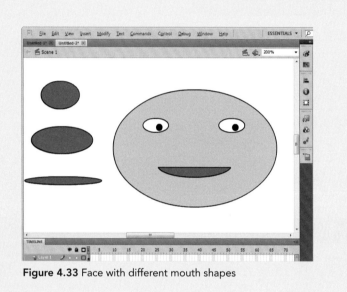

Figure 4.33 Face with different mouth shapes

Now you need to decide which mouth shapes to use.

- Find exactly where the first word occurs in the timeline, using the wave form and the playhead.
- Now insert another layer for the mouth (this needs to be above the face layer).

As you will be changing around the different mouth shapes needed, it is important that all the different mouth shapes are in the same place on the face. You can use guidelines to help you position the mouths.

How to position mouths

Step 1   Click on the **View** menu and then choose **Rulers** so the rulers are displayed at the top and left of the editing window.

Step 2   Now drag a guideline (shown in blue) from the top ruler and position it in the middle of the mouth. Do the same from the left ruler.

Step 3   Insert a keyframe in the frame where the first mouth shape of the first word is needed. Delete the existing mouth shape and insert the required mouth shape from the library.

Step 4   Now find within the audio track the next place where the mouth shape changes. Insert another keyframe there, delete the existing mouth shape and insert the new one. Repeat the process until the mouth shapes are added for the whole audio track. Figure 4.34 shows the technique in use.

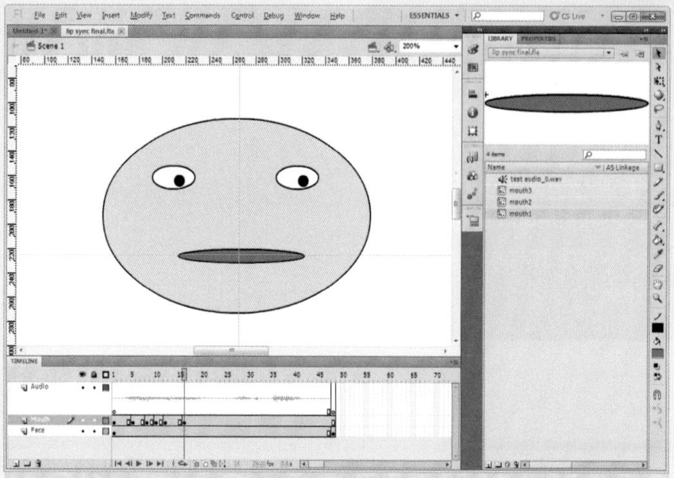

Figure 4.34 Synchronizing the audio track with the mouth shapes

An alternative to using pre-drawn mouth shapes from the library is to create a motion tween for the first mouth shape, insert a keyframe when each shape change is needed and adjust the shape of the mouth as required at each keyframe. This method gives a smoother, more realistic result.

Activity   4.9

1 To help you decide which mouth shapes to use, get someone else to say the words in the audio track and carefully watch their mouth shape as they do so (or do it yourself using a mirror). You will probably need to get them to repeat each word several times. Each word will probably be made up of a least two mouth shapes.

2 Try animating a cartoon face with a mouth to a short phrase like 'I love to make animations'. Record the audio first and then work out the mouth shapes. Animate the cartoon face using the appropriate mouth shapes to match the audio recording.

Testing the animation

Getting started ▶▶

Think about the different stages you work through when you are creating an animation. What sorts of things do you think you will need to test and record as you work through this process?

Introduction

Developing your final animation for assessment of this unit is likely to be a lengthy process. You will need to develop prototypes, practise techniques and refine aspects of the animation until you arrive at the completed product. Testing and previewing is unlikely to be a single event. You will need to think about this throughout the development process, testing and reviewing parts of your animation early on in the process to decide whether some parts need further work before they are acceptable.

Functionality

You will need to test the functionality of your animation. When doing this, ask yourself the following questions:

- Does it play properly?
- Is the animation reasonably smooth?
- Does the soundtrack play?
- Is it audible?
- Is it in reasonable synchronisation with the action?

Remember: your animation must be between 30 seconds and two minutes in length.

Fit for purpose

As well as testing the functionality of your animation, you also need to review if it is fit for purpose. For this, you must return to the original requirements you stated in the design of the animation. You need to consider if what you have produced meets the intended purpose of the animation and if it is likely to appeal to the stated target audience. For example, if your target audience is young children, you need to check that the content of your animation really will appeal to them, and that the language you have used is understandable for your chosen age group.

Getting feedback on your animation

It is often difficult to see flaws or weaknesses in your own work, but others can usually provide constructive feedback. For prototypes, this feedback can be informal. However, for your final version, you must get formal feedback by using either a written questionnaire or audio/video recorded interviews.

The questions you should ask your reviewers about your final product include:

- Will it appeal to its intended audience and how well does it meet their needs? (Make sure you tell your reviewers who your intended audience is.)
- Is the movement of the characters realistic? Are there some parts that are better than others?
- Is the timing of the movement and action appropriate, or do things happen too quickly or too slowly?
- Is the quality of the sound appropriate? Does it synchronise well with the animation?

Documenting improvements

Following the testing and feedback, you will need to make improvements to your animation and you should document the changes you make. The simplest way to do this is to take 'before' and 'after' screenshots.

Exporting and compressing animation files

Once your animation is complete, you will need to export it from Flash® into a format that other people (who may not have the full Flash® software on their computer) can view. Flash® animations are designed to be played using a web browser (such as Microsoft® Internet Explorer® or Google Chrome™). So that your animation can be played using a web browser, you need to export it as a SWF file.

When Flash® creates a SWF file it compresses the graphics in your animation. This avoids creating a very large file. The larger your SWF file, the longer it will take to download from a website. If your resulting SWF file is still very large, you can adjust the compression setting.

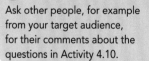

Did you know?

You can preview your animation from within Flash® Professional by choosing the **Control** menu and then selecting **Test Movie** from within the **Test** submenu. The keyboard shortcut to do this is Ctrl+Enter.

How to adjust the compression settings

Step 1 Choose **Publish settings** from the **File** menu.

Step 2 In the dialog box that appears, you can change the JPEG quality value. The default is 80. Choosing a lower number compresses your images more but results in a lower image quality. You will need to experiment with this setting to find the best compromise between file size and image quality.

Step 3 Now test your animation in a web browser:

Step 4 Go to the **File** menu in Flash® and choose **Publish Preview**, then **Default – (HTML)**. This will then create the SWF and HTML files in the same folder as the original animation file and will open them in your default browser.

Activity 4.10

Create a test document for your animation in which you list all the things you are going to test in a table, and then go through your animation writing the results and any other comments against each test.

- Does the animation follow your original design?
- Does it run smoothly?
- Is the animated movement realistic?
- Is the timing of the animation acceptable (e.g. do things happen too quickly or too slowly)?
- Is the overall length of the animation acceptable?
- Is the soundtrack audible and of acceptable quality?
- Is the soundtrack synchronised with the animation?

Take it further

Ask other people, for example from your target audience, for their comments about the questions in Activity 4.10.

Discussion point

What other questions can you think of to ask about your final product?

Just checking

1 When testing the functionality of a product what questions should you ask?

2 Where are final versions of Flash® animations designed to be viewed?

3 What problems can be caused if your Flash® SWF file is very large? What can you do about it?

Reviewing your finished digital animation

Introduction

For the assessment of this unit, you must write a review of the process you used to create your animation, and whether the end result met your original plan.

How to review your animation

The review stage is just as important as the design stage. This is the point at which you need to check that the animation you have produced is of a high standard, meets its original requirements, is suitable for the audience and is the best animation you can produce.

Table 4.2 explains the different things you should be checking for when you review your animation.

Table 4.2 The different areas you need to consider when reviewing your animation

Quality of the product	How good is the quality? You can't expect to produce material of professional quality, but comparing your animation against professional products can help you to identify its strengths and weaknesses.
	You need to consider things such as how well drawn your characters and backgrounds are, how good the animation is (how smooth, realistic, etc.) and how good the soundtrack is (synchronisation with the action, accuracy of the lip sync, etc.)
Fitness for purpose	How well does your final product match its original purpose? Will it really appeal to your target audience?
	You need to review the specific features in your animation and explain how they meet the purpose and audience requirements.
Suitability against the original requirements	How closely does your final product match your original design? You need to look back at the design you originally created for the animation. It is very likely that you did not follow the design exactly. Where there are differences, explain why they occurred.
Legal and ethical constraints	Did copyright constraints prevent you from using some assets you would have like to use?
	Did you consider general safety issues, such as taking care with downloads to avoid viruses, or specific health and safety issues, such as taking regular breaks when using the computer or keeping food and drinks away?
	Did you take regular backups of your work? Is the content suitable? (Is it likely to cause offence to anyone? Does it contain any personal information?)
Strengths and improvements	What was really good about your animation?
	How might you further develop the animation if you had more time?
	How would you do things differently next time to avoid the problems you encountered?

Assessment activity 4.3   *English*   1C.4 | 1C.5 | 2C.P4 | 2C.P5 | 2C.M3 | 2C.M4 | 2C.D3

Barry likes your design ideas and he would like you to create the animation.

- Source and file all of the assets needed. Edit as required.
- Create your animation using your design brief.
- Carry out checks to ensure that your animation plays and that there are no technical faults with it.
- Critically think about each element of the animation you have created and find out what other people think. Is there anything at this stage which you could improve on? If so, make the improvements.

Tips

- Make sure that all graphics and audio files are saved in the correct format.
- Keep notes explaining why you included each piece of material.
- Keep asking yourself, 'How could this be improved?' And ask for feedback from other people and use this to improve your animation.

Assessment activity 4.4   1C.6 | 2C.P6 | 2C.M5 | 2C.D4

Barry is very happy with your animation. But how do you think it went? Look back over the design process and the finished product to see if you could make any improvements.

- Compare your final animation with your design brief.
- Does the animation include the key points Barry wanted it to? Explain how.
- Do you think your animation will appeal to Barry's target audience?
- Where there any problems you experienced when sourcing graphics or audio for the animation?
- Identify some areas where you could improve your animation.

Tips

- Explain why you made any changes.
- Refer back to the feedback you received from other people to consider what further improvements you could make.

Introduction

Sound is extremely powerful – it provides the soundtrack to our everyday lives. It can be used to convey emotions, warn of danger, educate, inform and communicate.

Digital audio products can be found all around us, for example, music (radio, MP3 files, streaming); radio adverts; film and TV programme soundtracks; recorded announcements on public transport; audio books.

Technological advancements have radically impacted on how audio is produced and delivered. Computer software advancements have also helped shape the way sound is recorded and edited, and the internet has revolutionised how audio products are delivered (for example, downloading podcasts, streaming live concerts). How people access audio products has also changed, and there is currently a demand for products to be available instantaneously and while 'on the move'.

In this unit you will learn about the features and applications (uses) of digital audio and learn how to design, record and edit audio clips. This unit gives you the opportunity to develop your technical skills and to use creative skills in the production of audio clips.

Assessment: You will be assessed by a series of assignments set by your teacher.

Learning aims

In this unit you will:

A understand the applications and features of digital audio products

B design digital audio products

C create, test and review digital audio products.

I have really gotten into the digital audio unit, as it lets me combine my interests in music, computing and drama. I have managed to persuade some of the other guys who are studying drama with me to create a radio-style play. One of them has written a script and we have been rehearsing it, ready to make the final recording. It's also been fun sourcing all of the sound effects and suitable music to create the right atmosphere and make it sound realistic.

Ahmed, BTEC First in I&CT student

Creating
digital audio

5

This table shows what you must do in order to achieve a **Pass**, **Merit** or **Distinction** grade, and where you can find activities in this book to help you.

Assessment criteria

Level 1	Level 2 Pass	Level 2 Merit	Level 2 Distinction
Learning aim A: Understand the applications and features of digital audio products			
1A.1 Identify the intended purpose and features of two digital audio products. **Assessment activity 5.1, page 156**	**2A.P1** Explain the intended purpose and features of two different digital audio products. **Assessment activity 5.1, page 156**	**2A.M1** Review how the products are fit for purpose and their intended effect on the audience **Assessment activity 5.1, page 156**	**2A.D1** Discuss the strengths and weaknesses of the digital audio products. **Assessment activity 5.1, page 156**
Learning aim B: Design digital audio products			
1B.2 Identify the audience and purpose for the design of a digital audio product. **Assessment activity 5.2, page 161**	**2B.P2** Describe the audience and purpose for the design of a digital audio product. **Assessment activity 5.2, page 161**	**2B.M2** English Produce detailed audio designs, including reasons why alternative ideas have been discarded. **Assessment activity 5.2, page 161**	**2B.D2** English Justify the final design decisions, explaining how they will: • fulfil the stated purpose and requirements of the brief • meet the needs of the intended audience. **Assessment activity 5.2, page 161**
1B.3 Produce outline design(s) for the digital audio product(s). Each design must include: • an outline script • a timeline. **Assessment activity 5.2, page 161**	**2B.P3** English Produce designs for two digital audio products, each of at least three minutes duration, which together include speech, music and sound effects. Each design must include: • description of requirements from the brief • a script • a list of the ready-made digital audio assets to be used • a timeline. **Assessment activity 5.2, page 161**		
Learning aim C: Create, test and review digital audio products			
1C.4 Record audio and gather audio assets, with guidance. **Assessment activity 5.3, page 172**	**2C.P4** Carry out a soundcheck and record audio, demonstrating awareness of purpose, and prepare audio assets, listing sources used. **Assessment activity 5.3, page 172**	**2C.M3** Record high-quality original audio, demonstrating awareness of audience, with all sources of assets fully referenced. **Assessment activity 5.3, page 172**	
1C.5 Edit audio assets to create a digital audio product of at least three-minutes duration, and test it for functionality, with guidance. **Assessment activity 5.4, page 175**	**2C.P5** Edit audio assets to create two digital audio products each of at least three-minutes duration. Test the products for functionality, purpose and against the original requirements, making any necessary improvements to the products. **Assessment activity 5.4, page 175**	**2C.M4** Gather feedback from others on the quality of the digital audio products and use it to improve the products, demonstrating awareness of audience and purpose. **Assessment activity 5.4, page 175**	**2C.D3** Refine audio assets to create two high-quality digital audio products. **Assessment activity 5.4, page 175**

Assessment criteria			
Level 1	**Level 2 Pass**	**Level 2 Merit**	**Level 2 Distinction**
1C.6	2C.P6	2C.M5	2C.D4
For each of the final digital audio products, identify how they are suitable for the intended purpose. **Assessment activity 5.5, page 177**	For each of the final digital audio products, explain how the final product is suitable for the intended audience and purpose. **Assessment activity 5.5, page 177**	Review the extent to which each of the final digital audio products meets the needs of the intended audience and the purpose, considering feedback from others and any constraints. **Assessment activity 5.5, page 177**	Evaluate the final digital audio products against the initial designs and justify any changes made, making recommendations for further improvements. **Assessment activity 5.5, page 177**

English / Opportunity to practise English skills

How you will be assessed

This unit will be assessed by a series of internally marked tasks. You will be expected to show that you understand the features of audio products and the processes involved in creating them. The tasks will be based on a scenario for which you will need to develop two audio products, which need to be at least three minutes in length and which meet a particular brief. For example, you could be asked to produce a podcast on a particular subject and a radio advert or trailer.

Your assessment could be in the form of:

- a research report or magazine article reviewing existing audio products
- design documents or prototypes for the audio products you will be developing
- a completed checklist of your soundcheck, with supporting photographic or video evidence
- digital files of your original audio recordings and ready-made assets
- completed audio clips, which could be in a compressed file format
- a completed questionnaire or witness statement, as evidence of testing and feedback
- a written evaluation report of your final audio product.

Applications and features of digital audio 1

Getting started ▶▶

The ability to create audio is important in many jobs, including sound designer, sound engineer, music artist and music producer.

What other jobs do you think require digital audio skills?

Introduction

Digital audio is the preferred audio form for most professionals, as it provides a high-quality professional sound. Digital audio products can be used in a wide range of applications, both on their own and in combination with other media.

This section looks at some of the applications (uses) of digital audio and explores some of the main technical features.

◤ Applications of digital audio

Digital audio is used across multiple platforms (such as television, mobile devices and the internet) and sectors (such as business, media, transport, design and education). Some of the more common uses of digital audio are:

- **Radio.** Although many radio programmes are broadcast live, some are recorded. Live broadcasts usually include some recorded sections, for example 'jingles' and adverts. Because of the large number of radio stations broadcasting, the content is very diverse and can include news, comedy shows, 'soap' dramas, live artist sessions, book and poetry readings, political debates, sports events, and so on.

- **Podcasts.** A podcast is a multimedia digital file (audio or video) that is available to download via the internet. Podcasts are used for a wide variety of purposes: radio stations use them to compile the 'best bits' from a programme; health services use them to provide advice; entertainment companies use them for promotions (such as interviews with cast members before the release of a new movie).

- **Animations.** Because of the nature of animated features and films, the soundtrack tends to be recorded and edited separately from the creation of the animation.

Did you know? ?

There are a number of podcast directories on the internet that you can use to find podcasts you might be interested in. You can access the directory podcast.com by going to Pearson Hotlinks (www.pearsonhotlinks.co.uk) and searching for this title.

◤ Effect on audience

Sound recordings are used for all sorts of reasons. For example, sound effects can be used to add atmosphere or to create a mood. In a horror movie or radio play, sound effects such as a creaking door, approaching footsteps or a dripping tap may be used to create tension. In a romantic comedy, music may be used to help convey a romantic mood or setting.

The effect the audio recording has may depend on the age, gender or interests of the audience. For example, a series of jokes recorded for an audience of 5–8 year olds would not be suitable for an audience of 15–18 year olds. When designing an audio product, you need to be aware of who your audience is and then make sure that your product is tailored to meet their needs.

Activity 5.1

Make a list of all the applications of digital audio that you have listened to in the last month and say what effect they had on you, for example entertained, thought-provoking, energised, etc. Remember to include audio that is part of another media, such as the soundtrack to a film.

Technical features of digital audio products

Digital audio has a number of technical features that affect the quality of the product and its suitability for various uses.

Digital audio is created using signals from a microphone. Sound itself is created by pressure waves in the air around us. The pressure waves are converted to electrical **voltages** by a microphone. These electrical voltages are converted to **binary data** using a process called **sampling**.

Quality and file size

The two main aspects of the sampling process that control the quality of the resulting digital audio file are sampling rate and bit depth.

- **Sampling rate.** This is a measure of how often the samples of the incoming voltages from the microphone are taken. The sampling rate is measured in kilohertz (kHz) – 1 kHz is 1000 times per second. The sampling rate for audio CDs is 44.1 kHz and professional audio recording equipment often uses higher rates than this.

- **Bit depth.** This is a measure of how many **bits** are used to encode each sample. The more bits used for each sample, the better the quality of the recording will be. The bit depth used with audio CDs is 16 bits and this is widely used for high-quality recordings.

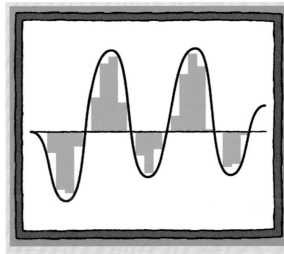

Figure 5.1 The sampling rate measures incoming voltages

With a high-quality digital recording taking samples 44,000 times every second and each sample consisting of 16 bits, it is not hard to see that a lot of data is collected. This can result in a large file being created. For example, a three-minute **stereo** (twin track) recording at 44.1 kHz, 16 bits will require 10,584,000 bytes of data, which is approximately 10 megabytes (MB).

For this reason, most audio recordings are **compressed**, although uncompressed audio recording can be saved using the WAV file format.

Just checking

1. What sampling rate is used for CDs?
2. What is the difference between a stereo audio recording and a mono audio recording?
3. How can audio be used to create an atmosphere in a radio play?

Key terms

Voltage – A measurement of the energy contained within an electric circuit at a given point.

Binary data – A set of binary files that contain data encoded in binary form.

Sampling – A technique used to convert analogue data to digital data. It involves taking a reading of the incoming data at fixed intervals (the sampling rate) and converting each reading to a binary number.

Bit – A unit of information expressed as either 0 or 1 in binary notation.

Stereo (short for stereophonic) – Describes audio that includes two channels or tracks, one for left and the other for right, to give the impression of directional sound. Mono (or monophonic) sound has only a single channel.

Compressed – This is when a recording is reduced (made smaller) in size, meaning that it takes up less space.

Discussion point

8 kHz is sometimes referred to as telephone quality. This rate can be used when high-quality music is not required. In small groups, discuss which types of application would require using a high sampling rate, and which applications would require lower rates.

Did you know?

Audio CDs were the first widely available digital audio media. They were developed by the electronics companies Phillips and Sony in the 1980s and were designed to replace analogue (gramophone) records.

Applications and features of digital audio 2

Introduction

In order to produce professional digital audio products, you need to know about the different features and be able to use them.

This section looks at some of these features, including the file types available, what soundtracks and voiceovers are, and the special effects that you can use to enhance digital audio products.

File types

There are a number of different compressed audio file formats, including:

- **MP3** perhaps the best-known format, due mostly to the fact that it was the first widely used compression method for audio files that maintained quality while significantly reducing file size. MP3 files are generally around only 10 per cent of the size of the same uncompressed audio file. MP3 works by removing parts of the audio signal that would be largely inaudible to the human ear.
- **WMA (Windows® Media Audio)** – is a Microsoft® Windows® compressed audio format. Microsoft® developed this format as a competitor to MP3 and it is the format used by the Windows® Audio recorder
- **AAC (Advanced Audio Coding)** – was designed as the successor to MP3 and achieves better-quality results at the same bit rates. AAC is the default audio format for the Apple® iPod®, iPhone® and iPad®.
- **WAV** – is an uncompressed audio format developed in the 1990s by Microsoft® and IBM. Unlike compressed formats, all the original sampled data is retained. This is what makes WAV the preferred format of some audio professionals, as it provides the highest quality. However, this is at the expense of file size.

The size of digital audio file depends on a number of factors. These include the length of the track and the type of compression used. Another factor is the quality of the recording. High-quality recording creates a larger file than low-quality recording, and stereo recording requires around twice as much space as mono.

Codecs

Key term

Codec – A program (or part of a program) that is used to encode and/or decode binary data into a particular format.

A **codec** is a program that is used to encode or decode binary data into a particular format. For example, to make an audio recording and save it as an MP3 file, a codec is needed to encode the resulting audio data into MP3 format. Similarly, to play an MP3 file, a codec is needed to decode the data.

Platforms and compatibility

The large number of different formats used for digital audio means that there is the potential for incompatibility. For example, the Windows® Sound Recorder can only save files in the WMA format. If you have recorded a soundtrack using the Windows® Sound Recorder and then want to add it to an animation you have created using Adobe® Flash®, you will find that Flash® cannot import WMA files. Fortunately, there are many applications available to convert from one format to another.

Soundtracks and voiceovers

A soundtrack is the audio accompaniment to a film or video, including both animation and live action. It is usually made up of live recorded dialogue spoken by the actors, mixed together with sound effects and music.

A voiceover is a spoken commentary that accompanies a film or television scene. It is not spoken by people who appear in the scene but by someone off-camera (not visible) who is commenting on the events shown.

Mixing and multi-track recording

A soundtrack is created by bringing together various elements such as music, sound effects, voiceover and live actors' speech. This process is called **mixing**. The different elements are usually recorded and edited on different tracks using a sound-editing application such as Audacity® or Power Sound Editor. This technique is sometimes referred to as **layering** or **multi-track recording**.

Different layers can be recorded at different times and then the volume or level of each layer adjusted when the layers are edited together. This technique is almost always used when recording modern music. Rather than having the whole band play the track together, different instruments are recorded separately and then mixed together to achieve the desired result.

Take it further

Find out what application programs are available to convert files to a different format.

Key terms

Mixing– The process of blending together two or more audio tracks, such as spoken commentary and background music.

Layering/multi-track recording – A technique in which separate audio recordings are imported into audio-editing software and then synchronised and mixed together to achieve the desired result.

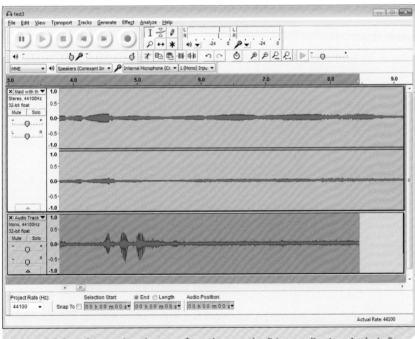

Figure 5.2 Sample sound track screen from the sound-editing application, Audacity®

Special effects

Digital audio-editing application programs allow you to add various special effects to your audio product.

- **Fade.** The gradual increase in the volume of an audio track as it is started is called fade in. The gradual decrease in the volume before it ends is called fade out.

CONTINUED ▶▶

- **Echo.** This is the effect of sound reflected off a surface. Because it takes time for the sound to reach the surface, you hear an echo shortly after the original sound. Adding an echo effect to a voice or other sound will help give the impression that the person is in a place where an echo would naturally occur (such as in a large, empty building or in a tunnel).

- **Distortion.** This effect reduces the quality of a sound recording. You might want to use it for a number of reasons; for example to give the impression that someone is talking over the telephone or to provide the voice of an alien or monster in a science fiction radio play or animation.

- **Pitch.** This is the **frequency** of sound. Higher-frequency sounds are of a higher pitch (treble) and lower-frequency sounds are of a lower pitch (bass). Audio-editing software allows you to adjust the pitch of tracks. You may want to do this for a variety of reasons, such as to add comic effect by making a man's voice sound like a woman's (women generally have higher-pitched voices).

- **Tempo.** This is the speed that an audio track plays at. Increasing the tempo will also typically increase the pitch (make it higher) and decreasing the tempo will decrease the pitch (make it lower). However, audio-editing software usually allows you to change the tempo while keeping the pitch the same.

> **Key term**
>
> **Frequency** – The pitch of a sound: high-pitched (treble) sounds have a high frequency, whereas low-pitched (bass) sounds have a low frequency.

Activity 5.2

Find examples of digital audio recordings that demonstrate some of these features:

- mixing of different voices and/or music tracks
- special effects, such as fade in/out and echo
- a voiceover
- different files formats, e.g. MP3, WAV
- tracks recorded with different sampling rates and/or bit depth.

Assessment activity 5.1   1A.1 | 2A.P1 | 2A.M1 | 2A.D1

Your local sports club wants to attract new members and promote the activities on offer. You have offered to help out by creating some audio for them. To help you prepare for this work, you have decided to investigate different types of audio products.

Choose two different audio products to evaluate and prepare a short document that covers the following:

- Who is their intended audience?
- What features do they each have?
- Is each product fit for purpose?
- What effect will it have on its intended audience?
- What are the strengths and weaknesses of each one?

Tips

- Identify the key elements of each product and consider them carefully in turn.
- Give a reason to justify each opinion you state.

Designing a digital audio product 1

Getting started ⏩

Think of a radio jingle or ad that you have heard. The version you hear is the final product. What information do you think the creative team behind the jingle or ad were given at the start of the process? What factors might they have considered when planning the design of the jingle or ad?

Key terms 🔑

Client brief – A document that explains what the client's expectations are. It should explain what the project is and what they expect you to do/create.

Target audience – The people who you are designing your product for. For example, you might decide that your target audience is females aged 16 to 19 who are interested in fashion.

Introduction

As with any product that is of professional quality, a digital audio product must be planned before work on recording it starts. The first stage of any audio product is the design.

The design stage is very important, as this is the point where you will need to plan and decide on what to include in your design. There are a number of different factors that you will need to think about when planning your design, and they are covered in this section.

▶ Purpose and audience

Before you can start designing your audio product, you need to establish the purpose of the product and who the target audience is.

Purpose

You must decide or identify the purpose of the audio product. If you are working to a **client brief**, the purpose should be clearly stated in the brief. If not, you must speak to the client and find out what the purpose of the recording is.

If the product you are creating is part of a bigger project, such as the soundtrack for an animated film, then your design for the audio product must integrate with the design for the associated product.

Audience

As well as clearly identifying the purpose of the audio product, you must make sure that you understand who the **target audience** is. These are the people who you think will use the product. You should define your target audience in terms of age group, gender, interests, etc. You will then need to consider the product features that will appeal to your target audience so that your design takes these features into account.

Activity 5.3

Imagine you have been asked to create a radio ad for a new product such as a new mobile phone or an event such as a football match. Identify a purpose and target audience for your audio product. Make a list of the features that you think would and would not appeal to your target audience. Aim for at least six features for each.

▶ Script

If your audio product contains scripted dialogue, then writing the script will be an important part of your planning for the product. Although your product can contain unscripted dialogue or interviews, scripted dialogue can be more effective and result in a more professional-sounding product. Your script should identify who is talking and what they will say, clearly laid out so it is easy to read.

CONTINUED ▶▶

Simon:	Dad – I think there is an alien in our back garden. And it's eating Mum's flowers!
Dad:	(Disinterested) I see.
Simon:	It's now trying on the clothes on the washing line. (Beat.) I think it has spotted us. (Beat.) It's now coming towards the house.
FX:	**Knock on the door.**
Dad:	(Annoyed) Honestly, Simon. Stop messing around.
FX:	**Door opens.**
Alien:	(Guttural alien language.)
Dad.	(Screams in disbelief)
Simon:	I told you so.

Figure 5.3 Example of a section from a radio play script

Activity ▸ 5.4

You have been asked to produce a short radio news article on something to do with your school (for example, a recent event or achievement at your school). Write a script for your news article. You might find it helpful to listen to some radio news bulletins to get an idea of how they are scripted. Most radio stations have news on the hour (although BBC Radio 1 has a news bulletin called *Newsbeat* at half past the hour).

Timeline

A script is one of the starting points you need when you are planning your audio product, but a script does not identify other aspects of your product such as timings and how you will integrate different elements such as scripted dialogue, interviews, music and sound effects. A timeline table is a useful planning tool, as it extends a basic script to cover all these additional aspects of your product.

The main elements of a timeline table are:

1 timings

2 direction

3 dialogue

4 effects.

An example timeline table for a short (one-minute) radio advert is shown in Table 5.1.

Table 5.1 Timeline planning table for a one-minute radio advert

Audio Timeline plan			
Description:	Northgate College radio advert		
Length:	60 seconds		
Author:	Wendy Smith		
Timing	**Direction**	**Dialogue**	**Effects**
8 secs	Introduction (spoken by presenter)	Thinking about your future? Qualifications can make all the difference. Studying at Northgate College certainly helped Amrita.	Background music: BGMusic.mp3
34 secs	Audio clip by Amrita, student at Northgate College		Amrita1.mp3 Background music continues.
15 secs	Summary (spoken by presenter)	So, to get ahead, get in touch! Call Northgate college now on 0208 8881111 or visit us at www.northgate.ac.uk	Background music continues
3 secs			Fade up background music

Just checking

1 What are the main elements of a timeline?
2 What is the purpose of a client brief?
3 What is a 'target audience'? Why is it important?

Take it further

Create your own timeline for a short radio advert. You should choose a topic, decide on the length of the advert and allocate timings to dialogue and effects.

Designing a digital audio product 2

Introduction

Once you have identified the purpose and target audience for your audio product and created a script and timeline, you will need to test out your ideas to make sure that they will work and will result in the product that you would like to create. You also need to produce a schedule for your recording sessions and consider the health and safety aspects involved in your recording.

The previous section covered what to include in your design. Figure 5.4 contains a reminder of what you need to include.

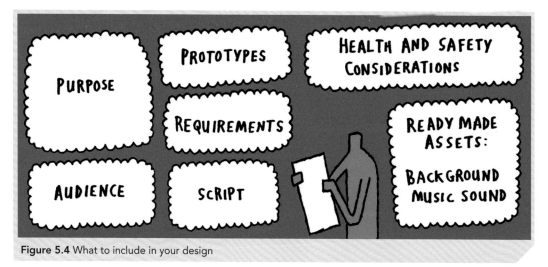

Figure 5.4 What to include in your design

Prototypes

You should test out your ideas for your audio products by creating a **prototype** for each of your ideas.

A prototype does not have to be polished or of high quality, as its main purpose is to test out ideas. For example, if you are creating sound effects for a computer game, you might want to try out various ways of creating the sound effects in order to find the most suitable method. If you are developing a voice for an alien character in an animation or science fiction play, you might try various combinations of audio settings to achieve the desired effect.

Recording schedule

In addition to planning the content of the audio product, you should also plan your recording sessions. This will help to ensure that the recording process runs smoothly and you don't forget anything. Your recording schedule should include:

- **Date and time.** You will need to consider how long you need to make your recording. You probably won't get the recording you want on the first attempt, so allow enough time for several takes.
- **Equipment and people.** Your plan should list the equipment and people you will need to complete the recording session so you can make sure they are all available on the day and at the time that you need them.

- **Location.** You will need to identify the location where you are going to record the material. For example, if you want to do a news-style outdoor interview, you will need to choose somewhere that is not very noisy. Alternatively, if you want to use a quiet room to do the recording, you may need to check with your teacher to arrange booking a room in your school. Make yourself a 'Recording in Progress – Do Not Disturb' sign to put outside the room.

Health and safety precautions

When planning a recording session, you also need to think about the environment around you and make sure that it is safe for the people involved in the recording.

Health and safety rules

1 Recording in an outdoor location can involve a number of dangers. For example, if recording near a road, you will need to take care, especially if you will be wearing headphones as you may be unaware of nearby traffic.

2 You need to take care with any trailing cables from headphones and microphones to avoid tripping hazards.

3 While wearing headphones, take care that the volume levels are not so high that they could cause damage to your hearing.

4 Take all the normal precautions when using electrical equipment, such as keeping drinks and other liquids well away from the equipment.

5 If you are planning a recording session outside, keep an eye on the weather – if it rains you will need to protect the equipment from getting wet.

| Assessment activity 5.2 | *English* | 1B.2 | 1B.3 | 2B.P2 | 2B.P3 | 2B.M2 | 2B.D2 |

For the sports club, you have decided to create two podcasts, which will be available to download from the club's website.

The first podcast will feature content about the club and will include interviews with some of the club's members. The second podcast will be a recording featuring two club members discussing a recent sporting event (e.g. a World Championship event or a premiership football game) and how the club's activities link to this.

- Identify the key points of this brief.
- Who is the podcast aimed at? How will you make it appeal to them?
- Create a timeline and scripts – make sure each podcast is at least three minutes long.
- Come up with some ideas for the design of the audio product. Think about the elements it will contain and how they could fit together. Select which elements you will use.
- Create a list of the assets you will use.
- Review your chosen designs and give reasons why you selected each element.

Tip

Always keep your audience in mind when making decisions. It's not about which things you like best (unless you're the target audience!).

Digital audio equipment 1

Getting started

In small groups, discuss the advantages and disadvantages of built-in microphones and external microphones. Create a list of situations where it is appropriate/not appropriate to use each type.

Introduction

You will need to be familiar with various tools and techniques in order to create, test and review your digital audio products.

If you are using a mobile phone to make your recordings, you will probably have to use the built-in microphone, but if you use a laptop or other recording device, you have the option to use an external microphone. This section looks at the different types of microphone available.

Figure 5.5 Examples of (from top to bottom) a dynamic microphone, an electret condenser microphone and a condenser microphone

Microphones

A wide range of microphones are available with many different features. Microphones can be classified by the technology that they use. Most microphones are one of three types:

1 **Dynamic microphones** are robust and relatively cheap. They are often used on stage by rock and pop music performers because they are not easily damaged.
2 **Electret condenser microphones** are very cheap to produce and provide good results. This is the type of microphone used in mobile phones and laptops.
3 **Condenser microphones** are often used where the highest quality is required, such as in a recording studio. Condenser microphones require a power source and so usually include a battery. If you are using a condenser microphone, it is wise to have a spare battery available.

Handheld or clip-on?

A handheld microphone is more flexible – you can hold it or place it into a microphone stand. There are many types of stand available, including desk stands and floor stands. You need to take care when using a handheld microphone, as it can easily pick up unwanted noises from being handled.

Clip-on microphones can be attached to the clothing of the person being recorded. While this frees up the person's hands, this type of microphone is only suitable for recording one person's voice.

Wired or wireless?

Wireless microphones are more convenient and avoid trailing wires. However, you must ensure the batteries in the microphone and the receiving unit are fresh (and that you have a spare), and that the reception is of good quality.

Wired microphones of the same quality are likely to be cheaper than wireless microphones, but you may need to use extension cables to allow you flexibility in positioning the microphone(s).

Link

See the section *Health and safety precautions* for advice on dealing with wires and cables.

Pickup pattern/directional response

It is important to know the **pickup pattern** of a microphone (also called directional response or polar pattern), as this will affect the choice of microphone for a particular situation.

- **Omnidirectional.** A microphone that has an omnidirectional response is equally sensitive to sound arriving from all directions. If you wanted to record a discussion with a number of people around a table, using a microphone with an omnidirectional response placed in the centre would be a good choice.
- **Unidirectional.** A unidirectional microphone is sensitive only to sounds from a certain direction. This type of microphone is used for recording one person speaking or singing.
- **Cardioid.** Various different patterns of unidirectional sensitivity are used, but one of the most common is known as the cardioid pattern. Dynamic microphones used by live stage musicians commonly use a cardioid pattern of sensitivity to reduce the problem of **feedback**. A cardioid pattern microphone would be a good choice when recording an interview with a single person in a location where there might be some background noise, such as in a busy shopping centre.

Figure 5.6 Cardioid pickup pattern

Connectors

Laptop and desktop computers have 3.5 mm stereo sockets for connecting microphones, headphones or speakers. Microphones (and headphones) that have been designed for use with computers have a matching **jack connector**. However, microphones and other equipment designed for professional audio use may have ¼ inch (6.3 mm) mono or stereo jacks. Some professional microphones may have a type of connector called XLR. You can purchase adapters for most of these types of connectors to fit the 3.5 mm stereo sockets on a computer at electronics stores or online.

Protecting a microphone

If you record a person's voice with a condenser microphone, especially while they are singing, you may need to use a pop shield. A pop shield minimises **plosives** and protects the microphone from saliva.

If you are using a microphone outside, you may have problem with wind noise, which can spoil a recording. In these situations, you should use a windshield. Windshields vary from small foam covers to large **zeppelins**, which are used to create an area of still air around the microphone.

Just checking

1 What is a microphone pickup pattern?
2 What types of pickup patterns do microphones typically have?
3 What is a zeppelin used for?

Digital audio equipment 2

Introduction

In addition to microphones, all sorts of equipment is used in the production of digital audio. You should be able to make recordings of adequate quality using a mobile phone or digital voice recorder. However, using additional equipment may make it more convenient and easier to make high-quality recordings.

Whatever equipment you are using, it is important to test it before you make your recording. This section gives details of some of the other recording equipment available and how you can test it before use.

Other recording equipment

- **Laptop.** This is probably the most convenient method of recording digital audio, although to get recordings of a reasonable quality, you must use an external microphone. Most laptops have internal fans, which make noise, so the microphone must be kept well away from the laptop. You must ensure that the microphone has a long enough lead or that you have an extension lead.
- **Mobile phone.** This is a convenient alternative to using a laptop, although you are limited by the quality of the internal microphone and you must hold the phone carefully to avoid adding unwanted handling noise to the recording.
- **Digital voice recorder.** Digital recorders are usually designed for making voice notes or recording interviews and have a built-in microphone. Some digital voice recorders have a socket to connect an external microphone. Many of these devices also allow you to select the quality of the recording, so make sure you set it to the highest quality.

Playback equipment

It is useful to be able to monitor a recording as you make it, so a set of headphones or earphones is a useful piece of equipment. These will allow you to check that the microphone is picking up the sound correctly and that there is not too much background noise. Headphones that fully cover your ears are the best choice, as they help cut out external sounds so you can concentrate on the sound picked up by the microphone. You should not try to monitor the recording you are making by listening to it on speakers, as this will interfere with the recording (and may cause feedback). However, once the recording has been made, you can listen to it using speakers.

Choosing equipment

Frequency response

One of the most important measures of the quality of a microphone or other recording and playback equipment is its **frequency response**. This is the range of sound frequencies that the device is able to capture or reproduce.

Humans are usually said to be able to hear sounds between 20 Hz (low frequency) to 20 kHz (high frequency), although this ability diminishes with age. Equipment used for recording or playing back human speech only (with no music) can have a much narrower range of frequency response, as speech is normally only within the range of about 200 Hz to 8 kHz. Equipment that will be used to record or play back music needs a wider frequency response, in line with what humans can actually hear.

Other things to consider

Other aspects of recording and playback equipment you need to consider include:

- **Cost.** You do not need to obtain a lot of expensive equipment, but really cheap microphones may not produce very good results.
- **Length of cord.** If you purchase a microphone, it will probably come with quite a short lead, which can make it inconvenient to use. You can, of course, use extension leads if needed.

Activity 5.5

Make a list of the equipment you have available to record and play back digital audio and the specifications of each piece of equipment. Include the response pattern (for microphones), frequency response and the type of connectors required.

Prepare and test the equipment

When preparing a recording session, especially if it will be 'on location' (away from your school, college or home), make sure you have all the equipment and cables you need. Make sure any equipment with rechargeable batteries (laptop, mobile phone) is fully charged up and you have spare batteries for any equipment that uses replaceable batteries.

Soundchecks

Before you start recording, you should carry out a soundcheck. This involves setting up all your equipment (laptop or other recording equipment, microphone, etc.) and making a short test recording. Ideally, your test recording should be with the same actors' voices as you will be using for the real recording and should be in the same location.

Once you have made your test recording, play it back and check that everything is as it should be. In particular, check that the actors' voices are clearly audible and that there is no background noise or other unwanted noises.

If the results of the soundcheck are not acceptable or you think you can improve on them, make whatever adjustments are necessary and do another soundcheck. You might find you need to adjust the position of the microphone, adjust the recorder settings or move to a different location to achieve better results.

> **Remember**
>
> Although you can make some adjustments to the recording after it has been made, it is wise to start off with the best possible recording. It is very difficult and time-consuming (and may not always be possible) to adjust a poor recording to achieve something that is of an acceptable quality.

Preparing for your recording will help ensure that everything goes smoothly

CONTINUED ▸▸

Did you know?

You can download a useful microphone technique manual from the Shure website, a well-known manufacturer of microphones. Go to Pearson Hotlinks (www.pearsonhotlinks.co.uk) and search for this title.

Audio recording set-up

Once the soundcheck is complete, you can make the actual recording. Professionals often need several 'takes' in order to get it right, so don't be concerned if it does not go well the first time. Listen to the recording as soon as you have made it to ensure it is of the required standard. Don't delete any recordings at this stage, as you may be able to use the better parts of an otherwise poor recording at the editing stage. If you have any doubts, try the recording again. It far better to have several good recordings to choose from than to have just one that is not really good enough.

Activity 5.6

Check out your equipment by doing a soundcheck. Connect the equipment together as required, then record some sample dialogue and play it back to check everything is OK. If you are recording using a mobile phone or digital voice recorder, copy the files across to a computer and check that they play.

Try several different recording locations with your microphone and try recording a single person speaking and a group (two or three people). Experiment with a number of recordings and attempt to find the best arrangement for each situation.

Did you know?

If your recordings are still quiet after setting the **Microphone** slider to maximum volume, you can use the **Microphone Boost** slider to further increase the volume. (See Figure 5.8.) Not all sound cards support this feature.

However, you may find that using too much microphone boost increases background noise or adds distortion. You need to experiment to find the best settings in a particular situation, which is why a soundcheck is important.

Microphone technique and settings

When recording spoken dialogue, keep the microphone between 15 and 30 centimetres from the speaker. Have the person speak directly into the microphone, as turning their head when they speak will change the way the recording sounds.

Making adjustments to microphone input

You can make some basic adjustments to the microphone input on a computer that has a Windows® operating system using the Control Panel. For example, if the soundcheck indicates that the recording sound is either too quiet or too loud, you might need to adjust the level up or down.

If you are using a computer as your recording device, you can use the simple sound recorder that comes with Windows® or you can use a more sophisticated audio application, such as Audacity®.

How to adjust microphone levels

Step 1 Open the **Control Panel**.

Step 2 Select **Hardware and Sound**, then select the **Sound** option. You will see a dialog box similar to Figure 5.7. The exact options you will see will depend on the type of sound card your computer has.

Step 3 Click the **Recording** tab.

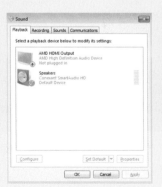

Figure 5.7 The Sound dialog box

Step 4 Select **Microphone** (in this example, this is the internal microphone in a laptop), then click the **Properties** button.

Step 5 In the **Properties** dialog box, click the **Levels** tab.

Step 6 Slide the **Microphone** slider up or down to adjust the level of the microphone (see Figure 5.8).

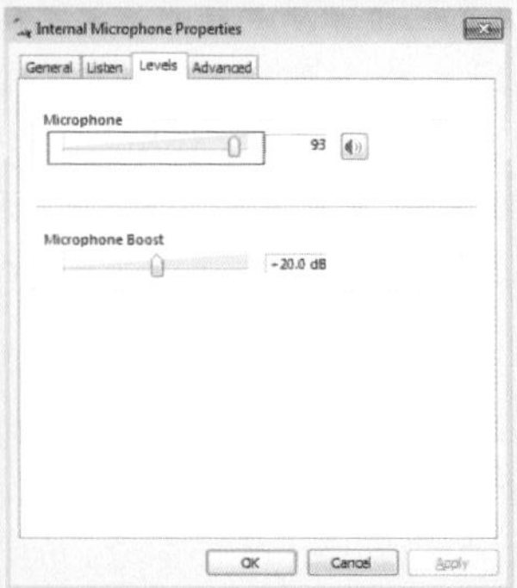

Figure 5.8 Adjusting the levels of the microphone

WorkSpace

▶ Sally Blake

Sound archivist

I work as a sound archivist at a museum in London. It's a fascinating job in general, but even more so for someone like me who is interested in history and enjoys a challenge!

The museum has a large collection of historical audio recordings, all of which are held on a variety of analogue media, such as gramophone records, reel-to-reel tapes and cassette tapes. Some of the very old recordings were made on wax cylinders and magnetic wires. Most of these recordings are in such poor condition that they will soon decay to the point where we can no longer save them.

Because some of the tapes are in such poor physical condition (due to age, dust and mould), they have to be cleaned up before we can even try to play them. I have a range of analogue playback equipment connected to my computer, including reel-to-reel and cassette tape players and gramophone turntables. Once I have converted the recording to digital format, I then have to adjust the recording to achieve the best possible result. I also have to update the file's metadata and add in details of what the recording is and when it was made. This enables historians to search for information relevant to their research.

Some of the material is really fascinating. The project I'm currently working on involves the recollections of a solider from World War I, recorded on a gramophone record in the 1920s, shortly after the war ended.

Think about it

1 What sort of skills (both technical and other skills) do you think Sally needs to do her job?

2 What challenges does she face in her day-to-day work?

3 What do you think she likes best about her job?

Using audio-editing software 1

Introduction

Once you have recorded your own audio and collected ready-made audio following the plan you created, it is time to edit these files to make your final product. There are many different audio-editing applications you could use to do this. Most computers will have audio-editing software installed on them, but you can also buy or download additional software packages to suit your requirements.

Gathering ready-made assets

You can find many ready-made audio assets such as background music and sound effects on the internet, and possibly other media such as CDs. You always need to check that the assets you want to use are copyright free before you download them.

If you use downloaded files, you will need to credit them and state where you found them. You should create a table listing all the ready-made clips that you use, including full details of where you obtained them.

Most ready-made files will be in MP3 or WAV format. Once you have downloaded these files, you can import them into your audio-editing software, and edit and mix them with the rest of your track to provide the desired effects.

Many sites will quote the sampling rate or bit depth of the files you can download. When you import the clip into your audio-editing software, it should show you the sampling rate and bit depth in the track header on the left. It is fine to use tracks with different sampling rates or bit depths, as the software should mix them all together. But you should choose the highest quality available for the clips you download, as editing and mixing will not improve the quality.

Importing audio files

Sound effects or clips you find on the internet are likely to be in MP3 or WAV format. You can import these file formats into your audio-editing software, but you may not be able to import WMA files as these are uncompressed files.

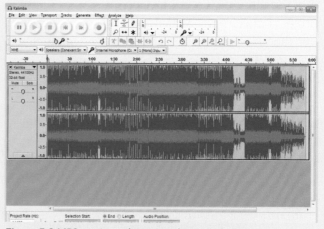

Figure 5.9 MP3 music track imported into Audacity

Cut, copy and paste clips

One of the first things you might need to do, especially with a clip you have recorded yourself, is to remove unwanted parts of the recording. The clip shown in Figure 5.10 has about a second at the start of the recording before the speech starts. Here's how to remove this silent part at the beginning of the clip.

How to remove unwanted parts of a recording

Step 1 Drag your mouse to highlight the portion you wish to remove. (See Figure 5.10)

Step 2 Choose **Cut** from the **Edit** menu.

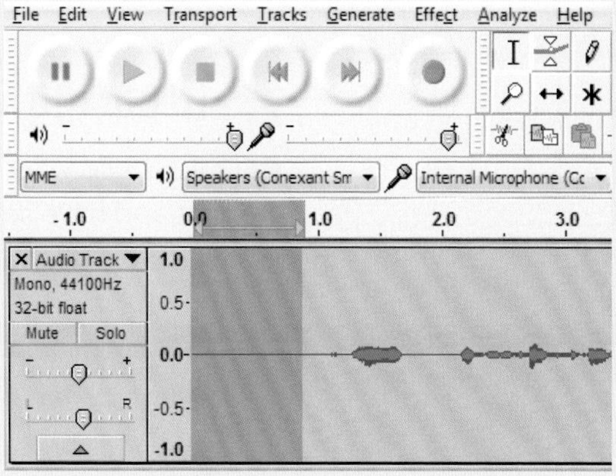

Figure 5.10 Selecting a portion of an audio track

You may also want to cut out portions of your recording and paste them into a separate track.

How to copy and paste between recordings

Step 1 Highlight the part of the track you want to copy by dragging your mouse across it.

Step 2 Go to the **Edit** menu and choose **Copy**.

Step 3 From the **Track** menu, choose **Add new**. This will create a new track for the part of the recording you have copied.

Step 4 Then select **Audio track** from the drop-down menu options.

Step 5 From the **Edit** menu, choose **Paste**.

If you click the **Mute** button on the original track, you can then play the new track without the original one playing (see Figure 5.11).

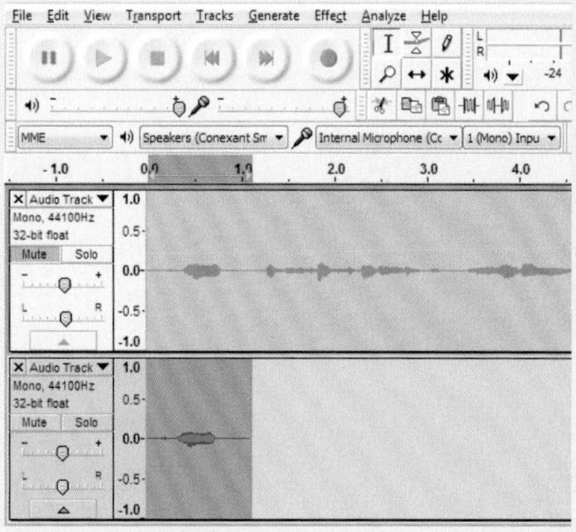

Figure 5.11 Pasting a portion of an audio track

To delete a track, just click the **X** icon next to the track name.

Just checking

1 Before you use an asset you have found on the internet, what should you check?

2 Is it possible to improve the quality of an audio clip once you have downloaded it?

Using audio-editing software 2

Introduction

Having imported your audio track, you will probably want to adjust the volume of your different tracks and apply other effects. The 'How to' features in this section explain how to make tracks start at different times within your product, how to adjust the volume of a track, as well as how to remove background noise.

Creating tracks for dialogue

You might also want to have a background track that plays throughout your audio product and have sections of dialogue playing at various times during the clip. If you do this, you won't want the dialogue to start at the same time as the background music.

How to make background music play before dialogue starts

Step 1 Copy the section of dialogue you want to use.

Step 2 Create a new track for your dialogue.

Step 3 Click at the point in the new track where you want the dialogue to start.

Step 4 Go to the **Edit** menu and choose **Paste**. Now you can paste in the section of dialogue you copied. (See Figure 5.12).

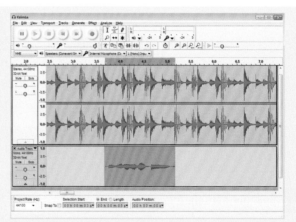

Figure 5.12 Background track with dialogue track added

Adjusting the volume of the background track

You might need to adjust the volume of the background music so that it is audible but quieter than the dialogue.

You can use the volume slider for the background track to reduce it to the right level. However, this will lower the volume of the whole background track. To lower the volume only when the dialogue is playing, you need to create an **envelope**.

How to create an envelope

Step 1 Click the **Envelope** tool. (See Figure 5.13.)

Step 2 Click and drag in the background track to create the point where the volume drops and the point where it increases at the end of the dialogue.

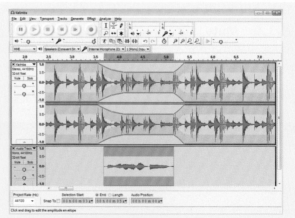

Figure 5.13 Using the Envelope tool

Fading the volume up or down

Audio-editing software can also be used to fade in or fade out tracks.

How to fade in or fade out of tracks

Step 1 To select the length of the fade in or out, select the part of the audio track over which the fade will happen.

Step 2 From the **Effect** menu, choose **Fade in** or **Fade out**.

Audacity® has an effect called **Auto Duck** that will automatically create an envelope for you, lowering the volume of a background track when there is dialogue in another track.

How to use Audacity®'s Auto Duck effect

Step 1 Make sure the dialogue track is below the music track.

Step 2 From the **Effect** menu, choose **Auto Duck**.

Other useful effects

Your audio software editing package also provides a number of other useful effects, including:

- **Normalise.** This will set the maximum volume of a track.
- **Change pitch.** This allows you to change the pitch of a track (or a selected portion of a track) without changing the tempo.
- **Change tempo.** This allows you to change the tempo of a track (or a selected portion of a track) without changing the pitch.
- **Echo.** You can add an echo effect to a track (or a selected portion of a track) using this option.
- **Reverse.** You can use this effect to reverse any track. This will make any speech unintelligible but can be used to provide a special effect.
- **Noise removal.** A track you have recorded may have background noise you want to remove.
- **Pan.** This controls the levels of the left and right tracks in a stereo sound clip (sometimes this is called balance). Your software will have a pan slider on the track header, normally located to the left of the track itself. Typically, you might want to adjust the relative levels of the left and right tracks to give the impression of movement, for example someone walking from left to right. In this case, their voice should start loud on the left track, and then you increase the right level until the levels are equal (when the person is in the centre). Then you decrease the left track level and increase the right level. You can adjust the relative volume levels of the left and right tracks using the envelope effect.

Remember

If you need to record a sound clip in a location where there is a lot of background noise, remember to record a few seconds of just the background noise, with nothing else. You can then use this to create the noise profile.

CONTINUED ▸▸

How to remove background noise

Step 1 Select the section containing just the background noise. (See Figure 5.14.)

Step 2 From the **Effect** menu, choose **Noise Removal**.

Step 3 The **Noise Removal** dialog box will appear (see Figure 5.15). Click the **Get Noise Profile** button.

Step 4 Make sure you don't have the section with just the noise selected.

Step 5 Return to the **Noise Removal** dialog box. Click **OK**. The background noise will be removed (see Figure 5.16).

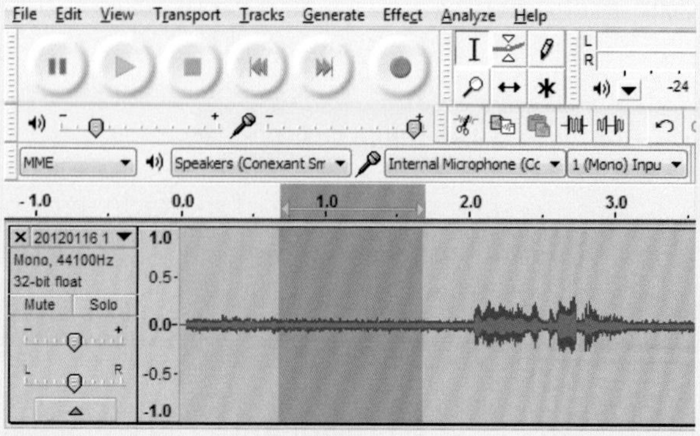

Figure 5.14 Track with noise

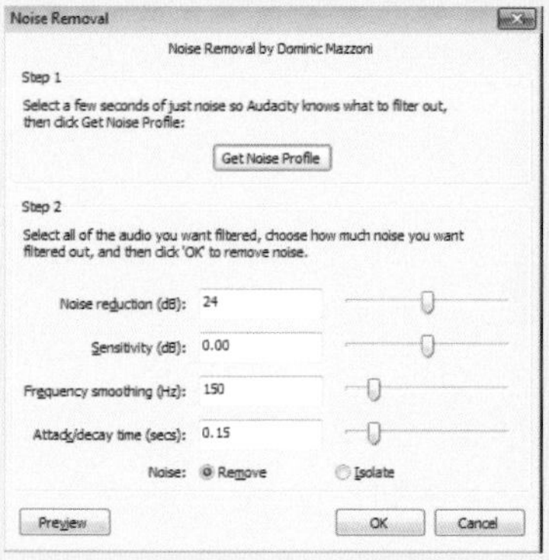

Figure 5.15 Noise removal dialog box

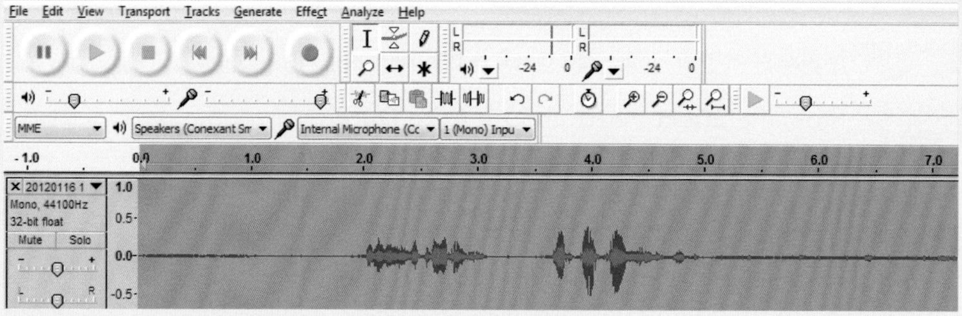

Figure 5.16 Noise removed

Assessment activity 5.3

1C.4 | 2C.P4 | 2C.M3

You have shown your design ideas to the sports club and they would like you to go ahead and create the podcast.

- Gather together all the equipment you need, using your timeline as a guide.
- Test the audio equipment and carry out sound checks before recording.
- Record the interviews for your podcasts and (if required) download them onto your computer.
- Find and download suitable, copyright-free, ready-made audio clips, including background or theme music and any sound effects that you need. Keep a record of the assets you are using and where you got them from.

Tips
- Make sure that all assets are saved in the correct format.
- Make sure you give yourself enough time for the recording – it will probably take a lot longer than you expect.

Testing audio products

Introduction

It is important to test and refine the audio products you have created. There are two main areas you need to test: the technical suitability of your product and how well your product meets your original intentions and audience requirements.

Test for functionality

You will need to test the functionality of your audio products to ensure they work properly. You should check that the sound levels are appropriate and that the different assets are edited together correctly with no long pauses or cut off words or music. You also need to check that the products meet the purpose you stated in your design documents and that they will appeal to your target audience.

Gather feedback from others

Before you started work on your audio products, you should have been clear about the purpose and audience for your products. You now need to consider if you have achieved your original intentions and how well your final products match your audience requirements. These questions are more subjective than the technical ones, so it is often a good idea to ask other people to comment on these issues.

To gather feedback from others about the quality and suitability of your products, you could create a questionnaire for people to complete or you could interview people and ask them a series of questions from a script. Here are some examples of the sort of questions you could ask:

- How do you rate the sound quality?
- Was the dialogue clear and audible?
- Are the different assets (dialogue, music, sound effects, etc.) mixed together effectively?
- Do you think the product will appeal to its target audience?
- Does the product meet its original requirements?
- What are the strengths of the product and how might it be improved?

It is also useful to have some questions that use a numeric scoring system, as this makes the results easier to collate. For example, you might have questions like: 'Rate the overall quality of the product on a scale of 1 to 5. 1 = very poor, 2 = poor, 3 = OK, 4 = good, 5 = excellent.'

If you use the interview method, you should record the interviews so you can listen to them later.

You should aim to gather feedback from around eight to ten people. Gathering feedback from too few people could mean that the views of one particular person take on too much importance. The more people you interview, the more likely it is that the results you get will be fair and accurate.

CONTINUED ▸▸

Link

Refer to section *Reviewing audio products* for information on the review process.

Once the questionnaires or interviews have been completed, you need to collate the results.

The final step is to write up a review of your product, based on your experiences and the feedback you received from others.

Exporting and compressing your finished audio product

Remember

A codec is a program (or part of a program) that is used to encode and/or decode audio data into a particular compressed format such as MP3 or WMA.

Once you are happy that you have completed the editing of your audio product, you should compress and export it. This will make it suitable for other people (who perhaps don't have the same editing software as you) to listen to.

Choosing a format such as MP3 to export your audio clip will mean that it can be played on almost any computer or music player. It will also compress the file to reduce its size, which will make it much quicker to download the file from a website.

How to export an audio clip

Step 1 Go to the **File** menu and choose **Export**.

Step 2 A dialog box will appear. In the dialog box, choose the file name, location and the format the file will be saved in. (See Figure 5.17.) Click **Save**.

Figure 5.17 Exporting a file from Audacity®

Step 3 You will be asked if you want to edit any of the metadata saved with the file. Click **OK**.

Step 4 Your software program will remind you that the various assets you have edited together will be mixed to a single stereo track. Click **OK**.

Step 5 If it is the first time you have exported an MP3 file, the software program will ask you where the codec for the MP3 conversion is located. Some programs use a free MP3 codec called LAME, which you can download. Once your software program knows where the MP3 codec is, it will not ask you again and your project file will be converted to an MP3 file.

Step 6 If you want to adjust the quality (and therefore the file size) of the MP3 file, you can click the **Options** button in the **Export File** dialog box (see Figure 5.17) and choose a different quality setting (bit rate).

Technical testing of your audio product

When carrying out your technical testing, ask yourself the following questions:

- Does the audio clip actually run?
- Is the sound audible (loud enough to be heard)? Is the volume equalised throughout the clip or are some parts louder than others?
- Is the clip of adequate quality? (With a low level of background noise, there is no noticeable distortion.)

- Are the different assets edited together in a professional manner? For example, are there any long pauses or sudden changes in quality or volume between the assets?
- Is the clip of the right length? (Remember: you are required to produce clips that are at least three minutes long.)
- Does the clip meet the original requirements of the brief?

You can use a simple test plan to make sure you have checked for each of these points. See Figure 5.18 for an example of a simple test plan.

	Runs?	Clip quality?	Edit quality?	Correct length?	Fits brief?
Clip 1					
Clip 2					
Clip 3					
Clip 4					
Clip 5					
Clip 6					
Clip 7					
Clip 8					
Clip 9					
Clip 10					

Figure 5.18 Example test plan

◤ Documenting improvements to refine your product

If your product fails any of the technical tests, you will need to correct the problem(s) and test the clip again. At the end of your test plan, add in the details of any changes you made to your product as the result of testing. You may also need to update the table of ready-made assets you used if you have to make any changes to these.

Assessment activity 5.4

1C.5 | 2C.P5 | 2C.M4 | 2C.D3

You now need to edit the assets and create your podcasts. Remember: your podcasts need to be at least three minutes in duration.

- Use audio software to edit the audio clips together. Add effects and adjust the sound quality as required.
- Create a test plan for the podcasts and test them to ensure they achieve acceptable levels of quality and are fit for purpose and your target audience.
- Note any changes you make as a result of testing.
- Gather feedback from a number of people about the clips and use this feedback to improve your products.
- Refine the audio assets to create high-quality audio products.

Tip

Keep asking yourself, 'How could this be improved?' And ask for feedback from other people and use this to improve your podcast.

Reviewing audio products

Getting started

In small groups, discuss what you think is meant by 'the review stage'.

Introduction

The final step in the process is to review what you have produced. This stage is just as important as the design stage, as you will need to evaluate your work and compare it against the original requirements. It is suitable for the target audience? Does it meet its original purpose? Is it of a high enough quality?

Reviewing your own work can be hard, so it is a good idea to ask others for their feedback. This can be very useful, as you will gain an understanding of how people engage with the product. It will also help you understand where improvements need to be made and what you could do better next time round.

Reviewing your finished product

Quality of the audio products

How good is the quality of your products? You can't expect to produce material of a professional quality, but comparing your audio products against professional products can help you identify their strengths and weaknesses. When reviewing the quality, be sure to consider:

- how good your recordings are (Is there any background noise? Can the people speaking be clearly heard? etc.)
- how well your different assets are edited together (Are the sound levels good? Is the timing good with no long pauses? etc.).

Fitness for audience and purpose

How well do your final products match their original purpose? Will they really appeal to you target audience? You need to review the specific features in your audio products and explain how they meet the purpose and audience requirements.

Meeting the original requirements

How closely do your final products match your original designs? You need to look back at the designs you originally created for the audio products. It is very likely that you did not follow the design exactly. Where are there differences? Be prepared to explain why they occurred.

Legal and ethical constraints

The reviewing stage should not just focus on how well your audio products function and meet their purpose. You should also consider the wider processes involved in creating the products, and where you sourced assets from. When reviewing your products from a legal and ethical constraints position, be sure to ask yourself the following questions:

- Did copyright constraints prevent you from using some assets you would have liked to use?
- Did you consider general safety issues, such as taking care with downloads to avoid viruses? Did you observe health and safety precautions, such as taking regular breaks when using the computer and keeping food and drinks away?
- Did you take regular backups of your work?
- Is the content suitable? For example, is it likely to cause offence to anyone? Does it contain any personal information?

Strengths and weaknesses

It is a hard skill to assess your own strengths and weaknesses, but it is a good exercise to do when reviewing your work and the processes involved in creating it. When reviewing your strengths and weaknesses, be sure to ask yourself the following questions:

- What was really good about your audio products?
- How might you further develop them if you had more time?
- How would you do things differently next time to avoid the problems you encountered?

Assessment activity 5.5

| 1C.6 | 2C.P6 | 2C.M5 | 2C.D4 |

You now need to review and evaluate your podcasts. Produce a document (it could be a report, or a presentation, etc.) that covers the following points:

- Does the podcast include the key points specified in the brief? Explain how it does this.
- Compare your finished podcasts with your initial designs – how do they differ?
- How successful do you think your podcasts will be in appealing to the club's target audience?
- Explain what changes you made as you developed your podcast, and give reasons why you made them.
- Where there any problems you experienced? How did you solve them?
- Identify some areas where you could improve your podcast.

Tips

- Give a reason for every change that you made.
- Refer back to the feedback you received from other people to consider what further improvements you could make.

Introduction

Digital graphics are images and/or text created on or scanned into a computer. Graphics are used to communicate messages in every part of our lives, including advertising, music, fashion, interior design and architecture. You will see them when you surf websites, play computer games, go shopping or read a user manual. They bring colour, information and interest to our lives.

Have you ever thought about how graphics are created? Who has designed them and who are they aimed at? When graphic designers are creating graphic products, they have to take into account the audience and purpose of their work. Are the graphics helping to promote retirement homes to older people or a new style of trainers to teenagers? How a graphic designer plans and designs a graphic will very much depend on what impact the graphic needs to make and who it is aimed at.

Most graphic products are made by using photo-editing and vector-editing tools and techniques on ready-made or original images. In this unit, you will investigate a range of applications and features of graphic products and consider their audience and purpose. You will be able to apply what you discover to your own digital graphic products.

Assessment: You will be assessed by a series of assignments set by your teacher.

Learning aims

In this unit you will:

A understand the applications and features of digital graphic products

B design digital graphic products

C create, test and review digital graphic products.

> *I'm a member of my school's fundraising team, and every year we choose a charity to raise money for. Using my graphics skills, I was able to design a series of promotional materials to help raise awareness. These were placed around the school and helped to make sure that the fundraising events were well advertised and well attended. The events were a great success and we raised lots of money!*
>
> *Tom, 16-year-old would-be graphic developer*

Creating digital graphics

6

This table shows what you must do in order to achieve a **Pass**, **Merit** or **Distinction** grade, and where you can find activities in this book to help you.

Assessment criteria

Level 1	Level 2 Pass	Level 2 Merit	Level 2 Distinction
Learning aim A: Understand the applications and features of digital graphic products			
1A.1 Identify the intended purpose and features of two different graphic products **Assessment activity 6.1, page 187**	**2A.P1** Explain the intended purpose and features of at least two different graphic products. **Assessment activity 6.1, page 187**	**2A.M1** Review how the products are fit for purpose and their intended effect on the audience. **Assessment activity 6.1, page 187**	**2A.D1** Discuss the strengths and weaknesses of the graphic products. **Assessment activity 6.1, page 187**
Learning aim B: Design digital graphic products			
1B.2 Identify the audience and purpose for the design of a graphic product. **Assessment activity 6.2, page 192**	**2B.P2** Describe the audience and purpose for the design of a graphic product. **Assessment activity 6.2, page 192**	**2B.M2** English Produce detailed graphic product designs, including reasons why alternative ideas have been discarded. **Assessment activity 6.2, page 192**	**2B.D2** English Justify the final design decisions, explaining how they will: • fulfil the stated purpose and requirements of the brief • meet the needs of the intended audience. **Assessment activity 6.2, page 192**
1B.3 Produce outline design(s) for the digital products. Each design must include outline product ideas. **Assessment activity 6.2, page 192**	**2B.P3** English Produce designs for two digital graphic products with different purposes and audiences. One design must be for a vector image and the other must be a bitmap image. Each design must include: • requirements of the brief • documented product ideas and/or prototypes • a list of any ready-made assets to be used. **Assessment activity 6.2, page 192**		
Learning aim C: Create, test and review digital graphic products			
1C.4 Prepare assets for the graphic products, with guidance. **Assessment activity 6.3, page 199** **Assessment activity 6.4, page 203**	**2C.P4** Prepare assets for the graphic products, demonstrating awareness of purpose, with a list of sources for ready-made assets. **Assessment activity 6.3, page 199** **Assessment activity 6.4, page 203**	**2C.M3** Prepare high-quality assets for the graphic products, demonstrating awareness of audience, with all sources of assets fully referenced. **Assessment activity 6.3, page 199**	**2C.D3** Maths Refine assets to create two high-quality digital graphic products. **Assessment activity 6.5, page 205**
1C.5 Maths Edit assets to create graphic products, and test them for functionality, with guidance. **Assessment activity 6.5, page 205**	**2C.P5** Maths Edit assets to create two graphic products that both include text. Test the products for quality, purpose and against the original requirements, making any necessary improvements. **Assessment activity 6.5, page 205**	**2C.M4** Maths Gather feedback on the quality of the products, and use it to improve the products, demonstrating awareness of audience and purpose. **Assessment activity 6.5, page 205**	

Assessment criteria			
Level 1	**Level 2 Pass**	**Level 2 Merit**	**Level 2 Distinction**
1C.6	2C.P6	2C.M5	2C.D4
For each of the final graphic products, identify how the final product is suitable for the intended purpose. **Assessment activity 6.6, page 207**	For each of the final graphic products, explain how the final product is suitable for the intended audience and purpose. **Assessment activity 6.6, page 207**	Review the extent to which each of the final graphic products meets the needs of audience and the purpose, considering feedback from others and any constraints. **Assessment activity 6.6, page 207**	Evaluate the initial designs and the final graphic products and justify any changes made, making recommendations for further improvement. **Assessment activity 6.6, page 207**

Maths ⟋ Opportunity to practise mathematical skills

English ⟋ Opportunity to practise English skills

How you will be assessed

This unit will be assessed by a series of internally marked tasks. You will be expected to show an understanding of the design and development of digital graphic products. The tasks will be set in the context of the marketing sector. For example, you might be given a scenario like the following: Your line manager is involved in promoting a new product aimed at certain audiences. She asks you to produce two graphic products to advertise the new product, one using bitmap images and the other using vector images.

Your assessments could be in the form of:

- a research report or magazine article reviewing existing graphic products
- a design log for your products
- any prototypes you have produced
- a sources table of ready-made assets
- digital files of ready-made and original graphic assets
- your completed digital graphic products
- a completed questionnaire or witness statement as evidence of testing and feedback
- a report to your line manager explaining your design choices and describing any steps that could be taken to improve the products.

Applications and purpose of digital graphic products

Getting started ⏩

Think about a journey that you have been on in the last few days.

How many graphic products (e.g. road signs, advertisements, logos, posters, magazine covers) did you see?

In groups, discuss all the different graphic products you have seen and ask yourselves:

- What are they for?
- Who are they for?
- What information do they provide?
- How did they affect me?

Draw up a table and compare it with other groups.

Link ◓

Being able to create effective digital graphics will help you in many areas. Your graphic skills will support work in several units of this course, particularly: *Unit 4 Creating digital animation*; *Unit 8 Mobile apps development* and *Unit 13 Website development*.

Take it further ↗

Find examples of graphics from the following media:

- print publications
- instruction/technical manuals
- web design
- advertising.

What is the purpose of the graphics? Do all media use graphics in the same way?

Introduction

Before embarking on designing and creating graphical images, you should first be aware of the applications of images – this means where and why images are used. You will also need to be able to identify the features of graphical images that are important to their construction (how they are made) and effect (people's reaction).

In this section you will develop your knowledge of digital graphics and how they can be used. This will help you later on when you come to design your own images.

The range of digital graphics

The term digital graphics is very broad and covers a very wide range of products that are created using digital tools. Two examples of graphic products are logos and signs (see Figures 6.1 and 6.2).

Figure 6.1 Examples of three types of logo

Figure 6.2 Examples of some common signs

Figure 6.3 An example of packaging

Graphics are also used in posters, magazine covers, packaging (see Figure 6.3), web graphics, engineering drawings, manuals, imagery in movies and computer games.

The purpose of graphics

Digital graphics are usually created with a specific purpose in mind and to appeal to a particular audience. The purpose will depend on a product's objective – it could be to inform, to entertain, to educate, to persuade, to produce emotion, or even to change people's opinions. For example:

- Signs inform us about things such as where a place is or that a certain area is dangerous. The road sign with a red circle and a number inside informs drivers of the maximum speed allowable by law. That is its specific purpose.

- Games and movies containing digital graphics are designed to entertain us. They may make us feel sad or happy or excited, or a mixture of all three.

- The purpose of manuals and magazines might be to inform and educate.

- Packaging and logos inform us about products and suppliers. The packaging is often designed to make us desire the product.

In many cases, a digital image will have more than one purpose. For example, a primary school safety campaign might feature a superhero character who gives advice on how to stay safe. The graphic of the superhero is multi-purpose, as it is used to inform, educate and entertain the children (the audience).

The effect of graphics on different audiences

All digital images are designed to target a particular audience, for example:

- interest groups – such as medical advertisements targeted at doctors (which might be very different from graphics for the same product that are targeted at patients)

- gender groups – such as magazines specifically for women

- age groups – such as comics for children under five.

All of these images will have a specific, and different, effect on each person or group.

Figure 6.4 The right image can evoke a particular reaction from viewers

---

Activity 6.1

Look carefully at the two images shown in Figure 6.4. They have been deliberately designed to be affecting and to evoke a reaction from people.

Write down your responses to the following questions:

- What do the images show?
- How they make you feel?
- Do you think the images contain a message?
- In what ways could be the images be used?

Just checking

1 Name five examples of digital products.

2 What is the purpose of using graphics?

3 Why is the selection of digital images so important?

Features of digital graphics 1

Introduction

A good graphic is made up of many components and features. In this section you will learn about different features and how you can use these to achieve different effects. Understanding what makes a strong graphic, and what effects you can add during the design process, will help you during the planning and design stages when you create your own digital graphics.

Key terms

Vector graphics – These are created using a series of commands or mathematical statements (algorithms) to place lines and shapes in a given two-dimensional or three-dimensional space. These graphics are scalable and do not pixelate when enlarged. They are used in CAD packages.

Bitmap graphics – These are created using a series of pixels (or bits) within a grid system.

Pixel – A small component (also known as a dot) that contains colour information for an image. When all the pixels are brought together, the image will be visible.

Figure 6.5 Vector (top) and bitmap (bottom) images are two types of graphics

Types of graphics

There are two main types of digital graphics – vector and bitmap.

- **Vector graphics** are made up of lines and standard shapes, which are called objects. Information about these objects, such as start point, end point and length, is held mathematically as a sequence of instructions that the computer must follow to recreate the image. Vector graphics take up less memory and storage space than bitmap graphics. They are good for drawings and simple illustrations but not for high-quality images.

- **Bitmap graphics** contain a full illustration **pixel** by pixel, with each pixel holding information on colour. This type of graphic can give very high-definition images, but the file size can be very large because of the large amount of information the file contains. Digital photographs are examples of bitmap graphics.

Text

Text refers to the characters (letters, numbers and punctuation symbols) that are used within an image. For example, an image used within a police campaign might contain the emergency telephone number 999.

Take care to make text relevant and easy to read. Too much text may result in loss of interest; too little text may make the image hard to understand.

Composition

Composition describes how objects are arranged within an image. For example, a photographer will consider the composition of a photograph they want to take: whether to have a tree in the middle of the photograph or to one side, where to position people, and so on.

Sometimes, images are made up of multiple layers of objects. In this case, composition also refers to the order in which objects are placed in the layers.

Colour and texture

Each pixel within a bitmap image contains colour. The **colour depth** refers to the number of colours that are available within the **colour palette** of the software that is being used to view the image. The colour depth is based on the number of bits in the memory used to hold the colour of each pixel. File types supporting 8 bits per colour will only support a total of 256 individual colours, while 16-bit file types will support 64,000 colours, and 24-bit or 'true colour' file types support 16.7 million different colours. But be careful: the more colours there are, the larger the file size will be. This is very important when preparing images for web pages, as loading images with many colours can be very slow.

You should use colour with care, as some colours just do not go well together (for example, lime green text on a bright yellow background).

Texture is a term that can be used to describe two different things:

1 It can describe an apparent 3D effect in a 2D image (for example, a texture that looks like a rough surface).
2 It can describe a patterned filler used within a standard shape (for example, you can fill shapes with dots, stripes, checks and even tartans, rather than using a plain colour).

Size and position

You need to give careful thought to the size of various objects in an image. Minor details must not swamp the image and hide the message.

Position is a very important part of composition and refers to where in an image a particular object is placed.

Characters and objects

- **Characters** are the elements that make up text. Each letter, number, punctuation mark and space is a character.
- **Objects** are the visual elements within a digital image that can be manipulated separately. You can select individual objects and change their properties. For example, if you want to superimpose a photograph of yourself onto a photograph of a landscape, the shape of yourself will be an object.

Standard shapes such as circles and rectangles, lines and text can all be called objects.

Figure 6.6 shows how a standard piece of **Microsoft® ClipArt** is made up from many objects. Each piece of the image is a separate object and has been placed into position individually.

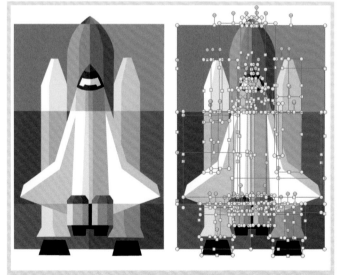

Figure 6.6 A number of objects have been used to create this digital image

Just checking

1 What is the main difference between vector graphics and bitmap graphics?
2 Name four other features of digital graphics.

Features of digital graphics 2

Introduction

Special files are used to hold digital graphics and in this section you are going to look at some of the different files used and the sizes of the different types of files. You will learn about how you can reduce the size of your files and some of the problems this may cause.

File types

There are a great many file types used for digital images, some of which are described in Table 6.1.

Table 6.1 Image file types

Type	Files produced	Description	Vector or bitmap?
Joint Photographic Experts Group	.jpg	Very popular format. Most digital cameras can save images in this format. Degrades on editing. 8 bits per colour.	Bitmap
Tagged Image File Format	.tif	Produces large files. Not well-supported by web browsers. 8 bits or 16 bits per colour. Compressed data.	Bitmap
Graphics Interchange Format	.gif	8 bits per colour (256 colours). Also supports animation. Good for limited colour use on web pages. Small files.	Bitmap
Portable Network Graphics	.png	Supports true colour (16 million colours). Replacement for GIF.	Bitmap
Windows® Bitmap	.bmp	Used within Microsoft® Windows®. Files are very large. Uncompressed data.	Bitmap
Corel PHOTO-PAINT®	.cpt	Default file format within Corel PHOTO-PAINT®.	Bitmap
Scalable Vector Graphics	.svg	Designed for use in web browsers.	Vector
Corel DRAW®	.cdr	Default file format within CorelDRAW®.	Vector
Corel® Paint Shop Pro®	.psp	Default file format within Corel® Paint Shop Pro®.	Vector and bitmap

Take it further

Use the internet to find out more about image file types. There are a number of informative websites that can help you, including Dan's Data: Graphic Formats Explained.

You can access this web page by going to Pearson Hotlinks (www.pearsonhotlinks.co.uk) and searching for this title.

Create your own copy of Table 6.1, adding some more image types.

File sizes

Generally, bitmap files are far larger than vector files, and bitmap files vary greatly in size depending on the type of bitmap. Table 6.2 gives an example of the different file sizes for the same bitmap image when saved as different types. It gives the approximate file size in kilobytes (KB).

Table 6.2 Bitmap file sizes in kilobytes (KB)

JPG	TIF	GIF	PNG	BMP
475	2500	225	375	2500

Compression

File compression techniques are used to reduce the size of bitmap files. Compression uses mathematical techniques to reduce the amount of 'waste' information held in a bitmap file. There are two generic types of compression:

- **Lossy compression** discards some of the information and so can lead to degradation in quality, but produces smaller files. It is used mainly, but not always, for multimedia files.
- **Lossless compression** systems allow the original file to be accurately and completely reconstructed from the compressed form. The files produced are larger than those produced from lossy compression.

Resolution

Resolution is the amount of detail visible in an image. With bitmap images, this is achieved by the number of pixels per unit of length (typically given as pixels per inch). The more pixels per inch, the higher the resolution, but also the larger the file in which the image is held.

Deciding on the best resolution for an image is often a trade-off between what is available (for example, the maximum resolution of your digital camera), what space is available to store the file, and whether or not it needs to be transmitted over a network. The larger the file, the slower the transmission will be.

Activity   6.2

Look at the examples of compression on the Image Compression Examples page of the PageTutor website. (You can access this web page by going to www.pearsonhotlinks.co.uk and searching for this title.)

Write a paragraph describing GIF compression and JPG compression, including when you would use each of them.

Assessment activity 6.1 | 1A.1 | 2A.P1 | 2A.M1 | 2A.D1 |

You have just started a work placement with a local graphic design company. The head designer is keen for you to develop your knowledge of the applications and features of digital graphics. He has asked you to find different types of digital images, e.g. a web page, a scene from a computer game, an advertisement, a sign.

Choose two different digital graphics to evaluate and prepare a short document that covers the following:

- What is the purpose of the digital graphics?
- Who is their intended audience?
- What features do they each have?
- Is each product fit for purpose?
- What effect will it have on its intended audience?
- What are the strengths and weaknesses of each one?

Tips

- Identify the key elements of each product and consider them carefully in turn.
- Give a reason to justify each opinion you state.

Key terms

Lossy compression – Compresses data by minimising the amount of data already there (by getting rid of some of it).

Lossless compression – Returns a compressed file to its original form without losing any of the information.

Did you know?

You can specify the quality percentage you want when you save a bitmap file. A .jpg image of around 115 KB will be reduced to around 15 KB at 10% quality reduction; 6 KB at 40% quality reduction; and 2 KB at 90% quality reduction.

It is often not until approaching 90% quality reduction that there is any noticeable difference in the photographic quality.

Remember

As a general rule, retain a high resolution (with larger file size) for products that are to be printed and a lower resolution (with smaller file size) for products that are to be viewed on screen.

Design documents 1

Getting started ▶▶

You are the owner of a chocolate factory and your team has created an exciting new chocolate bar. You hire a graphics design company to create the packaging for your new product. The designers would like some information on the product. What information do you think they need?

Discuss this in small groups.

Introduction

Getting the design of your digital graphics products right is essential and must be the first step in the development process, before you create them. It is impossible to create effective digital graphics products without first carrying out some good design work. To do this, you will need to use and produce a range of documents.

▶ The brief

Every project will start with the client giving you a brief description of the product(s) they would like you to produce. This document is called the brief, and will state the basic purpose, requirements and audience for the product that is to be developed. You will use some of this basic information to create your design brief. Figure 6.7 shows an example of a brief.

What information can you gain from this brief? Here is a summary of the information from the brief that will be useful for your design:

Client Brief for The Bredbury Little Theatre Company

The client requires a plan and drawings of the lounge area of 12 Assignment Street, a fictional address which is used as the set in a new play. The set has to fit the stage at the Bredbury Little Theatre, which has a width of 10 metres and a depth of 8 metres. The usable height is 4.5 metres.

These drawings will be outlines only and will be used by your client's set builders to build the set. It is therefore essential that the drawings are done to scale.

In addition, you are asked to give an artist's impression of what the finished set may look like. You will have to superimpose furniture, fabrics and fittings onto your drawings, and you will have to select suitable colour schemes. The play is a period drama set in the 1920s.

These images will be used by the client's props department to furnish and fit the set.

The client has asked you to design a few alternative styles of décor.

The final products must contain clear labels identifying the various parts.

Figure 6.7 Example client brief

1 Use vector graphics for the plan and drawings of the set. Use bitmaps (possibly photographs) for the artist's impressions of the finished set.

2 The client wants the images to be labelled, so you will need to include text.

3 The audience for your work will be professionals in:

   a) set design and manufacture.

   b) theatre properties and decoration.

4 The purpose of your work is to produce the essential basic set design from which your client can work.

5 The requirements are to include:

   a) drawings that are accurate and to scale

   b) illustrations of how the set could be decorated

   c) alternative solutions for the décor.

This brief is a very simple example, but it illustrates all of the basic points you will need to consider when you get a client brief. You should be able to identify the audience, purpose and requirements, which you will then include in your design documents. From the brief, you should also be able to develop a clear idea as to whether you will be using vector or bitmap graphics.

You must be absolutely certain that you know what the client needs. If this is not completely clear from the brief, you will need to go back and ask the client.

Intended audience, purpose and user requirements

Identifying the intended audience, purpose and user requirements will help make sure that you choose and create the correct digital graphics. You should think about the age and gender of your intended audience, as well as the purpose of the graphics product. For example, if the product is a range of leaflets to educate people about the dangers of swimming in rivers, you might use a cartoon graphic for a leaflet aimed at young children and a more serious graphic for an older audience.

Initial design ideas

Initial designs allow you to explore ideas. Have a look at other people's ideas and similar products that have already been created. In the case of the set design scenario (Figure 6.7), you could research other set designs to see the furnishing and decoration schemes used, or look at old photographs from the 1920s. The things that catch your eye and that you use for ideas are referred to as 'stimulus materials'.

Alternative design ideas

It is worth remembering that your vision for a design might be very different from what the client imagines. Even when you follow the design brief, your own interpretation of the design still might not suit the client. This is why it is a good idea to prepare some alternative ideas during the design stages. This does not mean you have to produce finished designs of lots of alternatives, but that you need to consider different ideas as you work on your design. This means that you are able to offer the client different options to choose from. These might be simple things, such as suggestions for different colour schemes, or they could be more complex, such as taking a totally different approach.

It is important to keep all of your notes and drawings of any alternatives that you think of. These will give you something to fall back on if, at the full design stage, your product is not exactly what your client wants.

Giving a client alternative options at various stages in the design will help the client to feel part of the design process.

? Did you know?

A client brief can contain very specific requirements. For example, the client might need you to create digital graphics that are compatible with particular web browsers or other software, or they might specify a maximum file size. They might also need graphics that fit their corporate style (for example, using exactly the same colours as their logo).

Remember

You cannot copy other people's designs without their permission. If you do so, you will be breaking the law. Although you cannot use their work, you may be inspired by what you see. This will help you develop your own ideas.

Design documents 2

Introduction

This section looks at other design documents you will need, including sketches of your ideas, prototypes and details of the ready-made assets you would like to use in your products. It also looks at the health and safety issues you will need to consider during the design stage.

Prototyping

Prototypes are samples or models created to test out your ideas. They are an excellent way of presenting an initial design and getting feedback on it. If you were designing the set for the Bredbury Little Theatre Company (see Figure 6.7), a visit to an exhibition at one of the world's grand theatres such as the Royal Opera House in London or the Palais Garnier opera house in Paris could provide you with inspiration. You would be able to see models of sets from famous productions. These perfect miniatures of the sets are examples of prototypes that were then used to produce the actual sets.

Activity 6.3

Read the following simple brief:

'I want a composite picture made up of photographs of red wild flowers. There must be a large caption in black that says "Red for rich pickings" and a further piece of text saying "Pick them, we lose them". The finished work will be used on a poster sent to schools to highlight the problem of picking wild flowers. It will be reproduced on A3 size paper.'

1 Identify the audience.
2 State the purpose of the picture.
3 Decide what you will need to create the picture.
4 State how you will get these materials.
5 Decide whether you will use vector or bitmap images.

Design methods

There is no set formula for producing a design and every designer will use their own preferred method. Some designers prefer to start with hand sketches, which are very rough drawings of what they are going to produce (see Figure 6.8).

Some designers might develop their sketches further by hand and then scan them in to a computer, while others may develop them by using digital editing software.

In this current age of digital technology, many designers skip the hand sketching phase and start their design work

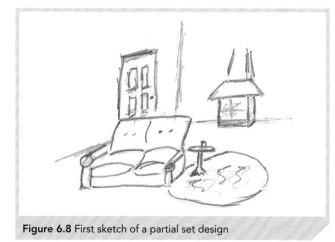

Figure 6.8 First sketch of a partial set design

using software. They then repeat and see their designs using the software tools and techniques.

The method that you use does not matter. What is important is that the design gives sufficient detail for the client to understand what you are proposing and to decide whether it will work for them.

You should keep all of your sketches and their developments and include them in your design documents.

Activity 6.4

Using the set design brief in Figure 6.7, draw sketches that you could use as the initial designs for this product. You will need sketches for both your vector and bitmap graphics. You could draw your sketches either by hand or using graphic software on the computer, or a combination of these.

Ready-made digital graphic assets

There are a great many existing shapes and images available, which you can add to your original graphic assets and use to produce a product. These are known as ready-made graphics.

If you use a ready-made graphic, even if it is free to download from the internet, you must give proper **acknowledgement** for the image in your final product. This means you have to say who owns the copyright to the graphic.

For example, the ClipArt image shown in Figure 6.9 comes from the Microsoft® suite of images and needs to be acknowledged accordingly.

Ready-made digital assets can include logos, cartoons, shapes and objects or even photographs. They are available for both vector and bitmap graphics.

You will need to decide which ready-made assets you would like to use and list them, together with their source details, in your design documents.

Copyright © Microsoft Corporation

Figure 6.9 Example of acknowledgement of an asset

Activity 6.5

In response to the set design brief in Figure 6.7, draw up a list of ready-made assets that you could possibly use in the design and creation of the products. Include proper acknowledgement for each ready-made asset you want to use.

Prepare a second list of assets that you will have to create yourself to complete the products required by the brief in Figure 6.7.

Key term

Acknowledgement – A full reference of the source of a ready-made asset, which gives proper recognition to the asset's designer and owner.

CONTINUED ▶▶

◤ Developing the design

Once you have done your initial sketches and chosen your ready-made assets, you need to develop your design. This involves tidying up your sketches, adding ready-made assets and suggesting colour schemes.

Remember that this is the design phase. Your work in this phase needs to give sufficient detail to indicate what the final product will look like, and no more. The final product will take shape in the product creation phase.

◤ Safety and hazards

Health and safety are always important. You will need to take health and safety issues into consideration when you are taking original photos (especially outdoors). Issues you will need to consider include:

- Some camera equipment can be heavy and difficult to carry. Not only could the equipment get damaged, but you could also hurt yourself if you are carrying too much weight. You could use trolleys to transport the equipment or ensure that there are enough people to carry it.

- The environment in which you are going to take the picture might present some health and safety issues. You may want to use interesting surroundings for your pictures and you need to make sure that you can do so without causing harm to yourself or others.

- Cables and tripods could easily cause problems with tripping. It is a good idea to keep cables tidy and visible. You can use cable clips to keep cables together or place traffic cones along the cord or at the base of the tripod to increase visibility.

- If you are using power, you need to make sure that live cables are insulated and sealed from moisture in case any liquid is spilled or if you are working outdoors.

Assessment activity 6.2   *English*   1B.2 | 1B.3 | 2B.P2 | 2B.P3 | 2B.M2 | 2B.D2

Produce full design documents that you can present to the client as the basis for further development. You can use:

- the set design brief in Figure 6.7
- your sketches from Activity 6.4
- the lists of assets (ready-made and those you will need to create yourself) from Activity 6.5.

Your design should include:

- a summary of the key points of the brief

- outline and detailed designs for one vector image and one bitmap image
- evidence of the alternative product ideas you had and any prototypes you created
- a list of all the ready-made assets you will be using
- notes of your alternative designs and reasons why you selected or discarded the alternatives
- an explanation of how your design will meet the requirements of the brief and the needs of the audience.

Tip

When considering which ideas to develop, always refer back to the brief – which elements would best fit the brief? Which would be best for the audience?

WorkSpace

Cyd Farleyhouse

Graphic designer

I can't think of a time when I didn't want to work with graphics. When I was in primary school I started to play with graphics programs and I used to design labels and posters for the teachers. I studied graphics and IT at GSCE stage and decided to do a National Diploma rather than A-levels, so that I could gain more practical experience in designing and creating graphics.

While studying for my National Diploma, I worked part time for an advertising agency. After I'd completed the Diploma, the company offered me a permanent job with the option to have time off to continue with my studies. Needless to say, I said yes! I'm currently taking modules that interest me in the hope of putting together a modular degree.

My work involves picking up an idea from the advertising team, who also give me an indication of the audience and purpose of the advertising campaign. I run up some designs, which tends to involve storyboards and prototyping. I also sketch out lists of what can be done based on existing assets and what we need to create from scratch. I then collate all of this information and pass it on for feedback. Once the campaign has been finalised, I then start to gather assets, create new material and assemble rushes of near final material. The final stages are quite adrenalin-fuelled, so it's easy to get swept away in the creative excitement and realise you've worked through lunch!

Communication is very important, as the wider team needs to be aware of what is happening during the different stages. In addition to the design aspects, I also need to be aware of things like health and safety, equality and diversity issues and so on, and build any requirements into my work.

The variety in my work seems endless, and every day brings new creative challenges.

Think about it

1 What skills do you think are necessary to do Cyd's role?

2 What type of campaigns do you think advertising agencies create?

3 Who are the main people that Cyd works with on a day-to-day basis?

Creating digital graphic products

 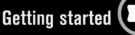
Introduction

Once you have carried out all of the relevant design work and produced a detailed design document, the next stage is to create your product. The first step in creating your digital graphic product is to gather together any ready-made assets you want to use, and prepare them for use.

You must create your own assets using graphics software.

Gathering assets

Before you start on the main creation activity, you will need to gather together the selection of ready-made assets that you are going to use in your finished product. These may be images, such as clipart, that you have found on the internet.

Make sure that each of the assets that you want to use is included in the list that you have already created and that the sources are correct. Make sure that your use of these assets will not break copyright laws by asking the following questions:

- Am I entitled to download the image free of charge?
- Am I entitled to use the image free of charge?
- If the answer is no to either question: Can I use the image by making a small payment?

If the answer to all three questions is no, you cannot use the asset in question and must find an alternative.

Having gathered together the ready-made assets you want to use, you will need to check that the file formats used are compatible with each other and with the file formats you are going to use for your original assets.

If there is any problem, you will need to try to convert all files to the same format or to **compatible formats**. If the file format of a particular asset is incompatible with the others and cannot be converted, you will not be able to use that asset.

Key term

Compatible formats – File formats that can be used together in the same graphics software. Formats that are not compatible with each other, or with the software, cannot be used.

Activity 6.6

Using the list of ready-made assets you produced in Activity 6.5, gather together the assets (vector and bitmap) and prepare them for use in the creation of your products.

Keep the prepared assets ready for use in your assessment.

Graphics software

As part of your assessment for this unit, you must use graphics software to create assets and to merge them with ready-made assets into the final products.

The features that you will be able to use will depend on the software that you have, and which version it is. (Newer versions will probably contain more features.) Whichever software and version you have, you should be able to use the majority of the tools and techniques described in sections *Vector-editing software* and *Photo-editing software*.

You will need to practise using these tools and techniques to become proficient in their use. These skills will help you to produce images with smooth edges and seamless joins where you have merged assets together, providing a more professional and polished finish.

Vector graphics

Vector graphics are suitable for illustrations that require accuracy, such as building plans and technical illustrations. They are easily scalable because they are based on mathematical properties. However, they are not good for displaying photo-realistic images because photos do not usually contain clearly defined shapes, lines and curves.

Bitmaps

Bitmaps are mapped into a pixel grid and are suitable for photo-realistic images that require complex colour variations. They are not easily scalable because the grids are not flexible. When a bitmap is enlarged, it loses its sharpness (it becomes pixelated), and edges within the image appear jagged.

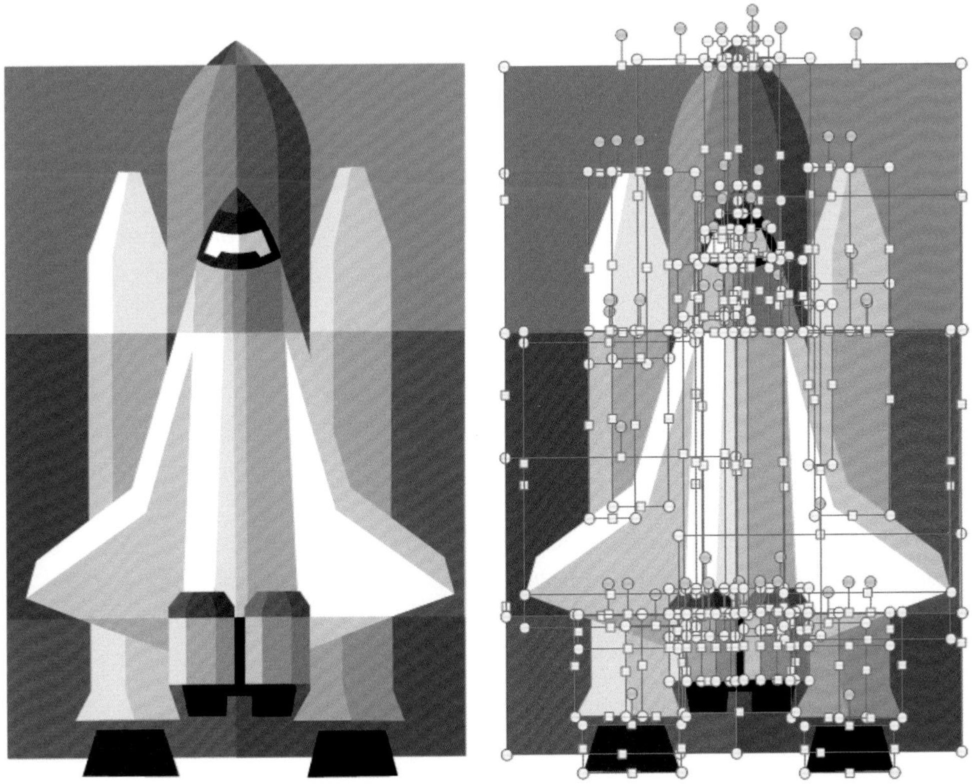

Figure 6.10 This image was created using graphics software

Link

Refer to section *Vector-editing software* for what you can do using vector-editing software.

Refer to section *Photo-editing software* for what you can do with bitmaps using photo-editing software.

Did you know?

Examples of vector graphics software include CorelDRAW®, Adobe® Illustrator®, Microsoft® Expression Design, Google™ SketchUp and the drawing tools in Microsoft® Word®.

Examples of bitmap software, also called raster software, include Adobe® Photoshop®, Corel® Paint Shop Pro®, Corel PHOTO-PAINT®, and Microsoft® Paint®.

Just checking

1 What questions should you ask to prevent you breaching copyright with ready-made images?

2 What is meant by 'seamless joints' when merging images together?

3 What is meant by a scalable graphic?

Vector-editing software

Link

See *Unit 4 Creating digital animation* to learn more about how to use vector-editing software.

Introduction

There are any number of vector-editing packages available. Some packages are better for producing creative freehand drawings, while others are better for producing technical drawings. However, most will share similar editing tools. These tools allow you to edit vector objects in various ways and add different effects. This section covers various software tools and techniques.

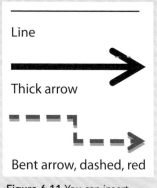

Figure 6.11 You can insert different types of lines and arrows

◤ Tools and techniques

In this section, we will look at the following tools and techniques:

- lines
- shapes
- text
- shading and effects
- colour fills, gradients and patterns
- shading and effects
- group and ungroup
- rotate and reflect
- duplicate and clone
- scale and dimensions
- combine shapes and paths
- edit and break apart paths
- layering.

Lines

You can insert lines and arrows into your image by marking the start and end points. You can define the thickness of the line, its colour and its style (solid, dots or dashes).

Shapes

You can create basic shapes including squares, rectangles, circles and ovals, triangles and block arrows. You can also create original shapes using the freehand tools.

Text

You can add text to vector images, and control whether it is drawn on top of or under the other components. You can also flow text around the edges of a shape so it doesn't overlap; imagine that the text is attached to a path it has to follow around a shape. (This is called wrapping text.)

WordArt and similar types of graphic lettering are also examples of text that can be used in vector images.

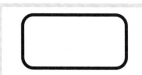

Figure 6.12 You can create a range of basic shapes

Figure 6.13 Example of WordArt

Colour fills, gradients and patterns

Any shape can be filled with colour. It can have a different coloured border for effect, and the colour can be faded across the shape in what is known as a **gradient**.

Shading and effects

There are standard effects that you can use with basic shapes. These include shadow, reflection, bevel and glow.

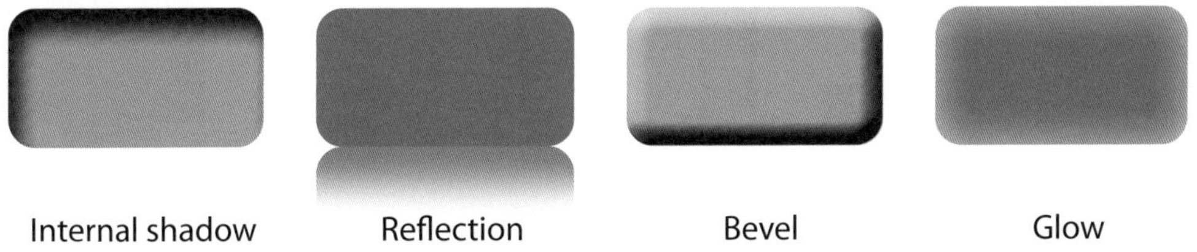

Soft gradient, dark outline

Internal shadow	Reflection	Bevel	Glow

Figure 6.15 Standard shading effects include internal shadow, reflections, bevel and glow

Dark gradient, no outline

Texture fill

Figure 6.14 You can select from a range of fill effects

Rotate and reflect

Rotate allows you to turn the image on the page. Reflect (sometimes called flip) gives a mirror image of the shape.

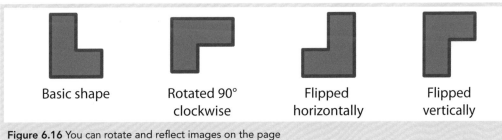

Basic shape	Rotated 90° clockwise	Flipped horizontally	Flipped vertically

Figure 6.16 You can rotate and reflect images on the page

Duplicate and clone

A duplicate is a single exact replica of an image, whereas a clone refers to one of many identical copies of an image.

Scale and dimension

Scale is used to enlarge or shrink an image relative to its original size. You can lock the ratio of height to width so that any change to the height will change the width in proportion.

Dimension is used to give actual sizes in centimetres to height and width. You can use this feature to change the **aspect ratio** between height and width.

Basic shape 1.25 cm × 1.5 cm	Increased by hand to 1.5 cm × 1.2 cm	Aspect ratio locked 1.5 cm × 1.75 cm

Figure 6.17 Scale and dimension options

Key terms

Gradient – A block of colour that is stronger/solid at one end and then gradually gets fainter towards the other end.

Aspect ratio – The relationship between an image's width and height. In still camera photography, the most common aspect ratios are 4:3 and 3:2.

CONTINUED ▶▶

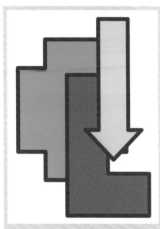

Figure 6.19 A simple example of image combination

Group and ungroup

The group feature allows you to group together images and to treat the grouped image as a single object, which you can then move, scale, flip, rotate, fill and duplicate as if it were a single image. For example, a diagram may contain several images that are grouped together as one, making it easier to work with.

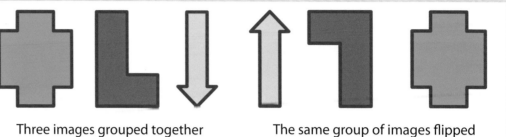

Three images grouped together The same group of images flipped horizontally and vertically

Figure 6.18 Grouped images can be flipped horizontally or vertically

Combining shapes and paths

Combining shapes and paths gives a single picture that can be treated as a single image.

A **path** is an image formed from a series of points (sometimes called **nodes**), each with its own vector properties and each of which can be edited individually. For example, if you draw a freeform shape using the pencil tool, when you convert it to a path, you will get a point wherever you clicked the mouse. Each point is described by vector information. (Refer to the section *Edit and break apart paths*.)

Combining shapes is different from grouping, which only groups together a number of separate images. When you combine shapes or images together, they form a single image, with shapes overlaying each other as in a real composition. For example, company logos are often made up of a combination of shapes and images.

Edit and break apart paths

Vector software that supports paths usually enables you to edit those paths or to break them apart into new paths.

Path-editing software allows you to do most of the things with objects that are described in this section, but at the node level. Because of the composition of the path, there are one or two extra things you can do, such as smoothing an angular shape into a curve, and then moving individual nodes of the curve.

You can also add extra nodes to a path, or you can break a path at a particular node, or delete a multi-node segment of a path. This enables you to fine-tune the design of your shapes as you go along, rather than restricting the path to the number of nodes that you originally used to draw the shape.

Paths can also be combined to give a compound path, which can be broken apart again later if necessary.

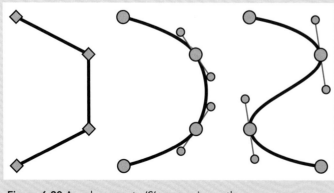

Figure 6.20 Angular curve to 'S' curve using paths

Layering

Layering is a technique used to build up complex images. Each different part of the image is created on a different layer, which is like a transparency (each layer is transparent, except for the image you have created on that layer). When you overlay all of the layers of 'transparencies' containing the parts of the image, you get a combination image.

The beauty of this technique is that you can lock the different layers and unlock only the layer that you want to work on. You can edit the image on this layer, and then recombine it without needing to work on the full finished picture.

You can usually set the amount of transparency that a particular layer has – this allows you to see only the part of the image that you want to work on.

Key term

Layering – A process that involves overlaying an image (or part of an image) on top of an existing image. This process can be repeated a number of times.

Activity　6.7

Using a subject that appeals to you, such as the layout of a sports field, a plan of a park or a drawing of a music venue, practise each of the vector-editing software techniques covered in this section.

- Use as many of these techniques as you can to create and edit individual assets.
- Practise the rotate and duplicate techniques.
- Group and combine images to form graphic products.
- If your software permits, try using paths.
- Practise layering.

Link

Unit 4 Creating digital animation explains how to use layers.

Assessment activity 6.3　　*Maths*　　　1C.4 ｜ 2C.P4 ｜ 2C.M3

Now you are ready to start creating the digital graphics products.

- Use the vector tools and techniques available to you to create and refine the vector assets you need for the set design products (those you listed in Activity 6.5).
- Gather them together and store them with the ready-made vector assets you gathered in Activity 6.6.
- Include the sources in the list of ready-made assets that you have already created.
- Annotate your designs to show that you are aware of the purpose of your products.
- Explain who the audience for your products is and how you have taken this into account in your design.

Remember

Graphics files can be quite large. If you are adding layers to an image, then the file size will increase. This can cause problems when saving it, when trying to email or share the file with another person, or when printing the image out.

Tip

Make sure that all assets are saved in the correct format.

Photo-editing software

Figure 6.21 Creating a simple combination from two images

Figure 6.22 Removing a section from one image and superimposing it on another

Introduction

Many of the tools and techniques used in photo-editing software are the same as those used in vector-editing software. In this section, we will look at the tools and techniques that are unique to photo-editing software.

Tools and techniques

In this section we'll look at the following tools and techniques:

- importing and combining images
- combining text and graphics
- selecting and removing parts
- cropping and resizing images
- duplicate and clone
- colour selection and palettes
- gradients and opacity
- brush and spray effects
- contrast and greyscale
- filters
- scale, rotate, reflect and distort layers.

Importing and combining images

Importing images is simply a case of moving the ready-made assets and original assets you have created into your photo-editing software. These assets may be in a variety of file formats, so you need to check that the software you are using supports the file formats of your chosen assets.

Image assets can come from many different sources, including:

- pictures held on your computer
- images from the internet
- scanned images from documents
- digital camera photographs
- mobile phone photographs.

Figure 6.21 shows a simple example of how images can be combined using photo-editing software.

Combining text and graphics

All graphic products are likely to include a combination of text and graphics. Think carefully about how you combine images and text to make sure that the information is clear and easy to understand. For example, if you want to display text over an image, you need to make sure the text can be read but that it doesn't block the image.

Selecting and removing parts

Photo-editing software has tools that will allow you to select parts of an image, remove them and use them elsewhere.

There are also tools that will let you mark the areas of a picture that you want to use and to discard other areas. The selected item becomes an object in its own right and can be used just like any other image. For example, you can superimpose it onto another picture.

The method of doing this will greatly depend on the software you use. Often you can select an area using a **marquee**. A **lasso** tool allows you to trace around an image to select it for use in other compositions.

Alternatively, you can use the eraser tool to erase small areas of your image, leaving only the part of the image that you want.

Cropping and resizing

Cropping is used to remove the areas from an image that you do not want. A cropping tool allows you to mark the area of picture that you want to keep, and then removes the rest of the image.

Figure 6.23 (a) A group of giraffes (b) Cropped to a single giraffe and resized

Resizing is used to make the whole image larger or smaller. You can do this in several ways:

- you can usually specify a height and width in centimetres
- you may also be able to do resize a selected image by using the handles on the image.

Duplicate and clone

As when speaking of vector graphics, a duplicate is a single exact replica of an image, whereas a clone refers to one of many identical copies of an image.

Colour selection and palettes

With photo-editing software, it is possible to create some different effects by using colour **filters**.

Figure 6.24 Warthog: (a) Original image (b) With green filter (c) With orange filter

CONTINUED ▶▶

Key terms

Marquee – A tool for selecting a simple shape, typically a rectangle or an oval.

Lasso – A freeform selection tool for drawing around the edge of a complex shape.

Filter – Application of a filter creates an image which appears to be viewed through coloured glass.

Remember

Vector graphics should resize without loss of quality. Take care when resizing bitmap images because the quality might get worse if you make the image larger or if you edit and save it several times.

▶▶ CONTINUED

Many colour palettes are available, from the basic 256 colours to the 'true colour' palettes of over 16 million colours.

Editing software often enables you to set two colours that you can work with at the same time: the foreground colour for drawing lines and shapes, and a background colour for when you are using the eraser. Dragging the eraser tool over an area will set it to the background colour.

Gradients and opacity

The gradient tool within photo-editing software is very similar to the tool used for colour fills in vector graphics software. It allows you to vary the depth of colour across the image.

Figure 6.25 (a) Original image and (b) with a grey gradient applied

Opacity allows you to make the image more or less transparent. For example, you can make text semi-transparent to create a **watermark** so that the background layer shows through the text.

Brush and spray effects

There are many tools for working freehand on bitmap graphical images.

You can use the brush tools for drawing and painting images. Rather like using a paintbrush, you can select different sizes of brush head to work with, depending on the effect that you want to get and the size of area that you are working with.

In addition to brushes, there are spray effects, sponge effects and smudging effects available.

Contrast and greyscale

Contrast and brightness are tools to lighten or darken the overall image. Brightness lightens or darkens the colours used, while contrast defines how the various images stand out from one another.

Figure 6.26 An image with varying brightness and contrast: (a) Original, 0% bright, 0% contrast (b) With 25% brightness, -12% contrast (c) With -40% brightness, -45% contrast

Greyscale is used to convert coloured images to shades of grey.

Figure 6.27 (a) A colour image (b) The result when it is converted to greyscale

Filters

We looked at plain colour filters in *Colour selection and palettes* in section *Vector-editing software*. There are other filters that you can apply for effects such as dots, clouds and blurring.

Scale, rotate, reflect and distort layers

Scale, rotate and reflect are identical to the techniques described in the *Rotate and reflect* and *Scale and dimension* sections in *Vector-editing software*.

We also looked at layering in section *Vector-editing techniques*. When an image is built up in layers, it is possible to use various effects on one of the layers and use this to distort the image in a variety of ways. For example, if you had a base layer showing a television at an angle, you could add a new layer containing a different television picture and warp it so that it fits the television screen on the base layer.

Activity 6.8

Load a photo into your bitmap-editing software and investigate the different filters that are available. Make a note of any filters that you think might be useful in your other work.

Activity 6.9

Using a subject that appeals to you, and for which you have photographs, practise each of the photo-editing techniques mentioned in this section.

- Use as many of these techniques as you can to create and develop individual assets.
- Practise using all of the colour features.
- Use as many of the texture features as you can.

Assessment activity 6.4   1C.4 | 2C.P4

- Use the photo-editing tools and techniques available to create the photo assets required in your designs for the bitmap graphic products (those you listed in Activity 6.5).
- Gather these together and store them with the ready-made photo assets you gathered in Activity 6.6.

- Include the sources in the list of ready-made assets that you have already created.
- Annotate your designs to show that you are aware of their purpose.
- Explain who the audience for your products is and how you have taken this into account in your design.

Tip

Make sure that all assets are saved in the correct format.

Testing and refining graphic products

Introduction

Once you have created your digital graphics products, you need to test them to make sure they are suitable. You then need to refine your products in line with the findings from your testing and feedback from other people.

Testing the properties of assets

You need to plan the testing of your digital graphics. You should create a simple test plan and list all of the things that you need to test. You can then make notes as you test each of the items. When creating your test plan, consider the following questions:

- Will the resolution be good enough on the client's system?
  - Will it be good enough when printed out?
  - Does the resolution support quick download speeds?
- Have I put all the assets into compatible file types so that they will work together on the client's system?
- Are the files of an efficient file size for loading and storing on the client's system?
- Is the compression used the maximum possible without distorting the image?
- Do the individual assets within layers and combinations appear with clean edges?

Gathering feedback

Asking for feedback is one of the best ways of reviewing a product to make sure that you have met the needs of the audience. Other people, such as fellow students, representatives of your client and members of the target audience, are more objective than you will be and can provide useful and constructive feedback.

A questionnaire is a good way of gaining feedback and so is an interview. Make sure you include enough people to get a good range of feedback and keep a record of the feedback for use in your assessments. Questions to ask could include:

- Are the digital graphics of a good quality?
- Is the resolution appropriate for the purpose of the digital graphics in terms of download speeds and print quality?
- Is the final image accurate?
  - Are all lines and shapes aligned correctly and smoothly?
  - Are the vector drawings accurate?
- How well do the graphic products meet the needs of the intended audience?

Activity   6.10

Obtaining and giving feedback about the work of friends is a good way of understanding what part this plays in final testing.

- Get feedback from your fellow learners on your final products (created for Assessment activity 6.4), either using a questionnaire or by discussing it with them. Document the feedback and keep your notes for use in your assessment.
- Give feedback on other learners' final products.

Update and improve

On the basis of the testing and feedback, make any adjustments and improvements to the products that are required.

If your product fails any of the tests, you will need to correct the problem and test the product again. It is important to record and document any improvements you make, as well as any you would like to make in the future.

Document the testing

Write down all of the results of your asset testing in your test plan and collate and summarise all of the comments received from the feedback.

Document all of the changes and improvements that you make to your products as a result of the testing and feedback. You can add the information about what you did at the end of the test plan.

Remember

If you change any of the ready-made assets, make sure that that you record the changes in your list of the ready-made assets you have used.

Exporting and compressing

Once you have tested your digital graphics, you will need to compress the files so that you keep the file size to a minimum, and then send them to other people for feedback.

To make the products accessible in terms of file size and loading speeds, they must be exported into suitable file types, such as .jpg or .gif. You must choose file types that your client can use.

Exporting will usually involve file compression and you will need to make some decisions about the amount of compression versus image quality. Your ability to do this will depend on the software you are using. Compression will be important to your client depending on what system they will be using to hold the graphics (for example, desktop, laptop, netbook, tablet or mobile phone).

Assessment activity 6.5 *Maths* 1C.5 | 2C.P5 | 2C.M4 | 2C.D3

Now you are ready to create your product and test it out.

Edit the assets you created in Assessment activities 6.3 and 6.4 to create two graphic products for the set design scenario (see Figure 6.7): one vector and one bitmap.

- Edit the assets to create your products including text.
- Test the products for functionality, quality and purpose. Ask other people for their feedback on these elements.
- Compare the product against the original brief.
- Make any improvements you have identified through the stages above.
- Refine the assets to create high-quality products demonstrating awareness of audience and purpose.

Tips

- Keep asking yourself, 'How could this be improved?'
- Ask other people for their feedback – they will spot things that you are too close to your product to see.

Reviewing graphic products

Introduction

Sometimes the review stage is called 'evaluation of product'. It is the final stage of the process, when you look at the finished products and the processes you used to create them.

How to carry out your review

A table is a good way to produce draft information for your report and to make sure you include everything in your review. You might like to base your review on Table 6.3, which lists the questions you need to ask during your review and provides space for you to enter your answers and to justify the decisions you made.

Table 6.3 Final evaluation

Question	Answer	Justification
Did the process I used to create the product go well?		
What would I do differently if I were to repeat the project?		
Are these products the best quality I could have produced?		
If not, what could I have done better?		
Are the products in the best state for use by the intended audience?		
Could I have done anything differently to improve the way they are used?		
Do the products meet the original need adequately?		
Do the products meet the original guidelines as established at the start of the project?		
What, if anything, has been missed?		

continued

Table 6.3 (*continued*)

Question	Answer	Justification
Do the products comply with copyright legislation?		
Did the process comply with health and safety practices?		
Do the products meet best practice methods?		
What are the strengths of the products?		
What are the weaknesses of the products?		
What can be done to improve the products?		

Having gathered this information in detail, you will need to produce a report headed 'Product review'.

Activity 6.11

Review both your vector graphic product and your bitmap graphic product by copying and completing Table 6.3.

Assessment activity 6.6   1C.6 | 2C.P6 | 2C.M5 | 2C.D4

Now it's time to review your graphic products you have created. Use the data you collected in your table to write a report that covers the following points:

- Identify and explain how the final product fits the brief. Discuss whether it is suitable for its intended purpose and its intended audience, and give reasons.
- Identify and consider any constraints you encountered.
- Compare the initial designs against the final product and justify any changes you made.
- Make recommendations for further improvements.

Tips
- Give a reason for every change that you made.
- Refer back to the feedback you received from other people to consider what further improvements you could make.

Introduction

Louis Lumière's first film camera, invented in 1895, allowed people to capture moving images in a way that had never been seen before. Eventually, film video became an exciting way to inform and entertain an audience. The advent of digital video production has been another revolutionary development in both how we view video but also in the way in which we create it. Digital video production uses digital cameras, digital storage devices and computers to create moving images that can be viewed in cinemas, on televisions and on the internet via computers or smartphones.

We now watch more video on more different platforms than ever before and this is because of the new ways of recording and publishing footage that digital video production provides.

Assessment: You will be assessed by a series of assignments set by your teacher.

Learning aims

In this unit you will:

A understand the applications and features of digital video products

B design a digital video product

C create, test and review a digital video product.

> *Creating a video was difficult, but being able to sit and edit the footage to produce the clip I wanted was rewarding. I've received really positive reactions to it, and have made the most of video sharing sites and my blog to publish it. I'm now able to pick up a camera and record material and edit it with ease.*
>
> *Ario, 16-year-old videographer*

Creating digital video

BTEC
Assessment Zone

This table shows what you must do in order to achieve a **Pass**, **Merit** or **Distinction** grade, and where you can find activities in this book to help you.

Assessment criteria			
Level 1	**Level 2 Pass**	**Level 2 Merit**	**Level 2 Distinction**
Learning aim A: Understand the applications and features of digital video products			
1A.1 Identify the intended purpose and features of two different digital video products. **Assessment activity 7.1, page 216**	**2A.P1** Explain the intended purpose and features of two different digital video products. **Assessment activity 7.1, page 216**	**2A.M1** Review how the products are fit for purpose and their intended effect on the audience. **Assessment activity 7.1, page 216**	**2A.D1** Discuss the strengths and weaknesses of one digital video product. **Assessment activity 7.1, page 216**
Learning aim B: Design a digital video product			
1B.2 Identify the audience and purpose for the design of a digital video product. **Assessment activity 7.2, page 220**	**2B.P2** Describe the audience and purpose for the design of a digital video product. **Assessment activity 7.2, page 220**	**2B.M2** English Produce a detailed video design, including reasons why alternative ideas have been discarded. The design must include: • logsheet • recce of filming locations. **Assessment activity 7.3, page 224**	**2B.D2** English Justify the final design decisions, explaining how the designs will: • fulfil the stated purpose and requirements in the brief • meet the needs of the audience. **Assessment activity 7.3, page 224**
1B.3 Produce an outline design for a video product. The design must include: • an outline script • an outline storyboard. **Assessment activity 7.3, page 224**	**2B.P3** English Produce a design for a video product of at least 5 minutes' duration. The design must include: • description of requirements from the brief • a script • a storyboard • a cast/crew list • a list of any ready-made assets if used. **Assessment activity 7.3, page 224**		
Learning aim C: Create, test and review a digital video product			
1C.4 Record video clips and, if required, prepare any other assets, with guidance. **Assessment activity 7.4, page 235**	**2C.P4** Record video clips and, if required, additional audio clips and prepare any other assets, demonstrating awareness of purpose, with sources of assets listed. **Assessment activity 7.4, page 235**	**2C.M3** Record high-quality video clips, demonstrating awareness of audience, with all sources for assets fully referenced. **Assessment activity 7.4, page 235**	
1C.5 Edit original video clips and, if required, any other assets to create a video product of at least 3 minutes' duration, and test for functionality, with guidance. **Assessment activity 7.5, page 237**	**2C.P5** Edit original video clips, if required, audio clips and ready-made assets to create a video product of at least 5 minutes' duration. Test the product for functionality and purpose, checking that it meets the original requirements, making any necessary improvements to the products. **Assessment activity 7.5, page 237**	**2C.M4** Gather feedback from others about the quality of the product and use it to improve the product, demonstrating awareness of audience and purpose. **Assessment activity 7.5, page 237**	**2C.D3** Refine video and other assets to create a high-quality video product. **Assessment activity 7.5, page 237**

Assessment criteria			
Level 1	**Level 2 Pass**	**Level 2 Merit**	**Level 2 Distinction**
1C.6	2C.P6	2C.M5	2C.D4
For the final video product, identify how the final product is suitable for the intended purpose. **Assessment activity 7.6, page 239**	For the final video product, explain how the final product is suitable for the intended audience and purpose. **Assessment activity 7.6, page 239**	Review the extent to which the final video product meets the needs of audience and the purpose, considering feedback from others and any constraints. **Assessment activity 7.6, page 239**	Evaluate the final video product and the initial designs and justify any changes made, making recommendations for further improvements. **Assessment activity 7.6, page 239**

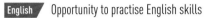 English   Opportunity to practise English skills

How you will be assessed

Devise, plan and produce an original video product using contemporary video capturing and editing software whilst working to professional standards and expectations. You will be asked to demonstrate an understanding of modern uses of video, and the purposes and effects that we require our products to have on specific audience. This may take the form of a written report, presentation or even a video-based submission in its own right.

The processes of shooting and capturing your own footage and editing it together into one final piece will be monitored and assessed by your tutors. You are expected to review and evaluate your digital video product throughout the production process.

Your assessments could be in the form of:

- a written report or multimedia presentation.
- a folder of design and project management work, including scripts, storyboards, schedules and logsheets.
- a digital video file.
- a recording of peer feedback.
- an evaluative report.

Applications of digital video products

Getting started

What sorts of video do you come across in your everyday life? Discuss all of the different ways that you see and use video both personally and as a student.

Introduction

Digital video has a wide variety of applications, a number of which are covered in this section.

Digital video applications

There have never before been so many ways in which we can capture and create digital video, from the video capabilities of mobile phones to the broadcast quality of professional HD video cameras. Video sharing sites such as YouTube have given videographers a place to publish their work, and receive feedback from anyone who seeks out their video or happens to stumble across it.

There are many different applications (uses) of digital video products (different reasons for creating digital videos). Some familiar examples of digital videos that have different applications include:

- a TV news segment or weather report
- a comedy sketch
- a documentary
- a reality TV show
- a TV advert
- a movie trailer
- a movie.

An application you may be less familiar with is Machinima. Machinima combines filmmaking, animation and game development to create videos in real time using 3D computer graphics. Machinima is widely used in the computer games industry. For more information on Machinima, please go to Pearson Hotlinks (www.pearsonhotlinks.co.uk), click on this unit and look for the link.

These different applications of digital video have different effects on the audience, depending on the purpose of the video.

Key term

Application – In this context, the specific use or purpose of a video product. (Application can also mean a program or piece of software that is designed to fulfil a particular purpose.)

Did you know?

The purpose of a video will have an impact on the type of video equipment used, how it is made, the number of people needed to make the video and the platform on which it is published.

You can now watch video wherever you are on mobile devices

Case study

YouTube is a video file sharing site. Since its launch, YouTube has had a major impact on the way in which we use video and incorporate it into our daily lives. Users can upload their clips and add them to the database of videos stored on the website, whether they are home videos, music clips, video blogs or television content.

Questions

1 What are the benefits of free distribution sites like YouTube?
2 What are the disadvantages of free distribution sites like YouTube?
3 Access to content can vary widely between countries. Why do you think the governments of some countries wish to temporarily or permanently block access to sites like YouTube? Discuss in small groups.

The effect of digital video products

Understanding the audience of any media product is key to its effectiveness and to how successful it is in achieving its purpose. It is important to ensure that you understand your audience: their age, gender and interests. By understanding your audience's needs, you can target a digital video at that audience to produce the effect you are looking for.

Some videos evoke emotion, while others are meant to educate, entertain or inform their audience. An ineffective video might bore an audience or leave them confused. In contrast, a poor-quality video might get a positive response, even though it lacks the quality of a big-budget movie.

Watching a film in 3D can enhance the effect of action and scenery on the audience

Purpose and effect are very closely linked. The purpose of a video is what you want to achieve by creating it, while the effect is how the audience react to the video. If the purpose of a video is to make the audience laugh and the effect it has on them is to make them cry, the video has not succeeded in its purpose, but the effect is still the effect.

Effect can be influenced by the platform that the video is watched on. For example, the experience of watching a horror file in a cinema may make it more effective, while watching an online promotional video is likely to be more direct and personal to an individual.

Just checking

1 Identify three different uses of video that are not TV, Film or YouTube.
2 Write down three different genres of movies and identify the key characteristics of each.
3 Select one video clip and identify both the purpose and the effect.

Discussion point

The move away from premium quality

There are several examples of television shows and films for which the director has chosen to shoot video so it appears informal, amateurish or even low quality. These have included using lower resolutions and camera shake. The docusoap genre of television uses a very relaxed way of shooting.

In what situations and for what purposes it is appropriate to use less than perfect footage?

Features of digital video

Introduction

This section examines the features you will need to consider in order to compare and describe digital video products.

Timing and length

The length of a digital video is determined by its purpose and platform. Television adverts are around 30 seconds long, while soap operas tend to be around 25–30 minutes. Although there are times when these conventions do not apply, such as in viral advertisements or short films. When planning the content of a video you should make sure you understand how long it should be to fit its purpose.

Timing concerns what content appears when in the sequence of footage, and for how long. For example, tension and comedy can be built up by holding back key information within a clip, while interest can be sparked by presenting masses of information and graphics within a short space of time.

Layers

You can easily combine many different elements within digital footage, such as audio soundtracks, sound **FX**, visual **SFX**, text (the narrative), transitions and animations. Music videos use a variety of editing styles to create interesting and unusual footage to match songs.

CGI and sound FX can be added to films to add more drama. This technique is known as 'layering' and involves stacking up different elements on a piece of footage to make a product that looks and sounds great and is effective.

Platforms and compatibility

When film was first invented, the only way for audiences to watch it was at a cinema because it required specialist equipment and engineers. When television sets became common, audiences could watch at home and eat meals in front of the television. Video recorders were developed so that people could buy films on video to watch in their homes. Originally, televisions used an analogue signal but nowadays they use a digital signal.

Digital signals can be transmitted via the internet. This advance in technology led to new types of video being created and a new type of audience. The Internet generation are able to seek out and watch television shows, films, home movies and advertisements outside of the confines of the television schedule.

We are now able to watch high-quality digital video from wherever we are on mobile devices. You can also create video on these devices and upload it directly to the internet without the need for specialist equipment or engineers. Video has never been so readily available or so easy to create.

File types

The file type you choose to use will directly affect the quality of your video and the platform(s) on which your video may be viewed. For example, a web-quality Flash®

video file (.flv) would not be suitable for high-definition (HD) broadcasting on a satellite network because it would appear pixelated, grainy and low quality. A broadcast quality MPEG2 file (see Table 7.1) would look great on the web, but would have a large file size that would require far too long to load on a web page. The most commonly used video file types are described in Table 7.1.

Table 7.1 Common video file types

File type	Description
.avi	This is the Microsoft® Windows® standard video format. It has less compression than .mov and .mpeg files.
.mov	This is a QuickTime® file type developed by Apple®. It can be used on both a Mac® and a PC and provides a good balance between high quality and small file sizes.
.wmv	This is a heavily compressed file type developed to work on Microsoft® Windows®.
.mpeg2	This is the file type commonly used in satellite broadcasting and on domestic DVDs and DVD players.
.mpeg4	This is a compressed file type that will be **lossy**, but is very effective across small bandwidths and with small file sizes.
H.264	A high-definition file type used for HDTV and Blu-ray, as well as for mobile devices such as the iPhone® or the PlayStation® Vita.
.flv	Nearly three quarters of all web videos are in the .flv format, as it has small file sizes but has a range of quality choices and is very good at retaining video quality.

Codecs

Choosing the right file type can be a complex decision. It can be made a little easier if you understand **codecs** and how they work.

If you have ever burned a DVD or played a CD, then you've used a codec. Codecs compress files so that they can fit on disks or hard drives and then be decoded by devices when you click play.

> **Key terms**
>
> **Lossy** – This is a type of file compression that results in a loss of data and quality.
>
> **Codec** – The way in which video is encoded and decoded to and from video files. For example, a high-definition H.264 file can be decoded on both Quicktime® and DivX® players, as they both have H.264 codecs integrated into them.

File size

File sizes are determined by the resolution of the video, the bit rate, and the codec used to encode the digital information. 640x480 uncompressed files need around 9 megabytes per second of video captured. The introduction of the H.264 codec gives us the opportunity to capture high quality footage at around 24 megabytes per second. A Blu-ray disk can store 25 gb or 9 hours of HD footage, whilst a standard DVD can store 4.7 gb or up to two hours of standard definition footage.

Resolution

Digital video resolution is displayed as the number of pixels in both the horizontal and vertical dimensions. For example, a HD recording has a minimum number of 1280x720 pixels, whereas 1920x1080 pixels provide even higher quality images.

The resolution of your final video product should depend on where you plan to publish it, and more pixels equal greater file sizes. Web videos used to be restricted to around 480x360 pixels, but increased bandwidth means we can now view very high-quality videos online, even if they take a little longer to load and stream.

CONTINUED ▸▸

Did you know?

You can turn the limitations of your project (such as having a low budget and few resources available) into key features of the video. Well-shot low-resolution images can create a unique effect and can encourage you to be more creative with your project than if you had a high-resolution camera.

Key terms

Bit rate – The amount of data stored for each second of footage, usually measured in megabits per second (Mb/s).

Frame rate – The number of still images that are recorded to make up the appearance of a moving image, usually measured in frames per second (FPS).

Quality

The quality of your footage matters, as it has an effect on how audiences perceive a video. Modern audiences are very aware of terms such as 'HD' and 'web quality'. The choices you make about video quality will be based upon:

- the resources available
- where and how (which platform) you plan to distribute your footage
- the desired effect of your video.

We measure quality in terms of **bit rate**. The bit rate of video on a DVD is around 10 megabits per second (Mb/s), while HD video has double the bit rate of around 20 Mb/s.

You should also consider the **frame rate** of a video when considering quality. The frame rate is measured in frames per second (FPS). This means the number of images in sequence presented for each second of a video. The standard FPS used in TV and film production are 24, 25 and 30 FPS, which allow for a smooth image. However, higher frame rates are used for HD video, extreme slow-motion capture and video games.

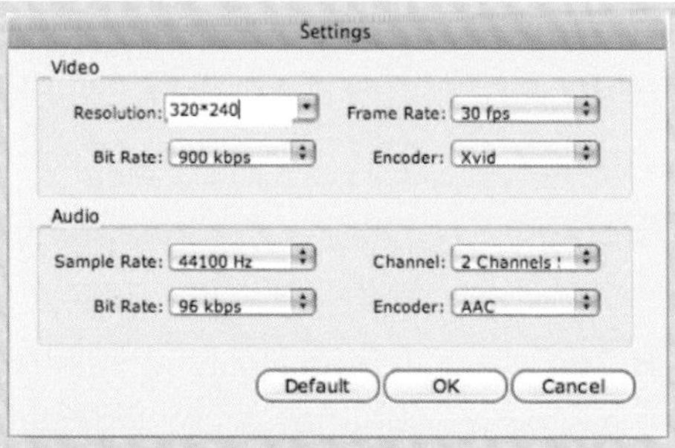

Figure 7.1 Setting the bit rate and frame rate in video-editing software

Assessment activity 7.1

1A.1 | 2A.P1 | 2A.M1 | 2A.D1

Parton Publishing Enterprises is a publishing company. They want to create a video campaign to promote their new range of digital books. The target audience is aged 18–25, and the company want to make use of online resources including social media and network platforms.

You work for the video production company hired to create the new campaign.

The first stage in the process is to consider the different types of video that you could produce. Select two different existing products (e.g. a news report and a viral video, or a movie trailer and a documentary). Compare them in detail to produce an illustrated report that covers the following:

- What is the purpose of the videos?
- Who is their intended audience?
- The features of each video (e.g. timings, length, layered elements, quality).
- The technical features (e.g. file type, file size, platform, resolution).
- Is each product fit for purpose and what effect does it have on its audience?
- What are the strengths and weaknesses of each one?

Tips

- Identify the key elements of each product and consider them carefully in turn.
- Give a reason to justify each opinion you state.

Design documents 1

Getting started ▶▶

Having an idea may be the most difficult step in creating an original video. Discuss all ideas with your peers and try to get as much feedback as possible to help guide your ideas and designs.

Introduction

The best videos are thought out in advance and planned to make sure they are fit for purpose. In the process of designing your digital video product, you will need to create a number of different design documents. These are discussed here and in the section *Design documents 2*.

Intended audience

The first thing you must consider when designing your video product is your intended audience. Who are you making the video for? What age group or gender is your video aimed at? Are you trying to attract people with a specific interest e.g. skiing or animal welfare?

Without a clear idea of how your audience is and their wants and needs, your video will probably not appeal to anyone and will not be fit for purpose. When producing your design brief, you should consider the intended age, gender and interests of your audience and think about where they will be watching your video. For example, a video that is to be shown to young adults in a cinema will need a different approach to a video shown to young children to introduce them to an online educational game.

Initial design ideas

Remember

Working in teams, every member should have a chance to be involved in the development of the idea. You should look to get the best out of every member in your team by sharing and discussing ideas.

You should brainstorm your initial design ideas with your team, perhaps using a spider diagram. Then you can group ideas into categories, such as ideas relating to the purpose and audience, the technical features of the video, the plot and characters, etc. Once you have done this, you can cut down your ideas until you have something you are happy with and can put the purpose and requirements of your video in a design brief.

You may wish to create a simplified version of your design idea that you can show to a test audience to get their reaction and feedback. This is known as prototyping. Your prototype could be an animated storyboard or a video recording produced without the technical care and consideration that you would use for your final video product. Prototyping gives you a valuable opportunity to make sure that your design idea:

- can be produced within the constraints of your project
- is of interest to the intended audience and fit for purpose.

Script

Take it further

It is worth looking at a professional script before you start your own. Look at the layout and how certain elements (such as instructions and stage directions) are labelled in a very particular way, using a key.

Even a film without any speech needs to have a script. Your script should detail what will be included in the video product: the sequence of events as well as the dialogue. Any instructions for the director, actors or support team should be clearly indicated, as should all movements (stage directions), effects and the changing of scenery.

You should aim to make your final script as accurate as you can before recording it. However, you will need to continually review and update your script during filming. After a filmshoot a producer's script will be full of pencil notes and changes.

CONTINUED ▶▶

Storyboards

Storyboarding is a very important part of the planning process and you should give it a lot of time and thought. A storyboard provides a visual explanation of the video using a series of drawings with plenty of written notes and details about the key aspects of the individual clips. The storyboard should cover these elements:

Figure 7.2 An example storyboard

- **characters** – the actors that appear within each scene
- **scenery** – the imagery that appears behind the characters and key objects
- **props** – the key objects and assets within the scene, including furniture, everyday objects and tools (e.g. the murder weapon in a crime thriller is a key object)
- **timing** – when certain events will happen within the sequence of footage and how long each camera angle or scene will be
- **camera angles** – how the cameras are to be positioned for each scene in relation to actors, scenery and props
- **FX** – any sound or video effects that are added to a scene.

You can use a storyboard as a way of sorting your ideas and getting a clearer idea of what you need to gather together and prepare for the project, including props, assets including those or which you will need to get permission to use and talent (actors and support staff). Your storyboard should also show the flow of your video (the order and suggested timings of each still image or scene) so that you can visualise your footage and film before you pick up a camera.

Gathering ready-made digital assets

There are many wonderful ready-made digital assets that you can source for your project, including audio (speech, music and sound effects), graphics and video recordings. You can download **licence-free** assets to use within your project from media libraries, stores and archives. You may wish to use a particular piece of music or clip from an existing film or TV programme. In these cases, you must obtain permission from the original author to do so because these assets are **licensed**.

Using pre-prepared assets can save you a lot of time and effort and also give you access to content that would be difficult to produce yourself because they require specialist equipment, talent or resources to create.

You should document and reference all assets that you are using in your video in a log. This should include the source of each asset. If any of the assets you need are licensed, then your log should state what each asset is to be used for. This will be useful when contacting the original creator of that asset and asking them for permission to use it.

Just checking ✓

1 Note the key information that should appear on a script.

2 Explain why it is important that storyboards are detailed and should be well presented.

Design documents 2

Introduction

Every video production, whether it is a large-scale film production or a short on-location news report, benefits from thorough planning and consideration of what needs to be captured. This reduces the chances of problems arising on the day and ensures you can put all of your effort into capturing the best possible quality footage.

Alternative design ideas

Considering other ways in which you could respond to a brief is an important part of the design process. It gives you an opportunity to look at alternative ideas and how you might produce a video for the same brief using different methods.

You may create your alternative design ideas in the form of a storyboard or script, or by creating another prototype to capture similar footage using different methods and approaches.

Even if you do not choose one of your alternative ideas, you may wish to use certain features of that design within your final design. This will strengthen the product and increase the likelihood that you are creating a product that an audience will want to see and that is fit for purpose.

Recording schedule and logsheet

These two documents will help you to plan your video recording. You will need to refer to your storyboard and script in order to create these documents.

A recording schedule sets out when you are shooting, the people needed and at what times, and any resources required. It should be set out in time order, from the first day of the shoot to the last. This should be finalised before the shoot begins, so that you can use it to gather together everything and everyone you need for the project.

You should use a logsheet throughout the shooting process to record what you film as you shoot it, plus any details about the scene (such as problems and notes for the editor). You should therefore create a simple layout such as the one shown in Figure 7.3.

Day 1	Time slot	Location	People required	Resources required
	9:00am–10:00am	Outside 1	Sam Helen	Back packs Hiking gear
	10:30am–11:30am	Outside 2	Riikka Saul	Emergency vehicle
	12:00pm–1:30pm	Inside 1	Simone Handan	Desk Chairs
	3:00pm–4:00pm	Inside 2	Sam Handan	Dining supplies
	4:30pm–6:00pm	Inside 3	Riikka Saul	Music

Day 2	Time slot	Location	People required	Resources required
	9:00am–10:00am	Outside 1	Sam Helen	Back packs Hiking gear
	10:30am–11:30am	Outside 2	Riikka Saul	Emergency vehicle

Figure 7.3 Example logsheet

CONTINUED ▶▶

◤ Health and safety considerations

It is very important to make sure that you understand the potential health and safety risks that you might face when filming a video production. If you do not carefully consider these health and safety risks beforehand, they might stop a shoot in its tracks.

Many productions make use of interesting locations and environments for filming and you must make sure that you consider what implications your chosen environment will have on filming. For example, filming near or on water might require specialist waterproof equipment. You also need to make sure that all of the actors and crew are able to work in the environment and can move around freely and that you have considered and planned for all potential risks.

Below are some of potential health and safety considerations to think about before you start filming.

- Are there any trailing cables?
- Have you got access to electricity and is it set up in a safe manner?
- Is there a risk of falling anywhere?
- Are there any slippery surfaces?
- Are there any sharp objects?
- Is there any heavy equipment and does it need to be moved? (You need to make sure it is moved in a safe manner.)

Assessment activity 7.2   1B.2 | 2B.P2

Parton Publishing Enterprises is pleased with your initial research. For the next stage, refer back to Assessment activity 7.1 for information about the publishing company. In addition, they want the video campaign to:

- contain a variety of audio-visual material, with the intention of both entertaining and informing
- showcase the company as an exciting and dynamic company
- showcase the new digital product range as 'must-have' products
- last at least five minutes.

Prepare a short report that outlines:

- the purpose of the video
- the intended audience
- features that the video needs to include.

Tip

Check your work by proofreading it for errors. It is best to leave at least a day between writing it and reading it, as you are more likely to spot things when reading something fresh.

Conducting a recce: scouting your locations

Key terms

Recce – Short for 'reconnaissance', which means an initial investigation. Filming projects use recces to obtain as much information about filming locations as possible prior to filming.

Scouting – The process of looking for locations.

Introduction

It is important to check in advance the suitability of the locations where you wish to film, so you need to conduct a recce of each one. If you just turn up with a video camera and start recording, you might run into all sorts of problems and won't get the best results.

Types of location

When planning a video shoot, you need to think about the location (where the shoot will take place). **Scouting** for suitable locations is an important part of the initial investigation for your project, and you should do this well in advance of the shoot itself. Although you may have a clear idea of where you want to shoot, it is possible that the location is not suitable for a film crew, filming equipment and actors to work there, for example it might be a dangerous derelict building site.

On a shoot, your focus must be on the video you want to make. Interruptions or distractions (for example, crowds of people or loud traffic noise) can interfere with a shoot and prevent the crew from working effectively.

There are three types of location:

1 **Exterior.** This is an outdoor space – it could be a natural environment or one that you have pre-designed for your video.
2 **Interior.** This means working in an existing room indoors.
3 **Stage.** You can design a stage for your video in the same way a theatre stage is designed. You could design it to look like an exterior or interior location. Using a stage can make filming quicker and easier. For example, many sitcoms and soaps use stages so that all the scenes, cast, crew and resources are centred in one place to make the filming process more efficient.

Each location type has strengths and weaknesses, and needs considered within the parameters of your project and what you want to get out of the shoot.

Considerations and factors

When planning a shoot and scouting locations, there is a wide range of factors to consider. Table 7.2 looks at eight of these considerations in a bit more detail.

Table 7.2 Considerations when planning a video shoot

Lighting	Lighting can be used not only to illuminate or show a scene, but also add to a particular effect that you want to achieve. Strength of light, colour and shadows are all tools that a director has to set the scene they want. Natural light can look fantastic on film, but it is often impractical – you can't ask an actor to look in the direction of the sun too long. Using additional light sources gives you a lot of control over illumination within your video, but can easily appear too strong or artificial.

continued

Table 7.2 (*continued*)

Ambient noise	Background noise can be used to add atmosphere to a scene (such as in cafés, at events, or on the street) but can also ruin the final sound of your film. The key question is whether it will prevent the audience hearing the dialogue (or any other sound) that you want them to hear.
	The choice of equipment will greatly affect this – many built-in microphones will pick up all sound from a range of directions, so you may need a targeted or directional external microphone to focus on the dialogue.
	You may consider dubbing sound in afterwards, re-recording speech or taking a separate sound recording of an environment and layering the soundtracks on top of each other so that you can control the levels and effects of each.
Weather	Exterior scenes can be interesting and unusual, but they are constantly under the threat of the weather at that particular time. Rain is not the only threat; strong sunlight, wind, snowy or frozen ground and fog can all prevent you from shooting.
	Using weather reports can help you predict when and where you will be able to shoot, but it is also worth having a backup plan just in case an unexpected rainy day ruins your plans.
	Rather than lose the planned shooting time (as you may have borrowed equipment and specialist talent may have given up their time), you may choose to shoot an interior scene rather than waste the day altogether.
Transport	Can you safely and efficiently get all of your crew and equipment to the location, ready to shoot at the same time? Can you get everyone and everything back to where they need to be at the end of the day?
	Clever use of interiors or stages may be the answer if the answer to either of these questions is no.
Security	Video/film shoots, no matter how large or small, attract attention. Whether it is due to the equipment, the lights, the actors or the action itself, people are always interested when they see people using a camera. You must make sure that your chosen location allows you and your crew to work without any threat of other people disrupting your filming and being a threat to the project or the team working on it.
Legalities	There are two key legal considerations you need to consider.
	1 Does the location have any health and safety issues that could have legal implications? For example, a crew member injured because of a slippery floor may make a claim against the production company.
	2 Does the location allow filming? Many locations, including public buildings, shopping centres and colleges/universities, will want to know what you are using the location for before they allow you to start filming. They can stop you publishing a video if you haven't obtained the correct permission.
Safety and hazards	If you want to use a busy environment, question how safe you are all going to be. This is particularly important when the environment is your subject and you need something specific within it, such as buildings or streets. You may need to capture an image of a moving tram or bus, but if getting a close-up shot puts you at risk and makes filming unsafe, you may have to look at alternative safer options such as filming it at a distance or when it is stationary.
	At no point should your film be more important than the people working on it. A good recce will make sure that no-one will feel unsafe during the filming process.
Indoor/ outdoor	How you approach and plan for an indoor scene will be different from how you approach and plan an outdoor scene. Be sure to think about how much equipment you have and how it fits in the available space, as well as about whether the indoor or outdoor location may cause you problems. The more issues with the location you can plan for in advance or avoid, the better prepared you will be on the day.

Just checking

1 Name the three types of location and give an example of each.
2 State three ways in which you could manage ambient noise when recording at an external location.

Recruiting a cast and crew

Getting started

There are many 'behind the scenes' videos available to watch online or provided as extras on DVDs, which show the parts of a video production not included in the final version. Watch several examples of these and make a note of all the different people involved in each production.

Introduction

Your video may involve many actors and crew members. You need to understand the role of each person before you begin.

Your cast

- **Lead actors** provide the main focal point of the video. The cast are the medium through which you tell your story and communicate it to the audience. Lead actors tend to be given the most dialogue and will likely be on the video more than any other actor.

- **Secondary actors** support the lead actor. Their role is to help explain the story, provide support to the lead actor or simply to fill the screen with something more interesting than empty space. Their presence is usually less important to the piece than lead actors.

- **Extras** fill screen space and make the scene look more real. For example, a shopping centre would look less realistic without staff and shoppers walking around with shopping bags. Extras tend not to have speaking parts (dialogue), but they will need instruction on what to do and when.

Your crew

Your crew should consist of five key members.

1 **Director.** This is the person in charge. They have responsibility for deciding how the story is told and presented to the audience, what shots to use and how the piece will 'feel' at the end of the production.

2 **Producer.** This is the person in charge of organising all of the personnel and resources involved in the project. They also make sure that all other crew members are in the right place at the right time. It is important that this person has strong organisational and communication skills.

3 **Camera operator/Cinematographer.** This person is in charge of the camera(s) and must be skilled in using them. They provide the technical skills needed to bring the director's instructions to life.

4 **Sound recordist.** This person focuses only on recording the sound needed for the video and maintaining quality throughout. They will focus on the sounds and background noises within a recording, and they will need to have the skills and knowledge to manage both.

5 **Lighting technician.** This person will have a similar brief to the sound recordist but with a focus on lighting and light levels. They should be able to add or remove light as the director wishes, and will be able to make decisions on what lighting is needed and what will produce the required effects.

CONTINUED ▸▸

Video shoots can be exciting, but a successful shoot requires a lot of planning and organisation

Assessment activity 7.3 — *English* | 1B.3 | 2B.P3 | 2B.M2 | 2B.D2

Parton Publishing Services has looked over your document and they are happy that you understand their requirements. Now they want you to prepare some design ideas. Use the brief you created for Assessment activity 7.2 as a starting point.

Your design should include the following elements:

- a proposal or presentation to describe the requirements from the brief
- a script that details exactly what each actor will say
- a detailed storyboard that covers the beginning, middle and end of the video and any key points. Aim for at least 12 panels and include notes on timings and transitions.
- a log sheet of the shots to be taken during the filming process
- a schedule for the shoots. This should include details of what you are going to shoot, the location, the cast and crew, and what assets are required.
- an outline of the job role of each of the crew members. Consider what your project requires them to do and assign a role to each person. Justify why you have selected each person for that job role.
- notes from your recce of each location, including any health and safety issues
- justification for each design decision. For example, annotate the storyboard with the reasons for your choice or shots, for adding certain sounds and for your choice of location(s).

Tips

- Make sure there is a clear link between your video and the intended target audience. For example, your proposal might state 'My target audience is … and so I must include … in my video.'
- Complete a recce for each of your locations you include in your design documents, even if the final shoot occurs at one location only.

Recording original video clips

Introduction

It is important to understand what digital video equipment is available and how to get the best out of it. In this section we will look at the type of camera equipment you will need in order to produce the best video you can make.

There are three main ways of obtaining footage for your video product:

1 Record your own using a digital video camera and produce a .dv stream using a tape-based camera or a digital file using a storage disk or card device.

2 Capture your own using screen capture software to produce a definite encoded (and probably) compressed but usable file type.

3 Obtain footage from an audiovisual library, with all relevant permissions. Make sure you are aware of the file format you will be given.

▼ Camera specifications

There are many types of cameras available. All will record footage and most will also record sound, but there are different ways in which recorded footage and sound are captured, stored and transferred to a computer.

Mini-DV cameras record to a small cassette tape that can be removed from the camera itself. These tapes can be either high or standard definition and are based on the **DV codec** developed in the mid-1990s. The **higher definition** (HD) version of these tapes is now widely in use within the TV and film industries. This type of recording equipment is low cost and very portable. Tapes can be shared between cameras and specialist **DV decks**. A DV tape can store around 60 minutes of footage in a **.dv stream format** and the footage must be captured to relevant software, usually in real time.

Some cameras store footage locally on a **hard drive** within the camera or to an **SD card**. The advantage of these types of cameras is that it is quicker to transfer files to a computer – you just plug a cable in to import the footage. Also, they can store large amounts of data so can record continuously.

Image sensors

Cameras contain a sensor that captures the light that passes through the camera lens and into the body of the camera itself. CCD (charge-coupled device) sensors tend to be able to capture a better range of light and colour than CMOS (complementary metal oxide semiconductor) sensors. However, CMOS sensors run slightly faster and are cheaper to produce, and so are more common in consumer-level equipment.

CONTINUED ▶▶

Professional camera operators use a range of different camera types depending on what the scene is

Connecting to video-editing software

Before you start shooting, it is worth looking at how your camera connects to a computer, and how it transfers footage into the editing software. You will usually use a USB or FireWire 1394 cable connected to the relevant port on a PC or Mac. Alternatively, you can remove the SD card and place it directly into the machine or in an external card reader.

Whatever equipment you have or want to use, do a **test capture** and make sure you can transfer that footage onto your computer before you proceed any further.

Cost

Digital video equipment has become more accessible in recent years, and there are many cameras that can record HD and have many professional features that cost less than a few hundred pounds. However, once you have added in a tripod, boom pole, microphone, lights and power sources the cost can rise rapidly. Alongside this, professional-level software and editing equipment add to the expense and you should also consider this when designing your own video product.

> **Key term**
>
> **Test capture** – Is when you record and capture a small amount of video to ensure you understand the process before working with larger recordings that may take much more time to complete.

> **Activity** 7.1
>
> Complete this activity before you start filming.
>
> 1 List the digital video equipment you have available to you.
> 2 What file format will you be recording to?
> 3 What quality of footage do you want? Can you achieve this with the equipment available?
> 4 How will you transfer your footage to a computer?

Workspace

▶ **Holly Samuel**

The Little Film Company

From the start of the project, all of my group had a clear aim and wanted to make a video with a simple level of content. I also wanted to shoot and edit it in an interesting way. The hardest part was deciding what we wanted in the film.

Our storyboard proved really useful. It helped us as a group work out what we wanted to achieve and let us plan out the footage before we even touched a camera. It also helped us to plan which assets we needed to gather and to identify the starting point for the shot list we created for the shoot.

The design process made sure we were clear on the technical aspects of the project, such as when we needed specialist kit and where it was to be used. It also allowed us to discuss the sort of film we were making and get all of our ideas out and then get rid of things that seemed to be unnecessary.

We completed most of the planning documents individually or in pairs. We then came together as a team and compared our work. This ensured continuity across all of our work and helped ensure we were planning the same film and were happy with what we were aiming for. It took a few tries to get everything to match up, but it's very satisfying to know that we're now ready to shoot with every little detailed planned out. Now we can concentrate on capturing the best possible footage.

Think about it

1 Why is a storyboard useful when planning a video?

2 Why is it important for a film crew to communicate with each other regularly?

Using the camera

Introduction

How you use the camera directly affects the style and purpose of your project. Static shots (looking at one thing in the same way for a set period of time) can be used very effectively, but you may wish to add interest to your scenes, and change the way the audience views the subject on their screens.

◤ Camera angles and camera placement

The position of the recording camera affects how the audience sees a subject. You can create drama, interest and emphasis by changing the image that the audience will see.

Low angle

Shooting from a low angle (see Figure 7.4) means that you place the camera below the targeted subject and look up. This technique can help add drama, as the subject looks down on you. It is also useful for removing distractions. For example, a person shot from a low angle will usually have just sky behind them, as this technique removes any background scene that might be visible if the camera was positioned at eye level.

Figure 7.4 Shooting from a low angle

Figure 7.5 Shooting from a high angle

High angle

If you are higher than your subject and look down on it, then you are shooting a high angle shot. (See Figure 7.5). This technique also adds drama to a scene, and takes in all of the floor and surrounding scene into the shot.

High angle shooting means you have to be higher than your subjects. However, it is very important to make sure that no crew member or equipment risks being hurt or damaged if you are working above floor level.

Tripods

Tripods are three-legged stands that allow you to stabilise the camera and remove the need for you to hold it continuously. All tripods have a standard fitting, which means that they can be attached to almost all devices. Cameras can be heavy and some tripods may be too light or unstable on some ground with heavier equipment.

Camera techniques

Two key types of camera movement are **zoom** and **pan**. These are described in Table 7.3.

Table 7.3 Explanation of camera movements zoom and pan

Camera movement and illustration	Description
Zoom	The camera moves closer to or further away from the subject or scene, changing the emphasis from the environment to the subject, or the other way round.
Pan	The camera moves sideways across a scene, either away from or towards a subject. This adds interest to a scene and shows that something significant is about to happen

Shot types

You can arrange your subject within the view of the camera to change the purpose or effect of a shot. Wider shots allow for more to be shown, while closer shots emphasise details. Combining shot types and using **contrasting** shots helps the director control the speed and mood. Table 7.4 describes a range of different shot types.

Table 7.4 Shot types

ECU **Extreme close up** Focuses on the detail of one part of the subject.	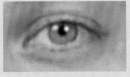	**MCU** **Mid close up** Shows the head and shoulders of an actor.	
CU **Close up** Focuses on one part or feature of the subject and will fill the frame.		**WS** **Wide shot** The subject is visible from head to toe and will usually fill the frame.	

continued

Table 7.4 (*continued*)

EWS
Extreme wide shot or **Establishing shot**

Sets a scene with the main subject barely visible. Gives a quick insight into where the scene is set.

POV
Point of view shot

Taken from the perspective of the subject – from their 'eyes'

OSS
Over the shoulder shot

Looks over the shoulder of one actor at a subject.

CA
Cut away

A shot of something that is not the main subject

Case study

Markins Kwai, Student, Manchester

On the first day, we were assigned our job roles. I was given the role of cinematographer, which meant I was in charge of using the camera and setting it up so we got the shots we were aiming for.

Quite early on it became clear that everyone had different ideas about what each shot should be and the content of each piece of footage we needed. Luckily, we had already planned out each shot using a storyboard and scripts. I used these to set up each shot and this meant that we got the shoot back on track and captured the right shots.

Our producer kept a log of every shot we took. I had to keep in constant communication with him, and take notes on what had and hadn't worked so well. The director allowed me to set shots and I was able to tell him then what else was needed to get the scene.

At the end of the first shoot, we had recorded just two of the three scenes we wanted. We had to adapt our shooting schedule to accommodate the missed scene. However, when we returned to the edit suite, we realised that we had taken some great footage. Although we had spent more time than planned, we had several good takes of each shot – which meant we could choose from a range of options.

Filming is a lot of fun and we had a lot of laughs, even when things went wrong. However, we also realised that unless the crew is really clear about what they want each time they click the record button, they won't have the footage they want. Planning everything out in advance is a very important aspect of a successful shoot, and it will save you time and effort in the long run.

Questions

1 If the role of the cinematographer is to set up and shoot footage, how can you ensure that other crew members have an influence of the 'look' of your footage? You may wish to review your planning documents and job roles in deciding this.

2 Why is reviewing footage after a shoot important to a production?

Using screen capture software

Using screen capture tools allow us to record what we see and do on computer, phone or tablet screens. Record yourself demonstrating a tool within graphics or animation software to become more accustomed to the methods and practices of capturing video in this way.

Introduction

Software such as CamStudio allows you to record the visual and audio elements of any image or footage on a computer screen.

▶ Capturing visual and audio elements

Imagine you want to feature footage of someone using the internet within your video. How do you go about doing this?

You could start with an over the shoulder view of the screen, with the user opening a search engine. But how do you capture exactly what is happening on the screen? Screen capture software will let you do exactly that. The software captures everything that happens on a user's screen, meaning that you can show on-screen footage without the distraction of the surrounding environment or computer user.

You can also capture sounds and narrate over these, although you may wish to see if your editing software can do this more quickly and easily. When including screen captures, you must consider:

- **The quality of the recording.** Check the resolution and quality of footage captured – it should be of a similar quality to the footage you have taken using your own video camera
- **The file format obtained.** This is usually a 'wrapped' format, encoded into a recognisable and usable format such as .avi or .mov. Not all formats work on all computers or within all software, so you must make sure that you understand the outputted file type before you capture.
- **The legal implications.** If you are using a particular website, you may need to look into whether your are free to publish that capture within your own film.

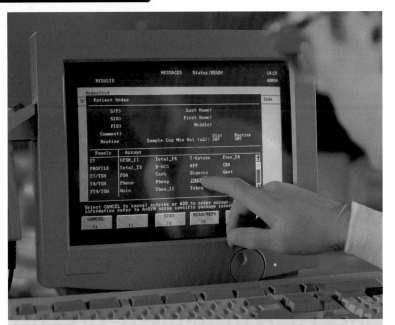

You can use screen capture software to capture what is happening on a person's screen directly, rather than filming it over their shoulder or have them point to things on the screen

Just checking

1 Identify three different video file formats and state when you may use each.
2 You have been asked to record a review of a new computer game. How would using screen capture software benefit the piece?
3 State two limitations on screen capture software.

Creating a video product 1

Introduction

Once you have captured all your footage and collected the sound and visual assets, you can start to look at bringing it all together within the editing process.

There are many pieces of software that allow you to edit your footage using PCs or Macs. Digital methods of video production allow you to take your footage, cut it up, rearrange it, add sounds, add visual transitions and effects, alter volume and colour levels and generally mix and mould it into the video clip you envisaged. Digital video-editing software allows you to do all this with a high level of control and organisation, and to delete and change it all if you wish.

Activity 7.2

Gather into a group with your class and ask the question: What should an editor do?

The editor can be seen as:

- someone who works strictly to the demands of the director and places audio and arranges audiovisual assets to meet these demands
- someone who has the creative freedom not only to meet the needs of a director, but also to apply their own creativity to the project and extend the vision of the director
- something in between, arranging the key components as demanded by a director, but also adding their own flair and originality to enhance the video.

1 What is the general consensus among your peers?
2 Consider how your view of what an editor should do affects your own approach to the edit process ahead.

There will be many different ways in which you can edit your footage, but you should remember what is was that you wanted to create at the start of the project, and not change the direction your project at this time.

Gather ready-made assets

Remember

You should look back at your design documents at the product you want to create. Think about how you will bring together all your work to make your product come alive.

Before you start to create your video product, ensure that all assets are ready to be edited within your chosen software. Collect all footage, music, sound and sound effects and save them together in a folder, so that they are stored in the same place. The software will usually have a method of managing these assets in a clear and organised way, especially if they are ready-made assets you have collected from another source.

Import video files and other files

Gather all of your video and sound files into your editing software, and double check that you have everything you need to start piecing your final product together. You can preview each asset to ensure they are as you expect and need them to be, and make a note of anything you have missed or that may need re-capturing or gathering.

Editing tools and techniques

When editing your video, you will need to be able to use some of the various editing tools and techniques available within your software.

Add your footage to the timeline that you have already created and start to lay it out into a rough outline of your video.

Table 7.5 Video-editing software tools and techniques

Cut, copy, paste and delete clips	You may choose to **cut** and **paste** or move clips to suit your ideas. Most software allows you to precisely select the part of a clip you want and drag that to the **timeline**, leaving behind what you don't want. Editing using digital methods is usually called 'non-linear' editing, as you can work across the frames within your piece and not in a chronological (linear) order.
Split and trim clips	You can add whole clips and break them into pieces and trim them to fit using the **Razor** tool.
Transitions	Transitions allow you to move from clip to clip (or sound to sound): • **Basic cuts.** Clips are placed next to each other without an additional transition added, so that an instant change from shot A to shot B occurs. • **Crosfades/dissolves.** Shot A will gradually change into shot B. Good for slowing footage down or indicating a change in time or location. • **Wipe.** Shot B will move across the screen to replace shot A. There are many unusual wipes, but you should use them carefully, as they can distract from the footage itself. • **Fade to/from Black.** Similar to a crossfade, but rather than mixing into another shot, shot A will blend into a plain black background. Can also be used to fade in a shot.
Text	You may also add text to be used as titles or subtitles, to assist and guide your audience through your piece.

Remember

Almost all modern editing is non-linear and makes use of computer-based editing software to move clips around a timeline and jump from frame to frame. Linear editing involves dealing with footage in sequence as it was shot, and not being able to jump across frames.

Key term

Timeline – A visual representation of the footage, which is usually arranged in chronological order. All of the edit happens within the timeline.

Did you know?

Editing software such as Adobe® Premiere® or Final Cut Pro has removed the need for large-scale, complex editing suites. Although professional editing companies will still dedicate whole rooms to editing equipment, using the suggested software is an excellent way of becoming more familiar with the tools of the trade and producing very high-quality video on a standalone computer.

Figure 7.6 Video-editing software packages like Adobe® Premiere® contain editing tools and effects which will improve the professional look of your video

Creating a video product 2

Key terms

Filters – These change the appearance of your clip, and are applied to the clip itself to work with the information within the chip.

Overlays – An overlay 'sits' over you clip, universally changing all data in accordance with the effect you have selected.

Introduction

Digital video methods allow is to quickly make dramatic and effective changes to our footage, and to alter and improve the appearance of the footage. Careful use of the tools available to use can turn well-captured video into a polished and professional product.

Effects

Effects can be produced by the software or by the skills of the user.

Filters and overlays

You can usually add **filters** and **overlays** within your chosen video-editing program. These add something to your clips that you could not always add in camera, such as altering the colour, converting to black and white, adding noise or ageing clips.

Layering and 'picture in picture'

You can add your own style to the piece by layering footage on top of other footage, or by adding sounds in very particular places. The way in which you introduced, or use a second can add drama or humour to a piece. Also, you may choose to use 'picture in picture', in which one layer is placed in a small section of another layer to create an effect similar to that used within the news. Placing two different clips next to each other or being creative with how your present small details or text can all alter the effect of your clip.

Video quality

One of the biggest advantages of using digital video is that you can improve or alter the footage within digital software. If you are familiar with image-editing software such as Adobe® Photoshop®, you will be used to altering the appearance of an image, and you can do the same with video.

Contrast

Contrast is the difference between the light and dark within an image. You can use digital video-editing software to increase or decrease the contrast originally captured.

Sharpen

You should look to have sharp and clean images within the original recording, but you can also add additional sharpening to improve them, or for dramatic effect.

Saturation

Digitally altering the saturation of an image allows you to increase or decrease the colour intensity of a video image, to improve the colour of the image or correct a flaw.

White balance

White balance is a big issue in video creation. It involves ensuring that the colours captured by a camera shot to shot are the same. Another issue is the way in which digital video is presented on a computer.

Although cameras and software have very effective automatic white balancing methods, you may wish to alter this using your video-editing software. This is a very precise tool that varies between software packages, so it is worth reading the Help section of your chosen software.

You can add many effects to your video using digital editing software

Assessment activity 7.4   1C.4 | 2C.P4 | 2C.M3

Parton Publishing Enterprises were very impressed with your design and they are now ready to move to the next stage – creating and producing the video product.

- Record all of the video clips and any additional audio clips required for the video product.
- Create a list of all the assets you are using in your video, including the source of each asset.
- Prepare any other assets you are planning to use in your video product (e.g. captures, sounds, music).
- Produce a high-quality audio and visual digital product – all sounds must be clear and video should only contain what is needed.

Tips
- Make sure your shoot takes place at the locations set out in the recce.
- Check how clear your list of assets is by asking someone else to locate the specified assets.

Testing your video product

Getting started ▶▶

Review your initial planning and design documents and remind yourself of your original intentions for your project.

Write a brief summary of your original intentions, setting out:

- the overall purpose of your video
- the key aims of your project
- the duration of your project
- the style you wanted to created.

Introduction

It is unlikely that your edited video will be perfect straight away. To make it as good as it can be, you must test and edit it to make improvements. Effective editing will enable you to achieve a polished outcome.

◤ Testing

When you have created your video product, you will need to check and test it. It is best to do this yourself in the first instance, so that you can try to remove flaws or mistakes while still in the editing software stage. Watching the video several times will help to reveal errors, or aspects of your edit that you are less happy with, as you will start to look beyond your intended narrative and notice the smaller and less obvious technical details.

When checking your video, be sure to test for:

- **functionality** – that all clips play and are shown correctly on screen
- **quality** – that the quality of the clips is appropriate for your purpose
- **volume** – that volume levels on all vocals, sound FX and music are correct
- **length** – that the video product is the correct length.

◤ Audience feedback

The testing stage should also include audience feedback. Initial feedback from your audience is vital in order to a digital video product that engages with the audience and meets your original aims. This type of feedback can help you refine and improve your final product before publishing it for general release.

When asking for audience feedback, consider the following areas.

- **Technical quality.** Is the picture of a good enough quality? Are the sounds and visuals appropriate and without flaws? Does the video flow or are there jumps between clips?
- **The purpose of the piece.** Do the audience understand what the video is trying to do? Does it make them think of a brand name or remember key information? Are they persuaded to agree or disagree with something because of your video?
- **Your intended aims.** Did the audience react as expected? Have you achieved the targets set by the brief?
- **The overall feel of the piece.** How professional is your video? How well does it compare to professional products? Is there anything within it that has stopped it being effective?

Consider how different methods of research may affect the quality of the feedback you obtain. Feedback from students who are also studying and making digital video may provide very specific, technical information, but it could lack the fresh set of eyes of your wider audience.

Discussion point 💬

If you worked in teams, compare clips with your peers and discuss the differences between individual edits. Why did you choose to present the same piece of footage in very different ways? Has this produced different effects?

Document any improvements

Did the video change as you were editing it? If you found that some of the footage was unusable, then you may have had to change your approach. You should compare the final video with your original intentions to make sure you have a video that you or the client wants. Additionally, if there are any ways to improve your video (based on your own conclusions and from audience feedback), be sure to document these. If any changes affect your assets, be sure to document these too.

Rendering

All of your transitions, effects, cuts, filters, music and titles will be rendered into one single file, so you need to ensure that they all appear as you want and expect them to. Have you used the correct file format, compression method and file size? Any errors will mean that you need to alter and re-render your video.

Remember

Within Learning aim A we looked at the types of video we use and can watch, and how they are put together to suit their individual aims. Review this for a reminder of what is needed from your own video product.

Assessment activity 7.5 | 1C.5 | 2C.P5 | 2C.M4 | 2C.D3

Before you can deliver the final product to Parton Publishing Enterprises, you need to edit your product and then test it to check that everything is working as well as possible.

- Edit your video. Remember: your finished video must be between 5 and 10 minutes in length.
- Once you have completed your editing, test the product for functionality, quality, volume and length. Be sure to check that:
  - there are no jump cuts or black empty spaces
  - all sounds and music are correctly cued and volumes are correct
  - the video follows the structure and intentions of your initial storyboard.
- Create a log of any improvements you made during the testing process.
- Gather feedback from others about the quality of the product and use this feedback to improve the product.
- Create a log of any improvements you make or would like to make to future versions and give a reason for each one.
- Refine your video and other assets to create a high-quality video product. You need to document how the changes you made have had a positive impact on your product.

Tip

You could produce 'before' and 'after' versions of your video as evidence for how your changes have improved it.

Reviewing the video product

Introduction

Once you have tested your product, you will need to review it. In this section we will look at the things you need to consider during the review stage.

You can evaluate your digital video product in terms of the constraints you had to work within when you created it.

Quality

The quality of your video will depend on where you plan to publish it. If it needs to be high-quality then all aspects of your video must be consistently well-presented, without pixelation or colour issues. Reduced-quality videos are more forgiving, but consistency is still key and any changes in ratio or resolution will be very noticeable.

Suitability

When reviewing your product, ask yourself the following questions:

- Is your video fit for purpose and audience? Does your video meet the needs of the brief you were working to?
- Have you included all of the required content originally asked for by the client or set by yourself and your team?

If the client has very specific targets, then your video must reflect these. Your video may be entertaining, but if it does not have a clear purpose, then it does not meet the targets you identified within the early stages of the project.

Also, consider the response of your audience, and use the feedback they provided to support your answer.

Legal and ethical constraints

A constraint is anything that prevents you making the exact product you want, to the highest possible standard.

The three main influences (and possibly constraints) on the success of your project are:

- **Technical constraints:** your personal skill and knowledge of digital video productions
- **Editing constraints:** the limitations of the available technology
- **Personnel constraints:** the limitations of working within a team.

In addition, you should review your video under the legal conditions that affect all creative media products. Have you infringed any copyright laws? You should be particularly careful with your screen captures. You must also be careful with any delicate or unsuitable content. Even if they are your main subject, you need to be sensitive in how you present them.

Strengths and improvements

When asked to review your own digital video, you need to think about its technical strengths and weaknesses. Ask yourself the following questions:

- are there any faults in your video?
- are all cuts and transitions appropriate and used correctly?
- are the levels of speech at the correct level?
- are there any technical errors that need correcting?

If you have used a combination of original and unusual editing styles, try to be objective about whether or not this approach has worked. While it's great to be creative and try new things, you need to make sure that the audience can follow and understand what is happening.

Changing the cuts, transitions, sounds and music to alter the pace or feel of a video is normal within an edit, so state what you changed and what effect these had on the piece. Again, refer to your audience's response: if they did not react as you wished, you may have had to re-edit your video to get the desired reaction.

Take It further

Now you have completed a video production, consider how you may apply the tools and techniques within your other work, either as methods of submissions or as tools to show individual development.

For example, you should be able to add video to podcasts to create multimedia podcasts in which you could talk about a product, while showing it on the screen.

Or you may wish to add text to an animated product as multimedia annotations, similar to adding notes to a YouTube video.

Assessment activity 7.6 | 1C.6 | 2C.P6 | 2C.M5 | 2C.D4

Parton Publishing Enterprises would like you to produce a report on your finished video product.

Create an illustrated report which includes:

- a review of the extent to which the final video product satisfies the brief and meets the needs of the audience. Include evidence of initial audience reactions and give examples of how they had an effect on the development of your video product.
- a comparison of your final product against the initial designs and justify any changes you made
- details of any constraints you came across during development. Specify whether this was technical, personal or editing.
- descriptions of three strengths of your product that make it a good example of a digital video production
- a recommendation for at least one area for improvement.

Tips

- Think about how you will structure your report. Break it down by using headings, so it is clear to the reader.
- Give a reason for every change that you made.
- Refer back to the feedback you received from other people to consider what further improvements you could make.

Introduction

With smartphones becoming the norm in modern society, people have become increasingly reliant on the mobile apps on their phones. These applications are used for all sorts of purposes, including playing games, reading books, downloading music, browsing the internet, sending emails, watching videos and viewing the stock market. Their popularity has resulted in a huge growth in the number of businesses specialising in the development of mobile apps, and with this growth has come a range of job opportunities. These include creative designers, artists and sound engineers.

This unit will enable you to learn about mobile apps and to look closely at their purpose, uses and features. You will also cover the mobile app development process, learning about how to design, develop and test an application to meet a specific need. You will not be expected to develop an application by programming it from scratch. However, you will develop an understanding of programming languages and be able to edit pre-existing code. Finally, you will learn how to evaluate the success of your mobile app. You will review its suitability and purpose, and assess how it meets user requirements. After obtaining feedback from others, you will be able to make final refinements to your mobile app.

Assessment: You will be assessed by a series of assignments set by your teacher.

Learning aims

In this unit you will:

A understand the characteristics and uses of mobile apps

B design a mobile app

C develop and test a mobile app

D review the finished mobile app.

I really enjoyed studying this unit as it was very practical, and after completing it, I knew how to make my own mobile app. I have now created a game that you can download from the Google™ Play store. Before studying this unit, I wouldn't have even known where to start.

Michael, 16-year-old future software developer

Mobile apps
development

8

This table shows what you must do in order to achieve a **Pass**, **Merit** or **Distinction** grade, and where you can find activities in this book to help you.

BTEC
Assessment Zone

Assessment criteria			
Level 1	**Level 2 Pass**	**Level 2 Merit**	**Level 2 Distinction**
Learning aim A: Understand the characteristics and uses of mobile apps			
1A.1 Identify the uses and features of two different apps. **Assessment activity 8.1, page 247**	**2A.P1** Explain the uses and features of two different apps. **Assessment activity 8.1, page 247**	**2A.M1** Review how the features of the apps affect the usability and intended use by the audience. **Assessment activity 8.1, page 247**	**2A.D1** Discuss the strengths and weaknesses of the apps. **Assessment activity 8.1, page 247**
Learning aim B: Design a mobile app			
1B.2 Identify the purpose and user requirements for the app. **Assessment activity 8.2, page 253**	**2B.P2** Describe the purpose and user requirements for the app. **Assessment activity 8.2, page 253**	**2B.M2** English Produce a detailed design for a mobile app, including: • alternative solutions • a detailed proposed solution using a range of design tools • test data. **Assessment activity 8.2, page 253**	**2B.D2** English Justify the design decisions, including: • how they will fulfil the purpose and the user requirements • any design constraints. **Assessment activity 8.2, page 253**
1B.3 Produce a design for a mobile app with guidance, including an outline of the proposed solution. **Assessment activity 8.2, page 253**	**2B.P3** English Produce a design for a mobile app, including: • a proposed solution • a list of any predefined codes/ programs • a test plan • a list of sources for any predefined code and assets. **Assessment activity 8.2, page 253**		
Learning aim C: Develop and test a mobile app			
1C.4 Prepare predefined code and assets with guidance. **Assessment activity 8.3, page 263**	**2C.P4** Prepare predefined code snippets and assets for the app, demonstrating awareness of purpose, listing sources for assets. **Assessment activity 8.3, page 263**	**2C.M3** Optimise assets for the app, demonstrating good awareness of the user requirements, with all sources for assets fully referenced. **Assessment activity 8.3, page 263**	**2C.D3** Maths Refine the app, taking account of the quality of the code and user feedback. **Assessment activity 8.3, page 263**
1C.5 Maths Edit predefined code and integrate with assets to develop an app, with guidance, containing: • one or more screens • constructs. **Assessment activity 8.3, page 263**	**2C.P5** Maths Edit predefined code and integrate with assets to develop an app which includes: • one or more screens • constructs • commentary throughout the code. **Assessment activity 8.3, page 263**	**2C.M4** Maths Develop a functional multi-screen app, containing original code, that meets the user requirements and purpose. **Assessment activity 8.3, page 263**	
1C.6 Test the app for functionality and purpose, repairing any faults and documenting any changes made, with guidance. **Assessment activity 8.3, page 263**	**2C.P6** Test the app for functionality and purpose, repairing any faults and documenting any changes made. **Assessment activity 8.3, page 263**	**2C.M5** Gather feedback from others on the usability of the app, and use it to improve the app, demonstrating awareness of audience and purpose. **Assessment activity 8.3, page 263**	

Assessment criteria			
Level 1	Level 2 Pass	Level 2 Merit	Level 2 Distinction
Learning aim D: Review the finished mobile app			
1D.7 For the final app, identify how the final app is suitable for the user requirements and purpose. **Assessment activity 8.4, page 265**	**2D.P7** For the final app, explain how the final app is suitable for the user requirements and purpose. **Assessment activity 8.4, page 265**	**2D.M6** Review the extent to which the final app meets the user requirements and purpose, considering feedback from others and any constraints. **Assessment activity 8.4, page 265**	**2D.D4** Evaluate the final app and the initial designs and justify any changes made to the quality of the code, making recommendations for further improvement. **Assessment activity 8.4, page 265**

Maths Opportunity to practise mathematical skills		**English** Opportunity to practise English skills

How you will be assessed

This unit will be assessed by a series of internally marked tasks. You will be expected to demonstrate knowledge of mobile apps, as well as the mobile app development process. The tasks will be based on a scenario for which you will need to develop a mobile app for a particular client. For example, this could be an IT services team that requires a mobile app for accessing requests for support and then marking them as completed.

Your assessment could be in the form of:

- a presentation on the purposes and features of existing mobile apps
- written design documentation for the mobile app you will be developing
- annotated programming code and screenshots of the developed app
- written review documentation, showing your completed test plan and the responses to feedback you have obtained
- written evaluation documentation, showing the strengths and areas for improvement of the app and improvements that you have made.

Why and how we use mobile apps

Introduction

When you are creating a mobile app, It Is Important to understand the purpose of mobile apps and to know the types of mobile app that are most popular with users.

The purpose of mobile apps

Originally, mobile phones were used simply to make phone calls and send text messages. Now they are powerful multi-purpose computer systems, much like your laptop or desktop PC.

Mobile apps are computer programs that instruct a computer's central processing unit (CPU) to carry out a set of instructions. These instructions are for a specific reason and use. A mobile app will tell the mobile device to carry out a particular task. For example, an email client app will turn your mobile device into a tool for sending and receiving emails. An e-book app will turn it into a tool for reading books, newspapers and magazines. Even the basic phone functions of your mobile phone are operated by a mobile app program. Everything your mobile phone or tablet can do is the function of a mobile app that either came with the device or you have downloaded.

Activity 8.1

1 In a small group, discuss why you use mobile apps on your personal smartphone or mobile tablet device. Produce a list of the purposes of mobile apps.

2 Compare these purposes with another group to see if they have thought of any that you haven't.

3 Use the internet to find out how many applications exist for each of the purposes that you identified.

Typical uses of mobile apps

We use mobile apps for a variety of different reasons.

To give and receive information

Some apps are designed to share information, for example photos, videos and music. Mobile apps for magazines, newspapers and news channels bring you the latest breaking news. There are also a number of apps that will give you up-to-date weather information or travel information (traffic updates, train times, flight times, etc.) Examples include FlightTrack for flight arrival times and The Trainline for train times.

For navigation (in the physical world)

There are apps to help you find your way to a particular point. They give step-by-step directions or show the location on a map. Your destination might be a restaurant, shop or a friend's house. Many smartphones contain **GPS chips**, which allow your location to be identified. Google™ Maps is a free app that uses GPS. It gives your position on a map and allows you to get directions from your exact position to where you want to go.

For entertainment

A smartphone is now a games console, MP3 player and portable TV, all in one. You can use music services like Spotify or Grooveshark to listen to music, the YouTube app for watching video footage or download and play games, such as *Angry Birds*.

For leisure and fitness

There are a number of mobile apps that allow you to track the exercise and sports that you do, so you can see how effectively you are training.

For communication

Mobile phones have always enabled you to communicate with others using calls and text messages. However, mobile apps have allowed us to use a range of other communications methods such as **VoIP** phone calls, instant messaging and emailing. Examples include Skype for making VoIP phone calls and K-9 Mail for sending and receiving emails.

For augmented reality

Augmented reality apps are a more recent development in mobile apps. These apps are designed to make use of the smartphone's built-in camera to overlay images created by the phone onto real objects. An example is looking at a famous landmark through your camera and a history of the landmark appearing next to it on your mobile screen. Applications such as Layar allow you to play games that appear in real world environments or to turn simple posters into animated 3D experiences.

> **? Did you know?**
>
> Many apps make use of the built-in GPS chip to automatically track your runs and cycle rides, in order to give an accurate recording of your speed, distance and calories burned. RunKeeper is an app that uses your GPS chip to track your runs this way.

Augmented reality apps overlay features onto real objects

Activity 8.2

1 Look at the list of different uses of mobile apps and discuss with a partner which of these you use.

 If you use your mobile in a different way from your partner, show them the app you use and explain why you use it.

2 What do you think is the most popular use for mobile apps? Try and find the actual answer using the internet.

Just checking ✔

1 What is the purpose of mobile applications?

2 What are the different uses of mobile applications?

3 Give an explanation of three uses of mobile applications.

Characteristics of mobile apps

Introduction

In this section, you will learn about the many different features of mobile apps. You will need to think carefully about these when developing your own app. You will also learn about the languages used to program mobile apps.

Features of mobile apps

Many apps perform the same task, such as providing news updates or entertainment services. However, each app will have its own features that make it unique and useful in different ways. There are a number of key features to consider when developing mobile apps, and seven of these features are described in Table 8.1.

Table 8.1 Features of mobile apps

Purpose	You must have a clear idea of what your mobile app will do, and how it will meet a need in the mobile app market.
User requirements	Many applications have the same use or purpose but are targeted at different audiences. These audiences may differ by gender, age, job, technical skill or many other factors. You must design your app for a particular audience, and consider what sort of content, features, colour schemes and styles they would like to see in a mobile app.
User-friendliness	This is the ease with which someone can use a mobile app. It is a key aspect of an app and you need to ensure that your mobile app is easy to use and that users can navigate through the content.
Dependence on particular hardware	There are many different mobile phones, each with different hardware. For example, the phone might have a touch screen that allows for multiple touch points. Or it might have a camera or a Wi-Fi internet connection.
Interface elements	The interface elements used within an app can alter its presentation, user-friendliness and the general experience of the user. Common interface elements include search boxes, drop-down menus, star rating systems and progress/loading indicators. You must ensure that you use these elements effectively and implement them in an attractive manner.
Integration with software	Most smartphones come with pre-installed software as part of the operating system. This can include contact lists, text-messaging services and notification areas. A mobile app can take advantage of these built-in facilities to give a better user experience. For example, a news app can indicate when new articles become available using your smartphone's notification area.
Platforms and compatibility	Operating systems for smartphone devices include iOS, Android, BlackBerry® OS and Windows® Mobile. A mobile app that has been developed for one operating system will not be compatible with other operating systems, and will usually require a significant amount of redevelopment in order to achieve cross-platform implementation.

Programming mobile apps

Mobile apps are developed using programming languages. A programming language is a language designed to communicate with computer systems. It can instruct the computer systems to complete a series of tasks.

Types of programming language

There are a number of different programming languages that can be used in mobile app development. Here are three programming languages that are commonly used:

- **C++.** This language can be used to develop mobile apps for a number of platforms such as Windows® Mobile and Palm OS. It can also be used in small parts for Android. C++ is a very powerful programming language that is used very commonly in large-scale software applications.

- **Java.** Java is the main language used to develop mobile apps for a number of major platforms, including Android and BlackBerry® OS. It is a very similar programming language to C++, but has some of the complexity of C++ removed.

- **XML.** This stands for Extensible Markup Language. While XML isn't a programming language as such, it is a markup language and can be used with a number of platforms. It is used to define data formats, particularly on the web. If you want your mobile app to access data stored on the internet, or other web services, then XML is the language you will need to use for this.

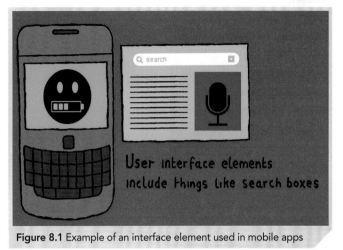

User interface elements include things like search boxes

Figure 8.1 Example of an interface element used in mobile apps

Reasons for compiling programs

When you create a mobile app using a programming language such as Java, that code needs to be translated into a language that the computer can understand, which is known as object code.

- If you **compile** your programs, this process will create an executable file that is already translated into the object code for your computer to use.

- If you do not compile your programs, then anyone wanting to run them will need special software. Also, people will be able to see your programming code and copy it to make their own version of your software.

> **Key term**
>
> **Compile** – To take the programming code you have written and turn it into a type of code known as object code, which the computer can understand. This is done by a program called a compiler.

Assessment activity 8.1 1A.1 | 2A.P1 | 2A.M1 | 2A.D1

You are on work experience with a small company which provides IT support to people in their own homes. The company is called ITsupport@home. Your work experience supervisor, Amit, is working on a project involving developing mobile apps and he is keen to involve you in the project.

Amit would like you to research two different types of apps; for example, an app which provides a business function and an app which provides an entertainment function. He would like you to produce an illustrated report on your findings.

Look at different websites that you can download apps from and select two different types of apps.

- Explain what each app does and why someone would want to use it.

- What is special about each app? What features do they include? How do the features differ between apps?

- Are the apps easy to use? Identify any problems you think users might have when using each app.

- Explain the strengths and weaknesses of each app.

Tips

- Structure your report to make it easy to follow. Use titles and sub-titles to help readers follow the flow of information. Be sure to provide a caption for any images and screenshots.
- Proofread all of your work and check for spelling and grammatical errors.

Designing a mobile app 1

Introduction

Before you develop a mobile app, it is important to think very carefully about its design. This will ensure that you have a clear idea of what you are creating, so that you do not continually change things or add new features during the development. In this section, we will look at what you need to do in the first stage of the design process.

Software development life cycle

There is a standard structure that people use when they develop software applications, known as the software development life cycle. You should use this structure when designing your app.

Stage 1 – Requirements of the problem

This stage involves meeting with your client and the users of the system. You can identify what they want and what they need to be included in the mobile app.

Stage 2 – Design specification

After you have a clear set of requirements, you will need to produce a design specification. This design should cover the scope of the application (exactly what it should do), the inputs, outputs, processing and the user interface design.

- **Scope.** The scope of the application is normally a list of what the application is required to do, for example, allowing the user to search for train times from two specific locations.
- **Inputs.** The inputs for the application are exact details of the data the app will need to collect from the user.
- **Outputs.** The outputs for the app are the data that will be presented to the user once it has been processed.
- **Processing.** The processing is what the app will do with the data entered by the user. For example, you may need to define how the app will perform calculations or how it will filter the data to produce a specific piece of information.
- **User interface.** This is how the user interacts with the mobile app. This is usually a graphical user interface which makes use of text, images and buttons to allow you to navigate through the app.

Stage 3 – Identify constraints

At this stage, you must identify anything that will affect the development of the application (these are known as constraints). Constraints could include the timescale or budget which you must develop the application within, or the programming languages you will be able to use for your given platform.

Stage 4 – Develop code

This is the stage where you develop your mobile app, using the programming language you have chosen and the graphics you have produced.

Stage 5 – Test

This stage involves checking that there are no errors in the final mobile app, and reviewing the application to ensure that it is of a high quality.

Stage 6 – Maintain code

Even after testing, it is very rare that an application is released completely error-free. If problems are discovered by the users, it is important that you provide ongoing support by repairing the code as necessary.

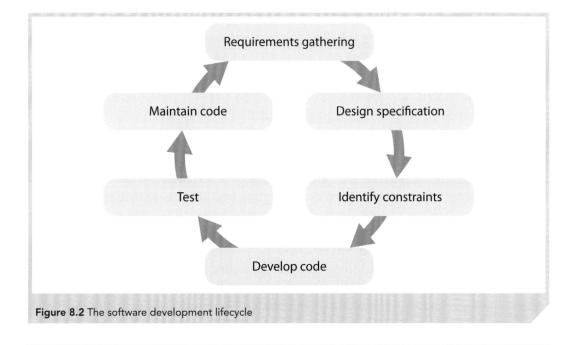

Figure 8.2 The software development lifecycle

Activity 8.3

1 Produce a diagram showing the software design lifecycle.
2 Expand on the diagram by identifying what you do at each stage of the lifecycle.

Just checking

1 What do we mean by the term scope?
2 What do we mean by constraints?
3 Why is it important to perform on-going maintenance of your app?

Designing a mobile app 2

Introduction

This section looks at the specific elements you need to include in your design so that your app meets the user requirements and can perform its main tasks. You need to be able to use a range of design techniques such as pseudo code, screen sketches and flow charts to help create a design document to show to customers and gain approval.

Purpose and user requirements

You need to define the purpose of your mobile app by describing exactly what it should do. You should have a good idea about what your app is aiming to achieve. For example, it could be to give directions to restaurants, based on the user's GPS position.

For a mobile app to be successful, it needs to solve an existing problem. You will usually get a range of requirements from the client that the application must meet. It is important to meet these requirements, as they are how your client will judge the success of the app.

You should also consider your intended audience – the type of people that you are developing the mobile app for. This audience can be classified in various ways, for example by gender, age group, geographical location or hobbies.

A proposed solution using design tools

Your design will need to include a proposed solution, which means a demonstration of how the system will look and work. When doing this, you will use a number of different design tools.

A description of the main program tasks

Any mobile app is programmed to perform certain tasks. These tasks will involve receiving some kind of input (such as entering a number), performing some processing (such as multiplying that number) and then showing some output (such as displaying the answer from the multiplication on the screen). The first thing you must do is describe all of the programming tasks that your application will perform.

Screen layouts and navigation, including prototypes

To ensure you have a well-designed user interface and a clear navigation structure, it is important to produce a drawing of the screen layout and a **structure diagram** (navigation hierarchy). You may also then create a prototype of the user interface. To do this, you create the user interface – but without the code in the background performing all of the tasks required. Screen elements you need to consider:

- **Initial splash screen.** This is the screen that displays while you load your app. It will often contain your logo and loading progress information.
- **Main activity screen.** This is your main screen where you interact with the app. It will often have input elements such as buttons or text boxes and a menu.
- **Over screens or screen elements.** There are many other screens you may include such as a help screen or warning screens. These will help the user to make use of your app and should be considered carefully.

<div class="key-term">

Key term

Structure diagram – Also known as a navigation hierarchy, this shows how you can get from a general category to a more specific one. For example, a drawing app could have a menu system where a user picks Tool, then Brush, then Thick Brush. At each stage, there are several options. You can draw all the options as a hierarchy.

</div>

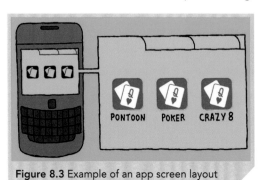

Figure 8.3 Example of an app screen layout

Algorithms and processing structure

An algorithm is a list of instructions for performing a task. Before you design exactly how your algorithms will specifically work, you must write a description of how the algorithms will produce your expected solution. You must also write a description of your processing structure.

Link

For more on flow charts and the symbols used to create them, see *Unit 2 Technology systems*.

The processing structure is how your code will actually perform the tasks that you have planned for. To do this, you will need to design the algorithms using techniques such as flow charts, pseudo-code and events.

- **Flow charts.** These are diagrams that show step by step how a program will work from a start point to an end point.
- **Pseudo-code.** This is where you describe step by step how the program will work, much like with a programming language, but using normal English instead.
- **Events.** These are the interactions a person will have with your user interface that will make it run the code. This could be clicking a button or entering some text.

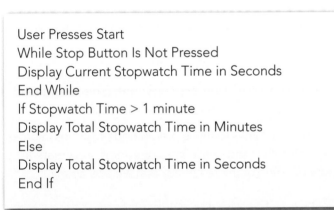

```
User Presses Start
While Stop Button Is Not Pressed
Display Current Stopwatch Time in Seconds
End While
If Stopwatch Time > 1 minute
Display Total Stopwatch Time in Minutes
Else
Display Total Stopwatch Time in Seconds
End If
```

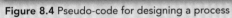
Figure 8.4 Pseudo-code for designing a process

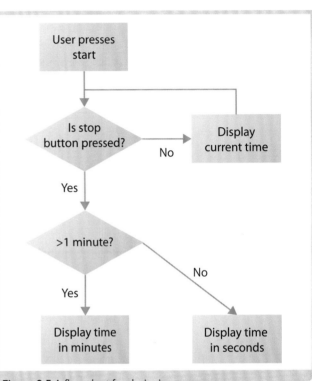
Figure 8.5 A flow chart for designing a process

Control structures

Much like with events, sometimes programming code will only run if certain criteria are met, such as a particular number being inputted. We make this happen using control structures. You need to document what control structures will be in place for your app.

Remember

When documenting your chosen design, make sure you list what other designs you came up with and why you rejected them.

Data validation

One of the dangers of any mobile app is that users might enter data that is incorrect, such as a name in a date field. You need to document what validation checks your system will have in place to prevent this.

Link

For more information about validation, see *Unit 10 Database development* and *Unit 12 Software development*.

Activity 8.4

Look at the user interface for several different mobile apps.

1 Re-create one of these user interfaces using graphics-editing tools.
2 Create your own version of the user interface to improve on it.
3 Create a hierarchy diagram to demonstrate the navigation of the mobile app.

Designing a mobile app 3

Introduction
There are further elements you can include in your design for your app, to help you ensure that it is the best solution possible.

Alternative solutions

Once you have planned and designed a solution for your mobile app, you should also describe an alternative solution. This is important, because it makes you consider whether the way you planned it is actually the best way for it to work. This could lead to your producing a more efficient, attractive and popular app. This alternative solution should consider all elements in the design as you would with your initial design such as screen layouts and navigation diagrams.

Predefined programs or code snippets

To save time on the development of the app, you may want to use programs that have already been created and are freely available to use. These might be from the internet or other media, such as CDs or DVDs.

It is important to ensure that you have permission to use the code snippets, as otherwise you will be breaching the original programmer's copyright. (This would lead to you having to remove the code and it could also lead to you being sued.)

You can then edit the code or create code that links to these predefined programs in order to produce your application. You need to collect the predefined programs and create a list of them so that you have a clear understanding of the resources that are available.

Ready-made and original assets

During the design stage, you will need to collect all of the video, graphics, audio and animations that you will be using to create the mobile app. These could include sprites (graphics that can be moved) for game characters, images that could represent backgrounds, movies to offer more exciting visual content and buttons to aid interaction between the user and mobile app. These may be ready-made and available through resources such as the internet. Be aware that while some will be freely available others may cost a fee. Alternatively, you can create these assets yourself, so that they meet your needs more effectively.

Remember

It is important to respect copyright. Documenting your sources makes it easier to show that you have the right to use these assets. If you feature a company's logo or brand, or music or sound clips from a TV show or film, then you will need to get copyright permission from the owner. While you may be able to find nearly everything on the internet, it does not mean that you have rights to copy it, reproduce it or use it.

Activity 8.5

Use the internet to search for free mobile app graphics. Visit some websites to look at the quality of the example graphics.

- Find the terms of use for the graphics to ensure that they are completely free to use for your mobile apps.
- Create a list of links to all the web pages that provide good-quality free graphics that you can use for the mobile app you will be designing.

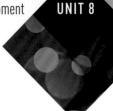

Document and reference sources

If you are using predefined programs or ready-made assets, it is important to document and reference where you collected these from. This will ensure that you give credit to the original creator of the content. You should include all credits in the documentation you create for the mobile app. Documenting the sources will also make it easier to find the content again at a later date if you lose the files.

◤ A test plan with test data

Your test plan is how you check to ensure the app doesn't have any errors or bugs in the code. Even if you have not created your app yet, you should be able to create a plan that you will be able to use to test your final mobile app. Your test plan will need to include a range of different inputs, and the outputs that you expect as a result. At this stage, you just need to identify what you are testing, what data you will be inputting to test it, and what you expect to happen as a result.

When compiling your code many errors will be identified by the compilers built in error checker. This will prevent you from being able to actually compile or run the code should there be a glaring programming error.

◤ Constraints

There will be a number of constraints on the development of your mobile app. These could include the programming languages you need to use for your chosen platform or the capabilities of the device you are developing the app for (such as the speed of its processor, the size of its screen or the capacity of its memory or hard drive).

> **Link**
>
> See *Unit 12 Software development* for an example of test plan that you can adapt for this unit.

Assessment activity 8.2 ◢ *English* | 1B.2 | 1B.2 | 2B.P2 | 2B.P3 | 2B.M2 | 2B.D2 |

Amit has asked you to help design one of the apps he is developing. The idea behind the app is to help ITsupport@home staff to log and track jobs in real time. You will need to:

- Gather information about the needs of the staff – what features would it be helpful for the job log app to include?
- Decide on the features and summarise this information in a document.
- Come up with a range of ideas of your design. Present your ideas and decide on the best option.
- Create a plan and identify what sources and assets your app will include.
- Identify any specialist tools or equipment you need to create your app.
- Design your app.
- Review your designs and explain why you selected them and how they are suitable for your intended audience.

Tips
- Keep in your mind the reasons why you are developing the app and who will be using it.
- Keep a record of any notes you made when considering sources and assets, and why you decided to include the ones you did.
- Consider what tools and equipment is available and which can aid the design and creation of your app.

Preparing content

Getting started

Using the internet, find examples of ready-made graphical assets that you could use in your application.

What are the benefits and disadvantages of using ready-made assets? Are there any restrictions with using these assets?

Introduction

Now that you have designed your mobile app, the next stage is to develop and test it. You will need to know how to develop the mobile app using predefined code, how to integrate and edit this code, and how to test it to ensure it works and is of good quality. In this section, we will look at preparing content to develop an app.

Key terms

Optimise – It is unlikely that an asset that you create or download will be suitable for use in a mobile app as it is. To optimise your assets, you need to make sure that they have a small file size but still look fine on a mobile device.

Subroutine – A set of instructions within a program that performs a specific task.

Copyright – A legal right that is given to someone who creates an original piece of work. This means that other people cannot use this piece of work without the creator's permission.

Prepare and gather programs and assets

In order to develop a mobile app using predefined programs and code snippets, you must first gather together all the material you need. Then you will be able to edit and **optimise** your assets to better meet your needs. To do this you will need to understand how to use graphic-editing programs, such as Adobe® Photoshop®, and understand the file formats that are available for you to use.

Using the internet, it is possible to find a wide variety of predefined programs, code snippets and **subroutines** that you can use to develop your mobile app. There is also a huge variety of ready-made graphical assets available that you can make use of in your application, as well as any original assets that you create yourself. You will need to gather all of these before starting to develop the application. It is important to be sure that you have permission to use these examples and assets, as otherwise you may be breaching the original creator's **copyright**.

Activity   8.6

Use the internet to search for code examples and tutorials for MIT App Inventor.

1 Try to implement the examples yourself to ensure that they work as you expect them to.

2 Save the web link for each example in a Microsoft® Word® document, and ensure that you have saved each of the examples you implemented.

3 Share the examples that you have found with others in the group and add other students' examples to your list.

Edit and optimise for a mobile platform

Once you have collected your graphical assets, you will need to use editing software to alter them to your needs. This might involve removing certain parts of the image, adding new parts or altering the colour scheme.

Graphics will have a big effect on the file size (and loading time) of your app, so you may also need to optimise them by reducing the quality of the assets. This will reduce the file size. As many mobile phones screens are very small, you don't need to have images of the highest quality.

Figure 8.6 Graphic-editing software packages like Adobe® Creative Suite provide you with a range of editing tools, effects and techniques

Use appropriate file formats

Not all file formats are appropriate for use in mobile apps. Some file formats cannot be used, as the device cannot understand these file formats. For example, you would not be able to use Shockwave Flash (.swf) file types for Apple® devices, because they do not support Flash® and therefore .swf files. Given the popularity of Apple® devices and the advent of HTML5, Flash®-based apps are in decline. Additionally, some file formats store the assets in very large file sizes because of the high-quality of the image, and so they are often not much use to you.

Did you know?

GIF and JPG file types are very commonly used for images, as they work on most platforms and have small file sizes.

Just checking ✔

1 What is a subroutine?
2 What do we mean by optimising assets?
3 Why is it important to choose appropriate file formats?

Develop and refine an app 1

Introduction

The next step is to actually develop the mobile app. This will involve using a development environment to integrate the predefined code snippets and assets to produce the final application and to refine the program by writing your own code.

Link

Having an understanding of the different types of technology and platforms available will be very useful when developing your mobile app. See *Unit 2 Technology systems* for a more detailed introduction to technology systems.

Use a development environment to write code

Depending on the programming language you are using to write code for your mobile app, there will be a variety of development environments to choose from. These development environments will provide you with the tools you need to create a working program. Some of the tools include code highlighting, code debugging and user interface designers. These tools will make it a lot easier to create a working program.

Activity 8.7

If you completed the starter activity for this unit, you should have MIT App Inventor set up for use on your PC.

1 Visit the MIT App Inventor website and complete the 'Hello Purr' tutorial. You can access this website by going to Pearson Hotlinks (www.pearsonhotlinks. co.uk) and searching for this title.

2 Try to make your own modifications to the code.

Integrate ready-made and original code

To use ready-made programs, code snippets and assets effectively, you need to be able to edit these and create some original code, to ensure that they integrate (work together) successfully. This will usually involve tweaking the code slightly, but it could also involve a large amount of original coding on your part, particularly if you can't find a code snippet that does what you want it to do.

Activity 8.8

1 Visit the MIT App Inventor website and complete the 'PaintPot' tutorials, parts 1 and 2.

2 Edit the code to add a fourth colour.

3 Think of other additions you could make to the program. Could you add the ability to draw shapes in different colours?

Program constructs to edit and create code

To create original programming code and edit ready-made code, you need to be able to use suitable programming constructs. These are the standard coding techniques used by software developers.

Command words

- **Comments.** These are used to describe your code and how it works. Comments are often added by using the symbol //. Anything written after these slashes is not actually part of the program but merely describes what is happening.

- **Constants.** Constants are used to store key information, such as words or numbers that are going to be used throughout the application. These are **variables** with a constant value that cannot change.

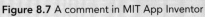

> This block of code changes the label 1 text to "Hello World" when you click the button.

Figure 8.7 A comment in MIT App Inventor

- **Operators.** These allow you to perform arithmetic or logical comparisons. The logical operators are usually used with **loops** or **sequences** (sequential statements) to check when to run the code. Table 8.2 outlines the arithmetic operators and the logical operators.

Table 8.2 Arithmetic operators and logical operators

Arithmetic operators	Logical operators
+ (plus symbol for addition)	< (less than)
- (symbol for subtraction)	<= (less than or equal to)
* (asterisk symbol for multiplication)	> (greater than)
/ (forward slash for division)	>= (greater than or equal to)
% (percentage symbol to find the remainder from a division)	'AND' to check when two different comparisons are true 'OR' to check when one of two comparisons are true 'TRUE' to check when a **Boolean variable** is set to true 'FALSE' to check when a Boolean variable is set to false

- **Reserved words.** All programming languages have reserved words that have special meanings in that programming language. These reserved words are usually commands already used by the programming language. Therefore, they are prevented from being used for variables, for example, as the compiler wouldn't be able to distinguish which is a command and which is a variable name. These include words such as 'if', 'case', 'for' and 'int'.

- **Input and output commands.** You will want your app to get input from your users and to give them certain outputs. You can use commands that will create input boxes for users to enter data and message boxes to feed back to them.

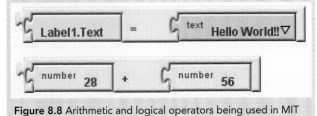

Figure 8.8 Arithmetic and logical operators being used in MIT App Inventor

CONTINUED ▶▶

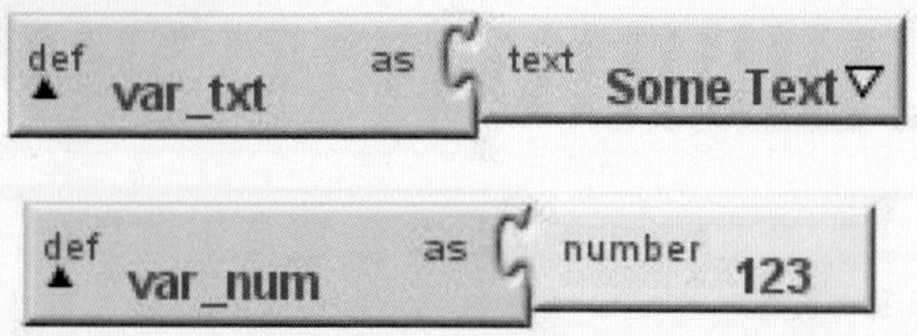

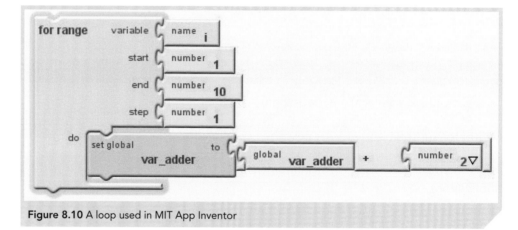

Figure 8.9 Two types of variables used in MIT App Inventor

- **Variables.** A variable is where you can store a piece of data and give it an identifiable name. These variables come in two varieties: local and global.

  - **Local variables.** Local variables are created within a subroutine and are only remembered in that subroutine. So if you tried to use the data in that variable in a different subroutine, it would cause an error, because it doesn't exist there.

  - **Global variables.** A global variable can be used in all parts of the program code, including all subroutines.

- **Assignment.** When you create a variable, you need to assign a value to it. To do this, you need to use assignment operators. The main kind of assignment operator is the = sign. This will allow you to give a variable a value, for example, $x = 10$.

- **Loops.** When you are programming, you will often require a piece of code to repeat a number of times. You can do this using loops. Examples of loops include 'For Loops', which will run a set number of times, and 'While Loops', which run until a certain condition is met, such as a button being pressed.

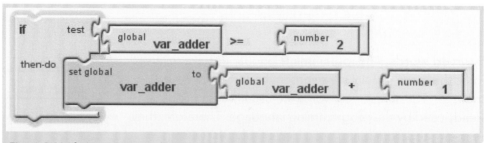

Figure 8.10 A loop used in MIT App Inventor

- **Sequential statements.** Sometimes you will want code to run only in certain circumstances. To achieve this, you can use sequential statements, such as the 'If… then…' statement. This will run the code only if a certain condition is met, such as a variable having a certain number assigned to it.

Figure 8.11 'If…' statement used in MIT App Inventor

Just checking

1 What is a variable?

2 Name three different types of loops.

3 What do we mean by sequential statements?

Develop and refine an app 2

Introduction

In this section, you will learn about further ways to edit and create programming code.

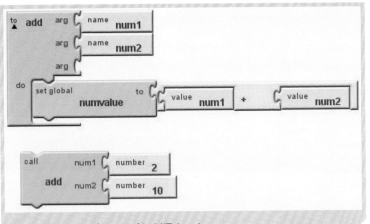

Figure 8.12 Procedure used in MIT App Inventor

Use other program constructs

Subroutines, functions and procedures

Subroutines, functions and procedures are sets of instructions that complete a specific task such as reading in data or printing out information. They are designed to be able to be used repeatedly and are assigned a name, so it is easy to refer to them within the main block of program code.

Use a range of data types

When you create a variable, you will need to give it a data type. The data type will define what sort of data a variable could store. Common data types include:

- **character** – an individual character such as a letter
- **string** – a piece of text such as a word or paragraph
- **integer** – a number with no decimal places
- **real number** – a number with decimal places
- **Boolean** – a 1 or 0 (true or false, yes or no).

Use basic string handling commands

There are a number of commands you can use to perform actions on strings. These can allow you to find the length of a string, find if a string is empty or turn a string into upper case or lower case.

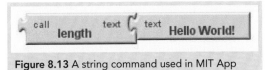

Figure 8.13 A string command used in MIT App Inventor

Event handling

- **Forms.** Events happen when you interact with your user interface. You create your user interface using forms. These forms can have buttons, text boxes, data validation, drop-down lists and many other items. When the user clicks on one of these, an event occurs.
- **Assigning actions and properties.** You can assign actions to these events. This could be a button that, when clicked on, will run code to add the values entered in two text boxes. It could also include drop-down lists to choose a country or county in an address. You can assign individual properties to these screen components as well. One of the key properties is its name. Always give your screen components good names, so that it is clear what you are referring to in your code. You could also set data validation processes in these properties to make sure what is entered is sensible.

CONTINUED ▸▸

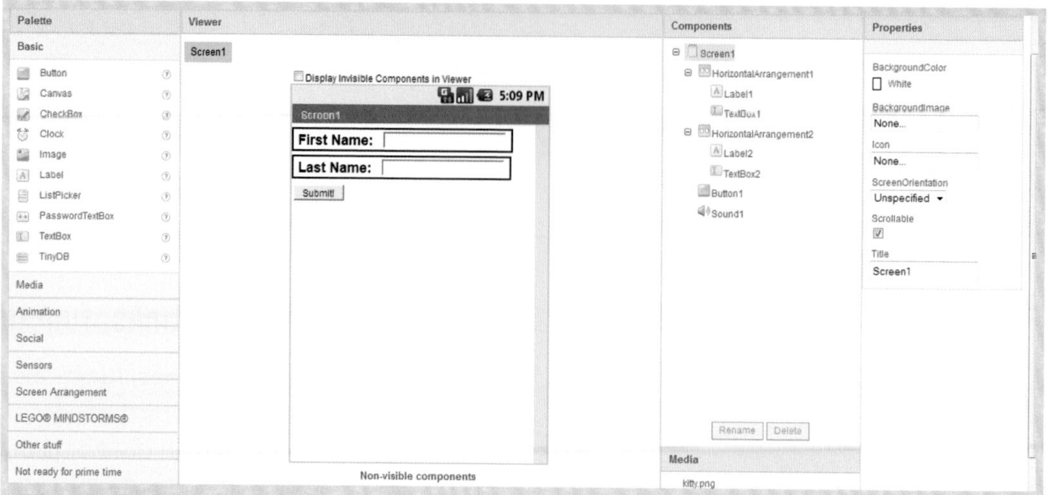

Figure 8.14 A form in MIT App Inventor

Figure 8.15 An event in MIT App Inventor

Annotate the code

You must always annotate your code using comments. Without comments, your code can be difficult to understand. If you look back at your code at a later date, or someone else needs to make modifications, these annotations will make it much easier to identify how the code works. It will therefore be much easier to repair or debug the program, should problems arise.

Compiling the program

You will need to compile the program into a suitable format to create an executable program. As covered in section *Characteristics of mobile apps*, a program called a compiler can take the programming code you have written and turn it into object code, which the computer will understand.

It is important to do this, otherwise people will not be able to run your program without special software. Also, your code will be clear to see for anyone who wants to copy it and make their own version of your software.

> **Just checking**
>
> 1 What are the different data types you can use when developing a mobile app?
> 2 What are events?
> 3 Why is it important to annotate program code?

WorkSpace

Matthew Lodder

Mobile app developer

I work for a software development company that specialises in the development of mobile apps for business use. I have a team of developers who all have their own specialist areas. I work with two other programmers to create the code for the application. There are also two designers who create the graphical elements of the application, such as designing and creating the user interface. Finally, there is a project manager who manages the team and works with the client to ensure that we are achieving the goals of the project.

In my role, I need to have an understanding of different programming languages, so that I am able to develop the application to work on a variety of platforms. It is important that I have designed the code properly to ensure that the application works the same on all of these platforms. I also need to check the code for errors and correct any problems that arise, so that the application won't be released with any bugs. I have to work closely with my team to ensure that the final application will come together effectively to produce a high-quality application.

Think about it

1. What skills and characteristics does Matthew need in order to be successful in his job? As well as his programming knowledge, does he also need graphical skills? Does he need good problem-solving and communication skills?
2. Do you feel you have any of these skills or characteristics? How could you develop them further?
3. Why do you think a project manager is required to make sure the app is a success?

Check and test a mobile app

Introduction

In this section, we will look at the ways in which you can assess the quality of your app. You will also learn how to test your app effectively, to ensure it functions well. This will include gathering feedback, making final improvements and documenting any changes.

Quality of software programs

The quality of software programs can be significantly affected by the software design and techniques used during development. You can judge the quality of your software applications using a number of different criteria.

Efficiency/performance

Your mobile app will use a certain amount of the system resources available (processor time, memory space, accessing storage media). You need it to use as little of these as possible so it will work effectively on the hardware being used. Designing your processing in detail can help to create the most efficient program code possible. You will have clearly thought through what needs to happen and can use this to produce the final code.

Figure 8.16 You need to make sure your app can run on different computer operating systems

Maintainability

At a later date, you may need to make modifications to the program to correct problems, improve the efficiency or add new functionality. By annotating the code and breaking it down into well-designed subroutines, you will make the program easier to maintain.

Portability

You will need your app to run on as many different hardware and operating system platforms as possible. This may require you to code the program in several different languages. It is much easier to do this if you have fully designed your code before implementing it.

Usability

Your app needs to be as easy to use as possible. If the program is too complex to actually use, then the app cannot be considered a success. By carefully designing your user interface and navigation, and by discussing your design with your client before implementing it, you can be sure that the app will be usable by your target audience.

Activity 8.9

1 In groups, choose a mobile app and review it against the quality criteria explained in this section. Give it a score out of five for each of the criteria.
2 Find a mobile app that rivals the first one you chose. Review it in the same way.
3 Which mobile app scored better? Which app do you use yourself? Is it the one you gave the highest score?
4 Compare your results with another group and discuss your findings.

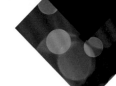

Test the program solution

Once you have created your app, you must test it to ensure that it works without any errors or bugs in the code and performs to a high standard.

- **Functionality.** You will first need to test the application against the test plan you created in the design stage to ensure that it functions as you expect it to.
- **Fit for purpose.** You must then test the program to ensure it is fit for purpose.
- **Quality.** Next you will review the quality of the program in terms of four key criteria: efficiency/performance, maintainability, portability and usability.
- **Feedback.** Finally you will gather feedback from others on the quality of the solution using the same four key criteria listed above.

Document any changes

You will need to document any changes made to the design, including changes to the source table of predefined programs/snippets and ready-made assets.

If you don't update the design documentation, it will be inaccurate. This could lead to problems for future development. Of particular importance is updating the source table, as you need to ensure that proper credit is given to the developers of the predefined programs/snippets and ready-made assets.

> **Remember**
>
> Unless the creator of an asset has given you permission to use it, don't assume that you are allowed to do so (even if you credit the source). Using an asset without permission will infringe (break) the owner's copyright.

Refine the software program

When you review the quality of your app, you will examine efficiency/performance, maintainability, portability and usability, as detailed above. If this review shows any clear weaknesses, you should make changes to improve your app before it is released. Once these improvements are made, you need to complete the testing process by ensuring no new problems have been created and the program quality has in fact improved.

Assessment activity 8.3   *Maths* | 1C.4 | 1C.5 | 1C.6 | 2C.P4 | 2C.P5 | 2C.P6 | 2C.M3 | 2C.M4 | 2C.M5 | 2C.D3 |

Amit presented your design for the job log app to ITsupport@home's Managing Director. She was very impressed by it and she would like you to work with Amit to develop an app containing multiple screens and constructs.

- Order, reference and file the asset sources to be used in the app. For each asset, record your reasons for selecting it and details of where you sourced it from.
- Prepare the code and integrate it with the assets. Carry out any editing if required.

- Annotate the code.
- Think about each element of the app. Is there anything at this stage which you could improve on? Ask other people to look at your app and ask them for feedback.
- Compare your app with your design brief. Are there any changes you want to make?
- Test your app to see if it works and make any necessary changes or improvements.

Tips

- Make sure that all assets are saved in the correct format.
- It is very important that you can explain and provide supporting evidence of your thought process and the different stages you went through over the course of a task.
- Ask for feedback throughout the process. Keep a record of the feedback and notes on how this affected your subsequent decisions.

Reviewing the finished mobile app

Introduction

Once your mobile app is complete, you should review it to decide how successful it was in achieving your goals.

What to include in a review

User requirements

During the early stages of the project, you identified a range of requirements for the mobile app. These were the specific things the app needed, according to your client and the end users of the mobile app. The most important measure of an app's success is whether or not you have met all of the requirements. You therefore need to compare each of the requirements for the app against the app itself and produce evidence to show clearly how it meets that requirement.

One important aspect of the user requirements was defining the intended target audience for your app. You must be able to show how the app appeals to the group of people you identified as your end users.

Fitness for purpose

Within the design brief, you defined the purpose of the app – what the app is supposed to be able to do. For example, the purpose of the app might be to allow users to watch and comment on videos uploaded by the general public. You now need to make a judgement on whether the purpose you defined has been met, and you must produce evidence to demonstrate this.

Constraints

There are a range of constraints that you defined which could potentially affect your app. For example, this could be the limitations of the programming language chosen, the time given for development, the copyright of the materials being used, or of the mobile phone's capabilities, such as connectivity available (Wi-Fi, 3G) and screen size. You should review your mobile app against these constraints to see how heavily it has been affected by them. Can your device actually run on the hardware available? Did you complete the project within the budget and deadline?

Quality of the program

You should review the quality of your mobile app using the following four criteria: efficiency/performance, maintainability, portability and usability.

Strengths and improvements

The final part of your review will be to look at the strengths of your mobile app and the improvements that you need to make. These strengths and improvements are likely to come from the earlier stages of your review. The areas you meet very effectively and can produce clear evidence for are your strengths. The areas you need to improve are the stages you cannot produce much evidence for or have not done at all. Perhaps there is a client requirement you have not met?

Assessment activity 8.4   1D.7 | 2D.P7 | 2D.M6 | 2D.D4

When you return to school, your teacher asks you to review the work you carried out during your work experience with ITsupport@home. He would like you to feed back to the rest of the class about the process of designing, creating and testing a mobile app. Decide how you will present your review to the class (e.g. a group presentation, an illustrated report, role playing a review session at the company). Whichever method you choose, include the following:

- The purpose of the app and how your design meets the requirements of the brief and the ITsupport@home staff.
- The process you went through when developing the app. Outline any instances where the app differs from your original design and explain why this is.
- Any problems you encountered and how you dealt with them.
- Identify any future changes you would make to the app to make it even better.

Tips

- Don't try to cover everything in one go. Apply a clear structure to your review and breakdown the information into topics.
- Give a reason for every change that you made.
- Refer back to the feedback you received from other people to consider what further improvements you could make.

Introduction

Numbers are part of our daily lives. We all need to be able to handle them, whether we are doing homework, working out home finances or running a business. Occasional one-off calculations might still be best with pen and paper or a calculator, but for repetitive or complex calculations with large quantities of numbers, a spreadsheet is essential. Once you have set up a spreadsheet, and added and checked the equations, you can make many calculations accurately and quickly.

One of the most powerful features of a spreadsheet is the ability to model situations using formulae. It allows you to trial changes and test possibilities.

You can format spreadsheets to create clear outputs, and you can sort, filter and update your data at the touch of a button. Spreadsheets are an invaluable software tool for a wide variety of situations and applications and are used extensively in many organisations.

In this unit, you will explore the wide range of uses for spreadsheets. You will discover the many tools and techniques available, and you will learn how to design, develop and test a spreadsheet solution. Once you have done this, you will review the finished spreadsheet solution and think about possible improvements.

Assessment: You will be assessed by a series of assignments set by your teacher.

Learning aims

In this unit you will:

A understand the uses of spreadsheets and the features available in spreadsheet software packages

B design a spreadsheet

C develop and test a spreadsheet

D review the finished spreadsheet.

I thought I'd find this unit a bit dull but, I was surprised. I had no idea that spreadsheets could be used in so many ways.

When my friends and I decided to take part in an enterprise scheme, I used a spreadsheet to help plan our finances. I was able to use the spreadsheet to analyse data and predict future growth. This really gave us the edge over other teams.

Oliver, 16-years-old

Spreadsheet development

9

Assessment criteria

Level 1	Level 2 Pass	Level 2 Merit	Level 2 Distinction
Learning aim A: Understand the uses of spreadsheets and the features available in spreadsheet software packages			
1A.1 Identify how spreadsheets are used for two different activities and how the features are used in the spreadsheets. **Assessment activity 9.1, page 273**	**2A.P1** Explain how spreadsheets are used for two different activities and how the features are used in the spreadsheets. **Assessment activity 9.1, page 273**	**2A.M1** Review how the features in the spreadsheets could improve productivity, accuracy and usability. **Assessment activity 9.1, page 273**	**2A.D1** Discuss the strengths and weaknesses of the spreadsheets. **Assessment activity 9.1, page 273**
Learning aim B: Design a spreadsheet			
1B.2 Identify the purpose and user requirements for the spreadsheet. **Assessment activity 9.2, pages 277–278**	**2B.P2** Describe the purpose and user requirements for the spreadsheet. **Assessment activity 9.2, pages 277–278**	**2B.M2** Produce detailed designs for a spreadsheet, including: • alternative solutions • detailed worksheet structure diagram • test data. **Assessment activity 9.2, pages 277–278**	**2B.D2** Justify final design decisions, including: • how the spreadsheet solution will fulfil the stated purpose and user requirements • any constraints to the design. **Assessment activity 9.2, pages 277–278**
1B.3 With guidance, produce a design for a spreadsheet, including: • worksheet structure diagram. **Assessment activity 9.2, pages 277–278**	**2B.P3** Produce a design for a spreadsheet, including: • worksheet structure diagram • how output data is to be presented • a test plan. **Assessment activity 9.2, pages 277–278**		
Learning aim C: Develop and test a spreadsheet			
1C.4 With guidance, develop a spreadsheet with a given realistic data set. **Assessment activity 9.3, page 300**	**2C.P4** Develop a spreadsheet with a given realistic data set, containing a user interface for data input and presentation of output data. **Assessment activity 9.3, page 300**	**2C.M3** Refine the spreadsheet to improve usability and accuracy using onscreen user navigation and guidance. **Assessment activity 9.3, page 300**	**2C.D3** Maths Refine the spreadsheet using automated tools/techniques to improve productivity, accuracy and presentation of output data. **Assessment activity 9.3, page 300**
1C.5 Maths With guidance, test the spreadsheet for functionality and purpose, and repair any faults, documenting any changes made. **Assessment activity 9.3, page 300**	**2C.P5** Maths Test the spreadsheet for functionality and purpose and repair any faults, documenting any changes made. **Assessment activity 9.3, page 300**	**2C.M4** Maths Gather feedback from others on usability, and use it to improve the spreadsheet, testing the additional functionality and repair any faults. **Assessment activity 9.3, page 300**	

Assessment criteria			
Level 1	Level 2 Pass	Level 2 Merit	Level 2 Distinction
Learning aim D: Review the finished spreadsheet			
1D.6 For the final spreadsheet, identify how the final spreadsheet is suitable for the purpose. **Assessment activity 9.4, page 301**	**2D.P6** For the final spreadsheet, explain how the final spreadsheet is suitable for the user requirements and purpose. **Assessment activity 9.4, page 301**	**2D.M5** Review the extent to which the final spreadsheet meets the user requirements and purpose while considering feedback from others. **Assessment activity 9.4, page 301**	**2D.D4** Evaluate the final spreadsheet against the initial designs and justify any changes that were made, making recommendations for further improvements to the spreadsheet. **Assessment activity 9.4, page 301**

Maths Opportunity to practise mathematical skills

How you will be assessed

The unit will be assessed by a series of internally marked tasks that together cover all of the criteria. You might be expected, for example, to show an understanding of the use of spreadsheets created by others, which allow them to solve problems. These may cover a range of scenarios. You might also then undertake a series of tasks to design, develop and review a spreadsheet of your own to solve a given problem.

The tasks could, for example, be based on the scenario that you are working in a local enterprise development agency that aims to help young people set up small business enterprises. Your manager might be concerned that some young people do not consider all the costs and the possible income for their new businesses. She asks you to create a spreadsheet model to allow the young people to explore their plans and make decisions that will allow them to produce a properly costed business plan.

Your assessment could be in the form of:

- written reports detailing the requirements and designs for your spreadsheet.
- a completed and documented working spreadsheet or series of spreadsheets that meets the user's need
- a presentation
- records of discussions with a teacher or supervisor
- a test plan
- an evaluation of your spreadsheet.

Uses of spreadsheets

Getting started ⏩

In many subjects that you study, you have to carry out calculations. With a partner, discuss the opportunities that you have had to use a spreadsheet to help you with your work. Make a list of the situations in which using a spreadsheet would have been valuable.

Introduction

In this section, you will learn about what spreadsheets are and how they are used in education and business. You will need to revise the spreadsheet skills that you developed in Key Stage 3, and develop a good understanding of the tools and techniques used to create efficient spreadsheet solutions.

What is a spreadsheet?

Spreadsheet applications are designed to carry out calculations quickly and accurately and to display the results in an easy-to-understand way. They allow users to make changes to the data and will automatically recalculate the results when changes are made.

Spreadsheets are used in many different types of organisations, in particular within small and medium enterprises (SMEs) where it may not be worth developing bespoke or tailor-made solutions. It is important for you to understand why they are so useful to organisations and the different ways in which they are used.

Reasons why spreadsheets are used in organisations

- **Improve productivity and accuracy.** It is important for commercial activities to be accurate, including the results of all calculations for invoices, salaries and tax returns. In an increasingly competitive world, it is also important that companies strive to be productive and not waste time or resources.

- **Support decision making.** Managers make decisions all the time. For example, they decide what products to make and/or sell and how to market them and at what price. In order to make good decisions, the managers need good information and this will often come from a spreadsheet. Spreadsheets provide a number of specialist techniques that help the user make decisions. One common technique is scenario modelling. Using this technique users can set up a model of how the situation behaves using equations and then by changing values in some cells, the user can follow the impact of the changes. Other techniques include data mining and goal seeking – these are described elsewhere.

- **Present information clearly and effectively.** Effective presentation of information improves communication between staff, suppliers and customers. Spreadsheets have powerful and flexible tools that can convert volumes of raw numeric data into more easily understood formats such as tables or charts.

- **Perform calculations and help with analysing data.** Decision making in organisations may require many complex calculations and then analysis of the data. Spreadsheets break down complex information into more readily understandable forms and have tools to enable data analysis. This allows an organisation to see longer-term trends in buying patterns, for example.

- **Manipulate large data sets.** A Microsoft® Excel® 2010 worksheet has up to 1,048,576 rows by 16,384 columns and a workbook can have multiple worksheets. This allows it to handle large volumes of data. However, it can require careful design and use of tools to manipulate such large volumes of data.

Activities where spreadsheets are used

Using spreadsheets is very helpful in a number of activities. These include:

- **Cost modelling.** Small businesses often create spreadsheet models to predict what will happen to their profits if they raise the price of their goods or invest in creating a new product. This is called cost modelling. Using a spreadsheet in this way is also known as 'what if' analysis or goal seeking. The process involves changing values in particular cells and seeing the change this has to values in all related cells.

- **Analysis of large data sets.** Spreadsheets are frequently used to analyse large sets of data, such as the results gathered during scientific experiments or large market research exercises. The format of the data to be gathered can be designed so that it can be directly imported into a spreadsheet model, ready to be analysed. The spreadsheet's ability to perform many calculations very quickly but also accurately is key.

- **Tracking progress and recording results.** Many teachers use spreadsheets to track learners' progress and record their marks. Some more complex functions such as IF statements can be used to flag up learners who are making good progress or those who may need extra help to reach their target grades.

- **Creating timetables and results.** Spreadsheets are often used to create timetables or fixture lists for sports clubs so that the information is clearly presented in tables. The spreadsheet can also perform calculations, such as work out points awarded and identify averages and goal differences. The information can be sorted to produce, for example, a league table, which someone in the club can easily update each week to show current league positions.

- **Stock control.** Small shops can use spreadsheets to control their stock. The number of items delivered by the manufacturers is entered into the spreadsheet model. When items are sold, the number of items in stock is decreased. The spreadsheet model can use IF statements to check if there are enough items left in stock. If the stock level is running low, the spreadsheet can warn the shopkeeper to order more.

Activity 9.1

A local fast-food outlet has asked you to conduct a survey of people's food and drink preferences. The manager would like you to find out about:

- people's preferred types of food and drink
- how much they are willing to spend on a meal
- if they prefer eating in or take-away
- preferred opening hours.

Initially, the manager assumes that you will only need access to word processing software to produce your feedback report.

Explain in a short report why you think you need to have access to spreadsheet software, giving some examples of its use in this situation.

Just checking

1 What does automatic recalculation mean?

2 Give three reasons why businesses might use spreadsheets.

Features of spreadsheet software

 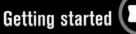
Introduction

The main feature of a spreadsheet is its capacity to perform complex sets of calculations repetitively, accurately and fast. Over time, however, other significant features and capabilities have emerged, such as the ability to convert numeric data into graphical formats and the development of specialist sets of analysis tools. Spreadsheets also have many other features using many detailed tools for sorting, formatting, cell protection, managing logical information, and so on.

Purpose of tools and techniques

There are a number of tools and techniques that help facilitate the use of spreadsheets. A selection of these are covered in detail in Learning aim B.

A good understanding of spreadsheets is necessary for people who work in business. Spreadsheets can help by:

- **improving usability** through the use of user interfaces that provide ways of navigating around large or complex spreadsheets
- **improving productivity** because the easier it is to do calculations, manipulate data and get the information you need, the more productive people in an organisation will be
- **improving accuracy** through the use of data validation or verification, which in turn helps managers to make good decisions
- **improving the presentation of output data** through the use of tables and/or graphs and charts.

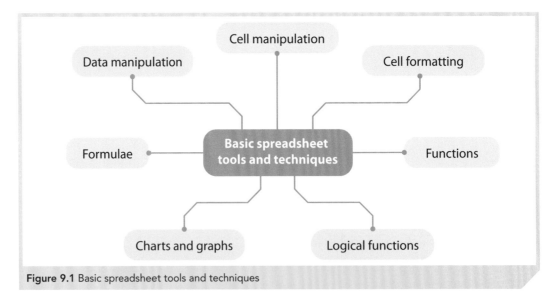

Figure 9.1 Basic spreadsheet tools and techniques

Just checking

1 What are the advantages of using a spreadsheet to analyse large data sets?

2 Why would small shops use a spreadsheet to control their stock? Would a large chain store use the same software?

3 What are the advantages to a football league of using a spreadsheet to store the fixtures, points and team league positions?

Assessment activity 9.1

| 1A.1 | 2A.P1 | 2A.M1 | 2A.D1 |

Just DVDs is a high-street shop that rents films to members of the public via a membership system. The shop's staff uses a paper-based system to track stock information, membership details and customer transactions. The manager would like you to upgrade the system and has asked you to create a spreadsheet solution which will make processes easier and more efficient for the staff.

You agree to create a spreadsheet solution which will contain three worksheets for the following areas:

a. **DVD stock.** This worksheet will contain information about each of the DVDs (e.g. a reference code for each DVD, title of DVD, rating, genre).

b. **Membership details.** This worksheet will contain information on members (e.g. name, address, phone number, membership number, member age/member category).

c. **Transactions.** This worksheet will contain information about each DVD (e.g. date take out, number of days rented for, return date, cost, paid/not paid, member who has taken it out, DVD reference code).

Tasks

The manager has never used a spreadsheet and he would like some initial training on the different ways they can be used and standard tools and features.

- Research which professions use spreadsheets and identify the common uses for spreadsheets. Create a simple poster to explain this information.

- Select two different activities and create an illustrated fact sheet which explains how and why a spreadsheet would be used for each activity.

- Make a list of the most well-known spreadsheet features. Compare this list with the features used in the two spreadsheets and add in any additional features. Beside each feature explain what it is used for and the ways in which it can improve productivity, accuracy or usability.

- Create a summary of the strengths and weaknesses for each spreadsheet.

Tips

- Be aware that different software packages include different tools and features. Make sure you know what the commonly used features are and how to use them.
- Present your information in a clear format.

Designing a spreadsheet

Introduction

This section looks at the issues you need to consider when designing a spreadsheet. It is very important to create a detailed design, so that you know that it is going to work before you build it. A detailed design will also enable someone else to use or adapt the model if circumstances change.

Intended purpose and user requirements

Spreadsheets are often designed for someone else to use. This person or organisation will provide you with a brief of their user requirements and will explain to you the purpose of the spreadsheet.

The **client** brief or the user requirements state what is expected from the spreadsheet model. Finding out what the client actually wants the model to do is an important but sometimes difficult stage in the design process. This stage can be difficult if the client does not have sufficient technical knowledge or a full understanding of what the software is capable of doing.

By analysing the client brief, you can identify what data is required for the spreadsheet, what processing of the data is needed and the output data that the client requires. You will also need to think about the user interface and facilities for input and output that will be required to satisfy the client brief.

Design documentation

Once the analysis of the client's brief/user requirements is clear, you can begin the process of creating a detailed design for the spreadsheet. Your design documentation should include the following information.

Worksheet structure diagram

When spreadsheets were first used, it was only possible to have one sheet in a file, but when multiple sheets in a file became possible it was necessary to introduce new terms such as **worksheets** and **workbooks**. Most IT people assume that a spreadsheet means the same thing as a single worksheet, but sometimes when a client asks for a 'spreadsheet' they may actually mean a collection of worksheets.

If the spreadsheet solution required by the client needs more than one worksheet, your design should include information about what is stored on each worksheet and the relationships or links between them. You will present this information as a worksheet structure diagram. For each worksheet, you will provide details of:

- **The proposed layout.** How many columns and rows there will be, whether any of the cells will need to be merged, etc.
- **Any text or labels.** This includes the headings.
- **The data input method.** This includes labelling, row and column use, forms, cell formatting, validation, conditional formatting.

- **Calculations or processes.** These are the formulae and functions. Before you can design the formulae and functions, you may need to work out how to carry out calculations by hand or by using a calculator. In this way, you will be able to identify how the problem can be solved. You can then translate these calculations into the formulae and functions needed for the spreadsheet. It is important that you end up with the correct formulae and functions. Otherwise, the model will not produce the results that the client/user needs.

User input interface

The client will want a user-friendly interface that is well laid out and easy to read and use.

At this stage, you also need to consider how the user will enter data into the spreadsheet model (the data input method). It is important that data in a spreadsheet is as accurate as possible.

To ensure accuracy, you can include a range of tools in the design to help users enter data correctly, such as drop-down list boxes, data forms and validation rules. These tools are often known as user input facilities. In addition, it is a good idea to include user instructions on the worksheet to guide the user.

You can set up drop-down list boxes to include allowable values for a cell that the user can choose. This means that the user can only choose from these values (although they still might choose the wrong one).

You can set up validation rules to ensure that data entered into a cell is within a set range, to ensure that the data entered is of the right kind, even if you cannot guarantee that the user has entered the right value.

User output data

You will need to think about how the data is output when designing your spreadsheet. How will the spreadsheet appear when you print it out? What other formats can you use to output data from spreadsheet (charts, graphs, etc.)?

The client will want the spreadsheet to produce professional-looking paper-based output. Spreadsheet packages have a range of features and formatting tools to improve the look of the worksheets. These include the use of borders, shading tools, fonts, colour and text alignment tools.

Onscreen user navigation and guidance

A spreadsheet solution that involves multiple worksheets may require navigation buttons or other techniques that allow the user to 'jump' to other worksheets or particular cells for ease of use. One commonly used technique is to provide a menu system on the first worksheet and navigation buttons elsewhere that allow the user to return easily and quickly to this main menu.

Even if the solution involves only one large worksheet, navigation buttons may still be useful, as the worksheet may well be made up of a number of areas of activity that have different purposes and perform different functions.

CONTINUED ▶▶

Remember

When spreadsheets were first used, only one sheet was possible for each but when multiple sheets in a file became possible it was necessary to introduce new terms such as worksheets and workbooks, Most IT people assume that a spreadsheet means the same thing as a single worksheet but sometimes when a client asks for a 'spreadsheet', they may actually mean a collection of worksheets.

You could provide onscreen guidance for users as they input data into the system. You might include a simple text box at the side giving instructions about what is expected or you could replace an open cell with a drop-down list box containing acceptable entries.

Adding such onscreen guidance and navigation tools will make the system easier to use, especially for inexperienced users, and will help to reduce errors.

Test plan

In your design documentation, you need to include a proposed test plan. It should include test data and details of the expected results. When you test the spreadsheet, you will add the actual results to the test plan. See section Learning aim C for more information on test plans.

Alternative design ideas

It is useful to think about different ways of reaching the same result. In your design plan, you need to include a brief outline of alternative design solutions. These may be a different choice of calculations from the ones you actually used, or an alternative formatting style for the solution.

Activity 9.3

Explain the value of:

- considering alternative solutions at the design stage
- formally creating a test plan before you begin to build the spreadsheet.

Constraints

As with all IT developments, there will be a number of constraints that will impact the development. Finance will be normally be a key one but in addition the new spreadsheet may have to be available by a certain date, or conform to certain organisational quality standards.

Just checking

1. Draw a diagram to show what a row, column, cell and cell reference are.
2. Explain why it is useful to create a detailed design for a spreadsheet model for a particular client/user.
3. Why is it important to check your formulae and functions at the design stage?

The manager of Just DVDs explains that the spreadsheet solution needs to be easy to use, as the shop is staffed by both permanent and temporary staff members.

Example data is provided here to help you with this activity.

a. DVD stock worksheet

Headings	Range of values	Examples	Validation
DVD code	DVD+number	DVD356	Must be unique
DVD name	Open text	Apollo 13	
Rating	Standard set	PG, General, 12A	Limited set of values
Genre	Type of DVD	Comedy, Sci-Fi, Horror	Limited set of values

b. Membership worksheet

Heading	Range of values	Examples	Validation
Membership ref	'M'+number	M56	Must be unique
Membership name	Open text	Jane Jackson	
Member address	Open text	13 The Drive, Whitsable	
Member postcode	Open text	WH6 7YH	
Member phone	Open text	01457 986677	
Member category	Student, Adult, OAP	S, A, OAP	Must be one of the three values

c. Transaction worksheet

Heading	Range of values	Examples	Comments
DVD code	Any valid DVD code	DVD196	A Lookup table would be useful to show DVDname for confirmation purposes
Date taken out	Date DVD taken out	03/06/2013	
Membership ref	Any valid reference	M310	
Number of days	Number	10	
Return date	Calculated	113/06/2013	
Cost	Calculated	£4.00	
Paid	Yes/No	Yes	

continued

CONTINUED ▶▶

Task

- Come up with a range of design ideas for each of the three worksheets. Discuss and compare them against the manager's requirements, and select the best options.
- Describe the purpose of each worksheet and explain how it will help the staff.
- Create a document for your manager that explains how you plan to create the three worksheets. Include a clear outline of the different stages and components of the design.
- Identify any problems or issues you foresee at this stage.
- Choose a design for each worksheet.
- Review your chosen designs and explain why you selected them and why they are suitable for your needs.
- You could include information about how the worksheets will help the business to run more efficiently.

Tip

Provide as much useful detail as possible about each of your worksheets and their structure. You can include drawings or screenshots to help explain how you want to structure them.

Cell manipulation and formatting

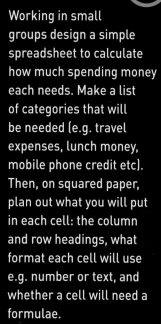

Introduction

To develop a spreadsheet solution to meet the purpose and user requirements of your client, you will need to use a range of spreadsheet software tools and techniques. In this and the following sections, we will look at the tools and techniques you may wish to use. In this section, we will focus on cell manipulation and formatting.

Cell manipulation

There are a number of techniques you can use to change how data will appear in a cell; ways in which you can manipulate cells.

Basic formatting

Here is some information that you need to understand about the basics of cell and worksheet formatting.

- Each cell within a worksheet is uniquely referenced by its column and row number. A1 is the first cell in the top left of the worksheet and the cell next to it across is B1. The cell under A1 is A2.
- Numbers can be formatted to display as currency, or with a certain number of decimal places. It is even possible to apply **conditional formatting** so that, for example, a number value is shown in red if it is negative and black if it is positive.
- Text or labels can be row/column headings or just titles or explanatory text.
- Equations range from simple sums such as =A1+B1 to very complex functions. Every equation must start with an equals sign, otherwise the spreadsheet engine might think it is just another piece of text.

Entering and editing data

If you have used any Microsoft® Office® applications before, you should find this process is quite instinctive.

If you want to change the contents of a cell, you can simply type over the existing contents.

If you want to change the contents of a cell, you can simply type over the existing contents. If it is a long piece of text or a complex equation, you can edit it directly. This is done by typing in to the space just above the actual spreadsheet area, which you'll find to the right of the tick, cross and function signs.

Cut or **Copy** and **Paste** work in exactly the same way as other Windows® software and use the same shortcuts:

- Cut is Ctrl+X.
- Copy is Ctrl+C.
- Paste is Ctrl+V.

Key term

Conditional formatting – This allows you to change the appearance of a cell or cells depending on certain conditions or criteria.

Remember

Formatting does not change the number. For example, if the number 1.276 is entered into a cell and formatted to 2 decimal places, it might now show as 1.28 but the number inside is still the same and it is the original number entered that will be used in calculations.

Did you know?

If you press the **Tab** key instead of the **Enter** key, the cursor moves to the next cell.

CONTINUED ▶▶

AutoFill

If you move the cursor over the bottom right-hand corner of a highlighted cell or cells, it changes to a **+** sign. This is called the **Fill handle** and it allows you to fill nearby cells (across or down) by holding the mouse button down and dragging across the cells you want to AutoFill. Here are some examples of how you can use AutoFill.

- If the first cell contains a month of the year, then the other cells will continue in the sequence of months.
- If the first cell contains a day of the week, then the filled cells will continue in the sequence of days.
- If two cells store consecutive values, then using AutoFill will continue the series within the filled cells.
- If the cell holds an equation, then the equation is copied into the filled cells.

Replication

Replication means copying. If a cell contains some text or a number, then replicating it will produce an identical copy of the first cell. However, if the cell contains a normal formula, then the copied cell will contain a similar equation but with the cell references suitably changed.

Table 9.1 Replicating a formula

	A	B	C
1	45.7	23.1	
2	78.9	35.8	
3	12.6	21.8	
4	=SUM(A1:A3)	=SUM(B1:B3)	

In the example shown in Table 9.1, copying or replicating the equation in cell A4 to cell B4 will change the equation slightly so it will add up the values in column B: =SUM(B1:B3).

If an exact copy of equations or parts of equations is required, then the cell references must be 'absolute'.

Link

Refer to section *Formulae and functions 2* for more information about absolute and relative cell referencing.

Activity 9.4

In a blank worksheet, place the following pairs into two cells next to each other, highlight both and then use the autofill to add values to subsequent cells. In each case, make sure you understand the outcome and check with a teacher if it is not clear.

- Monday   Thursday
- Monday   Tuesday
- 4/5/2013   7/5/2013

- 5   6
- 17   23

◣ Cell formatting

To format cells, select the cells you wish to format and choose from the options shown in Figure 9.2.

Figure 9.2 Formatting options

In the example shown in Figure 9.3, cells that contain a value greater than 1000 are formatted.

Colours and shading

Other formatting options available include changing the text and background colour of cells as well as changing the shading of cells.

Microsoft® Excel® provides a number of different ways of achieving the same thing. After first selecting the cell or cells to be changed, you can left click to bring up an editing window. Select the **Format cells** option and you are presented with a series of formatting choices including changing the colours and shading of the cells previously selected.

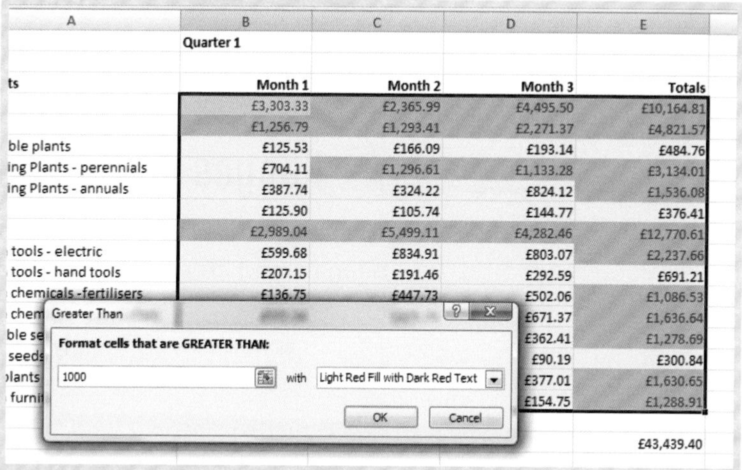

Figure 9.3 Conditional formatting in action

Merging cells

The contents of a number of cells can also be merged. This feature should be used with care and often best avoided as it can cause complications later if the cells are sorted or when the cells are being copied.

Alignment

Your software program will automatically align the data in the cells for you. The default setting for numbers is right aligned and the default setting for text is left aligned. You can change this so that the information displays to the right, centre or to the left of the cell edge. To change the alignment of a cell or group of cells, you first highlight the cell(s) you would like to change. Then go to your toolbar and click on the relevant icon.

Activity 9.5

On an example spreadsheet, highlight different cells (some with text and some with numbers) and experiment with the formatting options.

You can use conditional formatting so that only those cells that meet the condition are formatted, for example, to highlight certain chosen outcomes. You can access this through the Styles section of the format menu – see Figure 9.2.

Just checking ✔

1 You can change the colour of some title text in one of the cells at the top of a worksheet. Note three other formatting techniques that will also draw the attention of the user to the text.

2 If you put 'Day 1' into a cell and then use AutoFill to copy it into adjacent cells what will be placed into the new cells?

3 If you put 1.25 into cell A1 and then format it to one decimal place what will you now see in the cell? If you enter into cell B1 the equation =A1*2 what will you then expect to see in B1? Check out your thoughts on a real spreadsheet.

Ranges and range names

Introduction

In this section you will learn how to use ranges and range names, how you can use various tools to change the layout of worksheets, and about cell protection and macros.

Ranges and range names

You can name a cell or block of cells (a range). This can clarify equations. Cell B5 has been named 'tree_sales' and B6 named as 'Shrub_sales'.

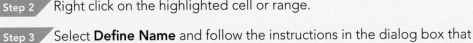

B7	▼	f_x	=tree_sales+Shrubs_sales
	A	B	C
3			
4		**Sales**	
5	Trees	£3,303.33	
6	Shrubs	£1,256.79	
7		£4,560.12	
8			
9			

Figure 9.4 Named cells

How to name a cell or range

Step 1 Highlight the cell or range.

Step 2 Right click on the highlighted cell or range.

Step 3 Select **Define Name** and follow the instructions in the dialog box that is displayed.

Without using names, ranges can be written using a colon to separate the first and last cell. For example, 'H6:H17' means all of the cells from H6 to H17 inclusively.

Worksheets

You can use the following tools to help lay out your worksheet and enhance individual cells.

Page layout and page breaks

To view how a spreadsheet will be printed, use **Print Preview** in the main menu. This also causes dotted lines to appear on the spreadsheet which help you check which portions will be printed on each page. If the natural page breaks are not appropriate, you can either change the column and row heights or insert page breaks, as shown in Figure 9.5.

Before pressing **Page Break**, select the cell in column A just below the row you wish to break at. If the cursor is not in column A, then you will insert both a horizontal and vertical page break, as shown in Figure 9.6.

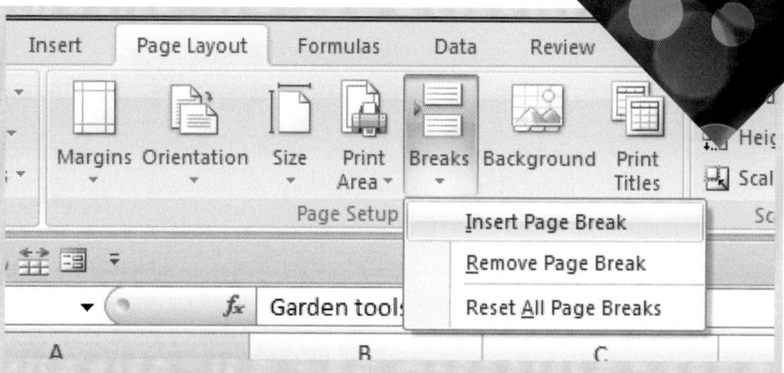

Figure 9.5 Page break options

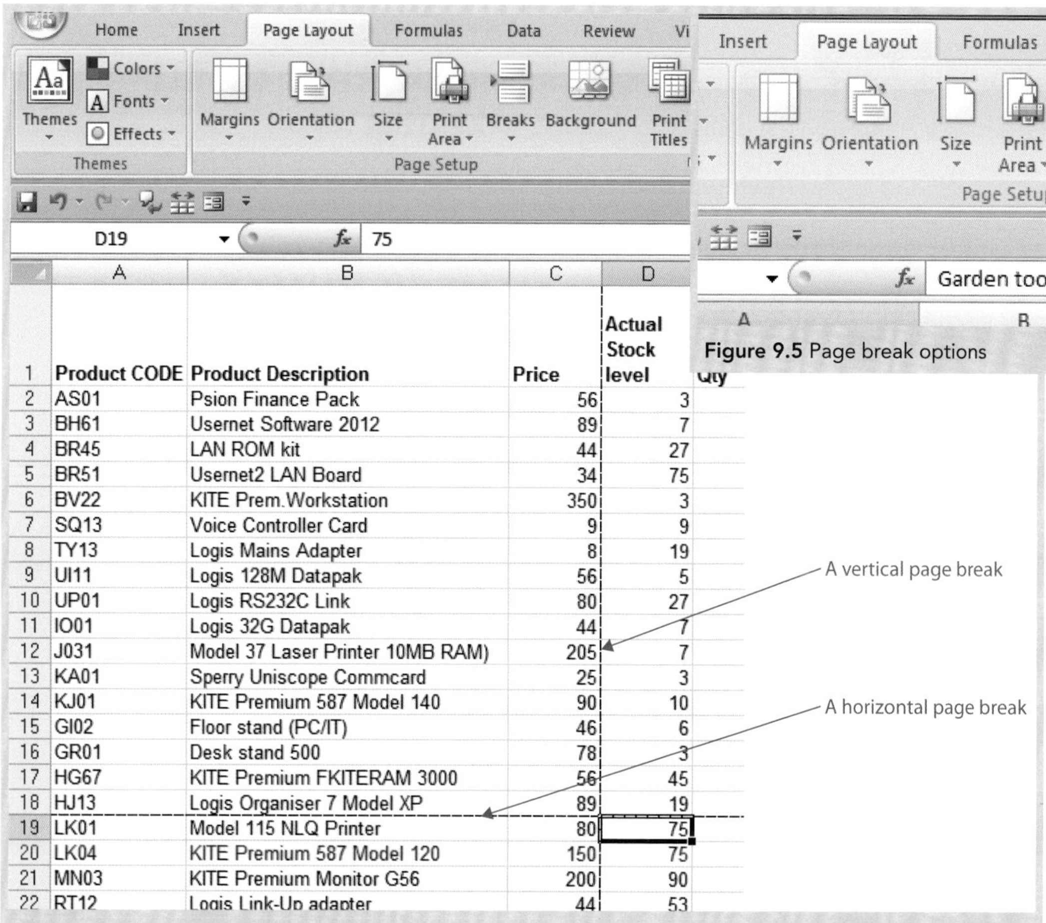

Figure 9.6 Inserting horizontal and vertical page breaks

Headers and footers

You can use the **Insert** menu to add headers and footers. The screen switches to a page layout view, so that you can see how the pages will be printed, and a header box opens to allow you to type in text. You can add other details such as the file name, date or page number.

Inserting hyperlinks

You can insert hyperlinks into cells. They can link to a web page or to somewhere in the spreadsheet. For example, you could provide a front 'Menu' worksheet that uses links to allow the user to jump directly to the various parts of the spreadsheet.

You will find the hyperlink feature in the **Links** section of the **Insert** menu.

▶ Cell protection

You can stop people changing the contents of individual cells or ranges of cells by applying protection to them. If you select **Protect Sheet** in the **Review** menu, then all of the cells are locked against change. In order to select cells or ranges that can be changed (the worksheet must be unprotected to start), highlight the appropriate cells then go to the **Format** menu, select **Protection** and then deselect the locked check box.

CONTINUED ▶▶

How to lock cells

To lock all cells against change:

Step 1 Go to the **Review** menu.

Step 2 Select **Protect Sheet**.

To select cells or ranges that you want users to be able to change, first make sure the worksheet is unprotected:

Step 1 Highlight the cells you want to unlock.

Step 2 Go to the **Home** tab and click on the **Format** menu. Select **Format Cells** and click on the **Protection** tab in the box that appears.

Step 3 Deselect the locked check box, as shown in Figure 9.8.

Step 4 Go to the **Review** menu and select **Protect Sheet**.

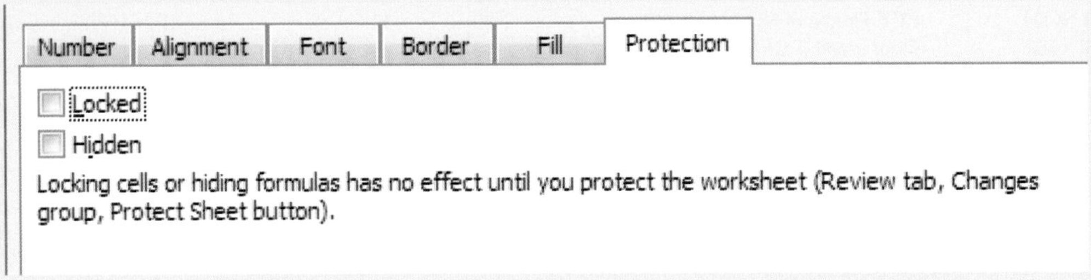

Number	Alignment	Font	Border	Fill	Protection

☐ Locked
☐ Hidden

Locking cells or hiding formulas has no effect until you protect the worksheet (Review tab, Changes group, Protect Sheet button).

Figure 9.7 Unlocking highlighted cells

Macros

A macro stores a series of actions. You can start recording a macro by going to the **View** menu and selecting the **Macros** drop-down option. You can assign the macro to a shortcut key and give it a name. When you stop recording, the actions are stored. When you later activate the macro by using the shortcut key, the actions stored will take place. Macros can be useful if you need to repeat a series of actions in the same order many times. Macros do, however, need careful testing.

Just checking

1 Give two specific examples of why you might want to protect every cell in a worksheet.

2 Note one advantage of naming cells and ranges.

3 Apart from allowing users to jump directly to another cell in the same spreadsheet, where else can a hyperlink take the user?

WorkSpace

► Caryl Stokes

Sales manager

I run a team comprising eight sales people. We sell windows to the trade and we operate throughout the UK and Ireland. Each member of the sales team covers a specific region and manages a client list within that area. It's my job to oversee everything and to ensure that the team is performing, clients are happy and that the company is making a profit.

Spreadsheets are integral to keeping track of everything. Each team member has their own spreadsheet which they use to record their daily progress. The spreadsheet contains information on each client (contact name/number, address, purchase history) and a record of communication (dates and details of the conversations). For each sale, the sales person will also record the following types of information: quantity of windows, style of windows, price of each item and any discount offered. I can then use this information to work out each sales person's commission per sale. I can also analyse this information to determine what style of windows is proving popular and which are not so popular. It's interesting, as this varies on a regional basis. What's popular in one part of the country is not always popular elsewhere.

It's very easy to spot trends and patterns as I can compare sales figures on a monthly basis from an individual sales person or across the wider sales team. This has helped enormously to anticipate when we might have quiet months or peak times. This helps us to manage our stock and ensure that we can negotiate on the best price for our clients.

There are lots of benefits to using spreadsheets to store this type of information. I can filter and sort information easily, and it can be converted to charts, tables or graphs. It is also an easy way to track and analyse sales by region, person, window type or sales per client.

In my role as sales manager, I have to report to the company's director and explain our sales performance. Using the data contained within the spreadsheets I'm able to create graphs and charts which present the information in a much more visual way. The company director then uses this to help plan the company's strategy over the coming months and year.

Think about it

1 Why would Caryl need to be able to sort the information captured within the sales team's spreadsheets?

2 What categories/fields do you think the sales team's spreadsheets need to include?

3 Are there any tools or techniques which Caryl could use to help make sorting and filtering the information more efficient and effective?

Formulae and functions 1

Introduction

You can use formulae and functions in order to do calculations in a spreadsheet.

Formulae

Formulae always begin with an equals sign (=). Once you have typed the equals sign, the spreadsheet will treat whatever is entered next as a formula rather than a piece of text.

For example, you might define cell F6 with the formula: **=A6+B6**

This means take the value in A6, add it to the value in B6 and store the answer in cell F6. The + (add) sign is an example of an operator. Other simple operators, that are used in a similar way are / (divide), * (multiply), - (subtract).

Functions

A function is a pre-set formula. Functions also begin with the equals sign, but are then followed by the function name and its arguments. Arguments are the part of a function enclosed in brackets. The arguments come after the function name to supply data to the function. Arguments are most likely to be cell references.

For example, the most commonly used function is SUM, which is used to add together numbers stored in cells. You might define cell H6 as: **=SUM(A6:G6)**

This means add up the numbers in cells A6 to G6 and store the result in H6. The sum function is very useful for adding up long columns or rows of numbers.

Logical functions

Sometimes you might want your spreadsheet to be able to check on the value of a cell and give different outcomes depending on the values given. Perhaps you need to know whether the cell contains a positive or negative number. To do this you will need to use an IF statement.

IF

The rule for the structure of an IF statement is: **=IF(criterion,TRUE,FALSE)**

For example, you might enter into D4: **=IF(C4<0,"Negative","Positive")**

If the value in C4 is less than zero, 'Negative' will be shown in D4, otherwise 'Positive' will be displayed.

One extension of the simple IF statement is the COUNTIF(range,criterion) function. This will count the number of cells in the range given that meet the criteria given.

In Figure 9.9, the COUNTIF function is used to determine how many of the learners' final marks are above the pass mark, which is a mark greater than 70.

Other logical operators include AND, OR and NOT. Read the following examples. Test them out and adapt them on a spreadsheet to make sure you know how they work.

	C17	▼	f_x
	A	B	C
1			
2	**Class test results**		
3			
4	Peter	Jones	45
5	Mary	Peters	56
6	Keith	Urquart	34
7	Hamid	Burrell	78
8	Lewis	Hall	79
9	George	Liverson	90
10	Lenny	Davids	70
11	Helen	Alavi	75
12	Allen	Kaye	71
13	Bessie	Severson	58
14	Dai	Morris	91
15	Vera	Williams	56
16			
17		**Number passed**	6
18			

Figure 9.8 Using the COUNTIF function

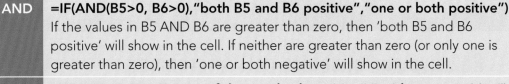

AND	=IF(AND(B5>0, B6>0),"both B5 and B6 positive","one or both positive")
	If the values in B5 AND B6 are greater than zero, then 'both B5 and B6 positive' will show in the cell. If neither are greater than zero (or only one is greater than zero), then 'one or both negative' will show in the cell.
OR	IF(OR(B5>0, B6>0),"one of them or both positive","neither are positive")
	If one of the values in B5 OR B6 is greater than zero, then 'one of them or both positive' will show in the cell (you'll also get this result if both of them are greater than zero). If neither are greater than zero, then 'neither are positive' will show in the cell.
NOT	=IF(NOT(B5>0),"B5 less than or equal to zero","B5 greater than zero")
	If the value in B5 is NOT greater than zero (i.e. zero or negative), then the message 'B5 is less than or equal to zero' will show in the cell. If the value in B5 is greater than zero, then you will see the message 'B5 greater than zero'.

Activity 9.6

Create a similar worksheet to the one shown in Figure 9.9 and test out the COUNTIF function. Change the formula to make the pass mark 70 or over (rather than greater than 70).

Nested IF

IF functions can be nested. This can be demonstrated using an IF function that identifies the tax rate that people pay based on their income.

First IF equation. Enter an income value in cell F8, then in another cell put the IF equation **=IF(F8>37400,40,20)** will result in either 40 or 20 being displayed according to whether the value in F8 is greater than 37,400 (after allowances). This means that everyone who earns more than £37,400 will be given a tax rate of 40%. Everyone how earns less than £37,400 will be given a tax rate of 20%.

Second IF equation. If a person earns over £150,000 they pay a tax rate of 50%. You can create another IF equation for this and nest it within the first IF equation:

=IF(A5<37400,20,IF(A5>150000,50,40))

This means that if a person's salary is less than £37,400 they pay 20% tax, if their salary is over £37,400 they pay 40% tax, unless their income is over £150,000 in which case they pay 50%.

Remember

Other functions that you are likely to use include:

• AVERAGE – Finds the mean (average) value of a set of values.

• MIN – Returns the smallest number in a set of values. Ignores logical values and text.

• MAX – Returns the largest number in a set of values. Ignores logical values and text.

• COUNT – Counts the number of cells in a range that contains numbers.

• LOOKUP – Looks up a value either from a one-row or one-column range.

• INDEX – Returns a value or reference of the cell at the intersection of a particular row or column, in a given range.

Take it further

Test out the nested IF function example on a new worksheet (the tax rates are valid at February 2012). Extend the worksheet to allow a user to enter their salary after allowances and for the worksheet to calculate and display the tax they should pay and the income left after tax.

Just checking

What formula or function would you need to use to:

a add together the numbers stored in cells A1 and A2?

b add together the numbers stored in cells A1 to A99?

c multiply the numbers stored in D4 and D5?

d divide the numbers stored in E4 and E6?

e add together the numbers in A3 and B3 and then divide the result by the number in C6?

f check whether the number in B5 is greater than 10?

Formulae and functions 2

Relative and absolute cell referencing

Relative cell referencing

In the worksheet shown in Figure 9.9, the next step is to add formulae to cells E4, E5, E6, etc. to calculate the totals for Months 4 – 6.

	A	B	C	D	E	F
	Sales	Quarter 2				
1	Sales	Quarter 2				
2						
3	Products	Month 4	Month 5	Month 6	Totals	
4	Trees	£1,531.61	£2,287.89	£4,711.32		
5	Shrubs	£1,500.50	£1,056.85	£1,530.10		
6	Vegetable plants	£94.89	£139.52	£122.92		
7	Flowering Plants - perennials	£340.41	£1,338.76	£1,260.61		
8	Flowering Plants - annuals	£207.30	£69.03	£662.26		
9	Bulbs	£37.75	£52.39	£49.40		
10	Café	£1,473.32	£1,126.68	£1,648.96		
11	Garden tools - electric	£577.06	£493.89	£606.63		
12	Garden tools - hand tools	£234.23	£223.15	£127.30		
13	Garden chemicals -fertilisers	£69.89	£403.21	£484.40		
14	Garden chemicals - weedkillers	£619.85	£369.90	£660.90		
15	Vegetable seeds	£301.01	£629.52	£77.10		
16	Flower seeds	£55.72	£92.23	£49.62		
17	houseplants	£163.13	£649.11	£265.54		
18	Garden furniture	£780.54	£252.61	£56.93		
19						
20					£0.00	

Figure 9.9 Garden centre worksheet ready for total formulae to be added

E6 — f_x =SUM(B6:D6)

	A	B	C	D	E	F
1	Sales	Quarter 2				
2						
3	Products	Month 4	Month 5	Month 6	Totals	
4	Trees	£1,531.61	£2,287.89	£4,711.32	£8,530.81	
5	Shrubs	£1,500.50	£1,056.85	£1,530.10	£4,087.45	
6	Vegetable plants	£94.89	£139.52	£122.92	£357.33	
7	Flowering Plants - perennials	£340.41	£1,338.76	£1,260.61	£2,939.78	

Figure 9.10 Copied formula

E5 — f_x =D5*E2/100

	A	B	C	D	E	F	G
1							
2				VAT Rate %	15		
3							
4	CODE	Description	Cost Price	Selling Price	VAT	Selling Price + VAT	
5	DF61	3.5 mm stereo jack lead	£4.90	£7.00	£1.05	£8.05	
6	SD02	Access 2010 software	£62.30	£89.00			
7	DS12	Apple earphones	£23.80	£34.00			
8	AS01	Apple iPOD case F1 Black	£10.50	£15.00			
9	UI11	Apple iPOD case F2 Green	£10.50	£15.00			

Figure 9.11 Calculating VAT to be paid on a selling price.

The formula in E4 could be **=B4+C4+D4**, but a better solution would be to use the summing function **=SUM(B4:D4)**. Once you have entered this formula and checked it is correct, you can copy it down the column using AutoFill.

As the formula is copied into the other cells, it adapts to the row number in each case. Figure 9.10 shows that the equation in E6 is now giving the total of the figures in row 6, which is exactly what is needed. When formulae are created in this way, they use **relative cell referencing**.

Absolute cell references

Sometimes you want to fix a cell reference in an equation so that it never changes as it is copied. This is called **absolute cell referencing**.

To turn a cell reference in an equation to an absolute cell reference, you use the $ sign. For example, in the equation **=G6*$B$3**, the cell reference B3 will always be the same no matter how often the equation is copied to other cells.

An example is shown in Figure 9.11. The first formula has already been entered into the cell in the normal way.

If the formula in E5 is now copied to cells below it, an error occurs – as shown in Figure 9.12.

You must replace the equation in E5 with one that uses an absolute address for E2 – as shown in Figure 9.13.

Activity 9.7

Create a similar worksheet to the one shown in Figures 9.9–9.11 and test out the use of absolute cell referencing. Add a few more rows and extend the worksheet to calculate the Profit (Selling Price – Cost Price). Check the answers using a calculator or pen and paper.

Lookup tables

Imagine you have been asked to add a series of standard postage and packing costs to the developing worksheet. A lookup table is ideal because:

- there will be a limited set of codes allocated
- it will be easy to make changes to the postage and packaging for all items.

Two functions for lookup tables are available: VLOOKUP and HLOOKUP. In most cases you will need VLOOKUP (V stands for vertical and is used when the values in the reference table are in columns). The operation of the VLOOKUP function is shown in the example in Figure 9.15.

The VLOOKUP function in H5 causes the software to look up the value in C5 and return the appropriate value in the second column of the lookup table, which is £2.50.

Figure 9.12 Incorrectly copied formula.

Figure 9.13 Correct formula entered into E5 and copied to other cells.

Figure 9.14 The VLOOKUP function

CONTINUED ▸▸

289

The VLOOKUP function takes three arguments:

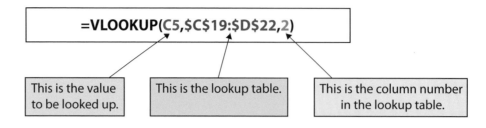

=VLOOKUP(C5,$C$19:$D$22,2)

| This is the value to be looked up. | This is the lookup table. | This is the column number in the lookup table. |

Activity 9.8

Explain the advantages of using a lookup table rather than entering each postage value directly.

Explain the reason why the lookup table needs absolute references.

Create a new spreadsheet using the data provided in Figure 9.14.

Add the packaging code to the worksheet and the lookup table and test that you can use VLOOKUP correctly.

Add a further packaging code (4) for heavy items that cost £7.25 to post and change the equations to include it. Test it out by changing one of the items to packaging code 4.

Take it further

Check out the operation of the HLOOKUP function and duplicate the outcome of the VLOOKUP using the HLOOKUP function instead. This will involve changing the layout of the lookup table itself.

	C4	▾	f_x	=B4*$C$1/100	
	A	B	C	D	
1		Donation rate %	4		
2					
3	Year	Lump sum	Charity donation		
4	2012	£20,000.00	£800.00		
5	2013	£19,200.00	£768.00		
6	2014	£18,432.00	£737.28		
7	2015	£17,694.72	£707.79		
8	2016	£16,986.93	£679.48		
9	2017	£16,307.45	£652.30		
10	2018	£15,655.16	£626.21		
11	2019	£15,028.95	£601.16		
12	2020	£14,427.79	£577.11		
13	2021	£13,850.68	£554.03		
14	2022	£13,296.65	£531.87		
15					
16			£7,235.21		

Figure 9.15 Calculating a charity donation

Figure 9.16 Setting up the goal seek

Goal seek

The goal seek function is an example of the analysis tools. It allows a user to see quickly what value an input value needs to be in order to achieve a particular output value.

An example is shown in Figure 9.15. In this example, a person has decided to give a certain percentage of a lump sum to charity every year for the next 10 years. At the moment the person has chosen to give away 4% each year so the amount they donate will reduce each year as the lump sum reduces. Currently at the end of 10 years the person will have £13,296.65 remaining.

The equation in B5 is =B4-C4. This gives a new value for the lump sum for 2013 (which has been reduced by the £800 amount given to charity in 2012). The equations below are replicated from B5 and C4. Note the need for C1 to be an absolute reference.

However, the person donating wishes to give away exactly £8000 in total and can use the goal seek to find out exactly what donation rate is needed.

Select **Goal Seek** from the **What-If Analysis** menu in the **Data Tools** section of the **Data** tab. The dialog window shown in Figure 9.16 is displayed. This allows the user to choose a cell to set to a certain value by changing another cell. In this case, we want to set the total donation value to £8000 by varying the donation rate.

After selecting **OK**, the system will display a further dialog window which should confirm that the goal has been found and what rate is required. If you choose not to accept the proposal, select **Cancel**, otherwise select **OK** and the spreadsheet changes accordingly – as shown in Fig 19.17.

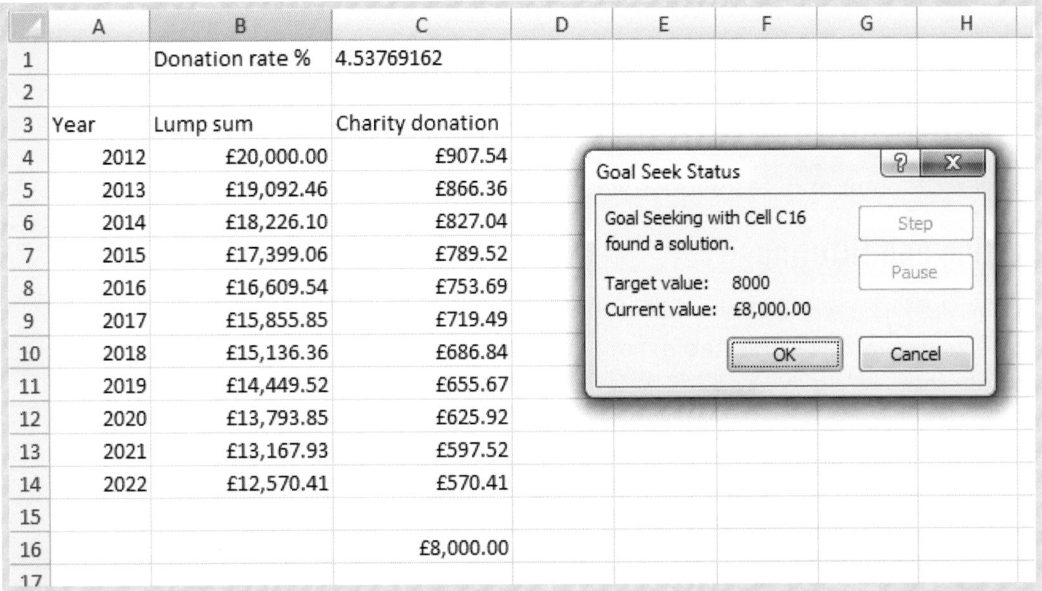

	A	B	C	D	E	F	G	H
1		Donation rate %	4.53769162					
2								
3	Year	Lump sum	Charity donation					
4	2012	£20,000.00	£907.54					
5	2013	£19,092.46	£866.36					
6	2014	£18,226.10	£827.04					
7	2015	£17,399.06	£789.52					
8	2016	£16,609.54	£753.69					
9	2017	£15,855.85	£719.49					
10	2018	£15,136.36	£686.84					
11	2019	£14,449.52	£655.67					
12	2020	£13,793.85	£625.92					
13	2021	£13,167.93	£597.52					
14	2022	£12,570.41	£570.41					
15								
16			£8,000.00					
17								

Goal Seek Status

Goal Seeking with Cell C16 found a solution.

Target value: 8000
Current value: £8,000.00

Step | Pause

OK | Cancel

Figure 9.17 Successful Goal Seek

In this situation, goal seek has found that the person needs to pick a donation rate of just over 4.53% each year in order to give £8000 to charity over the 10-year period.

Just checking

1 How can you tell if a cell reference in an equation is absolute or relative?

2 Explain with an example the use of the OR operator.

3 Explain with an example of the use of the AND operator.

Data manipulation

Introduction

There are various ways in which you can use a spreadsheet to help you change or manipulate a set of data.

Data manipulation

There are a number of techniques you can use to manipulate data.

Sorting and filtering

Tables such as the one shown in Figure 9.19 are also referred to as lists. In many respects they act as single-table, flat file databases and the rows in them can be sorted and filtered.

You can access sorting via **Sort & Filter** within the **Home** menu.

How to sort on a column

Step 1 Highlight any cell in the column.

Step 2 Select **Sort & Filter** and choose either **A-Z** (to sort from the smallest to largest) or **Z-A** (to sort from the largest to smallest) as required. (You can also get to these options within the **Data** menu.)

How to filter a list

Step 1 Make sure that the selected or active cell is somewhere within the list and then select **Filter** from the dialog box (Figure 9.19).

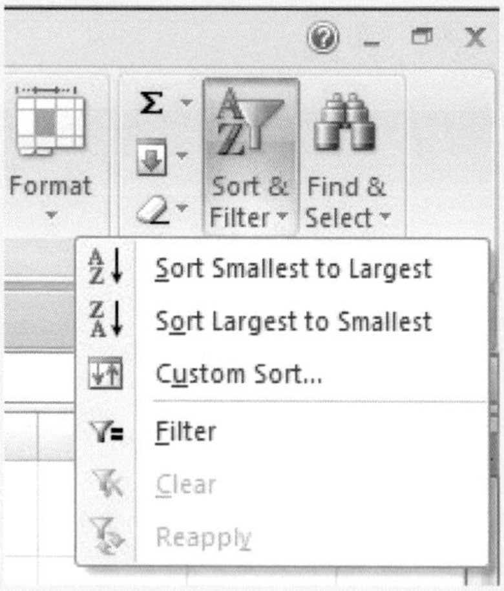

Figure 9.18 Sorting and filtering

Filters should appear at the side of each heading, as shown in Figure 9.19.

	A	B	C	D	E	F	G
1	Product CODE	Product Description	Cost Price	Selling Price	Stock leve	Supplier code	
2	AS01	Apple iPOD case F	£10.50	£15.00	3	S1	

Figure 9.19 Filters

To perform a filter:

Step 1 Choose the heading.

Step 2 Click on the filter and select from the list.

In the example shown in Figure 9.20, a filter is being applied that will only show rows where the Supplier code is S2.

The values shown will depend on the contents of each column.

The result of the filter having been applied is shown in Figure 9.21.

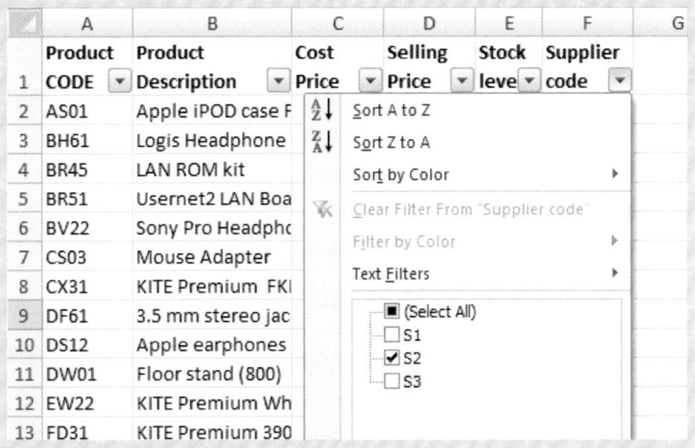

Figure 9.20 Filtering the list to show Supplier code = S2

Figure 9.21 List with Supplier code = S2 filter applied

Pivot tables

A pivot table is a tool that can sort, count, total or give the average of the data stored in a table. It always displays the results in a second table (called a pivot table).

An example use for a pivot table using the worksheet shown in Figure 9.21 could be to find out how much stock in total is being held for each of the three suppliers. The selected cell (or active cell) must be somewhere within the list first – select **PivotTable** from the **Insert** menu and choose the Supplier code and Stock level, as shown in Figure 9.22. This automatically generates the pivot table output, as shown in Figure 9.22, which displays each supplier and their stock level.

Although you can use normal spreadsheet equations to generate this output, pivot tables allow you to change the fields and calculations used quickly and easily, so you can explore the information and the relationships in the spreadsheet more readily.

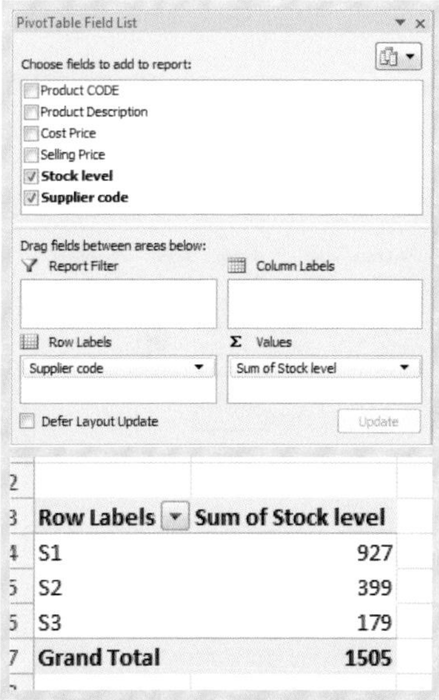

Row Labels ▼	Sum of Stock level
S1	927
S2	399
S3	179
Grand Total	**1505**

Figure 9.22 Pivot table design

▶ Data entry validation and data entry forms

As with all IT systems, the information being used must be reliable. In most cases, this means putting effective validation controls on the data as it is being entered into the system, so that a user cannot enter something incorrectly.

There are a number of different validation controls that work with different types of data. In the example in Figure 9.20, the Supplier codes are limited so a drop-down list is one way of ensuring that only acceptable values are input. In preparation for a drop-down list, you need to create a small table with these three codes in it – see Figure 9.22.

Highlight the cell that needs an input control, then select **Data Validation** from the **Data** menu (Figure 9.23) to display the dialog box shown in Figure 9.24.

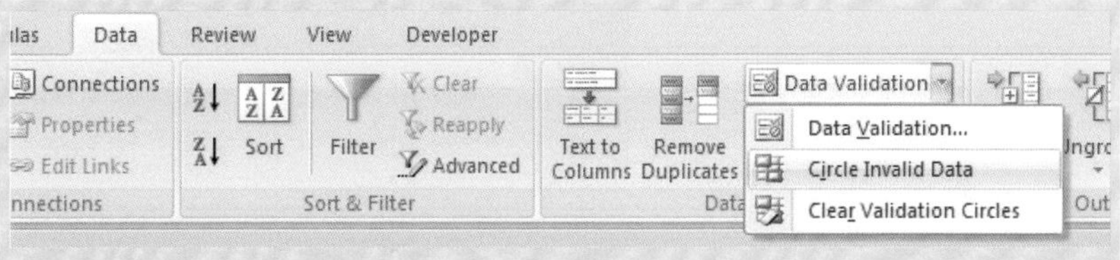

Figure 9.23 Selecting Data Validation

CONTINUED ▶▶

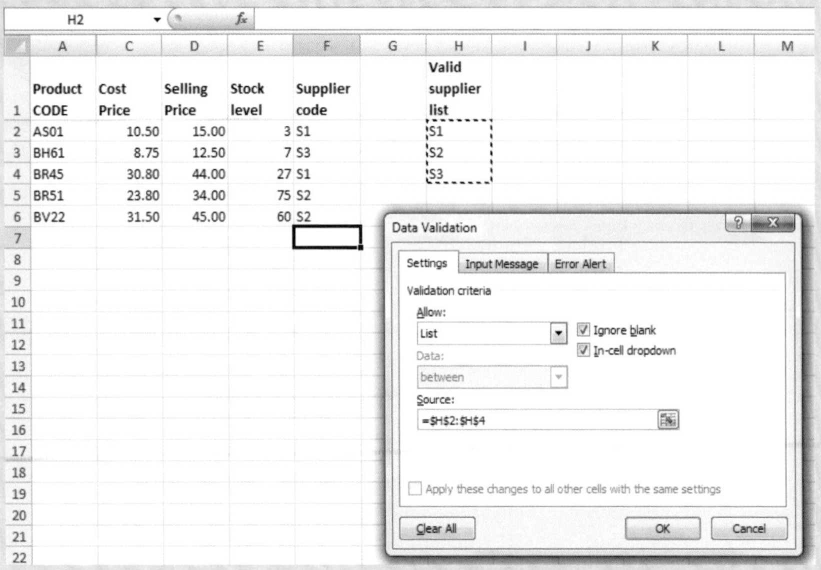

Figure 9.24 Using an existing table to provide a valid list of entries

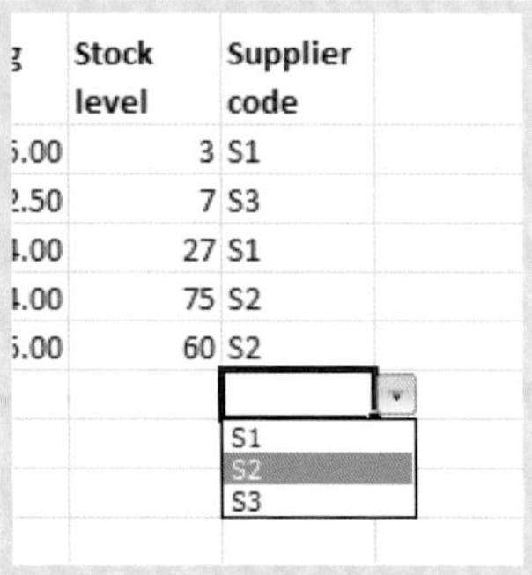

Figure 9.25 Input data validation using a list

Select **List** and enter the range in **Source**. Cell F7 will only be able to accept values of S1, S2 or S3. You can then copy F7 down the rest of column F. Figure 9.25 shows the resulting drop-down list. Users can select the supplier code they want from this list.

You can add similar controls to other cells using the same data validation dialog box. In the example shown in Figure 9.26, a control is being placed on the selling price. Only values that are at least 1.10 times than the value in C7 are acceptable.

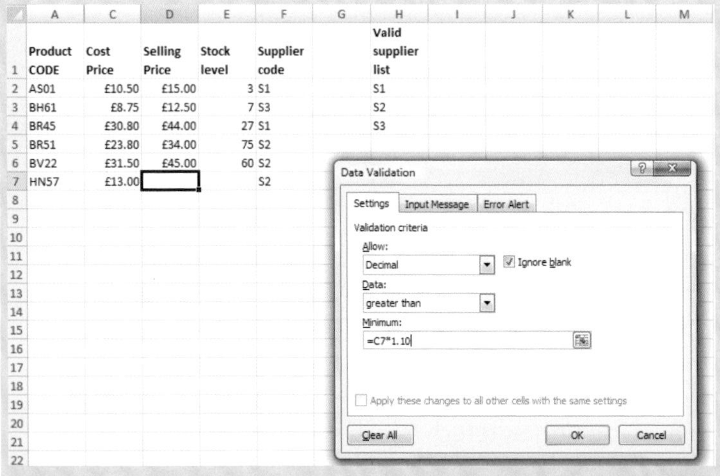

Figure 9.26 Validating the numeric input to D7 as being at least 10% more than C7

Activity 9.9

Create or adapt the worksheet shown in Figure 9.24 and test out the data validation controls.

Explain the effect of the validation that you have placed in D7.

Add a data validation control into E7 so that no negative stock levels or stock levels greater than 1000 can be entered.

You will notice when an invalid value is entered because a standard error message is displayed. Use the **Input Message** tab in the **Data Validation** box (see Figure 9.26) to give more meaningful messages, then test them.

Just checking

A manager of a second hand car garage finds that when staff enter details of the cars, they sometimes misspell the makes of the cars.

1 Explain what problems this can cause.

2 Describe an appropriate validation technique that could solve the problem.

Charts and graphs

Introduction

In many situations, displaying the contents of spreadsheets graphically in a chart or graph helps readers to understand the data more easily. There are a number of different types to choose from.

Types of charts and graphs

Bar graphs

A bar or column graph is a very common type of graph used to display numeric data. The amounts are displayed using vertical bars. The taller the bar, the greater the value. Bar graphs make it easy to see differences in the data being compared. One example would be to plot monthly temperatures.

Pie charts

Pie charts are good for showing the relative sizes of values that are part of a whole. The complete pie represents 100%, or the whole, and the segments represent the proportions of the whole. For example, a pie chart of monthly profits makes it very easy to see when the most and least profits were made and how they contributed to the whole.

Line graphs

Line graphs are often used to display continuous changes to a **variable** over time. Normally the time data is distributed evenly along the bottom x-axis and the other variable is plotted up the y-axis. Line graphs can be used to plot data recorded from experiments, such as the resistance measured in a wire when the electric current is gradually increased.

The individual data points are connected by lines. You can use this type of graph to predict future results.

Scatter plot graphs

Scatter plot graphs are used to find or show trends in data. They are especially useful when you have many pairs of data values. Like line graphs, they can be used to plot changes to a variable over time. Scatter graphs often use 'best fit' lines to try to identify the relationship between the two variables. The closer the actual points are to the best fit line, the more reliable the relationship. An example of a scatter graph might be the number of ice creams sold against temperature.

Creating a bar chart

Figure 9.27 shows a worksheet used to record average temperature and rainfull data over a year. It would be useful to show in a chart the changes in the average maximum and minimum temperature over the year.

Key term

Variable – A variable in maths is a changing quantity as opposed to a constant. For example, in this algebraic expression x and y are variables and 4 is a constant: $y = 4x$.

Take it further

Find some examples of charts and graphs used in newspapers. Explain for each one why you think that they have chosen that particular chart or graph type.

CONTINUED ▶▶

First you need to identify the data to be included in the graph. In this case, highlight (click, hold and drag) over the range A1:B13. Then select **Column** from the **Insert** menu and select the first **2-D Column**, as shown in Figure 9.28.

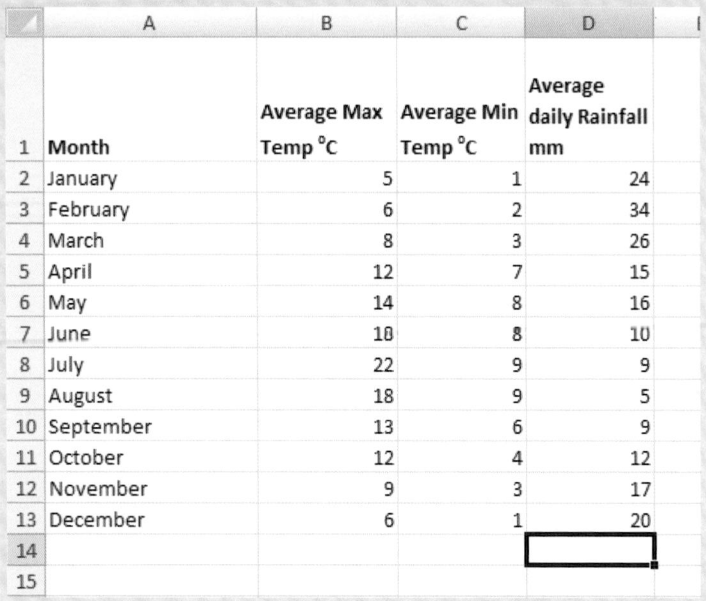

	A	B	C	D
1	Month	Average Max Temp °C	Average Min Temp °C	Average daily Rainfall mm
2	January	5	1	24
3	February	6	2	34
4	March	8	3	26
5	April	12	7	15
6	May	14	8	16
7	June	18	8	10
8	July	22	9	9
9	August	18	9	5
10	September	13	6	9
11	October	12	4	12
12	November	9	3	17
13	December	6	1	20
14				
15				

Figure 9.27 Temperature and rainfall daily averages table

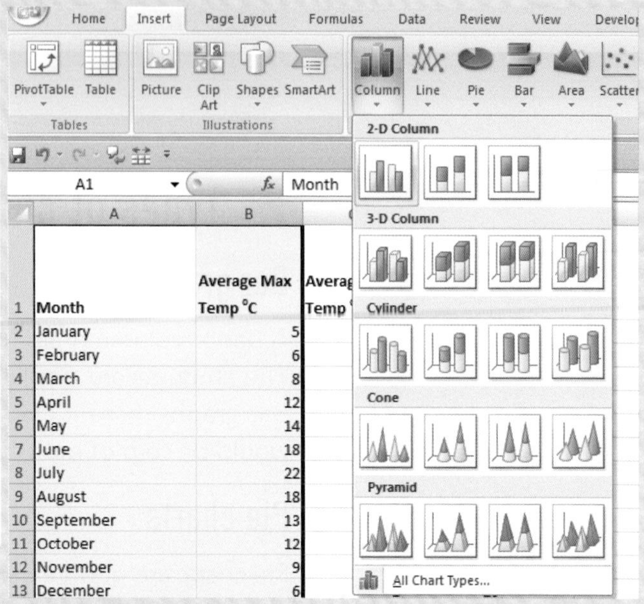

Figure 9.28 Selection of data and choice of chart type

A chart is then automatically created, as shown in Figure 9.29.

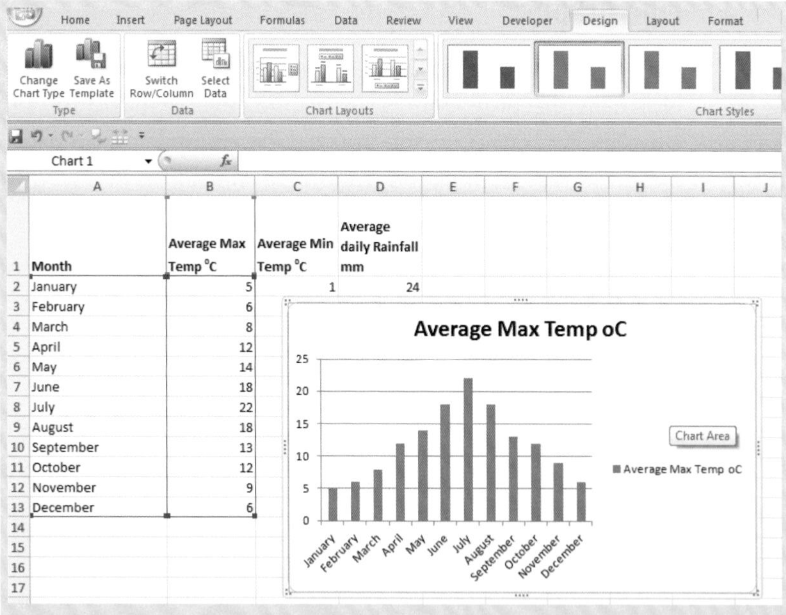

Figure 9.29 Column chart

Just checking

1 What is the best type of graph that will show how the sales of ice cream change according to the temperature.

2 What type of graph is used to show the relative sizes of values that make up a whole thing, for example the different costs involved in a holiday.

Formatting charts and graphs

Introduction

This section explain how to format charts and graphs.

Take it further

Right click on the temperature axis in the Average Max Temp graph, as shown in Figure 9.31, and select **Format Axis**. Use the options available to change the minimum to 5 instead of 0.

Describe the impact of making this change.

Formatting a bar chart

Once you have created a chart, you can format it as required. To change the characteristics of the whole chart, double click the chart to bring up a new chart toolbar. Alternatively, select the chart and right click on it to display the menu shown at the right of Figure 9.30.

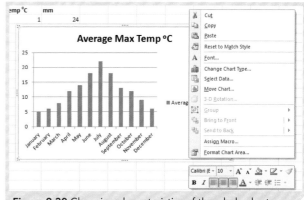

Figure 9.30 Changing characteristics of the whole chart

If you need to, you can change the type of chart to a 3-D column chart for example, or you can move them into a separate worksheet tab in the spreadsheet. If you click on particular areas of the chart, appropriate options are displayed. For example, if you select the y-axis area and then right click, another dialog box will open with options that relate to the axis. This is shown is Figure 9.31.

You can change the minimum and maximum axis values as well as changing colours, fills, etc.

Other charts and graphs can be generated in similar ways.

Figure 9.31 Axis formatting options

Activity   9.10

Create a 3-D column chart of the monthly rainfall.

Hint: to select data that is not next to each other, select (by clicking, holding and dragging) the first range and, then hold down the **Ctrl** key and select the second range.

Create a chart that displays both the average maximum and average minimum temperature on the same axis. Experiment with the different formatting options.

Creating and manipulating a line graph

The data in the worksheet shown in Figure 9.32 shows how the value of a new car bought in 2012 is expected to depreciate (reduce in value) over an eight year period.

This information is appropriate for a line graph, as the value depreciates continuously over time. Although the table of numbers does show the trend, it is not easy to see how the rate of depreciation changes as the years go by.

This time, to avoid the graph being created automatically, do not select the table first. Instead leave the cursor outside the table and then choose to insert a line graph from the **Insert** menu. This is shown in Figure 9.33.

	A	B	C	D	E
1					
2	Car Depreciation - Values over an 8 year period from new				
3					
4	**Year**	**Value**			
5	2012	21000	<--- price new		
6	2013	15800			
7	2014	13900			
8	2015	12200			
9	2016	10500			
10	2017	8800			
11	2018	7600			
12	2019	6500			
13	2020	5500			
14					

Figure 9.32 Car depreciation values

CONTINUED ▶▶

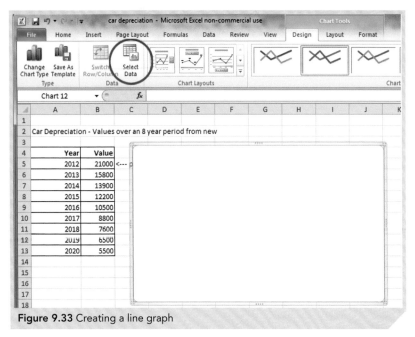

Figure 9.33 Creating a line graph

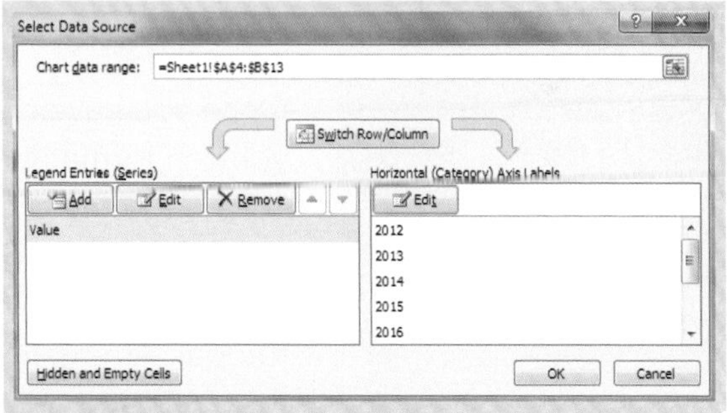

Figure 9.34 Data Source entries

Click on the **Select Data** option, also shown in Figure 9.33, and a **Select Data Source** dialog box is displayed. Choose to add a new legend entry, provide a title and make the series values the changing values. On the right hand side of the **Select Data Source** dialog box, select **Edit** for the Horizontal axis and use the years from 2012 to 2020. The final completed dialog box will be as in Figure 9.34.

Figure 9.35 shows the final graph after adding a title to the x-axis and changing the main title. All these and more options are available in the **Layout** menu, which is also shown in Figure 9.35.

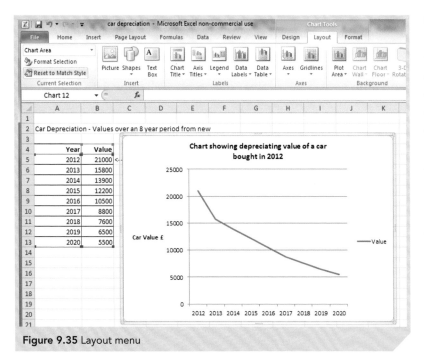

Figure 9.35 Layout menu

Just checking

Choose the best type of chart or graph to represent the following:

a the quarterly sales figures for a company

b the results of a survey asking people of different ages where they went on holiday

c cricket scores for a number of teams.

Test and refine a spreadsheet

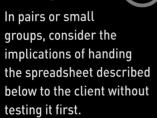

Getting started

In pairs or small groups, consider the implications of handing the spreadsheet described below to the client without testing it first.

The spreadsheet is a simple one designed to be used in the glazing section of a builders supply merchants. When customers come in and ask for the particular size and type of glass needed, the spreadsheet calculates the price.

Assuming that there are errors in the calculations that were not identified and fixed, list the potential consequences and further actions that will need to be taken if the spreadsheet has been in use for six months before the errors are discovered.

Introduction

It is important to test your spreadsheets to make sure they work as expected. When you come to testing and refining your spreadsheet, you need to think about the aspects covered in this section.

You will need to test all the features of the spreadsheet, such as formulae, functions, macros, printing and security features. Testing has to be a well-planned and structured process to make sure that all areas are fully tested. The easiest way to make sure that this is the case is to create a test plan (see Table 9.2).

Table 9.2 Test plan

Test number	Purpose of test	Test data	Expected result	Actual result
1				
2				
3				

At this stage, you can complete all sections except for the column for the actual results. For each test, the plan should describe the purpose of the test. This will help to ensure that a formula is correct and the right answer is produced or that a validation rule rejects incorrect values.

The design of the test data is important. You should choose the test data carefully to ensure that it tests the features thoroughly.

Test data comes in three forms: correct, erroneous (incorrect) and extreme. Correct data should produce the right answers if the spreadsheet has been designed correctly. Erroneous data should be rejected by validation rules. Extreme data will be very large or small values, depending on the rule or calculation being tested.

Activity 9.11

Working individually, create a test plan for a simple spreadsheet using some example test data supplied by your teacher.

Working with a partner, swap spreadsheets and test plans. Has your partner included enough tests to prove that the spreadsheet model works properly? Give your partner some constructive feedback on how they could improve their test plan.

▶ Functionality and usability

Functionality

The formulae and functions must perform accurately and correctly. You may think you only need to check the first formula in a column by hand, because the others have been copied from this one. However, you may not have copied the equation correctly. Some other sample cells need to be checked as well.

Usability

The users must be able to interact with the spreadsheet. They need to understand what they need to do to input data and what outputs can be achieved. Consistency of style is important.

You should have created a test plan during the design phase of your spreadsheet project. It is important to plan how your spreadsheet solution will met the user requirements before you create it. Once the spreadsheet have been created, you then need to test it using your test plan.

CONTINUED ▶▶

Link

Refer to section *Range and range names* for more information on inserting hyperlinks.

Onscreen user navigation and instructions

There are many techniques that you can use to help users interact and work with your spreadsheet. Providing onscreen guidance is crucial. Onscreen guidance could be explanatory text boxes, pop up error messages or you could even design special worksheets as help or reference pages.

Navigation around the various parts of the workbook is another form of onscreen guidance and the easiest way of doing this is to use hyperlinks.

Gather feedback

Formal testing is absolutely crucial to test your spreadsheet solution properly. However, informal feedback is also important as it can help to identify issues that might not be revealed in a formal test plan. In particular, it will give you feedback on the usability aspects, including the clarity of the instructions you have provided for the target user. User testing will also give you feedback on performance and the adaptability of the spreadsheet to different scenarios. The client may well want to comment on the visibility of any logos or the choice of styles used, to make sure they are consistent with the company's house style.

Make improvements

Some of the feedback may point to possible problems with the design or errors in development. In each case, you will need to make a decision about whether to make changes. The feedback might also point to improvements that could be made to adaptability, usability and productivity. Minor problems in the use of the spreadsheet need to be documented even if they are not significant enough to be fixed.

| **Assessment activity 9.3** | *Maths* | 1C.4 | 1C.5 | 2C.P4 | 2C.P5 | 2C.M3 |

You present your spreadsheet design to the manager of Just DVDs. He would like you to build the spreadsheet, which will be made up of the three worksheets.

The spreadsheet should contain a user interface for data input and presentation output data. Your teacher will supply you with a realistic data set.

- Build your spreadsheet.
- Test the functionality of your spreadsheet. Record your findings, fix any errors and make a note of any changes you made.
- Prepare a demonstration of the worksheets in your spreadsheet. Include information about what they do, as well as details of how to use them.
- Demonstrate your spreadsheets to others and ask them to feed back on how easy they found it to use.
- Based on the feedback you receive, identify and make any improvements.
- Using screenshots or a table, explain how you can use the features you identified in Assessment activity 9.1 to improve the data input and presentation output data.

Tips

- You could devise a short questionnaire to help you gather feedback, or ask questions about different elements (e.g. how easy it is to input data, titles for the entry fields, spotting information on the screen, what they find difficult about the system).
- When making changes or fixing errors you should log what you have done, why and the outcome. You should then check that the change or fix works and that it has resulted in an improvement.

Review the finished spreadsheet

 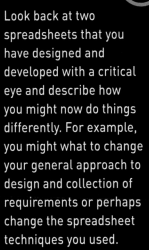
Introduction

Before handing over the final spreadsheet solution to the client, you will need to review and reflect on the finished product to be sure that it meets the client's purpose and the user requirements. You will also want to take an opportunity to reflect on your own work, your approach and the specific techniques you used in order to learn from the experience, so you are ready for your next project.

However well you have designed and developed your spreadsheet model, there will probably still be features that you can refine to improve its usability and performance. When reviewing your completed spreadsheet consider the following elements.

Table 9.3 Elements to consider when reviewing a spreadsheet

User requirements	Evaluate your solution against the user requirements set out in the client brief. Check that the user interface and the facilities for input and output meet the needs of the user.
Fitness for purpose	You need to ensure that all elements of the spreadsheet solution work well, and in the way you intended. If they do, then the spreadsheet solution will be fit for the purpose the client intended for its use. There may be differences between the design and the completed model that you introduced when making your prototype. Your review of the spreadsheet solution should include an explanation for and description of these changes.
User experience	It is crucial that users review the spreadsheet before it is put into use. They will be able to provide constructive feedback on the usability of the spreadsheet, its performance (how well it functions) and how adaptable it is.
Strengths and improvements	Once you have a finished product, it is useful to evaluate it. This involves identifying not only what its strengths are, but also the areas in which improvements can be made. This can lead to useful refinements or future developmental work.

Assessment activity 9.4   1D.6 | 2D.P6 | 2D.M5 | 2D.D4

You have completed and tested the spreadsheet for Just DVDs. The shop's manager would like you to produce a report reviewing the finished spreadsheet.

Your report can take any format but it will need to include the following:

- An explanation of the spreadsheet's purpose and how your design for each worksheet meets the requirements of the brief.

- The process you went though when developing each worksheet. Outline any instances where the worksheets differs from your original design and explain why this is.

- Any problems you encountered and how you dealt with them.

- Identify any future changes you would make to the spreadsheet to make it more efficient for the manager or user-friendly for the staff.

Tip

Your final product might differ from your original design. You need to be able to explain why this is and provide supporting evidence.

Introduction

Most people who use computers at work will probably use databases on a regular basis. In most situations, users will be interacting with an existing database, for example to add and amend records, to search for information or to produce reports. Some users, however, will need to be able to design and create databases – this unit covers the knowledge and skills required to do this.

The learning outcomes for this unit reflect the reality of commercial databases. They will help you develop the skills you need to design, develop and review database systems. You will learn how to create a relational database environment that incorporates a number of data tables. Relational databases are used because they can handle and manipulate large volumes of information. The tools needed to produce them are sometimes complex, but the benefits are huge.

Assessment: You will be assessed by a series of assignments set by your teacher.

Learning aims

In this unit you will:

A understand the uses of and tools/techniques used in databases

B design a relational database

C develop and test a relational database

D review the finished relational database.

> *Although I have only developed a couple of databases so far, I have learned how important it is to establish the requirements accurately. It is also crucial that the database contains accurate and reliable information, especially when the users of the database are not the same as the people who enter the data.*
>
> *Martin, junior database designer*

Database
development

BTEC
Assessment Zone

This table shows what you must do in order to achieve a **Pass**, **Merit** or **Distinction** grade, and where you can find activities in this book to help you.

Assessment criteria

Level 1	Level 2 Pass	Level 2 Merit	Level 2 Distinction
Learning aim A: Understand the uses of and tools/techniques used in databases			
1A.1 Identify the uses of databases and how the tools/techniques are used in two different databases. **Assessment activity 10.1, page 315**	**2A.P1** Explain the uses of databases and how the tools/techniques are used in two different databases. **Assessment activity 10.1, page 315**	**2A.M1** Review how the tools/techniques are used in two databases to improve productivity, accuracy and usability. **Assessment activity 10.1, page 315**	**2A.D1** Discuss the strengths and weaknesses of the databases. **Assessment activity 10.1, page 315**
Learning aim B: Design a relational database			
1B.2 Identify the purpose and user requirements for the database. **Assessment activity 10.2, page 318**	**2B.P2** Describe the purpose and user requirements for the database. **Assessment activity 10.2, page 318**	**2B.M2** Produce a detailed design for a relational database, including: • alternative designs • a detailed database structure • test data. **Assessment activity 10.2, page 318**	**2D.D2** Justify final design decisions, explaining how the relational database will fulfil the stated purpose and user requirements, and any constraints in the design. **Assessment activity 10.2, page 318**
1B.3 Produce a design for a database with guidance, including a single table database structure with a data entry form. **Assessment activity 10.2, page 318**	**2B.P3** Produce a design for a relational database, including: • a database structure • a test plan. **Assessment activity 10.2, page 318**		
Learning aim C: Develop and test a relational database			
1C.4 Develop a database with a realistic data set with guidance, including: • a single table structure • a data entry form. **Assessment activity 10.3, page 328**	**2C.P4** Develop a relational database with a realistic data set, which includes: • two tables • sort records • data entry forms. **Assessment activity 10.3, page 328**	**2C.M3** Develop the database demonstrating awareness of users' requirements and accuracy. To include: • customised data entry forms • queries and output data reports • onscreen navigation and guidance. **Assessment activity 10.3, page 328**	**2C.D3 Maths** Refine the database solution using automated tools and techniques to improve productivity, accuracy and the presentation of output data, taking account of user feedback. **Assessment activity 10.4, page 331**
1C.5 Maths Test the functionality of the database and repair any faults with guidance. **Assessment activity 10.4, page 331**	**2C.P5 Maths** Test the functionality and purpose of the relational database for functionality, repairing any faults. **Assessment activity 10.4, page 331**	**2C.M4 Maths** Gather feedback from others and use it to improve the database and test any additional functionality, repairing any faults. **Assessment activity 10.4, page 331**	

Assessment criteria			
Level 1	**Level 2 Pass**	**Level 2 Merit**	**Level 2 Distinction**
Learning aim D: Review the finished relational database			
1D.6	**2D.P6**	**2D.M5**	**2D.D4**
Identify how the final database is suitable for the user requirements and purpose. **Assessment activity 10.5, page 331**	Explain how the final database is suitable for the user requirements and purpose. **Assessment activity 10.5, page 331**	Review the extent to which the finished database meets the user requirements, considering feedback from others. **Assessment activity 10.5, page 331**	Evaluate the finished database against the design and justify any changes made, making recommendations for further improvements to the database. **Assessment activity 10.5, page 331**

Maths Opportunity to practise mathematical skills

How you will be assessed

The unit will be assessed by a series of internally marked tasks. You will need to show an understanding of the underpinning theory of relational databases, as well as the practical skills to use a software application package to create a working database.

You will be asked to describe the uses of databases, as well as the specific tools and techniques used in a particular database application package. You will also need to show that you are able to design a database that includes at least two tables, as well as a series of forms and reports that respond to the needs of a realistic scenario.

Your assessment could include combinations of the following:

- design documents and database structure
- written reports
- screen captures
- your database
- training materials, such as leaflets and Microsoft® PowerPoint® presentations
- annotated design documents and updated database files
- witness statements and observation records completed by your tutor, possibly based on demonstrations or discussions
- feedback from users.

Uses of databases in organisations

Uses of databases in organisations

Getting started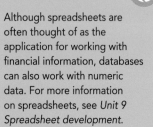

Identify three particular situations where a database could be used in the home. List the benefits.

Key terms

Relational database – A database that uses a series of tables to store information. The tables contain related information and are connected to each other.

Productivity – A measure of the efficiency of an orgainisation or individuals.

Link

Although spreadsheets are often thought of as the application for working with financial information, databases can also work with numeric data. For more information on spreadsheets, see *Unit 9 Spreadsheet development*.

Introduction

Every organisation needs to store, manipulate and access information relating to their business operations. This information used to be kept as paper-based records, but now most organisations use computerised databases.

Why are databases used?

Computerised databases offer a number of advantages when compared with paper-based records and physical filing systems. Well-designed database systems allow organisations to do the following:

- **Manage large amounts of data.** Databases make it much easier to keep records, as you can easily store, view, query, report on and analyse large volumes of information (data sets). Most databases are **relational** – that means that the information is stored in a series of tables that are connected or related to each other.

- **Improve productivity.** One main goal of organisations is to continually review and improve their **productivity**. Computerised databases have a set of searching and planning tools that allow organisations to do this.

- **Keep information safe and secure.** Information stored in computers can very easily and quickly be copied and backed up. Usernames and passwords can provide good (but not foolproof) security and can also give different levels of access to different people.

- **Help people work collaboratively.** Databases can be accessed by different people at the same time and a database used in a networked environment can be accessed by different people in different physical locations. This ensures that every user can potentially see the same up-to-date information.

- **Carry out calculations.** A database allows users to carry out calculations on the data accurately and quickly. Users can also produce reports to interpret a large volume of data. These reports provide insights and summaries that help organisations make decisions.

- **Produce accurate and regular financial reports.** Keeping track of the finances is crucial in the effective management of an organisation. Using a computerised database makes it easier not only to interpret data but also to present summaries of that information in clear numerical and visual formats. Some reports are required for external needs, such as tax returns, and others for internal use to help the managers make appropriate and timely decisions.

A small garage currently stores information in a paper-based filing system. They record details of:

- their customers
- regular car services undertaken and car service history of the cars they see regularly
- MOT details
- cars brought in for repairs, with dates, details of faults and work done
- invoices and payments
- details of the different car parts held in stock.

The garage owners are thinking of bringing in a specialist to advise them whether it is worth converting the paper-based system to a computerised one. Advantages that they have already considered are how easy it will be to produce accurate invoices and to manage payments. They can also see the possibility of improving their general record keeping.

Imagine you are the database specialist. Prepare a list of further advantages, giving some simple examples of how these relate to the garage business.

Types of databases

Flat and relational databases

The key difference between databases is whether they are flat or relational. Flat files store information in a table in a single file. Flat files are simple to implement, but the disadvantage is that they become increasingly inefficient as more data is added. Relational databases provide for multiple tables that can be related to each other – this type of database has significant advantages.

Local and networked databases

Another difference between databases is whether they are local or on a network. A local database will typically be saved and used on a single machine at home or in the office of a small company. Alternatively, the database could be put on a network to provide wider access for many people in different locations.

Online databases

Increasingly, databases are being used online, working behind the scenes of websites. For example, when using Amazon, you will want to be sure that the stock levels you see are up to date. To achieve this, the software running the website accesses the stock details in an underpinning database.

Relational databases

Introduction

Because of the significant advantages of relational databases, this is the type that is most commonly used.

Database examples and entities

Before you can create any database for an organisation, you need to divide the information into a set of tables.

For example, in a database for a library, at least three separate tables will be needed for the book stock, the members and the loans. These natural sets of things are called **entities**.

In practical terms, each entity becomes a table in the database.

Activity 10.2

The entities involved in a relational database for the garage in Activity 10.1 might include customers, vehicles, MOT appointments, services undertaken, employees, parts, etc.

Make a list of the possible entities for each of the following:

- a DVD rental store
- an estate agent
- an employment agency.

Types of relationships

Within a table, you will be able to see which fields are being used. However, this does not show you everything you need to know about the nature of the relationships between fields and data. This section explores different types of relationships and explains when they should be used.

One-to-many, many-to-many and one-to-one relationships

In the garage example (Activity 10.1), some of the customers may own more than one car and every car may have been serviced many times. This detail can be represented using **entity relationship diagrams (ERDs)**.

- **One-to-many.** Remember that the tables actually relate to entities. For example, the information about vehicles will be in one table and the information about services will be in another table. The fact that one vehicle can have many services over time is called a one-to-many relationship and is represented visually in Figure 10.1.

- **Many-to-many.** In many situations, the relationship is many-to-many. For example, the garage might have a database listing spare parts and suppliers. The spare parts will be in one table and the suppliers in another table. Each spare part might be in

Key terms

Entity – A real world thing about which information needs to be stored and maintained. Examples in the medical world are patients, doctors, appointments, treatments, drugs, etc. Each entity will have its own table in a database.

Entity relationship diagram (ERD) – A diagram that illustrates the relationships between entities (tables) in a database.

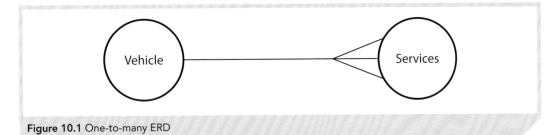

Figure 10.1 One-to-many ERD

stock at many suppliers, and each supplier has a stock of many spare parts. Many-to-many relationships are difficult to implement in a database, so to deal with this type of relationship, another intermediate table is created. This table breaks down the many-to-many relationship into two one-to-many relationships.

- **One-to-one.** In some situations, the relationship is one-to-one. One record in the first table corresponds to just one record in the other. For example, in a hospital database, the patient details (such as name and address) are stored in a different table to the patients' medical details (such as what medications they are taking). This is a one-to-one (1-1) relationship because each patient has only one set of medical details. A one-to-one relationship is represented visually in Figure 10.2.

One-to-one relationships are not good practice and can be quite inefficient. But in some cases there may be good reasons for using this type of relationship; for example, if both the administration staff and medical staff need access to the database, but only the medical staff should be able to see the medical details.

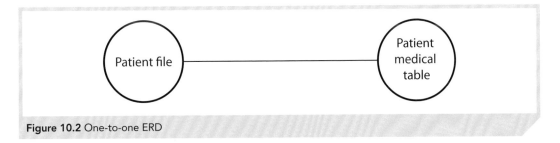

Figure 10.2 One-to-one ERD

Advantages of relational databases

Relational databases have many advantages, some of which are listed here.

- Simplicity of design – each table is about one thing.
- Modifications can be made with ease – new tables can be added without putting the whole database out of action.
- Complex relationships (one-to-one, one-to-many or many-to-many) between objects in the real world can be represented.
- Different 'views' of the database can be created for different users according to their need. For example, admin staff in a hospital might be allowed access to the patient details table but not to the medical details table.

Just checking

1 Give two examples of one-to-many relationships.
2 Explain why it is useful sometimes for different people to see different views of data in a database.
3 Give at least three examples of entities in a supermarket environment.

Tools and techniques used in a database 1

Introduction

Inside each database table is a series of records. Each record is divided into a set of fields that form the structure of the table. Each field stores a particular piece of information about each record in the table.

Table and record structures

An example of a table is shown in Table 10.1. This shows a vehicle table for a car retail business. It has 12 records and four fields. Each record is a row in the table and each field is a column in the table.

Field characteristics and validation rules

When you create a database table, you assign a data type (a characteristic) to each field. Common data types are text, numeric, currency, date/time and yes/no. Choosing the right data type helps to validate the input of information into the table. For example, you cannot type text into a numeric field. In addition, you can impose certain **validation** rules for each field. For example, if you extended the table in Table 10.1 to include a field for the mileage of the vehicle, you might add a rule to check that the value in this field is always positive (since a vehicle cannot have travelled a negative number of miles).

Table 10.1 Vehicle table with example records and fields

Reg. plate	Make	Model	Colour
AK57 YUP	BMW	Z4 Sport 2.5L	Blue
AW08 RTY	Ford	Galaxy Ghia	Red
S8 ODE	Ford	Focus ST-500	Black
SD60 NBV	Ford	Fiesta 1.6 TDCI	Silver
FG10 PLL	Ford	Focus Titanium	Silver
LP10 WER	Seat	Leon 1.6 TDI CR S	White
MS05 POW	Volkswagen	Passat	Silver

Activity 10.3

Look at the vehicle table shown in Table 10.1.

1 One field that is missing is the date the vehicle was registered. Make a list of other necessary and useful fields that you think should be included in this table.

2 Note the most appropriate data type for each field.

3 The company wants to add a field to store whether the vehicle has been sold or not. Choose and explain what data types could be used for this field. State which data type you think might be the best and explain your answer.

Primary keys

Each record (row) in the table must be distinct. No two rows can be the same or there could be confusion about which record you are accessing or updating. For this reason, the table requires a unique field (attribute) called the **primary key**. In most cases, the primary key is a single field. Sometimes there will be a natural choice for the primary key (for example, the vehicle registration number). Where there is no unique field for each record, designers often choose a new field and set it to be the **auto number** type, so that each new record gets a primary key value which is the next in a numeric sequence.

If an organisation already uses a particular combination of letters or numbers to uniquely identify records, such as a product code or student ID number, then it makes sense to use this as the primary key. This field will immediately be recognised and understood by people inside and outside the organisation.

Databases are used by educational providers to store students' details (e.g. name, address, student ID, classes they're taking)

Just checking

1 Note what data types you would best choose to store your name, phone number and date of birth.

2 Explain why a primary key is necessary for every table.

3 State whether you would store a telephone number in a number field or a date field. Explain your decision.

Tools and techniques used in a database 2

Building relationships using foreign keys

The primary key of one table can be placed in another table and used to link the tables together. In the other table, this field is called a **foreign key**.

Case study

Primary and foreign keys in practice

In colleges, one of the main entities will be 'students'. If each student in the college only does one course, the fields used for the student records might include:

- Student reference (Primary key)
- First name
- Second name
- Date of birth
- Address
- Postcode
- Telephone number
- Course code

However, if each student in the college can take a number of courses, this structure will not work.

The solution is to make a separate 'Student-Course' table and use the primary key from the 'Student' table as a field in this new table. This allows the two tables to be linked by a relationship.

Tables 10.2 and 10.3 show how these two tables look with example data in them.

Table 10.2 Three example records in the Student table

Student reference	First name	Second name	DOB	Address	Postcode	Telephone
S122	Roy	Peters	17/08/1992	14 The Slack	LP4 6HT	01367 987451
S323	Pat	Ibrahim	15/01/1993	6 High Street	LP5 4FR	01367 674355
S34	Neena	Shah	3/09/1992	Clinton Cottage	LP3 6GT	01367 874432

Table 10.3 Example records in the Student-Course table

Course code	Student reference
C23	S122
C23	S323
C23	S34
C24	S323
C26	S323
C24	S34

Figure 10.4 shows how the Student and Student-Course tables are linked by the primary and foreign keys.

continued

Case study (continued)

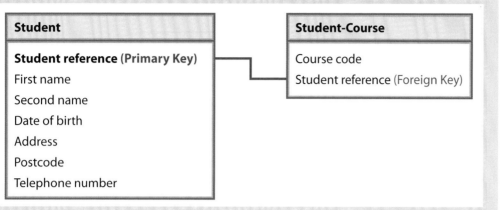

Figure 10.3 The Student and Student-Course tables

Now each course that a student is taking can appear as a separate record in the Student-Course table. At the moment the Student-Course table does not have a primary key.

Questions

1 Why can't the student name be used as the primary key in the Student table?

2 Most people now have two telephones, a home and mobile number. How can this be catered for in the Student table?

3 Course code C24 refers to GCSE Maths. Give the names of the students who are taking this course.

4 Make a list of other fields that it would be useful to add to the Student table. Suggest the best data type for each.

Indexing

If a table has only a few hundred records, finding and retrieving one record to look at or update will be very fast. If a table has many thousands of records, then this process can take much longer. You can set up indexes to make searching much faster. Indexes are typically set up on the fields that are searched on.

Just checking

1 Explain how one field can be both a primary key and a foreign key.

2 Explain one-to-many relationships and many-to-many relationships. Give an example of each.

3 Explore and describe the properties of different data types that help validate data entry.

Main constituents of a database

Introduction

In this section you will learn about the components that make up a database. The different components in a database are called objects.

Tables

You have already learned that a series of tables is an important part of a database. Tables store the raw data. Even small commercial databases will need perhaps dozens of related tables.

Queries

Queries are designed to show a specific view of the data that is needed for a particular user or requirement. You can develop queries from single tables or from a series of related tables.

For example, think about the college database from the Case Study in section *Tools and techniques used in a database 2*. This database needs a table listing all the students, a table listing all the courses, and a table listing which students are on which course. At the beginning of the academic year, the GCSE Maths tutor will need to know the names of all students on this course, and they can run a query to find out this information

Table 10.4 Query outcome showing all the fields of the Ford cars

Reg. plate	Make	Model	Colour
AW08 RTY	Ford	Galaxy Ghia	Red
S8 ODE	Ford	Focus ST-500	Black
SD60 NBV	Ford	Fiesta 1.6 TDCI	Silver
FG10 PLL	Ford	Focus Titanium	Silver

Table 10.5 Query outcome that shows just the registration plates and colour of the silver cars

Registration plate	Colour
SD60 NBV	Silver
FG10 PLL	Silver
MS05 POW	Silver

Another example concerns the garage database we looked at earlier. A supplier is offering a special deal on Ford spare parts and the garage owner wants to know how many Ford vehicles the garage has serviced. He can create a query to find out this information. Table 10.4 shows the result of running the query. The query outcome shows all the Ford cars from the database table in Table 10.1.

Then the garage owner hears about a new product for covering up scratches in silver paintwork. He remembers dealing with a scratched silver car recently, and thinks that the owner might be interested in buying the product from the garage. He decides to create a query to list the silver vehicles in the database – see Table 10.5. When you create a query, you can choose which fields you want to show.

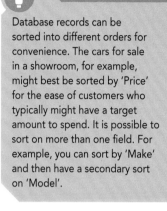

Forms

Data entry forms are an easy way for users to enter data into database tables. A series of validation and verification techniques ensures that the entered data is as accurate as possible. A car retail business might use a form to enter data about its stock, as shown in Figure 10.4.

Car Stock browse, amend and add

Registration plate	SD60NBV
Make	Ford
model	Fiesta 1.6 TDCI ECONETIC 3DR
colour	Silver
special features	CD Player
date purchased	15/11/2011
Sold	☐
Selling price	£8,700.00
First registered	2010
mileage	7500

Record: 7 of 22   No Filter   Search

Figure 10.4 Example form for a car stock table

Remember

Database records can be sorted into different orders for convenience. The cars for sale in a showroom, for example, might best be sorted by 'Price' for the ease of customers who typically might have a target amount to spend. It is possible to sort on more than one field. For example, you can sort by 'Make' and then have a secondary sort on 'Model'.

Link

See the section *Design documentation* for more information on validation and verification techniques.

Reports

Reports are the printed outputs from a database. Reports can be based on tables or queries. In addition, you can place other controls on reports, for example to give summary totals. For example, the car retail business could produce monthly reports listing all the cars they have sold each month.

Assessment activity 10.1

1A.1 | 2A.P1 | 2A.M1 | 2A.D1

A new library has opened in your area. They need a database to manage the book and DVD loan system. The library staff are unfamiliar with databases. You have volunteered to create a database for them.

Create an illustrated fact sheet for the staff explaining:

- what a database is
- the types of information stored using databases
- popular uses for databases
- common database tools and techniques and the strengths and weaknesses of each.

Create a section within the fact sheet that compares two different types of databases in more detail.

- Explain the purpose of each database and how people would use it.
- Explain how particular tools/techniques used by each database can help users; for example, when sorting or finding data. To help the library staff understand the importance of the tools/techniques, you could give them a rating based on different categories.
- Include the top three strengths and weaknesses of each database type.

Tips

- If you are including images, screenshots or reference material ensure that you credit all sources and check that you have permission to use them.
- When discussing database tools and techniques, you should provide evidence that you know the context for using them and how to use them.

Design documentation

Introduction

In order to ensure that a database is successful and meets its intended purpose, it is important to capture completely the customer requirements and understand how the system will be used. You can then use this information as the basis for your database design.

Overview of design documentation

The customer's requirements and the design documentation will vary for different companies and projects. The documentation should always include a clear brief that communicates the purpose of the database and the user requirements. The design documentation will also include:

- entities with field details (such as name, data type and length)
- entity relationship diagrams (ERDs)
- validation and verification requirements
- input and output screens, forms and reports
- resources needed (hardware, software and people)
- constraints.

In addition, the design documentation should include details of the test plans and a consideration of alternative design solutions.

Entity relationship diagrams (ERDs)

ERDs show visually how the entities in a database relate to each other. They also define the data storage in a precise way that you can use to generate and populate the tables of the database. When creating your ERDs, you should list all of the fields (attributes) of each entity, and give the properties of each field: the size, data type, format, etc. You need to consider what the relationships will be between the entities: one-to-many, many-to-many or one-to-one.

Validation and verification requirements

If users of a database cannot trust the actual content in the database, this can cause many problems. It can be very difficult to keep on checking the information inside a database, as users will be constantly changing and updating this information. It is much better to check that the information is correct as it is being entered into the database. You can do this using **validation** and **verification**.

- **Validation.** A drop-down list on a form is an example of simple validation – only valid items from a defined list can be entered into a field. An example of a drop-down list is shown in Figure 10.5. Other ways of validating data include setting the data type and size of a field; for example, the Price field in the Cars table might be a number field with no decimal places.

- **Verification.** This can be harder than validation to apply practically, but is especially important. In the drop-down list shown in Figure 10.5, although a user must enter a correctly spelt make of car from the list, it is still possible to choose BMW when the car is actually a Ford. Allowing the user to cross-check the information is a particularly good technique. For example, before printing a receipt for an MOT, the garage might ask the vehicle's owner to confirm the registration, make and model of their car to make sure the right record gets printed.

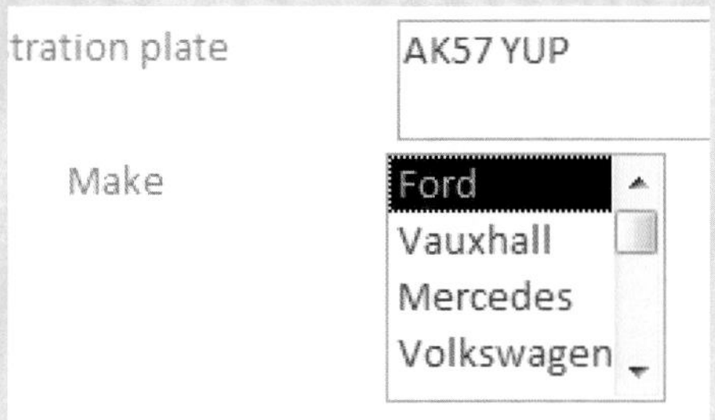

Figure 10.5 A drop-down list used to validate make of car

Activity　10.4

A hospital uses a database to store some vital details. The reception staff will enter the details for each new patient that is admitted. The nurses sometimes find that that the information in the Blood group and Allergies fields have not been entered correctly, so they always have to double-check these with the patients.

1　Explain possible situations or procedures where mistakes in these fields could generate serious problems for the patients concerned.

2　Describe any mechanisms that the database designer could use to make sure that this information will be entered accurately in future. Describe what needs to be done with the existing records.

Input and output requirements

In your design you will need to show how you will meet the input and output requirements for your database. The input screens will be the forms that you design for users to input data. The output will be the printed reports that users create from the data in the database. You can show your outline designs for these by drafting them on paper or creating prototypes.

Constraints

One of the most important constraints on a database design is often the money available to spend on it. At the design stage, you must balance the estimated costs of the project against the potential benefits. The costs are often difficult to estimate accurately and people are often over optimistic, thinking that the database will cost less than it actually does.

The costs you need to include are such things as hardware, software and development costs. The designer must also think more widely and consider the cost of training people to use the new system, any changes in employee costs and so on.

CONTINUED ▸▸

It might also be difficult to identify all the benefits. Some might be easy to measure, such as financial savings due to reduced staffing needs. But the requirements might also include less well-defined things such as 'improved customer service' or 'increased productivity', which are particularly difficult to measure.

Other constraints might be organisational policies, timescale, the need to integrate with existing systems, the available hardware platforms or having enough staff expertise in the organisation.

Activity 10.5

When asked to provide a test plan as part of the design documentation, a student responds by stating that the testing is all done at the end.

Write a short note to the student explaining the advantages of thinking about the test plan at the design stage before they create the database.

Assessment activity 10.2 | 1B.2 | 1B.3 | 2B.P2 | 2B.P3 | 2B.M2 | 2B.D2

Following on from your introduction to databases, the library staff discuss their requirements and decide that the database needs to include:

- a table of the books and DVDs in the library, including type [book/DVD], library catalogue number, title, author, ISBN, year of publication, genre
- a table of library members, including membership number, name, date of birth, address, phone number, email address
- a way to show whether a book/DVD is available or taken out on loan
- a way to show when a book/DVD has been taken out, by whom and when it is due back.

You decide to create a relational database.

- Describe the purpose of the database and explain how it will help staff.
- Come up with a range of design ideas for the database. Refer back to the staff's requirements and select the best option.
- Create a document for the library staff that explains your plan for creating and testing the database and clearly outlines the different stages and components of the design.
- Identify any problems or issues you foresee at this stage.
- From your design ideas, select the elements that best meet the brief, and give reasons why you selected or discarded each option
- Create test data that will be used during the testing stage.

Tip

Keep in your mind who the 'user' will be and how experienced they are using databases. You will need to tailor your structure around the users' abilities as well as their requirements. It's important that you demonstrate that you know what your users' requirements are and the different ways you have tailored your design to fit with these.

Tools and techniques: Tables

Introduction

This step-by-step activity demonstrates how to create a database for a company that sells IT and media products. You will see from this example how much planning is needed before you start work on the database itself.

Creating a database with tables

In this section you will create a database that contains tables. The software used is Microsoft® Access®.

How to create a database with tables

This example uses the information contained in Table 10.5 to create a Products table in a new database for a retail company called Kingsbury Media.

Table 10.6 Fields of the Products table

Field Name	Type	Description	Validation/verification
Product CODE	Text	Primary key	Two upper case letters followed by two numbers, e.g. HN67
Product Description	Text		Max 255 characters
Cost Price	Currency		
Selling Price	Currency		
Actual Stock Level	Numeric		Cannot be negative
Supplier Code	Text	Link to Suppliers table	Letter S followed by a number, e.g. S1, S2, S3, etc.

Step 1 Open Microsoft® Access®.

Step 2 Select **New** and choose to create a blank database, as shown in Figure 10.6.

Step 3 Select a location and give the database a meaningful name, in this case 'Kingsbury Media'.

Step 4 Click on **Create**.

Step 5 One new blank table is automatically created, as shown in Figure 10.7. This will have one ID field, but we want to change this and add more.

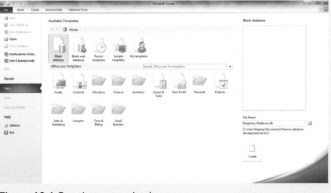

Figure 10.6 Creating a new database

continued

▶▶ CONTINUED

Remember

Modifying a table design has the greatest potential for causing additional work, as you may need to revisit and correct all of the relationships, queries and reports that depend on that table. It's very important to get it right first time!

Step 6 Select **View** and **Design View**. This will allow you to add fields to the table. At the start of this process, you are prompted to give the table a name. Name this table 'Products'.

Then you can add the fields required, as shown in Figure 10.8.

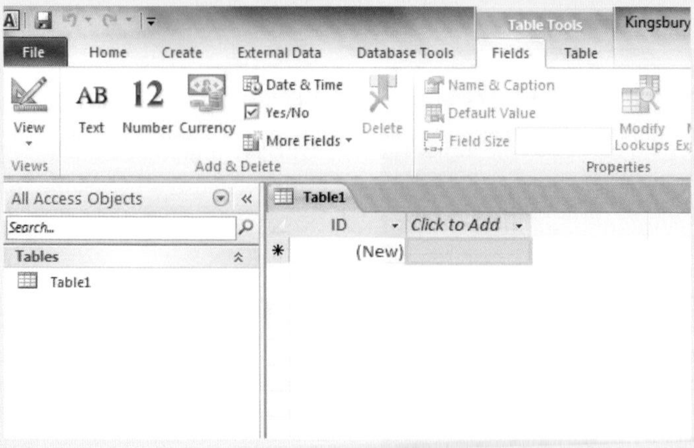

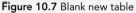

Figure 10.7 Blank new table

Did you know?

As in other software packages, formatting a field will only change the way the data is displayed. It does not change the actual stored values themselves. For example, some text may be actually stored in lower case but you want to display it as UPPERCASE text. Another example might be where you want negative numeric values to be displayed in red to highlight them in a field and this can also be achieved through formatting.

Step 7 An ID primary key field is automatically added. But this table will use a unique product code as the primary key. Change the **Field Name** from ID to Product Code and the **Data Type** to Text, as shown in Figure 10.9.

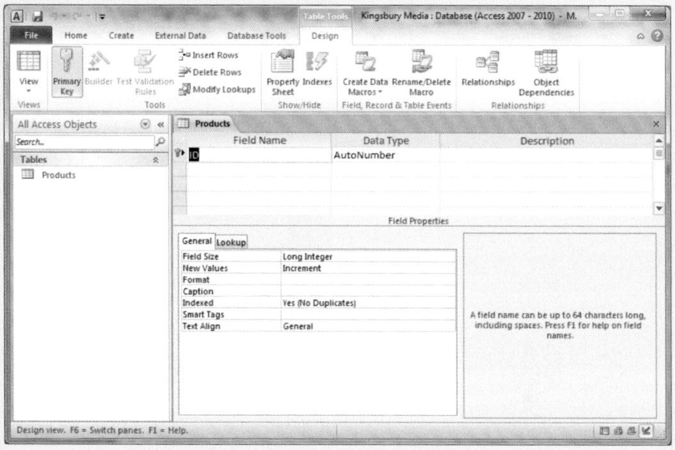

Figure 10.8 Design View ready to add fields

Step 8 The options on the **General** tab shown in Figure 10.9 allow you to control further the data entry. In this case, use an **Input Mask** to force the user to enter two characters and two letters. The mask LL99 accomplishes this.

Step 9 Enter the rest of the fields in a similar way. Figure 10.10 shows how to use a **Validation Rule** to validate the Supplier Code.

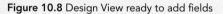

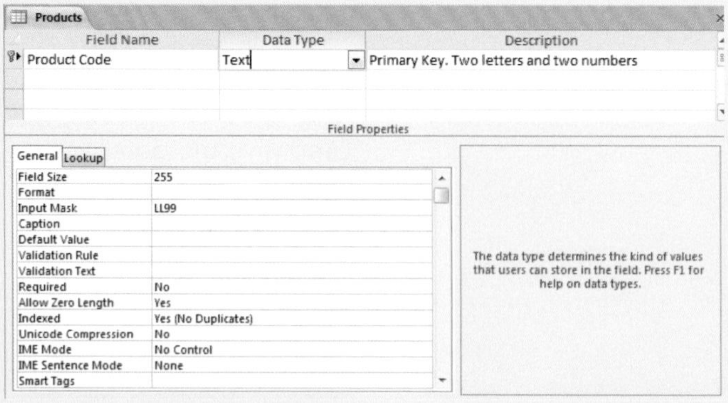

Figure 10.9 Amending Field Name and Input Mask

continued

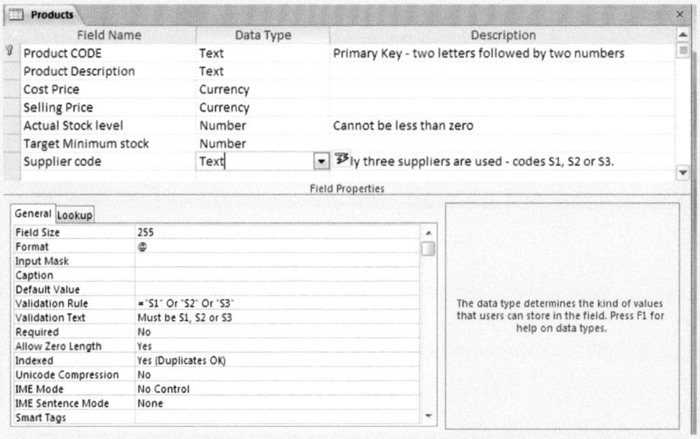

Figure 10.10 Setting a validation rule for the Supplier Code field

Step 10 The structure of the table is now complete. Close the table, saving your changes when prompted.

You can open this table to enter records by using either the **View** option in the **File** menu or by double clicking on the **Products** icon in the **Objects** list on the left hand side of the screen.

Activity 10.6

1 Open the table you saved as 'Products' and add the following two example records.

Product CODE	Product Description	Cost Price	Selling Price	Actual Stock Level	Supplier Code
AS01	Apple iPOD case F1 Black	£10.50	£15.00	3	S1
BH61	Logis Headphone Ear hook	£8.75	£12.50	7	S3

2 Add a third record and test out the validation rules by attempting to enter invalid values.

3 Close the table and reopen it in **Design View**. Add a new **Validation Rule** for the Actual Stock Level to ensure that users cannot enter a negative number. Use the operator **>=** which means 'greater than or equal to'. Add an appropriate comment in the **Validation Text** box.

4 Close the **Design View**. Open up the table and test out the new rule.

Did you know?

- You can set field sizes to match the expected data. For text fields you can enter the maximum expected number of characters of the longest entry. For numeric fields you can select from a wide range of number types as well as from 'number'. These include byte, integer, long integer, single, double and decimal.

- A Default value is one inserted into the field by the system as the record is created unless the user enters a new value themselves. If a sales record has a 'date sale took place' field, you might choose a default value of 'Today' because that will be the appropriate value for most of the entries.

Link

For a list of the operators you can use, see Table 10.7.

CONTINUED ▸▸

Activity 10.7

1 Create a second table in the 'Kingsbury Media' database called Suppliers, with the fields shown below. Add in a validation rule for the Supplier CODE.

Field Name	Data type	Description	Validation/verification
Supplier CODE	Text	Primary key	Letter S followed by a number, e.g. S1, S2 or S3
Supplier Name	Text		
Supplier Address line1	Text		
Supplier Address line2	Text		
Supplier Postcode	Text		
Supplier Phone	Text		

2 Add three records using realistic values.

3 Assume that all postcodes are in a similar format to AL8 6HY. Devise and test an appropriate input mask for the Supplier Postcode field.

4 Explain why the Supplier Phone field is not given a numeric data type.

5 Suggest some further fields you could add to the Suppliers table.

6 Delete one of your records.

Just checking

The validation rule '>5' is added to the selling price field in the example activity 10.6.

1 Explain what this means.

2 Devise an appropriate form of words to put into the validation text that relates to this rule.

Tools and techniques: Queries

Introduction

Queries are a very powerful method of allowing users to see different views of the information in a database. Once you have created a query, it acts as if it is a real table. For example, you can edit the results. However, the underlying information is not duplicated – if you edit a result in a query, you are really editing the original field in a table. You can create queries based on one table or on a number of tables that are linked together. The default type of query is the **select query**.

Key term

Select query – A query that selects the data from the fields that you specify and with the criteria that you set for those fields.

Creating a query

In this section we will open up the Kingsway Media database and create a query on the Products table. The query will select just the Product CODE, Product Name and Actual Stock Level for all the items with less than 10 in stock.

How to create a query

Step 1 Open the database and select **Query Design** within the **Create** menu. The dialog box shown in Figure 10.11 appears.

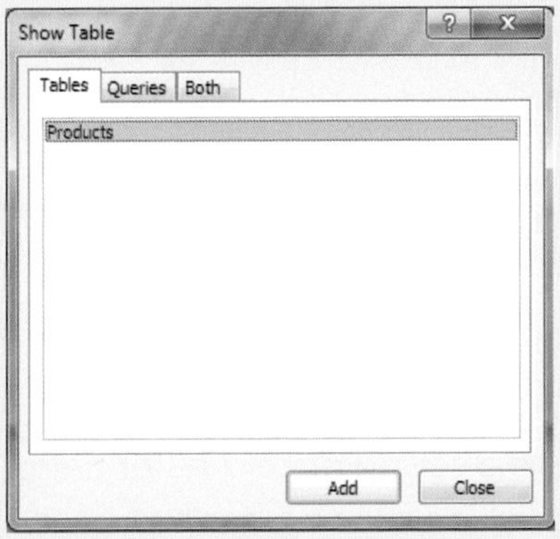

Figure 10.11 Creating a new query

Step 2 In the **Show Table** dialog box, select the Products table, Click **Add** and **Close**.

Step 3 The selected tables and fields from your database will be displayed at the top of the screen, as shown in Figure 10.12.

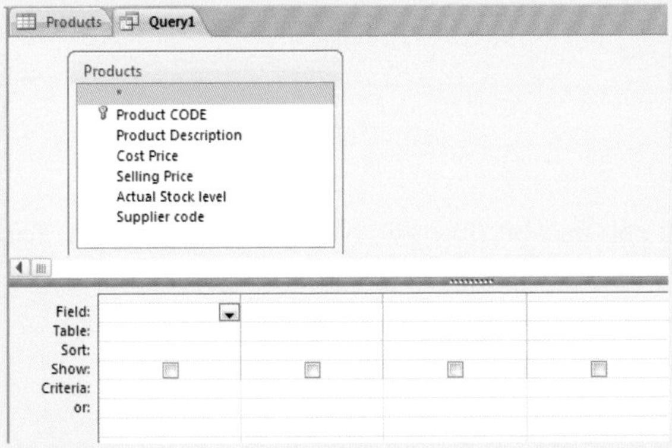

Figure 10.12 Table to be used in the query

Step 4 You create the query in the lower part of this screen. Drag down the field names that you want to use in your query. Make sure that the **Show** box is checked for all the fields you wish to display when you run your query.

The query shown in Figure 10.13 will display the three selected fields (Product CODE, Product Description, Actual Stock Level).

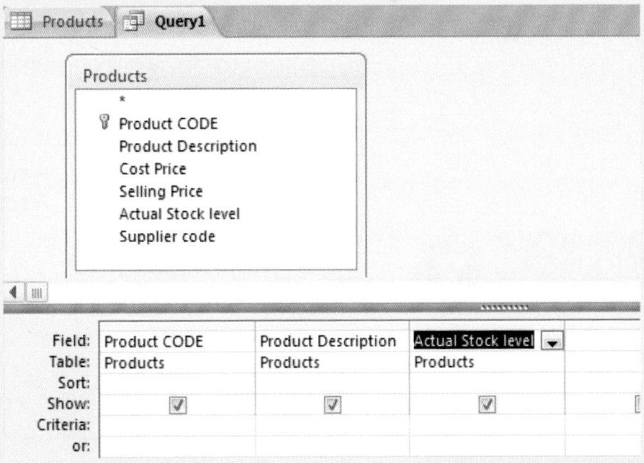

Figure 10.13 Selecting the fields to be used in the query

Step 5 You can set criteria for your query. Enter <10 in the **Criteria** box for Actual Stock Level, as shown in Figure 10.14. The query will now select only those records which have a stock level of less than 10.

continued

Products | Query1

Products

*
🔑 Product CODE
Product Description
Cost Price
Selling Price
Actual Stock level
Supplier code

Field:	Product CODE	Product Description	Actual Stock level
Table:	Products	Products	Products
Sort:			
Show:	☑	☑	☑
Criteria:			<10
or:			

Figure 10.14 Setting up a query with one criterion

Step 6 Close down the query, giving it a meaningful name when prompted. It will be displayed in the **Objects** list on the left hand side.

Step 7 Display the results of the query by either double clicking the query or right clicking and selecting **Open**. The query results are shown in Figure 10.15 – you can see all the products that have a stock level of less than 10.

Products | Products with less than 10 in stock

Product CODE	Product Description	Actual Stock
AS01	Apple iPOD case F1 Black	3
BH61	Logis Headphone Ear hook	7
SQ13	Voice Controller Card	9
J031	Model 37 Laser Printer 10MB RAM)	7
GI02	Floor stand (PC/IT)	6
GR01	Desk stand 500	3
SD09	Sony Headphone splitter 3.5 mm	6
YU11	Logis Maths Pack	5
CX31	KITE Premium FKITERAM 2011	5
DF61	3.5 mm stereo jack lead	8
DW01	Floor stand (800)	9
FD31	KITE Premium 390 90MB	0
FD81	KITE Workstation 205	0
GH81	Sperry Uniscope	0
NB11	Internal V21/23 Modem	5
NM01	Logis noise isolating earphone E12	5
QW12	Logis in ear earphone E4	3

Figure 10.15 Products with less than 10 in stock

Queries with multiple criteria

You can also create more complex queries using more than one criterion.

For example, the query shown in Figure 10.16 has two criteria. This query will select the records for products that have a selling price greater than £200 and that have more than 50 in stock. All of the fields will be shown when the query is run, apart from the Supplier Code, which hasn't been included in the query.

Field:	Product CODE	Product Description	Cost Price	Selling Price	Actual Stock level
Table:	Products	Products	Products	Products	Products
Sort:					
Show:	☑	☑	☑	☑	☑
Criteria:				> 200	> 50
or:					

Figure 10.16 Setting up a query with multiple criteria

Using operators

Table 10.7 shows the operators that you can use on numeric fields in your queries. You can also use operators that work on text fields. The query shown in Figure 10.17 uses the operator **Like** in the **Criteria** box to display records that have the word 'Apple' anywhere within the Product Description field.

In other systems, other logical operators such as **AND** and **OR** are also used to develop complex queries. However, in Access you don't need to enter AND and OR because they are implemented through the design of the query itself.

Did you know?

You can use the operators shown in Table 10.7 in your queries.

Table 10.7 Operators

Operator	Meaning	Opposite
=	Equal to	Not
Not	Not equal to	=
<	Less than	>=
<=	Less than or equal to	>
>	Greater than	<=
>=	Greater than or equal to	<

The examples so far have had the criteria on the same line (for example, Selling Price >200 AND Stock >50). When the criteria are on different lines, it means OR. The criteria shown in Figure 10.19 will select products supplied by S2 OR S3. The records will be displayed in ascending order of Product CODE because an additional requirement has been entered in the **Sort** box of the Product CODE field.

Field:	Product CODE	Product Description	Cost Price
Table:	Products	Products	Products
Sort:			
Show:	☑	☑	☑
Criteria:		Like "*Apple*"	
or:			

Figure 10.17 The Like operator

Field:	Product CODE	Product Description	Supplier code
Table:	Products	Products	Products
Sort:	Ascending ▼		
Show:	☑	☑	☑
Criteria:			="S2"
or:			="S3"

Figure 10.18 Products supplied by supplier S2 OR S3

Activity 10.8

For the following activity, you could give your answers on a blank criteria grid (you could copy the one from Figure 10.18 without the field names and criteria filled in). If you have access to a Products table in a database, you can create and test the queries.

1 Display the Product Code, Product Description and Selling Price for all products supplied by supplier S1.

2 Display just the Product Code for products supplied by supplier S3 with a Selling Price of more than £50.

3 Display all of the records using a multiple sort: the main sort is by Supplier Code and then by Product Code sorted within each supplier. (Hint: You may have to choose the order you bring down the fields into the criteria grid carefully.)

Did you know?

Wildcards allow the user to substitute symbols for one or more characters. They are used when you only know part of a field value or if you are not sure of the spelling used. The asterisk * will match any number of characters and the question mark (?) matches any single character. The search term 'BE?K' will find words such as BEEK, BERK and BEAK, however, BE*K will also find words such as BEDECK and BESERK.

Queries on related tables

When you have built a relationship between two tables, you can create queries using fields from both tables. When you create the query, you will be asked which tables you want to use. Select all the tables you need and pick the relevant fields from each.

Security considerations

A commercial database can have many users. Sometimes it is not appropriate for all users to be able to see all the data. Database administrators can use queries to control who has access to what data. For example, a business might have a database containing details about its employees with various queries set up. Everyone might be allowed to run the query listing employee names and departments, but only people in the Human Resources department might be allowed to run the query that shows how much each employee is paid.

Assessment tip

When you are designing your database solution, make sure you outline at least five queries to extract meaningful data.

Just checking

1 A criteria (AGE>65) uses the 'greater than' operator to find all records where the age of the employee is over 65. Develop another criteria that this time uses the 'greater than or equal to' operator that achieves the same purpose.

2 Apart from salary, give another example of a field in an employee record that you might not want everyone to see.

Tools and techniques: Forms

Introduction

It is usually best to create forms using the Form Wizard and then modify them as necessary. The wizard provides a number of basic design choices and then produces the final form automatically.

Creating a form using a wizard

In this section you will create a simple form for the Products table in the Kingsbury Media database.

How to create a form using a wizard

Step 1 Select **Form Wizard** from the **Create** menu. You will see the screen shown in Figure 10.19.

Step 2 At the top of the screen, you can choose which table or query to use as a basis for the form. Select the **Products** table. Then select the fields for the form using the > button. For this form, you want to use all fields, so use the >> button.

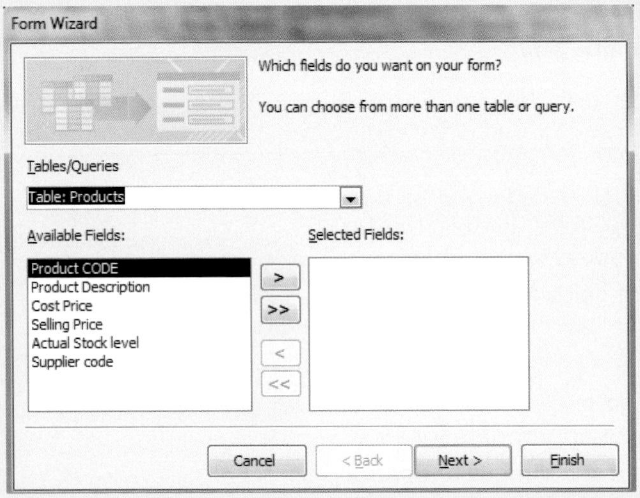

Form Wizard

Which fields do you want on your form?

You can choose from more than one table or query.

Tables/Queries

Table: Products

Available Fields:
Product CODE
Product Description
Cost Price
Selling Price
Actual Stock level
Supplier code

Selected Fields:

Cancel | < Back | Next > | Finish

Figure 10.19 Creating a form

Step 3 Click **Next** to go to the next stage in the wizard.

Step 4 Select the **Columnar** layout and then click **Next**. See Figure 10.20.

Step 5 At the next stage, you do not wish to modify the basic design, but you do want to view the form with data in it, so click on **Finish**.

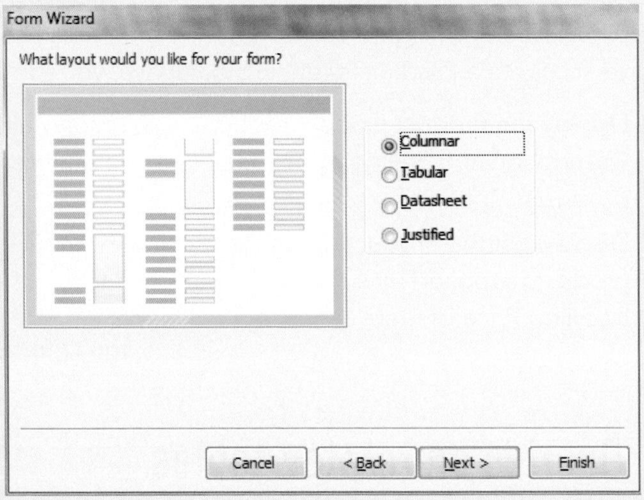

Form Wizard

What layout would you like for your form?

- ⦿ Columnar
- ○ Tabular
- ○ Datasheet
- ○ Justified

Cancel | < Back | Next > | Finish

Figure 10.20 Selecting the layout for a form

Step 6 You will see the basic form generated by the wizard, as shown in Figure 10.21.

Products

Product CODE   AS01

Product Description   Apple iPOD case F1 Black

Cost Price   £10.50
Selling Price   £15.00
Actual Stock level   3
Supplier code   S1

Record: I◄ ◄ 1 of 43 ► ►I ►❉ | No Filter | Search

Figure 10.21 Basic wizard-generated form showing one record

You can now use this form for a variety of tasks using the options in the bottom bar. You can add a new record, browse the database, search for a specific record and edit the records.

Creating a customised form

In this example, you will amend the form to improve how it looks and to aid the process of data entry. You will add useful text, a logo and replace the Supplier Code data entry box with a drop-down list.

How to create a customised form

Step 1 Open the existing wizard-generated form in **Design View**, as shown in Figure 10.22.

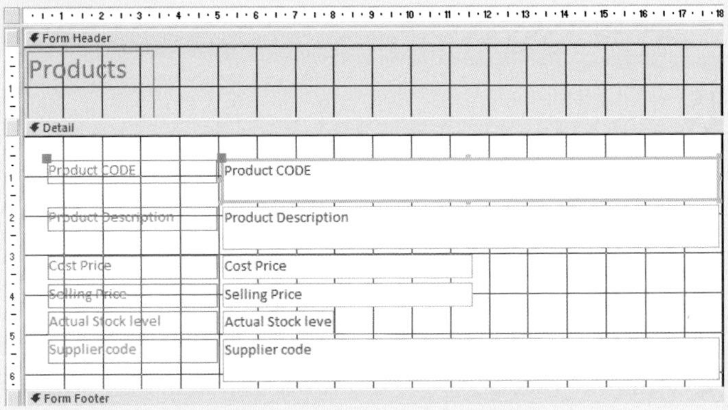

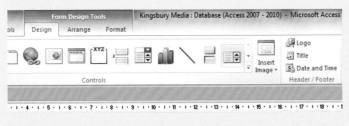

Figure 10.22 Wizard-generated form in Design View

Step 2 Highlight and delete the existing Supplier Code label and data entry box. Make more space at the bottom of the form by holding and dragging down the window edge.

Step 3 Select **List box** from the **Design** menu, as shown in Figure 10.23.

Figure 10.23 List box icon in the form Design menu

Step 4 The **List Box Wizard** is started and the first choice is whether to enter the list box contents directly here or take them from another existing table. It is better to take them from an existing table, so make this choice and press **Next**.

Step 5 Select the **Suppliers** table, as this contains the supplier codes. Select **Supplier Codes**, as shown in Figure 10.24, and press **Next**.

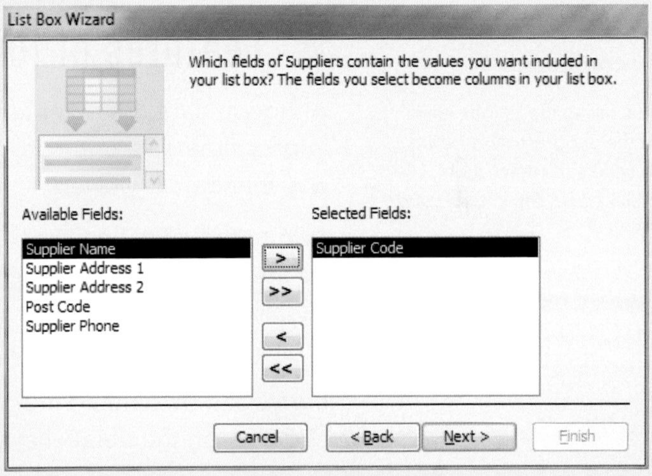

Figure 10.24 Selecting columns for the List box

Step 6 Continue with the wizard. Make sure that the value from the list box is stored in the Supplier Code field, as shown in Figure 10.25.

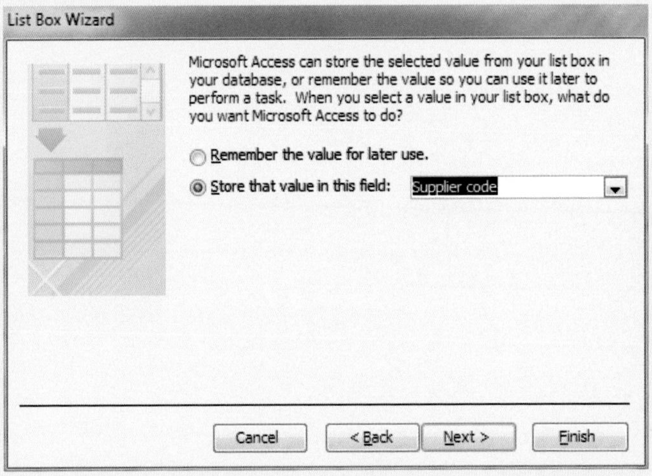

Figure 10.25 Storing the list box value in the Supplier Code field

continued

327

Step 7 Finish the wizard and give the list box the label 'Supplier Code'. If necessary, resize the list box and move it around on the form design to line it up with the rest of the data entry boxes.

Step 8 Close the form and save the changes. When you open the new form, it will display the Supplier Code list box, as shown in Figure 10.26.

Products

Product CODE	AS01
Product Description	Apple iPOD case F1 Black
Cost Price	£10.50
Selling Price	£15.00
Actual Stock level	3
Supplier Code	S1 / S2

Figure 10.26 Form with working list box

Discussion point

Why is taking the list box items from the Suppliers table better than typing in a new list of Supplier codes within the wizard?

Features of forms

Although data can be entered directly into tables and queries, the use of forms can improve the data entry process, allow you to choose which fields are included and the way that data is viewed.

Additional validation checks can be added through the form itself and the layout can be adapted to suit the fields to be displayed. Furthermore, additional explanatory text can be added to the form. Other features include the formatting of the screen and the addition of logos where necessary.

Forms can be deleted in a similar way to other objects, simply highlight the form name and click on the delete key. Deleting the form does not affect the data.

Just checking

1 Note what types of layout are available in the forms generated by the form wizard.

2 Apart from tables, what other objects in a database can forms be based on?

Tools and techniques: Sub-forms and reports

Introduction

Once you have learned how to create forms, you can make them more useful for the users of your database by adding programmable buttons and sub-forms.

Adding programmable buttons

Although it is possible to add records and to browse and search the records from the form, you can further improve the interface by adding buttons. You can insert a button onto the form using the button icon on the **Design** toolbar and then selecting from the choices in the menu. You then need to assign a function to your button.

Figure 10.27 shows a form with the following buttons from top to bottom: Record delete, Go to first record, Go to last record, Exit form.

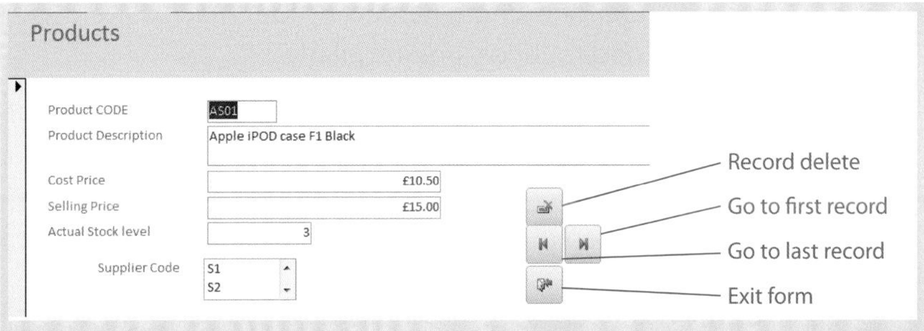

Figure 10.27 Adding programmable buttons to a form

Working with sub-forms

You can place one form inside another form and, as long as the tables or queries behind the two forms have a common field (such as primary key and foreign key), then they can usefully interact.

A useful application of sub-forms for the Products and Suppliers tables is a form that allows users to browse through the suppliers and see a list of the products available from each supplier as they do so. You can do this by creating a Suppliers form that incorporates a tabular Product sub-form.

Figure 10.28 Suppliers form ready for sub-form

Figure 10.28 shows a Suppliers form that displays just the supplier code and supplier name.

Figure 10.29 shows the same form with a Product sub-form added. In this screen capture, the user is viewing supplier S3 and all the products available from this supplier.

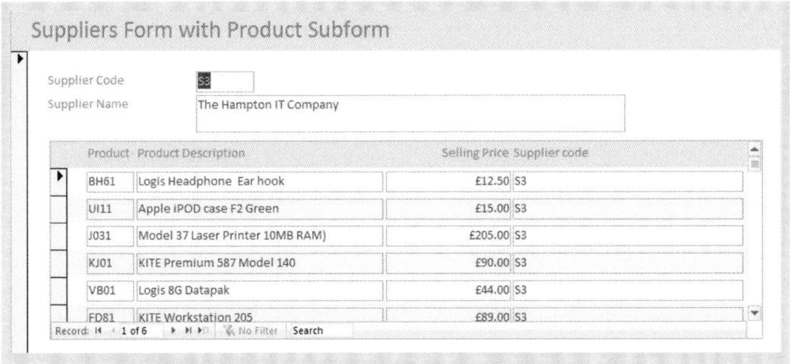

Six products are shown in the sub-form relating to supplier S3. You can enter new records for supplier S3 directly into the sub-form.

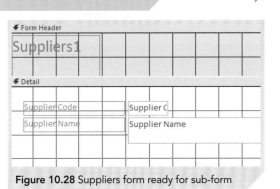

Figure 10.29 Product sub-form

CONTINUED ▶▶

▶▶ CONTINUED

Reports

You can design and create printed reports in a similar way to creating forms, using the Report Wizard. You make choices within the wizard to create reports in a number of basic styles, such as columnar and tabular, as with forms. In addition, reports can show grouped sets of records. However, you must apply an appropriate sort order to the records for the grouping to work. You can then refine the reports created by the wizard. Reports can be based on tables or queries.

Automation and usability

Being able to automate tasks within a database enables you to save time once you have it set up and makes using a database on a daily basis easier. Usability of a database is important to consider, as if it is difficult to use, then it will not fulfil its purpose, which is often to improve productivity and make data analysis simpler.

Automated tasks using macros

As described earlier in this chapter, a macro is a series of actions that is collected and stored under one single-named action. Macros are particularly useful for sets of actions that are used routinely and regularly.

Macros are typically recorded 'live'. Once you are sure what series of actions are to be recorded, you can start recording and then you run through the actions in sequence. Finish by stopping the recording. You are then prompted to give the macro created a name and then given a choice of assigning it to a key stroke, menu or button.

Usability

There are several things you can do to make your database easy to use. For example, you can add onscreen prompts and help screens, and you can make sure that navigation is consistent (for example, if you have a button for returning to the main menu, this should always appear in the same place).

> **Assessment tip**
>
> When designing a database solution, make sure you include at least three reports and that each report responds to the design requirements and is suitable for the intended audience.

> **Just checking**
>
> 1 Name three techniques that you can employ to make the database easy to use by inexperienced users.
>
> 2 Describe a situation when you might want to use a macro.
>
> 3 Two in-built actions that can be assigned to buttons and used on a form are 'Go to First Record' and 'Delete Record'. List four others.

Tools and techniques: Building relationships

Introduction

The main feature of relational databases is the use of simple named tables to store the information – the tables are created separately and then linked. This is the characteristic that distinguishes relational databases from other types of database.

The tables within a database are held together by the relationships between them and this is why this type of database is called relational.

Building the relationships

You can modify relationships between tables once a database has been constructed, but you have to do this with care. Once information has been added to tables, and a variety of other forms, queries and reports have been designed and created, changing one of the relationships can cause significant problems – it may be necessary to first delete a relationship and then recreate all of them again.

Creating a relationship

The step-by-step activity below is based on the Products and Suppliers tables (entities) in the Kingsbury Media database. The relationship between these two entities is one-to-many, as each supplier can supply many products. This relationship can be shown visually using the ERD in Figure 10.30.

Suppliers ——————< Products

Figure 10.30 ERD showing a one-to-many relationship

How to create a relationship

Step 1 Select **Relationships** from the **Database Tools** menu. You will see the screen shown in Figure 10.31.

Step 2 Add both of the tables – the **Products** table and the **Suppliers** table – to the **Relationships** and select **Close**.

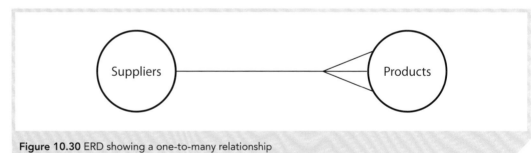

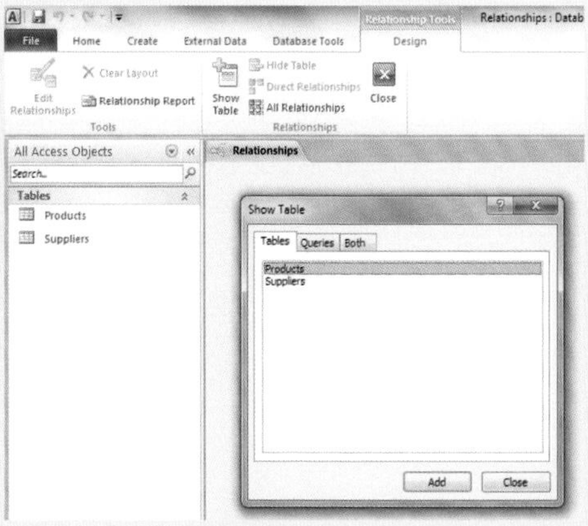

Figure 10.31 Choosing the tables to relate

continued

Step 3 Figure 10.32 shows the fields of the two tables side by side. The link between these two is Supplier Code. It is the primary key in Suppliers and a foreign key in Products. Click on Supplier code in Products and then hold and drag it over to Suppliers.

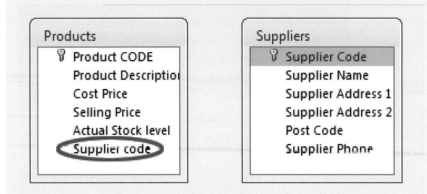

Figure 10.32 Creating a relationship between the tables

Step 4 A visual connection is made with a dialog box. In the dialog box, check the **Enforce referential integrity** box and then click **Create**. The final image will show that a one-to-many relationship has been established.

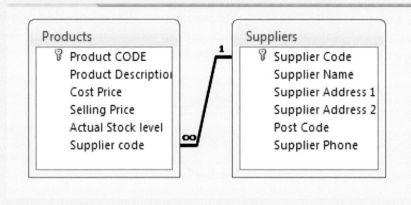

Figure 10.33 One-to-many relationship

Queries and relationships

Once you have created a relationship, it is visible to all other entities. This means that you can build queries across two related tables.

Figure 10.34 shows a query in the process of being created using the Products and Suppliers tables.

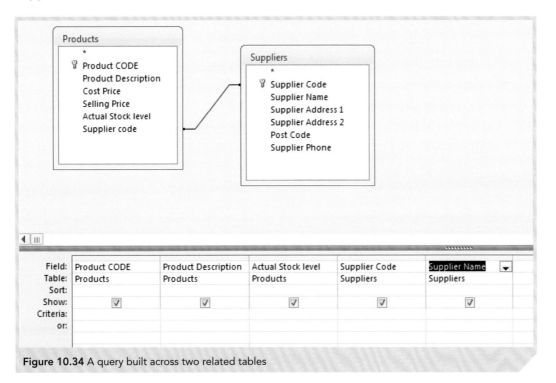

Figure 10.34 A query built across two related tables

Once you have created a query, you can use it as the basis for any subsequent forms or reports.

Activity   10.9

You are an IT technician working for a large company. You have been asked to computerise the records of the hardware faults and repairs completed over time.

You analyse the current paper-based records and work out that two tables are needed, with the following fields:

Machines table with the following fields	Faults table with the following fields
Machine Description	Fault Reference Number
Machine Code (primary key)	Date Fault Reported
Machine Purchase Date	Machine Code
Machine Location	Fault Description
	Date Fault Fixed

continued

Activity 10.9 (continued)

1 Design and create the two tables and link them using the Machine Code common field.

2 Then design and create a series of queries, forms and reports that meet the following requirements:

- a data entry form to view the machines in the company and allow machines to be added as they are purchased and deleted as they are decommissioned
- a data entry form to add details of the faults as they are reported
- a data entry form to update the record once the fault has been fixed
- reports that will produce:
  a) a list of machines with faults that have not been repaired
  b) the history of each machine showing the machine details and a list of past faults and dates. (Hint: use a sub-form for this.)

Assessment activity 10.3 *Maths* 1C.4 | 2C.P4 | 2C.M3

You have explained your database design to the library's staff. Now you are ready to develop your database. Your teacher will supply you with a realistic data set.

- Build your database, using the tables and data you have previously identified.

Tip

Be careful when using the data set or entering information into your database's fields. It's important to proof your own work and check that the data you're using is correct.

WorkSpace

▶ Mary Matheson

Owner of a high street printing shop

I own and run a high street printing shop. Together with my partner, we manage the whole business, but we do have some sales assistants who work for us at busy times. It is a franchise and most of the systems and procedures were provided to us when we set up the business. Each of us has focused on different aspects of the business. One of my roles is to manage the IT work – particularly the databases. We were given some blank databases at the start and some training to help learn how to use them. However, over time I have developed some new databases and also adapted the standard ones to give us more functionality and better reports.

The vast majority of my time on the databases is spent as a user – simply entering data or running reports. But occasionally, when I know the shop will be quiet, I take the time to look for improvements and added functionality – mostly by designing new queries and reports that we think will help us understand the business better. I have also added an extra field to the customer database that identifies the poor payers. This is quite useful now and I thought it would be easy to do, but in the end it was a lot of work to chase down all of the changes that needed doing to other objects to make it actually work!

The change that I am most proud of is when I added a menu system to the main database. I did this using a series of buttons on a menu form. The menu has made a huge difference to how easy it is to use the database. One additional benefit that I only realised later was that it restricted my partner's access to the underlying queries and reports – he had a tendency to 'tinker' with them and sometimes caused problems.

Think about it

1 What problems might Mary encounter when she does want to change forms and tables or add functionality? How can these problems be reduced?

2 What databases do you think the printing shop might need?

3 Do you think that Mary was sensible to add a menu system? What are the advantages and disadvantages of doing this in her situation?

335

Testing and reviewing

Getting started

Look at one of the test plans you developed earlier and consider if you think that it is sufficient to check all aspects of the database being developed.

Introduction

Once you have created your database you need to test it to see whether it fulfils its purpose, has all the required functionality and is usable. When you have finished testing your finished database, you will need to review the finished product.

Testing

When you plan your testing, you need to identify and list all the tests you will have to carry out on your database. You should create a test plan detailing how you will organise the tests and give an outline of all the tests that are needed. Your tests should check whether the database fulfils all of the original user requirements and the purpose for which it was created. You also need to check whether the database is usable by the people who will be using it on a regular basis.

You should plan out how you will test your database at the beginning of the design and development process, getting agreement for your test plan from the customer who briefed you to create the database. It is too important to leave to the end.

Link

See *Unit 9 Spreadsheet development*, Table 9.2 for an example test plan you can use.

Test cases

A typical test case includes:

- a unique name and number to make it easy to refer to the test
- a description of what is being tested
- expected results – for example, 'After clicking Delete, the record should no longer exist'
- actual results – what actually happens when the test is run
- comments – any other observations about the test (for example, 'It worked, but took a long time').

Test cases must be repeatable. You may need to go through the sequence of testing several times: carrying out the test, identifying any issues, resolving the issues, then retesting.

Assessment tip

If any of your tests fail, you should make improvements to your database so that they pass. Make sure you complete the test plan recording that the particular test failed. When you think you have fixed the fault repeat the same test formally and record the new outcome in the test plan.

Making improvements

Based on feedback from others and on the results of your tests, you should make improvements to your database. For instance, you could add additional tables, queries, forms and reports to enhance the data analysis or usability of the database. You could also improve the automation of the database to improve productivity or you could improve the security of the database.

Assessment activity 10.4   *Maths*   1C.5 | 2C.P5 | 2C.M4 | 2C.D3

You have developed your database. Now you need to test that it works.

- Test the functionality of your database. Record your findings, fix any errors and make a note of any changes you made.

- Demonstrate your database to some users and ask them to feed back on how easy they found it to use. You could devise a short questionnaire for them or ask them questions about different elements.

- Make any improvements you identify during testing.

Tips

- When testing the functionality of a product, it is important to use a methodical and logical approach. Be sure to record all of the steps you took and the outcome of each result.

- Be methodical when gathering feedback and keep a record of what questions you asked, who you asked and the responses you received. Good feedback can improve your product so it's important to ask the right questions.

Review and evaluation criteria

If you want to decide whether a database system is successful, you should ask whether it meets the user's requirements. You should ask the user to 'sign off' the finished database. This means that the user checks the database carefully for usability and reliability and formally agrees that it meets their needs. It will meet their needs if it has the features they asked for, is easy to use and works reliably. If this is the case, then the database is fit for purpose.

After the database is signed off, it is good practice to look back at the project and think about what went well and what could have been improved. You should also think about what database features you used and whether these were justified. This information will help you in your next database project. As well as the user requirements and experience and fitness for purpose, when reviewing your database you should also consider:

- **Constraints.** Were there any constraints on the hardware or software you had to use for the database? Did you have all the information and resources you needed to create a database that would be fit for purpose?

- **Strengths and improvements.** What were the strengths of your database? What part of the process went particularly well. Are there any solutions you came up with that you are particularly proud of? What were the things that could be improved about how you designed, created or tested your database?

Assessment activity 10.5   1D.6 | 2D.P6 | 2D.M5 | 2D.D4

You have completed and tested the library's new book/DVD database. Produce a report reviewing the finished database. Your report can take any format but it will need to include the following:

- An explanation of the database's purpose and how your design supports this and meets the requirements of the library staff.

- The process you went though when developing the database. Outline any instances where the design or functionality of the database differs from the original design and explain why this is.

- Any problems you encountered and how you dealt with them.

- Recommendations for any future improvements that you would make to the database.

Tips

- Give a reason for every change that you made.
- Refer back to the feedback you received from other people to consider what further improvements you could make.

Introduction

Networks are all around us and are a major part of our lives. We all use networks every day in many ways, particularly to send email, browse the internet, play online games, watch on-demand TV and to help us work.

A computer network can connect devices as diverse as your mobile phone and a massive computer data centre together using wired or wireless technologies.

In this unit, you will learn about different types of computer network and their hardware and software components. You will understand the uses of networks and how different systems, or elements in the system, affect the user experience. You will learn how to plan and design a network of your own to meet a client's needs.

You will build a network to fulfil your design using hardware and software components that you configure according to your design documentation. You will check that your network works well by using a test plan that you will draw up, and by reviewing it against the original requirements.

Assessment: You will be assessed by a series of assignments set by your teacher.

Learning aims

In this unit you will:

A understand the features and uses of computer networking

B design a computer network

C develop and test a computer network

D review the finished computer network.

> *This unit really helped me understand IP, and meant that I could set up the broadband router and network at home and in family and friends' houses. It was brilliant to see my parents' reaction when I configured their laptops to share files and link to the house printer and my dad's home office printer!*
>
> *Sam, 16-year-old would-be network administrator*

Computer networks

11

BTEC
Assessment Zone

This table shows what you must do in order to achieve a **Pass**, **Merit** or **Distinction** grade, and where you can find activities in this book to help you.

Assessment criteria			
Level 1	Level 2 Pass	Level 2 Merit	Level 2 Distinction
Learning aim A: Understand the features and uses of computer networking			
1A.1 Identify the uses and features of a different computer network. **Assessment activity 11.1, page 358**	**2A.P1** Explain the uses and features of a different computer network. **Assessment activity 11.1, page 358**	**2A.M1** Review how the uses and features of a different computer network affect the user experience. **Assessment activity 11.1, page 358**	**2A.D1** Discuss the strengths and weaknesses of the network. **Assessment activity 11.1, page 358**
Learning aim B: Design a computer network			
1B.2 Identify the purpose and 'client' requirements for the network. **Assessment activity 11.2, page 368**	**2B.P2** Describe the purpose and 'client' requirements for the network. **Assessment activity 11.2, page 368**	**2B.M2** Produce a detailed design for a computer network, including: • alternative solutions • an outline of how the computer network will be set up and configured • test data • costs involved with setting up the computer network. **Assessment activity 11.2, page 368**	**2B.D2** Justify final design decisions, explaining how the computer network will fulfil the stated purpose and 'client' requirements, describing the impact of any constraints on the design. **Assessment activity 11.2, page 368**
1B.3 Produce a design for a computer network, with guidance, including: • a list of hardware and software components • the number of network users • an outline network diagram. **Assessment activity 11.2, page 368**	**2B.P3** Produce a design for a computer network, including: • a list of hardware and software components, their role, and how they connect and communicate with each other • a network diagram • a test plan. **Assessment activity 11.2, page 368**		
Learning aim C: Develop and test a computer network			
1C.4 Develop a computer network, with guidance, that has: • at least two network users • network users sharing one folder and three files. **Assessment activity 11.3, page 374**	**2C.P4** Develop a computer network that has: • at least three network users • users sharing at least five folders and at least seven files. **Assessment activity 11.3, page 374**	**2C.M3** Develop a complex computer network with at least one additional shared hardware device and network utility software resource, demonstrating awareness of the original requirements. **Assessment activity 11.3, page 374**	**2C.D3** Refine the computer network in order to improve performance and reliability, taking account of feedback. **Assessment activity 11.3, page 374**
1C.5 Test the computer network for connectivity, with guidance. **Assessment activity 11.3, page 374**	**2C.P5** Test the computer network for functionality and connectivity against original requirements, and repair any faults as necessary. **Assessment activity 11.3, page 374**	**2C.M4** Test the computer network and gather feedback, and use it to improve the computer network on user experience for functionality and connectivity. **Assessment activity 11.3, page 374**	

Assessment criteria			
Level 1	Level 2 Pass	Level 2 Merit	Level 2 Distinction
Learning aim D: Review the finished computer network			
1D.6 For the final computer network, identify how it is suitable for the intended purpose and original requirements. **Assessment activity 11.4, page 375**	**2D.P6** For the final computer network, explain how the final computer network is suitable for the intended original requirements and purpose. **Assessment activity 11.4, page 375**	**2D.M5** Review the extent to which the final computer network meets the original requirements while considering feedback. **Assessment activity 11.4, page 375**	**2D.D4** Evaluate the initial designs against the final computer network and justify any changes that were made, making recommendations for further improvements to the computer network. **Assessment activity 11.4, page 375**

How you will be assessed

The unit will be assessed by a series of internally marked tasks.

You will be expected to show an understanding of the features and uses of computer networking, to practise your practical skills in designing, developing and testing a computer network, and to review the finished computer network.

Your assessment could be in the form of:

- written reports
- presentations
- web pages
- witness statements and observation records
- video recordings of your practical activities.

Computer networks

Getting started

Research both USB and PCI wireless network adaptors for computer system units.

How do they compare on price and speed?

Which would you buy for a computer upgrade? Why?

Introduction

Whenever you post a status or download music, the device you're using automatically connects to a computer network. A network enables information or data, in this case your status or music, to move from one place to another rather like delivery vehicles on a busy road network.

A computer network consists of hardware components and software applications connected together to enable computers and other devices to communicate and share data with each other.

In this section, we will look at how networks are connected together, using network cable or wireless technology.

Wired networks

A simple network, like the one you may use at home, usually consists of a desktop computer or laptop, printer, router and server. These devices need to be connected so that they can communicate with each other, allowing the user to send instructions from the computer to the printer to print the documents they create, or to connect the computer to the internet.

Devices can be connected in two ways, either through a wired network or a wireless network. In a wired network, cables link the hardware devices together. The cables are plugged into switches which then make the connection.

Wired networks today mainly use Ethernet technology. The switches in Ethernet networks have sockets for RJ45 plugs to connect the cables. The speed of a wired network – how quickly data travels – depends on the capacity of the cable. Ethernet cables have two different capacities:

- CAT5 (category 5) transmits data at 100 **mega bits per second (mbps)** and is now used mainly by older networks.
- CAT6 (category 6) transmits data at 1 **giga bit per second (gbps) (1000 mbps)**. This is a faster system and is used by most current networks.

Key terms

Mbps – The speed data travels through a cable or radio signals is measured in the number of bits that pass every second. A 100 mbps (mega bits per second) connection can handle 100 million bits in a second.

Gbps – A 1000 mbps connection is usually written as 1 gbps (giga bits per second). As there are 8 bits in a byte and data size is usually measured in bytes, the theoretical transfer time to move a 1GB file is around 8 seconds.

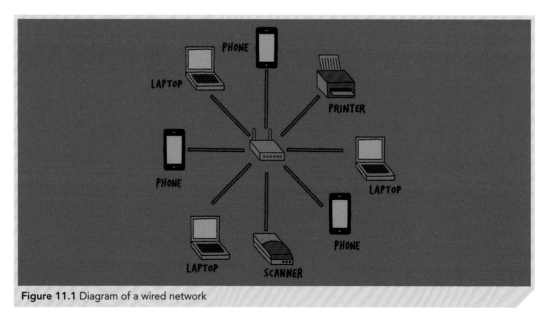

Figure 11.1 Diagram of a wired network

Wireless networks

Wired networks have one big disadvantage, computers have to be linked by cable to the network in order to connect to the internet. The wireless network, on the other hand, does not use cables to connect devices, and it is this technology that allows us to use smartphones, laptops, and tablets around the home, on public transport, in coffee shops, in fact pretty well wherever we happen to be.

Wireless networks can also be used in areas where it may be physically difficult to run cables. There are three main types of wireless network.

1. Wi-Fi networks

Wi-Fi networks can be accessed from anywhere so long as you have a connection. You can connect to a work, school or home network via a Wi-Fi connection and you can also use **Wi-Fi hotspots**. Wi-Fi uses wireless radio signals to connect to mobile devices such as laptops. Modern laptops usually have a wireless radio connection built in – this allows them to search for and then to connect to a wireless access point (WAP) on the Wi-Fi network.

Wi-Fi signals can only travel short distances, up to around 20 metres, so the device needs to be fairly close to the WAP to connect to it. This distance will vary, depending on where the WAP is located. The signal will be reduced if it has to travel through several walls in a building, and businesses often have several WAPs to ensure that all parts of the building have Wi-Fi access.

Wi-Fi speeds vary. It uses the **802.11 standards** developed for wireless technology: 802.11g transmits data up to 54 mbps, while 802.11n is much faster at up to 300 mbps.

Figure 11.2 Diagram of a wireless network

2. 3G and 4G networks

Third-generation (3G) mobile technology is a wireless network that allows mobile devices to connect anywhere using a mobile phone signal. Some devices such as tablets, netbooks and e-book readers have 3G built in so they can connect to the internet or download books, even when the user is on the move. Fourth-generation (4G) mobile services have been launched in the UK and aim to offer much faster speeds than 3G.

3. WiMAX

Similar to Wi-Fi, WiMAX (Worldwide Interoperability for Microwave Access) has a much wider range of around 30 miles. This technology can deliver speeds of up to 70 mbps.

WiMAX uses the IEEE 802.16 standard with a radio signal for transmitting data.

Features of computer networks 1

Introduction

In this section we will look at three more features of computer networks:

- the size of the network – from a small network that you might use at home to a large business network operating across many sites
- how networks are set up – this will depend on whether the network is for home use or for an organisation
- the different ways in which cabling can be organised to create a wired network and how networks communicate.

Scale of networks

Computer networks vary in size. Think of a typical home network of a computer, laptop, printer and other devices, and compare this with a very large business network, which may consist of thousands of computers and devices, often operating across several sites and sometimes across different countries.

The scale of a network then is how far its connections reach, from just a few metres to the other side of the world. This is sometimes called the scope of a network.

Here are some examples of different types of network connections.

- A **local area network** or **LAN**, is a small network which covers one building or sometimes several buildings on one site.
- A **wide area network** or **WAN**, connects LANs to a larger network. It can join other networks anywhere in the world.
- A **metropolitan area network** or **MAN**, can connect an area the size of a city, although sometimes it may only cover a group of buildings.
- A **personal area network** or **PAN**, is used to connect mobile devices such as your phone and laptop.
- A **storage area network** or **SAN**, connects data storage devices in a network to provide users with fast and secure access to their data.

Architecture

When we think of architecture, we are usually referring to the way a building has been designed to meet the needs of the people who live or work in it. But the term 'architecture' can also be used to describe computer networks. Network architecture is the way a computer system is designed to meet the needs of its users, from a simple network – known as **peer-to-peer** – to networks used in large organisations – called **client-server**.

Peer-to-peer network

This is the simplest type of network, and is used in homes and small businesses. Two or more computers are connected together to share resources such as the internet and printer (see Figure 11.3).

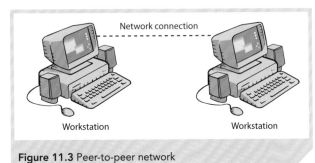

Figure 11.3 Peer-to-peer network

- In a peer-to-peer network, each computer – known as a workstation – has to be set up and configured individually, although a 'shared' folder can be set up enabling all users on the network to access the documents kept there.
- One disadvantage of peer-to-peer networks is that there are few security features.

Client-server network

Most larger businesses and organisations use a client-server network.

The network is controlled by one or more 'server' computers, which connect together all the workstations and devices on the network. The workstations are the 'clients'. To do their work, users login to the network through their workstation. The server is responsible for ensuring the security of data on the network and managing its resources.

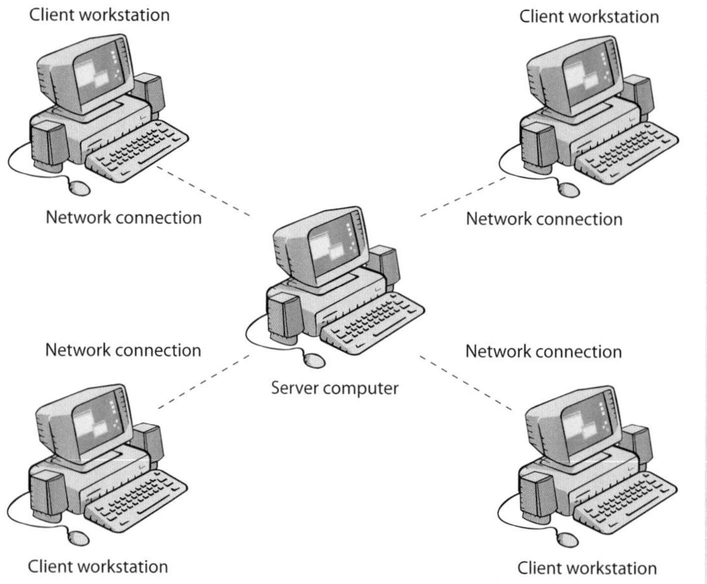

Figure 11.4 Client server network

Topology

Next time you're waiting for a train and glance at the electronic information monitor to find out when your train is expected, think 'topology'! The way information is sent and received on a wired network depends on how workstations, servers and other devices are arranged on the network cable – for example, in a line, a circle, or a star shape. The structure of the network is its **physical topology**. Its **logical topology** is the way in which workstations and servers communicate.

Physical topologies

Computers in a wired network can be arranged in several different ways, depending on the size of the network. The point at which workstations, servers and other devices connect to the network cable is known as the node.

There are several different types of network structure, or physical topology. Here are some examples:

- **Point-to-point** is the simplest physical topology, where a workstation connects directly to another using a **crossover cable**. It can be used to transfer a system from an old computer to a new one, for gaming or for a very simple network.
- **Star** topology is mostly used in homes and in small businesses. Workstations, printers and other devices are connected via cable to a central switch, hub or router. Imagine the switch in the centre, with spokes to the nodes forming a star shape.
- **Tree** topology links star topology networks together. It is used by medium to large businesses and organisations.
- **Ring** topology workstations are connected in a circle, with the server forming part of the circle. In the 1990s, ring topology was used by nuclear physics scientists in Switzerland to create a high-speed, long-distance network. Ring topologies are rarely used today.

Discussion point

Think of five groups of people who might use a computer network. For each case, discuss whether they should choose peer-to-peer or client-server networks.

Key terms

Physical topology – The design of how networked computers connect into a network.

Logical topology – Communication standards which specify how data may be moved across a wired network.

Crossover cable – A network cable that is used to connect two devices of the same type, e.g. two computers or two switches.

CONTINUED ▸▸

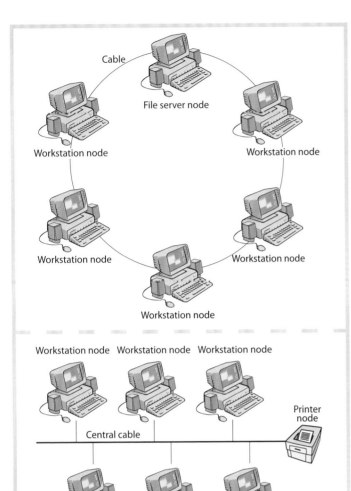

Figure 11.5 Example of a ring and bus topologies

- **Bus** topology workstations are connected in a line to a central cable, with the printer connected at one end of the cable (see Figure 11.5). This system used to be popular as a simple and cheap way of networking computers, but it is very slow and can be easily overloaded when a lot of data enters the system.

- **Mesh** topology is like a net – every workstation or device on the network is connected to each other, which means that there are many routes between the nodes. BT operates a mesh topology for the phone network we use for our voice calls and broadband – if there is a break in the system, voice or data can be routed around the problem.

Logical topologies

Earlier in this unit, we learned that wireless networks such as Wi-Fi use a set of standards developed for wireless technology which specify the different speeds at which data may be transmitted. Wired networks also have a set of standards that they use to communicate – this is known as logical topology. Standards are important in the computer industry because they help to maintain reliability and quality.

There are two main types of logical topology, or standard:

- **Ethernet** is the commonly used standard. It is used in modern networks where communications (data) are sent out directly from one computer to another, as in bus or star topology.

- **Token ring** is used in ring topology, where computers are arranged in a circle. Imagine a network of five computers, with computer 1 being the first in the network and computer 5 the last; computer 5 is connected to computer 4 and computer 1. A **token**, rather like an empty box, moves around the circle and is used to communicate (send data) between computers. Say computer 4 wants to send data to computer 1, it fills the empty token with the data, addresses the token to computer 1 and sends the token round the circle; now that the token is in use it cannot be used by any other computer in the circle. The token moves round the circle, only stopping when it reaches the computer it's addressed to, computer 1, which then empties the token of its data. The token is now empty and is ready for use once again to carry communications.

Key term

Token – A way of moving data between workstations and servers. The token is a signal that is continuously passed around the network and is able to carry data.

Activity 11.1

Team up with some others in the group to investigate how the network is set up in your school. Present your findings to the rest of the group.

Just checking

1 Which physical network topology is not much used in current systems? Why?

2 What is the biggest advantage of a mesh topology? Why?

3 What is Ethernet?

Features of computer networks 2

Introduction

There are three more features of computer networks that we need to look at:

- Security of the network – from the smallest home network to the largest corporate network, it is essential the network and the data it holds is kept secure, and that the system cannot be accessed by anyone who isn't authorised to do so.
- Software which is used to keep the network running smoothly – sometimes called utility software.
- Networks provide a range of services to their users, including resources such as software and access to the internet.

Security

Backing up data

If you or a family member have experienced a computer crash, and lost the work you've been doing, you will understand the importance of making backups. Imagine what would happen if a small business lost all its data as a result of a fire or flood in the workplace. If it cannot recover the data, the business may not be able to operate for days or even weeks, and might even have to close down.

On a network, data is usually regularly backed up centrally and the backup kept somewhere safe off site.

Network access and resources

If you use a social network site such as Facebook, you may be familiar with instances of people gaining access to other people's profiles without their permission. This can be a very upsetting experience for the person whose profile has been accessed. One way to prevent anyone unwanted accessing your social network account or other accounts you have on the internet is to keep your passwords safe and secure.

In a similar way, businesses try to keep their networks secure from unauthorised access. No business wants important documents or sensitive data to fall into the hands of its competitors. One way to make sure that authorised users only can access data on the network and other resources such as the internet, printers, scanners, and so on, is for employees to input a personal identity (ID) and password at login. The security of the network also depends on its users keeping their ID and password confidential.

In some organisations, not all employees will be permitted full access to the network, or there may be restrictions on the websites users can visit to prevent damage to the network from downloading **malware**. User permissions may be set to control access to the network and keep it secure.

It is easier to keep a client-server network secure than a peer-to-peer network, as there is far more control over user logins and the parts of the system seen by the users.

Key term

Malware – Any software that is designed to do something harmful. Examples of malware include viruses and 'trojan horse' software that steals users' passwords.

CONTINUED ▸▸

Utilities

So far, we've looked at the hardware components that make up a network, but the smooth running of any network relies also on system software – any program or suite of programs that analyse and support the operating system by keeping the network safe from threats and enabling technicians to sort out any problems. System software is often referred to as utility software, and includes:

- **virus protection software** – this helps to detect any malware that threatens the system or gets through the network's firewall (see Figure 11.6)
- **access control** – as mentioned above, this restricts the parts of a network that a user should not visit such as banned web pages
- **backup systems** – these regularly make copies, or backups, of data held on the network
- **remote desktop** – this allows a computer support technician to work remotely (without needing to visit the area) to locate and sort out problems on individual workstations or servers, or to install software. (See Figure 11.7.)

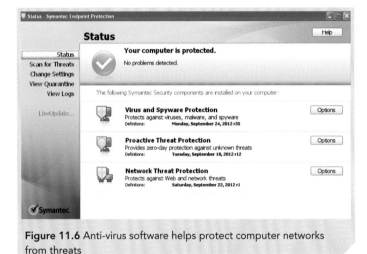

Figure 11.6 Anti-virus software helps protect computer networks from threats

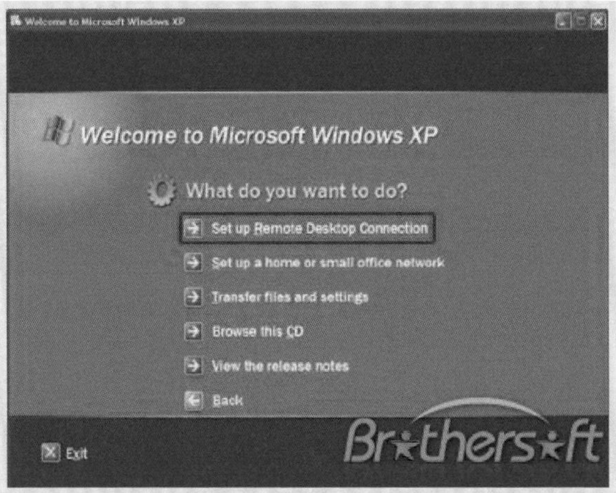

Figure 11.7 Remote desktop utility

Services

A network provides its users with a range of services. For example, when you use your school network, you may have a personal folder in which to store your work, and a shared folder in which your teacher puts documents to be accessed by the whole class. You may be able to email other students and teachers, and have access to the internet, but there are also areas which the network does not permit you to access, for example other students' personal folders, the school's administration, certain websites, and so on. These are the services of the network, and they can be tailored to meet the needs of individual users.

Network system login

When you login to your school's network, it's likely the first thing you do is to input your ID and a password. The network will use these to check that you are an authorised user before allowing you access to the system.

Once logged in to a network, the ID and password tell the network what services the user can access.

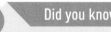

Account management

While many of the features of a network are built into the system, a network still requires a person to be in overall charge to ensure that the system is maintained and runs smoothly. This person is known as the network administrator, and in many organisations they are responsible for controlling what individual users can or cannot do when they login to the system. This is referred to as account management – every user on the network has an account which sets out what they are allowed to do on the network.

The network administrator can use account management software to set up a group on the network. The group may consist of users working in the same department who need access to each others' documents and data, or users across the organisation working together on a particular project. A user can be set as a group on the network, and account management software will be used to control the group settings. Any changes to these settings will apply instantly to all users in the group.

File and folder permissions

On your school network, you will be permitted to open some folders and use the files inside them. Sometimes you may be allowed to open documents but not to change them.

File and folder permissions can be set for an individual user or a group of users. If users are given full rights, they are able to make changes to the documents they open.

Security

We looked at some aspects of security earlier. A network is rather like a sports and leisure club – it's only open to members, and non-members may not use its facilities. An important function of network services is to set and maintain the security of the system, both to prevent unwanted visitors, such as hackers, and to ensure users have access to the parts of the network that are open to them and are blocked from entering restricted areas.

Software deployment

When you deploy something, you put it to use, so software deployment simply means the network provides application programs for authorised users.

Some organisations use software deployment to keep within the **software licences** that it has purchased. The network then ensures that only the permitted number of copies of the application can be run at any one time.

◤ Users

Computer networks are part of our everyday lives, and they cover a wide range of uses. Supermarkets, computer manufacturers, airlines, football clubs, health centres, construction companies, phone providers and call centres, all use networks for different purposes. A great feature of networks is that they can be set up to suit the needs of the organisation. A network may consist of individual users, and as we saw earlier, users can be linked together to form groups of users. A new user can instantly be given the same rights and permissions as other users, which saves time when setting up their account.

? Did you know?

Different users in different groups could believe they use a totally different network because the network services respond to their logins to provide their individual network environments.

Activity   11.2

Find out who the network administrator in your school is and ask them about administration and account management access controls for your school. Is there a difference between the access rights of staff and pupils? How do staff and pupils request for new software, for example, to be downloaded on to their systems? What licences does your school own? Does every department have access to these licences?

🔑 Key term

Software licence – when buying software a business may need several copies; it purchases a licence from the software manufacturer to allow it to run a certain number of copies of the application at any one time. It is illegal for the organisation to use any more copies than allowed by its licence. When you buy a software application for home use, the manufacturer gives you a licence to use it on your computer only.

Communication between computers

Introduction

When computers communicate across a network, they have to follow a set of rules to make sure they understand each other and that data is communicated as quickly and accurately as possible between them.

Protocols and services

What sports do you enjoy? Football, rounders, tennis, judo? Any others? The one thing all sports have in common is rules. In order to play any sport safely and for a game of football, rounders, and so on, to run smoothly, you need to know its rules.

That's the same for computer communications. When a computer communicates with another, it has to follow a set of rules, known as protocols. Computer protocols:

- specify how data can be transmitted from one system to another
- check for errors
- resend data if any problems are found.

Table 11.1 lists the three main types of protocols and services used by networks to communicate.

Table 11.1 Communication protocols and services

Protocol	What the protocol does.
Ethernet	Specifies how data should be sent between computers. Ethernet uses a **frame** to divide data up into small chunks, each of which is sent to the destination computer. The destination computer then rebuilds the frames into the data. Frames are a type of **packet**.
Internet Protocol (IP)	Specifies how data should be structured and sent over the internet. **IP** identifies where the other computer is and which route the frames or packets need to take to reach it.
Transmission Control Protocol (TCP)	A set of rules that allows all internet users to communicate whatever type of equipment they are using.

These protocols often work together: Ethernet cables make the physical connection to the communications system, IP handles the routing and TCP makes any translations needed for the systems and computers to understand each other. This is known as **TCP/IP** Ethernet, and is the system most commonly used when connecting to the internet or sending an email.

Key terms

Frame – A packet is known as a frame in Ethernet networks.

Packet – Computers transfer data by dividing each file into many thousands of packets. Each packet is individually routed to the destination computer where the packets are joined back into the data.

Internet Protocol (IP) – A set of rules that allow information to be transferred between computers on the internet. The protocols specify how data is to be structured and the control signals required.

TCP/IP – The combination of Transmission Control Protocol (TCP) and Internet Protocol (IP). TCP/IP is widely used by the internet to find websites and transfer their data to the browser so you can see the web pages.

Link

See *Unit 1 The online world* for more information on IP, TCP and TCP/IP.

IP addresses and subnets

IP addresses

When you post a greetings card to a friend or family member, you write their name and full address on the envelope. This enables the postal service to deliver it to the right person and address, even if they live thousands of miles away. Similarly, **IP addresses** are used inside networks to give each networked device an individual address, so that it can be quickly and easily identified.

An IP address has four sets of numbers (**octets**) separated by full stops, such as 192.168.1.1. If your family has a computer that can connect to the internet, it will have its own IP address.

There are two different types of IP address used by networks:

- **Static IP address.** Each computer in the network has its own individual IP address. In a home or business network, every IP address will have the same first three octets, for example 192,168.1, which identify the network. The last octet, for example 1, identifies the individual (host) computer within the network.
- **DHCP (Dynamic Host Configuration Protocol).** Here an IP address is given to computers as they join the network. In a client-server network, the IP addresses are allocated by a DHCP server. The router on your home network can be set to DHCP.

Subnets

At a whole-school assembly, the head teacher makes announcements that all students need to know. After assembly, the students split off into their individual lessons, where they are given information that is intended only for their class. A subnet on a network is similar to this. Sometimes groups of users on the network may need to have access to information that is not available to other users on the network. The network administrator can set up smaller sized networks within the main network by using IP addresses to identify different groups.

How a subnet mask works

To set up a subnet, the network administrator creates a **subnet mask**.

In a home or business network, the default subnet mask is 255.255.255.0 (255 = 11111111 in Binary Base 2 numbers). The first three octets are the network and the last one is the computer itself.

Computers use bytes, each of which has eight bits ('**binary** digits': 1 or 0). The value of a byte can be calculated by using a heading above each bit, then adding together every heading where the bit is 1. The heading we use is a sequence of numbers: 128, 64, 32, 16, 8, 4, 2, 1. If you add these together, they total 255. See if you can work out the following byte in binary:

128	64	32	16	8	4	2	1
1	0	1	0	1	0	0	0

Did you work it out? The value of the above byte is 168 (128 + 32 + 8).

continued

Did you know?

If you use a computer at home that can connect to the internet, you can find your computer's IP address by going to the Google™ search engine and typing IP address into the search box. When you press enter, Google™ will display your computer's public IP address.

Key terms

IP address – A unique address allowing a computer to be identified. Every computer on a network needs an IP address which is slightly different to the other computers, e.g. 192.168.1.5.

Octet – A number between 0 and 255 forming part of an IP address. It is called an octet, because it needs eight bits in binary (255 in decimal is 11111111 in binary).

Denary – A decimal system which has 10 as its base.

Binary – A system of writing and calculating with numbers. It only uses two digits, 0 and 1, and has 2 as a base. For example, 101 (1 four, 0 twos, 1 unit) = 5. This system is a lot closer to how a computer deals with numbers and data.

Subnet mask – Used to define how much of the IP address can change for computers that can see each other on the network.

Table 11.2 shows the subnet mask working on an IP address. Where the subnet mask has a 1, the IP network address is copied to the result. Where the subnet mask has a 0, the result is 0.

Table 11.2 The subnet mask working on an IP address

IP	192								168								1								1							
Mask	255								255								255								0							
IP	1	1	0	0	0	0	0	0	1	0	1	0	1	0	0	0	0	0	0	0	0	0	0	1	0	0	0	0	0	0	0	1
Mask	1	1	1	1	1	1	1	1	1	1	1	1	1	1	1	1	1	1	1	1	1	1	1	1	0	0	0	0	0	0	0	0
Result	1	1	0	0	0	0	0	0	1	0	1	0	1	0	0	0	0	0	0	0	0	0	0	1	0	0	0	0	0	0	0	0

This result from the subnet mask (11000000 10101000 00000001 in binary, 192.168.1 in **denary**) identifies the network part of the IP address for each of the connected computers in this network which are able to communicate with one another.

The host part of the IP address (00000000 in the result row of this example) will have a different pattern of 1s and 0s for each computer in the network.

Just checking

1 Why are computer protocols important?

2 What is TCP/IP?

3 What does DHCP provide to the network?

4 What use does a subnet mask have?

5 Name the two types of IP addresses used by networks.

Moving data across the network

Introduction

Data can be anything from a post to a spreadsheet or a web page. Moving data from one place to another is an important function of networks. In this section, we will learn how data is transmitted across the network using packet routing and the different ways or transmission modes in which data can travel.

Packets

Packet routing is the way in which data is transferred across computer networks and the internet. Data is divided into lots of small packets, which are sent individually from one system to the other. The router is a device used to find the best route or pathway for each packet to take.

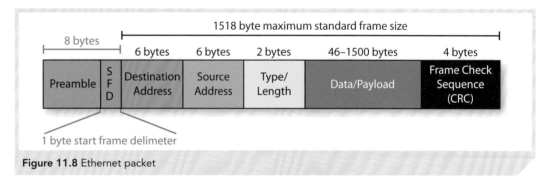

Figure 11.8 Ethernet packet

As explained in section *Communication between computers*, Ethernet packets are called frames. A frame has a similar structure to the packets used in other types of network. You can see an Ethernet packet in Figure 11.8. Here is what each part of the frame does:

- **Preamble** (the word 'preamble' means an introductory statement) – this is a regular 10101010 so that the receiving (destination) computer can get in time (synchronise) with the packet as it arrives.
- **Start of frame delimiter** – this is 11 at the end of the preamble and marks the beginning of the first byte in the frame.
- **Destination address** – the computer the packet is going to.
- **Source address** – the computer from which the packet is coming from.
- **Type/length of data field** – this gives the destination computer information about how to handle the data.
- **Data/payload** – the data being taken to the destination address. If the data is very small, then extra bits are sometimes included in a frame to make it big enough to send. This is called padding.
- **Frame Check Sequence (CRC)** – this comes at the end of the packet and enables error checking. The computer sending the data calculates the 'checksum' from the packet, so the receiving computer can do the same calculation to check for errors. If an error is found, the packet needs to be retransmitted.

CONTINUED ▸▸

Transmission modes and transfer rates

A transmission mode is the way data travels across the network. There are five main types.

Table 11.2 The five transmission modes

Simplex	This is where data travels only in one direction, from the transmitter to the receiver. For example, from your computer to a printer, or from your mouse to your computer.
Half duplex	This is where data can travel in both directions, but not at the same time, in a similar way to walkie-talkie radio. Half duplex was used in old coaxial network cables.
Duplex	This is sometimes known as full duplex. Data can travel in both directions at the same time. Duplex is used in modern UTP and STP network cabling.
Serial	Here data is sent down a cable a bit at a time. This technique is used in USB and many other types of cable. Serial transmissions can be very fast. This method is used in most modern data communications as these systems are good over distance.
Parallel	There are many strands inside the cable so a bit can travel down each strand alongside the other bits. This means that a whole byte can travel at the same time. Parallel is not used much, as there are problems with all the bits arriving at exactly the same time in a long cable. Modern serial cabling is a lot faster and better at distance. Parallel cables were used to join printers to computers.

Transfer rates

The transfer rate for any of these methods is how quickly data is transmitted. This is usually measured in bits per second, so a gigabit network connection can transfer up to a thousand million bits in a second.

Activity 11.3

Create a diagram of an Ethernet frame. Use callouts or another method to explain why the different parts of the frame are there.

Just checking ✔

1 What is a packet?
2 Explain the duplex transmission method.
3 What does a router do to packets?

Uses and benefits of a computer network 1

Introduction

Computer networks both at home and in the workplace have had a huge impact on the way we live. They've opened up a wide range of ways to communicate, allowed us to share hardware resources, exchange information electronically and benefit from a multi-user environment, both in our leisure time and in the workplace.

◤ Communication

If you have a home computer network, think of all the ways you and your family could communicate with others – you could send emails, order goods and services, make a doctor's appointment, chat online, blog, play online games with people around the world. In business, networks allow employees to communicate and exchange information with each other, and with customers and suppliers.

From this, you can see that communication is a major function of all networks. The different ways that people use networks to communicate is shown in Table 11.3.

Table 11.3 Different ways people use computer networks to communicate

Communication method	Description
Email	A popular and quick way to communicate. Documents can be attached to emails, making it an efficient way to send information. Distribution lists can be used to send emails to groups of people. Business networks often have an email server, and users select an email address from a list of people in the organisation.
Online chat tool	An online communication tool that allows users to chat to each other either through video calls or typing, and to exchange files and photos. Examples include Skype™ and Yahoo! Messenger. (See Figure 11.9.)
Social networking	You may well already use social networking sites such as Facebook, where you can set up a profile about yourself and visit the pages your friends and others have created.
Blogs	Discussion or information sites, with the most recent post listed first. Blogs are a great way of setting up web pages about something you care about, where others can visit and leave their comments.
Forums	These aim to provide answers to any questions you might have, such as how to fix your computer. Forums exist for just about anything. You can search them for information, create a new thread to ask your own question or respond to questions others have posted.
Wikis	These are websites where the users add their own information, e.g. Wikipedia.
Web conferencing	This enables businesses to hold a meeting without the need for anyone to actually travel. Each person in the meeting uses their computer to communicate with the others, usually with webcams, so they can see and be seen by the others.

CONTINUED ▶▶

▸▸ CONTINUED

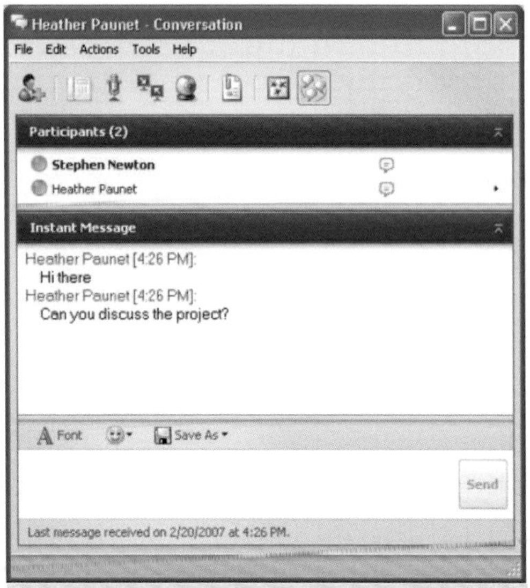

Figure 11.9 An instant messaging conversation

Sharing hardware resources

Computer hardware can be expensive to purchase and maintain, and takes up space in an office. Imagine a small business of six people, each with their own computer, printer and scanner. A network enables one printer and one scanner to be shared between all members of staff, and saves the business money only needing to buy two items of equipment instead of 12.

When someone wants to print a hard copy of their work or pages from the internet, they use the network to 'send' their work to the printer, where it prints or may wait for a short time in a queue if the printer is in use by another user. Similarly, a scanner can be shared by everyone on the network. Items scanned are saved to file and can be shared by other users.

The internet is another resource that can be shared. The network provides the connection and also provides security to protect the network from hackers and malware.

Another advantage of networks is that they offer huge amounts of storage space for a business' files and folders. Most have shared storage space, as well as private storage space in which individual users may keep their own work.

Discussion point

Can you think of any other forms of communication over a network?

Exchanging information

Businesses need to be able to share information between different departments and teams, and networks make it easy to exchange information with others in an organisation. For example, the managing director of a manufacturing company may want to know the latest sales figures. These can be easily accessed through the sales department's database stored on the network. Files of all types, such as word-processed documents and spreadsheets, can be saved to a shared folder, where others can open, view and change them.

Another way to exchange information within an organisation is through an **intranet**. This may include a list of employee contact details, important forms that can be downloaded, and to keep employees up to date with company news. An **extranet** is similar to an intranet but the users will be external to the company (rather than those with access to the intranet).

Key terms

Intranet – This is a type of communications system, rather like an internal internet, but set up and controlled by the organisation for the sole use of its employees.

Extranet – Similar to an intranet but it is designed to be accessed by authorised users from outside the organisation. It is often used for business or educational purposes.

Multi-user environments

When you login to a social networking site, you are logging into a multi-user environment, because, just like you, there are thousands of users all logged in at the same time.

Multi-user environments have two very different uses:

- **Gaming** can be more exciting on a network, because instead of playing just the computer, you can team up or compete with your friends using software to play games such as the *Halo* series.
- **Collaborative working** is highly valued in many organisations. People often make more of an effort when they work together on shared documents and projects. It can also be very practical, for example, a chain of shops might want to keep track of the money taken at each shop on a weekly basis. This can easily be done if the shops are linked by a network, as the shop managers can update their part of a shared spreadsheet.

Uses and benefits of a computer network 2

Introduction

All organisations need to have large amounts of storage space on their networks, while software applications available on a network will vary depending on the needs of the users.

Networked systems also have many features to help users be more productive at work and which can support the user experience.

Storage

Network servers have large amounts of disk space which can be used to store many files and folders containing a wide range of information. Storing data on the same server makes backing up much easier than if data is held on many computers.

Some organisations keep their files in a data centre which is usually off-site. A data centre offers a secure building in which server computers are set up with good communications links, and if there is a power cut, a backup power supply keeps the data centre up and running.

Applications

Workstations in a network usually run standard office desktop applications, such as word processing software. Depending on the type of business, specialist applications may also be available, for example, architects need design software. Users can save work to their network space or to areas shared with other users.

There are also networked online systems that can be run from individual workstations. Databases and spreadsheets are often shared by users in an organisation. The data they use is held on shared disk space.

Other applications include the organisation's intranet and extranet. When an intranet is opened up to authorised users outside the organisation, it becomes an extranet.

Productivity and user experience

Networks offer a range of features to help users improve their productivity and user experience.

- **Record keeping** is made easier, as several people can work on the same database together at the same time, and records are stored in a central place.
- **Speedy access to information.** A network enables information to be brought together quickly from different sources. For example, a user can get sales figures from a database on a computer on the same network, even if the sales team is in another building. Without the network, they would have to go and fetch the data by hand.
- **Information can be shared securely**. Files can be protected with passwords, or access to network folders can be restricted to a certain group of users.

CONTINUED ▶▶

- **Regular data backups.** These backups are not seen by users, but provide extra security. If you change or delete a file by accident, you can always restore the original version from the backup.

- **Networks can keep individuals informed.** In most organisations, the first thing users see after log in is the intranet, which often has news items on the home page to keep individuals up to date with information about the organisation. There are also network apps that allow users to talk to others, enabling instant communication.

- **Collaborative working**. See section *Uses and benefits of a computer network 1*.

- **Gaming in multi-user environment**. See section *Uses and benefits of a computer network 1*.

Assessment activity 11.1   1A.1   2A.P1   2A.M1   2A.D1

Select two computer networks that were designed for different purposes. For example, you could look at networks that are used for communication, sharing hardware resources, exchanging information, multi-user environments, data storage or distributing applications. Compare them in detail and produce an illustrated report that covers the following:

- The purpose of each network.
- An explanation and review of at least five of the following features of each network, and how they affect the user experience:
  - connection method
  - scope or scale
  - architecture
  - topology
  - protocols and their function
  - security
  - utilities
  - services
  - user groups.
- The strengths and weaknesses of each one.

Tips

- Choose two computer networks that have very different purposes.
- Include as much detail as you can about each feature.
- When reviewing how features affect the user experience, think about your own experience of using these networks.

Designing a network

Introduction

If you want to end up with a network that meets its users' needs, it is important to design it carefully.

Getting started

Most networks use switches to connect the components together using wired or wireless technologies. There is a massive range of switches available, with prices ranging from a few pounds to many thousands of pounds.

Research the switches that are currently available. Describe the extra features found in very expensive switches and the benefits they bring to an organisation.

Requirements

Designing a network is a skilled task. It usually requires a senior IT professional who can draw on experience and an up-to-date knowledge of network components to create a useful system.

The starting point for a network design should be a requirements document that clearly states everything required from the network. The requirements document can be created from a **client brief** or could be produced internally for a network designed in-house.

When designing your network, it is important to ensure that you follow the client brief. If you discover a problem with the brief, you should explain this to the client and discuss possible ways to resolve it.

The requirements document should include:

- ✓ the purpose of the network to summarise why the system is needed
- ✓ the requirements (detailed objectives) of what the proposed network needs to be able to do
- ✓ how many users there will be, with details of their roles
- ✓ the size of the network
- ✓ the location of the network, with any geographical issues
- ✓ the budget, setting out how much the network can cost
- ✓ any **constraints**, including the software and hardware you have available to implement the network.

Key terms

Client brief – The formal request from a client for you to do some work for them. The brief should include information concerning the aims of the project and clear client requirements. It should be written down so that both you and the client have something to refer back to.

Constraints – Limitations or restrictions, which make it harder to do something.

Initial design ideas

Your design for the network must include details of the following areas:

- **Users' needs.** This section in your design document describes what services and resources each type of user will need the system to provide for them.
- **Hardware components.** Your design must list the hardware components the network will need. These will include the computers, network cards, switches, cabling and any other peripherals or devices that you identify for your system.
- **Topology.** Think about the kind of topology that will be appropriate for your network.
- **Software resources.** Your design must list the software resources your network will need. You should identify the network operating system(s), applications and any utility software you think your network will require.
- **Names and roles of the network users.** Your design documentation must identify how many network users there will be for your system, with their names and roles. A table in your documentation is an effective way of doing this. You may identify one or more users who will be given administrator responsibilities for maintaining the computer network.

CONTINUED ▸▸

Did you know?

A network engineer designs, develops, tests, operates and supports computer networks and services. Other professionals who work with networks include network managers, who are responsible for ensuring that networks are secure and have sufficient capacity, and IT support technicians, who find and correct problems with the network.

- **Network diagram.** Your network diagram must explain the structure of your network and give a good guide as to how the network will be set up. This diagram needs to include the positioning of the network devices and other equipment, and show clearly how they are to be connected. The diagram should demonstrate that you have considered the IP addresses of the servers, workstations and printers in your network.

- **Test plan.** Your test plan needs to outline the tests you will perform when the network is up and running. You need to choose the tests carefully to prove that the computers connect to each other, the user logins work, and that users are able to access the necessary networked resources.

Alternative solutions

There will be more than one way in which you can design your intended computer network, using different topologies, hardware components or network architectures. You might, for example, design a cabled network and include wireless as an alternative solution.

It is always useful to think of alternative solutions when drawing up a design, as it makes you consider carefully the system you have chosen.

Activity 11.4

Swap your initial design ideas documentation with someone else in the group. Feed back to each other on the strengths and weaknesses in your designs.

Just checking

1 What is the purpose of the client brief?

2 What should be included in the requirements documentation?

3 What will be in the user needs sections of the network design documentation?

Hardware components in the network

Introduction

A network has both hardware and software components. This section looks at the hardware components used to create and run a network.

Features of hardware components

The hardware is there for the users so they can work and access the networked resources such as documents, emails, printing and the internet. Most organisations use network cabling and switches to connect the hardware together, although some networks use Wi-Fi to connect wirelessly.

How they communicate with other components

Table 11.4 explains how networks connect with different hardware components.

Table 11.4 How computer networks and hardware components communicate

Workstations	These are client computers on which users can log in to the network. Users are able to use software applications on their workstations. Each workstation connects to the rest of the system through a network adaptor.
Servers	Servers are powerful computers that control the network. A server also connects to the rest of the system through a network adaptor.
Network adaptors	Every computer in the system must have a network adaptor. The network adaptor can be wired with a network cable or be wireless with a small aerial to connect with a Wi-Fi system. A network adaptor can be a network interface card (NIC) plugged into the motherboard or can be integrated into the motherboard.
Router	A router connects the rest of the network to the internet. The router will use a cable to connect to the broadband socket. A wired router uses cables to connect to other devices in the system. A wireless router uses an aerial for Wi-Fi connections.
Hub	This is a box with sockets (ports) for the Ethernet cables. When data arrives at a port, the hub sends it to all the ports, so the data travels on to all attached devices. A hub connects networked devices together.
Switch	A switch is similar to a hub, but with better circuits inside. These circuits respond to the destination address when a packet arrives at a port. They route the packet through the switch to the port where the destination device is attached. This reduces data collisions and helps improve response times.

CONTINUED ▶▶

Network cabling

Network cabling is used in wired networks to connect components together by plugging the cables into switches or hubs.

- **Fibre optic cables.** These cables use light to transmit data. They offer a very fast connection and can travel long distances. Many organisations use fibre optic cables to connect switches together. There are many connectors in use for fibre optic, including:
  - **FC (Fixed Connector).** This is a popular connector used for telecoms distribution and LAN closets, but is now being replaced by SC and LC connectors.
  - **SC (Subscriber Connector).** This is often used for newer network applications.
  - **LC (Lucent Connector).** This is a small fibre optic connector with good performance.

Other network cabling uses electricity rather than light. This type of cabling is often called copper, as there is metal inside to conduct the electricity.

- **UTP and STP.** Ethernet is used by most modern networks with unshielded twisted pair (UTP) or shielded twisted pair (STP) cabling. Both of these types of cable have a twisted pair of wires inside the cable. STP also has a thin metal sheet wrapped around each pair to shield them from interference.
  - There is always a potential problem of interference with nearby metal cabling. Twisting a pair of wires is a very effective way of reducing interference, because interference in one wire is cancelled by the other.
  - The shielding in STP cables adds further protection. These cables are used in places with a lot of potential interference.
  - The connectors used by both UTP and STP are RJ45.
- **Coaxial.** The term 'coaxial' means that all the parts of the cable share the same axis (centre). If you cut a coaxial cable, you can see that every part is circular around the central core. Modern coaxial cables are used to connect routers to optical broadband.

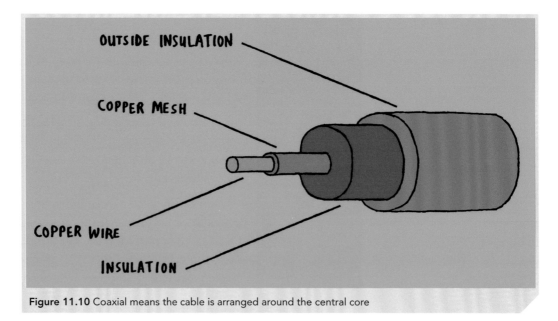

Figure 11.10 Coaxial means the cable is arranged around the central core

Wireless

Wireless connections offer a choice of technologies.

- **Infrared.** Infrared uses light to transfer data. This is a short-range slow method that has been used to transfer data between laptops and printing. It is not used much in modern systems.
- **Bluetooth.** This is a popular short-range and slow radio transmission method used between mobile phones and other devices, such as computers.
- **Lasers.** Lasers can be used in **free-space optical communication (FSO)** to transmit data fast and to link systems over a kilometre apart. This technology is good for making a connection that would be difficult for a cable and where there is direct line of sight between them.
- **Narrow-band (single-frequency) radio.** This is one of several radio technologies that can be used to transmit computer data. Most modern LANs use Wi-Fi for radio connections. Narrow-band radio is a slower radio connection that can connect up to around 3000 metres. This is more than 100 times further than most Wi-Fi systems can manage.

> **Key term**
>
> **Free-space optical communication (FSO)** – A way of transmitting data using a laser beam. It can be used for linking computer networks between buildings.

Wireless connections enable people to access computer and phone networks form practically any location in the world

> **Activity** 11.5
>
> Team up with another member of the group to work as a pair. Prepare and present a briefing for the rest on the group comparing wireless radio and light-based networks communications.

> **Just checking**
>
> 1 How can a network use laser technology?
> 2 What is STP?
> 3 How are switches and hubs different?

Software components in the network

Introduction

Once you have determined which hardware components you require, you need to think about the software components necessary to get your network up and running.

Features of software components

Software is there to run on the hardware so the users can work and the devices can communicate with each other. The network operating systems keep the communications working so the software apps can connect to shared documents and other resources.

Software components

Software components in a computer network will include a variety of applications, as well as an operating system with appropriate utilities.

Table 11.5 Network software applications

Internet browsers	These allow you to surf the internet.
Firewalls	Firewalls prevent unwanted intrusions from the internet. Note that many of professional networks use a hardware firewall, a device offering stronger protection than a software firewall can offer.
Email	Email is an essential part of a network system, used to communicate with people both inside and outside the organisation. A networked email system has advantages over a stand-alone system. For example, it provides a list of everyone inside the organisation, which is useful when you need to email somebody you have not emailed before. Also there are shared calendars, which can help you to arrange meetings and remind everyone to attend.
Anti-virus software	Network versions of anti-virus software offer features to help the administrators easily set up protection on thousands of computers and to receive notifications of threats as they are detected.
Network utilities	Many utilities exist to help run the network, including remote management, which the network administrator can use to control another computer from the IT support centre. This is useful for problem solving and for installing new software or updates, particularly if the network spans a number of locations.
Office applications	These help the user become productive. Networks can help you make better use of time and improve quality by sharing documents and configurations. You can store templates for new documents centrally, so every new document you start can be consistent with the documents of other users. Documents can be saved to shared folders, so other users can easily open and edit them for collaborative working.

Operating system

The operating systems in the network connect the computers and users together. A network operating system (NOS) will be on every computer connected to the network.

A client-server network needs a server NOS, such as Microsoft® Windows® Server, to run on the servers. It also needs a client NOS, such as Windows® 7 Professional, to run on each client workstation.

Every NOS has utilities to help it operate in the network environment.

- The server NOS has many utility software components that the administrator can use, such as the Active Directory to set up user accounts.
- An example of a client NOS utility software component is the login screen, where users enter their ID and password.

Figure 11.11 Second-user enterprise computer equipment in a warehouse

Constraints

There are usually some constraints that you need to consider when designing a network.

The cost of the components required for your intended computer network will be one of the most important factors you will have to consider. All organisations need to keep within the budget they have set for any particular area of the business or project. Usually the budget for a new network will be set by management. This will be the amount of money that can be spent on the new system.

To keep within budget, you may need to compromise on equipment that is purchased for the system. For example, you may need to buy cheaper or fewer components than you originally intended.

There may also be technical constraints due to the hardware and software that are available for the new system. For example, if an IT department has previously invested in particular equipment, you may have to reuse it, rather than buying replacements.

Old equipment can limit the functionality of a new network, due to performance limitations, such as lack of processing power, **RAM** or disk space.

Key term

RAM – Random access memory is used inside every computer to hold programs and data in current use. Data will be saved to the hard disk before switching the computer off, as the RAM will clear when power is off. RAM is often associated with volatile types of memory (where its stored memory is lost if the power is removed) but it can also be non-volatile.

Activity 11.6

Make an inventory of the hardware and software available for you to use in the computer build lab. Include in your inventory as much information as you can find about the make, brand and specification of each component.

You will be able to refer to this inventory when choosing components for your hands-on activities later.

Design documentation

Introduction

You must document your network design, so it can easily be shared and referred back to at a later date.

Setup and configuration

Your design documentation should include the configuration details of the network you have planned.

IP addressing

You need to record the IP addressing for your system. This should include the network address with either the static IP addresses of the other devices or how you will use DHCP to allocate dynamic IP addressing.

Subnet masks

If your planned design includes any subnet masks, you will need to identify them and explain how they will be used.

Security and access

You need to explain how security is to be configured in your network, with the network user rights for your users clearly shown, including:

- **access control rights** – the files and folders each user is able to access
- **shared resource rights** – list for each user:
  - the printer(s) and storage hardware resources they can use
  - whether they are allowed internet access
  - the software resources they are authorised to use.

Network user rights

You will need to set different access rights for different users. The rights for end users and administrators will vary, as administrators will have more privileges. You can present the access permissions using a table, with a row for each user and column headings for the resources and the user rights.

You should include instructions for how to manage user accounts. There needs to be enough detail here to be able to add, remove and amend user accounts on your network.

Network diagram

Your diagram must show how your network will be set up.

Structure and positioning

You will need to show the structure of your network, including a list of all the necessary components and details of how they will be positioned. Your logical diagrams should clearly show the devices with their connections. You may prefer to produce a floor plan, showing the positioning of the network devices and their connections.

IP addresses

If you are using a static IP network, your diagram must include the IP addresses of all the network devices. For a DHCP network, the addresses need to be identified in your planning documentation.

Connection medium

You should also show the connection medium/media for your network – for example, wired Ethernet or Wi-Fi.

◢ Test plan

Your test plan must test the functionality of the network and needs to outline the tests you will perform when the network is up and running. The tests need to be carefully chosen to prove that the computers connect to each other, the user logins work, and users are able to access the networked resources identified in the user needs section. Your test plan can include data such as user IDs, passwords and filenames used in the testing. Table 11.6 gives an example of a test plan.

Table 11.6 Example test plan

Test	Description	Data	Pass?	Comments
1	Kim login	ID: KimL Password: adfKL231X	Y	Password includes a mix of lower case, upper case and numerals.
2	Hasani login	ID: HasaniB Password: ekjOS973P	Y	

Connectivity

You can test the computer network for connectivity using the command prompt utilities **ipconfig** and **ping**.

Reliability

This is difficult to measure, so you could include this as your last test, with comments on any reliability issues found in the previous tests.

Performance

This can be tested by measuring the time it takes to transfer a large file using the network between computers. Your plan must test all the services required from the operating system, including shared resources, file/folder permissions and user accounts.

Key terms

Ipconfig – A command prompt utility, which shows the current IP address of a computer.

Ping – A command prompt utility, which proves that another computer can be seen on the network.

CONTINUED ▶▶

Assessment activity 11.2

| 1B.2 | 1B.32 | 2B.P22 | 2B.P32 | 2B.M22 | 2B.D2 |

You have been hired by a dental practice, Pearly Whites, to design a network for their office. The brief includes the following key points.

- The network is to be used by the dentist (Kim) and two receptionists (Hasani and Debbie). There will be a workstation with a printer in the reception area and another workstation with a printer in the office.
- Wireless access to the network is required.
- All staff should be able to print to either printer.
- Each computer will have an administrator account.
- The router needs to be separate from any of the users.
- All staff should have their own documents folder. Kim's will be on the office computer workstation, while Hasani and Debbie's will be on the reception computer.
- There should be shared folders on the reception computer for appointments, letters and client contact details.
- Both workstations will have word processor, spreadsheet, presentation and database software, as well as email installed. This software should be available to all staff members.
- Wireless internet access should also be available in the waiting area during treatment time.
- The hardware and software budget for this network is £2500, which needs to include delivery and VAT.

You need to do the following:

- Outline the purpose of the network you are going to design and the client's requirements. Consider the network brief, the users and their roles, the size of the network, the budget and any constraints.
- Produce some detailed design ideas for the network.
- Compare each design idea against the purpose and client requirements to help you choose the best one. Give a reason why you have chosen your ideas.
- Create a list of all the hardware and software components your chosen network will need. Include the role of each component (why it is needed) and describe how the components are connected and communicate with each other in the network.
- Using your list, calculate the costs involved with setting up the computer network and compare the total against the budget.
- Produce a network diagram showing how the computer network will be set up and configured. It should also indicate how many users will be using the network and the access rights of each user.
- Detail any constraints on your chosen design and what impact they will have on user experience.
- Draw up a test plan for your chosen network design and create test data including at least seven documents and five folders to test access controls, a user ID and password list to test logins and static IP addresses that you can use to test connections.

Tips

- Make sure that your design does not exceed the budget for the network. If it does exceed the budget, you should reconsider what hardware and software components you will use and find an alternative solution within the budget.
- When comparing your alternative network solutions, consider the strengths and weaknesses of each design, i.e. is it within budget, is the network speed fast enough for the use it is being put to?

Developing a peer-to-peer or client-server computer network

Getting started ▶

Discuss your network design with another member of the group to identify the hardware and software you will need for you build.

Introduction

In this section, you will work through the process of putting together a peer-to-peer network and a client-server network for two different clients. This will follow on from the designs you created earlier in this unit.

This section compares the type of hardware, software and devices you would need if you were:

- **Setting up a peer-to-peer network**. The requirements will be based on the components listed in Table 11.7.
- **Setting up a client-server network.** The requirements will be based on the components listed in Table 11.7.

Table 11.7 gives a breakdown of the hardware, software and devices you would need for each network.

Table 11.7 Comparing the hardware, software and devices required for a peer-to-peer network and a client-server network

Peer-to-peer network requirements	
Computer hardware	• Two computer systems, each with a mouse, keyboard and screen. These will be used as workstations. • Two printers for your system.
Network devices	• The system units each need a network connection. The network adaptors in this implementation are to be wired, so the system units need RJ45 network ports for the Ethernet cabling. • The printer also needs a network connection. If the printer does not have a built-in RJ45 network port, a printer server is needed to connect an Ethernet cable to the printer USB port. • Four Ethernet cables to connect workstations and printers to the router. • One 4-port router with cable to connect to the broadband socket.
Computer software	• Windows® operating system for each workstation and Kim's laptop. Your networked computers will use the operating system to perform many functions. These include adding or removing users, sharing files and folders, setting access permissions, installing applications and sharing the printer and internet. • Printer driver so your networked computers can print. • Print server configuration utility for if you have a printer that does not have a network connection RJ45 port built and you use a print server to connect the printer to the switch. • Anti-virus software with licences for each computer to protect against malware. • Access to the router configuration to set up the internet connection and Wi-Fi security.
Additional software	• Simulated software, such as Packet Tracer, if no hardware and software resources are available. • A variety of utilities, such as remote desktop management, user rights, access control, firewall configuration, scheduling.

continued

▸▸ CONTINUED

Table 11.7 (continued)

Client-server network requirements	
Computer hardware	• Two computer systems, each with a mouse, keyboard and screen. These will be used as workstations in two of the areas. • One computer server system with a mouse, keyboard and screen. • Two printers to be used for the workstation areas. • One laptop with built-in Wi-Fi.
Network devices	• The system units each need a network connection. The network adaptors in this implementation are to be wired, so the system units need RJ45 network ports for the Ethernet cabling. • The printer also needs a network connection. If the printer does not have a built-in RJ45 network port, you will need a printer server to connect an Ethernet cable to the printer USB port. • Four Ethernet cables to connect workstations and printers to the router. • One 4-port router with cable to connect to the broadband socket. • One 16-port switch to connect workstations, printers and the router to the server. A hub or router could be used if a switch is not available.
Computer software	• Windows® Professional® operating system for each workstation and the laptop so they are able to log in to the server. • Windows® Server® operating system for the server to control the network and user logins. • Microsoft® Office Professional® disk with licences for installations. • Printer driver so the users can use this device. • Anti-virus software with licences for the network to protect against threats from malware. • Access to the router configuration to set up an internet connection.

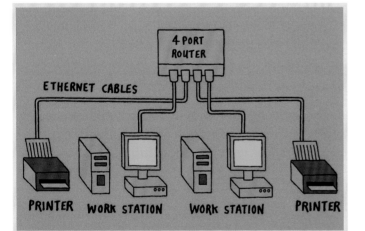

Figure 11.12 Components and network devices needed for the peer-to-peer network

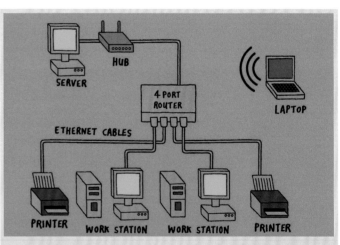

Figure 11.13 Components and network devices needed for the client-server network

Remember

Make sure mains sockets are switched off before connecting or disconnecting mains cables.

Always get help before lifting any heavy equipment.

Just checking

1. What hardware/software connections are needed for the computers to join the network?
2. What software configuration settings are needed for the computers to make their network connections?
3. How can a printer be connected and shared between peer-to-peer networked computers?

Health and safety when developing a network

Getting started

Static electricity builds up on everyone. It has the potential to damage a sensitive electronic circuit, such as a network card, if there is an electrostatic discharge (ESD) to ground through the card when it is installed into a computer.

Find some photographs of damage to electronic circuits from static electricity to use in a poster, warning of this danger.

Remember

Always look at electrical plugs and cables, and do not use if damaged.

Make sure wall mains sockets are switched off before connecting or disconnecting any mains cables.

Only switch a wall mains socket on when all cables are plugged in.

Introduction

Health and safety (H&S) is always important in everything you do and especially so when working with electrical equipment while developing a network.

Position of hardware

You need to site hardware carefully to ensure there are no H&S risks to their users. These risks include uncomfortable working positions, loose cables or equipment that might fall over.

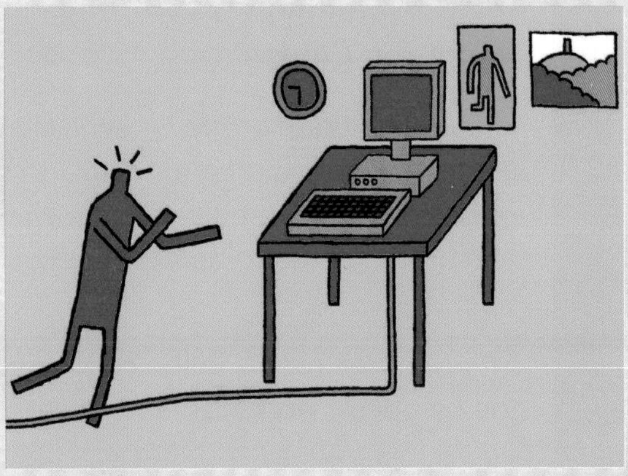

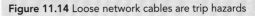

Figure 11.14 Loose network cables are trip hazards

Electrical risks

Electrical connections are potentially very dangerous:

- They can cause injury to people through electric shocks.
- Short circuits can severely damage hardware.
- Electrical sparks caused by poor or loose connections could cause a fire in the building.

You must always follow the health and safety guidelines or procedures provided by your organisation to ensure your safety and the safety of others.

Handling equipment

You must always get help if any heavy equipment needs to be moved or handled. It is dangerous to try to move heavy equipment on your own, because you could easily damage your back or drop it on your foot.

Activity 11.7

Work as a pair to research the health and safety (H&S) aspects of computer builds. Include mains and static electricity risks, as well as physical issues such as lifting. How would you communicate these to a workforce to improve their H&S awareness?

Just checking

1 How is mains electricity a risk?
2 What is a short circuit?
3 Why are sparks a risk?

WorkSpace

▷ Aiguo Tao

Network manager, Learning Resource Centre

I head up a team of five IT technicians. We are responsible for the running and support of nearly 800 workstations in the classrooms and offices of the three sites our college operates.

We use three rooms in the college main site: the helpdesk, workshop and server rooms.

The helpdesk room has our helpline telephone where users can ring in with problems. We have our desks in this room, and this is where we normally work.

The workshop is where we fix and upgrade our IT equipment. We have earth points around the benches to reduce the danger from static electricity and sensitive trips on the mains sockets to protect us.

We have a rota for the helpline telephone duty, so we take it in turns to answer calls in half-day slots.

Most of the routine network administration is to reset passwords, control internet access and to restore lost or deleted work.

The team and I train up staff in the Learning Resource Centre (LRC) on basic tasks, such as resetting student passwords. We have to assign network rights to the LRC team to enable this. About half of the password resets are by LRC staff, freeing up our time and improving the student experience. It's a win-win situation for everyone!

Our busiest time is the autumn term, when we need to create around 2000 new network IDs for the new students. User groups on the network are a massive help here, as we can process names from the enrolment system into new users.

Think about it

1 What other routine network administration tasks do you think are needed?

2 Identify the user groups within this college network.

3 What network rights would you allocate to these groups?

Testing the finished network

Introduction

Designing and installing a network is only part of the process. It is also important that you test the finished network to make sure it works and is suitable for its intended use.

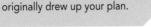

Remember

You can add to the test plan during testing, to include tests you did not think of when you originally drew up your plan.

Follow your test plan

You must follow your test plan to check all the network works as expected.

The test plan is there to make sure everything is tested, so it is important to follow your plan carefully to make sure that no test is missed.

You should carefully record in the plan the result of each test. If a test fails, you can record what happened in the comments box, along with the actions you took to resolve the problem. You should then take the test again to confirm that the fix worked. Record this in a new row added to your test plan.

Test for functionality

The testing should prove that the network functions and is fully connected, as you planned. Use command line tools, such as ipconfig and ping to test the connections and their performance. You should also use the full range of utilities and services provided by the operating system to test the network.

Make sure that you test the following:

- Computers can be seen on the network (for example, they appear in the list of networked computers viewed on another computer in the network).
- Computers can communicate through the network (for example, you can remote desktop from one computer to another).
- Performance is acceptable (for example, a remote desktop operates at a usable speed).
- Shared resources, user accounts, access control and file/folder permissions work (for example, you can print to a networked printer, and when you log in as a certain user, you only have the permissions you expect).

Client feedback

After you have set up and tested your network, you need to ask the client to test the system and provide feedback on how the networked system performs.

You should find it useful to hear this independent opinion of your system, as it might give you some ideas on how the network could be improved.

Feedback from the client needs to cover these areas:

- **Functionality**. The client must report on whether all parts of the system work as expected and if any problems are encountered.
- **Usability**. The client should give their opinion of how easy or difficult the system is to use.
- **Requirements**. The client must check your networked system against their original requirements and report on how well these have been met.
- **Performance**. The client should give their opinion of the speed of the system and whether the network is fast enough to be usable.

The role of the client could be carried out by other members of your class or the assessor.

CONTINUED ▶▶

▶ Potential improvements

Following your testing and the client reviews, you should be able to identify some improvements that could enhance your computer network. Table 11.8 sets out the key areas you should be thinking about when looking at how to improve the network.

Table 11.8 Improvements to the network

Performance	Performance can often be improved by using better hardware with a higher specification. This hardware includes the workstations, the server, the cabling or the switch used.
Capacity	This is the amount of available storage. It can be improved by adding another hard disk to the server.
Accessibility	Think about ways in which the network can be improved to make it easier for users. For example, you might include desktop shortcuts to shared resources or you could ensure that all font sizes are easy to read. You could also address any other usability issues identified in the testing and client feedback.
Portability	There could be scope to improve your networked system by setting up remote access for laptop users. This would enable them to log in from remote places such as home or Wi-Fi hotspots.
Reliability	Any reliability issues uncovered by the testing should be addressed (for example, machines disappearing from the network). You may be able to improve your network by replacing or reconfiguring unreliable components in the system.
Security	You might be able to identify improvements to the networked system security by adding biometric hardware, configuring strong passwords or implementing other measures.

Assessment activity 11.3   1C.4 | 1C.5 | 2C.P4 | 2C.P5 | 2C.M3 | 2C.M4 | 2C.D3

Now it's time to build your network.

- Using the network design you produced for Assessment activity 11.2, develop a complex computer network for Pearly Whites Dental Practice. Make sure that you implement your full network design, incorporating the hardware and software components listed in your design and created the network in your design.
- Using the test plan and test data you created for Assessment activity 11.2, test your built network for functionality and connectivity against the original client requirements.
- Record details of any faults you find, and fix them.
- Gather feedback from others on their user experiences of the functionality and connectivity of the network and use this feedback to refine the network's performance and reliability.

Tips

- Be sure to record all test results (keep a log of the tests you do) and the feedback you receive, and also what you changed as a result to improve the network.
- If users highlight problems in their feedback, ask them further questions to find out exactly what is at the source of the problem to help you fix them.

Reviewing the network

Introduction

At the end of the process, it is useful to review what you have done.

Formal review

You need to look back at the user requirements within your design documentation in order to compare them with the network you developed. You can then check whether your network provides all the services your client specified.

The purpose is similar to user requirements, but focuses on why the network was created. You need to include in your final review whether the network meets the original purpose.

An important part of your review will be feedback from the user on the network's reliability and performance.

- **Reliability.** Reliability can be judged by how easily the network connects to devices and if there are any problems with how any part of the network works.
- **Performance.** This is how quickly the system responds. Performance will significantly affect the user experience, as nobody wants a slow, sluggish system.

You may well have had hardware and software constraints when building your network. For example, you may not have been able to buy the exact equipment you specified or may have or not have had the hardware and software available in your centre.

During the review stage, ask yourself the following questions:

- What were the effects of these constraints?
- Was the network still able to deliver the services needed to meet the user requirements?
- What differences would there have been if you had been able to buy in new equipment?

Assessment activity 11.4

| 1D.6 | 2D.P6 | 2D.M5 | 2D.D4 |

Now it's time to evaluate the computer network you have created. Write a report that covers the following points:

- Consider the extent to which the final computer network you have built meets the original purpose and client requirements.
- Explain any changes you made during development and give a reason why you made them.
- Make recommendations for further improvements that could be made to the computer network that Pearly Whites may wish to consider implementing in the future.

Tips

- Whatever format you choose for your evaluation, make sure it is well structured and presented clearly.
- For each design element ask yourself: Have you included the design element? How well it fulfils the original requirements? Whether its performance or reliability be improved further?

Introduction

What do we mean by software development? You will have used many different programs, both in school and at home, for education and for entertainment. Have you ever wondered how they can make your computer or handheld device behave in such different ways?

Software development or computer programming is not about building computers or operating them, but is about giving the computer system a set of instructions that will tell it to carry out actions. These range from changing the font in a word-processing package to moving a character across the screen in a computer game.

In this unit, you will learn about developing software. By the end of this unit, you will understand the process of designing, developing, testing and maintaining a software program to solve a particular problem. You will also learn that in order to create successful software programs, you need to develop good problem-solving and creative-thinking skills.

Assessment: You will be assessed by a series of assignments set by your teacher.

Learning aims

In this unit you will:

A understand the characteristics and uses of a software program

B design a software program

C develop and test a software program

D review the finished software program.

> *I've enjoying playing around with computers throughout school. I really wanted to know much more about how computers process information to produce answers to problems, create screens for interaction and produce output. This unit really gave me the insight and grounding I was after!*
>
> *Annabelle, 18-year-old computing student*

Software
development

This table shows what you must do in order to achieve a **Pass**, **Merit** or **Distinction** grade, and where you can find activities in this book to help you.

Assessment criteria			
Level 1	**Level 2 Pass**	**Level 2 Merit**	**Level 2 Distinction**
Learning aim A: Understand the characteristics and uses of a software program			
1A.1 Identify the purpose of two simple programs and their characteristics, including tools and techniques used. **Assessment activity 12.1, page 385**	**2A.P1** Explain the purpose of two simple programs and their characteristics, including tools and techniques used. **Assessment activity 12.1, page 385**	**2A.M1** Comment on the quality of one of the given simple programs, suggesting any improvements and provide a flowchart to show the processing. **Assessment activity 12.1, page 385**	**2A.D1** Discuss the strengths and weaknesses of the software program. **Assessment activity 12.1, page 385**
Learning aim B: Design a software program			
1B.2 Identify the purpose and user requirements for the software program. **Assessment activity 12.2, page 388**	**2B.P2** Describe the purpose and user requirements for the software program. **Assessment activity 12.2, page 388**	**2B.M2** Produce a detailed design for a program, including: • alternative solutions • a detailed proposed solution using a range of design tools • test data. **Assessment activity 12.3, page 394**	**2B.D2** Justify the design decisions, including: • how they will fulfil the stated purpose and user requirements • any design constraints. **Assessment activity 12.3, page 394**
1B.3 Produce, with guidance, a design for a program, including: • a problem definition statement • an outline of the proposed solution. **Assessment activity 12.3, page 394**	**2B.P3** Produce a design for a program, including: • a problem definition statement • a proposed solution • a list of any predefined functions/ subroutines • a test plan. **Assessment activity 12.3, page 394**		
Learning aim C: Develop and test a software program			
1C.4 Maths With guidance, develop a program for a given brief, that contains: • a user interface (input and output) • constructs/techniques. (Please see guidance.) **Assessment activity 12.4, page 413**	**2C.P4 Maths** Develop a program for a given brief, which includes: • a user interface (input and output) • constructs/techniques • commentary throughout the code. **Assessment activity 12.4, page 413**	**2C.M3 Maths** Develop a functional program that meets the given brief. **Assessment activity 12.4, page 413**	**2C.D3 Maths** Refine the software program, taking account of the quality of the code and user feedback. **Assessment activity 12.5, page 413**
1C.5 With guidance, test the program for functionality and against the original requirements and repair any faults. **Assessment activity 12.5, page 417**	**2C.P5** Test the program for functionality using the test plan and against the original requirements and repair any faults. **Assessment activity 12.5, page 417**	**2C.M4** Test the program using the test data, gathering feedback from others on the usability and quality of the program, and use it to improve the software program. Repair any faults. **Assessment activity 12.5, page 417**	

Assessment criteria			
Level 1	Level 2 Pass	Level 2 Merit	Level 2 Distinction
Learning aim D: Review the finished software program			
1D.6	2D.P6	2D.M5	2D.D4
For the software program, identify how the final program is suitable for purpose and the original requirements. **Assessment activity 12.6, page 419**	For the software program, explain how the final software program is suitable for the original requirements and purpose. **Assessment activity 12.6, page 419**	Review the extent to which the software program meets the original requirements, considering feedback from others and any constraints. **Assessment activity 12.6, page 419**	Evaluate the final software programs against the initial designs and the quality of the code, and justify any changes made, making recommendations for further improvement. **Assessment activity 12.6, page 419**

Maths   Opportunity to practise mathematical skills

How you will be assessed

The unit will be assessed by a series of internally marked tasks. You will be expected to show an understanding of the characteristics and uses of software programs. The tasks will be based on a scenario. For example, you have arranged a work experience placement with a software development company. Your line manager has asked you to look at some software programs they have developed. Once he is happy that you understand how to write code, he will give you a brief to design, develop, test, and review a software program to solve a client's problem.

Your assessment could be in the form of:

- a report on existing programs
- a design for a solution to meet the brief
- a test plan and test data
- a working software program that fulfils the client's requirements
- changes you have made to the code
- a guide to using the software program, showing how it was created
- a presentation that reviews the software program against the client's or user's requirements and considers the quality of the code you have written.

Software

Getting started

What software do you use?

Think about the software programs you use at home, work, school or college. With a partner, discuss why you use those software programs. For example, you could talk about your favourite computer game.

Introduction

In this section, you will learn about software and why it is used.

Why is software used?

Software is a collection of computer programs (or sometimes one program) that tells a computer system to carry out a set of instructions. Software is used to provide a solution to a problem or to improve productivity. Computer hardware cannot function without software, and vice versa. They both rely on each other to be present for a computer system to operate in a normal way.

There are three main categories of software, as explained in Table 12.1.

Table 12.1 The three main categories of software

Application software	This type of software is intended to be run on a computer system with an operating system present. Application software includes word-processing, spreadsheets, databases, and email.
System software	This type of software is fundamental for a computer system to operate. System software includes the operating system, device drivers and any other software needed to operate specialised hardware devices or components.
Computer programming software	This type of software is used to help design and develop software programs. You will learn how to use computer programming software to write your own software programs.

Software is used for many different purposes:

- **Gaming and entertainment:** for example, computer games and social networking
- **Increasing productivity:** by using automated processing
- **Storing and managing information:** for example, using databases (telephone directories, product information, customer accounts)
- **Completing repetitive tasks:** for example, by using robotics in car manufacturing
- **Solving complex problems:** for example, stock control systems, booking systems, weather forecasting and flight tracking.

Software programs are developed using computer programming tools or specialist software. All software uses a programming language and is built using constructs and techniques. Programming languages will be discussed in this section, and constructs and techniques will be discussed in the section *Programming languages: constructs and techniques*.

Discussion point

Write a set of ordered instructions for how to make a cup of tea. Compare your instructions to another person's in the group.

Programming languages

A programming language is used to write software programs. A software program contains a set of instructions designed to carry out specific tasks on a computer system. Software applications, system software and utility software are examples of software programs written using a programming language.

There is only one programming language that computer systems can understand. This is called machine code. This language is represented in binary (1s and 0s). All other programming languages need to be translated to machine code before they are run. All other programming languages apart from machine code are considered to be low-level or high-level languages.

Low-level programming languages

Low-level programming languages allow programmers to interact with computer hardware directly. Programmers can write specific instructions (similar to machine code) that manipulate the behaviour in a computer system. Software programs can be **executed** far more quickly in low-level programming languages than in high-level programming languages, as they are very similar to machine code.

High-level programming languages

High-level programming languages are far easier to write because they use elements of our own spoken language. In this unit, you will learn how to design, write and test software programs using a high-level programming language. There are different types of high-level programming languages.

- **Procedural programming.** This allows programmers to write software programs that contain a set of instructions, which are followed in a sequence from beginning to end. Pascal, C and COBOL are examples of procedural programming languages.
- **Event-driven programming.** This allows programmers to write software programs that respond to events. Events contain actions that are performed by the user. For example, a user may click on a button in an application, which may play a sound. Visual Basic, Visual Basic.NET, and Visual C++ are examples of event-driven programming languages.

Link

See *Unit 2 Technology Systems* for more information about binary.

Key term

Execute – To perform or carry out a software program containing a set of instructions.

Link

Compiling is covered in more detail in section *Programming languages: constructs and techniques.*

Did you know?

Programming languages have been in existence since the 19th century. In 1801, Joseph-Marie Jacquard punched holes in cards to control movements by a weaving hook to create decorative patterns in fabric.

Activity 12.1

1 List as many examples as you can of procedural and event-driven programming languages.
2 Do you think writing software programs in a low-level programming language is easier than writing programs in a high-level programming language? Explain your answer.

Just checking

1 What is the difference between a high-level programming language and a low-level programming language?
2 Why can low-level programs be executed far more quickly than high-level programs?
3 What is the only programming language that computer systems can understand?

Programming languages: constructs and techniques

Introduction

Software programs are developed using a range of constructs and techniques. For example, if you develop a software program that adds two numbers together and displays the result on the screen, you need to use commands (constructs) that allow the software to store and manipulate numbers. Techniques are the ways in which you use commands to make software programs. The following constructs and techniques are used in most programming languages.

Command words

A command word is an instruction which usually forms part of a statement that tells the computer system to perform a specific task. For example, FOR… and NEXT… are command words used in Visual Basic.

Subroutines

A subroutine, function or procedure is a portion of code within a program that performs specific tasks, either separately or in connection with the main program. Subroutines, functions and procedures will be covered in detail later in this unit (see section *Variables, data types, assignments and structures*).

Basic string handling

String handling is a set of **predefined** functions that allow programmers to write software programs to manipulate strings. A string consists of one or more characters, including text and numbers. For example, 'I enjoy sport' is a string. You can manipulate string in the following ways: removing all spaces, replacing characters or changing lower case characters to upper case.

Basic file handling

File handling is a set of predefined functions that allow programmers to write software programs that open, read, write and close **files**. Information is stored in files that are saved on the computer system. Storing information in files allows users to retrieve data quickly. For example, letters, images and emails are saved in files.

Data structures

A data structure is the way in which data is stored, organised and accessed within a software program. **Arrays** and records are examples of data structures.

Event handling

Event handling manages and responds to the inputs received within a software program. For example, when a user clicks a mouse button (event), the event handler routine recognises this and performs the defined set of actions for that event.

Activity   12.2

1 FOR... and NEXT... are command words used in Visual Basic. What is the purpose of these command words?

2 Apart from file handling, can you think of another way data can be stored permanently in a software program?

3 What is the difference between string handling and file handling?

Compiling programs

A compiler is a software program that translates **source code** into machine code. It takes the software program code written in a high-level programming language and transforms it into a low-level programming language.

Low-level software programs interact with and control the hardware in a computer system. For example, if you want your software to read the contents of a DVD-ROM, the software must control the DVD-ROM drive. So, before any software programs can be executed by the computer system, they need to be compiled. You will be expected to write software programs that will go through this process.

One of the major functions of compiling is to check the source code for any errors that will prevent it from running. You will learn a lot more about this and how it is used to support the **debugging** of programs (see section *Testing the program solution*).

Key terms

Source code – The text that is used to create software programs in a high-level programming language.

Debugging – The process by which you can find errors in a software program.

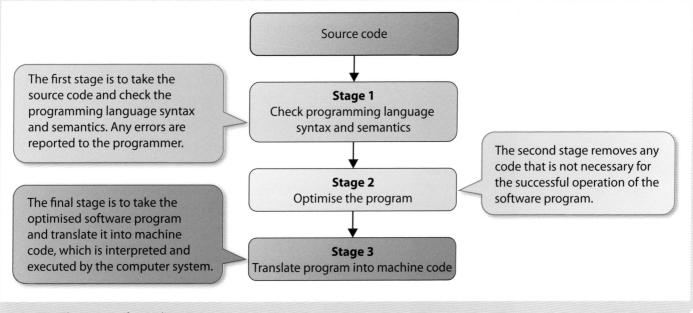

Figure 12.1 The process of compiling a program

Just checking

1 Why do software programs need to be compiled?

2 What happens to a software program if any errors are found?

3 What happens to the source code of a software program when it has been successfully compiled?

Quality of software programs

Introduction

Computer users expect software programs to be of a good standard. Therefore, it is important for programmers to think carefully about the design, and the techniques they use to develop the software. This section looks at the ways in which you can measure the quality of the software.

Table 12.2 Ways of measuring the quality of software

Efficiency/ performance	When you design a software program, a key feature will be how well it performs in terms of speed, processor time, memory space and interaction with storage media.
	The overall performance of a computer system and how fast the software program carries out its instructions will be a measure of the quality of your software. The way in which the code is written has a big impact on this. For example, a software program that has efficient and well structured code will perform better than one with poorly structured code which more lines of code than is necessary to get the same outcome.
Maintainability	A well-written software program can easily be modified in order to carry out any necessary alterations to the code. These could be in order to correct, refine or adapt the existing code.
	It is important that you write a software program that is easy for you or someone else to change in the future. For example, you should add comments and use meaningful names for variables.
Portability	Programmers must think about how software programs will run on different types of computer systems. Software can react and perform differently, depending on the type of computer system. Software is considered highly portable if it can execute any type of computer system.
Reliability	People depend on software to provide them with accurate information. The data is used to inform important decisions. For example, sales figures can determine whether or not someone receives a bonus. So the accuracy and reliability of a software program's outputs are another crucial measure of quality.
Robustness	Software needs to be able to cope with processing large amounts of data reliably. It must also be able to handle unexpected input values in a controlled way (for example, by displaying a warning instead of **crashing**).
Usability	It is important that a software program is easy to use for its intended purpose. You need to design your software carefully to guard against problems such as a poor layout of the user interface, a lack of instructions to help the user, or error messages which do not explain how a problem can be fixed. As part of the design, users should be involved in testing the software for usability.

Key term

Crashing – When a software program freezes or stops performing. There are many causes of software program crashes.

Assessment activity 12.1

You work as an intern for a software development company. You have been given the following programs to assess:

Program 1

Public Class frmCurrency

  Private Sub btnCalculate_Click(ByVal sender As System.Object, ByVal e As System.EventArgs) Handles btnCalculate.Click
    'Data Declaration
    Dim amount, rate, result As Decimal

    amount = CDec(txtAmount.Text)
    rate = CDec(txtRate.Text)

    'Calculate result by multiplying the amount with the exchange rate
    result = amount * rate

    'Display the result
    txtResult.Text = result

  End Sub
End Class

Program 2

Public Class frmSelection

  Private Sub btnSubmit_Click(ByVal sender As System.Object, ByVal e As System.EventArgs) Handles btnSubmit.Click
    'Data Declaration
    Dim Sales_Total As Integer
    Sales_Total = txtSalesTotal.Text
    'Amount entered into 'Sales Total' Text Box equal or exceeds 150,000 in the 'If Statement', Message Box to display 12,000.
    If Sales_Total > 150000 Then
      MsgBox("Bonus Achieved: 12,000")
      'Amount entered into 'Sales Total' Text Box ranges from 90,000 to 149,999 in the 'If Statement', Message Box to display 8,000.
    ElseIf Sales_Total >= 90000 And Sales_Total <= 149999 Then
      MsgBox("Bonus Achieved: 8,000")
      'Amount entered into "Sales Total' Text Box ranges from 50,000 to 89,999 in the 'If Statement', Message Box to display 5,000.
    ElseIf Sales_Total >= 50000 And Sales_Total <= 89000 Then
      MsgBox("Bonus Achieved: 5,000")
      'Amount entered into 'Sales Total' Text Box less than 50,000 in the 'If Statement', Message Box to diplay 0.
    Else : MsgBox("Bonus Achieved: 0")
    End If
  End Sub

End Class

Start by explaining the purpose and characteristics of each software program, including detail of the tools and techniques used.

Now carry out a review of the programs. Your review should include a discussion of:

- the strengths and weaknesses of the program
- the quality of the program
- any problems with it and any improvements that could be made to it. Include a flowchart showing the processing of the program once the improvements you have suggested have been made.

Tips

- Include as much useful detail as you can about the characteristics of each software program and the tools and techniques they use.

- You are expected to run the programming code, not just read it. However, if you do not have the facilities to run the code, you can do a dry run using a trace table.

Design a software program

Introduction

Program or software design is a fundamental part of the software development process. In this section, you will explore the types of design documents that typically fulfil the design specification. You will also learn about the software design process. The software development life cycle will give you an insight into how software programs are developed.

Software development life cycle

When designing a software program, you need to be aware of how long the process will take, from the starting point (inception) through to the end point (completion).

The software development **life cycle** is the approach adopted by programmers. Each stage of the software development life cycle is performed in a cyclical sequence. This is what gives the life cycle its name. There can be slight variations in individual software development life cycles, but all of them carry out the same processes.

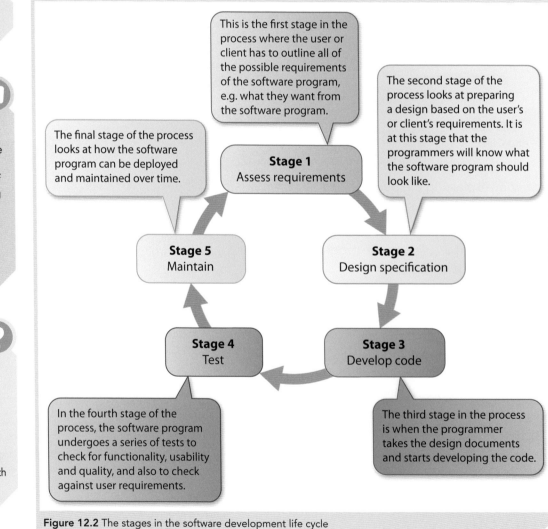

This is the first stage in the process where the user or client has to outline all of the possible requirements of the software program, e.g. what they want from the software program.

The second stage of the process looks at preparing a design based on the user's or client's requirements. It is at this stage that the programmers will know what the software program should look like.

The final stage of the process looks at how the software program can be deployed and maintained over time.

Stage 1 Assess requirements

Stage 5 Maintain

Stage 2 Design specification

Stage 4 Test

Stage 3 Develop code

In the fourth stage of the process, the software program undergoes a series of tests to check for functionality, usability and quality, and also to check against user requirements.

The third stage in the process is when the programmer takes the design documents and starts developing the code.

Figure 12.2 The stages in the software development life cycle

1   Can you think of any other information a client should give during the first stage of the software development life cycle?

2   Each stage of the software development life cycle has to be completed before the programmer can progress to the next stage. What are the potential problems with this approach?

3   The model shown in Figure 12.2 does not consider **iterations**. Redraw the software development life cycle to include iterations between stages.

Intended purpose and user requirements

Before you develop a software program, it is important that you gain an understanding of what needs to be done to fulfil the client's requirements.

You will be given a brief by the client. The brief will outline a problem for which you need to design and develop a software program. The brief should contain the intended purpose of the software program, with a list of the user requirements you should consider. In this unit, you will think about the intended purpose of the software program and user requirements for a given brief. This information will be used to translate your ideas into a design.

Design specifications

A design specification helps you to identify the different elements involved in the design process. It should outline the scope, inputs, outputs, processing, user interface and constraints for the intended software program. It is a good idea to refer to your design specification during the software development life cycle.

Table 12.3 Design specifications for software

Scope	Scope is about understanding the requirements of the software program, capturing all necessary information that will be used as part of the development of a software program.
Inputs	Inputs are the data you input into the software program after the software program runs.
Outputs	Outputs are the data which is generated by the software program after the software program runs.
Processing	Processing is often referred to as the main software program tasks, and will manage any inputs, outputs and storage to meet the ultimate aim of the software program.
User interface	The user interface is what allows users to interact with and use a software program. Graphical User Interfaces (GUIs) is mainly used in software programs.
Constraints	A constraint is considered to be anything that will prevent a software program from fulfilling its intended aim and purpose, and/or impacts upon the quality of a software program.

CONTINUED ▶▶

Problem definition statement

A problem definition statement outlines the issues that the client or user is experiencing in a particular area that they feel a software program could resolve.

Take it further

You can take your investigation further by interviewing the client so that you are absolutely clear about what the software program is intended to do. This will ensure that you do not spend many hours designing and developing a software program that does not meet the requirements. Many programming projects fail because of a lack of communication between the client and the software developer.

Assessment activity 12.2   1B.2 | 2B.P2

Dayce Travel Agency is a family-run travel agency business. The company currently uses a paper-based system to manage holiday bookings, but they would like to change over to an electronic system. Richard Dayce, the company's director, has asked for your help in setting up the system. He would like the new software program to allow staff to:

- create, amend and cancel holiday bookings
- search and browse for holidays
- print holiday bookings
- print sales reports.

To ensure that you have understood the brief, create a report for Richard explaining the intended purpose and user requirements of the software program.

Tip

Make sure that you present your report in a clear and professional format.

Planning your design 1

Introduction

Planning the design for a software program is a very important part of the software development process. The first part of design planning determines what the main software program tasks will be, and how the program will be presented to the client. This stage of the process also gives some thought about how information is going to be stored, managed and processed.

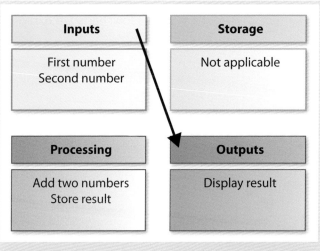

Figure 12.3 Diagram representing a series of inputs, processing, storage, and outputs

Description of the main software program tasks

Your description of the main program tasks should identify the inputs and outputs of the software program. Inputs are the data you input and outputs are the data shown after the software program has run. For example, in a software program that adds two numbers together and displays the result, the inputs are the two numbers, and the output is the result.

You need to know what information is going into and out of your software program. You will refer to this when you start writing the program. This series of inputs and outputs can be presented in a diagram. See the example in Figure 12.3.

Screen layouts and navigation

The client needs to know what the proposed user interface should look like. Using diagrams to sketch out the design is a good way of doing this. Navigation diagrams are also useful for seeing how the screens will be linked together. It is important to discuss your screen layouts and navigation diagrams with the client or user, so that they can provide you with feedback and check that you are meeting their expectations. User interfaces often make use of forms. For more information on forms see section *Event handling: forms*.

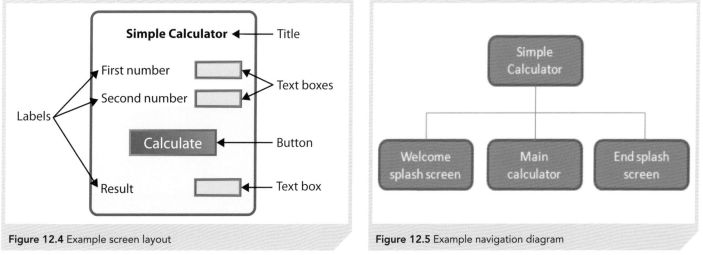

Figure 12.4 Example screen layout

Figure 12.5 Example navigation diagram

CONTINUED ▶▶

▶▶ CONTINUED

Prototyping is a technique that allows you to experiment with different ideas by producing alternative designs. You can then decide what design to take forward for development. Most designs will have some problems, so it is always a good idea to consider alternatives.

Algorithms

Algorithms are a series of step-by-step instructions written to solve problems. They can be expressed in many different ways, including **pseudo code**, flowcharts and programming code. Algorithms are useful for identifying the major functions of a software program, including the processing that takes place within them. You will refer to this processing when you start writing the software program. Flowcharts are explored in more depth in section *Flowcharts*. See the example in Figure 12.6.

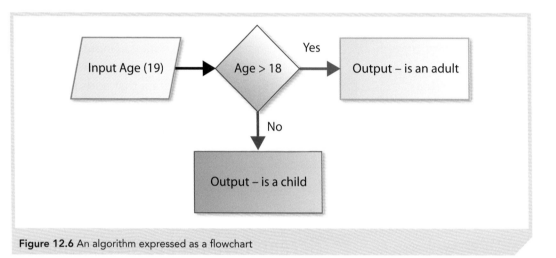

Figure 12.6 An algorithm expressed as a flowchart

```
Program Calculator
Start
    Ask user to enter the first number
    Accept and store the first number

    Ask user to enter the second number
    Accept and store the second number

    Add the two numbers together and store the result
    Display the result
End
```

Figure 12.7 Example program in pseudo code

Pseudo code

Pseudo code is used to show how the proposed software program will be written and presented. This form of code uses human language and contains a series of brief statements describing what the code will be doing. Pseudo code will help you understand the structure of the software program before you start to write it.

Figure 12.7 shows an example of pseudo code for a simple calculator software program, which adds two numbers together and displays the result.

Data structures

A data structure is the method by which information is stored and organised. There are many different types of data structures. Some examples include arrays, records, hash tables, lists, trees and graphs. The most common type of data structure used in software development is an array.

An array can store a large set of data in a single data structure, where individual elements can be accessed directly, based on their location in the array. You will learn how to implement data structures in a software program. Figure 12.8 gives an example of an array data structure. For more information on arrays, see section *Data structures*.

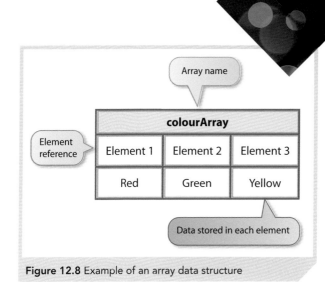

Figure 12.8 Example of an array data structure

Data storage

Data storage is a way to store data permanently after a software program has finished. There are two common types of data storage: databases and files. You will need to decide on the type of data storage that is most appropriate, depending on the problem and client's requirements. You will learn how to develop software programs that read/write information to a file.

Control structures

Control structure or control flow is the order in which instructions are performed. Software programs that make choices have a structure, which manages how these decisions are made. Examples of control structures used in software programs include IF, select and loop statements. These instruct the computer system to make decisions (IF) or to repeat specific functions (loop). You will need to decide on the most appropriate control structures to use, bearing in mind the quality of the software program. You will learn how to develop software programs that include selection and repetition statements.

Data validation

Data validation is the process of checking data. The data must undergo a series of validation checks, which make sure that the data is correct and presented in the right way. For example, entering text characters instead of numbers in a numeric field on a form should result in an error.

Before you write the code, it is important to think about the inputs of your software program and how you will validate them. This is so you can decide which type of validation check is most appropriate to the input data. The consequences of not doing so could lead to serious problems for the user, such as discovering that their name is spelt wrong or the wrong amount of money has been credited to their bank account.

Error handling and reporting

Error handling is thinking about the possible problems that could arise in your software program. If you can anticipate these errors at the start of the development, you can include additional code that will capture the errors and provide a means of stopping the software program. You will often see messages following a software program 'crash', which give you the choice either to stop/restart the software program or to search other sources for possible resolutions. This is how errors are reported back to their software manufacturers.

Planning your design 2

Introduction

The second part of design planning allows the software developer to think about some of the items covered in the first part, and determine whether or not there is a better way of delivering the same solution. Software designers also need to think about reusability and if there is any existing source code written by others that could be included in their software programs, providing that they have permission. They also need to give some thoughts about testing and any constraints.

Alternative solutions

It is good practice to consider alternative ideas and solutions as part of your design. There will always be a different way of achieving the same goal. You may even find that ideas you didn't think of at first turn out to be the best ideas that you then take forward in your development.

You can present alternative solutions in different ways using the following:

- screen layouts
- screen navigation diagrams
- algorithms

- processing structures
- data structures
- control structures.

You should comment on how each version of your design documents differs from the others. For example: 'I feel that Alternative screen layout 2 has a better user interface than Alternative screen layout 1, because the objects presented are not so close together, and there is some kind of visual process to follow.' (See Figures 12.9 and 12.10.)

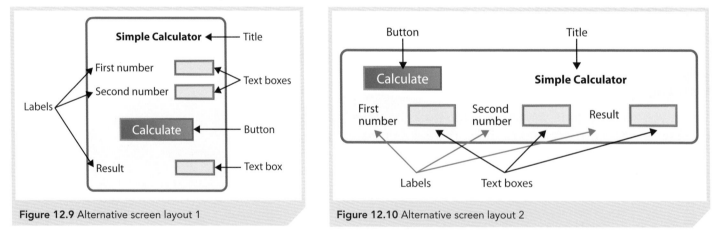

Figure 12.9 Alternative screen layout 1

Figure 12.10 Alternative screen layout 2

Predefined programs

One of the key benefits to software development is reusability. Reusability is the technique of reusing the same segment of code either in the same software program or in a completely different software program (provided that you have permission to do so). You will find that most software programs contain duplicate segments of code, with perhaps some tweaks made by programmers to customise it for their own purposes. One reason for reusing code is that time can be saved if the code has already been written.

It is important to emphasise that you need to seek permission to use code written by someone else, especially if you intend to use it in your own software program. If you are going to reuse code, make sure you acknowledge the source in your software program's comments.

You will need to spend time looking for any predefined code that would be useful in your software program. If you do find any useful code, it is important to explain how the code will help with the development of your software program, not forgetting to make a list of the sources where you obtained it. You should include this information in your design documents.

The internet provides a large resource bank for predefined software programs and code snippets.

Test plan with test data

Testing is a fundamental part of the software development life cycle, designed to make sure that all aspects of your software program work as they should.

You will need to produce a test plan, including test data, to outline the range of tests that you will carry out on your software program. Test plans with test data are explored in greater depth in section *Testing and refining the software*.

Constraints

Many programmers will be challenged by **constraints** that affect the way a software program is designed and developed. Sometimes it can be difficult to overcome these constraints, especially if the necessary resources are unavailable. Therefore, programmers often have to consider alternative solutions.

Here are some examples of constraints that are common in software development.

- **Time** – there is limited time to design and develop a complex software program.
- **Costs** – a programmer's fees for developing the software program could be considerably more expensive if it takes longer than expected.
- **Programming software and tools (availability)** – the programmer may not have access to a particular programming language.
- **Programming software and tools (limitations and capabilities)** – programming languages will have limited functionality, which may mean that the user requirements of the software program cannot be fully met.
- **Client's computer system (including hardware and software)** – limited memory and processor speed, for example, will affect the performance of your software program, while problems of connectivity to external devices could mean that printers are not available.
- **Frameworks** – for example, Apple™ applications can only be written using a Mac operating system.

You will need to consider whether there are any constraints that are going to prevent you from fulfilling the client's requirements. If there are, you should look into alternative solutions and discuss them with the client. Make sure you include this information in your design documents.

> **Key term**
>
> **Constraints** – Limitations that prevent a software program from fulfilling its intended purpose.

CONTINUED ▶▶

Link

For more information about using predefined code snippets, see *Unit 8 Mobile apps development*.

Activity 12.4

1 Use the internet to find free predefined software programs and/or code snippets, and explain their purpose.
2 Make a note of the websites where you found the predefined software programs and/or code snippets.
3 Can you think of any more constraints (other than those listed) that can affect how a software program is designed or developed?

Assessment activity 12.3

| 1B.3 | 2B.P3 | 2B.M2 | 2B.D2 |

The Dayce Travel Agency would now like you to design their new software program.

Use the original user requirements and the report you produced for Assessment activity 12.2 to produce a detailed design for the software program. Your design documentation should include the following.

- A problem definition statement showing your understanding of the original user requirements and intended purpose of the software program.
- A number of proposed solutions. Consider all your design alternatives in relation to the brief and decide which one will best fulfil the purpose and user requirements. Consider also whether there are any constraints on each design and what impact they will have on user experience. This will enable you to justify your final design decisions.

Once you have decided upon a solution, produce a detailed proposed solution report using a range of design tools. Your report should include.

- A description of the main software program tasks, including all inputs and outputs.
- Screen layouts and navigation diagrams.
- Pseudo code for the proposed software program.
- A list of data structures you would use, and how the data will be stored.
- An explanation of how you will validate the data.
- A list of any predefined functions/sub-routines or programs that you intend to use, with acknowledgement of the sources.
- A test plan for your chosen software solution design and test data that you have created that will enable you to test your software program.

Tips

- You can present your description of the main software program tasks (inputs and outputs) as a diagram.
- Make sure you annotate your screen layouts and navigation diagrams and explain the differences between each design.

Flowcharts

Getting started

Diagrams are a great way of solving problems easily and are used a lot in the IT and creative computing industries. When was the last time you browsed through a document, either paper-based or online, and found a diagram to help you troubleshoot a problem?

Using the internet, find a diagram which could help someone resolve a technical problem with their personal computer system.

Introduction

A flowchart is a diagram that represents a particular process in a system or software program. People use flowcharts to find solutions to problems, and they are often used in troubleshooting contexts.

Producing flowcharts is a very important activity in the design process. A flowchart contains a mixture of symbols, which are all connected together to illustrate how data flows throughout a process.

Figure 12.11 shows an example of a flowchart that calculates the additional premium for car insurance, based on the number of years' driving (D) experience, and the number of years of no claims (C). The flowchart shows the decisions to be made.

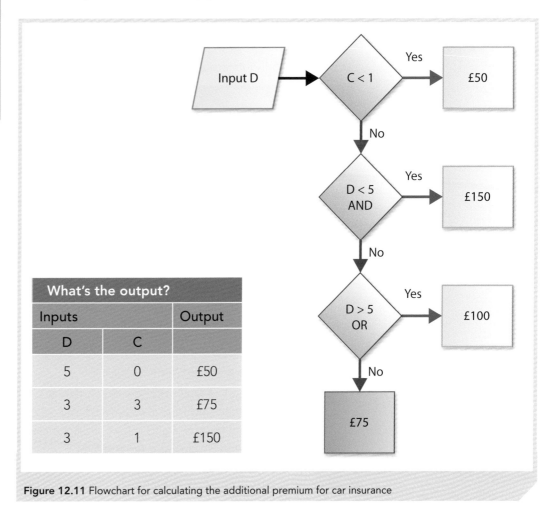

What's the output?		
Inputs		Output
D	C	
5	0	£50
3	3	£75
3	1	£150

Figure 12.11 Flowchart for calculating the additional premium for car insurance

The flowchart works by taking the input values in the table and feeding it through the process until a possible output can be determined.

CONTINUED ▶▶

Activity 12.5

Using the flowchart shown in Figure 12.11, determine the outputs for the following input values:

1 D is 6 and C is 1.

2 D is 3 and C is 4.

Activity 12.6

Dayce Travel Agency would like to tell customers the cost of flights to and from Switzerland on certain days, as well as the times of the week and the choice of airlines available.

There are only three airlines flying to/from Switzerland:

- Euro Airways
- Beta Air
- Tango Airlines.

Flights are operating Monday to Sunday between 7:00 am and 8:00 pm.

The following flights are available:

Days	Times	Cost	Airline
Friday to Sunday	7:00 am to 10:00 am	£500	Euro Airways
Friday to Sunday	10:00 am to 4:00 pm	£300	Beta Air
Friday to Sunday	4:00 pm to 8:00 pm	£400	Tango Airlines
Monday to Thursday	7:00 am to 10:00 am	£400	Euro Airways
Monday to Thursday	10:00 am to 4:00 pm	£200	Beta Air
Monday to Thursday	4:00 pm to 8:00 pm	£300	Tango Airlines

If a customer wants to fly to Switzerland on a Saturday at 9:00 am and return on a Thursday at 7:00 pm, it is going to cost them £500 to fly out and £300 to return. This is a total cost of £800. They would be flying with Euro Airways and Tango Airlines.

1 Create a design for a flight booking system, which can be added to the travel agency's management software program.

- Draw a flowchart to illustrate how the software program will find individual costs for flights to and from Switzerland, based on the day and time that the customer wants to fly out and return. Test the decisions made in the flowchart by inputting random day and time values.
- Show the outputs of these decisions.

Just checking

1 What is the purpose of a flowchart?

2 What are the main symbols used in flowcharts?

3 What is meant by a process?

Develop software

Getting started

Can you remember a time when you may have controlled an object on-screen using simple instructions? Or created a product on a Computer Numerical Controlled (CNC) milling machine?

Find or give some examples of how instructions have been used to create products or solve problems.

Introduction

In this section, you will learn how to develop and refine your own software programs using suitable constructs and techniques. As this unit is intended to cover the introductory concepts of programming, you will learn Visual Basic. Visual Basic is a high-level programming language and a perfect software tool for anyone wanting to learn programming. As you work your way through the activities in this topic, you will improve your understanding of using a development environment to produce code.

Discussion point

With a partner, discuss the benefits and drawbacks of developing software programs.

Key term

Integrated Development Environment (IDE) – A software tool that allows programmers to write software programs.

Creating a new project

To get started, you will learn how to create a new Visual Basic project, followed by a brief tour of Visual Basic's **Integrated Development Environment (IDE)**.

You will need to create a new project for all the software programs you write. The latest version of Visual Basic is available to download from the internet. For the purposes of these activities, you will need to have already successfully installed this product.

How to create a new project

Step 1 Open Visual Basic.

Step 2 Click the **File** menu and select **New Project** (see Figure 12.12).

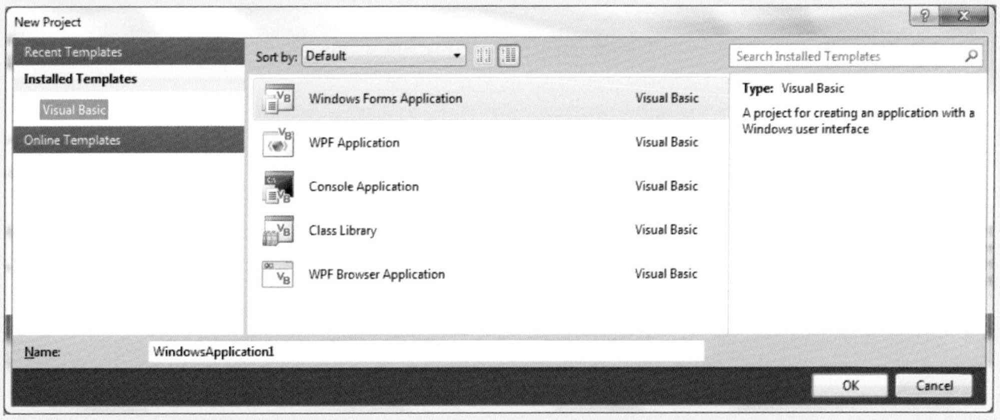

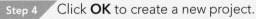

Figure 12.12 New Project screen

Step 3 Click **Windows Forms Application** and enter a name for the new project, such as 'Application1'.

Step 4 Click **OK** to create a new project.

CONTINUED ▸▸

Integrated Development Environment

Visual Basic's Integrated Development Environment consists of:

- a source code editor
- development tools
- a compiler
- a debugger.

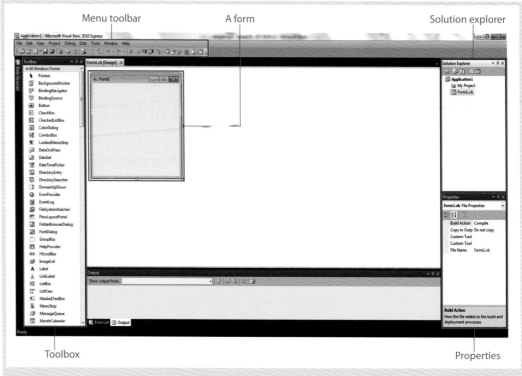

Figure 12.13 Visual Basic Integrated Development Environment

Forms

A Visual Basic software program can have multiple forms (or windows). A form allows programmers to design the graphical user interface for the software program. (See section *Event handling: forms* for more information on forms.)

Toolbox

The toolbox is a very important feature of Visual Basic. The toolbox contains a large collection of tools, objects, and controls, all of which have different functions in a software program.

Properties

The form and all objects placed on a form have a set of properties. Programmers can use properties to configure any settings, style or behaviour of any objects.

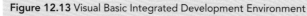

Just checking ✓

1 Visual Basic is what type of programming language?

2 What is the latest version of Visual Basic?

3 List the features of an Integrated Development Environment?

Event handling: forms

Introduction

A form is a collection of related user interface components. You will learn how to create a simple form, which uses one screen component.

Creating a simple form

A form allows programmers to design the graphical user interface for a software program. In this section, you will learn how to create a simple form containing a Label tool, and change the properties of this tool. You will also learn how to debug and run your first software program.

How to create a simple form

Step 1 Open your project and locate the **Toolbox**. Click on the **Label** icon (see Figure 12.14).

◂▸	HScrollBar
🗗	ImageList
A	**Label**
A	LinkLabel
▤▾	ListBox

Figure 12.14 The Toolbox window showing the Label tool highlighted

Step 2 Go to the form.

Step 3 Hold down the left mouse button and drag the mouse to create a label.

Step 4 Click on the **Label** and locate the **Properties window** (see Figure 12.15).

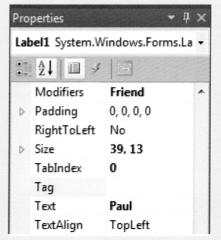

Figure 12.15 The Properties window showing a sample of properties associated with the label object

Step 5 Find the **Text** property and replace the current **Label1** text with your name, e.g. Paul.

Step 6 The label on the form will change to **Paul** (see Figure 12.16).

Figure 12.16 The form showing the label when the software program is running

Step 7 Click on the **Debug** menu and select **Start Debugging** (or press **F5**). The program should run by opening a new window, which displays your name. The form has now become a window, so you can move it and change the size or position.

Step 8 To stop the program, click on the **Debug** menu and select **Stop Debugging** (or press Ctrl+Alt+Break).

CONTINUED ▸▸

Assigning properties to screen components

The form and all objects placed on a form have a set of properties. Using the same software program as before, you will change the presentation of your form by assigning properties to some of the features, including the font, font size, foreground colour and background colour. You can also add a button object to your form.

How to assign properties to screen components

Step 1 Click the label.

Step 2 Go to the **Properties** window.

Step 3 Find the **ForeColor** property and change the current colour to a custom **Red** (see Figure 12.17). The label on the form will change colour.

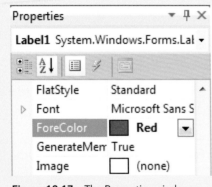

Figure 12.17 – The Properties window for the label object with the ForeColor property highlighted

Step 4 Find the **Font** property (see Figure 12.18) and change the current font to **Arial**, size **14 pt**.

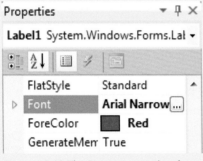

Figure 12.18 The Properties window for the label object with the Font property highlighted

The label on the form will increase in size and display in an Arial font.

Step 5 Using the toolbox, find and click on the **Button** icon.

Step 6 Go to the form and drag the mouse to create a button.

Step 7 Go to the **Properties** window.

Step 8 Find the **Text** property and replace the current Button1 with 'Click Me!' (see Figure 12.19). The text on the button will change to say 'Click Me!'.

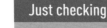

Figure 12.19 The Properties window for the button object with the Text property highlighted

Step 9 Find the **BackColor** property and change the current colour to a custom Pink.

Step 10 Debug and run the software program.

Did you know?

❓

You can also begin and end software programs by clicking on the play and stop icons on the toolbar.

Just checking

✔

1 What other properties can be changed for the Label object?

2 Which icon on the toolbar will allow you to run a software program?

3 What is the shortcut key for debugging and running a software program?

Event handling: user interface

Introduction

An event is something that a program can react to, such as the user clicking a button or a timer expiring. In this section, you will learn how to use output commands or tools to display a string (or text) on a form

Label tool

The Label tool is a toolbox feature in Visual Basic, which allows you to output information. You will add code to the button.

Using the same software program as before, you will instruct the computer system to output 'Hello, welcome to programming!' when a user clicks on the button. The user clicking on the button is one example of how Visual Basic handles an action to trigger an event.

How to use the Label tool

Step 1 With your new project open, double click on the **button** object, which is on the form.

Step 2 This action will display the **Code Editor**.

Step 3 Place the mouse cursor between **Private Sub Button1_Click** and **End Sub**.

Step 4 Type the command Label1.Text = "hello, welcome to programming"

```
Private Sub Button1_Click(ByVal sender As
System.Object, ByVal e As System.EventArgs)
Handles Button1.Click
        Label1.Text = 'hello, welcome to programming'
End Sub
```

Label1.Text is the name of the label object on the form. The text enclosed within the quotation marks will display in this label.

Step 5 This command will change the text of the label on the form when the software program is running and the user clicks the button.

Step 6 Debug and run the software program.

Step 7 Click on the **Click Me!** button to see what happens (see Figure 12.20).

Figure 12.20 The form showing some text when the software program is running

Displaying a message box

A message box is a separate dialogue box used to display a message to the user, which they either acknowledge or respond to.

CONTINUED ▶▶

Key term

Reserved word – A predefined word embedded into a programming language that has a specific purpose.

How to display a message box

Step 1 Replace the 'Label1.Text…' command with 'MessageBox.Show("Hello World")'

Step 2 See what happens to the software program when you click the button (see Figure 12.21). 'MessageBox.Show(…)' is an example of a **reserved word**. Reserved words are the commands used within a programming language.

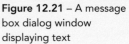

Figure 12.21 – A message box dialog window displaying text

Did you know?

There is predefined code within Visual Basic for you to work with. The predefined code prepares the methods for objects on the form, so when a user interacts with these objects, the instructions given will be carried out.

Input and output commands

You will learn how to use input and output commands in a software program. The text box object is also a toolbox feature in Visual Basic, which allows user to input or enter information.

Activity 12.7

1 Create a new project called 'TextDemo.'
2 Create a form that contains one label, one text box and one button.
3 Change the text property of 'Button1' to 'Click Me!'.
4 Remove the text property of 'Label1'.
5 Go to the code editor and locate the 'Button1_Click' method.
6 Type in the command 'Label1.Text = TextBox1.Text.'

```
Public Class Form1
    Private Sub Button1_Click(ByVal sender As System.Object, ByVal e As
    System.EventArgs) Handles Button1.Click
        Label1.Text = TextBox1.Text
    End Sub
End Class
```

7 Debug and run the software.
8 Enter some text into the textbox, and then click on the 'Click Me!' button.

Annotating the code

Remember

Remember to annotate your code throughout your software program to help you and others to understand what it is doing.

It is good programming practice to annotate your code so that it helps you and others to identify what your code is doing. In Visual Basic, you can add comments, which are ignored by the compiler.

To add a comment, include the comment character (') at the beginning of the line. The text will change to green.

Variables, data types, assignments and structures

Introduction

This section introduces some fundamental components of computer software.

Variables

Variables are used in software programs as a way of storing values that are accessed and changed during the software program. These values can consist of text or numbers, depending on the type of data.

There are two main types of variable:

- **Local.** A local variable is only accessible from the function, subroutine or procedure that it is stated within.
- **Global.** A global variable is stated outside of any functions, subroutines or procedures, and is accessible from any location in the software program.

It is possible to have a **constant** variable that has a value already assigned to it, which can never be changed during the software program.

Here is an example of a variable:

Dim number As Integer

Dim is used to state the variable. It is followed by a relevant name (e.g. number), and the type of data it will store is a whole number (**As Integer**). You cannot use reserved words as variable names.

Data types

The most common data types are listed in Table 12.4.

Table 12.4 Common data types

Data type	Description	Data type	Description
Boolean	True or false	Byte	1 byte
Char (single character)	2 bytes	Date	Date and/or time
Decimal	16 bytes including decimal place	Double	8 bytes
Integer	4 bytes	Long	8 bytes
String	0 to 2 billion Unicode characters	User-defined	Custom data types

CONTINUED ▶▶

Many programming languages, including Visual Basic, will allow you to create your own user-defined data types and record structures.

For example:

```
Private Type myTelephoneBook
    firstname As String
    lastname As String
    telephone As String
End Type
```

You can then state variables using this data type, as follows:

```
Dim telephonebook As myTelephoneBook
```

Record structures

Record structures similar to this can also be imported from outside the software program. These structures are usually created in separate files and are then shared with software programs. The advantage of this is that if you want to make a simple change to the structure, you only need to do this once, and all programs that depend on this structure will automatically be updated. Visual Basic uses the import statement to include structures.

Assignments

An assignment is where you assign (or give) a variable a value to store. The symbols used to represent an assignment are = and :=

For example:

```
number = 20
```

The value stored in this variable is 20. The value can change by using more assignments within the software program.

Subroutines, functions and procedures

A function, also known as a subroutine or procedure, is a segment of code that performs a specific task.

Before you start writing your software program, it is important to be aware of the arithmetic operators used in programming. (See Table 12.5.)

Table 12.5 Arithmetic operators used in programming

Operator	Description
+	Addition
-	Subtraction
*	Multiplication
/	Division
=	Equals
% (Mod in Visual Basic)	Modulus (remainder after dividing)

Activity 12.8

1 Create a new project called 'FunctionDemo'.

2 Create a form that contains three labels, three text boxes and two buttons.

3 Add the appropriate labels and titles to objects as shown.

4 Go to the code editor and type the following code. Some of the code will already be there.

```vbnet
Public Class Form1

    Dim number1 As Integer
    Dim number2 As Integer
    Dim result As Integer

    Private Sub Button1_Click(ByVal sender As System.Object, ByVal e As System.EventArgs)
    Handles Button1.Click
        number1 = CInt(TextBox1.Text)
        number2 = CInt(TextBox2.Text)

        AddNumbers()

        TextBox3.Text = result
    End Sub

    Private Sub Button2_Click(ByVal sender As System.Object, ByVal e As System.EventArgs)
    Handles Button2.Click
        number1 = CInt(TextBox1.Text)
        number2 = CInt(TextBox2.Text)

        SubtractNumbers()

        TextBox3.Text = result
    End Sub

    Private Sub AddNumbers()
        result = number1 + number2
    End Sub

    Private Sub SubtractNumbers()
        result = number1 - number2
    End Sub

End Class
```

5 Debug and run the software program.

6 Enter a number in the text box labelled **first number**, and a number in the text box labelled **second number**. Click either the '+' or '-' buttons to see the result appear.

Activity 12.9

1 Add two extra buttons to the form to allow the user to multiply and divide.

2 Add two extra functions that will allow the software program to calculate the result of two numbers by multiplication and division.

3 Add an extra function that will calculate the remainder if the first number is divided by the second (use the Mod operator).

4 Change the software program to allow three different sets of numbers to be calculated.

Link

See *Unit 8 Mobile apps development*, for further information on variables.

Counter controlled loops, conditional loops, iteration and recursion

Introduction

in this section, you will learn how to use counter controlled loops, conditional loops, iteration and recursion statements to change the behaviour of a software program. These terms all effectively do the same task of repeating a sequence of instructions many times. For, While, and Do are examples of commands that will allow you to repeat instructions without the need to duplicate the code.

Figure 12.22 The form showing a list of numbers between 1 and 8.

For statement

The For statement is very useful if you know the amount of times to loop instructions. In this activity, you will develop a program that will display the numbers 1 to 8 on separate lines.

How to use the For statement

Step 1 Create a new project called 'ForDemo'.

Step 2 Create a form that contains 1 text box and 1 button.

Step 3 Change the **Multiline** property of the text box from False to **True**.

Step 4 Add the appropriate labels and titles to objects as shown.

Step 5 Go to the code editor and type the following block of code in the 'Button1_Click' method:

```
Dim number As Integer

TextBox1.Clear()

For number = 1 To 8
        TextBox1.AppendText(CStr(number))
        TextBox1.AppendText(Environment.NewLine)
    Next
```

Step 6 Debug and run the software program.

Step 7 Click the button and see what happens.

You will now change the software program so that it calculates the sum of numbers between 1 and 8, and displays the result after each loop.

```
Dim number As Integer
Dim total As Integer

TextBox1.Clear()

For number = 1 To 8
        total = total + number
        TextBox1.AppendText(CStr(total))
        TextBox1.AppendText(Environment.NewLine)
    Next
```

Step 8 Change the software program to include the code shown to the right.

Step 9 Run the software program again and see what happens.

While statement

The While statement will repeat a set of instructions until a specific condition is met. In the 'How to use the While statement' activity, you will develop a software program that will keep looping until a variable reaches the value 100.

How to use the While statement

Step 1 Create a new project called 'WhileDemo'.

Step 2 Create a form that contains one multiline text box and one button.

Step 3 Add the appropriate labels and titles to objects as shown.

Step 4 Go to the code editor and type the following block of code in the 'Button1_Click' method:

Step 5 Run the software program and see what happens.

```
Dim total As Integer

TextBox1.Clear()

While total < 20

        TextBox1.AppendText(CStr(total))
        TextBox1.AppendText(Environment.NewLine)

        total = total + 5
End While
```

Do statement

The Do statement will also repeat a set of instructions until a specific condition is met.

You can use the 'ForDemo' software program you created in section *Counter controlled loops, conditional loops, iteration and recursion* to make changes using the following code:

```
Dim number As Integer
number = 0

TextBox1.Clear()

Do
        TextBox1.AppendText(CStr(number))
        TextBox1.AppendText(Environment.NewLine)
        number = number + 1
Loop Until number = 10
```

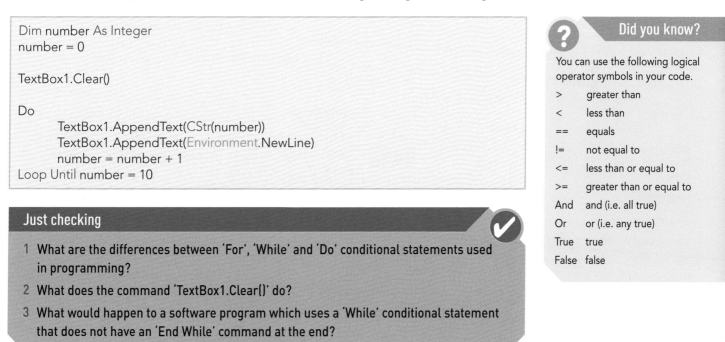

Did you know?

You can use the following logical operator symbols in your code.

>	greater than
<	less than
==	equals
!=	not equal to
<=	less than or equal to
>=	greater than or equal to
And	and (i.e. all true)
Or	or (i.e. any true)
True	true
False	false

Just checking

1 What are the differences between 'For', 'While' and 'Do' conditional statements used in programming?

2 What does the command 'TextBox1.Clear()' do?

3 What would happen to a software program which uses a 'While' conditional statement that does not have an 'End While' command at the end?

Sequential statements and selections

Introduction

In this section, you will learn how to use sequential statements and selections to change the behaviour of a software program. These statements are very common in software programs. A software program can test one or more values and, depending on the result, will perform one set of actions or another. You will learn how to use IF and selection statements.

Did you know?

When a customer enters a PIN number into a cash machine, the machine software has to test if the PIN number entered is correct. If it is, the customer is granted access. If not, they are given the choice to try again.

IF statement

The IF statement allows programmers to introduce decision-making into a software program. The 'How to' guide will show you how to create a software program, which will demonstrate how decisions are made based on what a user inputs into the program.

How to develop a login program that will authenticate users

Step 1 Create a new project called 'IfDemo'.

Step 2 Create a form that contains one label, one text box and one button.

Step 3 Add the appropriate labels and titles to objects.

Step 4 Go to the code editor.

Step 5 Type the following block of code in the 'Button1_Click' method:

```
Dim password As String
password = TextBox1.Text

If password = "puzzle" Then
      MessageBox.Show("Access Granted")
End If
```

Step 6 Debug and run the software program.

Step 7 Enter any characters into the password textbox and click the button. Nothing should happen. However, if you enter the word 'puzzle' and click the button again, a message box with 'Access Granted' should appear.

Figure 12.23 A message box window displaying 'Access Granted'

Step 8 You might want to display a message saying 'Access Denied' if an incorrect password is entered. If so, you need to introduce an Else command.

Step 9 Stop the software program and return to the code editor.

Step 10 Replace the IF statement with the following block of code:

```
If password = "puzzle" Then
      MessageBox.Show("Access Granted")
Else
      MessageBox.Show("Access Denied")
End If
```

Step 11 Run the software program again and see what happens when you enter an incorrect password. A message box with 'Access Denied' should appear.

Figure 12.24 A message box window displaying 'Access Denied'

Select statement

The Select statement is another way of combining multiple IF statements into a single statement.

How to develop a software program that demonstrates a Select statement

Step 1   Create a new project called 'SelectDemo'.

Step 2   Create a form that contains two labels, one text box and one button.

Step 3   Add the appropriate labels and titles to objects.

Step 4   Go to the code editor.

Step 5   Type the following block of code in the 'Button1_Click' method:

```
Dim dayNumber As String
dayNumber = TextBox1.Text

Select Case dayNumber
        Case 1
            Label2.Text = "Monday"
        Case 2
            Label2.Text = "Tuesday"
        Case 3
            Label2.Text = "Wednesday"
        Case Else
            Label2.Text = "Not a valid number"
End Select
```

Step 6   Debug and run the software program.

Step 7   Enter a number between 1 and 3 into the text box and click on the button. The day of week should display, depending on the number you entered.

Step 8   See what happens when you enter a different number.

Activity   12.10

Complete the rest of the Select Case statement for SelectDemo to include outputs for Thursday, Friday, Saturday and Sunday.

Just checking

1   What is the difference between an 'IF' and a 'Selection' statement used in programming?

2   AND, OR and NOT are examples of what type of operators?

3   How can you change a textbox property so that it displays password characters instead of ordinary text?

Data structures

Introduction

In this section, you will learn how to develop software programs that make use of data structures. There are many different types of data structures, including user-defined data types and record structures, and arrays. You will also learn how to use one-dimensional arrays.

Arrays

An array is a type of data structure which can store a large collection of data. You will create a software program, which will demonstrate how data can be stored and accessed in a one dimensional array.

How to develop a software program that will add multiple players to an array

Step 1 Create a new project called 'ArrayDemo'.

Step 2 Create a form that contains one button, one label and one list box.

Step 3 Add the appropriate labels to the objects.

Step 4 Go to the code editor and type the following code:

```
Public Class Form1
    Dim Players_Names(6) As String

Private Sub Button1_Click(ByVal sender As System.
Object, ByVal e As System.EventArgs) Handles
Button1.Click

    NewPlayer()
End Sub

Private Sub NewPlayer()
    Dim idx As Integer

    For idx = 1 To 6
        Players_Names(idx) = InputBox("Enter the
        players name", "Enter Name", "", 500, 500)

        If Players_Names(idx) <> "" Then
            ListBox1.Items.Add(Players_Names(idx))
        Else
            End
        End If
    Next
End Sub
End Class
```

Step 5 Debug and run the software program.

Step 6 Click the **Add Players** button. An input box window will appear, asking you to enter each player's name. This process will repeat until you enter all six names. As you accept each name, the list box on the form should display the player's name (see Figure 12.25).

Figure 12.25 The form showing six names added to an array.

Basic string handling

A string is a piece of text containing one or more characters (letters, digits, punctuation, etc.).

How to develop a software program to compare two words and place them in alphabetical order

Step 1 Create a new project called 'StringDemo'.

Step 2 Create a form that contains three labels, two text boxes, one list box and one button.

Step 3 Add the appropriate labels and titles to the objects.

Step 4 Go to the code editor and type in the code below. Some of the code will be predefined for you.

```
Public Class Form1
    Dim first_word As String
    Dim second_word As String

    Private Sub Button1_Click(ByVal sender As System.
    Object, ByVal e As System.EventArgs) Handles
    Button1.Click
        first_word = TextBox1.Text
        second_word = TextBox2.Text

        If first_word > second_word Then
            ListBox1.Items.Add(second_word)
            ListBox1.Items.Add(first_word)
        Else
            ListBox1.Items.Add(first_word)
            ListBox1.Items.Add(second_word)
        End If
    End Sub
End Class
```

Step 5 Debug and run the software program.

Step 6 Enter two words into the text boxes and click the **Compare** button. The list box should display the words in alphabetical order (see Figure 12.26).

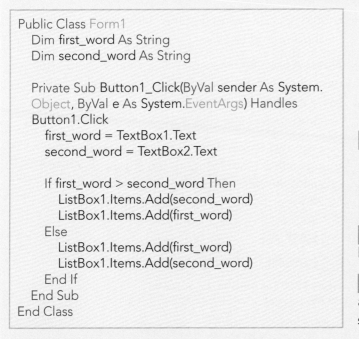

Figure 12.26 The form showing two words in alphabetical order.

Step 7 Find and replace this section of the code only.

```
first_word = TextBox1.Text.ToUpper()
second_word = TextBox2.Text.ToUpper()
```

Step 8 Run the software program again and see what happens.

Step 9 Declare a new variable called 'no_of_chars' as **Integer** and add the following lines of code to the software program:

```
no_of_chars = first_word.Length
MsgBox(no_of_chars)
```

Activity 12.11

1 Add a Clear button and function to the software program so this button will clear all information in the list box.

2 What happens to the software program if you change the ToUpper() method to ToLower() method?

3 Experiment with the software program and see what happens when you use the following string methods:

- Trim
- Remove
- Substring
- IndexOf
- IsNumeric
- Split

Take it further

Look at how you can develop the array software program to make use of two-dimensional arrays and to search for information within arrays.

Also, look into how you can insert individual characters into a string using the **Insert** method.

Basic file handling

Introduction

In this section, you will learn how to develop software programs that read and write information to and from a file. You will learn how to use the StreamReader and StreamWriter classes in your software programs to access files.

Writing to a file

The StreamWriter class has two methods. These are called **Write** and **WriteLine**.

How to write (output) information to a file

Step 1 Create a new project called 'OutputFileDemo'.

Step 2 Create a form that contains one button. Label the button 'Write Data'.

Step 3 Go to the code editor.

Step 4 Type the following block of code in the 'Button1_Click' method:

```
Dim fileReader As System.IO.StreamReader

fileReader = _
My.Computer.FileSystem.OpenTextFileReader
("d:\\demofile.txt", True)

Dim stringReader As String
stringReader = fileReader.ReadLine()

While stringReader <> Nothing
        TextBox1.AppendText(stringReader & vbNewLine)
        stringReader = fileReader.ReadLine()
End While

    fileReader.Close()
```

The name and location of the file

Step 5 Debug and run the software program.

Step 6 Click the button. A message box alert should appear saying that the software program has finished writing to a file.

Note: A warning message will appear if you do not have access to the folder where you want your file to be created. If this happens, choose an alternative location such as the USB drive.

You can test to see if the program has worked by going to the folder location (see Figure 12.27) and opening the demofile.txt file in Notepad (see Figure 12.28). You should see two lines of text.

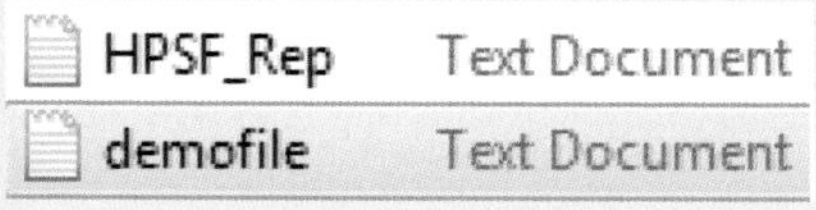

HPSF_Rep	Text Document
demofile	Text Document

Figure 12.27 The demofile text document has been created.

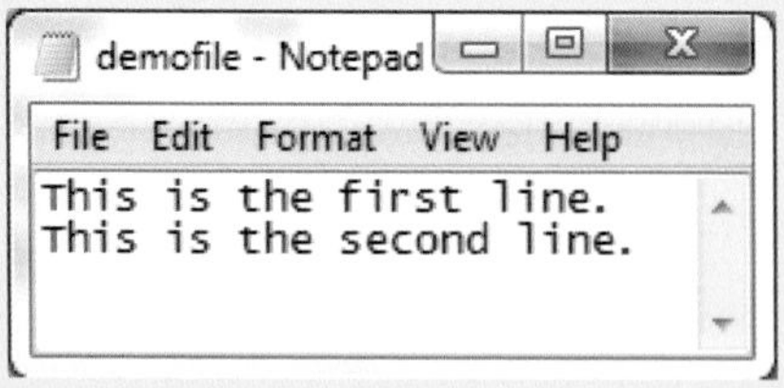

demofile - Notepad
File   Edit   Format   View   Help
This is the first line.
This is the second line.

Figure 12.28 The contents of the demofile text document.

Activity 12.12

1 Try replacing WriteLine with Write. What happens to the output text in the file?

2 What is the total file size of demofile.txt?

3 Write a software program that uses a FOR... NEXT... loop to write any single character (many times) to a file on either a single line or multiple lines.

How to create a multiline text box and button

Step 1 Create a new project called 'InputFileDemo'.

Step 2 Create a form that contains one multiline text box and one button. Label the button 'Read Data'.

Step 3 Go to the code editor.

Step 4 Type the following block of code in the 'Button1_Click' method:

Step 5 Debug and run the software program.

Step 6 Click the button. The contents of the file should appear in the multiline textbox.

Note: A warning message will appear if the file cannot be found.

```
Dim fileReader As System.IO.StreamReader
fileReader = _
My.Computer.FileSystem.OpenTextFileReader("d:\\demofile.txt")

Dim stringReader As String
stringReader = fileReader.ReadLine()

While stringReader <> Nothing
TextBox1.AppendText(stringReader & vbNewLine)
stringReader = fileReader.ReadLine()
    End While
fileReader.Close()
```

Activity   12.13

1 Write a software program that will write a line of text (entered by the user in a text box) to a text file called textfile.txt.

2 Using the same software program, add extra functionality to display the contents of textfile.txt in a multiline textbox.

3 What happens to the software program if it is unable to find the file?

Take it further

A database is another way of storing information. Most programming languages, including Visual Basic, support databases. Visual Basic has its own set of classes that work with databases. Explore and practise how you can work with information stored in a database.

Assessment activity 12.4   *Maths* | 1C.4 | 2C.P4 | 2C.M3 |

The Dayce Travel Agency would now like you to develop its new management software program. Develop a functional software program using the design documents you created for Assessment activity 12.3 and referring to the purpose and user requirements from Assessment activity 12.2.

Your software program must include:

• a user interface, including the inputs and outputs

• a range of constructs and techniques

• commentary throughout the code.

Tip

Work methodically and check your work as you go.

Testing and refining the software

Getting started

With a partner, discuss your experiences of software programs unexpectedly 'crashing' and think of why it happened in each case. Did the error occur at the same point every time? Did you fix the problem? If so, how?

Introduction

In this section, you will learn about the importance of testing and refining software. Testing can identify errors, bugs or defects that will or could occur during the software program. Testing can also ensure that your software is performing well and meeting the user requirements.

Failing to test software programs rigorously can lead to major problems.

Case study

In March 2011, it was reported in the media that more than 40 Commonwealth Bank ATMs (Automated Teller Machines) in Australia were dispensing large amounts of money to customers by mistake. The machines were reportedly in standby mode, which meant that customers were able to withdraw more money than they had in their bank accounts. As soon as this news was released, customers all over Australia were taking advantage of the computer fault. The police were called in and they made several arrests. It was reported that the bank was reluctant to shut down the entire network of ATMs, fearing that this would complicate matters even further.

Failure to test the software running ATMs can have serious consequences.

Questions

Using the internet, investigate this event in more detail, and then answer the questions.

1 List the main functions and features of an Automated Teller Machine.
2 List the problems with the Commonwealth Bank's system and the impact this had on customers.
3 What were the main reasons for the failure?
4 Who was responsible for the computer fault?
5 Did the Commonwealth Bank resolve the problems with the system? If so, how?

Test plan with test data

Testing is not a straightforward task and requires planning, especially at the design stage of the software development life cycle. It is good practice to think about the range of tests you will carry out on your software program in advance. This will help to highlight any issues that could quite easily be resolved at the development stage.

There are two parts to producing a test plan with test data:

- The first part looks at how you start to build up a test plan with test data covering a range of tests. This is completed at the design stage of the software development life cycle. The test data is the data you input into the software program.
- Once you have developed the software program, the second stage is to revisit the test plan, perform the tests and record the outcomes.

You should take screenshots of your test results to back up your test report and to provide evidence for assessment.

Table 12.6 An example of a test plan for a software program

Part 1			Part 2		
Test data	Test	Expected outcomes	Actual outcomes	Pass/Fail	Comments
	User selects the option Exit from the menu bar.	Program should close.	Program did not close.	Fail	Incorrect programming code behind this event.
ABC	User enters the test data into a numeric field on a data entry form.	A message box alert should appear warning the user not to enter any invalid characters.	A message box appeared.	Pass	
	Program presents a list of available reports.	Program should display a list of available reports	A list of available reports displayed allowing users to make a choice	Pass	
Apple1234	User enters an invalid password to access the program.	A message box alert should appear warning the user to enter a valid password.	A message box did not appear.	Fail	The program was accepting both valid and invalid passwords. The IF statement had the wrong relational operator.

Just checking

1 Why is it important to test a software program?

2 What is a test plan?

3 When should the testing stage be performed?

4 Explain the second part of the test.

Testing the program solution

Introduction

It is important to test your program thoroughly before it is released to your users.

Functionality

Test all processes by inputting data into the software program and validating the results. If you find any errors, for example if an incorrect result is displayed, change your software program to resolve them.

Errors

Even the best programmers cannot avoid errors as they develop and use their software programs, so it is likely that your software program will also contain some. Your goal should be to identify and eradicate as many as possible.

Visual Basic uses its own compilation feature to find errors as you type the code into the code editor. If the IDE knows you have made a mistake, it will underline the error for you. If you move your mouse cursor over the line, an explanation of the error should appear. Errors will also appear in the 'Error List' window.

The mistake in this code is in the **expression** 'MessageBox'. The IDE does not recognise it as a valid expression. The correct expression to use is 'MsgBox'.

Debugging

The role of the debugger is to find errors (bugs) in a software program and provide suggestions to fix them. Visual Basic has a menu option dedicated to debugging. Some of the menu options are explained in more detail in Table 12.7.

Key terms

Expression – An individual part of the software program code.

Run-time – When a software program is in use.

Table 12.7 Visual Basic debugging menu options

Start Debugging	By clicking **Start Debugging** or pressing the shortcut key **F5**, you will build your software program and start a debugging session for it.
Build	**Build** is the same as **Start Debugging**, except that it will not execute the software program. It will create an executable file of the software program, so that you do not need to use Visual Basic to run it later.
Step Into Step Out Step Over	**Step Into**, **Step Out** and **Step Over** allow you to execute the software program one step at a time. The code editor will highlight the section of the code that it is running. It is a good way of spotting errors at **run-time**, because you can identify what part of the software program is causing the problem.
Toggle Breakpoint	If you click on **Toggle Breakpoint** or press **F9**, a breakpoint will be placed in the software program where it will stop executing. This feature is useful, because it means you do not have to step through the software program one step at a time to reach a certain point in the software program. When the debugger has stopped at a breakpoint, you can step through the program from that point.

Reviewing the quality

When reviewing the quality of your software program, be sure to check its:

- reliability
- usability
- efficiency/performance
- maintainability
- portability.

Feedback

It is always important to gather feedback from others, particularly from the client and the people who will be using the software program. Their feedback can demonstrate that you have produced a software program that meets their requirements and expectations. Make sure that you consider all feedback and make any necessary amendments to your code.

Design changes

If you change your program, make sure you update your design documents to match. Don't forget to explain what changes you have made to your original design documents, including any items in your source table of predefined assets, if applicable.

Improvements/refinements

Changing several lines of code inevitably has a knock-on effect on other parts of the software program, which could cause the software program to fail. If you change your software program, carry out the testing again.

Activity 12.14

This code contains errors that will stop it from executing.

```
Public Class frmVariables

    Public Sub btnCalculate_Click(ByVal sender
    As System.Object, ByVal e As System.
    EventArgs) Handles btnCalculate.Click
        Data Declaration
        Dim new_mileage, cars_mileage, petrol,
        petrol_gallon As Integer

        new_milege = txtNewMileage.Text
        cars_mileage = txtMileage.Text
        petrol = txtPetrol.Length

        new_result = new_mileage - cars_
mileage
        petrol_gallon = new_result / petrol

        lblResult.Text = petrol_gallon

        lblResult.Items.Add(petrol_gallon)

    End Sub
End Class
```

1 Spot the errors in the program code and suggest how to fix them.

Assessment activity 12.5   *Maths* | 1C.5 | 2C.P5 | 2C.M4 | 2C.D2 |

It's time to test the management software program you have created for Dayce Travel Agency:

- Using your test plan and test data (Assessment activity 12.3), test your built software program for functionality against the original requirements.
- Repair any faults you find.
- Gather feedback from others on the usability and quality of the program and use this feedback to refine the quality of the code. For example, you could make the user interface more accessible, add extra functionality to support users, or improve security.

Tips

- Be sure to record all test results (keep a log of the tests you do) and the feedback you receive, and also what you changed as a result to improve the network.
- If users highlight problems in their feedback ask them further questions to find out exactly what is at the source of the problem.

Reviewing the finished software program

Introduction

In this section, you will learn the importance of reviewing a finished software program and understand how this process can influence the way you design and develop software programs in the future. This section looks at the six areas that you need to cover when you review your finished software program.

User requirements

The user requirements are a list of objectives that the user wants your software program to deliver. The final software program may not necessarily match all of those requirements, perhaps as a result of constraints. In your review, you need to state which of the requirements have not been covered and the reasons why. For example:

'I have not been able to include a function that allows users to save information to a file because security restrictions on the computer system prevented me from doing this.'

It is also good practice to highlight all the requirements you have met.

Fitness for purpose

In your review, you need to think about whether your finished software program does what it is meant to do. This might be, for example, adding two numbers together and displaying the result.

If it meets its intended purpose, explain how. If it doesn't, set out the reasons why not and describe the changes you could make to fulfil the original client brief.

User experience

It is important that your software program meets the user requirements and purpose. However, another important aspect to review is the user experience. You should therefore obtain feedback from the people who are actually going to be using the program. Check whether or not the program is easy to navigate and whether it performs in the way the users expect.

Constraints

Programmers are always faced with challenges. Many of these are to do with constraints of the programming language, the timeframe in which software programs must be developed and limited access to device capabilities. This part of the review is where you have the opportunity to talk about the challenges you have encountered, and how you have overcome them. Sometimes constraints are unavoidable, and alternative solutions need to be found.

Quality of the program

In order to ensure that you have developed a high quality software program, you can check it against the measures shown in Table 12.8.

Table 12.8

Reliability	Is the software program reliable? (Does it allow users to use the software program to get what they want from it? If so, it can be said to be a reliable solution.)
Usability	Is the software program easy to use and manage? Does it have a user-friendly interface that allows users to navigate through the screens?
Efficiency/ performance	Has the software program been developed in a way that allows information to be retrieved quickly? Is the information presented accurately? Are there any validation checks that would improve the performance of data?
Maintainability	Is the software program capable of being maintained over a period of time? Can the software program be modified to allow for additional functionality?
Portability	Is the software program capable of running within different environments, for example different platforms or operating systems?

Strengths and improvements

All software programs have their own strengths and weaknesses. Can you identify the strengths and weaknesses of your software program? You could present these in a two-column table with the strengths of the program listed in the first column and the weaknesses listed in the second column.

Assessment activity 12.6   1D.6 | 2D.P6 | 2D.M5 | 2D.D4

Carry out a review to measure the success of the management software you created for Dayce Travel Agency.

Review the extent to which the final software program meets the original purpose and user requirements.

- Compare the software program you have created to your original software design solution and the quality of the code. Give a reason why you made any changes during development.
- Identify and consider any constraints you encountered.
- Consider the feedback you received from others.
- Make recommendations for further improvements that could be made to the software program that Dayce Travel Agency may wish to consider implementing in the future.

Tip

Whatever format you choose for your evaluation, make sure it is presented clearly. Think about the structure, and tackle one design element at a time. For each design element ask yourself: have you included the design element, how well does it fulfil the original requirements, could its performance or reliability be improved further?

Introduction

Most of us use the internet every day and visit a whole range of websites in order to do business, to find out information, for entertainment and to keep in touch with friends. Many of these websites are visually stimulating, containing many different elements, such as text, graphics, animation, video and programs, as well as a number of sophisticated interactive features. The internet has become the prime way in which we communicate with one another. As a result of this, web development is a skill which is very much in demand, not just for people directly developing websites, but for almost anyone involved in developing IT products.

In this unit, you will investigate the features and uses of websites, and how their components and applications interact with each other. You will also learn how to design and develop effective websites using a range of tools and techniques. Finally, you will review your website and consider any improvements that can be made.

Assessment: You will be assessed by a series of assignments set by your teacher.

Learning aims

In this unit you will:

A understand the uses and features of websites

B design a website

C develop and test a website

D review the finished website.

> *I'm really interested in web development and am hoping to have a career in that area. I enjoy the way it allows me to combine creative and design skills with technical skills.*
>
> *'I used some of the graphics I developed for Unit 6 and also used the skills I learned to develop the website for my portfolio in Unit 3.*
>
> *Anita, 16-year-old web developer*

Website development

This table shows what you must do in order to achieve a **Pass**, **Merit** or **Distinction** grade, and where you can find activities in this book to help you.

Assessment criteria			
Level 1	**Level 2 Pass**	**Level 2 Merit**	**Level 2 Distinction**
Learning aim A: Understand the uses and features of websites			
1A.1 Identify the intended use and features of two websites. **Assessment activity 13.1, page 430**	**2A.P1** Explain the intended uses and features of two different websites. **Assessment activity 13.1, page 430**	**2A.M1** Review how the features in two websites improve presentation, usability, accessibility, and performance. **Assessment activity 13.1, page 430**	**2A.D1** Discuss the strengths and weaknesses of the websites. **Assessment activity 13.1, page 430**
Learning aim B: Design a website			
1B.2 Identify the purpose and user requirements for the website. **Assessment activity 13.2, page 435**	**2B.P2** Describe the purpose and user requirements for the website. **Assessment activity 13.2, page 435**	**2B.M2** Produce a detailed design for a website, including: • alternative solutions • aesthetic features • interactive components. **Assessment activity 13.2, page 435**	**2B.D2** Justify the final design decisions, including: • how the design will fulfil the purpose and user requirements • including any design constraints. **Assessment activity 13.2, page 435**
1B.3 Produce a design for a four page interlinked website, with guidance, including an outline of the proposed solution. **Assessment activity 13.2, page 435**	**2B.P3** Produce a design for an eight page interlinked website, including: • a proposed solution • a list of assets • a test plan. **Assessment activity 13.2, page 435**		
Learning aim C: Develop and test a website			
1C.4 Prepare assets and content for the website, with guidance. **Assessment activity 13.3, page 457**	**2C.P4** Prepare assets and content for the website, demonstrating awareness of purpose, listing sources of assets. **Assessment activity 13.3, page 457**	**2C.M3** Prepare assets and content for the website demonstrating awareness of the users' requirements, with all sources fully referenced. **Assessment activity 13.3, page 457**	**2C.D3** Refine the website, to improve accessibility and performance, taking account of user feedback and test results. **Assessment activity 13.3, page 457**
1C.5 Develop a website containing four interlinked web pages, with guidance. **Assessment activity 13.3, page 457**	**2C.P5** Develop a website containing at least eight interlinked web pages, demonstrating awareness of purpose. **Assessment activity 13.3, page 457**	**2C.M4** Develop a website including interactive components, demonstrating awareness of user requirements and taking account of usability. **Assessment activity 13.3, page 457**	

Assessment criteria

Level 1	Level 2 Pass	Level 2 Merit	Level 2 Distinction
1C.6 Test the website for functionality and purpose repairing any faults and documenting changes, with guidance. **Assessment activity 13.3, page 457**	**2C.P6** Test the website for functionality and purpose, repairing any faults, and documenting changes. **Assessment activity 13.3, page 457**	**2C.M5** Test interactivity and gather feedback from others on the quality of the website, and use it to improve the website, showing awareness of user requirements. **Assessment activity 13.3, page 457**	
Learning aim D: Review the finished website			
1D.7 Identify how the final website is suitable for the intended purpose. **Assessment activity 13.4, page 459**	**2D.P7** Explain how the final website is suitable for the intended audience and purpose. **Assessment activity 13.4, page 459**	**2D.M6** Review the extent to which the finished website meets the needs of purpose and user requirements, while considering feedback from others and constraints. **Assessment activity 13.4, page 459**	**2D.D4** Evaluate the final website against the design and justify any changes made, making recommendations for further improvements. **Assessment activity 13.4, page 459**

How you will be assessed

This unit will be assessed by a series of internally assessed tasks. You will be expected to show that you understand the uses and features of websites and the processes involved in creating them.

The tasks will be based on a scenario in which you will need to develop a website consisting of at least eight interlinked pages which meet a client brief. For example, this could be for a charity that has commissioned you to produce a website promoting its particular cause.

Your assessment could be in the form of:

- a report or magazine article on the use and purposes of websites
- written design documentation and prototypes for the website you will be developing
- the completed website
- annotated and updated design documents
- written review documentation showing your completed test plan, test outcomes and the responses to feedback you have received.
- written evaluation report showing strengths and weaknesses of your website and improvements made.

The uses of websites

Introduction

Websites are used for a very wide range of purposes.

Typical uses of websites

There are millions of websites on the internet. They are used for almost every conceivable purpose including business, personal and entertainment purposes. Some of the more common purposes of websites are described in the following sections.

Presenting information

Websites are commonly used both for presenting information, such as news, and for product advertising. Most companies have their own website. Some of the best known news websites are those of BBC News (www.bbc.co.uk/news) and Al Jazeera (www.aljazeera.com).

Storing information

Websites can be used to archive information. The 'cloud' concept is a relatively recent development in information storage. It involves using the internet to store information rather than using local storage (such as your computer's disk drive or a USB memory stick).

Browsing and searching for information

The internet search engine Google™ has become such a part of our lives that the verb 'to Google™' has been included in the Oxford English Dictionary. If you ask someone a question, you may get the response, 'Just Google it'. The internet has also become a useful source of real-time information. For example, if you are meeting someone at the railway station or airport, the quickest way to check real-time updated information is via the internet.

Improving productivity

Email has revolutionised personal and business communication, enabling people to share information and send documents to each other quickly and so improving productivity. Facilities such as video conferencing allow people to have 'virtual' meetings, enabling them to work collaboratively without having to spend time travelling.

Making decisions

Many websites provide information which helps individuals and businesses to make decisions. Price comparison websites like Compare the Market™ (www.comparethemarket.com) and Money Supermarket™ (www.moneysupermarket.com) help people to decide on the most suitable insurance policy, loan or other financial service.

Communication with people

Social networking sites, such as Facebook, have become very popular as they allow people to communicate with their friends. They can let all their friends know what they are doing with status updates and they are able to chat with friends though an instant messenger type interface. Many other instant messenger services, such as Yahoo™ Chat™, are popular and some include video chatting as well as text chat.

Media sharing

Another area that the internet has revolutionised is how we listen to music or live radio, and how we watch films. Sites such as Apple™ iTunes™ allow consumers to purchase and download music, while sites such as YouTube let people view and share videos on a wide range of subjects. Radio stations now broadcast digitally and so you can listen to them over the internet. Some radio stations are only broadcast digitally such as BBC Radio 6 Music.

E-commerce

There has also been a huge increase in the number of goods being bought online, both from online-only retailers like Amazon and high street chains, such as Tesco and John Lewis. A large proportion of trade business is now conducted online.

Education

The internet contains a vast resource of information on just about every subject imaginable. You can find information on encyclopaedia websites or specialist websites. Some of these, such as www.tomshardware.co.uk, which provides lots of information about PC hardware, give details on training courses and contains video instructions on how to do all sorts of practical things.

Downloading information

Many websites provide digital content for you to download. iTunes™ is one of the best known websites from which you can buy and download music. Many software vendors allow you to download their software products directly from their website.

> **Activity** 13.1
>
> Make a list of all the websites you visit in a week and classify each of them using the list above. What type has the most number of websites from your list? Which individual sites do you visit most often? What are the features of your favourite sites that attract you to them?

> **Just checking** ✔
>
> 1 How many websites are there now on the internet?
> 2 What is 'cloud' concept?
> 3 What is needed to set up a 'virtual' meeting?

Features of websites

Introduction

Websites are constructed on many different features. It can be useful to think about these when designing your own websites.

Target audience

Most websites will have a target audience and their content will reflect the interests of that group. For example, a site aimed at children may have bright colours, animation, lots of relevant images, clear simple text and simple, easy-to-use features. On the other hand, a website with support and resources for professional programmers might have plain colours and few, if any, images. The text would be technical and high level.

Websites run on a wide range of hardware and software platforms. You can view a website using a range of hardware devices, including mobile phones, tablet computers and laptops. There is also a variety of different operating systems and browsers that you can use to view websites. It is important to ensure that a website is compatible with all these different platforms, and this can sometimes be tricky to achieve.

Construction features

There are many different features that you can include when you're constructing a website to allow users to interact with it and to make it more interesting to use.

Hyperlinks and templates

These are links, which in the most basic form are displayed as underlined text. When you click a hyperlink, you are taken to another web page or to a different website.

Many websites use templates or styles to define the layout and formatting of all the pages on the site. This helps ensure consistent layout and formatting of the site.

Forms

Discussion point

Can you think of any other uses for forms on a website?

Forms allow users to make input and interact with the website. The simplest type of form is a search box which allows the user to input text which is then searched for on the site. More complex forms may be used, for example, to allow users to register their details with the site to receive updates. Forms can also provide a method for website users to feedback information (e.g. on a product or service they have received) to the people running the website.

Hot spots and action buttons

A hot spot is similar to a hyperlink, except that it uses an image rather than text.

Action buttons allow website users to access interactive features, such as submitting a form or searching for page content.

Interactive features

Registration

This allows the site to keep its users' details and to email them updates about the site. Registered users can log on to the site and do things that standard users cannot, such as review items, leave comments or add other information to the site (e.g. status updates). Registration is completed by filling in a form.

Email links

Some sites provide links that allow you to send emails to the site to request further information or ask a question.

E-commerce

Many websites sell goods or services online. E-commerce websites allow users to search for and view products, and place those they wish to purchase in a virtual shopping basket. When they have chosen all the items they want to buy, they can go to a 'check-out' page where they can enter delivery details and pay with a credit or debit card. E-commerce is the prime function of some websites, such as Amazon and online banks. Other websites use e-commerce as an added feature. For example, a rock band's website might have information about gigs, but also offer T-shirts and other merchandise for sale.

Online forums

Forums are very useful way to get questions answered about almost any topic. With a forum, you can place a question or comment (known as a posting) on the website, which all users can read. People will usually respond to your post if it contains a question or a request for help.

Aesthetics

The way a website looks is very important, both to encourage users back to the site and also to reflect the quality of the organisation it represents. There are a number of aesthetic aspects to the design of a website:

- **Colours**. These should be complementary rather than clashing. The target audience may dictate the choice of colours. If you are designing a website for children, for example, bright colours would be suitable, but more subtle colours may be a better choice for an adult audience. A consistent colour scheme across the pages that make up the site is important.

- **Layout**. Various layouts are possible with headers, columns, side bars and footers. As with colours, consistency is important.

- **Graphics and other media**. These need to be laid out neatly within the other features of the site. Images should be of good quality. The same applies to any video, animation or audio you add.

- **Text**. You should preferably use only one or two different fonts for your site, and you should have a consistent scheme of formatting for text which is used for headings, subheadings, plain text etc.

Remember

The best way to enforce a consistent design is to define style sheets which are used throughout the site. See section *Applying style sheets*.

CONTINUED ▶▶

◤ Accessibility

Not everyone who visits a website will have good eyesight. The needs of users with visual impairments must be considered. These users may need to use text readers, which convert text to speech, and the site should include alternative text which describes non-text items (such as images) to these users. See Unit 3 *A digital portfolio*, for more information on websites and accessibility.

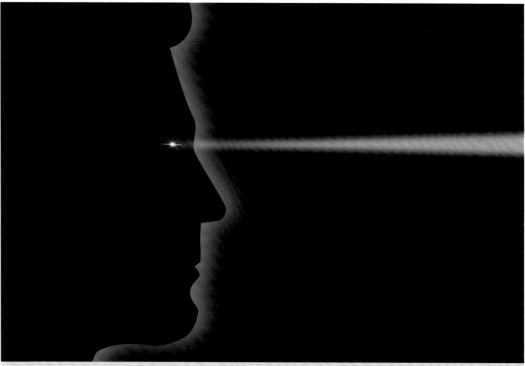

How people read information on computer screens differs hugely so it's important to make websites accessible

---

Activity 13.2

Revisit the list of websites created in the previous activity. For the sites you visited most often identify the following:

● Who do you think the target audience is for the website? What features on the website appeal to that audience?

● What interactive features do the websites have?

● How do the websites look, what features make them aesthetically pleasing?

Just checking ✔

1 Why can it be difficult to make sure people who view your website can see it the way you expect them to?

2 What is a hyperlink?

3 What are the benefits of getting your users to register with your website?

Types of websites and improving user experience

Introduction

Broadly speaking you can divide websites into two main types: static and dynamic. This section will discuss these two types of site and also what features you can add to improve the experience of users visiting your website, to make their visit more enjoyable and to give them a reason to come back to the website.

Static websites

A static website is one which is not regularly updated and does not have any dynamic content. When the internet was first used, a large proportion of websites were static: they presented unchanging information across a series of web pages. In fact, there are still many static websites, but they are no longer popular, due to the fact that they do not change very often and they do not have any interactive features to attract users. Static websites are created using **HTML**.

Dynamic websites

Dynamic websites include information which changes often, sometimes automatically using data feeds from other sources. Dynamic websites allow the user to select and view information based on the information they enter. Sites of this type include online banking sites, where users can see up-to-date information on their bank transactions and make payments and e-commerce websites, where users can search for products which match their requirements and purchase them online. These types of websites make use of web programming languages such as **PHP** and **ASP.NET**, as well as HTML.

Dynamic interactions

Social networking sites such as Facebook use dynamic interactions to allow users to customise their pages, to enter status updates, to see those of their friends and to share updates and media.

Interactivity through embedded digital assets

Embedding digital content including images, animations, sounds and videos makes a site more interesting and visually appealing.

For example, your favourite band probably has a website. A band website with photos, tour dates, their latest news and song lyrics is something you might want to visit once a week or once a month, depending on how often it is updated (this is **static content**). But if the website has a forum on it, where fans can post messages and discuss the band's latest album or recent gigs, then you might want to visit the site more often, because now it is interactive (this is **dynamic content**).

Key terms

HTML – HyperText Markup Language (HTML) is a coding language used to format web pages. HTML is read by your web browser (such as Microsoft® Internet Explorer® or Google™ Chrome™) which then formats the text and images etc which make up a web page based on the instructions in the HTML. HTML is not really a programming language, but just contains formatting instructions.

PHP and ASP.NET – These are just two of the many different web languages which are available to web developers. These languages allow HTML to be extended by inserting programming code in the form of scripts into the web page. They allow interactive and dynamic web pages to be created, which could not be achieved by HTML alone.

CONTINUED ▶▶

◤ Customer feedback forms

Forms that allow users to leave feedback or request further information are another way that can allow a site to interact with its users. Having a form to allow users to register with the site so email updates and other information can be sent to them is a way many websites use to keep in touch with their users and encourage them to come back to the site again.

◤ Applying style sheets

Another aspect of website design which can help attract people to the site is its visual appeal. A well-designed website with complementary colours, a consistent look and feel to all the pages and easy navigation is likely to give users a much more positive experience than a messy one with clashing colours, many different fonts etc. One method that is used by all professional websites to maintain consistency and to make updating easier is cascading style sheets (CSS). These specify the formatting of font styles and sizes, colours and backgrounds for each page of a site.

Assessment activity 13.1	1A.1	2A.P1	2A.M1	2A.D1

KidsSportingLife is a local charity that encourages young people to get involved in different kinds of sport. They have asked you to help them develop a new website. The management team at KidsSportingLife are unsure what style of website they would like. You have offered to produce a report to help them understand websites.

Choose two different types of website. Purposes could include: presenting, storing, browsing and searching, or downloading information; improving productivity; making decisions; communicating with people; media sharing; e-commerce; education. Present your findings in a report.

Research the two websites and prepare a short document that covers the following:

- The purpose of the website.
- An explanation of the intended uses and features of each website.
- A discussion on how the features of each website improves presentation, usability, accessibility and performance.
- A discussion of the strengths and weaknesses of each website.

Tips

- Make sure that you research two different types of website.
- Before you start writing, think about how you will structure your report so that it is clear.
- Include as much detail as you can about each feature.

Designing a website 1

Introduction

It is a good idea to think carefully about the design of a website before you try to implement it.

Did you know? ?

Several professionals might be involved in creating a website. A web developer will do the technical parts of designing the site. A separate content manager will be responsible for keeping the content up to date. There might also be an SEO (search engine optimisation) specialist whose job it is to encourage user traffic to the site from internet search engines.

Intended purpose and user requirements

Before you start work on creating a website, you must complete a design. Your first task is to identify the intended purpose of the website, the target audience and their requirements. If you are working to a client brief then you must read it carefully and ensure that all the details are clear. If they are not, you must clarify them with the client. If you are creating a website for yourself, then write down a clear statement of its purpose and the requirements of the intended audience.

Purpose

The purpose of a website may be stated as a problem it is intended to solve. This might be something like 'our high street shop sales are falling and we want a website to enable us to sell items online' or 'our rock band isn't as popular as we think it should be, so we want to promote ourselves and increase record sales in Europe and across the world'. Having a clear purpose to your site will provide focus when you are thinking about what features the site needs, what style it should have and how it will meet user requirements.

User requirements

Consider what features and functions your site needs to have in order to fulfil its purpose and meet the requirements of its intended users. Consider, for example:

- Will users have to register to see the site's content?
- Will users be purchasing items from the site?
- Will users want to be able to search the content of the site? Will users want to be able to feed back comments to the site, interact with one another through a forum or link to social networking sites?
- It is important to understand your audience (users) and what type of functionality and features they will need – and possibly expect – the site to have.

The user requirements might include the sort of language you use (for example, formal or informal, technical language or a more straightforward level of English), the colours and font styles you choose and the images and other media (such as videos) you include.

Activity 13.3

What sort of features would appeal to a target audience of students of your own age studying at school? What different features would you choose to appeal to male as opposed to female students? How would this affect the style of the site? You might find it helpful to discuss this in small groups of male and female students.

CONTINUED ▸▸

Design documents

Do not think of the design process as a one-time event where you sit down and create a design from start to finish within a couple of hours. Instead, it is a cycle in which you think up ideas, try them out and refine them, rejecting some ideas and developing others.

Site map

A site map is used to define the different pages on your site, their subject matter and how they are linked. Site maps are either hand-drawn or drawn using the simple graphics facilities in programs like Microsoft® Word®.

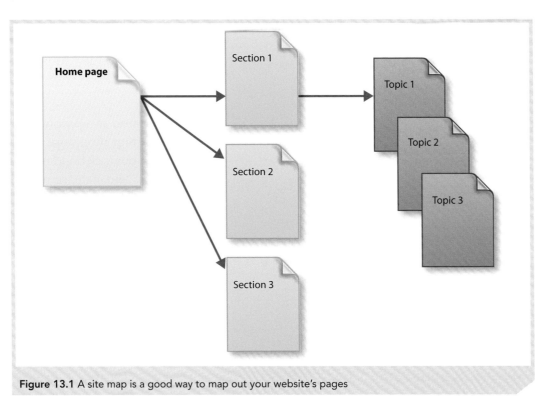

Figure 13.1 A site map is a good way to map out your website's pages

Design sketches or prototypes

As part of the design process, you may create hand-drawn sketches of page layouts or actual prototype web pages laid out using your chosen design, but containing dummy content. Your design should then be developed into style sheets and/or layout templates and a storyboard. It's a good idea to sketch out several different design ideas and then decide (perhaps with the help of others) which design you will go with.

Style sheets

A style sheet defines a hierarchy of formatting, to give your website a consistent and easily adjusted formatting structure. As well as defining text formatting, styles can also define page layouts and paragraph formatting, such as text and image alignment and spacing. You should create a table listing each type of style and the formatting that is associated with it. See the example in Table 13.1. You will cascade these styles throughout your website, this is why they are known as cascading style sheets (CSS).

Table 13.1 Style sheet formatting options

Style	Formatting
Page background	Light blue
Main heading	Arial 24 point, bold, dark blue, align centre
Subheading	Arial 18 point, bold, medium blue, align centre
Plain text	Arial 12 point, black, align left
Image captions	Arial 10 point, italics, black, align centre

An alternative to creating your own styles is to use built-in templates that are provided in Adobe® Dreamweaver® or obtained from other sources.

Storyboard

You will need to create a storyboard towards the end of the design process, as you finalise your design and decide exactly what you plan to have on each page. A storyboard is a multi-panel drawing or diagram of your website, showing its content and structure. You can draw storyboards by hand or using a computer.

Storyboards should be annotated to show the formatting being used for each element of your page (i.e. colours, fonts, sizes) and explain where hyperlinks will take the user. Assets such as photos or animations should be linked to the asset list by their asset number. Your storyboards don't have to show the actual assets and text content of your pages; you can use dummy content which you replace with the real content when you actually develop the pages.

Asset list

Your storyboards should enable you to list all the different digital assets you will need to complete the web pages you are designing. Digital assets can include things like images or diagrams, videos, animations and audio. You will need to create some of these yourself and others will be ready-made (for example, Clip Art). Your asset list is a list of everything you need and where you plan to get it from. You must document and reference the sources of any ready-made assets so that you know where they came from and can seek permission to use them. Your asset list can be used as a check list as you gather the assets during your construction of the site.

Link

Refer to *Unit 3 A digital portfolio*, for further information on storyboards, home pages and folder structures.

Just checking

1 What is the purpose of a site map?

2 What is CSS used for?

3 What information should you include in your asset list?

Designing a website 2

Introduction

In this section, you will consider the resources necessary for designing your website. You will also think about any constraints that may limit your design, you will devise a suitable test plan and you will consider alternative design ideas.

Resources

As part of the design process, you will need to consider the hardware and software that will be required to create the website. You can create simple web pages by entering the HTML codes in a text editor like Microsoft® Notepad®. However, professional web developers use more sophisticated tools like Dreamweaver® to create pages. You will also need additional software to edit image files and may need software to create and edit animations, sound and video files. To create images and video, you will need a digital camera. If you want to digitise existing artwork, you will need a scanner.

Hardware and software constraints

Designing and developing websites might seem a little like creating a brochure or booklet in a word-processing program. However, these documents are designed to be printed on paper, a process which will probably be controlled by you.

A website is fundamentally different in that it needs to be designed so it can be viewed by people anywhere in the world, using quite a wide range of different hardware and software over which you have no control. For instance, you don't know what screen size people viewing your website have (it can be anything from a very small screen on a mobile phone to a large monitor), you don't know what operating system they are using (it might be an Apple® Mac®, a Windows® PC or a PC running Linux®) and you don't know what web browser they are using.

All of these issues make developing a website more complex than you might first imagine.

Some features you might want to include in your website may require plug-ins to be loaded in the viewer's browser. For example, to play an animation created in Adobe® Flash®, the viewer must have the Flash® plug-in loaded. This may not be the case for every user as not all platforms support Flash® (Apple™ software, for example, doesn't). Some users might consider certain plug-ins (such as Active-X) as a security risk and might not load them. Because all users will have different hardware and software constraints, it's a good idea not to over-complicate your web pages and to work to the assumption that all users' systems are quite basic.

Remember

You don't know which web browser visitors to your website will be using. It could be Microsoft® Internet Explorer®, Google™ Chrome™, Firefox® or another browser, and you won't know which version of the browser they have installed.

Test plan

Towards the end of the design process, you will need to create a test plan for your website. Your test plan will define how you judge your website to be functional – or fully working – and should test each of the features of the site. At this stage, your test plan will just list the tests you plan to carry out and what you expect to happen for each test. When you have created the website, you will do the actual testing and record the results on the test plan. Your test plan should look something like the one shown in Figure 13.2.

Figure 13.2 Example test plan

	Home page	Contact page	About page
Internet Explorer			
Firefox			
Graphics			
Scripts			

The sort of things you should test for on every page on your site include:

- the page loads without any errors in a variety of different browsers
- each graphic on the page displays correctly
- text on the page is formatted and positioned correctly
- text is formatted in a consistent manner
- any tables on the page are formatted correctly
- all the links on the page (internal and external) work correctly
- any scripts you have on the page work correctly.

A brief outline of alternative design ideas

Rather than just adopting the first design that you think of, it is helpful to create a storyboard or even make a prototype page using a couple of different designs. You can then consider which one looks the best and provides the best user experience. You might find it helpful to ask other people what they think of your different design idea before making your final choice.

Assessment activity 13.2

1B.2 | 1B.3 | 2B.P2 | 2B.P3 | 2B.M2 | 2B.D2

KidsSportingLife would like you to design them a new website. It must have a minimum of eight interlinked pages. The aim of the website is to promote the range of activities on offer to children aged 6–16 and to encourage new volunteers to help out with running the activities. The charity would also like a section where people can make donations.

Your design documentation should include the following.

- A description of the purpose of the website you are going to design and the client's requirements.
- Some design ideas for the website.

- A comparison of the alternative solutions and reasons for each of your design decisions, with information about which one will be the best to fulfil the client's requirements.
- A consideration of any constraints on each design and what impact they will have on user experience.
- An account of the aesthetic features.
- An account of all the interactive components.
- A list of all the assets you will need, both ready-made and those you are going to create yourself.
- A test plan for your chosen website design and test data that you can use to test your website.

Tip

Make sure you include the source of all assets used in your asset list and to seek permission from copyright holders of any ready-made assets.

Starting to develop a website

Getting started

There are different software packages you can use to develop web pages. Using the internet, research web development software packages and then find some online tutorials which support the different packages. The relevant tutorials will also help you to develop your skills in this area.

Introduction

Once your site design is complete, the next step is to make the actual pages and link them together to create your website.

Use appropriate software tools and techniques

You can write HTML code with a simple text editor such as Notepad but creating sophisticated web pages is quite difficult. Web developers tend to use web development software such as Adobe® Dreamweaver®. You will also need access to a graphics-editing software (such as Adobe® Photoshop®) to prepare the images for your web pages.

Gathering and storing the assets for your web page

Eventually your website will be uploaded on a web server, and so it is important to create a folder where all the files for your site will be saved. Saving web pages and graphics and other elements you will use in your website in all sorts of different locations will not work when you upload your site to a server. This is why it is important to create a folder for all your site files at the outset.

How to create a folder

Step 1 In Adobe® Dreamweaver® go to the **Site** menu and choose **New site**. This will display the **Site setup** box as shown in Figure 13.3.

Step 2 Give your site a name and choose a folder where your site files will be saved. Then click **Save**.

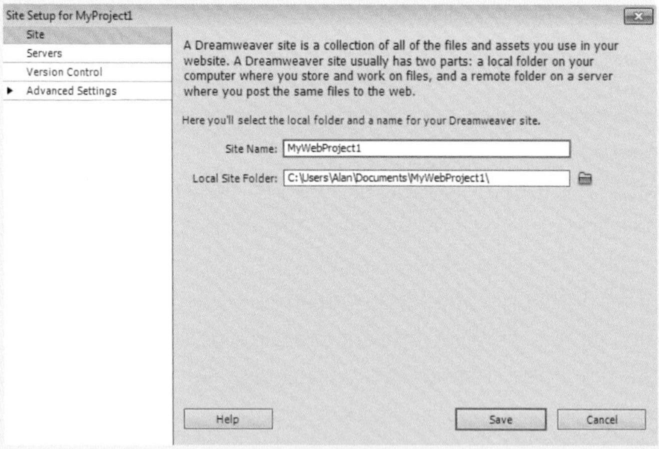

Figure 13.3 Site Setup

The design you created for your website should list the various assets you need, such as images, animations, video and sound files. You should now gather all these assets together and place them in a subfolder inside your site folder. You will need to create any assets that aren't ready-made digital assets yourself. You will also need to prepare text for your web pages and have ready any external links you need to include.

Naming your web pages

Next you should save the empty page Dreamweaver® has created for you. The home page on any site needs to have the name 'Index.html'. This also relates to when your pages are uploaded to a web server. Most web servers are set up to expect the first page in any website to be called 'Index.html'.

How to save a web page

Step 1 In Dreamweaver®, go to the **File** menu and select **Save**.

Step 2 Dreamweaver® will automatically choose the folder you defined in the Site setup, so all you need to do is to enter the name 'Index.html' and click **Save**.

Page properties

You can set page properties, which will control things like the default font, font colour and background colour.

How to set default fonts and backgrounds

Step 1 Click the **Modify** menu and choose the **Page properties** option. This will display the **Page properties dialog box** as shown in Figure 13.4.

Step 2 This is where you can set the default font, size and colour and the page background colour, or alternatively an image which will be displayed as a background for the page. Make sure you have the **Appearance (CSS)** option selected on the left side of the box.

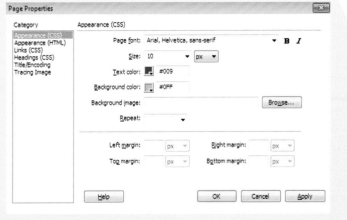

Figure 13.4 The Page properties dialog box

You can also do the following:

- **Adding text.** To add text to your web page, simply type in the design side of the screen display. You text will appear in the default font and colour chosen in the **Page properties** dialog box. You may have prepared your text in advance in which case you can copy and paste it in and then format it.

- **Headings and subheadings.** The best way to format headings and subheadings in a web page is to use the heading tags. This makes it easier to apply and change the formatting to the whole site using CSS.

  To apply a heading tag, simply select the text you want to make a heading. Then select the level of heading you want to apply from the format drop-down at the bottom of the screen (see Figure 13.5)

Remember

It is good practice not to use spaces in web page file names. Many web servers run software that will not allow spaces in file names, so you should avoid them. Give your web pages meaningful names by using capital letters or underscores, as in Contacts_Page.html or LinksToOtherSites.html.

CONTINUED ▸▸

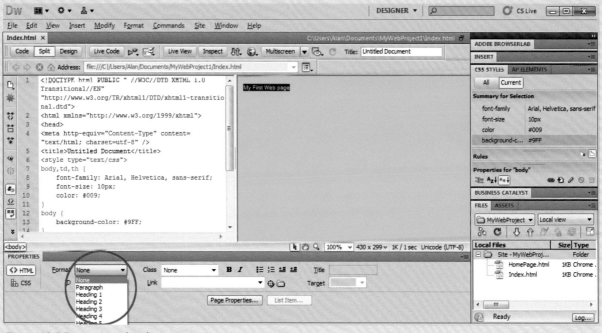

Figure 13.5 Formatting a heading

Heading 1 will be the largest text size, heading 2 is smaller and so on. Selecting
'paragraph' from the drop-down list will set the text in the default page font.

Activity 13.4

Create a simple 'My CV' web page with details about you and your qualifications.
Try out different background colours, text colours and fonts. Also try out the
different heading sizes on the content of your CV.

Just checking ✔

1 Why is 'My Page.html' not a good name for a web page?
2 What file name should be used for the first or home page of a website?
3 What is the difference between the <p> tag and the <br> tag?

Create and edit web pages 1

Introduction

Creating web pages involves many considerations. In this section we will look at the different software tools you can use and how to create the navigation for your website.

Formatting

There are a number of different ways you can create web pages.

HTML

You can type the HTML (HyperText Markup Language) code used to format a web page into a simple text editor like Microsoft® Notepad®. This is a good way to get familiar with HTML. However, writing and editing HTML like this is fiddly and not well suited to complex pages.

HTML is essentially a set of instructions which is sent to a web browser, telling it how to format a web page. These instructions are in the form of tags. Different tags tell the browser to format text, images or tables in different ways. For example, if you want some text to appear in bold, you use the <b> tag, and to switch off bold you use the </b> tag.

DHTML

In order to develop dynamic websites, web developers designed tools that were more sophisticated than HTML. DHTML (Dynamic HyperText Markup Language) is a general term for several technologies used to create interactive websites, including CSS (cascading style sheets), which we will look at later in this chapter, and JavaScript.

Adobe® Dreamweaver®

Many web developers use Dreamweaver® to create websites, and that's what we will use in the examples in this book. When you first open Dreamweaver®, you will see the welcome screen, as shown in Figure 13.6.

Figure 13.6 Adobe® Dreamweaver® welcome screen

Navigation

You will want to include navigation links to other pages in your site and also to external websites. The pages you want to link to don't have to be complete, but they must exist.

Menus

Many websites include some kind of menu bar, whether across the top or down the side of the page. This is to provide a consistent method of navigating around the site. The menus can be simple hyperlinks or more complex menus using forms with drop-down menus or scripts. Forms and scripts are covered later in this unit (see section *Create and edit web*).

CONTINUED ▶▶

Hyperlinks (internal and external)

Hyperlinks are one of the key features of the World Wide Web in that they allow links to be made from one page to another. Visitors to web pages can then follow the hyperlinks (by clicking on them) to take them to another page. Hyperlinks which link to another page within the same site are called internal hyperlinks, while those that link to a page on a different site are called external hyperlinks. A hyperlink can simply be some text on the page, or an image such as a button. Hyperlinks within text are normally shown by underlined text of a different colour to the standard text on the page.

How to create internal navigation links

This example shows you how to create a link to your website's contacts page from the home page.

Step 1 Start by creating a new page. Choose **New** from the **File** menu. This will display the **New document** dialog box (see Figure 13.7).

Step 2 Leave the **Page type** option set to **HTML** and click the **Create** button. This will insert a new web page.

Step 3 Type the heading 'Contacts' at the top of the page, then go to the **File** menu and choose **Save**.

Step 4 You will be asked to give your file a name. Enter the name for the page as 'Contacts.html', then click **Save**.

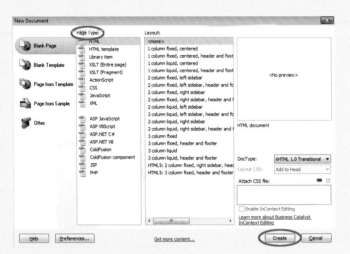

Figure 13.7 The New Document dialog box

How to create external navigation links

Step 1 Add some text that the user will click to follow the link. Then, as before, highlight the text and choose **Insert**, then **Hyperlink**.

Step 2 Now type the web address of the external page you want to link to. Note that you must include the 'http://' part of the address, otherwise the link will not work. See Figure 13.8.

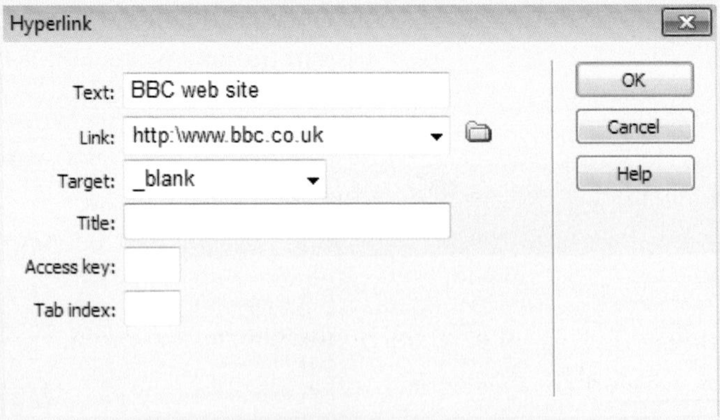

Figure 13.8 Adding an external link

How to link to a page from text or a graphic

You can link to a page from text or a graphic. In this example we just use text.

Step 1   Go to your home page by clicking on the **Index.html** tab.

Step 2   Under the heading, type 'Contacts page'. This is the text the user will click on to go to the Contacts page.

Step 3   Highlight this text. Go to the **Insert** menu and choose **Hyperlink**. This will display the **Hyperlink** dialog box (see Figure 13.9).

Step 4   Click on the **Folder** icon. The **Select file** dialog box will appear.

Step 5   Choose the **Contact page** option and then click **OK**.

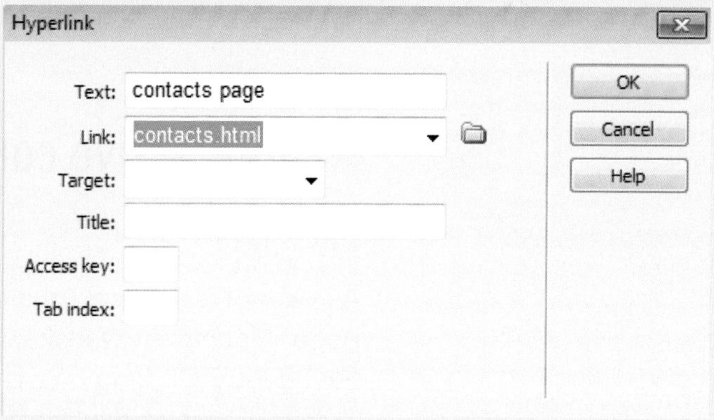

Figure 13.9 Hyperlink dialog box

Anchors

You can also create a link to a place within a page. This is useful if you have a long page and want to create a link to different subjects or headings within the same page.

How to create a named anchor

Step 1   Key click in the text you want to make a **named anchor**, and from the **Insert** menu, choose **Named Anchor**. This will display the named anchor dialog box.

Step 2   Type a name for your anchor in the box (don't use spaces in the name) and click **OK** (Dreamweaver® inserts an anchor symbol to show where the anchor is).

Step 3   To create a link to your new anchor, use the same procedure as with other hyperlinks, only this time when you enter the link details in the hyperlink dialog box, type a '#' symbol, followed by the anchor name you want to link to.

Activity 13.5

Using the CV web page you created earlier (in Activity 13.4), add some more pages (e.g. ones for personal interests, other work experience). Link these from you first page using hyperlinks.

Then create some external hyperlinks; for example, to your school website. Make the external hyperlinks open in a separate browser window.

Just checking

1 What is the difference between an internal and an external hyperlink?
2 How does DHTML differ from HTML?
3 What is the purpose of HTML tags?

Key term

Named anchor – This is a named location in a page that you can link to. You can create as many named anchors as you like within a page.

Did you know?

You can set the target of a hyperlink to '_blank', so that clicking the link opens the page in a new browser tab or window instead of replacing the current one.

Create and edit web pages 2

Introduction

In this section we will cover how to put interactive components into your web pages and how to embed digital assets.

Interactive components

Hot spots

A hot spot is an area, usually within an image, which contains a hyperlink to another page. A company website, for example, might have a map of all their offices across the country. Clicking on a particular office location on the map will open a page with details of that particular office. These are sometimes called image maps.

Buttons

The simplest way to add buttons to a web page is to have a graphic image of a button (for example, a windows 'OK' button) and then make the image a hyperlink. Clicking the button will then cause the browser to follow the hyperlink. However, this method is only suitable where you want to use buttons as hyperlinks. If you want a button to carry out some other function you will need to use scripts.

Menus

Dreamweaver® includes a selection of ready-to-use interactive components that you can add to your web pages. These are called 'Spry' features. You need to add programming code to your web pages to make these features work (see *Create and edit web pages 1*). One type of 'Spry' feature you can add is a menu bar.

How to add a Spry such as a menu bar to a web page

Step 1 Click in the page where you want the menu to appear.

Step 2 From the **Insert** menu, choose **Spry** then **Spry Menu bar**. You will then see the Spry menu bar dialog box. Choose the layout you would like and click **OK**. The menu bar will now be inserted.

Step 3 Click the blue bar at the top of the menu and the properties for the menu will be displayed in the Properties pane at the bottom of the screen (see Figure 13.10).

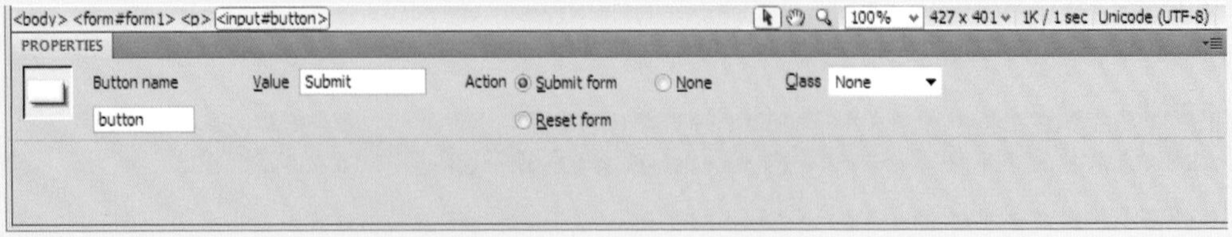

Figure 13.10: The Properties pane displays the properties for the menu

Each top level item (item 1, item 2 etc.) has a drop-down sub menu (item 1.2, item 1.2 etc.). You add or remove the top level and sub menu items using the + and – buttons in the properties panel. To change the item text click the item in the Properties panel, then type the text you want in the text box (see Figure 13.10). To choose what page the menu item links to, either type the URL in the link box or click the browser icon and choose the web page from your local site folder. Figure 13.11 shows one of the top level items has had its text and link changed.

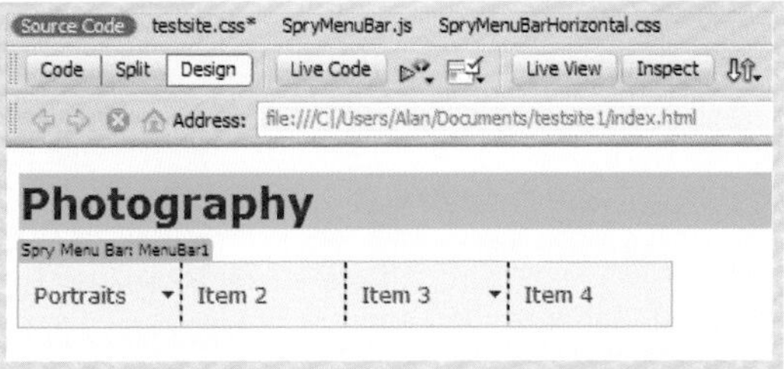

Image rollovers

Another type of interactive content is an image rollover. This is where you have an image in a website, and if the user moves their mouse over the image, it changes in some way.

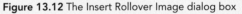

Figure 13.11: Editing the Spry menu bar

To create an image rollover, you need two images that are the same size. Both of these images need to be saved in your local site folder.

How to create a rollover

Step 1 Go to the **Insert** menu. Choose the **Image objects option**, and then choose the **Rollover image** option. The **Insert Rollover image dialog box** will now appear (see Figure 13.12)

Step 2 Enter the file names of both the original image and the one that appears when the mouse is moved over the image (the rollover image) and click **OK**. The original image is inserted in the web page and can be resized just like a normal image.

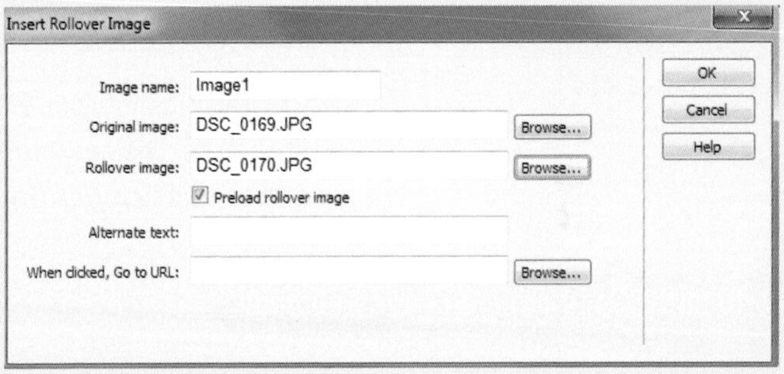

Figure 13.12 The Insert Rollover Image dialog box

Pop-up windows

Pop-up windows, or pop-ups, are another way you can add interactivity to your pages. Instead of a link going to a new page, it can open a new browser window, and you can specify the size of that window. This can be useful, for example, to allow a user to see a larger version of a thumbnail photo on your site. The page that will 'pop up' must already exist.

How to create pop-up windows

Step 1 Click on the text or image that the user will click to make the window pop-up.

Step 2 Go to the **Window** menu and choose the **Behaviours option**. This will open the **Behaviour panel**.

Step 3 Click the **+** icon in the **Behaviour panel** (see Figure 13.13) and choose **Open browser window**. The **Open browser window dialog box** will appear.

Figure 13.13 The open browser window behaviour

CONTINUED ▶▶

continued

Step 4 Enter the URL or filename of the page you want displayed and choose a size (in pixels) for the window. Then click **OK**. See Figure 13.14.

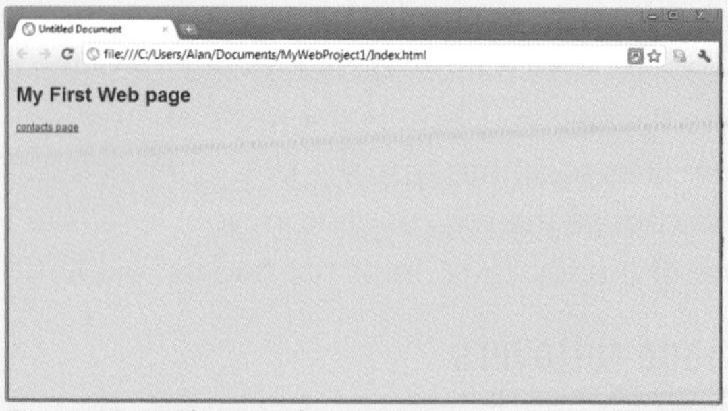

Step 5 If you now preview your page in a web browser (**File**, **Preview in browser**) and click the image. A new page will pop up (you may need to adjust your browser settings as they may prevent pop-up windows).

My First Web page

contacts page

Figure 13.14 The open browser window dialog box

Embedding multimedia or digital assets and graphics

To make your web pages more engaging you may want to include digital graphics, videos, audio or animations that you have either created yourself or ready-made assets that you have sourced.

To insert graphics in your web pages they must be in .JPG, .GIF or .PNG format. For the best results, resize your images in your image editing software to approximately the size they will appear on the web page and set their resolution to 72 **PPI**.

How to embed a graphic on your web page

Step 1 Position your cursor within the page where you want the image to appear.

Step 2 Go to the **Insert** menu and choose the **Image** option. This will display the **Select Image Source** dialog box (see Figure 13.15).

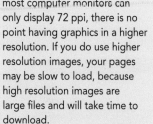

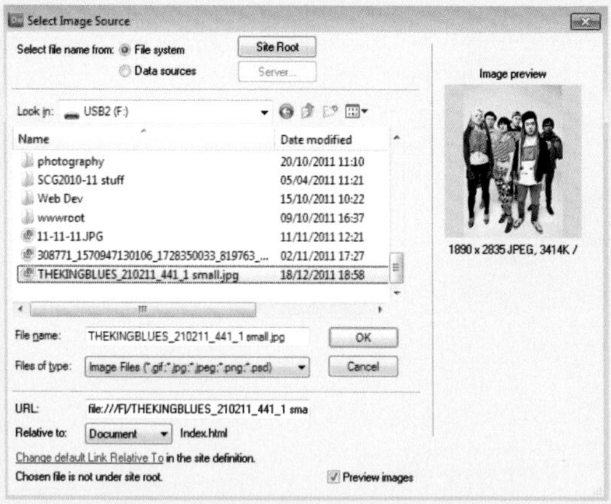

Figure 13.15 Select Image Source dialog box

Step 3 Find and select the image you want to insert and click **OK**. (If the file you select isn't located in the site folder, Adobe® Dreamweaver® will warn you that this is the case and ask you if you want to copy it there.)

Step 4 Choose the **Yes** option to copy the file to your site folder.

Step 5 Once you have saved your file, you will then see the **Image Tag Accessibility Attributes** dialog box (see Figure 13.16). This allows you to add alternative text which will describe your image.

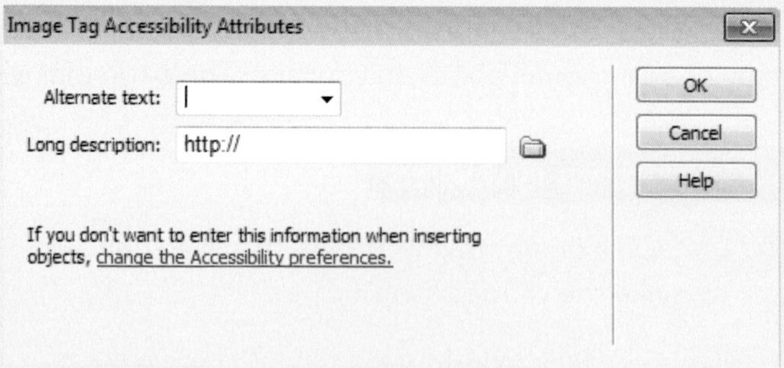

Image Tag Accessibility Attributes

Alternate text:

Long description: http://

If you don't want to enter this information when inserting objects, change the Accessibility preferences.

OK | Cancel | Help

Figure 13.16 Image tag accessibility attributes

Step 6 Enter a description of your image in the **Alternative** text box and click **OK**. The image will now appear in your web page.

You can adjust the way the image appears in your web page using the Properties panel at the bottom of the Dreamweaver® editing window, but it's a much better option to use cascading style sheets (CSS) to make these adjustments. CSS is described later in this section.

Figure 13.17 Once you have embedded graphics, you can edit how they appear

Activity 13.6

Using the CV web pages you have been working on, add in some images. Make one of your images a rollover. (If, for example, one of your hobbies is watching football, you could have an image rollover which shows photos of your team which changes to a photo of their ground when the mouse is moved over it.)

Just checking

1 What graphics file formats are supported by web pages?

2 What size (in pixels per square inch) should you resize images so they load quickly?

3 What is an image rollover?

Remember

Remember that all your website files must be in the same folder (or a subfolder under that folder), otherwise when you upload your files to a web server, your site will not work as you expect.

Did you know?

Adobe® Flash Player® animations use SWF files, while Flash® videos use FLV files. As with image files, these animations and videos should be saved in your local site folder and must be uploaded to the server along with your pages.

Create and edit web pages 3

Introduction

In this section we will look at how text, tables, forms and frames can be used in web pages.

Text

All websites contain a certain amount of text. The recommended way to format the text on a website is to use CSS (described later in the unit), rather than use individual text formatting options as you would in a word processing program. However, individual text formatting can be applied using to toolbar at the bottom of the Dreamweaver® editing window.

Tables

Tables are useful not only for displaying tabular information but can also be used to lay out your web page.

How to insert a table

Step 1 Go to the **Insert** menu, and choose **Table**, which will display the **Insert table** dialog box.

Step 2 Choose the number of rows and columns you want for your table, and adjust any other options you want. Then click **OK** to insert the table.

You can also add different options to your table. See Table 13.2 for these.

Table 13.2 Formatting options for tables

Table width	This is the width of the table across the web page. You can specify this in pixels or as a percentage of the user's browser window. If you choose a percentage amount, the table width will vary depending on the size of the browser window. If you choose a number of pixels then the table will be a fixed size.
Border thickness	This is the size of the border around the table. The larger the number, the thicker the border. If you set this value to zero, the border will be invisible.
Cell padding	This sets the space between the contents of a cell and its border.
Cell spacing	This sets the space between the table cells.
Header	This allows you to choose which rows or columns are formatted in a header style.

Forms

You can create simple forms easily with Adobe® Dreamweaver®, but to process the form entries once the user has completed them, you need to create programs which run on the web server that hosts the site. This is beyond the scope of this unit. However, it is useful to know how to create forms. Also you can use JavaScript in web pages to make sure the entries in a form are correct before it is sent to the server. For example, if a form field requires the user to enter a date, JavaScript can be used to check if the date is valid and display an error message to the user if it is not.

Text fields

There are a number of different types of input methods you can use on a form, the simplest being a text field.

How to insert a form text field

Step 1 Go to the **Insert** menu and choose **Form**. Then, from the menu that pops out, choose **Text field**. This will display the **Input tag** dialog box.

Step 2 Fill in an **ID** for the text field. This will be used to identify the field in any server- or client-side program which reads the form. The **Label field** is used to place text next to the field, so the web page user knows what to type in the text box. The **Style setting** controls if the label moves with the input box. The **Position setting** controls if the label is before or after the text box.

Step 3 Click **OK**. Adobe® Dreamweaver® will ask if you want to add a form tag. HTML forms should begin and end with a form tag, so click **Yes**.

Step 4 Your text box can now be seen in the preview window and the red dotted line around it shows that this is a form. In the code window, you can see that the orange colour form tags give the form a name and an ID. These, along with the method and the action, are used to process the form by client- or server-side programs. You can add other text fields and different form objects. Just return to the **Insert menu, form option** and choose the form object you want.

Text areas

Text areas provide a larger, multi-line area into which text can be entered.

Radio buttons

A radio button is a type of user interface feature which allows users to select only one option, not multiple ones. For example, a pair of buttons labelled Male and Female would allow a user to indicate their gender, and so only one button can be selected.

Did you know?

Radio buttons should be inserted in groups, since only one of the buttons in the group should be selected.

To create a group

Step 1 Choose **Radio button group** from the **Insert form** menu. This will display the **Radio Group** dialog box (see Figure 13.18).

Step 2 Figure 13.18 shows the Radio Group dialog box set up to display two radio buttons to select the user's gender. You can add more radio buttons (for a different application) by clicking the **plus** button.

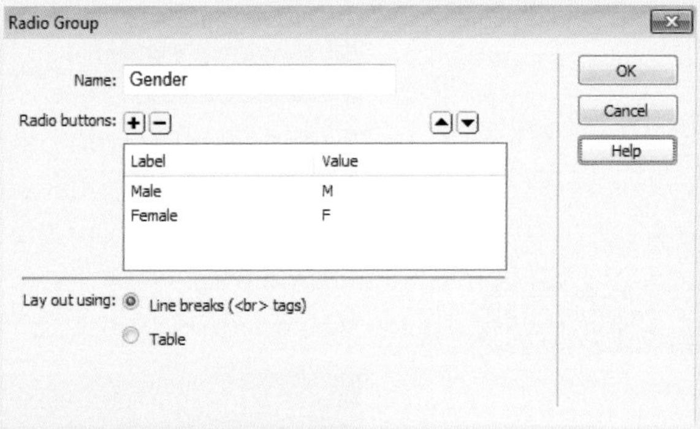

Figure 13.18 Radio group dialog box

CONTINUED ▶▶

Check boxes and select lists/menus

You can also add check boxes to your form. Unlike radio buttons, any number of these can be checked.

A drop-down box from which a user can select a single item.

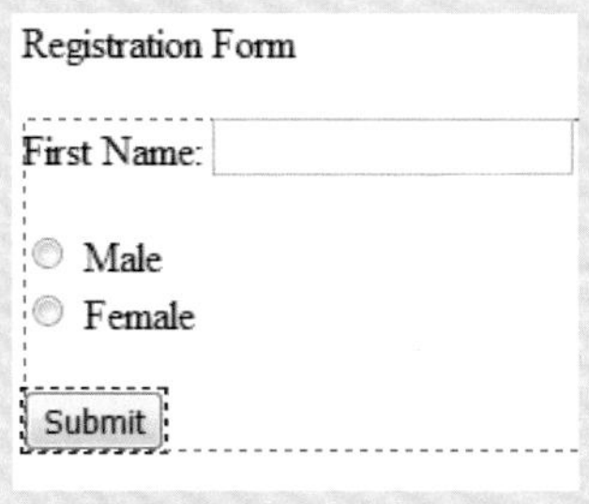

Buttons

Your form needs to end with a 'Submit' button. If you have a client-side script that validates the form, clicking the Submit button will link to the validation script. Clicking the button will also submit the form to the web server where the data the user has entered can be processed. Insert a button using the same method as the other input methods. You usually leave the label blank for a button. An example Submit button is shown in Figure 13.19.

Figure 13.19 Submit button

▌ Frames

In the past, frames were widely used to split web pages into sections, but they have now been replaced by better ways of formatting a page, such as cascading style sheets (CSS). Frames are essentially two or more web pages displayed together to give a layout effect, such as a header or a side bar.

How to create a page with frames

Step 1 Choose the **File** menu, then **New**.

Step 2 On the left of the **New document dialog box**, choose **Page** from **Sample**. In the **Sample folder** section choose **Frameset**, then on the right select the frame design you want. The design view will then show a grey line which divides the two frames. The HTML view will show only the HTML for the frame your cursor is currently in.

Activity 13.7

Using the CV web pages you have been working on, add a 'Contact page'. Via this page, potential employers will be able to contact you. Use a form to collect information about the employer (name, company, type of job – full time or part time etc.).

Just checking

1 What is a 'radio button'? How might a set of radio buttons be used on a web page?

2 In an HTML table, what does the 'cell padding' property do?

3 What is needed to be able to process the entries made on a web page form?

Create and edit web pages 4

Introduction

In this section we will look at how you can use colour schemes, styles and templates to create a consistent look and feel to your website and how accessibility features can be used to give all users a good experience of your website.

Accessibility features

Accessibility features are important as visually impaired people may wish to view the site using a text-to-speech reader. The text reader reads out the alternative text tags for the non-text features of your site including images, forms and tables.

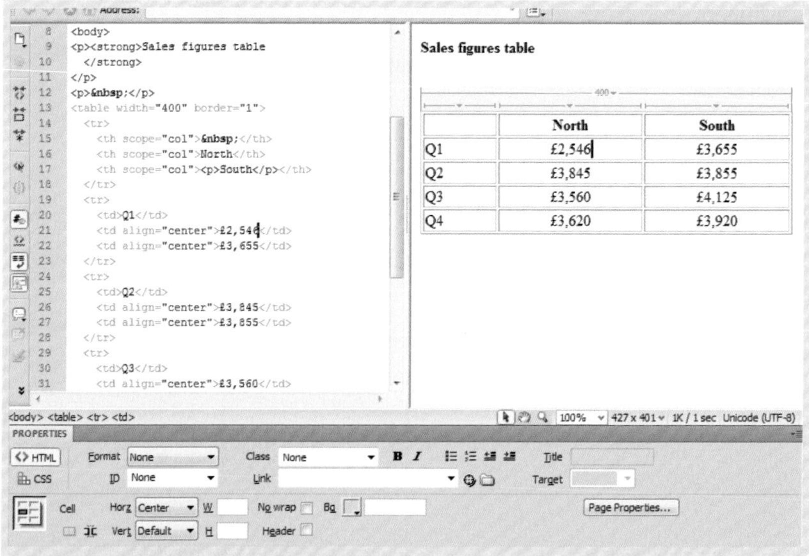

Figure 13.20 Table with properties shown

Figure 13.20 shows a table which is 400 pixels wide and contains three columns and five rows. When your cursor is in a table, the properties panel at the bottom shows the properties of the cell your cursor is in. To change the properties of more than one cell, select the cells you want to change.

You can change the text alignment and formatting of content. You can also resize columns and rows by dragging the borders.

Most modern browsers also allow users to zoom in and out of their view of the site. By zooming in, a user can view a site at a much larger size than normal.

Did you know?

Windows® 7 includes a basic screen reader. Choose **Start – All programs – Accessories – Ease of access – Narrator**. You can try out your web pages with it, but it takes some patience to use as it reads all the Browser menus first before it starts on your page content.

Colour schemes, styles and templates

Page layout

There are two main ways in which you can create multi-section page layouts for your web pages, including elements like title bars, side bars (content boxes which run down the side of the page) and main content areas. Using a table to achieve this type of page layout is fairly easy and individual cells within the table can be used to create each section of the page. You can use the table properties (e.g. table width) to set the size, position and colour scheme of each section.

An alternative method is to use cascading style sheets (CSS), although it is more flexible, this method is also more complex. You can set up CSS styles with colour scheme, width and alignment settings, and then use sections within your page formatted with these styles. Text will wrap within both a table cell and CSS section at the right-hand edge of the cell or section, and you can adjust the gap between the edge of the text and the edge of the cell or section using the cell padding (in a table) or padding (in a CSS style) property.

CONTINUED ▸▸

Background colours

See the section on *Page properties* for more information on background colours.

Cascading style sheets (CSS)

With cascading style sheets, you don't need to format the text and other items on each page individually. Instead, you create a single set of formatting styles in a separate file, which is then applied to all the pages in your site.

Dreamweaver® comes with some template style sheets for you to use, although you can also create your own. Try the sample ones included with Dreamweaver®.

How to try out sample style sheets

Step 1 Choose the **File** menu, then **New**.

Step 2 In the box that appears, choose **Page from Sample**.

Step 3 Make sure you have **CSS** selected in the middle, then preview the styles on the right and select the one you want (see Figure 13.21).

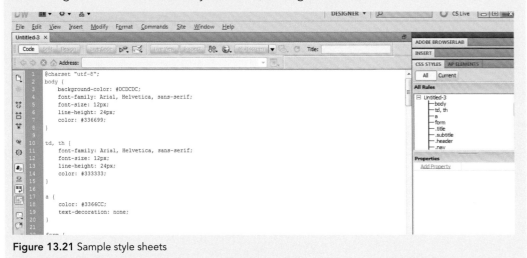

Figure 13.21 Sample style sheets

Step 4 Click the **Create** button and Dreamweaver® will create a new style sheet with the sample styles in it.

Remember this is not a web page – it's a style sheet that is used with a web page. Each style name is shown in purple and then in between the brackets, the formatting that applies to that style is listed in blue.

To use this style sheet, you need to save it in your local site folder.

How to use cascading style sheets

Step 1 Go to the **File** menu and choose **Save**, and give the file a name (no spaces in the name, remember).

Step 2 Now you need to attach this CSS file to the other pages in your site.

Step 3 Open the web page you want to attach the style sheet to, and make sure you have the CSS panel displayed on the right by choosing the **Windows menu** and **CSS styles**.

Step 4 Click the **Link** icon at the bottom right of the CSS pane. This will display the **Attach External style sheet** dialog box (see Figure 13.22).

Step 5 Use the browser button to locate your CSS style sheet. Then click **OK**.

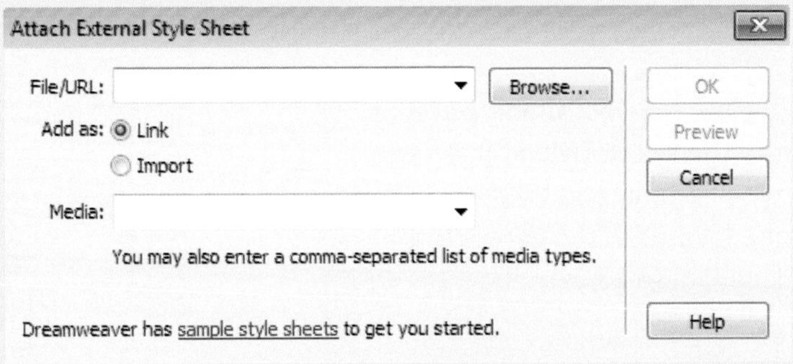

> **Remember**
>
> The extension for a cascading style sheet is not .HTML but .CSS.

Figure 13.22 Attach External style sheet dialog box

Step 6 If your page already has text on it then the text and the background colour will change to those set in the 'body' style of the style sheet you have attached the page to. To apply one of the other styles:

Step 7 Click in the text you want to apply the style to.

Step 8 In the **Properties** pane at the bottom choose the required style from the **Class** drop-down (see Figure 13.23).

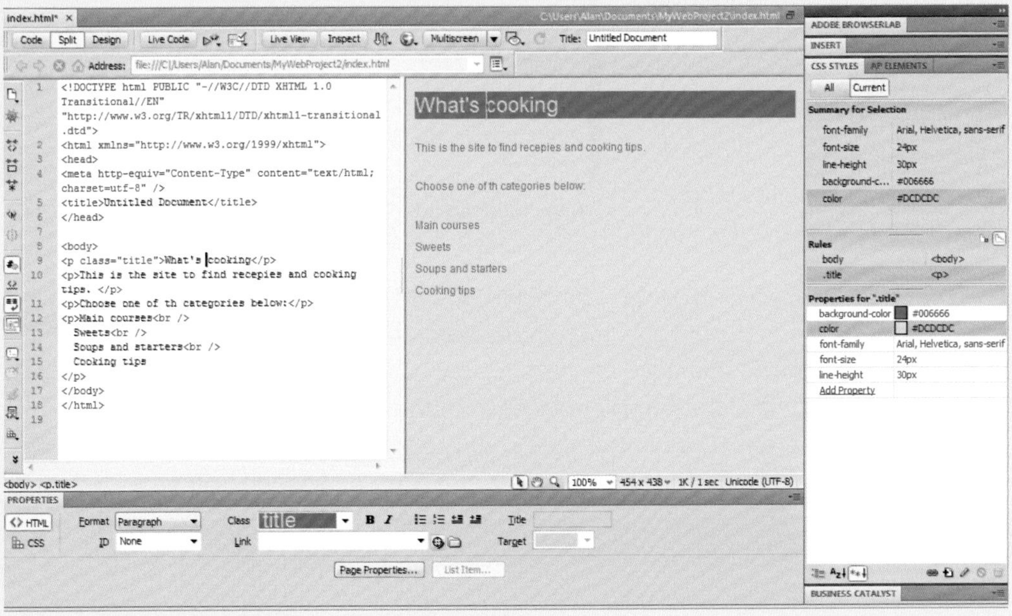

Figure 13.23 Applying styles

> **Remember**
>
> The idea of CSS is that you always use these styles to format your text rather than applying individual formatting. CSS makes it easy to change the formatting on your website. Suppose, for example, you wanted to change the formatting of all the headings. All you would need to do is change the heading style. Then all the headings formatted with that style would automatically change.

CONTINUED ▶▶

Key term

SECTION tags – These are used to create sections within your web page. By combining them with CSS styles, these sections can be used as page layout elements, or text boxes, with a specific size, position and formatting.

CSS can also be used to create sections or boxes within your web pages, such as headers, side bars and footers. You can use **SECTION tags** to create these sections in web pages, and CSS styles to format and position them.

Creating complex page layouts like this isn't easy, so Dreamweaver® comes with some pre-set CSS layouts.

How to create a new page using a pre-set page layout

Step 1 Go to the **File** menu and choose New.

Step 2 Select **Blank page** at the top left, **HTML** in the page type column and then one of the layouts in the centre left (see Figure 13.24).

Step 3 Then click the **Create** button and Adobe® Dreamweaver® will create the layout and fill it with instructional text.

Step 4 Read the instructions and then delete the text and replace it with your own website text.

Figure 13.25 shows the two-column fixed layout with a right side bar and header and footer.

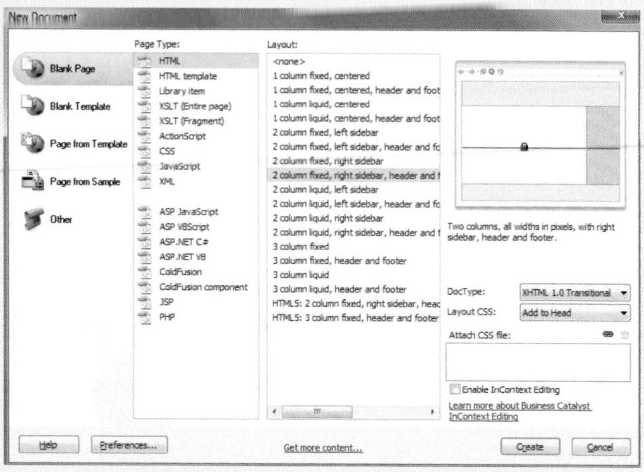

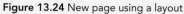

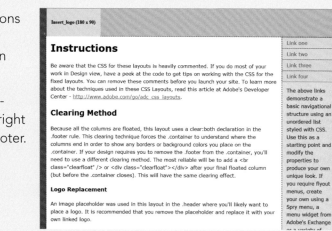

Figure 13.24 New page using a layout

Figure 13.25 Adobe® Dreamweaver® page layout

Activity 13.8

Using the CV website you have created in previous activities, apply a Dreamweaver® style sheet template to each of the pages. Experiment with applying the different styles in the style sheet to the text in your pages.

Just checking

1 What are section tags used for?

2 What file extension is used for CSS files?

3 How can a person with a sight impairment make a website easier to view?

Create and edit web pages 5

Introduction

In this section we will look at some simple client-side scripts, browser compatibility, exporting and compressing and suitable file types.

Client-side scripts

Scripts which run on the client's (user's) computer can do a number of things. We have already used built-in scripts to make a menu bar and open a browser window and there are quite a few others included in Adobe® Dreamweaver®, including ones to validate form entries. You can add your own scripts written in languages especially designed for web page scripts, like JavaScript and **AJAX**.

You can find many JavaScript examples on the internet. The very simple example shown in Figure 13.26 displays an alert box when the user clicks a button.

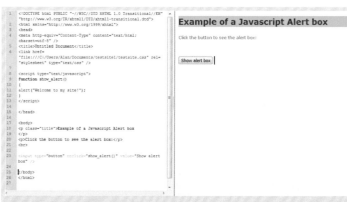

Figure 13.26 JavaScript example

If you preview this page in a browser then you will see something like Figure 13.27 when you click the button.

Browser compatibility

There are many different browsers in use (Explorer, Firefox, Chrome, etc.). Not all HTML features are supported by all browsers and older versions of browsers will not support the newer features. To ensure your web pages are compatible with different browsers, you need to load each page into a selection of the most popular browsers to see it they load correctly and display as you expect.

Export and compress/suitable file types

Digital assets such as images, audio clips and videos need to be prepared for inclusion in a web page. These assets often have large file sizes and may take a long time to download unless they are compressed. Image and video files need to be set to a suitable size and resolution to make sure their file size is not unnecessarily large.

Figure 13.27 JavaScript example in a browser

CONTINUED ▶▶

Web servers and web hosting services

Although you can preview your web pages in a browser locally on your computer, your web pages need to be uploaded on to a **web server** before they are available on the internet. In addition, you will need to choose a **web hosting** company.

Many organisations run web servers and offer a web hosting service. Most charge for this, although some offer the service for free (but include adverts in the pages).

Having chosen a web hosting company you will then need to upload your website files (everything contained in the local website folder, including images and other media) to the hosting company's servers. This is normally done using a web-based control panel program provided by the web hosting company.

Domain name

Simply uploading your pages on to a web server won't make them available on the internet, because no one will be able to find them. Your site will need to be assigned a **domain name,** which is unique to the site.

Activity 13.9

Research into different UK-based web hosting companies. How much to they charge, what facilities do they offer (e.g. do they offer server side processing, if so which programming language do they support)? Will they register a domain name for you?

Just checking

1 Where does a client side script run? On the web server or on the page viewer's computer?
2 Where is a good place to find JavaScript examples?
3 Why do you need to test your pages on different browsers?

WorkSpace

Ajay Singh

Junior web developer

I wanted to work in web development, as I think it is one of the fastest developing and most exciting areas in IT. I learned about the basics of web development when I studied for my BTEC First course and then I went on to study it in more detail at college and university.

After I left university I applied for a lot of jobs with no luck. After about three months, I found work at a local company which makes fashion wear. They were looking for a junior web developer to update their website and I got the job. Their website changes all the time, with new ranges of clothing coming out and old ones needing to be removed.

So far, I am happy with the job. Some parts of it are quite tedious, like uploading the new files, but I am learning new things all the time, and as I learn how to do more, I can get involved in the more interesting and exciting projects. We are currently looking at creating a version of our website for mobile users, which I am looking forward to working on.

Think about it

1 What sort of companies might want to employ a web developer?

2 If you wanted to become a junior web developer, what type of qualifications would be useful?

3 Why do you think Alex's employer wants to create a version of their website for mobile users?

4 If you got a job as a junior web developer, how might your career progress (i.e. if you got promoted, how would your job change)?

Testing the website

Introduction

Once the website is complete, you should test it using the test plan you created at the design stage.

Functionality

Check your website for basic functionality:

- the pages should load up and all the links should work
- the images should display well and all the formatting should be correct and consistent. You will need to check each page carefully to see if every element on the page is as it should be.

Quality

This is a fairly subjective measure, but you should compare the site to professional sites. Ask yourself the following questions:

- Does the layout and do your colour schemes have a quality look to them or are they messy with garish, clashing colours?
- Is all the spelling and grammar correct?
- Are the images of good quality (high enough resolution)?
- Does the home page load quickly?

Usability

Check that it is clear how to navigate around your site, and that there is a way back to the home page. You should check your website works correctly in all the commonly used web browsers, such as Microsoft® Internet Explorer®, Firefox and Google™ Chrome™.

Feedback

An important part of the testing procedure is to ask for feedback from others. Other users are more likely to be critical of your site than you are and they may spot things you have not noticed. You need to gather feedback on the following areas:

- **Content.** Is the content suitable for the site? Is the text free from spelling and grammar errors? Are the images suitable?
- **Presentation.** Is the content presented and formatted in a neat and consistent manner? Are the colour schemes complementary or do they clash? Are images and other assets sized and formatted appropriately?
- **Usability.** Usability will be extremely important for the intended audience of the website. If possible, ask some people from that group to give you their opinion of the site.
- **Performance.** How quickly does the site load? Do images load reasonably quickly or is there a noticeable delay before they load?
- **Purpose.** How well does the site meet the purpose that was stated at the design stage?

Improve accessibility

You should also consider if there are ways in which you can refine your site to make it more accessible to those with visual impairments. For example, have you provided alternative text for all your images, tables and forms? You can also try using a text reader to look at your site to see how easy it is to navigate. Have you enabled users to zoom in and out of the web pages?

Enhance performance

You may also be able to improve your website's performance, making it quicker to load if you adjust the size and degree of compression of, for example, the images, animations and videos included in your site. If you find that digital assets such as images, video or audio clips load too slowly you may need to return to the original files and see what can be done to make them smaller. With images you need to check that their actual size matches the size they will be displayed on the page and that their resolution is not higher than it needs to be. Videos also may need their resolution and size reduced to make the files smaller. Most graphics and video-editing software will allow you to adjust the amount of compression that is applied to the file when it is exported so you may need to increase the amount of compression by adjusting these values.

Add dynamic functionality

An important way you can refine and improve your website is to add dynamic functionality such as hot spots, rollovers, navigation menus and pop-ups. These provide additional ways for your users to interact with the site and make the site more interesting and engaging.

You should document any changes or improvements you make to your site, based on the testing you do, and any feedback you get from other people.

Assessment activity 13.3

| 1C.4 | 1C.5 | 1C.6 | 2C.P4 | 2C.P5 | 2C.P6 | 2C.M3 | 2C.M4 | 2C.M5 | 2C.D3 |

KidsSportingLife like your proposed idea and they would like you to go ahead and create the website for them. You will then need to test it.

- Prepare the assets for your website, including information about where they came from.
- Develop the website for KidsSportingLife, making sure that you implement your full website design (there must be at least eight interlinking pages), incorporating all elements of the original requirements. (Use the website design you created for Assessment activity 13.2 as your starting point.)
- Make any adjustments you identify to improve it.

- Using your test plan and the test data you created (see Assessment activity 13.2), test the functionality of your website.
- Check it against the original requirements: is it fit for purpose? Does it meet the client's requirements?
- Fix any faults you find and document the changes you make.
- Gather feedback from others on the interactivity and quality of the website.
- Use the feedback to refine the website's accessibility and performance, keeping the user requirements in your mind at all times.

Tips

- Be sure to record all test results (keep a log of the tests you do) and the feedback you receive, and also what you changed as a result to improve the website.
- If users highlight problems in their feedback, then ask them further questions to find out exactly what is at the source of the problem.

Reviewing the finished website

Introduction

The final stage is to review your website and the process you went through to complete it.

There are a number of things you should consider when reviewing your site.

Fitness for purpose and user requirements

You should go back and look at the original client or user requirements and consider whether these have been fully met. You should have had a clear statement of the purpose of the website and the audience it was targeted at. Have you achieved this stated purpose? Have you added features to your site which will appeal to the stated target audience? The feedback you should have obtained from members of the stated audience should help you here.

Functionality

Look carefully at each page of your site and check that it functions the way it should. Ask yourself the following questions.

- Do all the hyperlinks work correctly?
- Does any dynamic content (buttons menus, rollovers etc.) function as it should?

Information/content including digital assets

Review the content of your pages carefully. Ask yourself the following questions.

- It the text spelt correctly?
- Is it likely to make sense to the target audience for your site?
- Does it provide all the required information?
- Are the images relevant?
- Is the formatting you have applied to the content appropriate and consistent?

User experience

Your review should include looking at the feedback you obtained from other people who used the site. You should assess their comments on the following issues:

- **Usability.** Check their overall experience of using the website. Was it easy to navigate and understand?
- **Quality.** Check the user feedback to see whether the website gave the impression of being a quality product. See whether there were any issues which let the site down, such as inconsistent layout or formatting or spelling errors.
- **Purpose.** In the feedback, was the content of the site considered suitable to its purpose and audience?
- **Performance.** Check how the site performed: were the graphics and other media quick to download?
- **Interactive features.** Did the site have sufficient interactive features to make it interesting or did it consist of mostly static content?

Constraints

Review the constraints you faced in the development of the site. You may have been short of time and felt that you could have done much more with the site. Or you may not have known how to do some things and were therefore unable to include them in your site.

Strengths and potential improvements

Check how closely your final product matched the original design. It is quite normal to deviate from the design to a certain extent when you come to develop the product, but consider why these deviations were necessary. It might be that there were things you found you could not do, or that were too difficult to implement. Or perhaps in the process of developing your site, you thought of better ways of doing things.

Having considered all these issues, you should now be able to identify your website's strengths: the things it does well and that reviewers liked. You should also be able to highlight the areas where the website could be improved, given more time, resources or better knowledge.

Assessment activity 13.4   1D.7 | 2D.P7 | 2D.M6 | 2D.D4

Produce a report of your project that evaluates your website.

- Compare your website against your initial design.
- Review the extent to which the final website you have built meets the original purpose and user requirements, considering the feedback you got from others and any design constraints.
- Give a reason for any changes that you made during development of the final website.
- Make recommendations for further improvements that could be made to the website that KidsSportingLives may wish to consider implementing in the future.

Tips

- Whatever format you choose for your evaluation, make sure it is presented clearly. Think about the structure, and tackle one design element at a time. For each design element ask yourself: have you included the design element, how well does it fulfil the original requirements, could its performance or reliability be improved further?
- You can include annotated screenshots of your website in your evaluation.

Glossary

.dv stream format – Moving video from camera to computer using a DV format.

3G mobile photo technology – 3G stands for third generation and refers to technology which supports fast data-transmission speeds and increased network capacity and networks through a smart phone. 3G supersedes 1G and 2G mobile phone technology and precedes 4G technology.

802.11 standards – a set of computer industry guidelines, procedures and best practice that operators must follow when providing a wireless service. Standards help to guarantee reliability and quality.

A

Accessibility – A measure of how available and easy to use something is to all users.

Acknowledgement – A full reference of the source of a ready-made asset, which gives proper recognition to the asset's designer and owner.

Actuators – Motors that can be controlled by a technology system such as a motor used to move part of a robot arm.

Address book – An email tool that allows you to store the names, email addresses and other contact details of people.

Affiliate model – An 'affiliate' website is one that is attached to another company's website via a link. The affiliate website receives a percentage of the revenue from customers clicking through from their website to the other company's website.

AJAX (Asynchronous JavaScript And XML) – This is a relatively new web programming technology used to create sophisticated web applications like Google's™ Gmail and Google™ Maps. The 'Spry' features provided by Adobe® Dreamweaver® are written in AJAX.

Algorithm – A mathematical step-by-step sequence used to work out calculations or carry out instructions.

American Standard Code for Information Interchange (ASCII) – The system used in most computer systems to hold alphabetic and numeric characters. In this system, 01000001 (value 65) is used for A, 01000010 (value 66) is used for B, and so on.

Analogue data – Also referred to as analog data, is data represented by an electrical signal, and in the case of an ordinary internet user, travels down standard telephone lines.

Application – In this context, the specific use or purpose of a video product. (Application can also mean a program or piece of software that is designed to fulfil a particular purpose.)

Arrays – These store and arrange data.

Aspect ratio – The relationship between an image's width and height. In still camera photography, the most common aspect ratios are 4:3 and 3:2.

Assets – Things of value that you want to include in your portfolio. Digital assets can include images, sound and video.

Assignment – A statement that assigns a value to a variable.

Attachment – A file or document that you attach and send with an email.

Audio files – Any files containing sounds, speech and/or music.

Authoring software – A program used to create, edit and delete web pages.

Auto number – A data type used to generate a unique identifier for each record to create a primary key. This is used when there is no natural unique identifier.

Automated system – A system that uses technology and control systems. It doesn't usually require human invention.

B

Bandwidth – A way of measuring how much data can be carried over a network.

Battery life – How long the battery lasts in a mobile device.

BCC – Stands for blind carbon copy. You can copy in people to emails – but hide their identify and email address from other recipients – by entering them in this field.

Binary – A system of writing and calculating with numbers. It only uses two digits, 0 and 1, and has 2 as a base. For example, 101 (1 four, 0 twos, 1 unit) = 5. This system is a lot closer to how a computer deals with numbers and data.

Binary data – A set of binary files that contain data encoded in binary form.

Binary format – This format uses just two digits, 0 and 1. (The 'bi' part of 'binary' means two, as in a bicycle with two wheels.) Everything in a computer is in binary format, with groups of eight 1s and 0s held as bytes.

Bit – A place where either of the two digits 0 and 1 are kept. Bits are usually grouped into eight to make a byte. A byte is really useful, as there are 256 different ways the 8 bits can be arranged.

Bit rate – The amount of data stored for each second of footage, usually measured in megabits per second (Mb/s).

Bitmap graphics – These are created using a series of pixels (or bits) within a grid system.

Boolean variable – A variable that can have only two states: true or false.

Byte – In computing and telecommunications, a byte is a unit of digital information which commonly consists of eight bits.

C

Cabled topology – When devices connect using cable rather than wireless.

Cache memory – A fast memory that is used as a data buffer between the CPU and RAM.

Camera pan – Where the camera moves (usually horizontally) across a scene.

CC – Stands for carbon copy. You can copy in additional email recipients using this field.

Central processing unit (CPU) – The part of a computer that controls the entire system and processes the data.

CGI – Stands for 'computer-generated imagery'.

Characteristics – The properties that someone or something has. Usually these are things that are useful in certain types of work or situations. Characteristics that are not useful are known as negative characteristics.

Chat – In this context, refers to any kind of online real-time communication over the internet.

Chatroom – Large-scale interactive conferencing with many people involved in the same conversation at the same time.

Chip – A microchip, often called a chip, is an integrated circuit (IC). The IC is a single component that can be soldered onto an electronic circuit board to connect the chip to the rest of the device.

Client – The person or organisation that asks for a product to be built. They may or may not be the users of the finished product.

Client brief – The formal request from a client for you to do some work for them. The brief should include information concerning the aims of the project and clear client requirements. It should be written down so that both you and the client have something to refer back to.

Client-server – A computer system in which central server(s) control the networked workstations.

Client-side processing – When the interaction between a web page and code occurs directly on a user's computer.

Clock speed – How quickly a component works – the faster the better!

Cloud computing – This is when a computer uses services provided by another organisation's computer systems.

Cloud storage – This is when a computer's storage, access and retrieval facilities are hosted by another computer system.

Codec – A program (or part of a program) that is used to encode and/or decode binary data into a particular format.

Colour depth – The amount of graphics memory (measured in bits) allocated to each pixel. The more bits used the wider the range of colours that can be displayed in the colour palette. The number of colours displayed in a palette is often a function of the software being used.

Colour palette – The tool that contains the colour options.

Command line interface (CLI) – Used by older systems such as DOS, where you had to type commands into a prompt.

Compatible formats – File formats that can be used together in the same graphics software. Formats that are not compatible with each other, or with the software, cannot be used.

Compile – To take the programming code you have written and turn it into a type of code known as object code, which the computer can understand. This is done by a program called a compiler.

Compressed – This is when a recording is reduced (made smaller) in size, meaning that it takes up less space.

Compression – A method of reducing the size of files.

Compression ratio – The approximate percentage by which a file is reduced in size.

Computer aided design/computer aided manufacture (CAD/CAM) – A technology system used to design component parts on a computer and to send the design to robotic tools that manufacture the parts. CAD systems are also used to create plans for buildings. The plans are printed out using an inkjet plotter onto large pieces of paper.

Conditional formatting – This allows you to change the appearance of a cell or cells depending on certain conditions or criteria.

Consistency – When all similar pages look similar throughout the portfolio (e.g. all section pages have the same format).

Constant – Very similar to a variable, except that the constant is given a value in the declaration statement and that value is not changed by other parts of the program.

Constraints – Limitations or restrictions, which make it harder to do something.

Context pages – Pages that hold the content of the portfolio.

Continuity – When sections flow without major interruptions such as big changes in format or colour.

Contrast – A measure of the colour and brightness of an image, or set of images.

Coordinates – A set of values that relate to the position of an image or object. These values will tell you exactly where the image or object is positioned within a particular area.

Copyright – A legal right that is given to someone who creates an original piece of work. This means that other people cannot use this piece of work without the creator's permission.

Crashing – When a software program freezes or stops performing. There are many causes of software program crashes.

Crop – To remove parts of an image so that only the bit you want will remain.

Crossover cable – A network cable that is used to connect two devices of the same type, e.g. two computers or two switches.

D

Data – Any kind of information that has been formatted in a specific way. Different types of data include audio, video, images and monitoring signals, as well as text.

Database – A collection of data stored in a structured way.

Debugging – The process by which you can find errors in a software program.

Declaration – A statement that gives the name of the variable and states what type of data it can contain.

Denary – A decimal system which has 10 as its base.

Devices/components – Used as a generic term to mean computers, peripheral hardware, mobile telephones, manufacturing plant, environment monitors and many other things.

Digital data – Data transmitted or stored using bits and bytes.

Digital images – Diagrams, drawings, still photographs and clip art held electronically.

Digital portfolio – A collection of digital documents gathered together for a specific purpose.

Domain name – A domain name is a way of identifying your website and its location (which web server it is available from). A domain name consists of a URL (uniform resource locator) such as www.bbc.co.uk. Domain names have to be registered to ensure they are unique. Web hosting companies will normally arrange for your domain name to be registered.

Dongle – A small hardware device that plugs into the USB to provide functionality such as connecting to Wi-Fi.

Download – This is when you move files from a system to your personal computer.

DV codec – Digital video codec (DV codec), allows you to compress and store video digitally.

DV decks – A playback only device that can play digital video tapes.

Dynamic RAM – Or DRAM, is a type of memory that contains programs in use.

E

Encrypt – To protect data using a series of codes or passwords.

Entity – A real world thing about which information needs to be stored and maintained. Examples in the medical world are patients, doctors, appointments, treatments, drugs, etc. Each entity will have its own table in a database.

Entity relationship diagram (ERD) – A diagram that illustrates the relationships between entities (tables) in a database.

Envelope – A method of adjusting the volume of a track so it fades up and then down.

Ethernet – An ethernet cable is used to connect a user to a network.

Event handler – The event handler for an object is the code that runs when that event occurred. A button will have an event handler for the click event, with code that runs when the user clicks on the button.

Execute – To perform or carry out a software program containing a set of instructions.

Expression – An individual part of the software program code.

Extranet – Similar to an intranet but it is designed to be accessed by authorised users from outside the organisation. It is often used for business or educational purposes.

F

Feedback – The howling effect that can be heard when using a PA (public address) system if the volume of the amplifiers is turned up too high. It is caused by the output of the speakers being picked up by the microphone(s) and amplified again.

Field – A single piece of data within a record.

File – A type of data storage that holds data, which is often presented in coded form.

File permissions – Access rights granted to specific users and groups of users. These rights control which users can view or make changes to the contents of the system.

Filters – These change the appearance of your clip, and are applied to the clip itself to work with the information within the chip.

Flash memory – A type of memory which can be deleted and reprogrammed in blocks of memory.

Force feedback device – A device used to provide you with touch output from a computer device. A games controller uses this technology when it vibrates. An area for future development is a device to give surgeons feedback when carrying out an operation remotely using a robot arm.

Foreign key – A field in a table that matches the primary key column of another table. The foreign key can be used to link tables in a relational database.

Frame – A packet is known as a frame in Ethernet networks.

Frame rate – The number of still images that are recorded to make up the appearance of a moving image, usually measured in frames per second (FPS).

Free-space optical communication (FSO) – A way of transmitting data using a laser beam. It can be used for linking computer networks between buildings.

Frequency – The pitch of a sound: high-pitched (treble) sounds have a high frequency, whereas low-pitched (bass) sounds have a low frequency.

Frequency response – The range of sound frequencies that a device is able to capture or reproduce.

FX – Stands for 'effects'.

G

Gbps – A 1000 mbps connection is usually written as 1 gbps (giga bits per second). As there are 8 bits in a byte and data size is usually measured in bytes, the theoretical transfer time to move a 1GB file is around 8 seconds.

Gbps – Stands for gigabits per second. A medium with a transmission rate of 1 Gbps can transmit approximately one thousand million bits per second.

Geostationary satellite – A satellite orbiting the Earth at a height of 35,786 km and at the same speed that the Earth is rotating. It therefore appears to be stationary above a single point on the Earth's surface.

GPS chip – Global Positioning Satellite chip. This is a chip in a device that can communicate with satellites to give an extremely accurate location for your device.

Gradient – A block of colour that is stronger/solid at one end and then gradually gets fainter towards the other end.

Graphic assets – The digital images used in a product. You can create the graphic assets yourself or use ready-made assets from other sources, but you must have the right to use them.

Graphical processing unit (GPU) – A key component that supports the delivery and quality of graphics.

Greyscale – A monochrome image comprising only of many shades of grey varying from black through to white.

H

Hack – To use illegal means to access someone's email account or computer system.

Hard drive – Hard drive cameras do not need tapes, but store directly onto an in-built drive within the camera itself.

Hierarchical structure – An arrangement of items or data is a tree-like structure, which ranks the most important item or data in layers.

Higher Definition – Anything that runs at a resolution of above 1280x720 pixels.

Home page – The starting point for the portfolio and the page to which readers will return after completing a section.

HTML – HyperText Markup Language (HTML) is a coding language used to format web pages. HTML is read by your web browser (such as Microsoft® Internet Explorer® or Google™ Chrome™) which then formats the text and images etc which make up a web page based on the instructions in the HTML. HTML is not really a programming language, but just contains formatting instructions.

HTML element – An individual component of an HTML document.

Hyperlink – A link (which can be text or a graphic) that takes you to another web page or location within a document.

I

Identity theft – When someone steals your personal details in order to use them to open bank accounts and get credit cards, loans, a passport or a driving licence in your name.

Integrated Development Environment (IDE) – A software tool that allows programmers to write software programs.

Internet packets – A formatted block of data sent over networks and the internet. A packet contains the addresses of the sender and destination, the data itself and error checking.

Internet Protocol (IP) – A set of rules that allow information to be transferred between computers on the internet. The protocols specify how data is to be structured and the control signals required.

Intranet – This is a type of communications system, rather like an internal internet, but set up and controlled by the organisation for the sole use of its employees.

IP address – A unique address allowing a computer to be identified. Every computer on a network needs an IP address which is slightly different to the other computers, e.g. 192.168.1.5.

Ipconfig – A command prompt utility, which shows the current IP address of a computer.

Iteration – The act of repeating a process until a specific goal is reached.

Iterative process – This uses a series of repeated cycles of analysis to produce a result/finding.

J

Jack connector – The receptacle into which a plug is inserted to make an electrical connection.

K

Keyframe – A keyframe marks the start and end points of any significant change within an animation.

L

Landscape orientation – When the width of a page or image is greater than its height (i.e. it is short and wide).

Lasso – A freeform selection tool for drawing around the edge of a complex shape.

Layering – Layers are like transparent sheets layered on top of each other. Layers are shown in Flash® in the timeline. Graphic objects on the top layer will appear in front of those in lower layers. Parts of a drawing or character you want to animate must be on separate layers. Layering is when you place layers over the top of each other.

Layering/multi-track recording – A technique in which separate audio recordings are imported into audio-editing software and then synchronised and mixed together to achieve the desired result.

Licence-free – These assets are free and available for anyone to use within their own products.

Licensed – These assets are protected by copyright (they are owned by the creator of the assets). You will need to obtain the copyright owner's permission before you can use licensed assets and you may need to pay a fee.

Life cycle – The various stages required to produce new software.

Locked – When a document is locked, you won't be able to open it. It will only become unlocked once no users are accessing the document.

Logical operators – These operators refer to the use of AND, OR and NOT.

Logical topology – Communication standards which specify how data may be moved across a wired network.

Loop – A list of instructions that the computer keeps carrying out again and again until some condition becomes true.

Lossless compression – Returns a compressed file to its original form without losing any of the information.

Lossy – This is a type of file compression that results in a loss of data and quality.

Lossy compression – Compresses data by minimising the amount of data already there (by getting rid of some of it).

M

Machine code – A computer programming language consisting of binary or hexadecimal instructions that a computer can respond to directly.

Macro – A series of actions or commands that can be collected and stored under one single named unit. Macros are particularly useful for sets of actions that are used routinely and regularly.

Malware – A hostile, intrusive or annoying piece of software or program code.

Marquee – A tool for selecting a simple shape, typically a rectangle or an oval.

Mbps – Stands for megabits per second. A medium with a transmission rate of 1 Mbps can transmit approximately one million bits per second.

Microsoft® ClipArt – All Microsoft® programs come with ClipArt, that is a collection of ready-made graphics that can be used to illustrate documents or presentations.

Mixing – The process of blending together two or more audio tracks, such as spoken commentary and background music.

Mnemonics – Assembly language consists of a number of mnemonics (abbreviations) such as MOV (move instruction). Each mnemonic is equivalent to a machine code instruction.

Mouseover – Something that happens when you hover the mouse pointer over an item. Hovering your mouse over the top level of a menu, for example, might cause the menu to expand.

Moving images – Any images with movement (cartoons, video, film, etc.).

Multimedia files – Files that contain a mixture of digital images, sound or moving images.

Multiple processing core – Where multiple cores (central processing units) read and execute program instructions simultaneously.

N

Named anchor – This is a named location in a page that you can link to. You can create as many named anchors as you like within a page.

Navigation bar – A section of a web page that contains hypertext links, which connect you to other parts of the website.

Nested IF – A series of IF ... Else ... statements nested inside an IF ... Else ... statement.

Netiquette – Short for 'internet etiquette' or 'network etiquette'. It is a set of conventions covering the use of networks used to interact with other people. The conventions are designed to prevent people causing annoyance or offence to others.

Network – A group of computers that are connected together by communication channels and that have the capability of sending and/or receiving information between them.

Network of friends – A group of people who jointly keep up-to-date contact online. This may be a specific network, such as The National Youth Science Forum, or it may be more general, like a group of friends keeping in touch through Facebook.

Node – A control point that a path passes through.

O

Octet – A number between 0 and 255 forming part of an IP address. It is called an octet, because it needs eight bits in binary (255 in decimal is 11111111 in binary).

Online community – A virtual community which exists only online. It may be open to anyone (e.g. a bulletin board) or restricted by interest (e.g. various scientific communities).

Opacity – A measure of how transparent an image appears.

Operating system – The software that runs on computers and manages the computer hardware.

Optical media – CDs, CD-ROMs and DVDs are examples of optical media disks.

Optimise – It is unlikely that an asset that you create or download will be suitable for use in a mobile app as it is. To optimise your assets, you need to make sure that they have a small file size but still look fine on a mobile device.

Overlays – An overlay 'sits' over you clip, universally changing all data in accordance with the effect you have selected.

P

Packet – Computers transfer data by dividing each file into many thousands of packets. Each packet is individually routed to the destination computer where the packets are joined back into the data.

Path – A sequence of straight or curved lines.

Peer-to-peer – A simple network that can provide shared access to files, the internet and printing without a central server.

Peripheral – Any device, such as a printer, attached to a computer to expand its functionality.

PHP and ASP.NET – These are just two of the many different web languages which are available to web developers. These languages allow HTML to be extended by inserting programming code in the form of scripts into the web page. They allow interactive and dynamic web pages to be created, which could not be achieved by HTML alone.

Physical topology – The design of how networked computers connect into a network.

Pickup pattern – This is the microphone's sensitivity to sound and determines the direction that a microphone will pick up sound from. Different types of microphone are designed to pick up sound primarily from a single direction, from two directions, or from all directions.

Ping – A command prompt utility, which proves that another computer can be seen on the network.

Pixel – A small component (also known as a dot) that contains colour information for an image. When all the pixels are brought together, the image will be visible.

Pixelated – When an image is enlarged so much that it appears blurry.

Plosives – Letters such as P or B that, when spoken or sung, can cause popping sounds when recorded. Another name for plosives is oral stops.

Podcast – A download from the BBC, Apple® and many other providers in the form of video or audio. Once you have downloaded a podcast, you can play it at any time on your mobile phone or computer.

Point of sale (PoS) – Computerised tills that communicate with a database to keep track of stock. The information stored in the database updates with every item sold.

Portability – This is when you can view or use your portfolio across different systems, meaning that your portfolio is 'portable' and can viewed on systems using different browsers.

Portrait orientation – When the height of a page or image is greater than its width (i.e. it is tall and thin).

Power supply unit (PSU) – Every computer system unit has a PSU that plugs into the mains electricity socket. It converts mains electricity into low voltage electricity for the computer components. Every PSU produces the same voltage, but may produce a different amount of power (wattage). For example, a 600 W PSU is more powerful than a 400 W PSU.

PPI (pixels per inch) – This is a measure of the resolution of a graphic image. As web pages are designed to be displayed on a computer monitor, and most computer monitors can only display 72 ppi, there is no point having graphics in a higher resolution. If you do use higher resolution images, your pages may be slow to load, because high resolution images are large files and will take time to download.

Predefined – Refers to any items that are already prepared and made available.

Primary key – A field that uniquely identifies each record in a table, for example an ID number or product code.

Productivity – A measure of the efficiency of an orgainisation or individuals.

Profile – A user profile is a collection of personal data about a specific person. This may include biographical information, lists of interests and photographs.

Project lifecycle – The process of developing a project through a series of stages.

Protocol – Communications protocol is a set of rules that allows a computer system to connect with a different system to transfer data

Prototype – An original model of a new product. It can be either full size or scaled, depending on the project.

Pseudo code – A form of code that uses human language and contains a series of brief statements describing what the code will be doing.

R

Radio frequency identification (RFID) – The use of a wireless non-contact system that uses radio waves to transfer data from a tag attached to an object or person. The technology is mainly used for purposes of automatic identification and tracking.

RAM – Random access memory is used inside every computer to hold programs and data in current use. Data will be saved to the hard disk before switching the computer off, as the RAM will clear when power is off. RAM is often associated with volatile types of memory (where its stored memory is lost if the power is removed) but it can also be non-volatile.

Recce – Short for 'reconnaissance', which means an initial investigation. Filming projects use recces to obtain as much information about filming locations as possible prior to filming.

Record – A group of selected data that is associated in some way.

Referential integrity – A system of rules to ensure that relationships between records in related tables are valid and that you do not accidentally delete or change related data. For example, this prevents the problem of deleting a supplier when there are still products using the deleted supplier code.

Refine – To make things better in some way. This could be by careful selection of things (as in this case) or by changing things so they work better (e.g. a computer program) or by making things easier to read or access.

Relational database – A database that uses a series of tables to store information. The tables contain related information and are connected to each other.

Reserved word – A predefined word embedded into a programming language that has a specific purpose.

Resolution – Refers to the amount of information an image holds. The greater the resolution aspect, the better quality the image is.

Run-time – When a software program is in use.

S

Sampling – A technique used to convert analogue data to digital data. It involves taking a reading of the incoming data at fixed intervals (the sampling rate) and converting each reading to a binary number.

Scope – How much of the program can use a variable.

Scouting – The process of looking for locations.

SD card – Secure Digital (SD) cards allow you to store media on a small portable device that can be moved from a camera for example to a PC and other devices such as digital photo frames.

Search engine – A 'search and find' system into which you type what you are looking for and a series of 'best match' results will then be displayed.

Section page – The introduction page for each major section. It should describe the section and provide navigation through the section.

SECTION tags – These are used to create sections within your web page. By combining them with CSS styles, these sections can be used as page layout elements, or text boxes, with a specific size, position and formatting.

Select query – A query that selects the data from the fields that you specify and with the criteria that you set for those fields.

Sequence – In programming, a sequence is a list of instructions that the computer carries out in order.

Server-side processing – When the interaction between a web page and a computer is processed through a server.

Servers – A computer hardware system which acts as a host for other computers on the same network.

SFX – Stands for 'special effects'.

Software licence – when buying software a business may need several copies; it purchases a licence from the software manufacturer to allow it to run a certain number of copies of the application at any one time. It is illegal for the organisation to use any more copies than allowed by its licence. When you buy a software application for home use, the manufacturer gives you a licence to use it on your computer only.

Solid state – A component with no moving parts such as a solid state drive (SSD).

Solid state drive (SSD) – A data storage device.

Source code – The text that is used to create software programs in a high-level programming language.

Spam – Junk email where identical messages are sent to a number of recipients.

Static RAM – Or SRAM, is a type of memory that stores data, and which doesn't need to be continually refreshed.

Stereo (short for stereophonic) – Describes audio that includes two channels or tracks, one for left and the other for right, to give the impression of directional sound. Mono (or monophonic) sound has only a single channel.

Store and forward system – When an email is sent, it is stored on an email server and remains there until the recipient accesses their email account. It is at this point that the server forwards the message to them.

Storyboard – A sequence of sketches or images. Storyboards are used to plan out photo or video shoots, as well as to plan sequences in TV programmes and films.

String – A sequence of characters.

Structure diagram – Also known as a navigation hierarchy, this shows how you can get from a general category to a more specific one. For example, a drawing app could have a menu system where a user picks Tool, then Brush, then Thick Brush. At each stage, there are several options. You can draw all the options as a hierarchy.

Subnet mask – Used to define how much of the IP address can change for computers that can see each other on the network.

Subroutine – A set of instructions designed to perform an operation within a program.

Sun spot activity – From time to time there is the equivalent of a huge wave of flame released from the surface of the Sun. This releases millions of charged particles, some of which hit the Earth. These can cause disruption to data transmissions.

Sustainability – Using resources in such a way that we meet the needs of the present generation without affecting the ability of future generations to meet their needs. Sustainability involves protecting the environment so that we will continue to have the water, food and other resources that we need.

Switch – A box with ports (sockets) that are used to plug in the network cables. Cabled networks use switches to connect the devices together.

Synchronise – In this context, it means making the same data available using different devices. If you're using different devices, then each time you use a new device the data will need to 'sync' (i.e. update) so that you are using the most up-to-date version of the data.

System on a chip (SoC) – This is a single chip (integrated circuit) containing all the computer circuits an embedded device such as a microwave needs to control it.

T

Table – A two-dimensional representation of data in a database.

Target audience – The people who you are designing your product for. For example, you might decide that your target audience is females aged 16 to 19 who are interested in fashion.

TCP/IP – The combination of Transmission Control Protocol (TCP) and Internet Protocol (IP). TCP/IP is widely used by the internet to find websites and transfer their data to the browser so you can see the web pages.

Templates – Web pages that contain just the basic structure you want. You can then slot content into these templates to form the finished web pages. (Templates can also be used for items such as text documents, spreadsheets and slides.)

Test capture – Is when you record and capture a small amount of video to ensure you understand the process before working with larger recordings that may take much more time to complete.

Timeline – A visual representation of the footage, which is usually arranged in chronological order. All of the edit happens within the timeline.

Token – A way of moving data between workstations and servers. The token is a signal that is continuously passed around the network and is able to carry data.

Traditional platform – A computer system using mains power with system unit, keyboard, mouse, screen and hard drive.

U

Universal serial bus (USB) – A higher-speed serial connection standard that supports low-speed devices (e.g. mice, keyboards, scanners) and higher-speed devices (e.g. digital cameras).

Unsolicited bulk emails – Emails that are sent to a large number of people who haven't requested them.

Upload – When you upload a file you move it from one system to another system. For example, you can upload files from your computer to a web page.

URL – A unique string of characters that makes up a web page's address.

Utility application – A program which supports an app or operating system function.

V

Validation – The process of checking that data entered into a system is reasonable and is in the correct format.

Variable – A piece of memory that can be given a value (such as a number or word) and that is given a name to identify it.

Variable – A variable in maths is a changing quantity as opposed to a constant. For example, in this algebraic expression x and y are variables and 4 is a constant: $y = 4x$.

Vector graphics – These are created using a series of commands or mathematical statements (algorithms) to place lines and shapes in a given two-dimensional or three-dimensional space. These graphics are scalable and do not pixelate when enlarged. They are used in CAD packages.

Verification – A method of checking that the data entered into the system is correct and is the same as the information on the original source.

Version control – A way of tracking changes to documents and making sure that you are working on the most up-to-date version. Older versions of the document are kept as backup in case the most up-to-date version is lost or becomes corrupt.

Virtual world – An online community which meets in a computer-generated world, for example the large multi-player online games.

VoIP – Voice over Internet Protocol software allows you to make phone calls over the internet using a microphone and speakers connected to your PC.

Voltage – A measurement of the energy contained within an electric circuit at a given point.

W

Watermark – In digital graphics this a background image which shows through a foreground image. It can be used to identify images or to declare images draft or another status.

Web hosting – This is a service offered by companies that run web servers on behalf of people who want to have their website made available on the internet. Running a web server is a complex business, so very few small or medium size companies run their own web server. It's much easier and more economical to use a web hosting company.

Web server – A web server is a computer running software which stores web pages and sends them out over the internet in response to requests from users.

Wi-Fi hotspot – a site that offers internet access through a wireless network.

Wizard – A sequence of dialog boxes that lead the user through a series of well-defined steps.

Word – A fixed sized group of bits (binary data) that is handled as a group by the instructions set and the CPU

Workbook – The term used by Microsoft® Excel® to mean the collection of worksheets in a file. You will see this term when you want to print, as you are offered a choice of printing the active sheet or the entire workbook.

Worksheet – An individual sheet or grid that can be used to store data and equations. You can store many worksheets in the same workbook. See the Sheet1, Sheet2, Sheet3 etc. at the bottom left of the Microsoft® Excel® screen.

Z

Zeppelin – A microphone zeppelin is a kind of windshield. They are named after the cigar-shaped Zeppelin airships, as they resemble a miniature version of an airship. They completely enclose the microphone to protect it from wind noise.

Zoom – Where a camera starts with a wide view of a scene (sometimes called a wide angle shot) and then moves in to focus on a small part of the scene.

Index